THE MINOR PROPHETS

Old Testament Survey Series

THE
MINOR
PROPHETS

JAMES E. SMITH

COLLEGE PRESS
PUBLISHING COMPANY
Joplin, Missouri

Copyright © 1994
James E. Smith

Library of Congress Catalog Card Number: 94-72125
International Standard Book Number: 0-89900-423-7

DEDICATED TO

THE ELDERS OF

SOUTH SEMINOLE CHRISTIAN CHURCH
OVIEDO, FLORIDA

DOUG BRUMBAUGH
JAMES LESLIE, SR.
JAMES MONTGOMERY
HOWELL STARR
RAY WARMAN

MEN OF VISION
MEN OF WISDOM
MEN OF FAITH

CONTENTS

Chapter   *Page*

Preface 11

1. The Minor Prophets: An Introduction 13

The Early Prophets
Obadiah, Joel, Jonah

2. The Early Prophets: An Introduction 29
3. A Tale of Two Mounts (Obadiah) 49
4. The Day of the Lord (Joel 1). 61
5. The Day of Healing (Joel 2:1-27) 71
6. The Day of the Spirit (Joel 2:28-3:21) 85
7. The Saving of a Sinner (Jonah 1-2) 101
8. The Saving of a City (Jonah 3-4) 113

The Eighth Century Prophets
Amos, Hosea, Micah

9. The Eighth Century Prophets: An Introduction 127
10. The Approaching Judgment (Amos 1:1-3:8) 143
11. Prepare to Meet Your God (Amos 3:9-5:17) 157
12. Two Thundering Woes (Amos 5:18-6:14) 173
13. Visions of Judgment (Amos 7:1-8:3) 185
14. A Falling Temple and a Future Tent (Amos 8:4-9:15) . . . 195
15. The Tragedy of Unfaithfulness (Hosea 1-3) 209
16. The Lack of Knowledge (Hosea 4:1-6:3) 227
17. The Lack of Mercy (Hosea 6:4-8:14) 241
18. The Consequences of Sin (Hosea 9:1-11:11) 253
19. The Lack of Faithfulness (Hosea 11:12-14:9) 269
20. The Coming Judgment (Micah 1) 283
21. Present Corruption Condemned (Micah 2) 297
22. Man's Justice and God's (Micah 3) 307
23. Hope for a Better Day (Micah 4) 317

24. The Glory of Bethlehem's Ruler (Micah 5) 329
25. Present Repentance Pleaded (Micah 6:1-7:6) 341
26. The Outlook and the Uplook (Micah 7:7-20). 357

The Seventh Century Prophets
Nahum, Zephaniah, Habakkuk

27. The Seventh Century Prophets: An Introduction. 371
28. The Verdict of Vengeance (Nahum 1) 383
29. The Vision of Vengeance (Nahum 2). 391
30. The Vindication of Vengeance (Nahum 3) 397
31. The Coming Day of Yahweh (Zephaniah 1) 403
32. A Call for Repentance (Zephaniah 2). 413
33. The Results of the Great Day (Zephaniah 3) 425
34. Faith Out of Focus (Habakkuk 1:1-2:1) 437
35. Faith in Corrected Focus (Habakkuk 2:2-20). 449
36. 20/20 Faith (Habakkuk 3) 459

The Postexilic Prophets
Haggai, Zechariah, Malachi

37. The Postexilic Prophets: An Introduction 473
38. A Call to Action (Haggai 1). 491
39. The Great Shaking (Haggai 2) 503
40. Opening Words and Visions (Zechariah 1-2) 515
41. The Visions Continue (Zechariah 3-4) 531
42. Visions of Future Glory (Zechariah 5-6) 547
43. Fasting or Feasting? (Zechariah 7-8) 563
44. Yahweh's Triumphant Intervention (Zechariah 9:1-10:2) . 575
45. Messiah is Coming! (Zechariah 10:3-11:17) 587
46. The New Jerusalem (Zechariah 12-13). 599
47. The Triumph of Spiritual Jerusalem (Zechariah 14) 611
48. Divine Love Slighted (Malachi 1:1-2:4). 621
49. Broken Covenants (Malachi 2:5-16) 633
50. The People Sin Against Love (Malachi 2:17-4:6) 641

CONTENTS

Charts

1. The Minor Prophets by Size 14
2. Alternative Arrangements of the Minor Prophets 17
3. Pairing of Books in the Hebrew Arrangement 18
4. Predictive Element in the Minor Prophets 21
5. The Gist of the Minor Prophets 22
6. The Early Prophets 28
7. The Structure of Obadiah 34
8. The Structure of Joel 37
9. The Structure of Jonah 40
10. The Humbling of Pride 52
11. A Tale of Two Mounts 55
12. Fulfillment of Obadiah 17-20 59
13. Developmental Stages of Locusts 63
14. Eighth Century Prophets 126
15. The Structure of Amos 131
16. The Structure of Hosea 134
17. Comparison of Amos & Hosea 135
18. The Structure of Micah 138
19. Seventh Century Prophets 370
20. The Structure of Nahum 376
21. The Structure of Zephaniah 379
22. The Structure of Habakkuk 381
23. Postexilic Prophets 472
24. The Structure of Haggai 479
25. The Structure of Zechariah 483
26. The Structure of Malachi 486
27. Haggai 2:15-19 511

Maps

1. The World of Obadiah 48
2. The World of Joel 60
3. The World of Jonah 100
4. The World of Amos 172

5. The World of Hosea 208
6. The World of Micah, Nahum, Zephaniah and Habakkuk . 296
7. The World of Nahum. 396
8. The World of the Postexilic Prophets 490

Drawings

1. The Heavenly Reconnaissance Patrol 518
2. The Four Horns and Four Craftsmen 522
3. The Man with the Measuring Line 525
4. The Cleansing of Joshua 532
5. The Eternal Light. 538
6. The Flying Scroll 548
7. The Woman in an Ephah. 551
8. The Chariots of Wrath 554

PREFACE

If a prophet is one who received direct revelation from the Lord, then all the writings of the Old Testament were composed by prophets. Yet within the sacred canon are two sections of seventeen books which are designated "prophets" by modern students. The first five are designated Major Prophets because of their size. The twelve smaller books are called Minor Prophets. An earlier volume (1992) in this Old Testament survey series addressed the former. The focus of this present volume is on those twelve smaller volumes.

The format of this volume mirrors that of the other volumes in this series except in one important particular. The Minor Prophets are here discussed in what the author believes is the chronological order of their ministries. The twelve books are divided into four triads: the early prophets (Obadiah, Joel, Jonah), the eighth century prophets (Amos, Hosea, Micah), the seventh century prophets (Nahum, Zephaniah, Habakkuk) and the postexilic prophets (Haggai, Zechariah, Malachi). Each triad is introduced by a chapter containing background and introductory material as well as bibliography.

The following pages contain the fruit of some thirty years of teaching prophetic material. Every effort has been made to give credit to the numerous scholars whose brilliant insights have blazed the hermeneutical trails through the Minor Prophets. Here and there material found its way into class notes without documentation. Suffice it to say that after two thousand years of Christian reflection on these twelve books originality is an illusion. The goal has been to synthesize the best research and express it in a way which would be understandable and usable by those who might be exploring this portion of the Scriptures for the first time. In the notes which follow, the translation of Scripture is that of the author unless otherwise indicated.

Again on this volume as on the others in this series the editorial assistance of Linda Stark, Librarian of Florida Christian College, is gratefully acknowledged. The artwork which illustrates the visions of Zechariah was produced by Hope Wozniack Graves as part of a class project for the author.

CHAPTER ONE

The Minor Prophets
An Introduction

From very early days twelve smaller Hebrew prophetic writings are found united in one collection. In the Hebrew Bible this unified collection is positioned after the Book of Ezekiel.[1] The Book of the Twelve is the eighth component in the division of the Hebrew Bible known as the *Nebhi'im* ("Prophets"). The first four of these books—Joshua, Judges, Samuel and Kings—are known as the Former Prophets. The last four—Isaiah, Jeremiah, Ezekiel and the Twelve—are called the Latter Prophets.

PHENOMENOLOGY OF THE TWELVE

The constituent books in the Twelve are broken down into sixty-seven chapters, more than Isaiah (66 chaps.), Jeremiah (52 chaps.), or Ezekiel (48 chaps.). The total number of 1.050 verses, however, is less than any one of the three Major Prophets.[2] By word count the Book of the Twelve is eighteen percent smaller than Isaiah, the smallest of the three Major Prophets.[3]

Chart No. 1

THE MINOR PROPHETS BY SIZE			
BOOKS	**CHAPTERS**	**VERSES**	**WORDS**
1. Zechariah	14	211	6,444
2. Hosea	14	197	5,175
3. Amos	9	146	4,217
4. Micah	7	105	3,153
5. Joel	3	73	2,034
6. Malachi	4	55	1,782
7. Zephaniah	3	53	1,617
8. Habakkuk	3	56	1,476
9. Jonah	4	48	1,321
10. Nahum	3	47	1,285
11. Haggai	2	38	1,131
12. Obadiah	1	21	670
	67	1,050	30,305

CHRONOLOGY OF THE TWELVE

Two chronological issues need to be discussed by way of introduction to the Book of the Twelve. The first is the chronology of the individual writings, and the second is the chronology of the collection.

A. Chronology of the Books.

The individual books were produced in widely different periods of time. Among these books are some of the earliest and some of the latest of the Old Testament prophetic writings. In neither the Hebrew nor Greek arrangement of the books within the collection have strict chronological considerations been followed.

The twelve books come from four different periods. The earliest—Obadiah, Joel, and Jonah—appeared in the late ninth and early eighth centuries. This was the period prior to the rise of the great Assyrian empire. For that reason these three are sometimes called the pre-

Assyrian prophets. The second three—Amos, Hosea, Micah—come from the eighth century, the period when the Assyrian armies were dominating the scene in the ancient Near East. The third triad—Nahum, Zephaniah, Habakkuk—comes from the seventh century, when the power of the Assyrian empire faded rapidly and then was eclipsed by Babylon. The last three—Haggai, Zechariah, Malachi—come from the period after the exile when Judea was a province of the Persian Empire.

Were the books to be arranged in the order they were written the Book of the Twelve might look like this.

Obadiah	845 BC	Nahum	650 BC
Joel	835 BC	Zephaniah	630 BC
Jonah	755 BC	Habakkuk	609 BC
Amos	752 BC	Haggai	520 BC
Micah	735 BC	Zechariah	480 BC
Hosea	725 BC[4]	Malachi	432 BC

The prophetic literature in the Old Testament began to be produced in the days when the two Jehorams (Jorams) ruled, one in the north and the other in the south. At that time the prophet Elisha was still active in the kingdom of the ten tribes. The Joram of Israel (852-841 BC) was dominated by his fanatical mother Jezebel who was doing all within her power to convert the northern kingdom to the worship of Baal. Joram of Judah (848-841 BC) had married Athaliah, the daughter of Ahab and Jezebel. Through this marriage the pagan religious and social concepts of the north were transported into Judah. At one point Athaliah almost succeeded in exterminating all representatives of the house of David (2 Kgs 11:1-3; 2 Chr 22:10-12). Those were desperate days in both kingdoms. Yahweh countered the move toward idolatry with the miracles of Elijah and Elisha and the mighty messages of the succession of writing prophets.

B. Chronology of the Collection.

The twelve prophetic pamphlets were probably originally brought together because of their small size; at least that is an explanation found in the Talmud (*Baba Bathra*, 14b). Placing these separate works on one scroll helped preserve them from loss.

Probably the collection was assembled in the Persian Period, perhaps not long after Malachi's ministry had ended. Orelli thinks it is possible that the majority of these documents were found together in a special collection even before the Exile.[5] Rabbinic tradition held that the men of the Great Synagogue edited the Book of the Twelve (*Baba Bathra* 15a). This is probably referring to the collecting of the twelve books into one volume. The Great Synagogue was a body of learned scribes said to have been formed by Ezra. This body continued to exist into the early third century BC.

The collection of twelve prophetic pamphlets was known as "The Twelve" as early as the intertestamental writing of Ben Sirach (Ecclus 49:10). The twelve separate volumes were considered as one canonical book both by Josephus in the first century AD (*Against Apion* 1:8) and by the Talmudic scholars of the fifth Christian century.

ARRANGEMENT OF BOOKS

The issues of how, when and why the twelve books of the Minor Prophets were placed together in one volume have been addressed by only a few scholars. Actually the Book of the Twelve appears in two formats, viz., the Greek and the Hebrew.

A. The Greek Arrangement.

As noted above, in the Hebrew canon the Book of the Twelve was the fourth book in the Latter Prophets following Isaiah, Jeremiah, and Ezekiel. In some Greek manuscripts (e.g., Alexandrinus and Vaticanus) the Minor Prophets actually precede the Major Prophets. The logic of this placement probably has something to do with chronology. The Book of the Twelve begins with books which are older than Isaiah.

The order of the twelve prophets in the Septuagint differs from that of the traditional Hebrew text. In neither arrangement is chronology strictly observed. The English translations have followed the order of the Hebrew. A comparison of the two ancient formats of the Book of the Twelve is set forth in Chart No. 2.

Chart No. 2

ALTERNATIVE ARRANGEMENTS OF THE MINOR PROPHETS		
HEBREW ARRANGEMENT	**GREEK ARRANGEMENT**	**CHRONOLOGICAL ARRANGEMENT**
1. Hosea	1. Hosea	1. Obadiah
2. Joel	2. Amos	2. Joel
3. Amos	3. Micah	3. Jonah
4. Obadiah	4. Joel	4. Amos
5. Jonah	5. Obadiah	5. Hosea
6. Micah	6. Jonah	6. Micah
7. Nahum	7. Nahum	7. Nahum
8. Habakkuk	8. Habakkuk	8. Zephaniah
9. Zephaniah	9. Zephaniah	9. Habakkuk
10. Haggai	10. Haggai	10. Haggai
11. Zechariah	11. Zechariah	11. Zechariah
12. Malachi	12. Malachi	12. Malachi

The Hebrew arrangement seems to be more original; yet neither arrangement is decisive in determining the date of these writings. Both arrangements follow broad chronological principles in that the books of the pre-Assyrian and Assyrian periods are placed before the books of the Chaldean period (Habakkuk and Zephaniah). Both arrangements conclude with the triad of postexilic prophets (Haggai, Zechariah, and Malachi) in the order in which they appeared. Within the books of the pre-Assyrian and Assyrian periods, however, the chronological order was not strictly preserved. Other considerations appear to have outweighed chronology in the placement of books.

B. Explanations of the Arrangement.

Jerome addressed the issue of the arrangement of the books of the Minor Prophets in his prologue to this section. He conjectured that the prophets in whose books the time is not indicted in the title, prophesied under the same kings as the prophets whose books preceded theirs with the date of composition inserted. This would mean, for example, that Joel and Obadiah prophesied in the days of Uzziah of Judah and/or Jeroboam of Israel. No modern student of these books would ever concede such a thing. For Jerome's conjecture there is no evidence.

Keil has proposed the following plan by which the earlier Minor Prophets were arranged in this collection.[6] Hosea was placed at the head of the collection because it was the most comprehensive. The prophecies which had no date given in the heading were placed next. These non-dated books were always paired so that a prophet of the kingdom of Israel was always paired with one from Judah. For example, Joel of Judah was paired with Hosea of Israel. The complete scheme of Keil is displayed in Chart No. 3.

Chart No. 3

PAIRING OF BOOKS IN THE HEBREW ARRANGEMENT OF THE MINOR PROPHETS		
ISRAEL PROPHET	JUDAH PROPHET	ADDITIONAL CONSIDERATIONS
1. Hosea	2. Joel	Joel before Amos because Amos opens his books with the quotation of Joel 3:16.
3. Amos	4. Obadiah	Obadiah an expansion of Amos 9:12 which depicts the people of God possessing Edom.
5. Jonah	6. Micah	Jonah chronologically earlier than Micah. Jonah may be a specific example of the messengers sent to the nations in Obadiah 1.
7. Nahum*	8. Habakkuk	Nahum who predicted the fall of Nineveh (Assyria) must be earlier than Habakkuk who prophesied the coming of the Chaldeans.
*The location of Elkosh, Nahum's hometown, is uncertain. An ancient tradition places it in Galilee.		

Paul R. House[7] has proposed that the Minor Prophets have been placed in their present positions within the Book of the Twelve in order to highlight the main points of the prophetic message to Israel. The first six books focus on the sin of Israel and the nations. The next three books (Nahum through Zephaniah) highlight the punishment of sin. The last three prophets (Haggai through Malachi) emphasize the restoration which would follow the punishment.

House suggests that Hosea 1-3 forms an appropriate introduction to the entire Book of the Twelve. Chapter 1 sets forth the besetting sin of Israel, viz., God's people are not acting like his children. Chapter 2 announces that punishment for sin would be followed by reunification and multiplication of the nation. Chapter 3 depicts the purification which would be achieved through the punishment of exile. Thus these three chapters introduce the three major divisions of the Book of the Twelve. Though House has set forth his argument for the unity of the Book of the Twelve with great erudition, the scholarly world as a whole has not embraced his view of a carefully crafted and unified work.

PROFILE OF THE MINOR PROPHETS

Biographically little is known about any of the twelve Minor Prophets. Five of the writers reveal the names of their fathers. These were:

Hosea = Beeri	Zephaniah = Cushi
Joel = Pethuel	Zechariah = Berechiah
Jonah = Amittai	

Zephaniah traces his ancestry back four generations apparently to make the point that he was of the royal family. Nothing is known about the families of the other seven of the twelve Minor Prophets.

Three of the Minor Prophets are mentioned in the historical books of the Old Testament. From the reference in 2 Kings 14:25 it would appear that Jonah was a popular and influential prophet in Israel prior to his mission to Nineveh which is recorded in the book that bears his name. Haggai and Zechariah are mentioned twice in the book of Ezra. The rebuilding of the temple in postexilic Jerusalem is attributed to their dynamic ministries (Ezra 5:1 6:14). Micah is mentioned and quoted in the Book of Jeremiah (26:18).

Three of the prophets mention their hometowns. Amos was from Tekoa near Bethlehem on the edge of the Judean wilderness. Micah hailed from Moresheth-gath in the Shephelah, the rolling hills of Judah southwest of Jerusalem. To distinguish him from others of similar name the prophet was simply known as the Morashtite (Micah 1:1). Nahum is called "the Elkoshite" meaning that he was from Elkosh. Though the exact location of this town is not known, an ancient tradition places it in Galilee. The hometown of Jonah is identified in 2 Kgs 14:25 as being Gath-hepher, a town on Zebulun's border about two miles from Nazareth.

IMPORTANCE OF THE MINOR PROPHETS

Latin Christianity preferred to refer to the Book of the Twelve as the Minor Prophets. Augustine was quick to point out, however, that the term referred only to the literary extent of these books, not to the importance of their content.[8] They were called "minor" on account of the smaller bulk of the books which have survived when contrasted with the writings of Isaiah, Jeremiah and Ezekiel. Feinberg regards the assignment of the title Minor Prophets to this collection as "one of the literary ineptitudes of the centuries."[9] The main point is that these books are not of inferior authority to the Major Prophets.

The twelve authors of this collection preached and wrote at different periods ranging from the ninth to the fifth centuries BC. In this collection of books, then, are the earliest and latest prophetic testimonies concerning the future of the kingdom of God. Here also one can trace the development of that testimony. Taken together with the writings of the larger prophetic books they constitute the essentials of the prophetic word to ancient Israel. Here are the warnings that both the northern and southern kingdoms would fall to foreign powers. Here are the pleas for repentance as the only mechanism which might postpone those destructions. On the other hand, here the final touches are applied to the messianic portrait which began to emerge in rough sketch as early as the Garden of Eden (cf. Gen 3:15). To change the metaphor, these prophets "bring forth and sped on their way not a few of the streams of living water which have nourished later ages, and are flowing today."[10]

Chart No. 4

PREDICTIVE ELEMENT IN THE MINOR PROPHETS					
BOOK	DISTINCT PREDICTIONS	PREDICTIVE VERSES	% PREDICTIVE	PERSONAL MESSIANIC	FOCUS PREDICTION
Hosea	28	111	56%	4 vv.	Destruction of Samaria
Joel	25	50	68%	1 v.	Day of Yahweh
Amos	26	85	58%		Destruction of Samaria
Obadiah	10	17	81%		Edom Cut Off
Jonah	4	5	10%		Overthrow of Nineveh
Micah	40	73	70%	7 vv.	Fall of Jerusalem
Nahum	2	35	74%		Fall of Nineveh
Habakkuk	4	23	47%	4 vv.	Judgment on the Chaldeans
Zephaniah	20	47	89%		Judgment on Judah
Haggai	7	15	39%	6 vv.	The Great Shaking
Zechariah	78	144	69%	21 vv.	Temple to be Rebuilt
Malachi	19	31	56%	2 vv.	Coming of Messengers of Yahweh
	263	636	61% Avg.	45 vv.	
Statistics based on J. Barton Payne, *Encyclopedia of Biblical Prophecy* (New York: Harper and Row, 1973).					

The so-called non-literary prophets—those who preceded the Minor and Major prophets—focused on events of their own day. The literary prophets were more future oriented. According to Payne[11] 636 verses in the Minor Prophets—61% of the total—contain predictive material. Payne counts 263 separate predictions in these twelve books.

The most important contribution of the literary prophets was to recognize two important truths. First, Israel and Judah must politically

Chart No. 5

THE GIST OF THE MINOR PROPHETS				
BOOK	THEME	KEY VERSE	KEY THOUGHT	MESSIANIC PORTRAIT
Hosea	God's love for backsliders.	14:9	Return	Second Moses, David, Israel
Joel	The day of Yahweh is coming.	2:13	Repentance	Teacher for Righteousness
Amos	Prepare to meet your God!	5:24	Justice	Occupant of the Tent of David
Obadiah	The kingdom shall be Yahweh's.	v. 21	Pride Humbled	Savior & Judge par excellence
Jonah	Prejudice conquered.	4:11	Judgment Postponed	Resurrected Prophet
Micah	The triumph of hope.	6:8	Divine Expectation	Ruler from Bethlehem
Nahum	The overthrow of oppressors.	1:15	Nineveh Doomed	Bringer of Good Tidings
Habakkuk	Walking by faith.	2:4b	Faith	Conqueror of Satan
Zephaniah	The day of Yahweh's wrath.	1:4	Remnant	Witness against the Nations
Haggai	Courageous strength in discouraging times.	1:8	Build!	Desire of all Nations
Zechariah	Present distress and future glory.	4:6b	Visions	Enthroned Priest-King
Malachi	Divine love offended.	3:8	Robbery	Sun of Righteousness

INTRODUCTION

cease to exist. Both kingdoms would be carried away into captivity. Second, God would establish a new kingdom of a different kind, one which would attract all peoples. At the head of that kingdom would be that glorious king, priest and prophet who from the dawn of history had been promised to the human family.

The spoken words of these mighty prophets were committed to writing in order that, when fulfilled, these predictions might prove to future generations the righteousness and faithfulness of Yahweh. The Lord intended that these writings might serve as a lamp to the remnant of the faithful during the dark days of judgment and long years of waiting until the manifestation of the Sun of Righteousness (2 Pet 1:19).

The Minor Prophets generally have been considered more obscure and difficult to interpret than the other prophetic books of the Old Testament. The very brevity of these books results in the omission of historical allusions and details of description which would assist greatly in interpretation. Even the Books of Kings and Chronicles often are so brief that suggestions as to fulfillments are difficult. Hosea is particularly obscure. The visions of Zechariah are presented in simple language, but the symbolism there is difficult to ascertain. Speakers frequently change in Micah with no clear indication of who is speaking. Nonetheless, the overall message of each of these books is clear. The twelve themes of the Minor Prophets are indicated in Chart No. 5.

ENDNOTES

1. The Book of Daniel appears in the third division of the Hebrew Bible. Sometime after the time of Josephus Daniel was relocated from its position among the prophets to its present location following the *Megilloth* (Ruth, Song, Koheleth, Lamentations, and Esther).
2. Total verses in Isaiah = 1,292; Jeremiah = 1,364; and Ezekiel = 1,273.
3. Total word count in the Book of the Twelve is 30,305. Word counts in the three Major Prophets are Isaiah = 37,044; Jeremiah = 42,659; and Ezekiel = 39,407.
4. Hosea's ministry began before that of Micah and extended beyond it. Thus the Book of Micah would have been written before Hosea, but the ministry of Hosea chronologically would precede that of Micah.
5. C. von Orelli, *The Twelve Minor Prophets*. Trans. J.S. Banks. 1897 (Minneapolis: Klock & Klock, 1977 reprint), p. 1.

6. Keil and Delitzsch, *Old Testament Commentaries; Ezekiel XXV to Malachi* (Grand Rapids: Associated Publishers, n.d.), pp. 792f.

7. Paul R. House, *The Unity of the Twelve* (Sheffield, England: Almond Press, 1990), pp. 68-70.

8. Augustine, *The City of God* 18:29. In vol.2 of *A Select Library of the Nicene and Post-Nicene Fathers of the Christian Church*, ed. Philip Schaff (Grand Rapids: Eerdmans, 1956).

9. Charles L. Feinberg, *The Minor Prophets* (Chicago: Moody, 1976), p. 9.

10. George Adam Smith, *The Book of the Twelve Prophets* in "The Expositor's Bible;" 2 vols. (New York: Armstrong, 1898).

11. J. Barton Payne, *Encyclopedia of Biblical Prophecy* (New York: Harper and Row, 1973), pp. 674f.

INTRODUCTION

BIBLIOGRAPHY

Note: Listed below are important works which deal with all of the Minor Prophets. Subsequent bibliographies will list the works which focus on individual books or groups of books.

Boice, James Montogomery. *The Minor Prophets*. 2 vols. Grand Rapids: Zondervan, 1983, 1986.
Calkins, Raymond. *The Modern Message of the Minor Prophets*. New York: Harper, 1947.
Chisholm, Jr. Robert B. *Interpreting the Minor Prophets*. Grand Rapids: Zondervan, 1990.
Cohen, A. *The Twelve Prophets*. Soncino Books of the Bible. London: Soncino. 1961.
DiGangi, Mariano. *Twelve Prophetic Voices; Major Messages from the Minor Prophets*. Wheaton, IL: Scripture Press, 1985.
Feinberg, Charles. *The Minor Prophets*. Chicago: Moody, 1976.
Deane, W.J. "The Minor Prophets." *The Pulpit Commentary*. 2 vols. New Edition. New York: Funk & Wagnalls, 1909.
Hailey, Homer. *A Commentary on the Minor Prophets*. Grand Rapids: Baker, 1972.
Henderson, Ebenezer. *The Twelve Minor Prophets*. 1858. Grand Rapids: Baker, 1980.
Keil, Carl. "The Twelve Minor Prophets." Vols. 24 and 25 of *Biblical Commentary on the Old Testament*. Grand Rapids: Eerdmans, 1949 reprint.
Kelley, William. *Lectures Introductory to the Study of the Minor Prophets*. 1874. 5th ed London: Hammond, n.d.
Laetsch, Theo. *Bible Commentary; The Minor Prophets*. St. Louis: Concordia, 1956.
Lewis, Jack P. *The Minor Prophets*. Grand Rapids: Baker, 1966.
von Orelli, C. *The Twelve Minor Prophets*. Minneapolis: Klock & Kock, 1977 reprint of 1897 ed.
Pusey, E.B. *The Minor Prophets*. 2 vols. Grand Rapids: Baker, 1956 reprint.
Robinson, G.L. *The Minor Prophets*. 1926. Grand Rapids: Baker, 1978.

Smith, George Adam. *The Book of the Twelve Prophets.* "The Expositor's Bible." 2 vols. New York: Armstrong, 1898.
Tatford, Frederick. *The Minor Prophets.* 3 vols. 1874. Minneapolis: Klock & Klock, 1982.

PART ONE

THE EARLY PROPHETS

OBADIAH
JOEL
JONAH

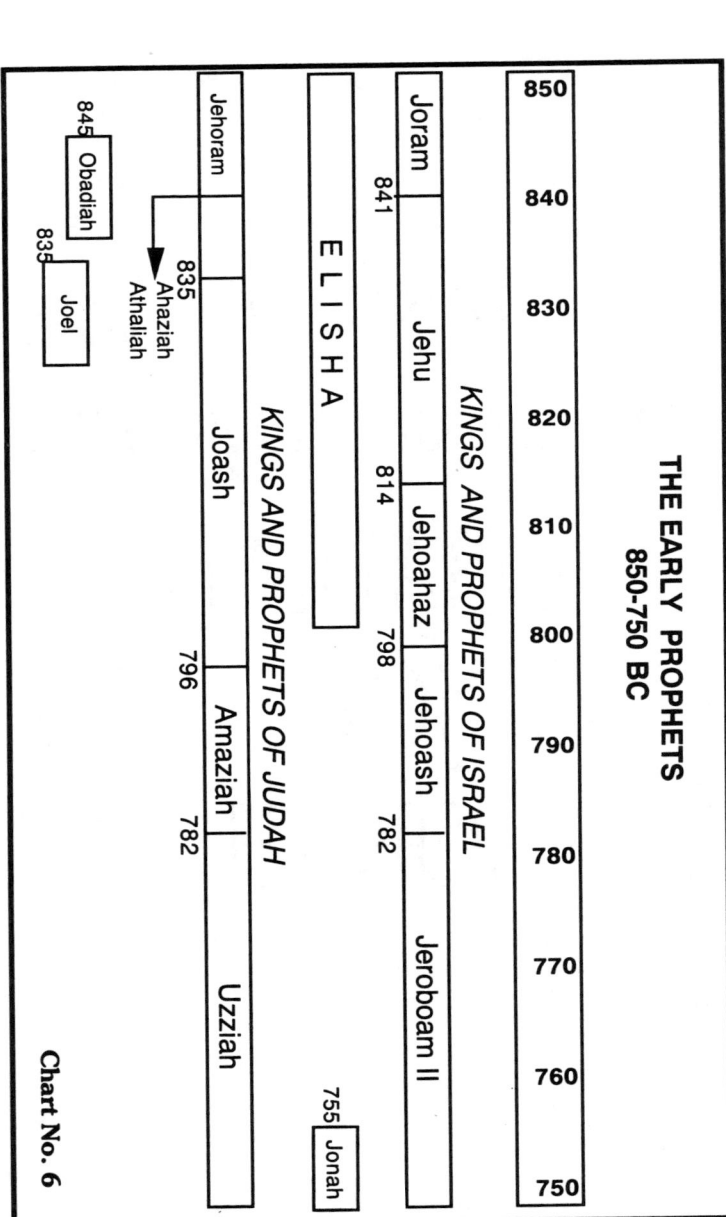

CHAPTER TWO

The Early Prophets
An Introduction

Liberal and conservative commentators assign widely different dates to the books of Obadiah, Joel and Jonah. While conservative commentators regard these books as the earliest of the Minor Prophets, the liberals tend to date them after the Exile at the very close of Old Testament history. In the pages which follow the arguments for the early date of these books will be presented.

HISTORICAL BACKGROUND

The great kingdom forged by the military genius of David split asunder after the death of Solomon in 931 BC. For about a half century, the two sister kingdoms took a hostile stance toward one another. Chronologically the first three of the Minor Prophets can be assigned to the century 850-750 BC. This was the Divided Monarchy period of Old Testament history.

A. Jehoram of Judah (848-841 BC).

When the Omri-Ahab dynasty took control in Israel (the northern kingdom), the two kingdoms entered an era of peace. Cooperative military and commercial ventures characterized this period. The ruling families even intermarried.

Until her death in 841 BC Jezebel, a zealot for the Tyrian god Baal, dominated both kingdoms. Her husband and two sons ruled the northern kingdom. Her son-in-law, grandson, and daughter ruled Judah. To counter the influence of this sinister woman, God raised up two powerful prophets in Israel, Elijah and Elisha. In the southern kingdom several political setbacks punished the alliance between Judah and Jezebel-dominated Israel.

King Jehoram of Judah walked in the way of the kings of Israel because he was married to Athaliah, the daughter of Jezebel (2 Chr 21:6). Yet Yahweh was not willing to destroy the ruling dynasty "because of the covenant which he had made with David" (2 Chr 21:7). God did permit, however, some disciplinary disasters to afflict Jehoram because of the direction of his reign.

Edom revolted against the rule of Judah in the days of Jehoram. The king almost lost his life attempting to put down this rebellion. Noting Edom's successful revolt, Libnah also rebelled against Jehoram "because he had forsaken Yahweh, God of his father" (2 Chr 21:10).

A letter from Elijah warned Jehoram of a worse calamity to follow. That calamity was not long in coming. "Yahweh stirred up against Jehoram the spirit of the Philistines and the Arabs who bordered the Ethiopians." This coalition came against Jerusalem. They carried off all the possessions found in the king's house together with his sons and his wives. Only one member of the royal family was left behind (2 Chr 21:16-17). This sack of Jerusalem about 845 BC is the background of the prophet Obadiah.

Jehoram died under God's judgment. "Yahweh smote him in his bowels with an incurable sickness." At the end of two years, Jehoram's "bowels came out" because of his sickness and he died in great pain (2 Chr 21:18-19).

B. Reign of Joash in Judah (835-796 BC).

Jehoram was followed on the throne by his son Ahaziah who was the grandson of Jezebel. His reign lasted but a portion of a year. Ahaziah died while visiting his uncle, the king of Israel, during the revolution of 841 BC (2 Chr 22:6-7). Forty-two members of the royal family of Judah who went to the aid of Ahaziah were also slain (2 Kgs 10:12-14).

The death of the king and so many members of the royal family created a power vacuum in Judah. Athaliah the queen mother in Judah seized power. This daughter of Jezebel was as ruthless as her mother. She destroyed all the royal offspring of the house of David. Only the infant Joash was spared by being hidden in the temple for six years (2 Chr 22:10-12).

In 835 BC Jehoiada organized a coup against Athaliah. The seven year old Joash was restored to the throne upon which his ancestors had ruled for several generations. During the minority of the king, Jehoiada served as regent. Joash did right in the sight of Yahweh "all his days in which Jehoiada the priest instructed him" (2 Kgs 12:2). Joash guided Judah in a national reformation. The temple was refurbished with monies contributed voluntarily by those who came to Jerusalem to worship. The prophet Joel should probably be assigned the period of the minority of Joash.

C. Reign of Jeroboam II in Israel (793-753 BC).

Both Israel and Judah were plunged into a time of political humiliation by the revolution of 841 BC. For almost half a century Hazael, king of Damascus, dominated the two kingdoms. In Israel Jehu (841-814 BC) and Jehoahaz (814-798 BC) were virtual vassals of Hazael (2 Kgs 13:3,7). All the territories east of Jordan were lost to the Arameans (2 Kgs 10:32-33). Jehoahaz "entreated the favor of Yahweh, and Yahweh listened to him; for he saw the oppression of Israel, how the king of Syria oppressed them" (2 Kgs 13:4).

A series of attacks by the Assyrians against Damascus culminated in a crushing blow struck by Shalmaneser IV in 797 BC. King Jehoash (798-782 BC) was able to win three victories over Benhadad II, the son of Hazael, and thereby recover cities which had been captured by the Arameans. With King Jeroboam II (793-753 BC) the recovery was completed.

Encouraged by the predictions of Jonah the son of Amittai, Jeroboam II restored the border of Israel from the entrance of Hamath in the north to the Sea of the Arabah (the Dead Sea) in the south (2 Kgs 14:25). This popular prophet, who had always predicted success for his country in campaigns against the Arameans, was dispatched by God to Nineveh to deliver a warning to the king of Assyria.

THE PROPHET OBADIAH
Herald of the Unshakable Kingdom

Obadiah has been called "the antagonist of Edom," "the censurer of ridicule," "the exposer of the gewgaws of worldly wisdom and power." He has been accused of "fatuous provincialism," and "intense sectionalism." His book—more of a tract than a book—is the shortest among the Minor Prophets. Yet the message of this unheralded herald is disproportionate to the length of his writing.

A. The Man.

The name Obadiah ("servant of Yahweh") was common in ancient Israel. At least twelve others by this name appear in the Old Testament. Jewish tradition is hardly correct in identifying the prophet Obadiah with the steward of King Ahab who hid a hundred prophets in caves during the Jezebelian persecution (1 Kgs 18:4). Others have suggested that the prophet Obadiah may have been the Obadiah sent out by King Jehoshaphat to teach the Law of God in the countryside of Judah (2 Chr 17:7). The Minor Prophet Obadiah, however, most likely is distinct from all the others by that name in Scripture.

Practically nothing is known about this prophet. He was probably a native of Judah. He lived through a humiliating sack of Jerusalem. He had tremendous faith to see the ultimate glory of God's kingdom. His personality, however, lies hidden in shadow. The message rather than the man is the focus of this book.

B. The Mission.

The major issue among students of Obadiah concerns the date of the book. Since the book makes no explicit claim regarding a date, even conservative scholars differ on this issue. Some hold to an early date of about 845 BC; others think the setting of the book is the

Babylonian destruction of Judah in 586 BC.

That Obadiah prophesied after a sack of Jerusalem is clear from verses 10-11 of the book. The sack which he describes, however, is not catastrophic enough to be the destruction of Jerusalem in 586 BC. Not one of the six characteristic marks of the 586 BC destruction of Jerusalem appears in Obadiah. Those six characteristics are: (1) the razing of the walls (2 Kgs 25:10; Jer 52:14); (2) the burning of the royal palaces and all houses (2 Kgs 25:9; Jer 52:13); (3) the burning of the temple (2 Kgs 25:9; Jer 52:13); (4) the capture and deportation to Babylon of the king (2 Kgs 25:7); (5) the deportation of the entire nation with few exceptions (2 Kgs 25:11,12); (6) the emigration of the Jews to Egypt (2 Kgs 25:26; Jer 41:16-43:22).

Other evidence also points to the earlier date for the book. Obadiah mentions Ephraim in such a way as to suggest that the northern kingdom was still standing. The position of the book in the canon—fourth in the Hebrew Bible, fifth in the Septuagint— suggests that Obadiah should be classified as one of the earlier Minor Prophets. Joel seems to quote from Obadiah 17 (cf. Joel 2:32).[1] Jeremiah, who prophesied just before the fall of Jerusalem, seems to quote from Obadiah 9.[2]

In a day when Judah had been brought low by military invasion and mocked by ancient enemies, Obadiah stepped forward to announce that the kingdom of God ultimately would be triumphant.

C. The Message.

The message of Obadiah might be titled "A Tale of Two Mounts." In this book Mt. Zion represents the people of God. Mt. Esau represents the adversaries of God's people. The same contrast is found in the terminology "house of Jacob" and "house of Esau." For the first group the present is bleak, but the future is bright. On the other hand, the adversaries of God's people have no future at all.

Payne has found ten distinct predictions in the Book of Obadiah. Seventeen of the twenty-one verses—81% of the contents—are predictive. The more important predictions are these: (1) Edom will be brought low; (2) Edom will be permanently cut off; (3) God's people will consume the Edomites and possess the Philistines; and (4) in due time Yahweh will be sole ruler over all. While some of the prophecies of Obadiah find fulfillment in the messianic age, there is no personal messianic prophecy in the book.

The message of Obadiah is illustrated in Chart No. 7.

Chart No. 7

THE STRUCTURE OF OBADIAH		
Pronouncement Against Edom vv. 1-10	Prediction Regarding the Nations vv. 15-16	Promise To Israel vv. 17-21
God's People Violated	→	God's People Vindicated

THE PROPHET JOEL
Prophet of Pentecost

Joel has been called "the prophet of Pentecost" (Robinson), "the prophet of hopefulness," and "the prophet of the Spirit." This man of God was privileged by God to see in prophetic prospect both the beginning and the end of the Christian age.

A. The Man.

The name Joel means "Yahweh is God." His name summarizes the bedrock conviction of his soul. Some thirteen other men by this name appear in the Old Testament. The most famous of the other Joels was a son of Samuel (1 Sam 8:2). The prophet Joel is said to be the son of Pethuel. He most probably was a native son of Jerusalem. He may have been a priest, though nothing he says nails this down conclusively. Nothing more is known about this prophet except what can be deduced from the message of his book. What is most important is that he was a true prophet of God, endowed with remarkable prophetic vision.

B. The Mission.

Placement of the ministry of Joel in the history of Judah is very difficult. Few other books in the Old Testament have been assigned to so many different dates as Joel. This book has been dated prior to 900 BC, down to as late as 350 BC, and virtually every century between. Some who deny the unity of the book place portions even later than 350 BC.

Most scholars have opted for one of two basic positions regarding the date of Joel. Some assign the mission of this prophet to the minority of King Joash of Judah, i.e., c. 835-817 BC. Others, usually of a more liberal persuasion, assign Joel to the period after the restoration of the Jews from Babylonian captivity, i.e., after 539 BC. Both groups of scholars place heavy emphasis on the fact that no king is mentioned in the book. Elders seem to be the real leaders. Does the absence of the name of a king, however, mean that the monarchy had ceased to exist? or does it mean that a boy king who was not really in control was sitting on the throne? Joel reflects the fact that the temple had been plundered. He does not, however, indicate that the temple had been destroyed. A plundering of the temple by the Philistines about 845 BC is probably intended (2 Chr 21:16f.).

The placement of the book among the Minor Prophets—second in the Hebrew and fourth in the Septuagint—suggests that Jewish scribes placed this prophet's ministry earlier rather than later. For the purposes of this study a date of 835-817 BC for Joel is assumed.[3]

A severe locust plague formed the background out of which the ministry of Joel emerged. This prophet was commissioned to use this plague as a springboard to announce the day of Yahweh, an even worse judgment to come. The locust plague would be removed. The Teacher for Righteousness would then appear. This would be followed by the outpouring of the Spirit upon all flesh and the terrible judgment upon physical Jerusalem.

The social and religious conditions reflected in the book are the following. The people have experienced poverty and suffering brought on by the locust plague. Offerings have been cut off from the house of God. Both leaders and people are in need of genuine repentance.

C. The Message.

The second book of the Minor Prophets contains seventy-three verses. This material is divided into three chapters in the English Bible, but four chapters in the Hebrew Bible. Though a small book, Joel bristles with so many complex problems that it has been called "sorrow's child" of Old Testament exegesis.[4] The teaching here is at once simple and profound. Joel presents his message in majestic verse. He is regarded as one of the greatest poets in the Old Testament. If in fact this book is among the earliest of the Minor Prophets, it contains the foundational statement of many of the most fundamental truths expressed in prophetic literature. Amos seems to have been dependent on Joel in at least two passages.[5]

Joel pleaded eloquently and effectively for genuine repentance. His call to repentance is one of the truly grand pemmican passages in the Old Testament. Yet he is even more noted for his eschatological thought. In majestic strokes this prophet paints the mural of the entire sweep of the messianic age from its beginnings in time and space to its culmination in eternity, from Pentecost to Paradise restored.

The doctrine of the day of Yahweh is the centerpiece of Joel's theology. Joel's outline of this event is expanded by later prophets, but these eight elements are part of the picture in this book: (1) the signs and wonders in heaven; (2) the day of Yahweh is eschatological as well as historical; (3) great judgment is associated with that day; (4) the final defeat and punishment of God's enemies; (5) the ultimate redemption of the remnant of believers; (6) the prominence of Zion; (7) Yahweh's triumphant and peaceful reign; and (8) the finality of this consummation.

Joel also paints a beautiful picture of the New Jerusalem, one which is further developed in the New Testament. Six leading elements of his teaching in this regard are these: (1) the eternal safety of those who inhabit that city; (2) the holiness of Zion; (3) the absence of any stranger (unbeliever) there; (4) the presence of the river of the water of life; (5) the theme of eternal life; and (6) the fact that Zion is the habitation of Yahweh himself.

The content of the Book of Joel is displayed in Chart No. 8.

Chart No. 8

THE STRUCTURE OF JOEL				
GOD'S JUDGMENT		GOD'S SALVATION		
Devastation Present & Future	Exhortation To Repent	Restoration of Blessing	Vindication Thru Judgment	Glorification At The End
1:1-2:11	2:12-17	2:18-29	2:30-3:15	3:16-21
JOEL SPEAKS 37 vv.		GOD SPEAKS 36 vv.		

Payne discovered predictive material in fifty of the seventy-three verses of Joel (68%). By his count, the book contains twenty-five distinct predictions.[6] Among the more important predictions are these: the day of Yahweh is at hand (1:15; 2:1-11); pouring out of the Spirit on the day of Pentecost (2:28-29); the heavenly phenomena which will prelude the day of divine judgment (2:30-31; 3:15f.); and the salvation of those who call on the name of the Lord (2:32).

THE PROPHET JONAH
The Prejudiced Prophet

The Book of Jonah is perhaps the most controversial book in the Old Testament if not the entire Bible. The book is full of miracles, and that offends the rationalistic mind of modern man. This book, however, emphasizes more than any other the universal love of God.

Jonah has been called "the vacillating prophet" (Ward). More positive designations are "the prophet of God's mercy" (Scofield Bible), "the prophet of catholicity" (Robinson), and "the first foreign missionary" (Bryan).

A. The Man.

The name Jonah means "dove." The prophet was the son of Amittai. Nothing more is known about his family.

Jonah was the most prestigious prophet of his day. He aided the great Jeroboam II in his military campaigns to recover the territories which Israel had lost to the Arameans. According to 2 Kgs 14:25 Jeroboam "restored the border of Israel from the entrance of Hamath as far as the Sea of the Arabah, according to the word of Yahweh, the God of Israel, which he spoke through his servant Jonah the son of Amittai, the prophet, who was of Gath-hepher." The town of Gath-hepher was located in the territory of the tribe of Zebulun about 2.5 miles northeast of Nazareth.

The character of Jonah has been described as self-determined and self-centered. Two commendable characteristics of the man were his frankness and his honesty. Whatever negative assessment is made of Jonah's life, he was not guilty of hypocrisy. He was narrow in his outlook. In fact he was nationalistic, totally unconcerned about the spiritual condition of those outside Israel. With all of his faults, however, Jonah was still teachable.

B. The Mission.

Besides the one reference in 2 Kgs 14:25, all that is known of the ministry of Jonah is reported in the book that bears his name. He was called away from his popular ministry of national recovery to deliver God's word of judgment to the most ruthless people history had every known. Prophetic oracles against foreign nations appear in every prophetic book except Hosea. These oracles, however, were spoken on Israelite soil primarily for the benefit of Israelites. The closest parallel to Jonah's journey to Nineveh was the political mission of Elisha to Damascus (2 Kgs 8:7-13).

Jonah rebelled against this call. Many men—e.g., Moses, Elijah, Jeremiah—were reluctant to shoulder the responsibility of prophetic ministry. Jonah, however, went beyond their hesitation. Instead of traveling east to Nineveh, Jonah bought a ticket to Tarshish in the distant west. Not fear of failure, but fear of success prompted Jonah to run from his calling. He did not want these heathen to be saved from God's wrath.

On the sea the delinquent prophet slept while Gentile seamen rowed desperately through a mighty storm. Finally Jonah was awakened. He told the crew that the calamity was upon them because of his presence on the vessel. For the sea to be calm they must throw him overboard. Still the seamen rowed on, not wishing to follow such desperate advice. Finally they were forced by the severity of the storm to follow that advice.

Jonah was swallowed by a great fish. Three days later he was vomited up on the shore. He had learned his lesson. Jonah went immediately to Nineveh. Through the length and breadth of that great city he preached a five-word message of doom. The entire city, from the king to the lowliest handmaid, responded to Jonah's preaching in a dramatic demonstration of repentance. God relented concerning the announcement of destruction. On the outskirts of the city Jonah sat and pouted. He really wanted to see the Ninevite repentance short-lived so he could witness the destruction of the place. The book closes with the Lord teaching Jonah a lesson about his mercy and compassion.

The date of Jonah's ministry to Nineveh probably fell within the reign of Jeroboam II of Israel, who began to reign as co-regent in 793 BC. His absolute rule began in 782 BC and terminated in 753 BC. Three Assyrian kings were contemporary with Jeroboam. Adad-nirari III (810-783 BC) made a move in the direction of monotheism. Some think this may have been the result of the mission of Jonah. Little is known about his successor Shalmaneser IV (783-773 BC). During the reign of Ashurdan III (773-755 BC) the nation was psychologically prepared to expect a great catastrophe. Serious plagues fell on Assyria in 765 BC and again in 759 BC. A total eclipse of the sun, always viewed with great alarm by the ancients, was visible in Assyria January 15, 763 BC. Taking all these data into account, Jonah's trip to Nineveh probably fell between 780 BC and 755 BC.

Jonah's ministry invites comparison with that of Elijah. The accounts of both prophets are thoroughly supernaturalistic. Both had their lives preserved by miracles. Both converted large numbers. God found it necessary to discipline Elijah. The same is true of Jonah. Both prophets were impatient with God. Both desired to see the wicked suddenly and miraculously overthrown. Both accounts end with the prophet engaging in personal conversation with God. Neither account explicitly mentions a change of negative attitude on the part of the prophet.

C. The Message.

Even a cursory reading of the Minor Prophets indicates that the Book of Jonah is different from the other eleven books. Whereas the other books are full of oracles against Israel and neighboring nations, Jonah contains but one oracle, and it is but five words long in the Hebrew. The Book of Jonah is mostly narrative. It is more similar to the Elijah-Elisha stories of the Book of Kings than it is to Amos or Hosea.

The theme of Jonah is God's concern for the lost. The book is a bifid. In the first two chapters God saved a sinner; in the last two chapters he saved a city. The book has been called "a model of literary artistry, marked by symmetry and balance."[7] Chart No. 9 diagrams the structure of the Book of Jonah.

Chart No. 9

THE STRUCTURE OF JONAH	
The Saving of a Sinner Disobedience (1:1-3) Discipline (1:4-16) Deliverance (1:17) Declaration (2:1-9 Discharge (2:10)	The Saving of a City Jonah and Nineveh (ch. 3) Jonah and the Lord (ch. 4)
Chs. 1-2	Chs. 3-4

✗Only half of one verse in Jonah is a verbal prediction. This is by far the least amount of prediction to be found in any of the Old Testament prophetic books. The three days and nights Jonah spent in the fish, however, are symbolically prophetic of the stay of Christ in the tomb (Matt 12:40).

The Book of Jonah is full of important lessons for believers. Here are a few of them. (1) The book is a rebuke to those who long for the conversion of sinners provided that only certain types of sinners come. (2) The book also rebukes those who do not have the passion to win people to Christ. (3) The person who questions the wisdom of God posits for himself a wisdom that exceeds omniscience. (4) The way to Nineveh may seem hard, and the way to Tarshish full of promise; but God knows best. (5) Human beings and even dumb beasts are all precious in the sight of God. (6) Are believers more concerned about plants or people? (7) God's love is great in its downward reach and in its outreach. (8) No preacher is qualified to preach to all men if he is not ready to preach to any man.

D. The Method.

The major issue facing the student of Jonah is the identity of the genre or category of literature into which this book fits. It has been described as (1) legendary, containing a kernel of truth expanded and exaggerated by the author; (2) allegorical, in which all of the leading features are symbolic;[8] (3) historically accurate in all its details; and (4) didactic fiction. The latter view is most popular today. Those who hold to this view employ one or more of the following phrases to describe the book: "a parable in ethics;" "a fiction in poetic dress;" "a moral or didactic fable;" "a parable;" or "a short story with a moral."

Why are modern scholars reluctant to accept the Book of Jonah as historical? The following arguments have been advanced:

1. The book lacks historical particulars. The author, for example, has not pinpointed the spot where Jonah was ejected from the fish, the specific sins of the Ninevites, or the name of the king of Nineveh. Yet a critic could make this argument against any historical work. No historian relates all the facts about any event. The Book of Jonah does in fact cite a number of very specific details which would be superfluous in a parabolic narrative.

2. The book ends abruptly, thus signaling that the author was trying to teach a truth and not necessarily relate true facts. Recognizing the didactic purpose of the book, however, does not prove that the book is unhistorical. An historical episode can be related for didactic purposes.

3. If taken as sober history, the behavior of Jonah is incomprehensible. On the other hand, however, would any writer slander a prominent prophet by attributing to him such negative actions? The account

makes sense only if Jonah himself is the author of this material, and if he is writing this account as a confession of sinful attitudes and actions.

4. If Jonah is history, why was this material not placed with the historical books? The history of the organization of the Old Testament canon is quite complex. The early historical books of Joshua, Judges, Samuel and Kings were considered to be prophetic books in one early arrangement.

5. The king of Assyria is inaccurately designated "the king of Nineveh" in Jonah. Biblical writers, however, sometimes called kings after the name of their capital. Ahab the king of Israel is called "king of Samaria" (1 Kgs 21:1), and Ben-hadad king of Syria is called "king of Damascus" (2 Chr 24:23).

6. The conversion of the Ninevites is historically improbable. History, however, is full of improbabilities. To be sure the Ninevite conversion must have been short lived. While to date no concrete evidence of even a temporary change of heart in Nineveh has been discovered, neither is there any data which would refute this claim of Jonah. In truth the history of Assyria during the period of Jonah is virtually a blank.

7. The circuit of the city of Nineveh was only about eight miles, a size which hardly would have required a three day walk (3:3). The language of Jonah, however, may have included the cluster of villages which surrounded Nineveh; or the length of time required to preach to all the people there.

8. The book contains an overabundance of the miraculous —twelve miracles in forty-eight verses. This more than any other reason causes modern scholars to question the historicity of Jonah.

While the arguments against the historicity of Jonah are not decisive, several arguments can be advanced to support the historical nature of the book.

1. Argument from style and language. Simply stated, the book appears to be historical. Technical language, totally out of place in a parable, is used in the sailing episode and in the decree of the king.

2. Argument from didactic purpose. Without question this book has a didactic purpose. It teaches God's universal love for all humankind. Only if the story is actually true, however, would it have had much of an impact.

3. *Argument from canonicity.* The book practically slanders a prophet. It would not have been allowed to remain in the canon unless it was regarded early on as true.

4. *Argument from historical accuracy.* Jonah was a historical character. Nineveh was notorious for moral depravity. The description of the size of Nineveh in the text is accurate. The mourning of men and cattle is documented by the Greek historian Herodotus (9:24). Joppa and Tarshish were historical cities.

5. *Argument from tradition.* The Book of Tobit (14:4-6,15), written during the intertestamental period, understood Jonah as historical. Josephus (*Antiquities*, 9:10,2) the Jewish historian also interpreted the book as sober history.

6. *Argument from analogy.* The analogy between the Book of Jonah and the account of Elijah is striking. Certainly the Elijah record was meant to be taken historically.

7. *Argument from the behavior of Jonah.* It is unlikely that an eminent prophet would have been selected to be represented as so foolish, so wayward and so out of harmony with God if in fact he had not so proved himself.

8. *Argument from authority.* Jesus referred to Jonah's stay in the belly of the great fish (Matt 12:39ff.; 16:4) in such a way as to indicate that he regarded it an an actual occurrence. Even more decisive is Jesus' reference to the men of Nineveh "rising up in the judgment" to condemn those who had rejected him (Luke 11:32). Men in a parable will not be present in the resurrection. Thus Jesus puts his endorsement upon the historical understanding of the Ninevite conversion. Sandwiched between the reference to the "sign of Jonah" and the reference to the Ninevites in the resurrection Jesus mentioned the visit of the Queen of the South to the court of Solomon. Certainly this was an historical incident. Jesus regarded the references to Jonah to be just as historical as that to the Queen.

ENDNOTES

1. C.F. Keil, "Obadiah" in *Old Testament Commentaries: Ezekiel XXV* to Malachi (reprint; Grand Rapids: Associated Publishers and Authors, n.d.), p. 1053. Cf. F. Meyrick, "Obadiah" in *The Holy Bible Commentary* (New York: Scribner's Sons, 1892), 6:562.

2. Meyrick, *op. cit.*, 563-64; E.B. Pusey, *The Minor Prophets* (reprint; Grand Rapids: Baker, 1956), 1:344ff.

3. Statements in the book which are alleged to indicate a postexilic date are these: "bring back the captivity" (3:1); "I will no more make you a reproach among the nations" (2:19); and "sons of the Grecians" (3:6). In the comments of the following chapters these phrases will be shown to be compatible with a ninth century date for the book. For an excellent statement of the arguments for the early date of the book see A.F. Kirkpatrick, *The Doctrine of the Prophets*, reprint of the 3rd ed. (London: Macmillan, 1920), pp. 57-73.

4. Merx, cited by James Robertson, "Joel" in *The International Standard Bible Encyclopedia*, ed. James Orr (Grand Rapids: Eerdmans, 1956), 3:1688.

5. Joel 3:16 compared with Amos 1:2; Joel 3:18 compared with Amos 9:13. See G.L. Archer, *A Survey of Old Testament Introduction* (Chicago: Moody, 1985), p. 311.

6. J. Barton Payne, *Encyclopedia of Biblical Prophecy* (New York: Harper and Row, 1973), pp. 406-411.

7. Leslie C. Allen, *The Books of Joel, Obadiah, Jonah and Micah* in "The New International Commentary on the Old Testament" (Grand Rapids: Eerdmans, 1976), p. 197.

8. E.g., *The Abingdon Bible Commentary* (p. 790). Jonah is said to represent Israel; the great fish is the exile. So following release from exile, Israel was to carry the message of ethical monotheism to the Gentiles.

BIBLIOGRAPHY
The Early Prophets

Note: Listed below are works which relate to one or more of the earlier prophets treated in this unit. For general bibliography on the Minor Prophets see at the conclusion of Chapter One.

Alexander, Desmund, David Baker and Bruce Waltke. *Obadiah, Jonah, Micah.* "Tyndale Old Testament Commentaries." Downers Grove, IL: InterVarsity, 1988.

Allen, Leslie. *The Books of Joel, Obadiah, Jonah, and Micah.* "The New International Commentary on the Old Testament." Grand Rapids: Eerdmans, 1976.

Coffman, James Burton. *The Minor Prophets: Joel, Amos and Jonah.* Abilene: ACU Press, 1981.

DiGangi, Mariano. *The Book of Joel.* "Shield Bible Study Outlines." Grand Rapids: Baker, 1970.

Driver, S.R. and H.C.O. Lanchester. *The Books of Joel and Amos.* "The Cambridge Bible for Schools and Colleges." Cambridge: University Press, 1915.

Excell, Joseph. *Practical Truths from Jonah.* 1874. Grand Rapids: Kregel, 1982.

Kirk, Thomas. *Jonah: His Life and Mission.* 1903. Minneapolis: Klock & Klock, 1983.

Kohlenbergber III, John R. *Jonah and Nahum.* "Everyman's Bible Commentary." Chicago: Moody, 1984.

Lanchester, H.C.O. *Obadiah and Jonah.* "The Cambridge Bible for Schools and Colleges." Cambridge: University Press, 1915.

McGarvey, J.W. *Jesus and Jonah.* Murfreesboro, TN: Dehoff, 1952 reprint.

Marbury, Edward. *Obadiah and Habakkuk.* Sovereign Grace, 1960 reprint.

Marten, A.D. *The Prophet Jonah; the Book and the Sign.* London: Longmans, Green, 1926.

Martin, Hugh. *Jonah.* 1866. Banner of Truth Trust, 1982.

Varney, George J. ed. *The Story of Jonah.* (Boston: Christian Witness, 1897

Wade, G.W. *Micah, Obadiah, Joel, and Jonah.* "Westminster Commentaries." London: Methuen, 1925.

Watts, John D.W. *Obadiah; A Critical and Exegetical Commentary.* 1969. Winona Lake, IN: Alpha, 1981.

Wolff, Hans Walter. *Obadiah and Jonah, a Commentary.* Trans. Margaret Kohl. Minneapolis: Augsburg, 1986.

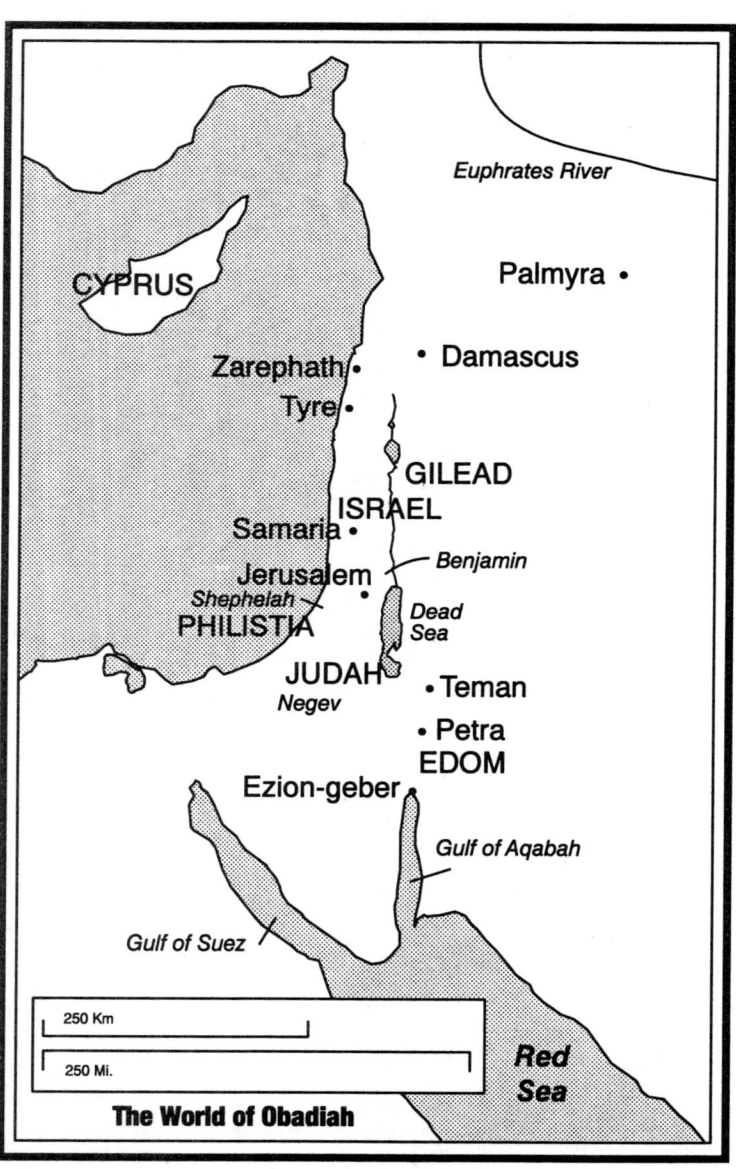

CHAPTER THREE

A Tale of Two Mounts
Obadiah

The first of the Minor Prophets to proclaim the word of God was the most focused. In his short book he blasts Edom, Israel's neighbor to the south, for violation of common decency and covenant loyalty. The book revolves around two mountains Mt. Zion which represents the people of God and Mt. Seir which represents the Edomites. The essence of his message is that God's people have a glorious future, while those who are hostile to the kingdom of God are destined for eternal ruin.

OBADIAH'S CLAIM
Obadiah 1a

Obadiah began his brief book by underscoring the source of his message. First, he refers to his book as a "vision" (*chazon*). The term refers to visual and audio-visual revelations (Dan 8:1; Isa 29:7) and to oral revelations which were "seen" by the ear (1 Chr 17:15; Ps

89:19; Hab 2:2f.). By extension, the term "vision" is also used of the written record of such revelation (Nah 1:1; Isa 1:1; 2 Chr 32:32).

Second, Obadiah used the ancient messenger formula ("Thus says the Lord Yahweh") to make another claim to divine revelation. The term "Lord" *('adonay)* emphasizes the absolute authority or sovereignty of God as creator. The term is used exclusively of Yahweh in the Old Testament. The name "Yahweh" underscores God's covenant relationship with Israel.

Third, Obadiah's God-given message is directed "to Edom." Yahweh is not a local deity who exercised sovereignty only over the land of Palestine. He is the Lord of all the earth who is cognizant of all that takes place among the nations of the world.

Fourth, Obadiah affirmed "a report we have heard from Yahweh." The plural pronoun may be a reference to the prophets collectively, or to Obadiah and all who hear or read his prophecy. The term "report" *(shemu'ah)* stands first in the Hebrew sentence for emphasis. Obadiah is again stressing the divine source of his message.

A PRONOUNCEMENT AGAINST EDOM
Obadiah 1b-2

Obadiah learned through revelation that an envoy or ambassador *(tsir)* had been sent among the nations. This ambassador must have been an angelic being. Through such spirit beings God persuades men and nations to do his bidding (cf. 1 Kgs 22:19-38; Dan 10:10-21). This envoy had the assignment of persuading the nations to join Yahweh in an attack against Edom. These conspiring nations had their own agendas, but they would be used like pawns by the sovereign Yahweh to bring about his purpose regarding Edom (v. 1b).

The result of the attack against Edom is not in doubt. By means of the word "behold," Obadiah announced the shocking outcome of the attack. Yahweh would make Edom "small among the nations." The verb in Hebrew is in the perfect tense which normally indicates completed action. Prophets often used the perfect tense to indicate an outcome which was so certain to be accomplished that it could be spoken of as already accomplished.[1] God saw Edom already humbled.

THE PRIDE OF EDOM HUMBLED
Obadiah 3-9

Like all unbelievers, the Edomites were so filled with pride that they paid no attention to the divine warning. They had been deceived—lulled into a false sense of security—by the arrogance of their heart. Five sources of Edomite pride are identified.

A. Pride of Location (vv. 3-4).

The geography of Edom gave the inhabitants of that land confidence that no foreign power could overpower them. Edom was a land of lofty mountains, steep crags, stifling heat and scarcity of water. Innumerable caves both natural and man-made offered the defenders cool sanctuaries from which to launch surprise attacks against invaders. To supplement these natural military advantages, the Edomites constructed fortresses at virtually every occupied site in the land.

A rhetorical question capsulizes the arrogant pride of Edom: "Who shall bring me down to earth?" Yahweh had an answer for them. Though they should build their dwellings as high as the eagles or even among the stars, "from there I will bring you down." To underscore this dramatic announcement, Yahweh appended his signature, as it were. The expression "oracle of Yahweh" (*ne'um Yahweh*) is the strongest possible claim that the pronouncement came directly from God.

B. Pride of Wealth (vv. 5-6).

Edom controlled the great trade route known as the King's Highway which connected Damascus in the north with the seaport Eziongeber on the Red Sea. Rich copper and iron mines in the area also provided a source of wealth. All the treasures stored in their mountain fortresses would be plundered. "Esau," i.e., Edom, would be ransacked. Thieves and grape gatherers normally leave something behind. Yahweh's agents, however, would confiscate all of Edom's hidden treasures.

C. Pride in Alliances (v. 7).

Edom felt secure because of her various commercial and military alliances. Their allies, however, would turn on them. Fugitive Edomites would be treated as strangers at the borders of allied nations. The allies would deceive and overpower Edom, i.e., join forces with the enemies. Obadiah states literally "your bread they shall place as a boil under you." The "bread" may be a figure for those who eat bread, i.e., familiar friends, turn against Edom.²

D. Pride in Wisdom and Armies (vv. 8-9).

The Edomites were noted for their wisdom in the ancient world. When judgment is unleashed, however, confusion will reign supreme in the mountain of Esau. No counselor will have any useful advice as to what course to follow to cope with the invasion. The "mighty men" of Edom will be dismayed by events to the point of incapacitation. They will not be able to fight. The slaughter will spread from one end of the land to the other. Even in Teman, in the southern region of the land, the slaughter would spread unchecked. Every one would be "cut off" from the mountain of Esau. None will be able to give a credible explanation as to how such a powerful nation could have been so completely destroyed.

Chart No. 10

THE HUMBLING OF PRIDE	
Sources of Pride	**Humbling of Pride**
Location (vv.3-4)	"I will bring you down."
Wealth (vv.5-6)	Treasuries searched out.
Allies (v. 7)	Allies deceive you.
Wisdom (v. 8)	Wise men destroyed.
Armies (v. 9)	Mighty men destroyed.
"The arrogance of your heart has deceived you" (v.3).	

THE EXPLANATION OF EDOM'S JUDGMENT
Obadiah 10-14

Having described how Yahweh would humble the pride of Edom, Obadiah next discusses four areas of transgressions which necessitated this judgment.

A. Covenant Abuse (v. 10).

Edom would be put to shame "because of violence to your brother." The term "brother" was part of the vocabulary of covenant formulation. Two nations with a treaty between them were called brother nations. Thus the crime here charged against Edom is that the terms of the covenant with Jacob, i.e., Israel, had not been observed. In fact, the "brother" Jacob had been treated with "violence," i.e., wrongful, hurtful action, especially cruelty and oppression.

Genesis records the struggle which marked the relationship between Jacob and Esau in their youth (Gen 25:21-34; 27:30-40). The Edomites were the descendants of Esau. They refused to allow the Israelites to pass through their territory as they were making their way toward Canaan (Num 20:14ff; 21:4). In the monarchy period Saul fought against Edom (1 Sam 14:47), and David conquered that land (2 Sam 8:13-14). Hadad the Edomite was one of the adversaries of Solomon (1 Kgs 11:14). The king of Edom was an ally of Israel and Judah during an invasion of Moab (2 Kgs 3:9). Some time later the Edomites were part of an invasion of Judah (2 Chr 20:1-30). In Obadiah's own time Edom revolted against King Jehoram of Judah (2 Kgs 8:20,21) and probably joined the Philistines and Arabs in an attack on Jerusalem (2 Chr 21:16).

Obadiah predicted that Edom would be "cut off forever." Subsequent to the time of Obadiah these were the highlights of Edomite history: (1) Edom was conquered by King Amaziah of Judah (2 Kgs 14:7 2 Chr 25:11). (2) The Edomites attacked Judah in the days of King Ahaz (2 Chr 28:17). In the fifth century BC Edom fell into Arab hands. In the third century BC Edom was overrun by the Nabataeans. In the second century the Edomites who resided in southern Judah were subdued by Judas Maccabaeus (1 Macc 5:65) and compelled by John Hyrcanus to be circumcised.

B. Callous Non-involvement (v. 11).

A particular example of the violence done by the Edomites is a non-action. Jerusalem was in desperate straits. Strangers had entered the city. They had carried away the wealth of the place. The conquerors were casting lots over the city, dividing it up for the purposes of taking plunder. As a "brother" or ally Edom should have rendered assistance to Judah. That, however, was not the case. The Edomites "stood aloof," (lit., on the other side, opposite, making no effort to aid). By failing to come to the aid of the oppressed "brother," the Edomites were "as one of them," i.e., they were as guilty as those who actually plundered Jerusalem.

C. Malicious Gloating (v. 12).

Obadiah was an eyewitness of the transgressions of the Edomites. The compassionate Yahweh seeks to save Edom from destruction by warning them to discontinue their malicious conduct. At the same time, the warning is an implied reproof. Obadiah ordered Edom not to "gloat" (NASB), "rejoice," or "boast" (lit., make the mouth large), over the day of Jerusalem's calamity. An ascending scale of guilt is here outlined. The complacent look led to malicious pleasure, and finally to actual words of insult and derision.

The word "day" is used four times in verse 12 to refer to the calamity experienced by the people of God. Obadiah refers to (1) "your brother's day;" (2) "day of his misfortune;" (3) "day of their destruction;" and (4) "day of their distress."

D. Ruthless Exploitation (vv. 13-14).

Not only had they gloated over the calamity, they had joined in the looting of the city. The Edomites had also stood at the crossroads to cut off those individuals who tried to escape the city. The fugitives were being captured to be sold as slaves. The fourfold repetition of the phrase "day of their disaster" in vv. 13-14 underscores the pitiful circumstances of Jerusalem.

Chart No. 11

A TALE OF TWO MOUNTS	
MOUNT ZION (Present Day)	**MOUNT ESAU** (Future Day)
Day of Misfortune (v. 12).	Covered with Shame (v. 10).
Day of their Destruction (v. 12).	Cut off forever (v. 10).
Day of their Disaster (vv. 13,14).	"As you have done, it will be done" (v. 15).
Day of their Distress (vv. 12,13,14)	Wine of God's Wrath (v. 16).
	No Survivor (v. 18).
	Submissive to Zion (v. 20).

A PREDICTION REGARDING THE NATIONS
Obadiah 15-16

Obadiah now states the grounds upon which the warning to Edom was based: The "day of Yahweh" is coming. This is the first use of this phrase in the Old Testament, but the concept is much older (cf. Num. 24:14-24). The "day of Yahweh" is that time when Yahweh comes into prominence, when the God of Israel manifests himself in a special way. Every heathen power eventually experiences a day of Yahweh. The "day of Yahweh" is a day of judgment for Yahweh's enemies and a day of vindication for his devoted worshipers. Every local judgment is a harbinger of that final day when all sinners meet their doom at the judgment bar of God (v. 15).

The standard which God will use in that day of judgment is this: As you have done, so shall it be done to you. Obadiah tells Edom, "Your deeds will return on your own head." The Edomites had committed sacrilege in God's sanctuary by drinking to the point of intoxication. In the day of Yahweh all the nations (Gentiles) will be forced to drink the wine of God's wrath. The nations will drink that wine and "become as if they had never existed," i.e., they would utterly perish (v. 16).

Thus Obadiah broadens the blast against Edom to include all

those who manifest the same behavior. Those who stand aloof from God's people, those who mock or persecute the church, those who desecrate sacred things shall all face the burning wrath of the Holy One of Israel!

A PROMISE TO ISRAEL
Obadiah 17-21

If the future of Mt. Esau is bleak, that of Mt. Zion is bright. Obadiah sketches a beautiful picture of the nature of God's kingdom on earth. He projects the ultimate triumph of this kingdom over all the earth.

A. Pictures of the Kingdom (vv. 17-20).

Five phrases describe the nature of the kingdom which will ultimately triumph. First, that kingdom would be a place of safety. "On Mt. Zion there will be those who escape." That place so despised and desecrated by the Edomites would become the seat of Yahweh (Joel 3:17) and his kingdom. Mt. Zion in Old Testament prophecy is used as a symbol of spiritual Jerusalem (Gal 4:25f.; Heb 12:22-25), the church triumphant (Rev 21-22).

Prophetic Mt. Zion is the place of salvation. A steady stream of desperate people will escape the devastation of sin and dread of death by seeking refuge on Mt. Zion, the spiritual kingdom of Christ (v. 17a).[3]

Second, prophetic Mt. Zion is a holy place, set apart from the world. Those who come out of the world to find salvation on Mt. Zion will be a holy people (v. 17b).

Third, Mt. Zion is an endowed place. The "house of Jacob," i.e., the inhabitants of Zion, "will possess their possessions" (v. 17c). Those who come out of the world to find salvation on Mt. Zion will be endowed with an abundance of spiritual gifts (cf. Acts 2:38).

Fourth, Mt. Zion is a unified place. The inhabitants of Mt. Zion are referred to as "the house of Jacob" and "the house of Joseph." Since 931 BC the people of God had been divided into two kingdoms. Obadiah, however, foresees the day when the twelve tribes once more would be united. The salvation which people seek on Mt.

Zion will break down all barriers (v. 18a).

Fifth, Mt. Zion is a victorious place. The unified people of God would consume the Edomites as easily as fire consumes stubble. No one would survive the onslaught against Edom, "for Yahweh has spoken" (v. 18b). This prediction began to be fulfilled during the intertestamental period when the Jews defeated the Idumeans. The complete fulfillment, however, is yet future. The spiritual kingdom of Christ is ultimately victorious over all opposition. Those who attack and harass the people of God will be destroyed completely.

Obadiah depicts in military terminology the expansion of God's kingdom on every side. The mountain of Edom would fall to the those who dwelled in the Negev, i.e., the southern part of Judah. Those who lived in the foothills of the Shephelah would push down into the coastal plains. Judah and Benjamin between them would possess the whole territory that once belonged to the northern kingdom of Israel, i.e., Ephraim, Samaria, and Gilead. Even Jewish captives who had been sold to Phoenician merchants would have a part in the great expansion which Obadiah predicts (vv. 18-19).[4]

Obadiah's purpose here is not so much to describe the changing map of Palestine, as it is to depict in concrete terms the majestic progress of the kingdom of God. The inhabitants of Mt. Zion do not maintain a defensive mode. They go on the offensive to spread the message of salvation "in Jerusalem, Judea, Samaria, and unto the uttermost parts of the earth" (Acts 1:8).

B. Prophecy Concerning the Kingdom (v. 21).

During the course of the struggle against Mt. Esau (the world), "saviors shall ascend on Mt. Zion." The term "saviors" (*moshi'im*) is used of those God raised up during the Settlement Period to rescue his people from oppressive foreign powers (Judg 3:9,15; cf. Neh 9:27). Yahweh also gave to his people a "savior" in the days of King Jehoahaz (2 Kgs 13:5). The term is broad enough in scope to include all the political and spiritual leaders who arose in the days subsequent to Obadiah who were successful in giving deliverance to the people of God. The work of the Maccabees during the intertestamental period particularly may be in view. These saviors, however, were but shadows of that greatest of all Saviors, even Jesus.

The saviors are said to ascend "On Mt. Zion." The Hebrew preposition is *beth*, not *'el* (unto) or *'al* (upon). The idea is that from among the citizens of Mt. Zion saviors would emerge. This prophecy is but a further development of the thought of v. 17 which spoke of Mt. Zion as the home of "those who escape." Obadiah began his prophecy by describing how Mt. Zion had been defiled. The saviors would be able to preserve the holiness of the people of God. Mt. Zion here is the abode of God's people over against Mt. Esau which represents the world.

The saviors who arise on Mt. Zion would "judge the mount of Esau." The term "judge" here means "punish" (cf. 1 Sam 3:13). Esau here is the nation Edom, which in turn is a type of Israel's and God's last foe (cf. Isa 63:1-4). Those who are able to deliver God's people from oppressors would also execute God's judgment upon Mt. Esau, the enemies of the redeemed. Again the Maccabean rulers are in view. They conquered several surrounding nations including the Idumeans or Edomites. John Hyrcanus compelled the defeated Idumeans to accept circumcision and incorporated them into the kingdom of Judah (cf. 2 Macc 10:15,23). In this respect also these saviors foreshadow Christ who is the ultimate Judge as well as Savior.

Obadiah concludes his prophecy with a magnificent three word (in the Hebrew) declaration: "The kingdom shall be Yahweh's." Here the prophet is quoting David (Ps 22:28). This is the bottom line of all history. The struggles between Mt. Zion and Mt. Esau, the world and the church, fade from the prophet's view. He sees the kingdom of Yahweh ultimately triumphant, surviving all the powers which have tried to destroy her. These words are the polar star to guide God's people through whatever dark days may arise.

The rest of prophetic literature is to a certain extent an exposition of the last line of Obadiah. Daniel declared to Nebuchadnezzar: "The God of heaven shall set up a kingdom, which shall never be destroyed" (Dan 2:44). To the pitiful remnant which returned from the captivity Zechariah would declare: "Yahweh shall be king over all the earth" (Zech 14:9). The angel declared to Mary that Christ would "reign over the house of Jacob forever, and his kingdom will have no end" (Luke 1:33). The volume of sacred literature concludes with these similar declarations: "The kingdom of the world has become the kingdom of our Lord and of his Christ; and he will reign forever and ever" (Rev 11:15). "Hallelujah! For the Lord our God, the Almighty, reigns" (Rev 19:6).

Chart No. 12

FULFILLMENT OF OBADIAH 17-20			
VERSE	**AREA**	**NT REF.**	**FULFILLMENT**
v. 19	Philistia	Acts 8:40 9:32-43	Philip preached from Azotus to Caesarea; Peter preached in Lydda and Joppa
v. 19	Samaria	Acts 8:5-17	Philip preached the Gospel to the Samaritans.
v. 20	Zarephath (Phoenicia)	Acts 11:19	Jerusalem Christians traveled as far as Phoenicia, Cyprus and Antioch.
v. 20	Sepharad (Asia Minor)	Acts 13-16	Church in Sardis; Paul traveled extensively in Asia Minor.
v. 17	Edom	Acts 15:13-18	Conquest of Edom in Amos is interpreted by James to refer to the conversion of Gentiles.

Basic idea. God's people in the future will experience growth and expansion which will embrace Gentile territories.

ENDNOTES

1. The NASB renders the perfect in v. 2 as a future in English.

2. Laetsch thinks the "bread" refers to the copper and iron which comes back against Edom in the form of weapons like a festering sore which saps the life from Edom. *The Minor Prophets* (St Louis: Concordia, 1956), p. 199.

3. The Hebrew imperfect tense describes the successive flow of this stream of salvation. New Testament references to the spiritual Mt. Zion are these: Rom 9:33; 11:26; Heb 12:22; 1 Pet 2:6; Rev 14:1.

4. Zarephath (v. 20) was located in Phoenicia between Tyre and Sidon. This is the Sarepta (ASV margin) of Luke 4:26. Sepharad is thought by some to be Spain, by others to be Sparta or Sardis in Asia Minor.

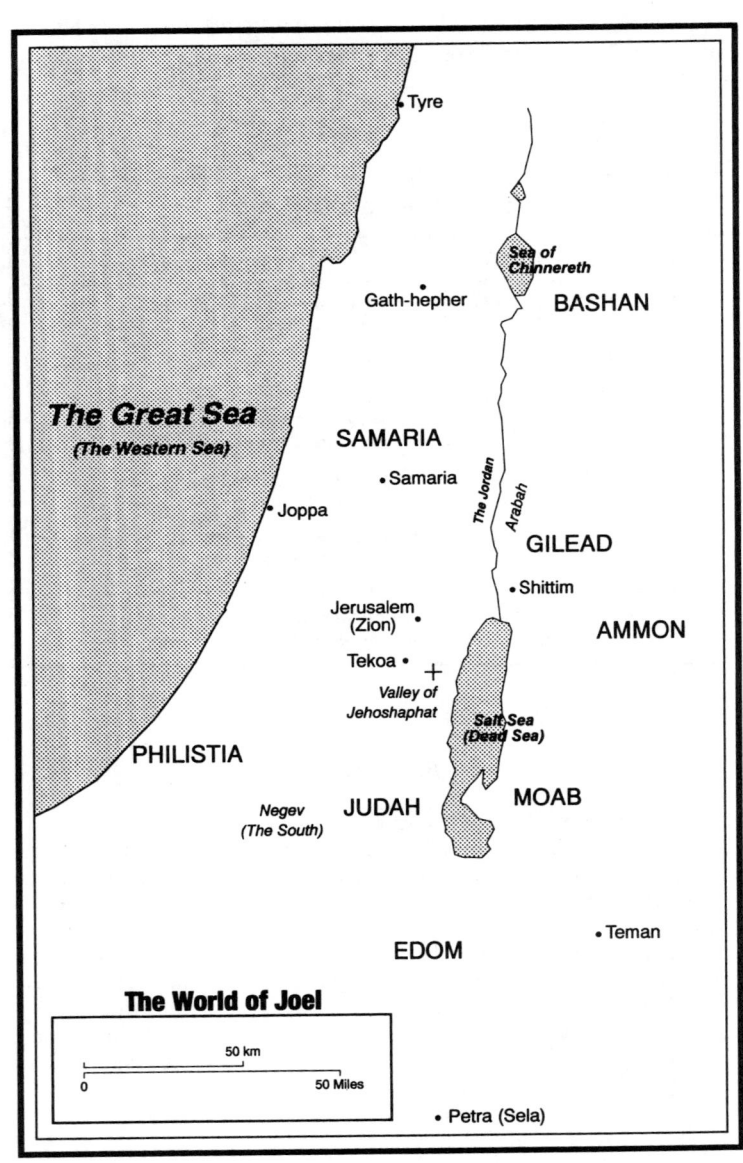

CHAPTER FOUR

The Day of the Lord
Joel 1

The judgment of God assumes many forms in Scripture. Yahweh is the Lord of nature. All the forces of nature are at his disposal in bringing discipline to wayward peoples. In the days of Joel, Israel experienced a devastating plague of locusts. The prophet interpreted this disaster as an effort to move Israel to repentance. At the same time this plague was a harbinger of a worse judgment to come.

A TRAGEDY TO MOURN
Looking Around
Joel 1:2-13

The Israelites had a tradition of holding special services of national lament in response to a variety of misfortunes (cf. Judg 20:26). Joel was convinced that the time had come for the community to meet in Jerusalem to hold such a service of lamentation in the temple. He addresses himself to five different groups within the community. The attention of each group is drawn to the way the locust plague impacted them.

A. Summons to the Elders (1:2-4).

The opening words of Joel are a call to receive instruction designed to arouse attentiveness: "Hear this!" Joel had a vital message for the people of Judah. He demanded the attention of his fellow citizens because his message came from God.

Joel first addressed the elders, who appear in this book as the real leadership group. Elders always were prominent in Israelite society; but in Joel's day they seem to have governed the land. During the minority of King Joash (835-817 BC) this would have been the case. The elders would have as their uppermost concern the well being of the entire community. Through the elders, Joel was addressing "all inhabitants of the land." His message was not a secret to be shared only with the elite. The entire community and its official leadership had a right and obligation to hear this word (1:2a).

Joel attempted to engage the attention of his audience by posing rhetorical questions, a technique used effectively by Isaiah and Jeremiah. Rhetorical questions challenge listeners to form their own independent judgment on issues. Joel wanted his audience to agree with him that the current crisis in Judah was unprecedented. He challenged the elders to search their national history for any incident which paralleled the current disaster (1:2b).

The momentous history which was unfolding before their eyes should be passed on to the coming generations. Posterity should remember this disaster. The directive to pass on the report of this calamity makes sense only if in this disaster people could perceive a word from Yahweh. A disaster of this magnitude must have some meaning. Somehow God's providence must be at work (1:3).

In verse 4 Joel finally describes the disaster. Israel had been hit by a fourfold blast. Joel uses four Hebrew words to designate the locusts. Scholars debate whether the prophet was thinking in terms of four waves of locusts, four species of locusts, or four stages of locusts' development. Modern scholarship prefers the latter interpretation.[1] Though the precise meaning of the four Hebrew terms used here is uncertain, the NASB attempts to bring out the connotation of the original: (1) gnawing locust, (2) swarming locust, (3) creeping locust, and (4) stripping locust. Three times Joel states that even the leftovers had been "devoured." The main point is that the locusts have left the land barren (1: 4).

Chart No. 13

DEVELOPMENTAL STAGES OF LOCUSTS Joel 1:4; 2:25			
HEBREW	**NKJV**	**PHYSICAL STAGE**	**EATING HABITS**
yelek "the lickers"	crawling locust	Hatchling	Consumes tender ground vegetation.
chasil "almost complete"	consuming locust	Hopper	Completes the destruction of tender vegetation.
gazam "branch snippers"	chewing locust	Winged Hopper	Attacks branches.
'arbeh "multiplying"	swarming locust	Mature Locust	Strips even bark.

B. Summons to the Drunkards (1:5-7).

After addressing those who were officially concerned about the current disaster, Joel issues a wake-up call for those who would be least concerned. Ordinarily drunkards care little about what goes on around them. They are content as long as they can have another shot of booze to numb their brains. Joel aimed to shock Judah's drunkards out of their stupor. No longer would they be able use alcohol as an escape mechanism. "Sweet wine" was the first product of the winepress. It was evidently a delicacy among these boozers. The locusts had snatched the wine from their lips by destroying the vineyards (1:5).

In explaining the disaster to the vineyards, Joel first emphasizes the colossal numerical strength of the locusts. An enemy "nation" was to blame for the devastation. This "nation" was "mighty and without number." Next Joel describes the enormous capacity of the insect army to inflict damage. Their powerful saw-edged teeth were as strong as those of a lion. Judah's vineyards were a waste. The locusts had stripped the bark from fig trees which often grew in the vineyards, leaving the branches white (1:6-7).

The emphasis here on *My* land, *My* vine and *My* fig tree gives the first hint that prayer for relief from the plague might be given a favorable hearing by Yahweh. God himself was involved in the suffering of his people. He was the landlord; Israel was the tenant. Therefore Yahweh had a vested interest in the devastation which the land was experiencing. Vine and fig tree were gifts bestowed on Israel by the heavenly Giver. Yet those gifts had now been taken away. The personal pronouns hint that the Creator himself is distressed by the devastation of the land which he loves.

C. Summons to City Dwellers (1:8-10).

The third group which Joel addresses is left unidentified except that the verbs are feminine singular. This suggests that Jerusalem is in view. The citizens of the city collectively are here regarded as a virgin daughter. Joel insists that a tragedy of monumental proportions had occurred which should evoke most bitter lamentation (1:8a).

The agony is compared to that which a betrothed virgin might feel at the death of her "husband," i.e., her fiancé (cf. Deut 22:22-29). Such a maiden would put aside her brilliantly ornamented wedding gown for sackcloth, the symbol of bitter agony. Sackcloth was a coarsely woven piece of material, generally made of goat's hair and therefore usually black. It was put on the bare body around the waist. Sackcloth was a visible representation of distress and humiliation.

For a young woman to lose to death the "bridegroom of her youth" (NASB) would be quite rare, but most bitter. The boisterous merrymaking of wedding preparation would give way to shrieks of emotional pain. Such is the lamentation which Joel urges upon the inhabitants of Jerusalem. The figure emphasizes the extremely rare, yet bitter, nature of the distress over which Jerusalem should now lament (1:8b).

The daily sacrifices at the temple gave rhythm to life in Jerusalem. Every morning and evening a lamb was sacrificed as a burnt offering. This was accompanied by an offering of meal moistened with oil and by a libation of wine. The locusts, however, had so devastated the land that the temple worship had been interrupted. The priests who found their joy in being "the ministers of Yahweh," i.e., the caretakers of his house, could no longer perform the required rituals. The priests lived on their portion of the daily offerings. So the priests mourned for themselves, as well as for all those who wished to reach out to God through the sacrificial system (1:9).

A drought[2] accompanied and intensified the locust invasion. Joel imagines the land itself mourning. The countryside joined the priesthood in lamenting the loss of oil, wine and grain. All three of the products were essential to the maintenance of the cultic activities of the temple. The ruined fields, however, could produce no grain. Olive groves and vineyards likewise failed to produce. The priests lamented because there was nothing to offer to the Lord (1:10).

D. Summons to the Farmers (1:11-12).

Joel next addressed those most immediately affected by the locust plague. He challenged those engaged in agriculture and viticulture to "be ashamed." Those being addressed—the "tillers" and "vinedressers"—were the landless peasants. For them life was defined by the annual production of the crop. Lack of a harvest was as much a disgrace for farmers as childlessness was for parents (cf. Ps 127:3-5). Failure to produce a crop was viewed as evidence that divine blessing had been withdrawn.

Joel reminded the farmers of the failure of their *wheat* and *barley* crops. Both of these cereals were among the most important crops in Palestine. Wheat was more highly valued because from it a better bread could be produced. Barley was the major component of the diet of the poorer people. Vines and fruit trees had "withered" and "dried up." Their roots could find no moisture with which to replenish the damage caused by the locusts (1:11-12a).

If the devastation in the fields, orchards and vineyards was not sufficient to move the farmers to tears, then Joel offers one more thought. Harvest time was the most joyous time of the year. Now there was no prospect of a harvest. As the crops gradually dried up, so did also the joy which the farming community anticipated all year (1:12b).

E. Summons to the Priests (1:13).

Joel called upon the priests to humble themselves. In the light of

1:9, this appeal is to be regarded as an encouragement to continue in the rites of lament in which they were already engaged. They should remove their ministerial robes and put on sackcloth (cf. 1:8). To dramatize the exceptional nature of the calamity, the priests were urged to wear the sackcloth during the night as well as the day. These actions would demonstrate the distress of the priests over the disruption of sacrificial ritual. Grain offerings and drink offerings could no longer be presented in the temple. With the daily sacrifice halted, so too was regular communion with God (v. 13).

Several phrases in 1:13 are especially noteworthy. The phrase "my God" underscores the authority of the prophet. Like all the prophets, Joel claimed a special insight into God's will. He therefore had the right to direct the priests in regard to national rites of mourning.

The suspension of the daily offerings has already been mentioned (cf. 1:9), but now Joel drove home how that affected the priests personally. The priests could no longer function as "ministers of the altar." The temple which now had been deprived of sacrificial gifts was "the house of your God." The maintenance of the sacrificial system was the main responsibility of the priests, and now that responsibility could no longer be fulfilled.

F. Issues in Interpretation.

The opening paragraphs of Joel raise two questions over which commentators are divided. First, is the account of the locust plague descriptive of something which already had happened, or predictive of a coming judgment? Second, is the description to be taken literally or are the locusts symbolic of great armies which would devastate the land? Nothing in the text suggests that the four kinds of locusts are symbolic of actual armies, e.g., the armies of Assyria, Babylon, Macedonia and Rome as suggested by Pusey. The best view is that Joel began to prophesy in the midst of an actual plague of locusts.

Researchers who have experienced twentieth century locust plagues in the Near East confirm the accuracy of Joel's graphic depiction. The mature desert locust has a wingspan of about four inches, and a body length of about three inches. Locusts look like large grasshoppers. Technically, what distinguishes a true locust from a large grasshopper is behavior. When conditions are right, grasshoppers that normally act as solitary individuals begin to swarm. Great clouds of the insects will rise during daylight hours in search of moist green vegetation. The sky can be blackened to an altitude of five thousand feet over tens of square miles. A swarm can contain over a billion creatures that, all together, can weigh more than three million pounds. When a species of grasshoppers exhibits this type of behavior they are called locusts.

Israel is the northernmost range of the migratory desert locusts. During a single day a locust swarm can travel sixty miles. During the course of a migration a swarm may move up to six hundred miles. In 1959 a locust plague in Ethiopia lasted six weeks. A conservative estimate is that these locusts consumed enough food to feed one million people for a year.[3]

Newly hatched locusts resemble ants or tiny roaches. Fully developed, these "hoppers" as they are called form marching bands up to ten miles wide and ten miles long. These bands move forward at a slow pace of about 250 feet per hour. Within their path they consume virtually every blade of grass or legume. No obstacle can stop this irresistible insect army.

A TIME TO PRAY
Looking Upward
Joel 1:14-20

Joel continued to address the priests. Now, however, he is no longer concerned about their own demonstrations of penance, but with those which they were to encourage the people to perform.

A. The Exhortation (1:14).

The priests were urged to "sanctify," i.e., set apart by solemn ceremonies for a solemn purpose, a fast for the entire nation. Only one fast was mandated in the Law of Moses. On the annual Day of Atonement every Israelite was to "afflict" his soul, i.e., his appetites. Fasting on other solemn occasions can be traced back to the period of the Judges (Judg 20:26; 1 Sam 7:6). Fasting was a sign of submission to the decreed calamity.

The priests were to summon all citizens, including the elders, to the temple. Usually such assemblies were limited to the elders or the heads of households. In this assembly (*'atsarah*) even sucking infants (cf. 2:16) would participate. The temple was the appropriate place for such an assembly because it was here that Yahweh as King of Israel gave audience to his subjects.

This assembly should "cry out unto Yahweh." Obviously they would pray for relief from the locust infestation. Surely they would also beg forgiveness that they might avoid an even worse calamity (v. 14). The verse underscores the power of fasting, assembling, and serious prayer in the midst of great loss. In this invocation of God the goal of the first chapter has been reached. Joel's main purpose has been to drive his audience to reach out to God.

B. The Explanation (1:15-18).

Joel next explained why a communal lamentation was necessary. He began his explanation with a cry of terror: "Alas for the day!" Things were bad in Judah. They would get worse. The dreadful "day of Yahweh" was near, the day in which God would settle accounts with his enemies (cf. Obad 15). The term *"day"* does not refer to a definite period of time but rather to an event. For those living in opposition to the will of God, that day would come as "destruction." As terrible as the locust plague had been, it was only a partial destruction. The day of Yahweh, however, would be a destruction from *Shaddai,* the Almighty.[4] An omnipotent destruction is a total destruction. Obadiah had spoken about the day of Yahweh affecting the Edomites. Here Joel insists that the inhabitants of Judah would also experience judgment on that day. The locust plague was but the harbinger of national destruction (1:15).

Joel again drew attention to the present calamity which was the prelude to "the day of Yahweh." First he alludes to the crop failure. The seed grain had shriveled under the clods of earth. This suggests that the seed had been plowed under before the beginning of the rainy season, or that it was sown as summer seed into parched land. Here drought is the cause of the distress (cf. 1:10,12). Since no harvest was anticipated, the flimsy storage bins had been allowed to fall apart. Such grain as did grow in the field had "dried up" (1:16-17).

Even livestock suffered because their pasture had been consumed. The large "beasts" were first affected. Eventually, however, even "herds of cattle," i.e., the smaller domesticated animals like goats and sheep, experienced the pangs of hunger. Joel thought of the groans of the suffering animals as a kind of prayer to the Creator for food. Thus sin indirectly affects all creation. These verses demonstrate the prophet's and Yahweh's sympathy for suffering animals (1:18).

C. The Example (1:19-20).

Whether or not the priests heeded Joel's call for national fasting and prayer, Joel prayed. Intercessory prayer was an essential part of the ministry of the Biblical prophets. His prayer is a model which others can follow in the national assembly for which Joel calls. While animals groan in complaint to the Creator, humans engage in rational communication with the deity. "To you, O Yahweh, I continue to call." The desperate conditions in Judah due to the double blast of locusts and drought compelled him to lift up his voice in narrative prayer. This type of prayer describes desperate conditions to God and obliquely requests relief.

Joel alludes to the "fire" and "flames" which had destroyed pastures and fruit trees. This may be a reference to the use of fire to divert the locusts. On the other hand, the prophet may have used fire as metaphorical of the drought or of the sound of the locusts in movement, i.e., they sounded like a forest fire driven by the wind. In any case, burnt pastures and dried up streams of water caused even the hardy wild animals to suffer. These animals were panting "for you," i.e., God. So men cry out to God, and animals pant after him. The point is, both are dependent upon the intervention of their Creator (1:19-20).

ENDNOTES

1. Hans W. Wolff, *Joel and Amos* (Philadelphia: Fortress, 1977), p. 27.
2. The Hebrew root *yabhash*—"dry up, wither"—is used seven times in Joel 1.
3. Harold Brodsky, "Locusts in the Book of Joel," *Bible Review* (Aug. 1990) pp. 33-39. The most authoritative discussion of a locust plague in

Palestine is by John D. Whiting, "Jerusalem's Locust Plague," *The National Geographic Magazine* 28 (Dec. 1915) pp. 511-550.

4. The term *Shaddai* is an ancient title for God associated with the Patriarchs (e.g., Gen 17:1). It appears occasionally also in the Psalms (e.g., Ps 68:14). Although the exact meaning of the term is unknown, an ancient tradition relates it to the concept of omnipotence.

CHAPTER FIVE

The Day of Healing
Joel 2:1-27

Chapter 1 addressed the current crisis of the locust plague. Chapter 2 anticipates a worse disaster to come, viz., the dreadful day of Yahweh. This impending judgment calls for repentance on the part of the people of Judah.

A TIME TO TAKE HEED
A Vision of Judgment
Joel 2:1-11

Joel 2:1-17 should not be viewed as a restatement, albeit in intensified form, of the call for national lamentation found in the first chapter. While it is clear that the locust plague shaped some of Joel's language in chapter 2, it is equally clear that he is describing a judgment which is subsequent to the locust plague. His essential message may be paraphrased like this: a worse "locust" plague is coming.

A. The Cry of Alarm (2:1-2).

Joel called for the trumpet *(shophar)* or ram's horn to be sounded. During the wilderness period the trumpet (1) summoned people to the tent of meeting; (2) signaled the start of camp movement; (3) sounded an alarm; and (4) announced a "holy convocation" (Num 10:1-10). Here the trumpet blast served as a warning.[1] The wall towers of ancient cities were manned by guards whose responsibility it was be on the alert for enemy attack and to sound the alarm when any suspicious movements were spotted. Here God himself functions as the watchman of Jerusalem. Through Joel he sounded the alarm for all to prepare for the approach of the enemy. God did not look for the city to respond by manning the ramparts, but by flocking to the temple for services of repentance and recommitment.[2]

The trumpet was to be sounded "in Zion." Zion in the Bible is used in several different senses. Geographical Zion was a rocky summit or fortress which David conquered from the Jebusites and on which he built his palace. After David's day the term "Zion" came to symbolize Jerusalem as the center of true worship. In the prophetic literature the term sometimes is used in a corporate sense, for the community, the government, the nation, or the kingdom whose earthly king resided in the place once called "Zion." Joel calls Zion "my holy hill," the only sanctuary of Yahweh recognized by the prophets.

The blast of the trumpet was to be a warning to "all the inhabitants of the land," i.e., citizens of both northern Israel as well as Judah. All who heard that sound should "tremble." The recent locust plague should have been Israel's wake-up call.

The alert was motivated not by the approach of just any powerful enemy; rather "the day of Yahweh" was coming, and that coming was near at hand. Some in Israel understood the "day of Yahweh" to be a time when Israel would triumph gloriously over all foes (cf. Amos 5:18). Not so! For impenitent Israel and Judah that day would be one of darkness and gloom, of clouds and blackness (cf. Zeph 1:15). Subsequent prophets used Joel's language in describing the day of God's judgment (1:1-2a).

As in the locust plague, in the day of Yahweh Zion would be approached by "a great and mighty people" (cf. 1:6). This coming enemy had never appeared before, nor would it ever appear again.

The recent locust plague was *unusual*; this future disaster would be *unique*.[3]

B. The Description of the Foe (2:3-11).

A "fire" burned before and behind this enemy army. The concept that when Yahweh approaches in judgment a fire burns before him is as old as Ps 97:3. The beautiful farm lands—like the garden of Eden in the eyes of farmers—would become a desert waste once God's judgment army had passed through. No escape from that judgment would be possible (2:3).

Having described the effect of the judgment army upon the land, Joel next described the army itself. This description is influenced strongly by the locusts which had already appeared. First, the enemy power looked like horses galloping across the ground. If Israel could barely stand before a hoard of tiny locusts, how would they endure the trampling of Yahweh's war horses? The terms "horses" and "war horses" here may designate the invincible chariot corps of Yahweh's army (2:4).

Second, he mentions the sound of the judgment army. As they came across the brow of a hill they sounded like chariots rumbling into combat or like a raging forest fire driven by the wind, or like a battle line surging forward in great tumult to the fray. These similes are intended to make the current buzzing of the locusts, as tremendous as it was, pale in insignificance (2:5).

Third, he describes the reaction to the judgment army. The approach of this dreadful army throws all peoples living in a region into panic; literally they writhe in terror. This language is elsewhere used of the day of Yahweh (cf. Isa 13:8; Ezek 30:16) and the approach of the enemy from the north (Jer 4:31). Joel is using language appropriate to a theophany or manifestation of Yahweh (cf. Ps 96:6). Thus the judgment army derives its significance from the presence of Yahweh himself (2:6).

In the course of its advance the judgment army shows itself to be a disciplined, irresistible conqueror. The focus shifts from the army collectively to the individual members of that army. Each has the skills of "mighty men" and "warriors." They "run" and "scale walls" and "march" in ranks never deviating from their course. Yahweh's judgment army cannot be stopped by acts of man any more than Judah had been able to stop the current locust plague. Joel says nothing here about the devastation done by the actual locust plague of his day. Nonetheless, he used the ceaseless advance of those insects as a model to describe what the day of Yahweh would be like for unrepentant sinners (2:7-8).

Yahweh's army would be skilled in the conquest of fortified cities. They would surmount walls and tear through defenses. They would run along the walls of the city. Like locusts searching out the last source of sustenance, they would force their way into houses. Barricaded doors would not deter them, for they would climb into houses through windows like thieves. No obstacle could stand in their path (2:9).

Cosmic upheavals accompany the approach of Yahweh with his judgment army. The "earth" would quake and then "heavens" would tremble. Sun, moon and stars would cease to give light. This is Joel's way of saying poetically that judgment day is a dark day, a tumultuous day (2:10).

In 2:11 Joel reaches the climax of his description of the judgment army. At the same time, this verse interprets what has been presupposed in the previous ten verses. First, the judgment army would be marshaled by Yahweh himself. He "utters his voice" (lit., "thunders") at the head of his army. He who in time past had been Jerusalem's protector, would now direct the attack against the city. Second, the numerous and powerful people of 2:2 are now identified as "Yahweh's camp." Third, this army is strong in the execution of the word of Yahweh. Fourth, what has been described in the preceding verses is the great and terrible "day of Yahweh." This explains the reaction of the nations in 2:6 and the universe in 2:10.

The description of the coming day of Yahweh concludes with this startling question:"Who can endure it?" (v. 11b). Merely raising that question suggests that those to whom Joel spoke were in no condition to survive that dreadful day. Judah had shown little ability to withstand the onslaught of insects; how much less would they be able to survive the march of Yahweh's army of wrath. Joel, however, did not mean to leave his people without hope. His question was more than rhetorical. In the next unit he will answer his own question.

A TIME TO REPENT
A Vision of Contrition
Joel 2:12-17

As terrible as the locust plague had been, this was not the last day, the final judgment. The devastating results of that plague should make all Israel aware of the need to repent.

A. The Nature of Repentance (2:12-13a).

The present crisis and impending day of Yahweh required immediate action. The term "now" establishes an agenda for the citizens. There is a logic to this word. There is also an urgency here. The action about to be recommended is the only one that can stem the tide of judgment. Should they fail to follow the prophetic prescription immediately, they will be swept away in the devastation described in the preceding verses. This was Israel's last chance.

The prophet stresses that his call for spiritual action is not merely a pragmatic suggestion by which they might postpone national destruction. Joel was presenting Yahweh's own summons to action. This he indicates by the words "declares Yahweh" *(ne'um Yahweh)*, the most solemn declaration of divine revelation possible in the Hebrew language. That the Lord himself invited repentance is an indication that real repentance would serve to assuage his holy anger.

The Hebrew word "return" *(shubh)* has the basic connotation of going back to the point where one got off the track. The word presupposes a covenant relationship with the Lord into which they should return. The preposition used here *('ad)* connotes arrival at the goal. Hence the Almighty called here for his people not just to turn in his direction, but to reestablish a shattered spiritual relationship.

Biblical repentance is not just a feeling or a fear. It is more than remorse and confession of sin. It goes beyond merely cessation of some conduct which may be causing personal distress. Repentance is a radical change of moral purpose implied in an honest renunciation of all sin and full surrender of heart and life to God. It is not just trimming the tree of sin, but cutting it down. It is not just turning over a new leaf, but casting away the old book.

Their "return" must be wholehearted. Yahweh would not be placated with a perfunctory show of repentance. Fasting and weeping would be outward manifestations of the sincerity of their repentance. Care, however, must be exercised that they do not substitute outward symbols for inward sincerity. Hence God called upon them to go beyond the traditional rituals of lamentation such as the tearing of their clothes. The classic cry of God through Joel is "rend your heart and not your garment." The "heart" to Joel was the center of moral purpose and resolve. Thus Yahweh was calling for a resolution of the will, a stout determination to obey the word of God.

True heart-felt repentance would display itself in various outward acts. In ancient Israelite culture heart-deep repentance surfaced in demonstrations of humility and distress. Here Yahweh called for three signs: fasting, weeping, and lamentation. Joel had already called for fasting as part of a national service of lamentation (cf. 1:14). In ancient Israel fasting served the purpose of indicating (1) self-renunciation; (2) submission to God and circumstances; and (3) earnestness in the petition which grew out of the fasting. Weeping and lamentation were evidence of sorrow over a life of sin.

A missing ingredient in this particular call for repentance is the mention of any particular sins of which Israel should repent. Obviously Joel viewed the locust plague as a punishment for violation of covenant stipulations. He apparently left it to the people to search their own hearts for evidence of the sin for which they had been suffering. A humble heart engaged in introspection will not be long discovering that which offends the Lord.

B. Inducements to Repentance (2:13b-14).

The Lord always accompanies demands for radical change with inducements of sufficient weight to persuade sinners to submit to his will. First, he speaks the wonderful name. They should return to Yahweh. That name had particular significance for the Israelites. Under that name the Almighty delivered Israel from Egyptian bondage. Under that name he entered into a covenantal relationship with that nation. That glorious name would evoke in the minds of Joel's audience recollections of past deliverances, triumphs and blessings.

Second, the special relationship between Israel and Yahweh is indicated in the phrase "your God." Yahweh had a special claim upon

Israel and vice versa. For better or worse he had married Israel at Sinai. As sinful and rebellious as they had become, they were still his people.

Third, Joel speaks of the nature of Yahweh (cf. Exod 34:6). He is "gracious and compassionate" to those who seek his face. The word "gracious" points to the favorable disposition which a superior party shows to one who is inferior. "Merciful" describes parental care for the life of one who is helpless and endangered. He is "slow to anger," i.e., he exercises great patience with the fallen sons of Adam. He is "abounding in covenant faithfulness." This expression refers to the abundance of kind deeds, great and small, by which relationships are built and affirmed.

Fourth, Joel reminds his audience that Yahweh "relents concerning calamity." He acknowledges a change on the part of his people by canceling or postponing a threatened calamity.

Fifth, sometimes God goes beyond mercy (i.e., withholding a punishment justly due) and bestows grace upon his people, i.e., he gives them something they do not deserve. Joel cannot guarantee God will so act in this present situation. His nature and past record would suggest the great possibility that sincere repentance on the part of Israel would cause Yahweh to "return" to a previous positive disposition toward them and to "relent" (NIV "have pity") respecting the present calamity and threatened worse calamity to follow.

Yet God is sovereign. Past experience is not an infallible guide to what God might do in the present or in the future. Perhaps Yahweh would cause his locusts to leave behind a small blessing—enough grain for an offering and enough wine for a libation in the temple. Even in that dark hour worship was uppermost in the mind of the prophet. "The 'perhaps' of hope is appropriate to the humility of one who prays; in the proclamation of the messenger it underscores the fact that the one called to return stands, for the time being, under the message of judgment and has to face up to it."[4]

C. Prescription for Repentance (2:15-17).

Joel did not leave his audience in the dark as to exactly what steps should be taken to demonstrate national repentance. Speaking specifically to the priests, he repeats the instructions of 1:14 and 2:1.

They should (1) blow the trumpet *(shophar)* in Zion; (2) sanctify a fast; and (3) call an assembly (2:15).

They should "sanctify the congregation" *(qahal),* i.e., the people assembled for worship. The term "sanctify" in this context means to make complete preparations for worship. In the Old Testament dispensation that would involve such things as desisting from work, food, and sexual intercourse (cf. 1 Sam 21:5). The holy assembly should include (1) the people, (2) the elders—here probably the older citizens rather than the office holders, (3) the children, (4) the infants, (5) the newly married, and, of course, (6) the priests. The entire population must be involved. All joyous activity must cease. Even the newly married, generally excused from civil responsibility for one year, are to be present. National repentance was the necessity of the hour, and all segments of society must be present (2:16).

The priests should lead out in the national mourning. As those who "minister before Yahweh" the priests led the great festivals when joy was the order of the day. So now they must officiate when the national mood should be one of sorrow. The priests were to stand in the temple court "between the porch and the altar." The priests were to congregate in their customary place in the inner court, while the laity assembled in the outer one. Presumably they directed their prayer of intercession toward the temple in the spirit of 1 Kings 8 (2:17a).

Joel leaves nothing to chance. He even structures a prayer for the priests to use at the solemn assembly. The prayer contains two petitions. First, they should begin with the strongest possible appeal to Yahweh: "Spare your people!" In the Hebrew this is an emphatic imperative. Second, they should plead that Yahweh would not cause them to be put to shame by permitting foreign nations to "rule over them" (NKJV).[5] The focus of the prayer which Joel recommends is "the destruction of Jerusalem as the people of God in the midst of the surrounding nations."[6]

The two petitions are linked with phrases which form oblique incentives for Yahweh to act. The phrase "your people" acknowledged their relationship to Yahweh, and at the same time used this relationship as an inducement for the Lord to respond favorably to their cry. The phrase "your inheritance" likewise reminded the Lord had he had a vested interest in the fate of this people. Yahweh's inheritance was the land of Israel.

The end of national Israel as the covenant people is involved in the threat of the day of Yahweh. If both the people of Israel and the land of Israel were totally destroyed, then Gentiles would conclude that the God of Israel must be impotent. They would mockingly ask "Where is their God?" The essence of this priestly prayer recommended by Joel is that God's honor is at stake in the fate of his people (2:17b).

This model prayer is the climax of Joel's efforts to move the people from indifference to the things of God. The tone of the prayer suggested urgency. The content of the prayer underscored their inability to save themselves. Only Yahweh can save them. They must therefore cast themselves upon his mercy and trust his grace.

The second half of Joel answers the mocking question which Gentiles would ask when the nation of Israel experienced destruction and exile. God's program and people in this world would not come to an end. After judgment would come restoration, vindication and glorification.

A TIME TO HEAL
A Vision of Restoration
Joel 2:18-29

Joel envisioned how Yahweh would respond to national repentance. The immediate result of repentance would be the removal of the locust plague. In the more distant future, God would send a wonderful teacher to those who were humble of heart to receive him.

A. The Plague Removed (2:18-22).

First, Yahweh would be "zealous" for his land, driving out the locusts which were devastating it. Second, he would take "pity" on his people. Immediate physical needs would be supplied first—grain, wine and oil. Third, Yahweh would answer his people, i.e., respond to their cries for help, with a positive word. The divine proclamation is introduced with a formula pledging immediate intervention. Joel uses the interjection "Behold! (*hineni*) plus a participle to express imminent action: "I am about to send you grain, etc." Once Yahweh's people have enough to fully satisfy them, the reproach of the land and people would be removed. The coming deliverance would prove to the heathen that Israel's God can indeed do mighty things (2:18-19).

The change of fortune envisioned by Joel would come about because God would drive "the northerner," i.e., the locusts, out of the land. Apparently the locust plague of Joel's day, like the similar plague of 1915, came from the north. That insect army would be driven into "the parched and desolate" desert, into "the eastern (Dead) sea, and into the western (Mediterranean) sea. The stench of decaying locusts would be a pleasant odor to those who had suffered such devastation in this plague. The destruction of this innumerable army will enable believers to declare that "he has done great things" (2:20).

In view of the impending deliverance from the locusts—the "great things" which God was about to do—Joel bids the land to replace fear with gladness and rejoicing. "Do not fear" is the traditional introduction to an oracle of salvation with which Yahweh might respond to a lamentation by his people (cf. Lam 3:57). The command to end fear occurs frequently in the context of an enemy attack (e.g., Num 21:34; Josh 8:1). The land and indirectly even the animals have been attacked by the locusts. Neither had anything further to fear from the insect invaders. The open pastures would again become green, the fruit trees would again produce in abundance (2:21-22).

Joel intends in this paragraph to reverse the bad news which he was forced to deliver in the opening chapter of the book. Whereas joy and gladness were absent from the land (1:16), now he twice urges both upon the people (2:21,23). Whereas the land had experienced a drought (1:17-20), now an abundance of rain would fall (2:23). The wild beasts which had suffered (1:20) would now have abundant pasture. The pastures which were barren (1:19-20) would again be clothed with green verdure (2:22). Fruitless trees (1:19) would again produce fruit (2:22). Repentance is the key which unlocks the bounty of God's grace. In chapter 1 Joel called upon drunkards, farmers and priests to lament (1:5,8,11,13). Now he calls on land, beasts and people to rejoice (2:21-23).

B. The Coming Teacher (2:23-27).[7]

Joel exhorted the "sons of Zion," i.e., covenant people (cf. Lam 4:2; Ps 149:2), by faith to join the animal and vegetable kingdoms in celebrating the blessing which God had in store for the land. Their joy should first of all be in Yahweh himself, and especially in the fact that he was, in a very special way, *their* God. The primary reason the sons of Zion can confidently endure the temporal calamities is because of their longstanding messianic hope. God would some day give to them the "Teacher unto righteousness." None of the standard modern translations have rendered accurately the Hebrew text at this point.[8]

That Joel 2:23 contains personal messianic prophecy was the dominant view of the early Jewish and Christian writers. Modern authorities have tended to shy away from this position because of the problem of relating a personal messianic interpretation to the context. The text, however, brings out several wonderful truths regarding the promised Messiah.

1. Messiah would be a teacher (*hammoreh*). The Hebrew text actually uses the definite article. He would be *the* Teacher *par excellence*. Teaching would be part of his priestly function.[9] In some passages God himself is called Teacher (Job 36:22; Isa 30:20) or is said to exercise the teaching function (Isa 2:3).

2. Messiah is a divine *gift* to God's people. This thought is echoed by Isaiah: "Unto us a child is given" (Isa 9:6); and "I have given him as a Witness to the peoples" (Isa 55:4).

3. The object of Messiah's coming is *righteousness*. The Teacher would be virtually a personification of what is right. Later prophets would refer to him as "the righteous servant" (Isa 53:11), and as one who would usher in "everlasting righteousness" (Dan 9:24).

4. Joel depicts the blessing which results from Messiah's coming in terms of rain and resultant physical prosperity. Yahweh would give the people the Teacher, and then he would let the rain come down, the *early rain* and the *latter rain*. Through this rain he would give to the land fertility and life.[10] Threshingfloors and vats would overflow (2:24). Jesus used a similar figure to describe the blessings which would come to disciples who generously shared in the work of the kingdom (Luke 6:38).

In that day of great blessing, past judgments would be forgotten. The damage inflicted by the locusts on vineyards and orchards over the years would be recompensed a thousand fold. Instead of the locusts eating the land, God's people would eat and be filled with the good things provided by the Teacher.[11] The sons of Zion would praise the name of Yahweh who provided through the messianic Teacher such abundant blessing. Never again would God's people have reason to be ashamed because of the apparent withdrawal of divine favor. To all those who would live to see that day it would be clear that the Lord was in their midst (2:25-27). Because of his words, his deeds, his death and subsequent resurrection the early Christians became convinced that God had visited them in a very special way in the person of Jesus. He was Immanuel, "God with us" (Matt 1:23).

ENDNOTES

1. The raucous sound of the *shophar* may have been used in an attempt to drive away the locusts. Harold Brodsky, "Locusts in the Book of Joel," *Bible Review* (Aug. 1990) p. 39.

2. Leslie Allen, *The Books of Joel, Obadiah, Jonah and Micah* in "The New International Commentary on the Old Testament" (Grand Rapids: Eerdmans, 1976) p. 67.

3. Hans Wolff, *Joel and Amos* (Philadelphia: Fortress, 1977) p. 42.

4. *Ibid.,* p. 50.

5. The Hebrew expression elsewhere is always rendered "to rule over" and that is how the ancient translations have rendered it. NIV and NASB have followed the modern trend which interprets 2:1-17 as referring to the locust plague. Wolff (*op. cit.,* p. 52) has argued that the "the numerous and mighty people" of 2:2 is the judgment army led by Yahweh himself. There is therefore no reason to depart from the usual translation in 2:17.

6. Wolff, *ibid.*

7. The discussion of Joel 2:23-27 is a summary of the discussion in the author's *What the Bible Says About the Promised Messiah* (Nashville: Nelson, 1993) pp. 220-229.

8. For example, KJV = "he has given you the former rain moderately;" ASV = "he has given you you the former rain;" RSV = "he has given you the early rain;" NIV = "he has given you a teacher for righteousness;" NASB= "he has given you the early rain." For a discussion of the translation of Joel 2:23 see Smith, *ibid.* pp. 225-227.

9. In Ps 84:6 *moreh* is translated *rain* in KJV and NIV. Even here the meaning *teacher* seems preferable.

10. The word for *early rain* is *moreh*, the same word which was translated *teacher* in the previous line. The usual word for former rain is *yoreh*. This deliberate play on words—in fact the creation of a new word—may be Joel's signal that the rain of which he speaks is metaphorical. It is Messiah's rain.

11. Cf. John 6:27,33,35,48-51,53.

CHAPTER SIX

The Day of the Spirit
Joel 2:28-3:21

The closing unit of Joel answers the mocking question which Gentiles would ask when the nation of Israel experienced destruction and exile. God's program and people in this world would not come to an end. After judgment would come restoration, salvation, vindication and glorification.

RESTORATION
A Vision of Blessing
Joel 2:28-29

After the coming of the Teacher unto righteousness, God promised to send his Spirit *(ruach)*. The reference is to the Holy Spirit, the third person of the Godhead. Old Testament prophets regarded the Spirit as the hallmark of the messianic age. The Spirit would effect a new creation (Isa 32:15; 44:3f.). Messiah himself was depicted as anointed with God's Spirit (Isa 42:1; 61:1). Joel now explores the ramifications of that coming day of the Spirit.

A. The Outpouring of the Spirit (2:28-29).

The Spirit would be "poured out." This verb *(shaphach)* points to the abundant measure of the gift. The verb is used figuratively, for it would not be possible literally to "pour out" a person, and the Holy Spirit is a person. Peter declared that on Pentecost the enthroned Messiah had "poured out" all which was seen and heard in the temple courts (Acts 2:33).

The Spirit would be poured out "on all flesh," i.e., all kinds of people, Jew and Gentile alike.[1] Needless to say the gift is only available to those who receive it. In Old Testament times the Spirit endowed chosen individuals for leadership or other skills. In the messianic age a more general dispensing of the Spirit was anticipated by the prophets (cf. Ezek 39:29; Zech 12:10). Joel stresses that the Spirit would be poured out regardless of sex, age, or societal status. Even lowly servants would receive the Spirit in those days. Paul would later echo the same thought with regard to those who are in Christ (Gal 3:28). Peter was probably alluding to the phrase "your sons and your daughters" when he told the Jews on Pentecost that the promise [of the Spirit] was "to you and to your children" (Acts 2:39).

The outpouring of the Spirit would inaugurate a new age of revelation. Recipients of the Spirit would "prophesy." The Spirit is frequently linked to prophecy in the Old Testament (Num 11:25; Mic 3:8). Visions and revelatory dreams would also be evidence of the commencement of that Spirit age. Visions and dreams were two means by which God revealed his will to prophets (Num 12:6).

B. The Fulfillment of the Prophecy.

The Apostle Peter identified the fulfillment of Joel's prophecy of the outpouring of the Spirit. The crowds heard the Apostles speaking in the temple courts in languages they had never studied. Some among the perplexed multitude thought the Apostles were drunk. Peter pointed out that the early hour made it highly improbable that they were under the influence of wine. He then went on to affirm that "this is what was spoken of through the prophet Joel" (Acts 2:16).

Those witnessing the Pentecost demonstration realized that Joel's prediction involved much more than they were witnessing that day. Joel's prophecy contemplated an outpouring of the Holy Spirit,

THE DAY OF THE SPIRIT   JOEL 2:28-3:21

not only on the men then before them, but on "all flesh," i.e., persons of all nationalities. Peter must have meant—and his audience must have understood him to mean—that the age of the Holy Spirit began on that Pentecost. Within a decade the household of Cornelius, a Gentile soldier, received the same outpouring of the Spirit experienced by the Apostles on Pentecost (Acts 11:15). Philip had four virgin daughters who prophesied (Acts 21:9). Certain women in the church at Corinth also prophesied (1 Cor 11:5). Thus Pentecost marked the beginning of the fulfillment of Joel's words.

SALVATION
Vision of Deliverance
Joel 2:30-32

The age of the coming of the Teacher and the outpouring of the Spirit would also involve a time of judgment. Many rejected the message of the Teacher and the witness of the Spirit. Upon these a terrible judgment would be poured out. This judgment would be preceded by warning signs. Those who called upon the name of the Lord in those days would be spared the ordeal of this judgment.

A. Warning Signs (2:30-31).

Warning signs in both heaven and earth would call sinners to repentance. On earth [or "in the land"] men would see "blood, fire and billows of smoke," i.e., bloody wars accompanied by burning cities. Jesus warned of wars and rumors of wars which would precede "the end," i.e., the destruction of Jerusalem by the Romans. Jesus warned his disciples to flee Jerusalem when they observed certain signs unfolding (Matt 24:15-21). That is exactly what the Christians did. They escaped the carnage of that terrible AD 68-70 tribulation by fleeing to Pella across the Jordan river.

In the heavens "the sun will be turned to darkness and the moon to blood." Some take this language literally. They point to Josephus and Tacitus for testimony that before the fall of Jerusalem to the Romans in AD 70 ominous heavenly signs were witnessed by both Jews and Romans. Those physical omens betokened the greater tragedy which was taking place, viz., "the Jewish church and Hebrew commonwealth went out in darkness."[2] Based on Gen 1:16, the sun and moon would represent rulers both superior and inferior. Jesus added that the stars would fall from the sky (Matt 24:29). These words recall Dan 12:3 where God's people are likened to stars (cf. Rev 12:4).

The signs on earth and in the heavens would precede "the great and awesome day of Yahweh." These words have been variously interpreted as a reference to the Roman destruction of Jerusalem, the final day of judgment, or even to the day of Pentecost itself. The immediate reference here is to the Roman destruction of Jerusalem in AD 70. Yet every judgment in history is a forerunner of the final eschatological judgment with which time ends and eternity begins.

B. Wondrous Salvation (2:32).

During the period preceding the ultimate rejection of national Israel (AD 70)—the period of signs and wonders—"whoever calls upon the name of Yahweh will be delivered" (2:32). The action of "calling" on God involves faith, repentance, and baptism (cf. Acts 22:16). On the day of Pentecost Peter quoted these verses from Joel. When pressed by his audience, the apostle told his auditors how to call upon the name of Yahweh. "Repent and be baptized each one of you in the name of Jesus Christ for the forgiveness of your sins; and you will receive the gift of the Holy Spirit" (Acts 2:38; cf. 22:16). He urged those Jewish sinners to "be saved from this perverse generation" (Acts 2:40).

In those days of the outpouring of the Spirit, the signs and wonders God would gather "those who escape." Those who are saved from coming judgment—who escape the wrath of God—would be gathered into a body. In Old Testament language Joel is announcing the establishment of the church of Jesus Christ.

Joel depicts the body of the saved being "on Mount Zion and in Jerusalem." Certainly on that Pentecost when the Gospel was first proclaimed in its fullness, the three thousand who responded in obedient faith were literally in Jerusalem and on Mount Zion. The words of Joel, however, have a deeper meaning. "Zion" and "Jerusalem" were types of the church of Christ. As God had his temple—his sanctuary and earthly habitation—in geographical Jerusalem in Old Testament times, so in the messianic age his temple is the church. Thus wherever the church is, there is Zion and Jerusalem. New Testament writers are not reluctant to proclaim this truth. Christians are said to have "come to Mount Zion" (Heb 12:22) and to be part of the "Jerusalem from above" (Gal 4:26).

The saved who are gathered to spiritual Mount Zion come from among "the survivors whom Yahweh calls." Peter on Pentecost incorporated this phrase into his appeal for commitment to Christ on the part of his audience. "For the promise is for you and your children, and for all who are far off, as many as the Lord our God shall call unto him" (Acts 2:39). Through presenting the facts about the enthronement of Christ and his plan of salvation, God had been calling those who assembled on Pentecost. The 'promise" of salvation—the forgiveness of sins and the gift of the Holy Spirit—could be claimed by subsequent generations ("your children") and even by "all that are afar off," i.e., Gentiles who heeded God's Gospel call. Paul makes it clear that the call of God to salvation comes through human messengers who are sent forth to preach the Gospel (Rom 10:10-13).

Joel was not the first to speak of the saved gathered together on Mount Zion. The phrase in 2:32 "as Yahweh has said" is probably a reference to the prophecy of Obadiah 17: "And on Mount Zion will be those who escape."

VINDICATION
A Vision of Judgment
Joel 3:1-15

A glorious future for God's people must include a removal of the enemies which constantly threaten, harass and persecute them. The events predicted in Joel are connected to what precedes by two devices. First, the word "for" suggests a logical connection between chapters 2 and 3. Joel would now amplify the glories of messianic salvation to which he just alluded. The phrases "in that day and at that time"[3] ties chapter 3 to chapter 2 time-wise. The events recorded here take place in the dispensation which followed the outpouring of the Spirit on Pentecost. The plural "days," however, suggests that a period of time rather than a specific point in time is in view. This makes it impossible to identify the judgments with specific events in history.[4]

A. Future Enemies (3:1-3).

For God's people the future was bright. God would "turn the captivity of Judah and Jerusalem" (3:1) This language does not refer to a restoration of the Israelites from captivity in foreign lands. Both the prophetic context here (the messianic age) and the usage of this language elsewhere in prophetic literature (e.g., Amos 9:14) require another explanation. The language basically suggests the elevation to a higher position of dignity and greater prosperity than had previously been experienced.[5] Thus in the messianic age Israel experienced metamorphosis. The old nationalistic Israel with its physical temple gave way to a new Israel of the Spirit, an Israel without geographical boundaries, an Israel that embraced all who declared faith in Jesus Christ.

While God's people ("Judah and Jerusalem") have a great future, "the nations," i.e., Gentiles, do not. All the nations will be brought down to the "valley of Jehoshaphat" (3:12).The reference seems to be to the valley or plain *('emeq)* where some fifty years before Joel, God had annihilated an enemy which was invading Judah (2 Chr 20:1-30). For Joel the valley of Jehoshaphat represents defeat for enemies and the deliverance of the people of God. Manifestly Joel was not thinking geographically.[6] No valley in Palestine could contain *all* the nations. His point is that God would subdue Gentiles in the future who attack his people just as he did in the days of good king Jehoshaphat.

The Lord would enter into judgment with the Gentile nations. The Hebrew verb form points to a lawsuit in which Yahweh is at first not the judge, but the plaintiff. Yahweh enters judgment "on behalf of my people and my inheritance" (3:2). As the people of God, Judah and Jerusalem also bear the name "Israel" (3:2a).

The question here to be resolved is whether this prophecy should be interpreted specifically of some group which attacked God's people, or whether it merely sets forth a principle which is always true, viz., that God will protect his own. The time frame of this judgment is "in those days," i.e., the days of the outpouring of the Spirit, the wonders in the heavens, the wars on earth, and the darkening of sun and moon. The enemies which came against God's land and people in this period were the Romans.

Three charges are leveled against those nations which God would judge in the valley of Jehoshaphat. First, they had scattered Israel, like sheep (cf. Jer 50:17), among the nations. In Joel's day the great scattering by the kings of Assyria and Babylon were many years in the future. Yet the scattering of the covenant people among the nations had been anticipated as early as the days of Moses (cf. Lev 26:33). The terms "my people and my possession" convey the divine outrage at the audacity of the heathen. They had taken away that which belonged to the Lord. Yahweh deeply resented the way his private possession had been treated. The traditional Old Testament enemies, Assyria and Babylon, practiced mass deportation of captive peoples.

Second, the enemies had "divided up my land." Here again Yahweh was directly affected by violence done by the Gentiles. Often soldiers of a conquering army were rewarded by being assigned plots of ground in the captured territory. Such confiscation of land accompanied the Babylonian conquest of Judah in 586 BC (Lam 5:2).

Third, they had shown no respect for life. They "cast lots[7] for my people." God's people were regarded as loot to be apportioned by lottery. The lives of Judean children were considered cheap. Little boys were sold as payment for a brief fling with a prostitute. Little girls were regarded as worth no more than the temporary gratification afforded by wine (3:2b-3).[8]

B. Present Enemies (3:4-8).

Before Joel describes the final judgment, he pauses to point out the bitter hostility of the neighboring nations of his own day, viz., Phoenicia and Philistia. Though much stronger than Judah, these nations were worthless and despicable in Yahweh's sight. "What are you to me?" God asks. The Living God was not impressed with the resurgent military power of the Philistines or the burgeoning commercial empire of Tyre and Sidon. In attempting to repay Judah for past actions, these Gentiles were in reality "recompensing" Yahweh himself. The point is that to attack God's people is to attack God. The spiteful deeds of these Gentile peoples would be swiftly repaid by Yahweh (3:4).

In 3:4 Yahweh plays the role of a prosecuting attorney. He fires indignant questions at the defendants (Philistia and Phoenicia). Then in his role as judge he announces the retribution upon them. Two charges are lodged against these nations. First, these neighbors had looted God's temple. Yahweh's gold and silver and other treasures now adorned pagan temples (3:5). Putting that captured temple treasure in the shrine of an idol signaled in the ancient mind the victory of the pagan god over the God of Israel. The background here is probably the same as that of Obadiah. See 2 Chr 21:16,17.

Second, Joel accuses the neighbors of slave trade at the expense of the sons of Judah and Jerusalem. Jewish slaves had been sold to Greek traders. That was sin enough. The guilt was double, however, because these captives had been far removed from their territory. By sending them so far away from Judah any chance of their return had been minimized. No divine mandate authorized that these neighboring nations deprive God's people of their God-given land and liberty (3:6). Amos would later condemn this same sin in these two peoples (Amos 1:6,9).

The judgment against Philistia and Phoenicia would be most appropriate. First, God would "arouse" those captive Jews in distant lands. The arousal may be spiritual as well as physical. Alexander and his successors set many Jews free within their empire. A restoration and empowerment of Jews is thus envisioned. By means of this revitalized Jewish community, God would "return your recompense on your head," i.e., they would experience the same indignities at the hands of the Jews which they had inflicted upon them. Philistines and Phoenicians would be sold to wealthy Jews who in turn would sell them to the desert dwelling Sabeans (3:7-8).[9]

In this passage the mistreatment of God's people is redressed, but not the sin of temple looting. In the announcement of judgment that sin is passed over. Perhaps this is a subtle suggestion that with God people count more than things.

The threats against Philistia and Phoenicia conclude with a formula of divine attestation: *Thus has Yahweh spoken.* What has just been expressed is not the consensus of contemporary opinion, nor the personal malicious desire of Joel. This threat is an expression of the solemn decree of God. Thus it most certainly would be fulfilled.

In Old Testament times both Uzziah and Hezekiah warred against the Philistines. During the intertestamental period the Maccabean rulers did the same. Philistia was totally dominated by Judea. As for the Phoenicians, they were cruelly conquered and enslaved by Alexander the Great in 332 BC and by Antiochus III in 245 BC. Thousands were taken captive. Many, no doubt, were sold to Jews who prospered greatly in the early Greek period.

C. All Enemies Summoned (3:9-11).

The doom of all those who attack God's people is announced in a somewhat unusual way. Messengers—probably angels—were to summon all Gentiles to prepare for war (cf. Jer 6:4). The command to "draw near" is used for the advance into battle (cf. Jer 46:3). The command to "come up" means to ascend into the mountains of Israel in the direction of Jerusalem (3:9). The ultimate battle is in view, the final showdown between good and evil.

The battle summons is full of irony. The coming conflict is so serious that these adversaries are urged to secure as many weapons as possible. They should even beat their plowshares into swords and their pruning hooks into spears. All available manpower would be needed. A total mobilization of surrounding nations against God and his people is envisioned. Even the physically weak and psychological misfits were not to be exempt. This huge army represents all the forces—physical, spiritual, intellectual—which have been hostile to God's people. These forces had many times separately attacked Jerusalem. Now they unite and hasten to return to the venue of their sin where they will face their doom (3:10-11a).

Some think that Joel contradicts the message of Isaiah (2:4) and Micah (4:3). Those eighth century prophets envisioned the Gentiles coming to Jerusalem in great numbers to learn from the God of Jacob. They would beat their swords into plowshares and their spears into pruning hooks. Those nations which came to that glorious Jerusalem would be at peace with one another. They would become citizens of messianic Jerusalem. Yet neither Isaiah nor Micah said that all nations would come. Joel contemplates the fate of those Gentiles who remain hostile to Jerusalem even after the glorious age of Messiah began.

As Joel in his vision sees the vast host approaching Jerusalem he offered up the second intercessory prayer attributed to him in the book: "Bring down, O Yahweh, your mighty ones." (3:11b). He prays that the Lord of hosts, the mighty divine warrior, would use the vast power of invisible armies to defeat Jerusalem's adversaries. At this point the text begins to make clear that the summons to battle is in reality a summons to doom (cf. Isa 8:9-10; Jer 46:3-6, 9-10).

D. All Enemies Destroyed (3:12-15).

Following his call for the nations to assemble against Jerusalem, Joel presents several pictures which reveal what would befall those enemies.

1. A judicial scene (3:12). The first picture is a judgment scene. The locale as in 3:2 is the "valley of Jehoshaphat." The Lord himself urges the hostile nations to enter that valley. There Yahweh would sit to judge all surrounding nations. "To judge" in Hebrew means not only to listen to evidence and deliver the verdict, but to execute the sentence as well. Here the emphasis of the word is clearly on condemnation and punishment (cf. 1 Sam 3:13). Ancient rulers would sit to render judgment. Joel is claiming that Yahweh is the king of all nations. The means of judgment is not clearly stated here, but the larger context suggests that war is envisioned. The Old Testament often depicts war as the medium of God's justice against wicked peoples.

This picture of the destruction of approaching armies may be based on the record of 2 Chr 20. A coalition of enemies bent on overrunning Judah met with calamity in the valley of Jehoshaphat. They destroyed themselves before the army of Judah arrived to confront them. All those who would harm God's people would meet with similar fate.

2. A harvest scene (3:13). The second picture is that of a vineyard ripe for harvest. Angels are directed to "put in the sickle, for the harvest is ripe." The term "sickle" (*maggal*) in this context probably refers to a vintage knife. The verb "to ripen" (*bashal*) suggests ripening of grapes. Clusters of grapes were piled up in a wine press, ready to be crushed. Both the cutting of the grapes as well as the subsequent treading of them symbolize punishment. The "wine press" (*gat*) was an upper basin where the grapes were smashed usually by treading upon them with bare feet. The "wine vat" was a receptacle at a lower level into which the juice from the press flowed by gravity. The overflowing vat symbolizes the excessive sin on the part of these nations.[10]

3. *A crowd scene (3:14).* The third picture is a crowd scene. Joel sees uncounted multitudes. The Hebrew noun contains sound effects as well as a visual image. It is repeated ("multitudes, multitudes") to stress the size of the crowd and the tumult which was being made. All of these stand in the "valley of decision," or "Verdict Valley" as Allen calls it. This is a new designation for the valley of Jehoshaphat in 3:2. God must render the final decision regarding the fate of these enemies. That is "the day of Yahweh" to which all temporal judgments throughout history have pointed.

4. *An astronomical scene (3:15).* The fourth picture is an astronomical one. Sun, moon and stars go dark (3:15). The association of darkness and final judgment is frequent in the Bible (e.g., Matt 8:12; 22:13, 25:30). The idea is that nature is horrified at the approach of Yahweh in judgment. Joel does not dwell on the carnage which would accompany the Gentile attack against Zion. It was enough to depict the reaction of the heavenly bodies. If sun, moon and stars shrink before the approach of Yahweh, mere mortal man would have no chance of success. Thus the darkening of the heavenly bodies signals a terrible slaughter upon which the creation itself does not wish to gaze.

GLORIFICATION
A Vision of Ultimates
Joel 3:16-21

The closing verses of Joel draw a sharp contrast between the fate of the wicked and the righteous. Zion would enjoy God's richest blessings. Zion's enemies would experience desolation and devastation.

A. The Strength of Zion (3:16).

The thunder of Yahweh's voice which was sounded in connection with the locust plague (2:11) is now heard again. This thunderclap sounds the death knell for enemies who were attacking

Jerusalem. It is from *Zion,* the center of God's earthly revelation, that the voice of Yahweh sounds forth. Heaven and earth tremble at his mighty voice. For his people, however, Yahweh is a "refuge." He is "a stronghold" to the sons of Israel, i.e., the true people of God. He is both the strength and hope of his people.

B. The Holiness of Zion (3:17).

The goal of Yahweh's dealings with the nations in the "day of Yahweh" is that all men—especially those of the covenant people—might recognize Yahweh's unique relationship with Israel. Zion is Yahweh's holy mountain. The entire city would become his sanctuary.

By virtue of being the dwelling place of God, Zion would be "holy." In this context the word does not stress so much the undefiled character of the city. Rather the idea is that "holy" Zion belongs exclusively to Yahweh the God of the covenant. The city is therefore a refuge for all the people of the covenant. No "strangers" would pass through Zion again (3:17). Joel is describing in Old Testament language what John pictured in language more familiar to Christians. "Nothing unclean and no one who practices abomination and lying, shall ever come into that city, but only those whose names are written in the Lamb's book of life" (Rev 21:27).

C. The Prosperity of Zion (3:18).

Joel brings his work to a grand conclusion by showing how the previous disastrous conditions of God's people would be completely reversed. The phrase "In that day," points to the messianic age. In this section Joel pictures the prosperity of Zion in terms of agricultural abundance. Finding refuge in Zion, the people of the covenant find an abundance of provisions.

As a result of the locust plague and drought Judah had experienced a scarcity of new wine (1:5). Now Joel foresees a day when the vineyards would yield rivers of grape juice. Lush pastures would cause the cattle to produce so much milk that it would seem to flow from the ground. Once again the land would be "a land flowing with milk and honey." This is a way of saying that the hills would be covered with vines, and the hills with luxuriant pasture, clothed with flocks. Agricultural abundance in Old Testament prophecy symbolized the spiritual blessings of the New Covenant age (cf. Col 2:10; Eph 3:19).

In 1:20 Joel had complained that the river beds were dry of water as a result of the drought. Now he foresees a day when the streams of Judah would flow the year around. Divine blessing replaces the curse of the opening chapter. Spiritual blessing is here represented by physical imagery.

A spring would go out from the house of Yahweh. The temple of Joel's day had suffered from the locust plague. Various offerings had been suspended due to lack of sacrificial materials. Thus joy and gladness had been cut off from the temple (1:9,13,16). Yet Joel could foresee the day when Yahweh's temple would become a source of fertility. Obviously Joel is not speaking about the physical temples built by Solomon or Herod, for those temples were destroyed, the former in 586 BC, the latter in AD 70. Nor is it likely that Joel is referring to some future millennial temple. Joel is thinking spiritually, not geographically. The temple must be the heavenly sanctuary of God, the holy of holies of that spiritual temple which is represented on earth by the church of Christ.

The temple stream would water the "valley of Shittim," i.e., valley of acacia trees. This valley is not mentioned elsewhere in the Old Testament.[11] If Joel had in mind a definite place it was probably that rugged part of the Kidron Valley east of Jerusalem which runs down to the Dead Sea. What is more important here, however, is the theme of the water of life, a theme later taken up by Ezekiel (ch. 47), Zechariah (14:8) and the Apostle John (Rev 22:1ff.). In this context the valley of Shittim represents what is dry and infertile, for in such soils the acacia managed to grow.[12] Joel is symbolically announcing that the Gospel would bring newness of life to a dying world.

D. The Security of Zion (3:19-21).

While God's people inherit a land of wonderful abundance, the unbelievers dwell in desolate places. Joel used Egypt and Edom, traditional enemies of ancient Israel, as types of the worldly powers in every age which have been at enmity with God. "Desolation" (*shemmah*) is the Old Testament equivalent of the "destruction" experienced by the disobedient in the New Testament (cf. Matt 7:13; 2 Thess 1:9). Two of the reasons for this sentence are stated here.

First, these enemies had done "violence" to the sons of Judah, i.e., the people of God. Second, they had shed innocent blood (3:19).

The aim of the divine judgment on Egypt and Edom is that the people of God might enjoy peace and tranquility. While the kingdoms of this world experience desolation, "Judah shall be inhabited forever, Jerusalem for all generations." In Old Testament language, the contrast here is between eternal life and eternal death (3:20).

The eternal endurance of Judah and Jerusalem would be made possible by two circumstances. First, Yahweh would pardon the blood guilt which he hitherto had not forgiven.[13] Blood guilt refers to any sin worthy of death (cf. Rom 6:23). Spiritual Jerusalem would be declared by God to be innocent, free from all guilt. Second, Yahweh would continue to dwell in Zion. His presence would give permanence to that place (3:21).

ENDNOTES

1. Acts 2:8-11,39,41; 10:34-47; 11:20,21; 15:7-12.
2. W.J. Deane, "Joel" in *The Pulpit Commentary* (New York: Funk & Wagnalls, 1909), p. 28.
3. The combination "in that day and at that time" occurs elsewhere only in Jer 50:4,20; 33:15. The point in these passages, as in Joel, is the security of God's people. The terminology seems to point to the messianic age.
4. Homer Hailey, *A Commentary on the Minor Prophets* (Grand Rapids: Baker, 1972), p. 56.
5. Deane, *op. cit.,* p. 47.
6. "The change of name to *Verdict Valley* in v. 14 suggests that the present name is intended as a theological symbol rather than a topographical identification." Leslie Allen, *The Books of Joel, Obadiah, Jonah and Micah* in "The New International Commentary on the Old Testament" (Grand Rapids: Eerdmans,1976) p. 109.
7. The expression "cast lots" is found elsewhere only in Obad 11 and Nah 3:10, both in reference to the actions of foreign nations against conquered peoples.
8. The Romans were guilty of all of these crimes against the Jews following the destruction of Jerusalem in AD 70. See Josephus, *Wars* 6.9.2-3.
9. The Sabeans were the traders of the land of Sheba in Southwest Arabia. They controlled the eastern trade routes by their caravan routes in North Arabia. Cf. Jer 6:20; Ezek 27:22.
10. The figure of the wine press of God's wrath appears also in Isa 63:1-6;

Jer 25:30; and Rev 14:19,20; 19:15.

11. Abel-shittim was the last camping spot of Israel before crossing the Jordan into the promised land (Josh 2:1). Perhaps this suggests a further application of the prophecy. The spiritual Israel—the church of Christ—is camped, as it were, beyond Jordan at Shittim. Even here believers experience the wonderful water of life. This, however, is but a foretaste of that glorious land for which believers long.

12. Allen, *op. cit.* p. 124.

13. Verse 21 is very difficult. NASB renders: "I will avenge their blood which I have not avenged." This translation requires an emendation of the text and does not relate well to the immediate context.

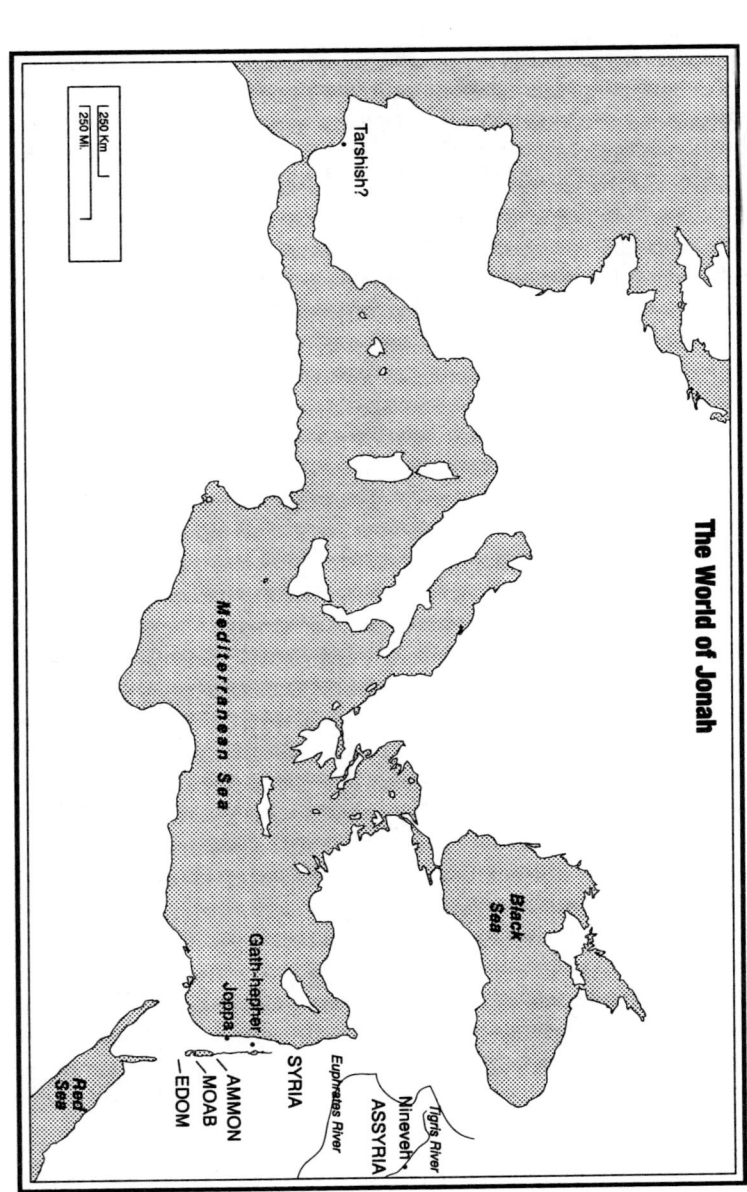

CHAPTER SEVEN

The Saving of a Sinner
Jonah 1-2

The first two chapters of the Book of Jonah focus on the prophet personally, how he sinned against God, experienced judgment and then was rescued by the grace of God from certain death.

JONAH'S DISOBEDIENCE
Jonah 1:1-3

About the year 755 BC the "word of Yahweh came to Jonah the son of Amittai." Jonah was in the midst of his prophetic career. He was the most popular prophet of his day due to his consistently optimistic forecasts regarding the military successes of Jeroboam II (2 Kgs 14:25). On this occasion, however, the directive which Jonah received differed from any previous divine communication which he had received (1:1).

Jonah was told to "arise and go to Nineveh." The formula is somewhat common in the Old Testament as a divine directive for a prophetic mission (cf. 1 Kgs 17:8). Concerning Nineveh, his appointed destination, these things can be said. First, it was a foreign city. Normally the prophets of Israel did not leave their native land to pronounce the judgment of the Lord on Gentile nations. Elisha once visited Damascus in Syria, but he was not sent there with a message for the entire city. Here, then, is the first of many surprises in this book of surprises, viz., that God would dispatch a prophet to preach his word in a Gentile city.

Second, Nineveh was a "great city" politically, demographically and geographically. It was one of the main centers of the Assyrian empire, although at the time of Jonah it had not reached the prominence which it later would receive under King Sennacherib.

Third, Nineveh was a wicked city. In fact God declared that "their wickedness has come up before me." Their wickedness was so great that God himself had taken judicial note of it. Escalating wickedness in society demands heavenly censure. The wickedness of the Assyrians included idolatry and pride (Isa 10:5-19; 36:18-20), cruel oppression (2 Kgs 15:29; 17:6; Isa 36:16,17), and especially inhumane warfare.

Fourth, Nineveh was a city under divine condemnation. Jonah was to "cry against" the place, i.e., announce God's judgment there (1:2).

The name Nineveh struck terror into the hearts of all those living in western Asia in this period. The Assyrian records bear testimony against them. This citation from the annals of Ashur-nasirpal II is typical.

> I stormed the mountain peaks and took them. In the midst of the mighty mountains I slaughtered them; with their blood I dyed the mountain red like wool. With the rest of them I darkened the gullies and precipices of the mountains. I carried off their spoil and their possessions. The heads of their warriors I cut off, and I formed them into a pillar over against their city; their young men and their maidens I burned in the fire! . . . I built a pillar over against the city gates, and I flayed all the chief men who had revolted, and I covered the pillar with their skins; some I walled up within the pillar, some I impaled upon the pillar on stakes, and others I bound to stakes round about the pillar.[1]

The theological implications of Jonah's commission should not be overlooked. Yahweh is represented here as the Lord of all nations who holds all the world morally accountable. "Their wickedness *has come up before me.*" Nineveh may be great, but God is greater, for he speaks from his heavenly throne. The language here is reminiscent of that which was used in Genesis of the wickedness of the cities destroyed by brimstone (cf. Gen 18:20-21). Nineveh was a second Sodom, the epitome of wickedness, which merited divine retribution. What an honor was bestowed on Jonah to be the first Israelite prophet to announce the divine word to a foreign city. He was called of God to be the first foreign missionary!

Now comes the second surprise in the book. Jonah, a genuine prophet with a bona fide commission rebelled against the directive of the Lord. He arose, not obediently to go northeast to Nineveh, but to flee west to Tarshish.[2] This was an ancient Phoenician colony on the southwest coast of Spain. It was about the farthest city to the west known at that time. The reason for Jonah's reluctance to proceed immediately to Nineveh is not stated at this point. That will be divulged in the concluding chapter as one of the last great surprises in the book. Here Jonah is simply branded as a deserter from the army of the Lord.

Jonah's purpose is twice stated in a verse which is marvelously structured. He wanted to flee "from the presence of Yahweh." The charge has been made that Jonah believed that Yahweh was a tribal deity confined to the territory of Israel. That is clearly not the case, for later in this chapter Jonah refers to Yahweh as "the God of heaven." To stand in Yahweh's presence means to serve him. The language is derived from the custom that servants always stood in the presence of seated royalty. Thus the text intends to relate that Jonah was resigning his prophetic office. He no longer wished to serve as God's messenger.

Jonah traveled some sixty miles from his home in Gath-hepher to Joppa, the only quality seaport on the coast of ancient Israel. There he found, as he knew he would, a Phoenician cargo ship about to sail for Tarshish. Jonah made no effort to board the ship as a stowaway. He paid the fare—the full fare. At least nothing is said about any "clergy rate." Jonah was not poor of purse, only poor of spirit. Since the

Israelites were not noted seamen, Jonah's willingness to embark on such a long and dangerous voyage is evidence of his stubborn determination to abandon his ministry.

Jonah might have argued that the circumstances seemed providential. Circumstances, however, are often deceiving. No matter how Jonah might have rationalized, minimized or whitewashed his doings, the stark and horrible truth remained that he was disobeying the God of heaven and earth. Neither prophets nor preachers have any more right to disregard the word of God than other men. Believers today are under a commission to carry God's word to distant lands as much as was Jonah.

JONAH'S DISCIPLINE
Jonah 1:4-16

The first of a series of supernatural events in the book is now related. Yahweh "hurled a great wind on the sea." This produced "a great storm on the sea." The Tarshish bound ship was "about to break up," i.e., be dashed in pieces. Even the experienced seamen (lit., salts) were afraid. Every man cried out to his god. When prayer is not a way of life it becomes a last resort. At the same time the crew jettisoned the cargo so as to lighten the ship in the hope they would be able to ride out the storm. They tried to counter the storm which God had thrown against the sea by some throwing of their own. Works, however heroic and sacrificial, cannot save from God's judgment (1:4-5a).

Now comes the third surprise in the book. Throughout this violent storm Jonah was asleep in the hold of the ship. The word used here implies a deep, even supernatural sleep such as Adam experienced when God took the rib from his side. Apparently the spiritual stress of his disobedience to God, and the hasty trip from Gath-hepher to Joppa had drained all the energy from the prophet. He was exhausted! (1:5b).

In the process of bringing up the cargo, the ship's captain discovered Jonah. He was aroused and rebuked for sleeping during the crisis by means of a rhetorical question: "How is it that you are sleeping?" He was ordered to "arise and call on your god." The verbs used by the captain (*qum qera'*) are the same as those used by God in his original commission to Jonah (cf. 1:2). Those words have now come back to haunt Jonah, to remind him of his present estrangement from Yahweh (1:6a).

The captain had by now concluded that none of the various gods worshiped by his crew could or would rescue the ship. He thought perhaps Jonah's God might be behind this unusual storm. "Perhaps," he suggested, Jonah's God might show compassion on all those whose lives were in jeopardy. Though an idolater, the captain had the correct perspective on prayer. Even many believers think of prayer as a mandate, as furnishing an agenda for divine action, which they have every right to demand and expect that God should follow. The captain's humble submission to the sovereign decisions of deity stands in stark contrast to Jonah's arrogant refusal to submit to that will (1:6b).

Did Jonah pray? Not likely. Prayer and other religious exercises cannot cancel the effects of deliberate disobedience. Jonah was smart enough to understand that. He was now learning, however, that his disobedient actions were placing many other lives in jeopardy.

The sailors concluded that the storm must have been sent against them to punish someone on board. They decided to "cast lots" to determine the guilty party. Casting lots was practiced by Israelites as well as by the heathen. From time to time God graciously condescended to declare his will through visible, external means. The Lord commanded lots to be cast only in matters of great importance. In order to prevent confusion and quarrels the lot was quite frequently utilized in Israel without divine command in matters of minor importance (e.g., 1 Chr 24:5,7,31). The only New Testament example of casting lots is the selection of a candidate to replace Judas (Acts 1:26). The important thing here is that Jonah knew he was the guilty party, yet, like Achan at Ai, he did not confess until God directed the lot (Prov 16:33) to fall on him (1:7).

Once his guilt was exposed, the sailors fired questions at Jonah. They did not wish to condemn the man until he had had the opportunity to present testimony in his own defense. First, they urged him to tell them on whose account the calamity had befallen them. They wanted to know what there was about Jonah that made him so offensive to the sea god. Then they asked in rapid succession about his occupation, his town and country and ethnic origins. From his answers they would be able to deduce what God he served, since in those days most nations had their own set of deities (1:8).

Jonah then told the sailors that he was a Hebrew. This term is frequently used when Israelites describe themselves to foreigners (e.g., Gen 40:15). Jonah told the crew that he "feared" (i.e., worshiped) Yahweh. Compared to the genuine fear of the sailors (cf. vv. 5,10) Jonah's "fear" of Yahweh was a mere formality. The prophet identified Yahweh as "the God of heaven." This title for God can be traced back to the age of the patriarchs (Gen 24:3,7), but it became more popular toward the end of Old Testament history (1:9a).

Jonah described Yahweh as the one who had "made the sea and the dry land." In spite of his reluctance to preach to Gentiles, Jonah, under the pressure of the moment, was bearing witness to the claims of Yahweh to a group of pagan men. His confession of faith in God is at the same time an admission that Yahweh is responsible for the storm. The reluctant missionary also told them that he was fleeing from the presence (i.e., service) of Yahweh (1:9b).

The sailors became frightened when they heard Jonah's explanation. They rebuked the prophet with a question: "How could you do this?" The greatest humiliation in the life of any believer is to experience a justly deserved spiritual rebuke from those who have made no commitment to the Lord (1:10).

When the sea became even more boisterous, they pled with Jonah to tell them what they could do that the sea might become calm. They assumed that if he was a prophet of Yahweh he should have some wise counsel for them in this respect. Jonah directed them to throw him into the sea. Only then would the sea become calm. Jonah must have been acting on some prophetic impulse here. His repentance was complete and sincere. He would not allow these sailors to suffer any longer on his account. Jonah was acting out of compassion for these Gentiles. Jonah committed himself to the will of God. He demonstrated heroic faith. Here is another surprise in the narrative (1:11-12).

Now comes the fourth great surprise in the book. The Gentile sailors were reluctant to throw Jonah to the sea in order to save their own lives. They had high standards. The sixth commandment was written upon their hearts. They rowed desperately to return to land. They could make no progress, however, because the sea was becoming still more tumultuous. They then turned to Yahweh in prayer. First, they prayed that they might not perish in the storm. Second, they asked that they might not be held guilty of shedding innocent blood. Third, they acknowledged that all that had befallen them had been the will of God—that God had the right and privilege of doing as he pleased. These heathen men experienced a kind of conversion. The very thing that Jonah did not want to happen at Nineveh was starting to happen on board that ship (1:13-14).

Viewing themselves as agents of divine justice, the sailors picked up Jonah and threw him into the sea. Immediately the sea stopped its raging. This is the second great miracle in the book. When the sailors witnessed the instantaneous calming of the water, they "feared Yahweh greatly," i.e., they worshiped him. They offered a sacrifice to the Lord and made vows of allegiance to him. The irony here is that Jonah fled because he did not want to preach God's word to a Gentile city. Now inadvertently he has been the instrument to bring the knowledge of the true God to a number of Gentiles (1:15-16).

JONAH'S DELIVERANCE
Jonah 1:17

Now comes the third great miracle of the book. Yahweh "appointed" (*minneh*) a great fish to swallow Jonah. This word never appears in the sense of prepare or create as the KJV translates. The Creator of the sea is also the Master of its creatures. They do his bidding. Here the great fish became the instrument of God's grace. The good Lord saved this rebellious prophet from certain destruction in the water of the sea (1:17a).

Jonah survived three days and nights in the stomach of the fish. Those who take the parabolic approach to the Book of Jonah have great difficulty suggesting a significance for the three days and three nights. The fact is that Jonah actually spent that amount of time in the sea creature. God left the prophet in the fish long enough to establish the fact that his survival was totally a supernatural event. It was a miracle (1:17b).

The credibility of the fish account in Jonah has been discussed thoroughly by several writers.[3] That God used a special creation to produce the fish which swallowed Jonah is certainly possible, although nothing in the Hebrew text points in this direction. Any one of several sea creatures known today could have been the agent appointed by God for this mission. A sperm whale, for example, has a mouth large enough to swallow a man. This animal has the habit of swimming rapidly near the surface with its mouth hanging open. Several writers recite the details of the celebrated case of James Bartley. In 1891 this seaman on the whaler *Star of the East* fell overboard. According to reports published at the time, Bartley survived two and a half days in the belly of a sperm whale.[4] The fact that sperm whales do not inhabit the Mediterranean Sea today in no way precludes the possibility that they did so in ancient times when the number of ships on the sea was far less.

Sharks are more common in the Mediterranean. At least two species of sharks seem to have the capabilities of swallowing a human being. The great white shark, in spite of its terrible teeth, might be a candidate for the sea creature of Jonah 2. *Smith's Bible Dictionary* cites one report of the whole body of a man in armor having been found in the stomach of a white shark. The same source mentions a report of a white shark which swallowed a horse.[5] The huge Rhinodon shark—as much as fifty feet in length—has also been known to have swallowed a man.[6]

The fish event occupies only three of the forty-eight verses in the Book of Jonah. Obviously the author did not see this as the main emphasis of his book. G. Campbell Morgan observed that "men have been looking so hard at the great fish that they have failed to see the great God" which is the main burden of the book.[7]

"Then Jonah prayed." It was about time. He prayed "from the stomach of the fish." A believer cannot come to a place so abnormal that he cannot not pray to God there. The belly of the sea monster became Jonah's prayer closet.[8]

JONAH'S DECLARATION
Jonah 2:1-9

If in chapter 1 Jonah ran away from God in chapter 2 he ran to God in prayer. Critics object that what is recorded in Jonah 2 is not actually a prayer. Prayer, however, is any conversation addressed to God. Petition is but one aspect of prayer. Though there is no petition here, there certainly is praise and thanksgiving Again the critics argue that thanksgiving is inappropriate here because Jonah had not yet been delivered. He had been delivered, however, from the sea, and he is confident that his deliverance will be made complete. Finally, critics criticize Jonah's prayer because it is made up of quotes from the Book of Psalms. Yet in times of desperation one often prays in the language of Scripture. Another possibility is that this prayer may have been composed afterwards expressing the sentiments he felt at the time.

A. Answered Prayer (2:1-4).

The prayer begins with an acknowledgment that God had answered his earlier prayer in the sea. Jonah had prayed out of his "distress" to Yahweh. He had "cried for help from the depth of Sheol." He was as good as dead when he lifted up his desperate cry. God heard the voice of Jonah, i.e. he granted the petition for help (2:2).

To magnify the marvelous grace of God in hearing his prayer, Jonah describes in narrative prayer the distress out of which he cried out to the Lord. He does not blame the sailors for his plight. Yahweh had cast Jonah into the deep in the sense that he had revealed that was the only means by which the raging storm could be calmed. The sailors were merely the instruments used by God on this occasion. It is to Jonah's credit that he did not have bitterness toward the sailors for throwing him into the water (2:3a).

Jonah vividly describes being sucked into the current and battered by the waves. Again he emphasizes that the sea was God's means of disciplining him when he refers to "your breakers," i.e., waves, and "your billows" (2:3b).

Jonah felt cut off from God. Being cast into the sea, he had been "expelled" from Yahweh's sight. Yet he was confident even in his dire straits that he would "look again" toward Yahweh's "holy temple." He anticipated renewed fellowship with his God. These words suggest that Jonah had experienced a change of heart. Arrogance had given way to humility, rebellion to submission (2:4).

B. The Crisis and the Rescue (2:5-7).

Jonah felt himself sinking into the watery grave. The water encompassed him "to the point of death." Seaweed wrapped about his head. He descended "to the bottoms of the mountains." This was the point of no return. "The earth with its bars" was around me forever, i.e., he was as good as buried in the earth, imprisoned by the bars of death. There was no hope of return apart from divine intervention. By means of the great fish, however, God had brought up his life from "the pit," i.e., from Sheol as in v. 2 (2:5-6).

While he was "fainting away," i.e., about to lose consciousness from lack of oxygen, he "remembered" Yahweh, i.e., he turned to the Lord for help. His prayer reached the heavenly temple, the dwelling place of Yahweh (2:7).

C. Commitment to Praise (2:8-9).

Jonah is aware of how much he was indebted to divine grace. His prayer concludes with a declaration of commitment. He notes first that idolaters eventually forsake their "vain idols." He, on the other hand, pledges to sacrifice to Yahweh and pay his vows. He recognizes by personal experience that "salvation" is from Yahweh. Jonah now realized that he needed salvation as much as the Ninevites. He also now realized that salvation was by grace (2:8-9).

The first two chapters of Jonah both conclude with sacrifice and vows. Both Jonah and the Gentile sailors had faced peril from the sea. Both had cried out to Yahweh. Both offered worship to him after being physically preserved. The proud and prejudiced prophet finally had matured spiritually to the level of the Gentile sailors. In chapter 1 Jonah had left the praying to the ship's crew. Now he shared their spirit of supplication and submission. He who thought that preaching the divine word to the heathen was beneath him, now had learned that Gentiles quickly and sincerely respond to divine interventions in the affairs of man.

JONAH'S DISCHARGE
Jonah 2:10

Yahweh responded to Jonah's prayer by commanding the great fish to vomit Jonah up on the dry land. No doubt the creature was most happy to rid himself of this indigestible lump in his stomach. Not even a great fish can stomach a man who is not missionary minded! (2:10).

ENDNOTES

1. Luckenbill, *Ancient Records of Assyria and Babylonia*, pars. 447,443. Quoted by J. Finegan, *Light from the Ancient Past*, p. 170.
2. Tarshish is usually located in southwest Spain near the mouth of the Guadalquivir river. Tarshish was a source of silver (Jer 10:9) as well as tin, iron and lead (Ezek 27:12). Others have located Tarshish in Cilicia (=Tarsus), Sardinia and even India.
3. W. Arndt, *Bible Difficulties* (St. Louis: Concordia, 1962), pp. 127-131; Harry Rimmer, *The Harmony of Science and Scripture* (Grand Rapids: Eerdmans, 1936), pp. 161-190; Bernard Ramm, *The Christian View of Science and Scripture* (Grand Rapids: Eerdmans, 1956), pp. 296-298.
4. F.E. Gaebelein, *The Servant and the Dove* (New York: Our Hope Press, 1946), pp. 88-89.
5. William Smith, *A Dictionary of the Bible* (New York: Revell, n.d.), p. 749.
6. Rimmer, *op. cit.*, pp. 188-89.
7. G. Campbell Morgan, *The Minor Prophets* (1960), p. 69.
8. Theo. Laetsch, *Bible Commentary:The Minor Prophets* (St. Louis: Concordia, 1956), p. 230.

CHAPTER EIGHT

The Saving of a City
Jonah 3-4

The material in Jonah 3-4 parallels to a certain extent that of the first two chapters. Jonah receives a second commission in language very similar to the first. In both sections Jonah encounters Gentiles who are in peril. His witness to the few sailors on board the ship in chapter 1 becomes preaching to the inhabitants of a great city. Just as the men on board ship cried out to Yahweh for deliverance, so also the Ninevites sincerely sought from Yahweh deliverance from impending calamity. The Lord responded to the prayers of the Ninevites just as he had responded to the prayers of the sailors. In chapter 1 God appointed a great fish as his agent in the underwater rescue of Jonah. In chapter 4 the Lord appoints a plant and a worm to rescue Jonah from the sea of despondency and bitterness. While Jonah celebrates his personal deliverance from death in chapter 2, he prays for death in chapter 4. The first half of the book ends on a triumphant note; the second half does not indicate how Jonah responded to divine discipline.

JONAH AND THE NINEVITES
Jonah 3

Jonah learned a great deal about himself, about Gentiles, and about his God through his harrowing experience on and in the sea. Jonah's recalcitrance in no way moved the Lord to change his mind about reaching out to Nineveh with a message of warning designed to elicit repentance. Jonah was now ready to listen. Experience had taught him the harsh consequences of deliberate disobedience to Yahweh's commands.

A. Jonah's Commission Renewed (3:1-4).

"The word of Yahweh came to Jonah a second time." Thank God for second chances! The marvelous grace of God seeks to find effective service even for those who once were rebellious to the divine calling. How gracious is this second call! There is no remonstrance and no mention of the first call and Jonah's reckless abandonment of responsibility. There was no need to make Jonah feel more guilty than he already felt (3:1).

The language of the commission is the same as earlier: "Arise, and go to Nineveh" (cf. 1:2). Some see in the command to "arise" a hint that Jonah had returned to his home in Gath-hepher after his ordeal in the sea.[1] The Lord did not wait for Jonah to go to Nineveh on his own initiative. God cannot compromise with the prejudices of his spokesmen. Though Jonah was reluctant to preach there, Nineveh was "the great city," literally, a great city to God, i.e., great in God's eyes as an object of loving concern. God was determined that this great city should have the opportunity to repent. Nineveh was on God's agenda, and that agenda is always non-negotiable (3:2a).

Jonah was to "proclaim to it the proclamation which I am going to tell you." God has never sent a messenger without a message. Those who make the claim to be spokesmen for God had better make sure that what they speak comes from God. Only this kind of preaching accomplishes the divine purpose. The language here is slightly different from the original commission ("cry against it") and is more specific (3:2b).

This time Jonah obeyed the divine directive. He arose and went to Nineveh "according to the word of Yahweh." How far he had to travel cannot be determined since the text gives no indication of the spot where Jonah made landfall after his harrowing voyage in the fishy submarine (3:3a).

Jonah found Nineveh, not just to be a great city (1:2, 3:2), but "an exceedingly great city." The greatness is geographical as is indicated in the phrase "a three days' walk." In Jonah's day the circumference of the city was about three miles, hardly a distance that would take three days to travel. [Later Sennacherib enlarged the city to the size of about eight miles in circumference.] Either Jonah is including the suburbs of greater Nineveh, or he is indicating that it would have taken three days to deliver his message in all sections of the city (3:3b).

Soon after his arrival Jonah "began to go through the city one day's walk." This suggests that Jonah's entire mission lasted three days. It took that long to deliver the message to all parts of the city. He "cried out" his message, i.e., raised up his voice. His proclamation was bold, plain, uncompromising: "Yet forty days and Nineveh will be overthrown." This term, which is used of ancient Sodom (Gen 19:21,25,29), suggests a complete destruction. The message in the Hebrew consists of only five words. Whether or not this was his total message or only the gist of it cannot be determined (3:4).

The "forty days" was a grace period. Often in the Scriptures "forty" is used for a period of waiting and testing.[2] Though the oral word made no mention of the possibility of reprieve, the Ninevites realized that they were being given an opportunity to repent. If God was irrevocably determined to destroy their city, why would he send a messenger to warn them?

B. Nineveh's Conversion Effected (3:5-9).

Jonah does not narrate the many questions he must have been asked. His abbreviated account simply states that "the people of Nineveh believed in God." The Hebrew term means literally "to regard or make firm by saying yea and amen." To "believe" God means to say yea and amen to God's word as it is revealed to someone.

Superstitious by nature, the Ninevites would shocked by the blunt announcement of judgment spoken by a man whose skin must have been shriveled and bleached by the gastric juices of the fish. Jesus declared that Jonah became "a sign" to the Ninevites (Luke 11:30). Perhaps some who had seen him spit out on the shore had preceded him to the city. Had Jonah gone to Nineveh when he was first called to do so, his message might have fallen on deaf ears. Here then is the supreme irony of the book. Jonah wanted to see Nineveh doomed, so he fled to Tarshish. In so doing, however, he set in motion a chain of circumstances which actually gave his message credibility.

For whatever reason, the Ninevites believed that their city was under a threat of divine judgment. So they expressed their contrition and sincerity with fasting. The entire population put on coarse sackcloth as another outward manifestation of their repentance (3:5).

Even the king of Nineveh was moved to repentance by Jonah's message of doom. He arose from his throne, put aside his royal robe, covered himself with sackcloth and sat on a heap of ashes. From that lowly spot he issued a proclamation in his own name and that of his nobles. The king called for an absolute fast. Neither man nor beast should eat anything or drink any water. For how long? The text is silent. The king may have heard the message only after several of the forty days had already elapsed. In any case, both man and beast were to be covered with sackcloth.[3] Men were to call on God earnestly (3:6-8a).

The king was not satisfied with mere ritual manifestation of repentance. He ordered a change of conduct on the part of his people. Every person was to turn from "his wicked way." In this demand the pagan king of Nineveh sounds very much like an Israelite prophet. Yahweh is never satisfied with religious ritual devoid of ethical conduct. The God of the Bible always demands personal reformation as the price of restoring fellowship with sinful persons.

The particular wickedness of which Nineveh was guilty was "violence." The king demanded that each person turn "from the violence which is in his hand." "Violence" is social injustice, it is trampling the rights of other people, it is man's inhumanity to his fellowman. In their foreign policy the Assyrians were more ruthless than any people in the ancient world (3:8b). The king, however, is referring to individual behavior within the city. Biblical prophets condemned violence in the cities of Judah as well (e.g., Jer 6:7). Such violence seems to be characteristic of those who dwell in overcrowded cities.

The perceptive reader will note the parallel between the role of the king in chapter 3 and that of the ship captain in chapter 1. Both leaders emerge to lead their followers in humble submission to Yahweh. Prejudiced Israelites would have had their negative assessment of Gentiles jolted by the actions of the kindly sailors. Now the accursed king of Nineveh is responding like the ship's captain with wise and perceptive actions in the face of a judgment by Yahweh.

The king was not sure that even these drastic measures would avert the calamity. Perhaps God would withdraw his burning anger and spare Nineveh. The king, though he was a pagan, recognized the sovereignty of God. Man's action does not dictate divine action. It only makes possible a change of disposition which might lead to the revoking of a threat (3:9). In this recognition of the sovereignty of God the king again is the parallel of the ship captain in chapter 1 (cf. 1:6).

Historical documentation of a mass Assyrian conversion in this period is lacking. For many years, however, no historical evidence of the Assyrian king Sargon (Isa 20:1) had been discovered. Given the nature of archaeological investigation, insisting on extra-Biblical confirmation for every statement of Scripture simply camouflages a hardened heart of unbelief. Jesus certainly viewed the repentance of the Ninevites as historical (Matt 12:41). The text does not necessitate that all the Ninevites who repented remained faithful to the Lord the rest of their lives.

C. God's Compassion Granted (3:10).

God saw the deeds of the Ninevites. They had experienced a genuine change of heart. They had turned from their wicked way. "Then God relented concerning the calamity which he had declared he would bring upon them." Repentance opens up the possibility of reprieve if not pardon. Yahweh did not do as he had said he would do (3:10). Because his grace never changes, Yahweh can change his threatened judgments. The principle later would be articulated clearly to Jeremiah: "At one moment I might speak concerning a nation or a kingdom to uproot, to pull down, or to destroy it; if that nation against which I have spoken turns from its evil, I will relent concerning the calamity which I planned to bring on it" (Jer 18:7-8).

The point is that a prophecy of doom is not absolute. Prophetic warnings of judgment are actually designed to elicit repentance. God is not so insecure that he must execute his every threat in order to establish his immutability. In his abundant compassion Yahweh looks for the slightest reason to delay judgment. His threats are actually a tool in his program to reach the hearts of people and lead them to his salvation.

JONAH AND THE LORD
Jonah 4

The battle for the souls of the Ninevites was not nearly as difficult as was the battle for the mind and heart of Jonah. The last chapter of Jonah relates how Yahweh, building upon the experience of divine grace, reasons ever so gently with his pouting prophet. By irrefutable logic he helps Jonah see that he is concerned about all his creation, even vicious Gentiles and dumb animals.

A. Jonah's Complaint (4:1-5).

That Yahweh would relent concerning the destruction of Nineveh displeased Jonah. For the first time in his prophetic career one of Jonah's predictions had failed! His reputation as a prophet had been ruined! Jonah was angry! Furthermore, those Ninevites deserved judgment. Wickedness should be punished, and no one disputed that those Ninevites were wicked. This was no momentary outburst on Jonah's part. He had felt this anger for a long time. Yet his outburst and childish conduct in chapter 4 is another one of those surprises that keep surfacing in this book. Should not a man who so recently had experienced God's grace want others to experience it as well? What a shock his anger is! He who praised the gracious mercy of God in chapter 2 now deplores it in chapter 4!

If there is anything at all commendable about Jonah's conduct in chapter 4 it is that he prayed. To be sure his prayer is the very opposite of the one he prayed in chapter 2. Nonetheless, prayer is a safety valve for believers to express their frustrations, their complaints to the Lord. That Jonah did.

THE SAVING OF A CITY

JONAH 3-4

Now comes another surprise. Jonah confesses that he feared all along that God in his patience would grant a reprieve to Nineveh. This was the very reason he had rejected the first commission. He fled to Tarshish because he anticipated that the Ninevites would repent. The ugly truth is that Jonah was so prejudiced against the Ninevites that he wanted to see them destroyed. He had purchased a ticket to Tarshish in order to frustrate divine grace (4:2a).

In his prayer Jonah recites a litany of the gracious attributes of Yahweh. Jonah knew that God was gracious and compassionate, slow to anger and abundant in lovingkindness. What he says here sounds much like what Yahweh said about himself in Exodus 34:6f. Jonah knew that God would look for any reason to relent concerning calamity. Jonah's words, however, are not words of praise. This prophet is registering his total lack of appreciation for these attributes which most sinners find eminently praiseworthy. Perhaps he even regarded these attributes as character weakness on the part of Yahweh. At the very least Jonah felt that grace should have borders, and those borders should correspond to the territory occupied by Israel (4:2b).

Feeling as he did about the grace of God as it had been extended to the Ninevites, Jonah knew he could no longer continue to represent Yahweh as his prophet. He became depressed. He echoed the prayer of Elijah in 1 Kings 19:4: "Please take my life" (4:3). Elijah prayed that prayer because he thought he had failed in his battle against Baalism in Israel. Jonah, however, wanted to die because he had succeeded. Elijah had not hesitated to minister in the name of Yahweh in Gentile Phoenicia (1 Kgs 17:8-24). Jonah was no Elijah. "The echo of Elijah's prayer is but another nail in the coffin of Jonah's reputation."[4]

The Lord responded to Jonah better than he deserved. Like a parent gently chiding a child, Yahweh directed a question to Jonah designed to make him reflect on his disposition: "Do you have good reason to be angry?" God's question is but three brief words in the Hebrew. Yahweh was dealing with Jonah more gently than he deserved. He did not condemn the prophet, although Jonah's attitude deserved condemnation. The question is designed to lead Jonah to see his fault and condemn himself. Jonah had just experienced the grace of God in his rescue from the sea. Now he resented the extension of that same grace to other sinners. No answer to Yahweh's question is recorded. Jonah was still not ready to repent of his attitude (4:4).

Then Jonah went out from Nineveh and took up a position on the east side of the city. There he made a crude shelter of a few intertwined branches to protect himself from the sun by day and the chill at night. He sat there "until he could see what would happen in the city." Whether Jonah went out before or after the end of the forty days is not clear. God may have revealed to him before the end of the forty days that the punishment had been canceled. Apparently Jonah did not believe that the repentance of the Ninevites would last the forty days. This hell-fire preacher wanted to see the fire fall. He was confident that it would once God saw that the manifestations of repentance in the city were phony. So he sat and pouted in his smug, self-righteous indignation (4:5).

B. Yahweh's Action (4:6-8).

The Lord was determined to rescue Jonah a second time, this time from a sea of discouragement, self-pity and depression. Again he employed a miracle. Yahweh God, i.e., Yahweh in his capacity of Creator, "appointed" a plant which miraculously grew up over Jonah to be a shade. Yahweh proved that he was God of the sea in the first half of the book when he orchestrated a storm and appointed a great fish. Now he shows himself to be Lord over the dry land as well. He controls the plants and insects as well as the sea monsters.

The plant "delivered" Jonah from his discomfort. Apparently the branches of his shelter were not sufficiently dense to protect him from the heat of the sun. The prophet was extremely happy about the plant. The castor oil plant has been nominated as the particular plant which God caused to grow up overnight (4:6).

In spite of God's efforts to comfort Jonah, the prophet remained sullen. For this reason the Lord employed sterner measures against him. He "appointed" a worm when dawn came the next day. The worm attacked the plant and it withered and died. When the sun came up God "appointed" a wind off the desert—the so-called sirocco. The sun beat down on his head causing Jonah to be faint. The scorching desert wind hurling bits of sand at him made the heat unbearable. His little shelter felt like an oven. Jonah begged with all his heart (lit., he wished in himself) to die. He had come to the point where he believed that death was better for him than life (4:7-8).

C. The Logic of Grace (4:9-11).

God nudged Jonah again with a probing questions about the dead plant. "Do you have good reason to be angry about the plant?" His first anger had been because Nineveh had not been destroyed; his present anger was because a vine had been destroyed.[5] People have a tendency to become extremely perturbed when even small things which directly affect their lives are touched by the finger of providence. On the other hand they can be coldly and criminally indifferent concerning matters of infinitely greater importance when these matters do not impinge upon their life.[6]

The gentle question ignited Jonah's simmering anger like gasoline poured on an open flame. Jonah shot back, "I have good reason to be angry, even to death." He had lost all patience with God. Those who are victims of self-pity are not hesitant to defend their negative attitude even to deity! The important thing here, however, is that God did not give up on Jonah even when he was acting like a royal jerk! (4:9).

Yahweh then pointed out how inappropriate Jonah's anger was. Jonah had "compassion" on the plant which he did not plant, cultivate and make grow. In that plant he had invested nothing. His concern for the plant was dictated by self-interest, not genuine love such as a gardener might have for his plants. That plant was here one day and gone the next. It had no lasting significance. Yet Jonah was sorry it had died. Should not then Yahweh have compassion on Nineveh? He created all those people. He loved them. That Yahweh should show compassion on them would be most natural.

Yet another reason motivated Yahweh's compassion on Nineveh. More than 120,000 people lived in the city and they did not know the difference between their right hand and their left, i.e., they were spiritual children, totally unlearned in the things of God.[7] People are more valuable than plants. Surely Jonah could see that. God had invested much time and patience on that city. Besides the multitude of people the city also contained "many animals." They were also precious in God's sight.

The book concludes abruptly with these words. The reader is left to ponder what might have become of the prejudiced prophet. Did he repent of his sinful attitude? Did he beg God's forgiveness? Did he re-enter Nineveh to encourage and instruct these baby believers? The text is silent about such questions. Most likely Jonah intended this account which puts him in such a bad light to be a confession. If that is true, then Jonah straightened out his thinking. He conquered his prejudice.

The Book of Jonah focuses on the saving work of God. Here the Lord deals with three classes of sinners all desperately in need of his grace. Jonah was a sinner in attitude and action even though he professed to be a worshiper of Yahweh. The sailors were heathen men who had never received any knowledge of the Living God. They were basically good men as the world counts goodness. Considering their lack of exposure to the written word of God, these sailors display some spiritual sensitivity. The Ninevites were also idolaters, but no one considered them "good." Even their king recognized the besetting sin of his people was violence—man's inhumanity to man. On the scale of sin, they were at the Sodom level. Yet they too responded to the word of Yahweh. They too experienced his grace. Thus the Book of Jonah would underscore that God loves sinners of all kinds. He reaches out to them. He offers them his mercy and his forgiveness.

ENDNOTES

1. Homer Hailey, *A Commentary on the Minor Prophets* (Grand Rapids: Baker, 1972), p. 75.

2. Israel spent forty years in the wilderness (Exod 16:35), and Jesus forty days (Matt 4:2). The rains came for forty days at the time of the Flood (Gen 7:12). Moses was in the mount forty days and nights receiving the Law (Exod 24:18).

3. The Greek historian Herodotus (9.24) documents that the Persians included animals in the mourning rites. The Assyrians seem to have also followed this custom.

4. Leslie C. Allen, *The Books of Joel, Obadiah, Jonah and Micah* in "The New International Commentary on the Old Testament" (Grand Rapids:

Eerdmans, 1976), p. 229.
  5. Hailey, *op. cit.*, p. 80.
  6. *Ibid.*
  7. Keil argued that the 120,000 were literal children under the age of seven. They would represent about one-fifth of a total population of about 600,000.

PART TWO

THE EIGHTH CENTURY PROPHETS

AMOS

HOSEA

MICAH

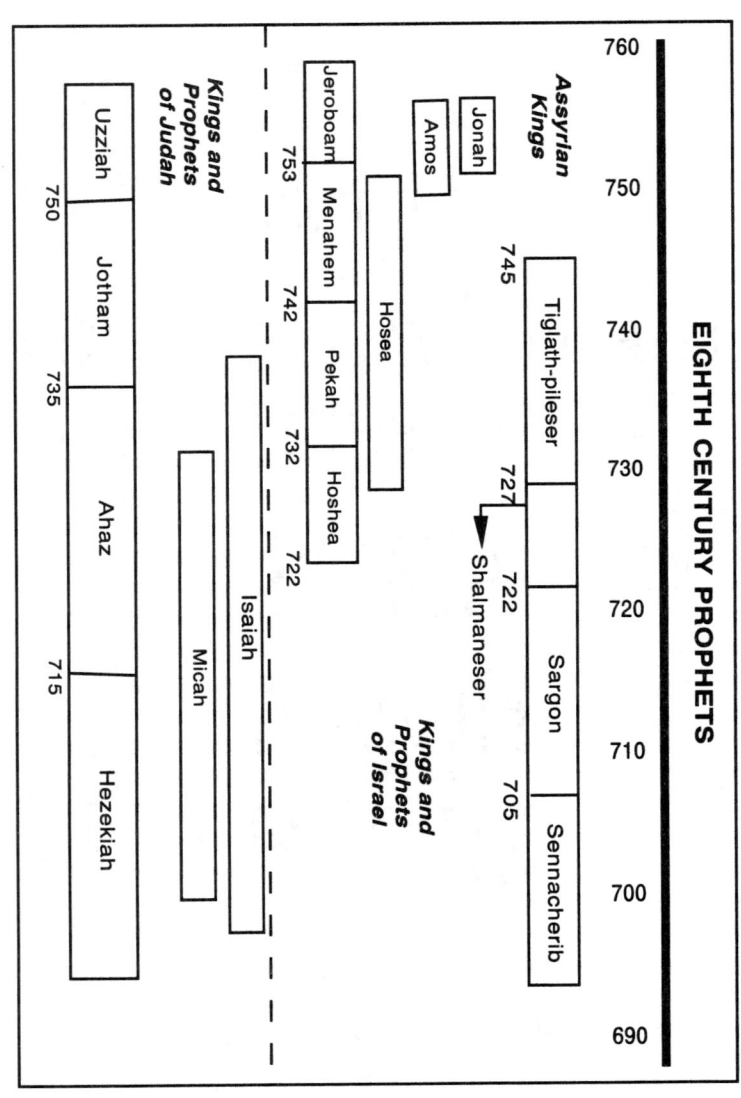

Chart No. 14

CHAPTER NINE

The Eighth Century Prophets
An Introduction

The eighth century BC is known as the golden age of Hebrew prophecy. Jonah's successful trip to Nineveh occurred early in this century. From about the mid-point to the close of the eighth century four other great prophets walked across the stage of history. Though he lived in Judah, Amos was dispatched to preach the word of God in Israel, the northern kingdom. About the same time a native of that kingdom, Hosea, was called to preach. In the year King Uzziah of Judah died (739 BC) Isaiah was called into prophetic ministry. His contemporary in the south was Micah the Morashtite.

THE PROPHET AMOS
Prophet of the Plumb Line

He has been called "the cowboy prophet" (Phillips), "the Salvation Army prophet" (Kelso), and "the backwoods prophet" (Chappell). At best these designations are misleading, and at worse totally false.

More appropriate would be these designations: "the prophet of justice" (Robinson), "the prophet of righteousness," or "conscience incarnate."

A. The Man.

The name Amos means "burden bearer." The prophet is not mentioned outside his book, although there is another by the same name in Luke 3:25. Amos is probably a shortened form of the name Amasiah which means "borne by Yahweh."

No mention is made of Amos' parentage. This has been taken by some to mean that he came from a well-known family, by others that his family had no social status.

Amos came from the village of Tekoa about ten miles south of Jerusalem on the edge of the Judean wilderness. The place is mentioned several times in Biblical and intertestamental history (e.g., 2 Sam 14:2). The village was some 2,500 feet above sea level. It commanded an awesome view of the Judean Wilderness, the Jordan Valley and the Dead Sea.

In three places Amos speaks of his life prior to his prophetic mission to Israel. In 1:1 he says he was among the *noqdim*. This word appears elsewhere only in 2 Kgs 3:4 where King Mesha of Moab is said to have been a *noqed*. He gave as annual tribute to the king of Israel 100,000 lambs and 100,000 rams. A *noqed* was thus a sheep raiser, as opposed to a shepherd who might work for someone else. Some have tried to read additional significance into this term, but these efforts are not convincing.[1]

In 7:14 Amos refers to himself as a *boqer*. This word occurs only here in the Old Testament. It seems to be related to the word *baqar* ("cattle"). This in no way contradicts the picture presented in 1:1. Apparently Amos kept cattle as well as sheep.

Also in 7:14 Amos says that before his prophetic call he was a *boles* of sycamore figs. The English versions have widely different translations of this once-used term. Thus Amos was a "dresser" (ASV, RSV), a "gatherer" (KJV), or a "grower" (BV; NASB) of sycamore figs. The NIV renders "he took care of sycamore figs." The ancient versions suggest that the word means something like "scrape" or "pinch" or "nip." Thus Amos was a fig nipper! Exactly why he nipped figs is not clear.[2] The sycamore figs grew in the lowlands region of Judah about twelve miles from Tekoa. Thus Amos would appear to have been a man of substance, but not necessarily wealthy. He was not the uneducated herdsman that popular preaching has made him to be.

The book which Amos left for posterity reveals several important conclusions about this prophet. (1) He was well acquainted with the world of his day. He mentions the names of at least thirty-eight towns and districts of the ancient Near East. (2) He had a keen awareness of the history, not only of his own people, but of foreign peoples as well. (3) He possessed a note of objectivity and sternness. (4) He was forthright in the presentation of the word of God. (5) He was a literary master and an incomparable preacher.

B. The Mission.

Amos explained his preaching ministry in Israel as due to the fact that "Yahweh took me from behind the flock" (7:15). The three visions recorded in the opening verses of chapter 7 may have constituted the call of this man. In the first two visions he saw the impending destruction of the northern kingdom. Amos prayed, and the blow was withheld. In the third vision, however, Amos learned that Israel did not measure up to the unalterable standard of God's plumb line, i.e., his law. The northern kingdom must therefore be destroyed. This certain knowledge of the doom of the sister kingdom to the north catapulted Amos into his prophetic ministry. This man felt a divine compulsion to preach God's warning. "Yahweh God has spoken! Who can but prophesy?" (3:8b).

Amos' ministry is dated to the reigns of Uzziah of Judah and Jeroboam II of Israel. His ministry must then be placed between 792 and 753 BC. Of course it is possible that Amos, like Hosea, omits the mention of the kings who followed Jeroboam since they were products of anarchy. If that is the case, then the possible parameters for the ministry of Amos would be 792-740 BC.

Amos further explains that his mission to north Israel transpired "two years before the earthquake." Over two centuries later this earthquake in the days of King Uzziah was still remembered (Zech 14:5). A tradition in Josephus (*Ant.* 9:10,4) relates that this earthquake occurred on the day that Uzziah attempted to usurp the office of the priests and was smitten with leprosy (2 Chr 26:16ff.). If that tradition is true, the earthquake occurred in 750 BC. Two years before the earthquake would date Amos' ministry to the north (or perhaps the conclusion thereof) to 752 BC.

No specific evidence indicates the length of Amos' ministry. Agreement generally exists that his ministry was very short. Guesses of one half hour (Morgernstern) or a few months (Smart) are probably too short. More likely his ministry extended for a few years. The years 754-752 BC for his mission to north Israel would not be far off.

Economically Israel was riding the crest of a wave of prosperity. Morally and spiritually, however, the nation was bankrupt in the mideighth century. Israel had grown prosperous, "pious," presumptuous, and pitiless. Amos was a keen and perceptive observer of Israelite life. He knew a mirage when he saw one.[3] The land was ripe for judgment.

Chapter 7 suggests that Amos was expelled from the northern kingdom by the religious authorities there. Chapters 8-9 may represent his preaching after his return to Judah. That phase of his ministry probably lasted from 752-750 BC.

C. The Message.

The Book of Amos contains prophetic oracles, visions, and hymn fragments (4:13; 5:8f.; 9:5f.). Amos uses certain key phrases to mark divisions of thought in his message, for example, "Hear this word (3:1; 4:1; 5:1); and "woe" (5:18; 6:1). He uses repetition to great advantage, as for example, the expression "Yet you have not returned unto me, says Yahweh" which is used five times in chapter 4. Few modern scholars would agree with Jerome's assessment that Amos was "unskilled in speech."

The opening message of Amos is a sermonic masterpiece. The prophet warms up his hostile audience by pronouncing doom upon all their national enemies one by one. He uses a traditional wisdom school formula to introduce each of these brief oracles of condemnation: "For three transgressions, yes for four, I will not reverse it," i.e., the judgment.

The Book of Amos stands third in the Hebrew canon (after Joel) and second in the Greek version (after Hosea). The structure of the Book of Amos is indicated in Chart No. 15.

Chart No. 15

THE STRUCTURE OF AMOS					
Ministry in Israel Chs. 1-6 755-752 BC		3 Visions Reflecting Amos' Call	Amos' Expulsion from Israel	Ministry in Judah Chs. 8-9 752-750 BC	
Judgment on the Nations Chs. 1-2	Indictment Against Israel Chs. 3-6	7:1-8	7:9-17	4th Vision + Message Ch. 8	5th Vision + Message Ch. 9

THE PROPHET HOSEA
Prophet of the Broken Heart

Hosea has been called "the Jeremiah of the northern kingdom" (Kirkpatrick) and "the St. John of the Old Testament." His personal family tragedy has earned him the title "the man of the shattered romance" (Ward). Because of his tender and earnest appeals for repentance he has been called "the home missionary," "the evangelist" and "the prophet of grace." His literary skills are recognized in the title "Israel's poet laureate."

A. The Man.

The name Hosea means "salvation" or "help." The eighth century prophet is one of four men of this name mentioned in the Old Testament. The last king of the northern kingdom was also called Hosea (2 Kgs 15:30), although in the English Bible this king's name is spelled Hoshea. The prophet Hosea was the son of Beeri. Nothing further is known of Beeri.

Hosea was apparently a citizen of the northern kingdom. This conclusion is based on the fact that he makes numerous and minute references to the events in that kingdom. He mentions, for example, Gilead (6:6), Mizpah (5:1), Tabor (5:1), Shechem (6:9), Gilgal and Bethel (4:5). Jonah is the only other prophet of the northern kingdom whose writings have survived.

Nothing conclusive can be said regarding the occupation of Hosea prior to his call to be a prophet. Because of his allusion to baking procedures some have suggested that he was a baker. Others have suggested that he was a tradesman or a priest. The silence of the Scriptures in this respect suggests the lesson that a prophet's message was more important than his personal background and personality.

Hosea was married. His wife Gomer bore three children to whom the prophet gave prophetic names: Jezreel, Lo-ruhamah, and Lo-ammi. These are the more or less indisputable facts about Hosea's marriage. A host of questions, however, has been raised about this man's family life. What was the status of Gomer at the time of the marriage? Was she a whore? a temple prostitute? a virtuous woman? Did Gomer already have children at the time of the marriage? Did Gomer become unfaithful to Hosea? Is the unnamed woman in chapter 3 Gomer? If so, was the marriage with Gomer ever reconciled? These questions will be addressed in the discussion of the relevant passages.

B. The Mission.

Hosea's call to ministry took the form of a command to "marry a wife of whoredom." No little discussion has centered on these words. The problem of the status of Gomer prior to her marriage to Hosea probably never will be settled to the satisfaction of all interpreters. The issue will be addressed in comments on chapter 1.

Hosea mentions four kings of Judah during whose reigns he was preaching in northern Israel: Uzziah, Jotham, Ahaz, and Hezekiah. At the same time he mentions only one king, Jeroboam II, who ruled in Israel. Jeroboam was the last great king to rule in the north. Apparently Hosea did not regard those who followed him on the throne as legitimate, or at least significant, monarchs.

Using these data which Hosea himself supplies the maximum chronological parameters of his ministry can be determined to be

767-686 BC. Jewish tradition regarded Hosea as the earliest of the Twelve. The rabbis based this conclusion on the language of 1:2, 'When Yahweh spoke *at the first* by Hosea' *(Baba Bathra* 14a). Modern scholars, however, hold to the temporal priority of Amos. No conclusive argument, however, substantiates the priority of Amos.

Hosea probably began his ministry prior to the assassination of King Zechariah in 752 BC. This conclusion is based on his prediction of judgment upon the Jehu dynasty of which Zechariah was the last representative. Probably his ministry extended only into the years of Hezekiah's co-regency with his father Ahaz, about 727 BC. The fact that Hosea makes no mention of the destruction of Samaria which he had prophesied suggested that his ministry terminated prior to that event.

Hosea's long ministry began in the prosperous reign of King Jeroboam II. From the heights of national glory the prophet rode with his countrymen the roller coaster headed for national destruction. Those were difficult times, times marked by deep spiritual apostasy and moral corruption. The hopeless political anarchy which followed the death of Jeroboam should have created a positive climate for the message of God. Unfortunately Hosea was greeted by hardened hearts, closed minds and clogged ears.

Logsdon has charted Israel's descent to destruction. The prophet alludes to the lack of spiritual knowledge (4:6,11), growth (4:16), dedication (4:17) and satisfaction (4:18). He documents their lack of devotion to God (5:4), their lack of humility (5:5), and their lack of consideration of others (7:2). Hosea stresses their lack of separation (7:4) and earnestness (7:14).[4] Robinson presents a similar list of chief problems: pride (5 5); instability (6:4); worldliness (7:8), corruption (9:9), backsliding (11:7); and idolatry (13:2).[5]

The immediate purpose of Hosea was to set forth before Ephraim (northern kingdom) the tragedy of their apostasy and the need for repentance. In carrying out his mission to his contemporaries Hosea at the same time rendered invaluable service to truth seekers throughout the centuries. In the context of Hosea's unfathomable love for his wife is revealed God's faithfulness in spite of human unfaithfulness. Perhaps no message in the Bible other than John 3:16 sets forth more clearly the grace and compassion of God for his people.

The fact that Amos and Hosea were contemporaries in the northern kingdom ministry invites a comparison between the two men. Chart No. 17 illustrates the similarities and differences between these two great prophets.

C. The Message.

The theme of the Book of Hosea is God's love for backsliders. Hosea expresses his message brilliantly. Few writers in the Old Testament can equal his skill and beauty. He uses clear and striking figures of speech. For example, to depict the instability of Israel's foreign policy he pictures a silly dove fluttering back and forth between Assyria and Egypt (7:11). The futility of trusting in human resources is likened to "feeding on the wind" (12:1).

Hosea employs a variety of tone and style. For example, in one place he uses the language of the law court (4:1), in another, the language of military commanders (5:8). This prophet had the marvelous ability to convey the anguish within the heart of a rejected God (cf. 2:14,15). What he says is made memorable by the way he says it.

Chart No. 16

Hosea and his Faithless Wife	THE STRUCTURE OF HOSEA		
	Yahweh and His Faithless People		
	Lack of Spiritual Knowledge	Lack of Brotherly Love	Lack of Covenant Faithfulness
A Sin Against Trust	Appeal (6:1-2)	Appeal (10:9-11:11)	Appeal (14:1-8)
Chs. 1-3	4:2-6:3	6:4-11:11	11:12-14:8

The Book of Hosea is second only to Zechariah in size among the Minor Prophets. Hosea is arranged generally in chronological order. The message is especially hard to outline. The rapid change of subject matter suggests that what is now called the Book of Hosea is really a collection of preaching notes from his long ministry. Two major divisions are in evidence. The first three chapters are a personal introduction. Chapters 4-14 are the sayings of Hosea which are loosely organized in three main divisions. Chart No. 16 displays the structure of the Book of Hosea.

Hosea contains twenty-eight distinct predictions. These are found in 111 verses of the book. This means that the predictive element in the book accounts for over half (56%) of the material. The focus prediction is that of the fall of Samaria. Hosea paints three pictures of the coming Messiah. He will be (1) the second Moses (1:11); (2) the second David (3:5); and (3) the second Israel (11:1).

Chart No. 17

COMPARISON OF AMOS AND HOSEA	
SIMILARITIES	
Israel's Unique Relationship to Yahweh Demands Responsibility.	
Assyria will be Yahweh's Tool to Punish Israel.	
Opposition to Hypocritical Formalism.	
A New Beginning on the Other Side of Judgment.	
CONTRASTS	
AMOS	HOSEA
Broad International Outlook.	Focus on Israel.
Focus on Social Sins.	Focus on Political Sin, Internal Intrigue and Assassination.
Preacher of Righteousness.	Preacher of Mercy and Lovingkindness.
Yahweh's Universal Sovereignty.	Yahweh's Unique Relationship with Israel.
Focus on the Outward Conduct of Life.	Focus on Inward Springs of Life.
The Voice of Conscience.	The Expression of Emotion.
Man's Inhumanity to Man.	Israel's Infidelity to God.
Love was Exhausted.	Love was Inexhaustible.

THE PROPHET MICAH
Prophet of Bethlehem's Savior

He has been called "the homely country prophet," "worthy champion of the poor" (Yates) and "the spokesman for the common people" (Blackwood). Perhaps of all the prophets Micah is the one whose contributions have been least appreciated. Yet in Micah the Morashtite there is combined Amos' passion for justice and Hosea's heart of love. In this book are some of the most outstanding prophecies in the Old Testament.

A. The Man.

Micah is the shortened form of a name which means "Who is like Yahweh?" The name is appropriate for a book whose peaks of prophecy point heavenward to the majestic wisdom and power of the Creator. The name has at least five spelling variations. Six other Micahs can be identified in the Old Testament. The Minor Prophet Micah, however, is not to identified with any of these.

Micah came from the rural area of Judah. His home village was Moresheth-gath (1:1,14), about twenty-five miles southwest of Jerusalem on the Philistine border. As the crow files this would be about seventeen miles west of Tekoa, the hometown of Amos.

Nothing is known about the life of Micah except what may be deduced from the book which he left behind. Some have concluded that he was a man who lived close to the soil. Others see in Micah a small-town artisan. In any case, Micah was the kind of person who would have felt more at home in a labor hall than in a cathedral.[6] He was truly the blue collar prophet!

No call for this prophet is recorded. An earlier prophet—Eliezer son of Dodavahu—came from the same village as Micah (2 Chr 20:37). This Eliezer some twelve decades earlier had "prophesied against Jehoshaphat" asserting that Judah's commercial fleet had been destroyed because the king of Judah had entered into an alliance with Ahaziah of Israel. Micah may have been a descendant of this courageous man of God. A more immediate stimulus for Micah's ministry may have been the bold preaching of Amos who lived only a few miles away. Amos had concluded his ministry about fifteen years before Micah began to preach. In any case the Morashtite claims in no uncertain terms his inspiration and therefore his authority as a spokesman for God.

B. The Mission.

Micah prophesied in the days of "Jotham, Ahaz and Hezekiah" kings of Judah (1:1). The earliest possible date for Micah's ministry would be 750 BC. The latest possible date would be 686 BC. Micah's ministry appears to have begun before the destruction of Samaria In 722 BC (1:5) and after the commencement of the ministry of Isaiah. A date of 735-700 BC for the ministry of this man of God would not be far off.

The immediate purpose of Micah's mission was to correct inequity and injustice in the land of Judah through censure and threats of judgment. The ultimate purpose of this ministry was to announce the future government of God in the land through a coming Ruler.

Chronologically Micah was the fourth great prophet to arise in Judah, following Obadiah, Joel, and Isaiah. Together with Amos and Hosea in the north and Isaiah in Judah, Micah formed a quartet of great prophetic spokesmen who produced in the eighth century BC the golden age of Hebrew prophecy.

Micah's sermons were delivered, not for the most part in his home village, but on trips to the capital Jerusalem. There at the same time Isaiah was delivering his sermons stressing total reliance on the Lord. If Isaiah stressed faith, Micah stressed works. Perhaps here is an Old Testament example of the contrast in emphasis between Paul and James. Did the two great prophets know each other? There is no direct evidence that they did. Yet it is difficult to imagine that they did not. Like his great contemporary, Micah saw Yahweh as Ruler of nations and men. Both prophets recognized the absolute holiness and majesty of the Lord. The vision of the exalted temple mount is presented verbatim by both prophets (Isa 2:2-4; Micah 4:1-3).

International events had a profound influence on the ministry of Micah. The Assyrian Tiglath-pileser III launched an imperialistic campaign in 745 BC. The great Aramean city of Damascus fell to him in 732 BC. Israel to the north and Judah were now vulnerable. Already before Micah rose to preach the Assyrians had made several thrusts toward Palestine and Egypt. Micah realized that unless Judah quickly became realigned with the Lord, disaster would befall that land.

Judah in the eighth century has riding the crest of national prosperity. Morals, however, were appallingly low. Governmental officials were dishonest. The "prophets" were nothing but windbags. Religious commitment was superficial and totally divorced from moral fortitude. Judah had become sinful, soft, and ripe for conquest.[7] These conditions combined with the divine compulsion to cause Micah to devote his energies to calling this wayward people to repentance.

C. The Message.

The Book of Micah contains 3,153 words, which have been organized into 105 verses and seven chapters. The book stands sixth in the Hebrew prophetic canon after Jonah and before Nahum, and third in the Septuagint arrangement after Amos. The Septuagint arrangement was probably based on the length of the various books. In many respects the Book of Micah is a miniature of the Book of Isaiah.

Chart No. 18

THE STRUCTURE OF MICAH				
FIRST DOOM-HOPE CYCLE			SECOND DOOM-HOPE CYCLE	
Imminent Judgment Declared	Present Corruption Condemned	Ultimate Blessing Promised	Present Repentance Pleaded	Sustaining Hope Displayed
1:2-2:5	2:6-3:12	Chs. 4-5	6:1-7:6	7:7-20
Message to the Nations Chs. 1-2		Message to the Rulers Chs. 3-5	Message to Israel Chs. 6-7	

As with most prophetic books, the liberal critics question the genuineness of large chunks of what has survived under the name of Micah. While chapters 1-3 are usually taken to be from the pen of Micah, chapters 4-5 are questioned by some, and chapters 6-7 by others. With the arrogant dogmatism which often characterizes literary critics one writer declares that the book contains materials dating to as late as 200 BC![8] No substantial reason has ever been presented for denying any of the words of the Hebrew text to the eighth century prophet.

The theme of Micah is present judgment but future blessing. The book is structured around alternating passages reflecting doom and hope. Chapters 1-3 and 6:1-7:6 spell out doom for Judah; chapters 4-5 and 7:7-20 offer hope. The oracles were probably not delivered in this order. So Micah chose to arrange his book in this order to make a point.

Some outline the book according to the imperative "hear" which appears in 1:2, 3:1, and 6:1. Thus the book contains (1) a message to the nations (chs. 1-2); (2) a message to the rulers (chs 3-5); and (3) a message to Israel (chs. 6-7). Baxter has offered an appealing outline which follows a slightly different breakdown of the content: (1) imminent judgment declared (chs. 1-3); (2) ultimate blessing promised (chs. 4-5); and (3) present repentance pleaded (chs. 6-7).[9] Chart No. 18 displays the structure of the Book of Micah.

The Book of Micah contains several contrasting theological emphases. To Micah Yahweh is the God of Israel, yet at the same time the God of all nations. Yahweh is judge, yet he is also savior. He is majestic in wrath, yet astonishing in compassion. He demands and executes justice, yet promises forgiveness. Yahweh scatters, but also gathers his flock. He destroys Zion, yet he also resurrects Zion. The God of Micah threatens the nations with humiliation, yet offers those same nations peace.[10]

According to Payne[11] the Book of Micah contains forty specific predictions. These predictions involve seventy-three verses or about seventy percent of the book. The major prediction—about a fourth of the predictive verses—focus on the single episode of Sennacherib's invasion of Judah in 701 BC. Other important predictions include the total destruction of Samaria (1:1-7); the birth of Messiah in Bethlehem (5:2-5); and the exaltation of messianic Jerusalem (4:1-8).

ENDNOTES

1. Some trace the term *noqdim* to Akkadian or Ugaritic parallels which refer to those who raise large temple herds. Would there, however, have been several of these high ranking overseers in the small town of Tekoa? Others trace *noqdim* to Arabic cognates which refer to a special breed of dwarfed-sized sheep especially prized for their wool. Still others think that *noqdim* is related to the Hebrew *naqod* which refers to "speckled" sheep and goats (Gen 30:32).

2. The nipping has been explained as follows: (1) to allow the juice to run out (Howard) or (2) insects to escape (Kelley) in order to hasten the ripening process. Honeycutt has proposed that hand pollination of the tree is involved.

3. George Adam Smith, *The Book of the Twelve Prophets* in "The Expositor's Bible" (New York: Armstrong, 1903), 1:85.

4. S. Franklin Logsdon, *Hosea: People who Forgot God* (Chicago: Moody, 1959), pp. 7-15.

5. George L. Robinson, *The Minor Prophets* (Grand Rapids: Baker, 1978 reprint), pp. 23-25.

6. Rolland E. Wolfe, "Micah" in *The Interpreter's Bible* (New York: Abingdon, 1956), 6:898.

7. *Ibid.*, 6:898f.

8. *Ibid.*, 6:899f.

9. J. Sidlow Baxter, *Explore the Book*; six vols. in one (Grand Rapids: Zondervan, 1966), 4:188.

10. James L. Mays, *Micah* in "The Old Testament Library" (Philadelphia: Westminster, 1976), p. 1.

11. J. Barton Payne, *Encyclopedia of Biblical Prophecy* (New York: Harper and Row), pp. 424-434.

BIBLIOGRAPHY
Eighth Century Prophets

Auld, A.G. *Amos.* "Old Testament Guides." Sheffield, England: JSOT Press, 1986.

Barton, John. *Amos's Oracles against the Nations.* Cambridge: University Press, 1980.

Cheyne, T.K. *The Book of Hosea.* "The Cambridge Bible for Schools and Colleges." Cambridge: University Press, 1913.

———. *Micah.* 1882. "The Cambridge Bible for Schools and Colleges." Cambridge: University Press, 1921

Coffman, James Burton. *The Minor Prophets: Hosea, Obadiah, and Micah.* Abilene: ACU Press, 1981.

Cripps, Richard S. *A Commentary on the Book of Amos* (1929). Minneapolis: Klock & Klock, 1981.

Emmerson, Grace I. *Hosea: An Israelite Prophet in Judean Perspective.* Sheffield, England: JSOT, 1984.

Garland, David. *Amos.* "A Study Guide Commentary." Grand Rapids: Zondervan, 1966.

———. *Hosea.* "Bible Study Commentary." Grand Rapids: Zondervan, 1975.

Hagstrom, David G. *The Coherence of the Book of Micah.* Atlanta: Scholars Press, 1988.

Hammershaimb, Erling, *The Book of Amos; a Commentary.* New York: Schocken, 1970.

Harper, William R. *A Critical and Exegetical Commentary on Amos and Hosea.* "The International Critical Commentary." Edinburgh: T. & T. Clark, 1979.

Hayes, John H. *Amos the Eighth Century Prophet.* Nashville: Abingdon, 1988.

Honeycutt, Roy L. *Amos and his Message.* Nashville: Broadman, 1963.

———. *Hosea and his Message.* Nashville: Broadman, 1975.

Hubbard, David Allan. *With Bands of Love* (Hosea). Grand Rapids: Eerdmans, 1968.

Kapelrud, Arvid S. *Central Ideas in Amos.* Oslo: University Press, 1961.

Kelley, Page H. *The Book of Amos.* "Shield Bible Study Outlines." Grand Rapids: Baker, 1966.

Kidner, Derek. *The Message of Hosea.* "The Bible Speaks Today." Downers Grove, IL: InterVarsity, 1981.

King, Philip J. *Amos, Hosea, Micah; an Archaeological Commentary.* Philadelphia: Westminster, 1988.

Knight, G.A.F. *Hosea; God's Love.* "Torch Bible Paperback." London: SCM, 1960.

Logsdon, S. Franklin. *Hosea: People Who Forgot God.* Chicago: Moody, 1959.

Lüthi, Walter. *In the Time of the Earthquake.* Trans. J.L.M. Haire and Ian Henderson. London: Hodder & Stoughton, 1940.

Mays, James L. *Amos* in "The Old Testament Library." Philadelphia: Westminster, 1969.

_____. *Hosea.* "The Old Testament Library." Philadelphia: Westminster, 1969.

_____. *Micah.* "The Old Testament Library." Philadelphia: Westminster, 1976.

Morgan, G. Campbell. *The Heart and Holiness of God.* Grand Rapids: Baker, 1974 reprint.

Motyer, J.A. *The Message of Amos.* "The Bible Speaks Today." Downers Grove, IL: InterVarsity, 1974.

Scott, Jack B. *The Book of Hosea.* "Shield Bible Study Outlines." Grand Rapids: Baker, 1971.

Snaith, Norman. *Mercy and Sacrifice; a Study of the Book of Hosea.* London: SCM. 1957.

Ward, James M. *Amos, Hosea.* "Knox Preaching Guides." Atlanta: John Knox, 1981.

_____. *Hosea: a Theological Commentary.* New York: Harper & Row, 1966.

Wolfe, Rolland E. *Meet Amos and Hosea.* New York: Harper, 1945.

Wolff, Hans Walter. *Micah a Commentary.* Trans. Gary Stansell. Minneapolis: Augsburg, 1988.

_____. *Hosea.* Trans. Gary Stansell. Philadelphia: Fortress, 1974.

_____. *Joel and Amos.* Trans. Janzen, McBride, Muenchow. Philadelphia: Fortress, 1977.

CHAPTER TEN

The Approaching Judgment
Amos 1:1-3:8

The opening verse of Amos is a superscription such as appears over several of the prophetic books. It contains five vital pieces of information concerning the Book of Amos. First, it identifies the contents of the book. It contains for the most part "the words of Amos," i.e., his proclamations, oracles and sermons.

Second, the superscription identifies the one who spoke those words. The name Amos does not occur outside the book, although a longer form of it (Amasiah) appears in 2 Chr 17:16. At the time he was dispatched on his mission Amos was "among the sheepherders from Tekoa." On the significance of his occupation and hometown, see the introductory notes on Amos in Chapter Nine.

Third, the superscription speaks to the origin of these words. Amos "saw" these words, i.e., he received these words in divine revelation before he spoke them to his people. This idiom goes back to the visionary experience of the earlier seers (cf. Num 24:2f.; 1 Kgs 22:17). Five visions are described in the book.

Fourth, the superscription identifies the subject matter of the book. Amos spoke "concerning Israel." Though Amos lived in Judah, the main burden of his ministry was Israel, the northern kingdom.

Finally, the superscription places the ministry of Amos in an historical context. He mentions the names of two kings, Uzziah of Judah and Jeroboam of Israel. To pinpoint the time of his ministry further, the text declares that he preached "two years before the earthquake." For a discussion of these chronological data, see the introduction to Amos in Chapter Nine.

THE WARNING ROAR
Amos 1:2

The Book of Amos begins with a warning roar: "Yahweh from Zion roars, and from Jerusalem he gives forth his voice." This is not the roar of thunder (Keil; Deane), but of a lion (Harper; Lehrman). A lion roars when it is about to pounce upon the prey. Here the roar signals a imminent judgment. Amos has borrowed these words from Joel (3:16). Amos intends to summarize his message in this single verse.

The name Yahweh literally means "he who is" or the Eternal One. The name is associated with Moses and the Exodus. The name has connotations of holiness (cf. Exod 3:5) and redemption.

Yahweh roars "from Zion," i.e., Jerusalem. In the time of David Yahweh had chosen Zion as the place of his altar. That altar was the place of both wrath (death) and mercy (atonement). Amos' opening words were a rebuke to the northern tribes who had broken away from the God-ordained center of worship in Jerusalem.

The entire land would be affected by the judgment which God's warning roar heralded. "The pastures of the shepherds shall mourn." Some take these words metaphorically. The "pastures" are the nations of the world; the "shepherds" are their kings (cf. Jer 25:34ff.). "Carmel" would represent the land of Israel, and its "top" would be the royal house. Amos, however, probably only meant that the entire land would be devastated by blast. The picture is one of drought. The land shrivels up as a result of Yahweh's judgment.

THE ROAR AGAINST THE GENTILE NATIONS
Amos 1:3-2:3

Amos began his ministry with a series of blasts against foreign nations. One thing is clear in this section: nations are accountable to God for their conduct even if they have not had the benefit of special revelation.

Much discussion has centered on the order in which Amos addresses the nations. Some think that subject matter has determined arrangement. They point out the chiastic arrangement of sandwiching two slave trade denouncements between two war brutalities denouncements. Others think the arrangement is based on geographical considerations. They see here an outer square (Damascus; Gaza; Tyre; Edom) and an inner square (Ammon; Moab; Judah; Israel). Still others think that national relationships is the key: two neighbors of Israel, two allies of Israel, and two cousins of Israel.

The individual oracles have similar structures. First they each begin with a declaration of divine hostility. "For three transgressions, yes for four, I will not reverse it." This so-called X + 1 formula appears several times in the book of Proverbs (e.g., 30:15). This pattern appears also in the Ugaritic (Canaanite) literature. The idiom is intended to produce a cumulative effect. The cumulative effect of national sin is judgment. Second, God declares that he will not "reverse"[1] that sentence of judgment. The warning roar would not be canceled. Third, Amos sets forth the reason for divine hostility against the nation. In fourth place stands a stereotyped announcement of the sending of fire against the place. Finally, the oracles speak of the removal of the king and the captivity of the people of each nation.

A. Judgment on Damascus (1:3-5).

Damascus was condemned for having "threshed Gilead with threshing instruments of iron." The reference is probably to the war atrocities perpetrated by Hazael and his son Ben-hadad during the years of their ascendance over Israel (cf. 2 Kgs 8:12; 13:7). The threshing instrument was a drag of heavy boards armed beneath with sharp stones or iron points weighted with a driver who stood on it. Apparently the Arameans would arrange prisoners on the ground, then drive this instrument over them. Such brutality demands condemnation (1:3).

Yahweh declares his intention to send the fire of judgment against "Hazael," i.e., the current dynasty of Damascus. The fire of war would consume the palaces of "Ben-hadad," one of the popular names for the rulers of Aram (1:4).

Yahweh would "break the bar of Damascus," i.e., that which secured the defenses of the city. Thus the city would be defenseless before an invading army. The rulers would be cut off from Bikat-aven (Valley of Vanity) and Beth-eden, secondary capitals of the Aramean kingdom. "The people of Aram will go into captivity unto Kir," i.e., they would return to their ancestral home (cf. 9:7) as captives (1:5).

B. Judgment on Philistia (1:6-8).

The Philistines were guilty of slave trade. "They carried away a whole captivity to deliver them up to Edom." Without regard even for women and children the Philistines handed these captives over to the Edomites who dispersed them to distant lands (1:6).

For their participation in slave trade the great Philistine cities would be assaulted by the fire of God's judgment. The rulers of Ashdod and Ashkelon would be "cut off." Yahweh would "turn his hand" over the city of Ekron, i.e., continue to demonstrate his power over that place. "The remnant of the Philistines shall perish," i.e., the Philistines as a people would be destroyed (1:7-8).

C. Judgment on Phoenicia (1:9-10).

The Phoenicians had also been involved in slave trade, delivering up an entire captive population to Edom. Their sin, however, went beyond that of Philistia because Phoenicia "did not remember the brotherly covenant." They had violated a sacred treaty. Thus the moral principle to which God holds all peoples accountable is that the pledged word is inviolable (1:9).

Tyre was the leading city of Phoenicia. God's judgment fire would destroy that place with its palaces (1:10).

D. Judgment on Edom (1:11-12).

Twice Edom has already been indicted for slave trade (cf. 1:6,9).

Now a new dimension to the national guilt of this nation is added. Edom is accused of pitiless pursuit of his brother nation Israel. "He pursued his brother with the sword and destroyed his compassions." Here is a crime of the heart. Edom harbored hatred toward a nation with which a sacred treaty was in force. The Lord accused Edom of perpetual anger and wrath. God does not tolerate ethnic or racial hatred. Without forgiveness towards others, there can be no forgiveness from God. God's judgment fire would be poured out upon Teman and Bozrah, the major cities of Edom.

E. Judgment on Ammon (1:13-15).

The Ammonites were guilty of attempting to expand their territory at the expense of Israel. In so doing, they had committed unspeakable atrocities, especially in the area of Gilead. In an attempt to wipe out the entire male population, they had even gone after the little babies in the wombs of their mothers. Here is raw ambition trampling on the rights of the helpless—women and the unborn. God expects all nations to respect basic human rights, including the right to be born (1:13).

The fire of war would be unleashed against Rabbah, the capital of Ammon. The forces of nature would assist the armies in dashing the place to pieces. The royal family of Ammon would be taken into captivity. Nothing moves God to punish so much as wanton cruelty to the helpless (1:14-15).[2]

F. Judgment on Moab (2:1-3).

The Moabites are condemned for having "burned the bones of the king of Edom to lime." To open a tomb and desecrate a corpse was considered the ultimate sacrilege in the ancient world. Obviously the Moabites were taking vengeance on the royal family of Edom. Perhaps the Moabites were taking revenge for the attack recorded in 2 Kgs 3:26-27. The king of Moab had immolated his son, the crown prince, during the pressure of an attack by the combined forces of Israel, Judah and Edom. In any case, the Lord could not overlook sacrilege (2:1).

The fire of God's judgment would be directed against Moab. Their capital Kerioth would be consumed. Their land would be overrun by armies which would come "with shouting and with the sound of the horn." The "judge," i.e., ruler, of Moab would be cut off along with all the members of the royal family (2:2-3).

Amos' God was God of all the earth. Surrounding Gentile nations are all condemned by a "Thus says Yahweh." He had seen the monstrous atrocities of the Arameans of Damascus. He took note of the slave trade of Gaza and Tyre. He knew of the commitments made between nations which had been broken. He even observed the sins of the heart—hatred, ambition, vengeance.

THE ROAR AGAINST JUDAH
Amos 2:4-5

The warning roar of divine judgment has been hurled at six foreign nations. Syria, Philistia and Tyre belonged to Israel's political environment. Edom, Ammon and Moab were Israel's "cousins." The "noose of judgment"[3] was tightening around the neck of the covenant people. Now the focus is on the people of God. They had misunderstood the doctrine of election to be a declaration of favoritism. Amos first addressed Judah (2:4-5) and then the northern kingdom of Israel (2:6-16).

Judah falls under condemnation for despising then dismissing divine truth. "They have rejected the law of Yahweh and did not keep his statutes." The term "statutes" comes from a verb meaning to carve out or engrave. The term points to the imperishable and unchangeable nature of God's truth. The "statutes" were the separate precepts contained in the Torah or Law. Whereas the Gentiles had sinned against natural law, Judah had sinned against written law. This oracle demonstrates Amos' impartiality (2:4a).

Amos also charged Judah with falling into idolatry. "Their lies," i.e., idols, had caused them "to err." The idols made false claims and false promises and consequently are called "lies." Yet the citizens embraced those idols as their fathers before them had done. Like their fathers, they "walked after" those idols, i.e., allowed those false religions to guide their daily lives. "The popular error of one generation becomes the axiom of the next. The children canonize the errors of their fathers."[4] While Judah possessed God's Law, they preferred the traditions of men (2:4b).

The judgment against Judah is stated in language which had already been employed against the nations. God would send the fire of his wrath against Judah. It would consume the palaces of Jerusalem. These words were literally as well as figuratively fulfilled by Nebuchadnezzar in 586 BC (2:5).

THE ROAR AGAINST ISRAEL
Amos 2:6-16

In his oracle against Israel Amos draws two contrasts. First he contrasts the deeds of Israel with those of Yahweh. Then he makes a similar contrast between the words of Yahweh and those of Israel.

A. Israel's Sinful Acts (2:6-8).

Amos first sketches the sinful deeds of Israel. He speaks of four sins in particular.

1. Covetousness (2:6-7a). The wealthy landowners in Israel "sell the innocent for silver and the needy with a transfer of shoes." This was definitely, as Kelley observes, the survival of the slickest.[5] The "innocent" can refer to one who is right in a lawsuit, or more generally, one who is right with God. The "needy" are those who were in no position to offer any resistance to legal abuse. For a small bribe the judges would pronounce the innocent guilty, even for such a small bribe as a pair of shoes. Others think that the needy were being taken into debtor's slavery for a debt as small as as a pair of shoes (2:6).

The wealthy land owners in Israel are described as those who "pant after the dust on the head of the poor." The lust for land was so great that Amos (humorously) depicts the wealthy of panting like an excited dog after the dust that a poor man might sprinkle on his head as a sign of mourning. Others think the meaning is that they long to see the poor brought into such misery that they pour dust upon their head. The "poor" here are the poverty stricken.

The powerful land owners would "turn aside the way of the humble" or "meek." These were the underdogs of Israelite society. Their "way" is the legal process. They "turn aside" these underdogs, i.e., they denied the legal rights of these people (2:7a).

2. Immorality (2:7b). Amos charges that "a man and his father," i.e., the whole male population, "go unto the same maid." The prophet is alluding to the immoral practices associated with Baal worship (cf. Hos 4:13f.). The terminology used here is not that which is usually used to depict sexual intercourse. This suggests that these men had lost all sense of disobeying the commandments of their God (cf. Exod 20:14). Visiting the prostitutes at the local shrine was routine behavior. For a man to have sexual intercourse with a prostitute was bad enough; for a man and his son to have the same woman was a monstrous abomination. Such action would be considered incest under the Law. The language here implies that these men deliberately committed these sins in order to "profane" Yahweh's "holy name," i.e., to bring discredit upon true faith and worship. Sexual gratification had replaced divine holiness as the guiding principle of life (2:7b).

3. *Heartlessness (2:8a).* The sinners in Israel would "stretch out beside every altar upon garments taken in pledge." Amos refers to the sacrificial feasts held in the shrines at Dan and Bethel. The garments mentioned here were the large outer garments which formed the poor man's dress by day and cover by night. The Law required that if these garments were pawned, they were to be returned by nightfall (cf. Exod 22:26; Deut 24:12). The altar, the symbol of divine mercy, was desecrated by such heartlessness on the part of the "worshipers." One cannot be right with God if he is wrong with men. When divine compassion finds no reflection in human compassion, then the altar is visited in vain.[6]

4. *Hypocrisy (2:8b).* "In the house of their God they drink the wine of them that have been fined." In the temples where supposedly they were worshiping Yahweh they mocked his Law. There they drank the wine purchased by fines unjustly charged the poor in court. Thus their worship was hypocritical. They went through the motions of worship, but they ignored the demands of the Law for justice in the courts. The charge may hint of intemperance as well, but this is not in the forefront.

B. The Saving Acts of Yahweh (2:9-11).

Alongside the shameful picture of the sinful acts of Israel, Amos places the gracious acts of God on behalf of his people. This juxtaposition highlights what surely must be regarded as the root sin of the covenant people, viz., ingratitude. In these verses the first person singular verb occurs five times, and twice it is reinforced with a personal pronoun.

1. God had destroyed the Amorite (2:9). Here the term "Amorite" is used in the broad sense for all the inhabitants of Canaan (Deut 1:20). The Lord emphasizes the magnitude of this intervention by two similes. First, the height of the Amorite "was like the height of the cedars." The extraordinary stature of some of these people had terrified the spies which had been sent into the land from Kadesh (Num 13:32; Deut 1:28). Second, the strength of the Amorite is likened to the mighty oaks. The inhabitants of Canaan were a powerful people.

Without divine intervention Israel could have never dislodged the Amorite from Canaan. Yet God graciously did intervene. He "destroyed his fruit from above and his roots from beneath," i.e., Yahweh completely destroyed this people.

2. God had brought them out of Egypt (2:10). The language reflects the fact that Palestine is a mountainous land, and Egypt is at a lower elevation. Through a mighty confrontation with Pharaoh and the gods of Egypt, Yahweh had liberated his people. To reach their destination the Lord had to lead his people through the wilderness. There he provided for them literally every day "for forty years." The mention of the duration of the wilderness wandering is a subtle reminder that those four decades were punishment for faithlessness on the part of Israel. Yahweh, however, continued to bear with them in spite of their disobedience. Israel came to possess "the land of the Amorite." God had given them the land in which they were living as an inheritance.

3. God had raised up spiritual leaders (2:11). "Prophets" brought divine revelation to Israel. "Nazirites" through their vow of abstinence from the fruit of the vine (cf. Num 6) set an example of consecrated living. The divine guidance which Israel had experienced in the Exodus and wilderness was continued once they were in Canaan by means of these prophets and Nazirites.

The unit concludes with a rhetorical question designed to engage the minds of the apostates in Israel: "Is this not so, O sons of Israel?" The authority of this contrast between the saving acts of Yahweh and the sinful acts of Israel is further underscored by the use of the formula "declares Yahweh" or oracle of Yahweh.

C. The Ultimate Ingratitude (2:12).

Israel showed no appreciation for the gracious act of Yahweh in raising up prophets and Nazirites. They manifested their wretched ingratitude in two ways. First, they "gave the Nazirites wine to drink." Instead of striving to follow the example of these holy men they tried to seduce them into breaking their vow. They may have used compulsion as well as persuasion. Second, they issued orders against the prophets forbidding them to prophesy. They tried to silence the voices which were a continuous rebuke to them. Amos himself is an example of one such effort to silence a prophet (cf. 7:10-17).

The covenant people are distinguished from the surrounding nations by the fact of divine revelation. God had given them his Law (2:4), prophets and Nazirites (2:11). Yet this people refused to listen. They ignored revelation. That monstrous ingratitude necessitated severe divine discipline.

D. The Impending Discipline (2:13-16).

Israel had forfeited God's favor. That is the theme of the final unit of Amos 2. An illustration of judgment (2:13) is followed by a description of that same judgment (2:14-16).

1. An illustration of judgment (2:13). The announcement of impending discipline begins with "Behold!" This word often introduces statements which are shocking or at least unexpected. In this case the same God who had twice spoken emphatically of what he had done *for* Israel (2:9,10,13), now speaks of what he would do *to* them.

God announces that he will "press down" Israel like "the cart presses which is filled with sheaves."[7] The picture here is of a heavily loaded cart which smashes the earth under its wheels. Thus Israel will be crushed by God's judgment.

2. A description of the judgment (2:14-16). In the face of the divine discipline native ability would avail nothing. The fleet of foot would not be able to flee. The strong one would not be able to "confirm his strength," i.e., use his strength to any advantage. Even the mighty man would not escape with his life (2:14).

In that day acquired skill would avail nothing. Skilled bowmen would not be able to stand before the enemy. Trained horsemen would not escape with their lives (2:15).

In that day outstanding qualities would avail nothing. The "stout hearted" among the mighty men, i.e., the bravest warrior, would flee "naked," i.e., stripped of weapons and heavy garments. "In that day" brings to mind the similar language of Joel. This discipline of Israel will be the day of Yahweh for that nation.

The argument of this Israel oracle has been this: Israel had sinned grievously against God. The disobedience of the people was due to no lack of effort on God's part to aid his people. Because of their sins Israel must suffer. No one would escape.

A DEFENSE OF THE WARNING ROAR
Amos 3:1-8

At this point Amos may have been challenged by his auditors. What right did he, a man of Judah, have to condemn the society in Israel? In defending his ministry Amos spoke of (1) the source (2) grounds, (3) logic and (4) compulsion of his message.

A. The Source of his Message (3:1a).

In the first of three "Hear ye" oracles Amos called upon the citizens of Israel pay attention to the word "which Yahweh has spoken concerning you." This is a clear and dramatic claim to divine inspiration. The message is addressed to "the children of Israel." The term "Israel" recalled that this was the people of covenant and promise. They were the elect of God. The term "children" identifies the present generation as the physical descendants of Israel or Jacob.

B. The Grounds of his Message (3:1b-2).

Israel had a special relationship with Yahweh. Israel and Judah combined were one "family" which Yahweh had brought up from the land of Egypt. Through Amos the head of the family was now about to speak, hence the first person pronoun. As a redeemed people, Israel was also a privileged people. "You only have I known of all the families of the earth." In this context, the verb "know" suggests the ideas of loved, acknowledged, or chosen. The language suggests an intimate relationship between God and his people (3:2a). In Hittite treaties the word is used in the sense "to recognize by covenant."

The belief that Israel had been chosen by God for a particular service to the rest of the world lies at the heart of every expression of Hebrew thought. Such a concept is without parallel among other nations of the ancient Near East.[8] In the popular theology of the day "favored" meant that Israel was exempt from punishment. The prophets, however, emphasized that Israel's selection by God meant that the nation must live by a higher standard. Since Israel had sinned against light, knowledge and love, her punishment must be the heavier. "Therefore I will visit upon you," i.e., punish, "all of your iniquities" (3:2b).

C. The Logic of his Message (3:3-6).

Before making any further announcement of judgment, Amos pauses to establish his right and duty to prophesy. He uses a series of chain-like similes drawn from life to establish a law of cause and effect which is true as much in the spiritual realm as in the physical.

1. Relationships are not accidental (3:3). "Will two walk together unless they have made an appointment?" At the very least this question means that it is not likely that two men will meet in a trackless desert. If they do walk together it is safe to assume that they do so because of a prior appointment. Is there more in this question? Some think the reference is to the covenant relationship between God and his people Israel, a relationship which was in jeopardy.[9] Others think that Amos is referring to his calling as a prophet.

2. Threats are not idle (3:4). Two rhetorical questions are based on the habits of lions. A lion does not give forth his voice until his quarry is in sight. The roar means the lion has sprung upon his prey. The point is that prophetic warnings of judgment are as ominous as the roars of lions.

3. Traps are triggered (3:5). Two additional rhetorical questions come from the realm of the fowler. Birds were caught by spring nets which were triggered by the bird when it went after "the snare" or bait. The exact mechanics of these two illustrations is not clear. The point, however, is that judgment is triggered by the actions of the people. Their sin has drawn them to destruction. God's judgment would spring up and catch all sinners.

4. Alarms produce fear (3:6a). "Is a trumpet blown in a city and the people are not afraid?" The trumpet was the signal of impending danger. The instrument was not blown unless the city was facing potential calamity. The prophetic message was like an alarm sounding throughout the land. Israel had heard, but chose to ignore the warning.

5. God brings judgment (3:6b). "Shall evil," i.e., calamity, "befall a city and Yahweh has not done it?" This question stresses the sovereignty of God. He is the author of all fortune, good and evil. All that happens must be assigned either to the active or permissive will of God. If evil befalls Israel it will not be due to chance, but to divine will.

D. The Compulsion of his Message (3:7-8).

Yahweh is a God of compassion. He never brings calamity upon a city without warning the people. He reveals his "secret purpose" (Heb., *sod*) unto his servants the prophets. He reveals to them the certainty and significance of the coming calamity (3:7).

Like a mighty lion about to pounce on the prey, Yahweh had roared forth his warning to Israel. This warning roar should cause every citizen of Israel to be afraid. The "roar" here refers to the word Yahweh Elohim had spoken. Amos had heard that word. Whether or not men feared, a necessity was laid on Amos to prophesy. Like Jeremiah, Paul and other great preachers, this prophet felt a compulsion to share the divine message (3:8).

ENDNOTES

1. The LXX reads "I will not turn away from it " i.e., I will no longer disregard its sins.
2. J.A. Motyer, *The Message of Amos* in "The Bible Speaks Today" (Downers Grove, IL: InterVarsity, 1974), p. 43.
3. *Ibid.,* p. 50.
4. E.B. Pusey, *The Minor Prophets, a Commentary* (Grand Rapids: Baker, 1956 reprint). 1:260.
5. Page H. Kelley, *The Book of Amos* in "Shield Bible Study Outlines" (Grand Rapids: Baker, 1966), p. 42.
6. Motyer, *op. cit.,* p. 60.

7. This translation is essentially that of the NIV. The Hiphil form of the verb weighs against NASB "I am weighted down beneath you as a wagon is weighed down when filled with sheaves."

8. W.R. Harper, *A Critical and Exegetical Commentary on Amos and Hosea* in "The International Critical Commentary" (Edinburgh: T. & T. Clark, 1966), p. 66.

9. Harper, Lehrman, Henderson, and Pusey hold that Amos is referring to the covenant between God and Israel in 3:3.

CHAPTER ELEVEN

Prepare to Meet Your God
Amos 3:9-5:17

After defending his ministry, Amos continues to expose the sin in Israel in two oracles. This exposure is followed by a lengthy call for repentance.

DIAGNOSIS OF ISRAEL'S AILMENT
Amos 3:9-15

Amos makes the point that God can become the enemy of those who once were his people. The God who had entered into a covenant with Israel at Mt. Sinai now announces his intention to smite and punish his people (3:14,15). Israel was alienated from God. She had become powerless before her enemies. Three formulas of introduction outline the prophet's diagnosis of the spiritual condition of the nation.

A. The Social Dimension (3:9-11).

God had become the enemy of his people because they had not maintained the standard of God's law in their social relationships. To make his point Amos rhetorically summoned the neighboring nations to come and bear witness against Israel. Amos then specificies what the heathen would observe in Samaria. This is followed by an announcement of judgment.

1. The summons of the heathen (3:9a). Ashdod of the Philistines and Egypt were chosen because they were the chief enemies of Israel. From the flat roofs of the palaces of these lands the summons went out for the witnesses to gather. Perhaps the thought is that only those in palaces were capable of pronouncing a correct sentence as to the mode of life commonly adopted by the wealthy of Israel. The heathen were to assemble on "the mountains of Samaria." This capital of Israel was situated in the center of an amphitheater of mountains. From this vantage point these witnesses could gain a clear view of all that transpired within the city.

2. The observations by the heathen (3:9b-10). First, the heathen observed in Samaria "great tumults" (*mehumah*). The word refers to the turbulent life of the nobles which included oppression, confusion, overturning of justice, arbitrary deeds of might, strife between poor and rich. A city of "great tumults" is a city in a state of confusion in which everything is turned topsy-turvy and all justice and order are overthrown by open violence. Second, the foreign witnesses observed "oppressions," i.e., acts of violence against the powerless (3:9b).

Third, they observed a people who did not know how to do right. Injustice had become second nature for them. They could no longer distinguish between right and wrong. Fourth, they observed that the affluent stored up "violence and destruction," i.e., the fruits of their violent robberies (3:10).

3. The punishment on Samaria (3:11). Because of these social evils, Yahweh Elohim would bring punishment upon Israel. First, the land which they had defiled would be surrounded by an adversary. The Assyrian army fulfilled this prophecy. Tiglath-pileser overran Israel in 734 BC. Shalmaneser attacked Israel more than once. Sargon presided over the siege and capture of Samaria itself in 722 BC.

Second, the power they abused would be smashed, for the adversary would "bring down from you your strength." Third, the palaces which they filled with ill-gotten gain would be plundered.

B. The Spiritual Dimension (3:12).

A direct utterance of Yahweh announces the total destruction of Israel as a political entity. Israel could no more escape God than a sheep could escape a lion. The shepherd may indeed "rescue" two shank bones or a piece of an ear from the beast to prove that he had not stolen the animal from the owner (cf. Exoc. 22:13). To this extent the "children of Israel" would "be delivered." The point is that only a pitiful remnant of the nation would survive the judgment which Yahweh was about to unleash (3:12a).

The last phrase of this announcement of judgment indicates the spiritual condition of the nation. Amos again employs humor to depict those being taken away by the great lion (Assyria) as clinging for dear life to that which they most prized. They would be be taken away "with the corner of a couch and part of a bed."[1] A sensual and worldly people cannot part with their material possessions even in the judgment. They would cling to broken beds and couches, symbols of their luxury and idleness.

C. The Religious Dimension (3:13-15).

The heathen who were called to witness the sins of Samaria (3:9) were now instructed to announce her punishment. The witnesses were to address this oracle to "the house of Jacob." The traditional title for the people is used to remind them who they were. They were God's people. Therefore they were held to a higher standard of accountability (3:13a).

What the heathen witnesses were about to announce is an "oracle of Yahweh Elohim, the God of hosts," i.e., Yahweh the God of covenant, Elohim the Creator, the God of all armies earthly and heavenly. These names underscore that the judgment about to be announced was both purposeful and powerful. The God they were about to face was not the anemic Yahweh worshiped at the northern shrines at Bethel and Dan. The calf worship of Jeroboam made Yahweh a divine bellhop to do the bidding of the state (3:13b).

The heathen were to announce the day of Yahweh's visitation of Israel for the purpose of judgment. The "transgressions" of the nations would be punished, especially those deliberate departures from the Law with respect to religious practice. Yahweh would "visit," i.e., punish, the "altars of Bethel." Apparently additional altars had been erected in the city since 931 BC when Jeroboam I had built the first altar there. Even the most sacred part of those altars where the sacrificial blood was sprinkled—the horns—would be broken off and fall to the ground. Yahweh had no respect for the most sacred shrines in Israel. Those "holy" places would afford no sanctuary in the day of his wrath (3:14).

Private dwellings as well as shrines would be devastated in that day. Yahweh would smite "the winter house along with the summer house." These were probably not two separate buildings, but the exterior and interior portions of a palace. The former would be used in the summer, the latter in the winter (cf. Jer 36:22). The "houses of ivory," i.e., palaces with ivory inlaid walls (cf. 1 Kgs 22:39), would also perish. These "great houses" of the king and nobles would come to an end (3:15).

FOCUS ON CONDEMNATION
Amos 4:1-13

In his first "Hear ye" oracle Amos had done two things. He had defended his right to preach (3:1-8) and he had announced the judgment on Israel (3:9-15). The second "hear ye" oracle focuses on condemnation. Here Amos brings the picture of Israel's sin into sharper focus as he targets Israel's women, worship and waywardness. Unlike the previous message, however, this one concludes with an appeal.

A. Condemnation of Women (4:1-3).

Amos addressed the women of Israel as "cows of Bashan."[2] Though the cows of Bashan were some of the best in the land, this title was not intended to be complimentary. Rather it points to the self-indulgent lifestyle of the women who reside "in the mountain of Samaria." The strength of that city created the climate where these women gave little concern to the possibility of national judgment (4:1a).

Three participial phrases present an unflattering picture of the way these women customarily acted. First, they "oppress the poor." Through their husbands they extracted from poor working people the wherewithal to subsidize their extravagances. Second, they "crush the needy." They walked all over the little people. After all, was it not their place in life to serve the cause of the well-to-do? Rank had its privileges, and those with no rank had none. Third, they nagged their husbands to provide the wine for their debauchery. They even urged their husbands to join them in the revelry (4:1b).

The women of Samaria were destined to face the wrath of Yahweh Elohim. He had sworn by his own holiness that the days of judgment were coming. Men swear by God, but God swears by himself. His holiness cannot tolerate the iniquity of these women (4:2a).

Yahweh threatened to take these women away "with hooks" and "fish hooks." Assyrian monuments depict captives dragged along by a rope fastened to a ring in the underlip. Thus these words could be taken literally (cf. 2 Chr 33:11). Others, however, think Amos is employing a metaphor taken from fishing practice. These women would be utterly helpless, taken away for destruction like fish caught with hooks (4:2b).

The women would "go out through breaches" in the wall of Samaria "everyone before her." The wall would be filled with so many holes that each would go straight forward from the place where she was captured. The women would then be "cast away toward Harmon," i.e., their corpses thrown down in the direction of a place called Harmon. Many think the reading should be "Hermon," a reference to the famous mountain in Bashan. Thus the irony here. The cows of Bashan would end up as carrion on the mountains of Bashan! (4:3).

B. Condemnation of Worship (4:4-5).

In condemning Israel's worship, Amos employs the language of priestly exhortation, but with a twist of bitter irony. This is a "shocking parody of ecclesiastical language that must have sounded like irreverent blasphemy" to Amos' audience.[5] He may have spoken these words during one of the great festivals at Bethel.

1. The places of worship. He begins by condemning the places of worship. "Come to Bethel and transgress, to Gilgal and multiply transgression." The corrupt calf worship practiced in the name of Yahweh at these places was an abomination to God. Gilgal was the first camping spot of Israel after entering Canaan. Apparently the place had become a shrine frequented by the calf worshipers of the north. The prophets viewed Jeroboam's calf as a violation of the Second Commandment. Furthermore, in order to be legitimate all public worship had to be conducted at the place God had chosen, viz., the temple in Jerusalem (4:4a).

2. *The acts of worship.* Next Amos uses his sarcasm to condemn the acts of worship being performed in Israel. He urges his auditors to bring their tithes "every three days." Normally they were brought annually (Lev 27:30). The point is that even exaggerated tithing would avail nothing with God. He cannot be bribed with donations (4:4b).

Second, he urged them (sarcastically) to offer thank offerings of leavened as well as unleavened bread. Such offerings would violate the law of Moses (Lev 2:11; 7:12). A different custom, however, may have been followed in the north. In any case, Amos' point is that such religious zeal would avail nothing. Third, the prophet urged them (sarcastically) to "proclaim freewill offerings." Is he urging them to boast of these private offerings? (Harper; Lehrman). Or is Amos urging the priests to make freewill offerings compulsory? (Deane; Keil) Again the point is that all the worship which they could muster would not thwart the judgment of God (4:5a).

3. *The motives of worship (4:5b).* "For thus you love, O house of Israel." Their worship was man-centered. They loved the rituals and ceremonies. The implication is that God did not. In this paragraph many different aspects of religious devotion are mentioned. Religious privileges—visiting the house of God and offering sacrifices; religious duties—tithes; religious joys—the sacrifice of thanksgiving; religious devotion—freewill offerings. All together they were pointless.[4]

C. Condemnation of Waywardness (4:6-13).

Chapter 4 concludes with a narrative intended to serve as further indictment of Israel. This unit contains five distinct sayings, each opening and concluding in the same manner. Amos artistically utilizes repetition to drive home his point.

1. Former judgments on wayward Israel (4:6-11). In the law God had told Israel exactly what the consequences of waywardness on their part would be (cf. Deut 28:15-29:28). The Lord had done exactly what he said he would do. A whole series of disciplinary disasters had been sent upon Israel—*musar* judgments—designed to bring the nation to repentance. Had the people been more perceptive they would have recognized in the recent national disasters the covenant curses which had been pronounced by the Lord more than six hundred years earlier.

The first blow was famine. When there is a scarcity of food in the land the citizens have "cleanness of teeth." God speaks here in the first person, and the first person verb is reinforced by means of the pronoun. Perhaps the thought connection is like this: While they have been busy with their religious exercises, God was using national calamities to bring about their true commitment to him. Famines are documented during the reign of Ahab (1 Kgs 17:12) and his son Jehoram (2 Kgs 4:38; 8:1). The famine mentioned by Amos, however, is probably an unrecorded one. In spite of this blow, Israel did not return unto Yahweh (4:6).

The second blow was untimely drought. Yahweh had withheld the so-called latter or spring rain "when there yet remained three months before harvest" which occurred in May or June. As proof that it was not due to the blind laws of nature, the drought hit only selective cities. In some areas the situation was desperate. Two or three cities "wandered" to one city to find drinking water. They were not able to find enough water to satisfy their needs. Yet Israel did not return unto Yahweh (4:7-8).

The third plague was blight. The scorching east wind off the desert withered the crops (cf. Isa 27:8; Ezek 17:10). Crops were ruined by mildew which was caused by dampness and heat (cf. Jer 30:6). Insect infestation destroyed gardens, vineyards, and fig and olive trees. Still Israel did not return unto Yahweh (4:9).

Pestilence and war constituted the fourth blow against Israel. "Plague in the manner of Egypt" is a plague as severe as the pestilence sent upon Pharaoh (Exod 9:3ff.). Egypt was notorious for its plagues in the ancient world (cf. Deut 7:15; 28:27,60). Israel's young men were slain by the sword. Probably the reference is to the repeated wars with the Arameans which characterized the latter half of the ninth century BC. While the soldiers were slain, their war horses were captured. Decaying human flesh caused a stench throughout the land. Yet Israel did not return unto Yahweh (4:10).

The fifth blow was earthquake. Yahweh "overthrew" some of their cities with such devastation that the cities were obliterated as thoroughly as Sodom and Gomorrah in Genesis 19. Some cities just barely survived. They were "like a brand snatched from the fire," i.e., blackened, diminished, worthless. Yet Israel did not return unto Yahweh (4:11).

2. *Future judgment on wayward Israel (4:12).* The *musar* judgments had failed to produce the desired results. Therefore, Yahweh announced a new kind of judgment, one much worse than any of the five blows just mentioned. "Thus will I do to you, O Israel." Do what? Yahweh does not specify what that final judgment would be. He uses the device of aposiopesis, a sudden breaking off of the sentence as if the speaker is unwilling to express his mind.

Because God anticipated one last, terrible judgment, Israel needed to "prepare to meet God." This short statement, the most famous in the book, is also one of the most controversial. Some see it only as a sarcastic challenge: Endure this judgment if you can! (Kelley). On the other hand, the statement has been taken to be simply an announcement of judgment (Mays). The term "prepare" implies warning. It also suggests the possibility of repentance.[5] The word is used before Israel's encounter with Yahweh at Mt. Sinai (cf. Exod 19:15).

Israel should prepare "to meet your God." They would not return to him, so he would come to them in a terrifying judgment which no Israelite would be able to avoid. The judgment would be more awesome than any of the blows which had already been sent their way. Yet the idea of meeting God in Scripture always has a connotation of grace.[6] Certainly the personal possessive pronoun seems to point in the direction of grace. Thus, those who see in Amos 4:12 both a warning and a call for repentance are no doubt correct.

3. *The God with whom they must deal (4:13).* Amos enforces his threat and appeal with a description of God. The God they

expected to meet was nothing like the great and awesome God whom they would encounter in judgment. This description of God appears to be a fragment of an ancient hymn which Amos himself may have composed. Five dimensions of Yahweh's power are praised in this piece.

First, Amos mentions Yahweh's *creative power*. In the visible realm he forms the mountains. He also creates the wind in the invisible realm. Second, the hymn alludes to Yahweh's *discerning power*. He "declares to a man what is his thought." The point is that God knows the thoughts of men. Through his prophets he reveals secret thoughts and motives.

Third, the *transforming power* of Yahweh is praised. He "makes dawn into darkness." Yahweh changes the day into the night (Harper) possibly by blotting out the sunlight by means of storm clouds (Lehrman). Fourth, Amos speaks of Yahweh's *triumphant power*. He "treads on the high places of the earth." He reigns over the earth as well as the heavens. Fifth, the name "Yahweh of hosts" suggests his *redeeming power*. Faith can cling to this covenant name. Perhaps this great God would yet intervene on behalf of his people, if they would only repent.

A CALL FOR REPENTANCE
Amos 5:1-17

Having in detail set forth the case against Israel, Amos now began to plead for repentance. A terrible disaster was about to befall the nation. Only by seeking Yahweh with contrite hearts did this people stand any chance of survival.

A. An Ominous Threat (5:1-3).

To dramatize the desperate situation in Israel—the northern kingdom—Amos takes up a lamentation over the nation. He mourns over the fall of "the virgin of Israel." This poetical personification of the population of the nation is designed to point to political chastity. Israel was a "virgin" in the sense that the nation had not yet been conquered by any other country. The title also points to the defenseless condition of the land. That a "virgin" should die also hints at a premature national death (5:1-2a).

The virgin of Israel "shall fall." The word suggests a violent end for the nation. That virgin "shall rise no more," i.e., Israel as a political entity would not have the strength to recover from the blow which would be inflicted upon her. She would be "stretched out upon her land," abandoned by her former allies and left to die where she fell. She aroused no sympathy. No one would or could extend to her a helping hand. While Amos always held out hope of pardon and mercy to penitent individuals, Israel as a nation would be dead permanently (5:2b).

Amos now abandons the figurative language for a more literal explanation of the fate which awaited Israel. As always, these words are couched in the form of a "thus says Yahweh." He depicts the troops mobilizing from the various cities of the land marching forth to confront the unnamed enemy. Whereas the basis of military enrollment in Israel's earliest days was the tribe or clan, in this period the city or village supplied the manpower for the army ranks. Throughout the land the cities would experience a ninefold decimation of their forces. Such staggering losses would mean the complete overthrow of any nation (5:3).

B. An Urgent Appeal (5:4-5).

A call for repentance is at the same time a rebuke and a warning. Amos' appeals are a double imperative in the Hebrew. This construction has conditional force in which the second imperative is like a promise which is based on compliance with the first imperative. The first appeal with its promise is: "Seek me and [you shall] live." The verb "seek" (*darash*) often has the meaning of going to the holy place in order to get a divine word from the priest or prophet (cf. e.g., Gen 25:22; 1 Sam 9:9). If this is the sense in which Amos is using the verb, then the implication is that they would not be able to find divine counsel at the shrines of the north. Only at Jerusalem would they be able to "seek" a divine word. It is possible, however, that Amos is using *darash* in a more general sense. To seek Yahweh would be to learn his word and apply it to one's life. Taken in this sense the term would involve worship and fellowship.

What is involved in the promise, "you shall live"? Does it mean only to be preserved from the coming calamity? Or does it mean to obtain possession of the more abundant life? Probably both ideas are included. If Israel began to adhere to the principles of God's ancient covenant they would indeed enjoy divine blessings. Surely the hint is here that the impending disaster could be averted through seeking Yahweh in sincerity (5:4).

Amos quickly added a word of caution. He was not advocating more of the same kind of worship which was so popular in the northern kingdom. They were not to seek Yahweh at Bethel where Jeroboam had erected his golden calves in 931 BC. Nor were they to seek Yahweh at Gilgal, the shrine which memorialized the crossing of the Jordan under Joshua. Nor were they to make the long trip to Beersheba some fifty miles southwest of Jerusalem. Were northern kingdom worshipers making the long trip to the Beersheba shrine? Or are these words aimed at citizens of the southern kingdom? In any case seeking Yahweh did not mean visiting popular shrines (5:5a).

To underscore how worthless the worship at Gilgal and Bethel was, Amos made a prediction. He announces first that "Gilgal shall surely go into captivity." The Hebrew employs paronomasia which might be paraphrased like this: Gilgal shall taste the gall of exile. Bethel as well would "come to nought." *Beth-el* in Hebrew means "house of God." Again using paronomasia Amos is declaring that "the house of God would become a house of *aven*," i.e., iniquity, idolatry, delusion (cf. Hos 4:15). The omission of Beersheba in the announcement of judgment supports the conclusion that the citizens of Judah were frequenting this shrine. The primary aim of Amos was to predict overthrow of the northern kingdom (5:5b).

C. A Second Urgent Appeal (5:6-9).

The second appeal is structured like the first, as a double imperative. One must deliberately set himself to live the way God has outlined in his word. "Seek Yahweh and live." The second imperative in Hebrew expresses what would automatically follow upon compliance with the first imperative (5:6a).

The second appeal is accompanied by a word of warning. Failure to seek Yahweh would mean that he would "break out like fire in the house of Joseph," i.e., the northern kingdom. Yahweh is a consuming fire (Deut 4:24). His wrath is frequently represented by fire (Deut 32:22; Ezek 22:21). In this case the fire of God's wrath is directed against religious sham, hypocrisy, ritualism, and phoniness. Nothing which might be done in Bethel, the religious capital, could quench this fire (5:6b).

A series of participles describes the actions of the house of Joseph for which they would face the fire of God's judgment. First, he accuses them of turning "justice to wormwood." The bitter wormwood plant is a figure here for wrongdoing. Justice is sweet; injustice is bitter. Second, they "cast down righteousness to the earth," i.e., they trampled under foot what was right (5:7).

With the words from another hymn Amos described the God which the citizens of the northern kingdom should seek. First, he is the Creator of the constellations Pleiades and Orion.[7] Pleiades was connected with the coming of spring and the setting of Orion was connected with the coming of winter. For this reason some see here the principle that Yahweh changes the seasons.

Second, Yahweh "turns the shadow of death into the morning and makes the day dark with night." This refers either (1) to the power of God to obscure the sun by thick clouds or an eclipse (Lehrman); or (2) to his control over the interchange between day and night (Keil).

Third, Yahweh calls for the waters of the sea and "pours them out upon the face of the earth." This refers to the normal water cycle in which evaporated waters are returned to earth in the form of rain. The reference may also be to judgmental inundations like that of Noah's Flood (5:8).

Fourth, Yahweh brings lightning swift judgments upon evil doers. The result is the destruction of even the strongest fortresses (5:9).

D. A Serious Accusation (5:10-13).

At this point Amos returns to the theme of Israel's guilt. He makes four charges against Israel. His purpose here is to demonstrate further the need for repentance. By reversing these condemnations they would have some idea of where repentance should lead their society.

1. Hatred of reproof (5:10). The citizens of Israel "hate the reprover in the gate," i.e., a prophet or judge or anyone wise who might raise his voice to condemn injustice. Amos may even be referring to the way he was being treated in the north. The following verses, however, seem to focus on the judicial system. The "gate" was the public forum for business or the administration of justice, or simply for gossip. In that place they "abhor him that speaks uprightly," i.e. what is true and right. Reversing this condition would suggest that what God wanted was a love of the truth and support for those who speak it.

2. *Oppression of the poor (5:11)*. The sinners of Israel "trample upon the poor," i.e., upon their rights. They took "exactions of grain" as bribes before they would render a just verdict for a poor person. With this illicit gain they had built "houses of hewn stone" for themselves. Since ordinary houses were made of mud brick, such houses would be a mark of luxury and wealth. Yahweh declares that these wicked leaders would never dwell in their dream houses. Nor would they ever taste the wine from the vineyards they had planted with the bribes they had taken from the poor. God would not allow them to enjoy the fruits of wealth they had illegally obtained (5:11).

3. *Manifold transgressions (5:12)*. The sins of Israel are described as "mighty." Specifically, they afflict the just, i.e., persecute them. Judges accepted bribes (*kopher*) for the souls of murderers in violation of Numbers 35:31. They "turn aside the needy in the gate." People could receive justice only if they could pay for it (5:12).

4. *Evil times (5:13)*. The fourth charge is that the times were evil. A "prudent person," i.e., anyone who wanted to succeed in life, knew that he would have to "keep silence in such time."All who under ordinary circumstances might be expected to rebuke the public iniquity remained silent. This was "an evil time." Not only was it futile to speak out, it was dangerous because of the ruthlessness of those in high places. The implication here is that a messenger of God cannot be prudent. He must speak out regardless of the cost (5:13).

E. The Final Appeal (5:14-15).

Amos urged his audience to "seek good, and not evil, and live." The two previous appeals to "seek God" (vv. 4,6) are now explained as "seeking good" and shunning evil. Thus holiness has both a positive and negative aspect. Amos assured his auditors that if they embraced good, then Yahweh would "be with you as you say." Israel thought they stood in fellowship with the Lord because they were biologically descended from the covenant people. They thought their many sacrifices were pleasing to Yahweh. They thought that Yahweh would never allow any foreign power to conquer them. They thought their present national prosperity was evidence that God was with them. All of this was self-deception. Yahweh the God of hosts will only walk with those who embrace the values which he loves (5:14).

Amos now amplified his appeal. "Hate evil, and love good." The godly life is concerned with both actions and emotions. Action, however, is put before emotion. Believers must not wait until they "feel led" to do what is right. Emotion often follows duty; but even if not, believers are bound to obey the commands of the Lord. (5:15a).[8]

Amos leaves nothing to the imagination. He spells out what he means by hating evil and loving good. The leaders of Israel must "establish justice in the gate." Among the people of God holiness has a social dimension. The present condition of things must be reversed if there was any hope for deliverance.

Even if Israel should repent, the question of relief was not absolutely certain. "Perhaps Yahweh God of hosts may be gracious to the remnant of Joseph." The nation as a political entity was doomed. Deliverance, however, might be possible for the penitent and purified few mentioned by Isaiah and Micah, i.e., those who would be saved after heavy chastisement (5:15b).

F. A Sad Conclusion (5:16-17).

The conclusion of Amos' third "hear ye" oracle begins with a logical connector and a strong assertion of authority. The word "Therefore" seems to link this conclusion with the assertion in verse 13 that the time was evil. The implication is that the appeal for repentance in verses 14-15 was futile. The conclusion is undergirded by a triune title for God. He is *Yahweh,* the God of the covenant. He is the all-powerful "God of hosts." He is *the Lord,* the sovereign master (*'adonay*). This is the one who now pronounced judgment on Israel (5:16a).

Yahweh describes the complete despair which will come upon Israel as a result of the widespread disregard for covenant responsibility. He pictures wailing everywhere in the land, especially in the towns with their "broad ways" and "streets." Even the vineyards which were normally places of mirth would become venues of wailing. Everyone would engage in lamentation. Professional mourners—those to whom tears come easily—would lead the lament. These were employed during funerals to stimulate appropriate lamentation. The "farmers" would mourn the loss of their occupation as well as the death within the family. Using the traditional expression of mourning for the dead (cf. 1 Kgs 13:30), they would cry "Alas, alas" (5:16b-17a).

Why such lamentation? Yahweh declared his intention to "pass through the midst" of his people. They assumed that Yahweh was already in their midst (cf. 5:14). He was not. He was, however, coming soon. Merely walking through the midst of his people would bring a national disaster the likes of which Israel never before had experienced (5:17b).

ENDNOTES

1. The last half of 3:12 has received a wide variety of translations. ASV has "in the corner of a couch and on the silken cushions of a bed." NASB has "with the corner of a bed and the cover of a couch." NIV translates "on the edge of their beds and on the corner of their couches."
2. Some think that the *nobles* of Samaria, not the women, were called cows because they are effeminate and licentious. This position is based on the fact that in the Hebrew the genders interchange. In Hebrew, as in English, however, a masculine suffix can have a feminine antecedent on occasion.
3. James L. Mays, *Amos, a Commentary* in "The Old Testament Library" (Philadelphia: Westminster, 1969), p. 74.
4. J.A. Motyer, *The Message of Amos* in "The Bible Speaks Today" (Downers Grove, IL: InterVarsity, 1974), p. 95.
5. *Ibid.*, p. 100; and Theo. Laetsch, *Bible Commentary: The Minor Prophets* (St. Louis: Concordia, 1956) p. 158.
6. Motyer, *op. cit.*, p. 123.
7. The constellations Pleiades and Orion are also mentioned in Job 9:9 and 38:31.
8. Motyer, *op.cit.*, p. 123.

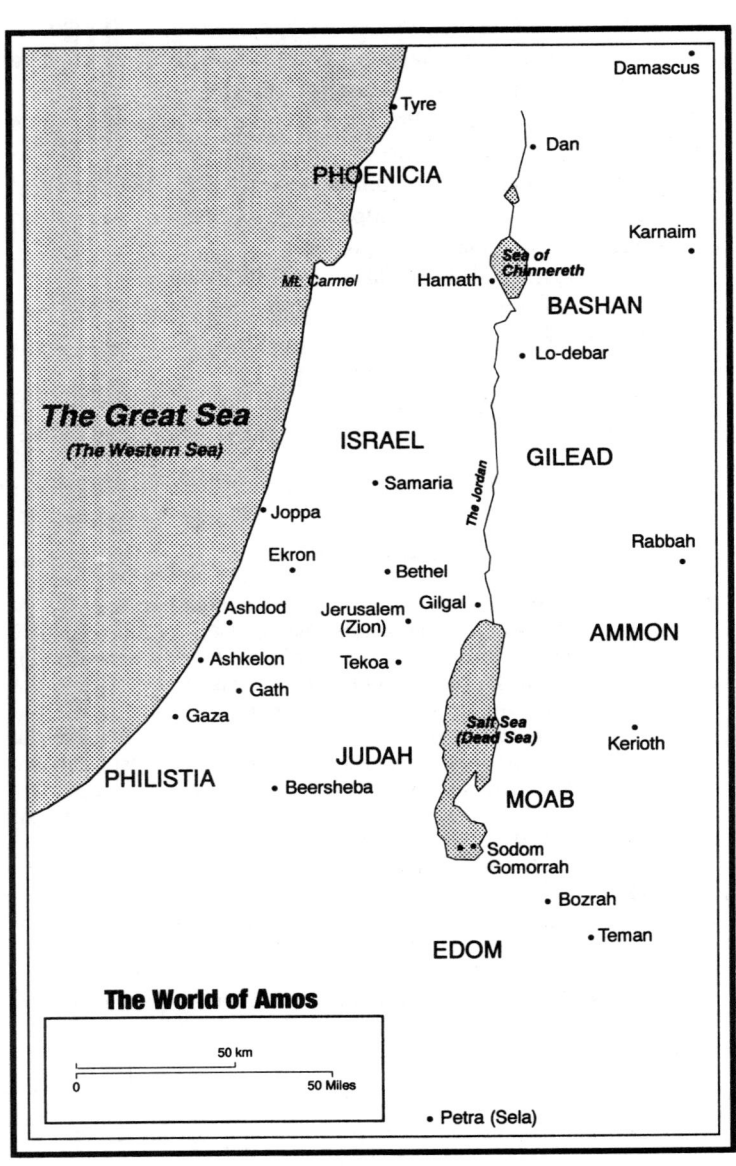

CHAPTER TWELVE

Two Thundering Woes
Amos 5:18-6:14

Following his detailed call for national repentance, Amos again focused on condemnation and proclamation of judgment. To accomplish this end he employed two "woe" oracles, the second of which is expanded by a detailed description of judgment.

THE FIRST WOE ORACLE
Amos 5:18-27

The first "woe" oracle exposes the presumptuous attitude and unacceptable worship of the northern kingdom.

A. Presumptuous Expectation (5:18-20).

The first "woe" is pronounced against those who desired for the day of Yahweh to come. They wrongly interpreted that day to be a day of judgment upon the heathen. They anticipated that in that day Israel would be vindicated and exalted. This day of Yahweh theology may have been based on a misapplication of Joel 2:32. Amos challenged this presumptuous doctrine by asking a rhetorical question: "Why would you have the day of Yahweh?" (5:18a).

Amos declared that the day of Yahweh would be a day of darkness and not light for Israel. That day would bring them harm and destruction, not vindication, prosperity and salvation. "Darkness" here may be literal as well as figurative (5:18b).

In a powerful and humorous illustration Amos drove home the truth that no sinful person could escape the judgment of the day of Yahweh. A man flees from a lion, then encounters a bear. He rushes into the house, leans breathlessly against the wall, and is bitten by a serpent. One danger after another would befall the wicked. Just when they thought they might have escaped disaster, they would experience a fatal calamity (5:19).

A second rhetorical question reinforces the view of the darkness of the day of Yahweh. "Shall not the day of Yahweh be darkness, and not light, even very dark, and no brightness in it?" Here Amos uses stronger words for darkness and light. The darkness would intensify with the passage of time. There would not even be a ray of light (*nogah*). That would not be a day for the sinners of Israel to anticipate (5:20).

B. Unacceptable Worship (5:21-27).

Amos now returns to the theme of the unacceptable worship in Israel. He makes three charges against that worship.

1. Unacceptable gatherings. The worship gatherings were unacceptable. Yahweh declares, "I hate, I despise your feasts." Outward formal worship will not avert the danger nor secure the favor of God in the day of visitation. God hated these feasts—Passover, First Fruits, Tabernacles, et al.—for three reasons: (1) The festivals failed to comply with the law of a single sanctuary; (2) the golden calf symbol was unauthorized and in fact had become an idol; and (3) the celebrations of these festivals tended to get out of hand especially as regards drunkenness (5:21a).

Yahweh also declared "I do not delight in your solemn assemblies" (*'atsarot*). The word appears in the plural only here. It refers to the times of worship at the festivals, particularly at Passover and

Tabernacles (Lev 23:36; Num 29:35; 2 Chr 7:9). The term "delight" literally means "smell." Yahweh would not smell with satisfaction, i.e., accept, the offerings which were presented to him at the festivals (5:21b).

2. *Unacceptable offerings.* Their worship offerings were unacceptable. The burnt offering symbolized complete consecration of the worshiper. For these hypocrites to offer this offering was an abomination. The meal offering primarily expressed thanksgiving to Yahweh. Thanksgiving must be translated into thanks-living or it too is abomination. The peace offering was an expression of the communion between the worshiper and God. Light and darkness, however, can have no fellowship. Amos made no mention of the sin offering. These people, apparently, did not see themselves as sinners before God! (5:22).

3. *Unacceptable music.* Their worship music also came under the condemnation of this prophet. The temple singing was a wearisome noise (*hamon*) to God, clashing sounds. The objection here is not to the music in worship, but to the entire worship of which music was a part. Instrumental music was no more acceptable than their singing. Yahweh declares: "I will not hear the melody of your harps."[1]

C. Dearth of Justice (5:24).

Israel's worship was devoid of application. Instead of elaborate ritual, God wanted justice and righteousness to prevail in the land. Martin Luther King, Jr. was fond of quoting Amos 5:24 during the civil rights movement of the 1960's. This may well be the golden text of Amos: " But let justice roll down as waters, and righteousness as a mighty stream." These words are more likely an exhortation than a threat.

"Justice" goes beyond fairness. It is that correct moral practice in daily personal and social life which is clearly observable to others. ""Righteousness" is mainly internal. It is that disposition to do what is right. Righteousness expresses itself in society as justice. God wants an abundance of both qualities rather than the formalistic and corrupt worship of the northern kingdom. In a water-starved country, a perennial stream was a delight. Righteousness and justice are such a delight to God (5:24).

D. Pervasive Idolatry (5:25-26).

A rhetorical question called attention to the Israel's checkered past. "Did you present me with sacrifices and grain offerings in the wilderness for forty years, O house of Israel?" Scholars are sharply divided on whether Amos anticipated a positive or a negative answer to his question. He probably anticipated a "yes."[2] During the forty years of wilderness wandering Israel did bring sacrifices, but they were unacceptable because of clandestine worship of idols (5:25).

The standard English versions differ widely on the translation of Amos 5:26. The verse charges Israel with carrying two objects. First, they took up a shrine or tabernacle (*sekhuth*).[3] The reference is to a portable shrine such as ancient nations used to transport their gods. This shrine belonged to "your king," a title sometimes given to the pagan god Molech.[4]

Those wilderness wanderers also carried about "the pedestal of your idols" (NIV).[5] Essentially this would be the same kind of portable shrine mentioned earlier in the verse. These idols are further described as "your star god." They were worshiping astral deities during that forty year period. Astral worship in the wilderness period is attested in Deut 4:19; 17:2f.; Josh 24:2,14.

Israel's tainted worship was useless for protection. The idolatry which had begun in the wilderness clandestinely continued to Amos' day. This people would be sent into exile "beyond Damascus," lit., from afar with respect to Damascus. Stephen correctly identified the specific area of the exile as Babylon (Acts 7:43). Yahweh, the God of redemption, had brought Israel into Canaan centuries before. Now Yahweh, the God of covenant, would expel this persistently apostate people from that land just as he had threatened to do in the Sinai covenant.

THE SECOND WOE
Waking up an Indifferent People
Amos 6:1-14

The citizens of Israel were more indifferent than hostile to the truths which Amos proclaimed. The prophet blasted that indifference in his second "woe" oracle.

TWO THUNDERING WOES AMOS 5:18-6:14

A. Description of the Indifferent (6:1).

Amos pronounced his second woe of lament on "those who are at ease in Zion," i.e., those who were secure, or careless. "Zion" here could be Jerusalem; more likely it is used here, as frequently in the Scripture, for the people of God collectively. The particular part of the nation which is being targeted is indicated by the next phrase: "those who are secure in the mountain of Samaria." These words suggest that it was military security which gave these sinners a sense of carelessness (6:1a).

Those who were at ease are described as 'the notable men of the chief of the nations." From the earliest times Israel had regarded herself as the most exalted of nations. The entire house of Israel would come to these national leaders to have their affairs regulated. These members of the aristocracy were at ease in eminent responsibility (6:1b).

B. Challenge to the Indifferent (6:2).

Amos challenged the indifferent leaders of Israel to take a tour of surrounding nations, especially Calneh, Hamath, and Gath. The exact location of Calneh is uncertain. Assyrian records indicate that a place of a similar name was located north of Hamath in Syria. Gath was a leading city of the Philistine plain of Palestine. Though these were great cities in Amos' day, they in no way exceeded Samaria in prestige.[6] From north (Calneh) to south (Gath) there were no kingdoms in the area superior to Judah and Israel in quality or size.

The leaders of Samaria ignored the basic fundamentals of real leadership. They were content with the status quo. They were more concerned with privilege (dwelling in the capital) than performance, with reputation than with responsibility. By comparing themselves to those less fortunate, they lost their vision and goal. All of this led to complacency.

C. Sins of the Indifferent (6:3-6).

Six word pictures describe the sin of those indifferent leaders of Samaria. First, they were guilty of hardened unbelief. They "put far away the evil day." They refused to take seriously the voice of warning. They did not deny that a day of judgment was coming, but not in their day. No end was in sight to the economic prosperity of Israel (6:3a).

Second, heartless oppression characterized these sinners. They "cause the seat of violence to come near." In the seats of authority violence, not justice, was encouraged. (6:3b).

Third, they were guilty of sinful self-indulgence. They sprawled on their ivory couches, i.e., couches inlaid with ivory which were the mark of opulence in this period. Looseness of gesture often goes with looseness of morals. They consumed the finest foods: "lambs out of the flock and calves out of the midst of the stall," i.e. fresh lamb and fatted veal. This is a picture of wantonness, extravagance and perhaps drunkenness (6:4).

Fourth, they indulged in profane revelry. They "sing idle songs to the sound of the harp." The word "sing" appears only here in the Old Testament. It seems to suggest the bawling of those who are drunk.[7] The sinners even "invent instruments of music like David." King David apparently devised stringed instruments for use in the temple music program. While he invented instruments for the praise of the Lord, these sinners used their musical skills for their god, the belly (6:5).

Fifth, the sinners in Israel were guilty of shameful debauchery. "They drink wine in bowls," not goblets or cups. The word used here is elsewhere used of the large sacrificial bowls used in the temples for libations of blood and wine. The language may hint of sacrilege. At the same time they were consuming this wine in such enormous quantities, the revelers would "anoint themselves with the chief oils." Anointing oneself with oil was a sign of joy. Oil refreshed the skin and protected it from the sun. Since oil was also used as a symbol of the Holy Spirit in sacred rites of consecration, here there may also be a hint of sacrilege (6:6a).

Finally, the leaders of Israel showed calloused unconcern. "They are not grieved for the affliction of Joseph." They were so preoccupied with sinful self-indulgence that they could not see the approaching ruin of "Joseph," i.e., the northern kingdom. Since the two most prominent tribes in the north were descended from Joseph, the entire nation is here designated by the name of that Patriarch. Leaders in God's kingdom must always put the welfare of the people of God above their own selfish interests (6:6b).

D. Punishment of the Indifferent (6:7).

The indifferent leaders of Israel would lead the way into captivity. The "revelry" (*marzeach*) of those who stretched themselves out would pass away The drunken shouts of those sprawlers would not be heard again. The *marzeach* was a pagan ritual banquet or a memorial meal (cf. Jer 16:5,7-8). Such banquets often lasted several days and were accompanied by excessive drinking. Few social institutions in antiquity have been so well illuminated by archaeology as the *marzeach*, although many aspects of it are still debated among scholars.[8]

ANNOUNCEMENT OF JUDGMENT
Amos 6:8-11

Having set forth the basis for condemnation, Amos proceeded to announce the judgment upon Israel. He speaks of the basis, course, and cause of that judgment.

A. Basis of Judgment (6:8a).

Amos' attack on the luxury-loving northern tribes cannot be dismissed as the ravings of a conservative country bumpkin against urban society. His condemnation of the evils in Israel was not based on his cultural biases. Yahweh was genuinely offended by the conduct of these people. In revelation to Amos Yahweh had taken an oath regarding his attitude toward the moral climate in Israel. He had "sworn by himself" since there was no one higher by whom an oath might be taken (cf. 4:2).

Under oath Yahweh swears in the first person "I loathe the arrogance of Jacob." Here the entire nation is called by the name of its progenitor. The name "Jacob" recalls the pre-conversion period of that Patriarch's life when he was a worldly schemer. The participle used here implies that the divine abhorrence is a lasting feeling and not merely a passing emotion. God declares that he "hates" the palaces of Jacob. Everything of which this nation was so proud disgusted and angered Yahweh. He totally rejected the opulent lifestyle of the leading citizens.

B. Course of Judgment (6:8b-11).

Since Yahweh so detested the conditions in Israel, he declared his intention to "deliver up the city with all that is therein." Most likely Samaria, the northern capital, is in view. Though the massive walls of the place might deter an attacker for some time, ultimately the city would fall. The Lord would see to that. All of the city's inhabitants would suffer in that day (6:8b).

Those who survived the slaughter of war would face death by pestilence within the city. Those who lived in humble houses would perish as well as those who occupied the palaces. Amos depicts ten survivors—perhaps a large family—huddling in one of the few remaining houses. They too die (6:9).

Because burial grounds were inaccessible during siege, bodies had to be cremated for sanitary purposes. Cremation was extremely rare among Israelites, but was practiced in emergency situations.[9] Amos depicts a man's uncle—the term can be used for any near relative—coming to the house to do his duty. The corpse had decomposed to the point that only bones were left. Apparently these bones were placed in a front room of the house where the cremation team might easily find them. The picture is meant to be gruesome (6:10a).

The "uncle" shouts into the innermost part of the house to ascertain if any other survivors were there. A voice from the inner chamber answered in the negative. Then the "uncle" would respond with a warning: "Hold your peace; for we may not make mention of the name of Yahweh." Apparently the "uncle" was afraid that in the desperation of the hour the victim within, who perhaps was suffering the effects of the plague, would curse God's name or recklessly blame God for his suffering. This might call down immediate retribution from on high.[10] Hence the warning not to mention the name of Yahweh (6:10b).

Amos concluded this section with a shocking declaration. The gruesome depiction of the plague-ravished city would come about as a result of the active will of God. Amos introduced this announcement with "behold," a word often used by prophets to point to the unexpected. For Yahweh to withdraw and refuse to aid Israel when under massive attack would be bad enough. Amos, however, declared that "Yahweh commands" the destruction. Those who orchestrate the destruction of Samaria would be agents of the God of Israel! In that day the "great house," i.e., the palaces, would be "smashed to pieces." Likewise the "little house" would be demolished. The houses of the rich and poor are intended. The singular is used with indefinite generality, i.e., every house (6:11).[11]

C. Cause of Judgment (6:12-14).

Worldly pride was the root cause of the impending judgment against Israel. That pride manifested itself in Israel's deeds and words.

Two rhetorical questions are raised in order to make Israel realize the stupidity of their present course of life. "Do horses run upon the rock? Will one plow there with oxen?" Both questions point to actions which are both stupid and dangerous. Turning "justice to gall," and "the fruit of righteousness to wormwood" is similarly stupid and dangerous. Gall and wormwood were poisonous and bitter plants (cf. Hos 10:4; Amos 5:7). The "fruit of righteousness" is the impartial administration of justice. The leaders of Israel had done something very dangerous in turning that which was good and right to that which was bitter and injurious. The point here is that in the moral realm, as in the physical realm, there is an inexorable law which cannot be violated with impunity (6:12).

The words of Israel as well as their deeds demand judgment. They were rejoicing in "Lo-debar," lit., a thing of nought. Lo-debar appears to be the name of a village in Transjordan (2 Sam 9:4f.; 17:27). They boasted, "Have we not taken to us Karnaim (lit., horns) by our own strength?" This appears to be the name of another village in Transjordan. Israel was boasting over two of the recent military successes of King Jeroboam of Israel.[12] (6:13).

The arrogant deeds and words of Israel were premature. Again Amos makes the shocking ("Behold!") announcement that Yahweh would bring judgment. This statement goes beyond what the prophet said about Samaria in verse 11. First, this announcement is more specific. Yahweh would raise up "a nation" against the house of Israel. The reference is undoubtedly to Assyria, though Amos never mentions the enemy by name. Second, this announcement is reinforced with two formulas which underscore the solemnity of it. "Oracle of Yahweh" (*ne'um Yahweh*) is the strongest possible assertion of divine authority. "God of hosts" is the strongest possible assertion of divine power. The doom of Israel is sealed because it is the God of all armies in heaven and on earth who engineers the catastrophe.

Third, this announcement is directly addressed to the "house of Israel." The entire nation, not just the capital city (v. 8) fell under the condemnation of the Lord. Fourth, this announcement spelled out geographically the extent of the disaster. The invaders would afflict Israel "from the entrance of Hamath unto the brook of the Arabah," i.e., the whole kingdom as it had been expanded under Jeroboam II (cf. 2 Kgs 14:25). The "entrance of Hamath" refers to the pass between the Lebanon mountains which led north to Hamath. The city of Dan stood at the southern end of that pass. The "brook of the Arabah" was most likely a stream flowing into the north end of the Dead Sea (6:14).

Amos 6 offers a prophetic analysis of why Israel, the northern kingdom would fall. Blame is placed on a foreign invader (v. 14), on the leaders of the nation (vv. 1-3; 4-7), and the ungodly pride of the populace (v. 8). Ultimately, however, it was Yahweh himself who would orchestrate the collapse of the northern kingdom (vv. 8,11).

ENDNOTES

1. Only here does the Hebrew *zamarah* refer to instrumental rather than vocal music.

2. Usually in Hebrew a question anticipating a positive answer is couched in the negative: "Did you not..." For this reason the majority of scholars conclude that Amos is denying that Israel brought sacrifices during the wilderness period. Henderson, Young and Archer think that the anticipated answer is "yes."

3. This translation is defended persuasively by Gervirtz, JBL 87:1968, 267-76 who connects the word *sekhuth* with a Ugaritic word meaning "shrine." KJV, ASV and NIV understand the text in this way.

4. So RSV, NASB, BV, ASV. The KJV understood the term to be the proper name of the god Molech. The suffix, however, weighs against its being taken as a proper noun.

5. The term translated "pedestal" *(kiun)* is regarded as a proper name by KJV, RSV, BV, NASB.

6. Calneh, Hamath and Gath were not cited as examples of fallen greatness as Lehrman contends. The Assyrians did not destroy these places until long after the time of Amos.

7. O. Bussey, "Amos" in *The New Bible Commentary* ed. F. Davidson (Grand Rapids: Eerdmans, 1954), p. 706.

8. Philip J. King, "The *Marzeach* Amos Denounces," BAR July/August 1988, pp. 34-44.

9. On cremation, see Lev 20:14; 21:9; Josh 7:15,25; 1 Sam 31:12; cf. Gen 38:24.

10. Other interpretations of this difficult admonition: (1) In view of our violation of the covenant, do not provoke Yahweh by continuing to pray to him (Deane); (2) the speaker blames everything on Yahweh and cannot stand the further mention of his name; (3) it is too late to call on the name of Yahweh since it is now the time of vengeance.

11. Harper follows the Jewish Targum on the passage in understanding the "great house" to be Israel and the "small house" to be Judah. The former suffered under the Assyrian Shalmaneser, and the latter under Sennacherib.

12. So NIV, NASB and NKJV. Harper defends the rendering of the KJV "thing of nought" and "horns." The idea is that the people were flattering themselves with self-deception and boasting of the power ("horns") they had acquired under Jeroboam II. The ancient versions support the rendering of KJV.

CHAPTER THIRTEEN

Visions of Judgment
Amos 7:1-8:3

The content of Amos 7-9 is very different from that which precedes it. Visions are the dominant literary form in this section. The title Lord Yahweh appears frequently, eleven times of a total of twenty times in the book. Five times in the final forty-six verses of the book he speaks of Israel as "my people." This theme reaches its climax in 9:15 with "your God."

The five visions of chapters 7-9 together with the narrative which is inserted after the third vision, may be a clue to the entire ministry of this prophet. The first three visions may have constituted Amos' call to preach the word of Yahweh in Israel, the northern kingdom. The fourth and fifth visions may point to a Judean ministry on the part of Amos after he was expelled from the northern kingdom.

VISION ONE: LOCUSTS
A Burden for the Lost
Amos 7:1-3

Amos' visions came from Lord Yahweh, i.e., the sovereign Yahweh. The first four visions have a uniform introduction: "Thus the Lord Yahweh showed me." Whether this was a kind of inward illumination, or whether the vision was seen with the physical eye is impossible to determine (7:1a).

"Behold!" introduces the shocking scene which Amos saw in his first vision. Yahweh was forming locusts. The participle indicates continuous action. The reference may be to the larval stage of this insect. Some commentators see in these locusts a veiled reference to the Assyrian invasion of Israel. The vision is best understood, however, as the threat of a literal locust attack.

The time of the appearance is crucial: "in the beginning of the shooting up of the latter growth." In Palestine the first growth begins in October and continues through the winter. The latter growth comes in spring after the latter rains. If this herbage was destroyed there would be no hope of recovery for the rest of the year because the rains were all past and the heat of summer was starting.

The appearance of the locusts is further specified as "after the king's mowings" or as others prefer "shearing." This seems to be nothing more than an effort to pinpoint the time of year when the locust judgment would fall. The "mowings" might refer to tribute levied by the king on the spring herbage as provender for the royal cavalry. Since, however, there is no biblical mention of such a tax policy, some prefer to think that the spring sheep shearing is what is intended.[1]

Amos watched in his vision the devastation which the locusts were inflicting. When the insects had made an end to eating the grass of the land Amos fell to his knees in prayer. He begged the Lord Yahweh to forgive Israel. In Old Testament vocabulary only God can forgive. He based his intercession on the fact that Jacob (i.e., Israel) was but a small nation with meager resources. It could not stand (lit., rise up or recover from) such a devastating blow. As an outsider, Amos' view of Israel as "small" was more realistic than the inflated opinions which the northern natives had of their own situation (7:2).

Amos was a man of prayer before he was a prophet. He prayed for this people long before he preached to them. His intercessory prayer was effectual. Yahweh "relented" concerning this threat. He declared that "it shall not be," i.e., the utter destruction which had been proposed would not take place.

A locust plague was listed among the *musar* judgments sent against Israel in 4:6. The sending of the plague in that passage is viewed as an act of mercy with the purpose of bringing Israel to repentance before Yahweh poured out total devastation. Here the removal of the locust plague is the act of mercy. Placing the two passages in juxtaposition helps point out two aspects of God's mercy, the active and the passive.

VISION TWO: FIRE
Persistence in Prayer
Amos 7:4-6

At some unspecified time later Amos saw a second vision. In it he saw Lord Yahweh in open contention with his people. The Lord called forth fire to be used in the conflict. The all-devouring fire represents a much more severe judgment than that depicted in the first vision. This was no ordinary fire. It "devoured the great deep," the subterranean waters which supply waters for fountains and rivers. Then Amos saw the resulting drought beginning to consume "the portion." This may refer to the land occupied by Israel, the people of God, or to both the land and the people (7:4).

Again Amos went to his knees in intercessory prayer. He begged Lord Yahweh to cease the devastating blast against Israel. He again pled Jacob's (i.e., Israel's) helplessness and weakness in the face of such a devastating supernatural judgment. Once again Yahweh "repented," i.e., relented, concerning this impending judgment. "This also shall not be," declared Yahweh (7:5-6).

Commentators differ over the significance of the first two visions. Some take the visions as predictive of two invasions by the Assyrians under Tiglath-pileser when he carried away captive some of the citizens of northern Israel (cf. 2 Kgs 15:19, 29). Others think these visions are parallel to the list of afflictions in 4:6-11. The first two visions represent all the efforts which God had expended in an effort to get Israel to repent. Still another view is that the first two visions were the first stage of Amos' call to be a prophet. God was showing Amos actual judgments which Israel was facing in the future. Amos's intercessory prayer actually gained two reprieves for Israel.

VISION THREE: THE PLUMB LINE
The Urgency of Proclamation
Amos 7:7-9

Since what follows is shocking, the third vision is introduced with "Behold!" The unit unfolds in two stages focusing first on what Amos saw, and then on what he heard.

A. What Amos Saw (7:7-8a).

Amos saw Yahweh standing beside a wall. While no person has seen God at any time in his heavenly glory, several in biblical history saw theophanies, i.e., visible manifestations of Yahweh usually in a human-like form.

Yahweh had a plumb line in his hand. The plumb line was simply a line with a weight on one end. This simple device placed alongside a wall measured perpendicularity. The plumb line was a symbol of judgment in the Old Testament (cf. 2 Kgs 21:13; Isa 34:11).

Yahweh was standing alongside a wall which had been built with the aid of a plumb line. This wall symbolizes Israel and the plumb line, God's law. Established by the law of God, Israel had been an upright nation. Now, however, that wall showed signs of deviating from the perpendicular. Such a tottering wall was a public menace and must be destroyed.

To focus his attention on the plumb line, Yahweh asked Amos what he saw. Mention of the prophet's name adds a warm and personal touch to an otherwise grim scene. Amos perceived that the key to this third vision was the plumb line. So he responded to the Lord's question by mentioning that device (7:8a).

B. What Amos Heard (7:8b-9).

Yahweh responded to the prophet's observation with a shocking

("Behold!") double declaration. First, he declared: "I will set a plumb line in the midst of my people Israel." The law of Moses was the yardstick by which God measured his people. The plumb line is set in the midst of his people so that each individual might be measured thereby. All would be forced to acknowledge the justice of the sentence.

Second, Yahweh announced the verdict regarding the fate of Israel: "I will not pass by them any more." This is equivalent to saying, I will not again pardon this people. Why does not Amos offer up a third intercessory prayer? He must have interpreted Yahweh's declaration as meaning that prayer at this point would be useless. In a moral universe, judgment on sin is inevitable at some point. The words of Yahweh sealed the doom of Israel (7:8b).

Yahweh followed his decision regarding the destiny of Israel with a description of the judgment. The "high places of Isaac," i.e., Israel, would be the first to fall before the test of the plumb line. These illicit shrines were a direct transgression of the commandments of the Law. The use of the name "Isaac" to designate the nation here suggests a contrast between the deeds of the people and the blameless life of the Patriarch.

Next the "sanctuaries of Israel"—the official shrines at Dan, Bethel, Samaria and Gilgal—would experience the judgment of Yahweh. They would be "laid waste" by an unnamed foe.

Finally, Yahweh declared that the ruling dynasty in Israel would experience his judgment. "I will rise against the house of Jeroboam with the sword." The political structure was as crooked as the religious structure. These words are probably not to be restricted to the house of Jeroboam, but rather the entire Israelite monarchy. With the fall of the house of Jeroboam—the Jehu dynasty—the Israelite monarchy in effect came to a close. The sword which God would use against the monarchy in the north would be Assyria (7:9).

CONFRONTATION IN BETHEL
Amos 7:10-17

Students of Amos have puzzled as to why a narrative has been inserted at this point in the book, between the third and fourth vision. First, the Bethel episode is chronologically in place. The prediction of

7:9 regarding the royal family triggered this confrontation. The passage also has an illustrative function. Heretofore the plumb line of God's truth has been applied to the state religion, the wealthy and the ruling family. Here is an example of the use of the plumb line on an individual level. Furthermore, this episode may narrate the termination of Amos's ministry in northern Israel. The fourth and fifth visions may represent a later phase of Amos' ministry in Judah.[2]

A. The Opposition (7:10-13).

Amaziah ("Yahweh is strong") was the leader of the state religion headquartered in Bethel. He sent a messenger to King Jeroboam to warn him of the impact which Amos was having in his kingdom. Obviously Amaziah had influence in the royal court. In his communique Amaziah charged that Amos had "conspired" against Jeroboam. Certainly this was a fabrication. Amos had no political ambitions. He had come to Israel to foment a spiritual revolution, not a political one. Amos may, however, have started to attract some disciples. Amaziah may have worried that the spiritual fervor generated by Amos' preaching might take on political overtones at some point.

Amaziah unwittingly commended the courage of Amos when he noted that he was preaching "in the midst of the house of Israel." Bethel was the religious capital of northern Israel. The priest bore witness to the effectiveness of Amos' preaching when he stated that "the land is not able to bear all his words." The prophet from Judah obviously was causing discontent among the parishioners of Amaziah (7:10).

To substantiate his charge against the prophet, Amaziah quoted Amos, but not precisely. "For thus Amos says: Jeroboam shall die by the sword." Actually Amos had said that the "house" of Jeroboam would so die. Jeroboam died a natural death; but his son Zechariah died by sword in a coup (cf. 2 Kgs 15:10). Then Amaziah accused Amos of saying: "And Israel shall surely be led away captive out of his land." In essence Amos indeed had said this (7:11).

Amaziah was determined to put Amos in the worst possible light. He did not mention to the king the sins which Amos had specified as being the cause of the impending judgment. He did not mention all the efforts which God had made in recent years to lead this nation to repentance. Nor did he mention Amos' calls for repentance. Amaziah represented Amos to the king as hostile to the crown and the people of Israel.

At some point Amaziah directly confronted Amos. Was he acting on his own authority? Or had he received a directive from the king? The text does not answer these questions.

Amaziah addressed Amos as "seer" (*chozeh*). Certainly this title is used elsewhere as an honorable designation for those who brought the prophetic word.[3] By use of this term Amaziah may have meant to mock the three visions which Amos had just reported in his preaching.

Amaziah ordered Amos to leave Israel, to flee to the land of Judah. This is not the friendly advice of one religious leader to another, but the command of one who was in a position of authority. The idea is that Amos' message of Israel's destruction would be readily accepted in the rival southern kingdom. It certainly was not welcome in the north. (7:12a).

Amaziah insinuated that Amos preached only in order to earn a living. In Judah he could "eat bread and prophesy." Phony religious leaders always assume that all others who serve in like capacity are only in it for the money (7:12b).

Amaziah then ordered that Amos refrain from preaching at Bethel. That city was "the king's sanctuary," i.e., a sanctuary founded by the king, principal headquarters of the national religion. That city was also "a royal house," i.e., the capital, a royal residence (7:13).

B. The Response (7:14-17).

Amos was faithful in defending his calling. First, he described to his antagonist the circumstances before his call. The Hebrew reads literally, "No prophet I, nor a son of a prophet." The translator must supply some form of the verb "to be" to make sense of this. Some wish to insert the present tense. They thereby make Amos disassociate himself from prophets. He supposedly saw himself as a new breed of prophet. A better proposal is that the past tense should be inserted. "I was no prophet." The idea is that he became a prophet only after God called him. To be a prophet's "son" was to be a student of a prophet. Amos is saying that he had not studied at the feet of some prophet (7:14a).

Before his call to ministry Amos had been a "herdsman" and "a fig nipper." For a discussion of Amos' occupations prior to his call see the discussion in Chapter Nine.

Amos gave no details of his prophetic call. He simply said, "Yahweh took me from following the flock." The command came to him to "go, prophesy unto my people Israel." That divine command may have come after the third vision. In any case, once Amos had heard that awesome directive he could no longer continue his business enterprises (7:15).

Amos then issued a prophetic utterance directly to Amaziah personally. Whereas Yahweh had called Amos to prophesy, the priest had ordered him not to prophesy. He was not to "drop" his word against "the house of Isaac," i.e., the northern kingdom. The verb used here *(nataph)* pictures the word of prophecy dropping refreshingly like dew upon the obedient, but like monotonous water torture upon the disobedient. By directing this oracle to Amaziah, Amos was violating the gag order (7:16).

Because Amaziah had dared to try and silence the living word of Yahweh, he would face a terrible personal judgment. First, his wife would become a harlot in the city. In the economic extremities which Israel would face during the days of the Assyrian invasion, his wife would voluntarily enter into whoredom to obtain her accustomed luxuries. Second, Amaziah's children would fall by the sword of those same Assyrians. The fact that daughters would be included in the slaughter would indicate abnormal cruelty. Normally the Assyrians spared the women to become wives for their soldiers. Third, the real estate owned by Amaziah would be "divided by line," parceled out to others, probably colonists settled in the area by the Assyrians. Fourth, Amaziah himself would die "in an unclean land," on foreign soil. Thus Amaziah would be carried away into captivity. Foreign lands were considered by Israelites "unclean" because of the idolatry practiced there (7:17a).

Amos concluded his message to Amaziah by reasserting the same prediction which got him into trouble with this priest in the first place. "Israel shall surely be led away captive out of his land."

Whether Amaziah liked it or not, whether he believed it or not, this was the word of God regarding the fate of Israel. God's purpose remained unchanged (7:17b).

In his confrontation with Amaziah Amos overcame two temptations. He resisted the temptation to change his message or to plead misunderstanding, or to apologize for anything which he had said. Second, he resisted the temptation to act in his own self-interest, to preach where he would be economically comfortable and physically secure.

VISION FOUR: ROTTEN FRUIT
The Necessity of Judgment
Amos 8:1-3

Amos may have been expelled from Israel after his confrontation with Amaziah. If so, the visions and prophetic oracles continued to come to him. The fourth vision was not as dramatic as the first three. Yahweh showed Amos a basket of summer fruit. A question from the Lord fixed Amos' attention and elicited from him the utterance of the word "basket." That was the key word. Then by means of a play on words Yahweh explained to Amos the significance of the vision. The "end is come upon my people Israel." The word for "end" (*qets*) sounds in Hebrew very much like the word for "summer fruit" (*qayits*). The political end of northern Israel would come about because Yahweh declared that he would "not again pass by them any more." He would not overlook their transgression any longer (8:1-2).

While the word "basket" is the key to the fourth vision, the significance of the summer fruit well along in the ripening process should not be overlooked. The ripening process is (1) gradual in its outset, (2) swift in its conclusion, (3) ruinous in its end, and (4) is irreversible. So this basket of late summer fruit was a good illustration of the corruption of Israel.

Amos then explained what he meant by "the end of my people Israel." In the temple the songs would be turned to wailing, joyous worship to lamentation. Why? Because "the dead bodies shall be many." So numerous would be the corpses that burial would be impossible. The dead bodies would be unceremoniously "cast forth" with silence.

ENDNOTES

1. Keil proposed an allegorical interpretation for this allusion. The king is Yahweh. The mowings are past judgments on Israel. The growing of the second crop is the prosperity which Israel regained after those judgments.

2. John D.W. Watts, *Studying the Book of Amos* (Nashville: Broadman, 1966), pp. 13-16.

3. In pre-exilic literature *chozeh* is used only of Gad (2 Sam 24:11). In Chronicles, however, the term is used of several prophets.

CHAPTER FOURTEEN

A Falling Temple and a Future Tent
Amos 8:4-9:15

Students of Amos have suggested that Amos may have been expelled from northern Israel after his confrontation with Amaziah. The fourth vision and all that follows in the book would then represent the ministry of Amos after he returned to Judah. Following his fourth vision Amos has incorporated an extended oracle on the theme of covetousness. This is followed by the fifth vision in which Amos saw the collapse of the temple. In the future, however, he anticipated the resurrection of the fallen tent of David.

ORACLE ON COVETOUSNESS
Amos 8:4-14

The oracle which follows the fourth vision may have been delivered in Judah during a second phase of Amos' ministry. In any case, these verses contain one of the strongest indictments against covetousness found anywhere in the Bible.

A. Condemnation of Covetousness (8:4-6).

The oracle begins with "hear this" which is very similar to the earlier "hear this word" (3:1;4:1;5:1). Covetousness stands condemned in this oracle for four reasons.

1. Covetousness harms innocent people. The "needy" and the "poor" suffer as a result of this sin. The first term (*'ebhyon*) often has spiritual connotations. It frequently refers to those who are meek and humble. The second term (*'anav*) refers to those who are physically destitute. The oracle is addressed to those who "pant after" ("trample" NASB) the needy. The verb conveys the picture of a vicious beast after its prey, eager to swallow him. The metaphor probably refers to the land barons forcing people into debtors' slavery so that they could confiscate their small holdings. Through both legal and illegal means these powerful landholders were causing "the poor of the land to fail" (8:4).

2. Covetousness despises sacred things. The new moon and sabbath were sacred days under the law of Moses. Normal commerce was suspended. Yet instead of focusing on worship, the greedy merchants were calculating the profits from future sales. The sacred days were an annoying interruption to their business. They could not wait for the holy days to be over so they could market their wheat and other grains. They loved grain, gain and gold more than they loved God (8:5a).

3. Covetousness employs unscrupulous practices. In their business dealings the wealthy merchants used every trick in the trade. They made the ephah—the dry measure which was about a bushel—small. The buyer got less of the commodity than he had purchased. They also made the shekel great. The buyer would have to place more gold or silver in the balances to equal the heavier weight on the other side. So the customer got less product for more exchange. In addition Amos accuses these merchants of "dealing falsely with balances of deceit." Apparently they also rigged the scales in their favor (8:5b). Verification of the situation described by Amos was discovered by archaeologists in Tirzah, one of the leading cities of northern Israel. Two sets of weights were found, one for buying and one for selling. The find dates to the time of Amos.[1]

4. Covetousness results in cruel oppression. The wealthy were determined to "buy the poor for silver." By cheating the poor man they made him so poor that he would be obliged to sell himself to them from want and distress. For the smallest debt—no more than the price of a pair of shoes—they would be sold by the court into slavery. In addition to everything else, the poor man only got "the refuse of the wheat" for his hard-earned money. Thus the merchants were falsifying the product they sold. They were selling as good wheat ephahs mostly filled with the wheat which fell through the sieve. This refuse wheat was normally given to the animals (8:6).

B. Curse on Covetousness (8:7-10).

Judgment against covetousness among God's people was certain. Yahweh "has sworn by the pride of Jacob," i.e., the pride of the nation Israel. In 6:8 Yahweh swore by himself; in 4:2 he swore by his holiness. In 6:8 Yahweh expressed contempt for the pride of Jacob; here by way of contrast is the true pride of Jacob, i.e., Yahweh himself (8:7a).

Yahweh had sworn that he would never forget any of their deeds. The Lord can never show mercy to those who cannot bestow mercy on others (8:7b).

The judgment against covetousness would be terrible. By means of a negative rhetorical question Amos underscored the certainty of the calamity. "Shall not the land tremble for this?" The demonstrative refers either to the sins of the people (Harper) or to the substance of the oath (Deane; Keil). The trembling of the land refers to an earthquake, perhaps the one mentioned in 1:1 (8:8a). The reference may be to the massive earthquake in the days of King Uzziah which was still remembered two hundred years later (Zech 14:5).

The severity of the earthquake is likened to the annual inundation of the Nile river. The rising of the Nile takes a month or so, and the sinking of the river a similar amount of time. Thus the earthquake envisioned by Amos would not be a momentary tremor. It would be prolonged shaking (8:8b).

That day of judgment would see "the sun go down at noon." Thus Yahweh would "darken the earth in the clear day." An eclipse of the sun was visible in Palestine June 15, 763 BC. That event may have been the background for this utterance of Yahweh. The language here, however, is metaphorical for the sudden destruction of the nation at the height of prosperity (8:9).

As the judgment began to unfold the people of God would make a conscious effort to show an awareness of sin. Their feasts would be turned into mourning, their songs into lamentations. All would put on "sackcloth," the coarse cloth made of goat or camel hair which was worn by mourners. They would shave their heads, a mourning sign forbidden in the law of Moses because of its heathen association (Deut 14:1). The mourning of that day would be as intense as that for an only son. "The end thereof," i.e., of the mourning, would be "a bitter day." The cessation of the mourning would not mark the dawn of better times, but of even more suffering (8:10).

C. Consequences of Covetousness (8:11-14).

Another shocking announcement about that day of judgment is introduced by the word "behold!" The bitterness of suffering in that day of punishment is amplified by the fact that God would withdraw his word of revelation from them. There would be a famine in the land, not a famine of bread or water, but of "hearing the words of Yahweh." Those who presently spurned the prophetic word would then earnestly long for a comforting word from the Lord (8:11).

Amos pictures distraught Israelites wandering about in search of a word from heaven. The word "wander" literally means to reel, to totter. It expresses their uncertainty. They would be like a drunk staggering about. The expression "from sea to sea" probably refers to the Dead Sea and to the Mediterranean Sea. They would search "from the north even to the east." This is probably an abridged version of "from the north even to the south, and from west to east." In their eagerness to seek the word of Yahweh they would "run to and fro." Part of the punishment on those who will not listen to the Lord is to put them into circumstances where they cannot listen (8:12).

The young people would suffer most in that day of spiritual famine. The "fair virgins and young men" would "faint for thirst." Older people looking back can survive great hardship because they remember the word of God from earlier days. The young, however, would faint because there was nothing to revive them. If these vigorous young people succumb to the unquenchable thirst for God's word, how much more the weak (8:13).

In that desperate day when Yahweh would cut off from Israel his living word, those who were most involved in the calf cult would taste God's judgment. These calf worshipers are here designated as "they that swear by the guilt of Samaria." Samaria was the political capital of the northern kingdom. By the time of Amos a temple for the calf cult may have been built in Samaria. Or it may be that Amos is referring to the calf temple in Bethel. Swearing in the name of the deity held in highest regard was part of the worship of Old Testament peoples (cf. Deut 6:13; 10:20). These calf devotees would "fall and never rise up again." This prediction was fulfilled when the northern kingdom of Israel was destroyed in 722 BC and its citizens carried into captivity (8:14a).

A condensed version of the oath which the calf worshipers used is cited by Amos: "As your God lives, O Dan.' This is an obvious reference to the calf located in the far northern city of Dan. What is meant by the second oath formula is not as clear: "As the way of Beersheba lives." The "way" would be the actual road to Beersheba or perhaps the whole system of worship at that place. Nothing is known about the worship at Beersheba or its connection with the northern kingdom. Apparently some religious merit or benefit was thought to accrue from merely making the journey to Beersheba in southern Judah. This type of superstition stood condemned as much as the outright worship of the calf in Bethel and Dan (8:14b).

The main point of these last verses is that in a time of crisis false cults, superstition, and corrupt worship can never satisfy.

THE FINAL VISION
Yahweh Beside the Altar
Amos 9:1-10

In his fifth vision Amos saw Yahweh "standing beside the altar." Probably the altar at the Jerusalem temple is intended. The Lord issued the order, probably to some destroying angel, to "smite the capitals." The capitals were the knobs or ornaments on top of the pillars which supported the roof of the temple. The result of that smiting would be that the thresholds would shake. The smashing blows from above on the capitals would drive the pillars down upon their own thresholds. The entire edifice would crumble "on the head" of all those worshiping within (9:1a).

A. The Certainty of Judgment (9:1b-4).

Those that escaped the collapse of the temple would be slain by the sword, every last one of them. Not one would escape. The sinners would not have a "fugitive" who would flee or "a refugee" who would escape (9:1b).

Using hyperbole Amos underscores the fact that none would escape no matter what efforts they might make. Though "they dig into Sheol," the abode of the dead, here the symbol of extreme depth, "there shall my hand take them." Even if they could climb into heaven, symbol of extreme height, "there will I bring them down" (9:2).

Some might try to take refuge in the forests on top of Mt. Carmel. There Yahweh says he would search out the sinners. Though they took refuge in "the bottom of the sea" there God would "command the serpent" to bit them. These sea-serpents were popularly believed to be extremely dangerous (9:3).

Though they go into captivity before their enemies, there God would command the sword to slay them. Some may have thought that Yahweh was impotent outside Palestine. Even on foreign soil, however, he was sovereign. Again the point is that there would be no escape. Wherever they were Yahweh would set his eyes upon them "for evil, and not for good." He had taken these sinners under his special superintendence for evil, i.e., to punish them (9:4).

B. The God of Judgment (9:5-6).

Amos concludes his discussion of Yahweh's judgment with another hymn fragment which praises the power of God. He is indeed able to bring about such an inescapable punishment because he is "Yahweh of hosts," i.e., he has at his disposal all the power of the armies of heaven and earth. When this mighty God merely touches the earth it melts causing all who dwell in the earth to mourn. Mighty earthquakes cause the earth to rise and fall like the Nile river in its annual inundation (cf. 8:8). Thus Yahweh has absolute power over the dry land (9:5).

Likewise the Lord has power over the sea "He builds his upper chambers in the heavens." The word usually refers to the means of ascent, hence stairs. The visible heavens are but the steps leading to the eternal throne room of Yahweh. He has "founded his vaulted dome over the earth" (NASB). The metaphor refers to that which is elsewhere in the Old Testament called the expanse (*raqia*). According to Genesis 1:7 this expanse divides the water above from the waters beneath. The upper chambers of God are built in or out of the waters above this expanse (9:6a).

From these heavenly chambers Yahweh calls for "the waters of the sea." The water cycle is here suggested. Through evaporation God brings moisture from the seas. He then "pours them out upon the face of the earth" in torrential downpours. Yahweh is the God who sends these rains, not Baal who pretended to be the storm god in Canaanite theology (9:6b).

C. The Aim of Judgment (9:7-10).

The prophet next began to explain the aim of the judgment which he has been describing. Amos engaged the thought processes of his auditors by means of rhetorical questions designed to indicate the present condition of Israel, a condition which was quite perilous.

"Are you not as the children of the Ethiopians unto me, O children of Israel?" This question no doubt would have provoked the arrogant Israelites to anger. Amos is not denying here that Yahweh had a unique relationship with Israel (cf. 3:2). Since Israel was now in open rebellion against God they were no better than the Cushites who, as descendants of Ham, were brethren of the accursed Canaanites (Gen 9:18ff.; 10:6). With these words Amos tore away from Israel the last support of carnal security. No longer could this nation rely upon its election as the special people of God (9:7a).

While it was true that Yahweh had brought Israel out of the land of Egypt, the covenant between God and the nation was forged at Mt. Sinai. The Exodus lost its spiritual significance when the covenant obligations were ignored by this people. Yahweh had also orchestrated the movement of other ancient peoples—the Philistines from Caphtor (the island of Crete) and the Syrians from Kir (east of the Persian Gulf). He had brought these neighbors of Israel from distant lands to their present homes. These sinful nations, like Israel, were under the sovereign rule of Yahweh. No longer, however, did Israel have any special claim on the covenant blessings. They had spurned their God for years. Now he would withdraw his grace from them (9:7b).

Arrogant Israel argued that the eyes of Yahweh were upon them. They were right about that. "Behold, the eyes of the Lord Yahweh are upon that sinful kingdom." He saw only sin, rebellion, immorality and hypocrisy. The singular "kingdom" probably encompasses both Israel and Judah. Yahweh solemnly declared that he would destroy that sinful kingdom "from off the face of the earth." Thus his eyes were on that kingdom for calamity, not for blessing (9:8a).

The absolute declaration of destruction was tempered a bit by a wonderful gem of grace: "except that I will not utterly destroy the house of Jacob." The announcement of judgment was sealed with the solemn signature of Yahweh: "oracle of Yahweh." So also this gracious promise. The kingdom—the monarchy—would be utterly destroyed from off the face of the earth. The northern kingdom was destroyed in 722 BC, the southern kingdom in 586 BC. The "house of Jacob," the descendants of Israel the Patriarch, would not be totally destroyed along with the kingdom. Thus a remnant would survive the destruction of the monarchy, and that remnant would include some from both Israel and Judah (9:8b).

Amos used the illustration of a sieve to make clear what the coming destruction of the kingdom would accomplish. A sieve is ordinarily constructed in such a way that the good grain is retained while the light grain, the dust, and chaff fall through to the ground when the sieve is shaken. Yahweh would sift the house of Israel among all the nations, like grain is sifted in a sieve. "Yet not the least kernel will fall upon the earth." The good grain would remain for a time in the sieve (the exile) while the bad would fall to the ground (i.e., perish). The basic idea here is that in exile Israel would be purged from her ungodly members, but not one truly righteous person would be lost in the process (9:9).

Lest there be any misunderstanding of the illustration of the sieve illustration, Amos added a clear explanation. "All the sinners of my people shall die by the sword." The "sword" represents a violent death, perhaps by the army which would destroy the sinful kingdom. Amos immediately qualified his "all" by limiting the threat to one class of sinners: "those who say, the evil shall not overtake us." Presumptuous sinners always seem to think that they will escape any judgment which God may pour out.

BEYOND THE JUDGMENT
Amos 9:11-15

At some point after the destruction of the sinful kingdom and the sifting of all its citizens in exile, wonderful blessings awaited the faithful.

A. A Glorious King (9:11).

"In that day" after the judgment had fallen upon national Israel and all the sinners of God's people had been destroyed, Yahweh would initiate a great work of restoration. Yahweh promised that he would "raise up the hut of David." The word "hut" (*sukkah*) is a symbol of frailty, a temporary booth at the mercy of the elements. The once powerful Davidic house was but a hut in the days of Amos. Ten of the tribes had refused to recognize the authority of the Davidic rulers in 931 BC.

The Davidic hut, as pitiful as it was in the days of Amos, would experience yet further calamity. At some point it would totally collapse. The last descendant of David to rule in Jerusalem was Zedekiah. He was removed from the throne and was carried into captivity in 586 BC. At that point it could be said metaphorically that the Davidic hut had fallen.

Yahweh would one day "wall up their breaches." The plural suffix suggests that the term "hut" in the previous line actually refers to the kingdom of God which was then divided into two kingdoms. In the future the nation would be united again under one king who is called "David" (cf. Hos 1:11; 3:5; Ezek 37:22). That future "David" was Jesus Christ.

Yahweh also promised to "raise up his ruins." The singular suffix refers to David, i.e., a descendant of David, under whom the destroyed kingdom would rise to new power and prestige.

The Lord would "build it [the hut of David]." The term build (*banah*) here means to finish building, to carry on, enlarge, beautify the building. Though David's house had received and would yet receive considerable blows, it would not utterly perish. The Lord would honor the word of promise which he had made through the prophet Nathan (cf. 2 Sam 7:11,12,16). Early Jews recognized this passage as messianic and coined a term for Messiah from this verse: Son of the Fallen, a reference to the fallen "hut."

The promise goes one step further. Yahweh would build the house of David "as in days of old." The reference is to the glorious days of David and Solomon when the Davidic kingdom was the leading kingdom of the Near East. He who would be the fulfillment of these promises went even beyond Amos when he declared that "a greater than Solomon is here" (Matt 12:42).

B. An Expanding Kingdom (9:12).

The purpose of the restoration of the Davidic kingdom was so that the true sons of Israel—those who survived the sifting of judgment—would take possession of "the remnant of Edom." Edom, Israel's neighbor to the southeast, would go through their own national judgment (cf. 1:11f.). This taking possession of the remnant of Edom is very different from the subjugation of Edom and other surrounding nations to David. Here the remnant of Edom is incorporated into the kingdom of Messiah. This is an example of New Testament evangelism expressed in military metaphor (9:12a).

The remnant of Edom in this promise is but a specific example of a general principle. The restored Davidic kingdom—the church of Christ—would take possession of "all the nations." The reference is to all those who hear the word of the Lord and who, by faith, are incorporated into the true Israel of God. The messianic kingdom would become the means of reaching the nations of the world with the claims of Messiah.

Those nations which would become part of the messianic kingdom would be those which "are called" by Yahweh's name. To be called by someone's name is to belong to that person. A conquered city is called by the name of its conqueror (2 Sam 12:28); the wife is called by the name of her husband (Isa 4:1). The expression is also used of adopted sons (Gen 48:16). Thus to be called by one's name means to have an intimate association with that person, to belong to them in a special sense.

Those who accept Christ through faith are incorporated into the family of God. They become part of a group which is the special possession of God (1 Pet 2:9). Thus Amos is declaring that a day would come when the people of God would be reconstituted under a Davidic king. Gentiles would be very much a part of that kingdom. Through the Gospel they become fellow heirs and partakers of the promise. At the Jerusalem conference this text was cited to furnish Scriptural justification for Gentile evangelism (Acts 15:16f.).

The opening word of 9:12 should be noted. The word "for" (*lema'an*) suggests the purpose for the restoration of the Davidic kingdom under Messiah, viz., that Gentiles might be included within the family of God. Thus world evangelism was part of God's plan from the very beginning.

C. A Bountiful Land (9:13).

Having described the messianic kingdom in its outward expansion, Amos next stressed the inward bounty of that kingdom. Agricultural metaphors depict the abundance of blessing in that future day. The land occupied by the restored Davidic kingdom would experience amazing ("Behold!") fertility. The days would come, declares this solemn oracle of Yahweh, when "the plowman shall overtake the reaper, and the treader of grapes him that sows seed." The crops would be so abundant that harvesting would continue up to the time of sowing for the next season. In that messianic kingdom the citizens would enjoy the blessing which Moses promised to Israel if they were faithful to the covenant (Lev 26:5). The immediate context suggests an evangelistic emphasis in this figure. In the kingdom of Christ preparation, planting, cultivating, and harvesting would all be going on simultaneously. Perhaps Amos is describing poetically what Luke reported in Acts 2:47: "And the Lord added to the church daily such as were being saved."

In that messianic age the Lord declares that the "mountains shall drop sweet wine, and all the hills shall melt," i.e., dissolve into streams of wine, milk, honey. Truly this kingdom of grace would be a land flowing with milk and honey. To a farming community this language would suggest utopia. This language symbolizes the rich blessings which would follow the establishment of Christ's kingdom. "Under the figure of a supernatural fertility are represented the victories of grace."[2] In Luke 6:38 Jesus also used a figure of agricultural abundance to represent spiritual blessings.

D. A Restored People (9:14).

Yahweh promised that his people would inherited the glorious kingdom which he has been describing in the previous verses. He declares his intention to "restore the captivity of my people Israel." This metaphor appears frequently in prophetic literature. It means something like "change the fortunes of a people for the better." The statement does not necessarily require a literal restoration from a land of captivity. The idea is that a people once humiliated and oppressed would experience a wonderful new day.

The curse of Amos 5:11 would be reversed in that day. Frustration and disappointment haunt the life of those who violate the covenant of God (Deut 28:30, 38-41). That would not be the case with the citizens of Messiah's kingdom. Not only would they build up ruined cities, they would enjoy the fruit of their effort and actually dwell in those cities. Not only would they plant vineyards, they would enjoy the wine thereof. Not only would they make gardens, they would eat the fruit of them. Amos was declaring that the frustrations of a life of rebellion against God would not be a part of the experience of the citizens of Messiah's kingdom.

E. A Permanent Inheritance (9:15).

The last of the great metaphors of Amos stresses the permanence of the inheritance of God's people in the messianic age. Yahweh declares that he will "plant them upon their land." The picture here is of a tree firmly rooted in the ground. Messiah's kingdom is an everlasting kingdom (Dan 7:18,27). The people of God would "not again be rooted out from their land." That land or kingdom was their inheritance. What is being described here in Old Testament language is equivalent to what Jesus declared in John 10:28, "And I give eternal life to them, and they shall never perish; and no one shall pluck them out of my hand."

ENDNOTES

1. James L. Mays, *Amos, a Commentary* in "The Old Testament Library" (Philadelphia: Westminster, 1969), p. 144.
2. W.J. Deane, "Amos" in *The Pulpit Commentary*. New edition. (New York: Funk & Wagnals, 1909), p. 178.

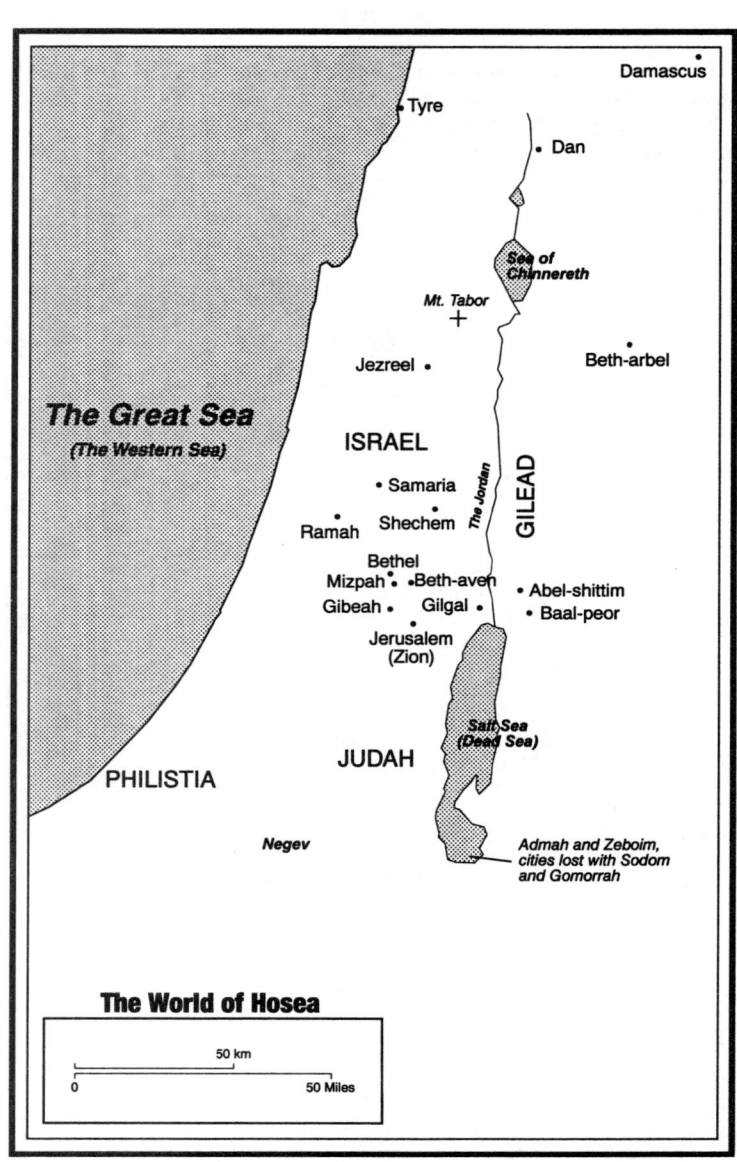

CHAPTER FIFTEEN

The Tragedy of Unfaithfulness
Hosea 1-3

In the days of the great Jeroboam II God raised up another mighty prophet. Through personal tragedy in his own life Hosea son of Beeri learned the pain which Israel's waywardness caused Yahweh. The first three chapters introduce the major themes of the entire book. Israel's sin is grievous, like adultery. Israel's punishment is certain. Yet beyond the judgment there was hope for a glorious future.

AN UNUSUAL MARRIAGE
Hosea 1:2-3

Hosea's ministry began when Yahweh "spoke by (lit., in) Hosea." The Lord directed him to go and "take," i.e., marry, "a wife of whoredom." To escape the moral implications of such a command some have suggested that this is actually a parable or a vision. Nothing in the text suggests either interpretation.

What is meant by "wife of whoredom?" Is this a woman whose business or livelihood consisted of prostitution? (Keil; Laetsch). Or is this a woman that Yahweh knew would lapse into harlotry? According to this view the woman had the potential of becoming a harlot. Or is this phrase neutral as to the character of the woman? (Snaith; Paterson; Yates). The phrase seems to be explained in the clause "because whoring, the land whores away from Yahweh." Any female citizen of the northern kingdom would be a wife of whoredom simply by virtue of living in the apostate northern kingdom. Therefore the phrase "wife of whoredom" does not indicate anything regarding the character of the woman.

Hosea was also told to take "children of whoredom." Are these children already born to a whore? (Keil). Probably not. The verb "take" has two objects in verse 2, but it undergoes a slight change in meaning in the second clause. The prophet would take a wife of whoredom and take (i.e., beget) children by her. Again, the children are called "children of whoredom" because they would be citizens of an apostate kingdom, not because their birth was illegitimate in any way.

Hosea did as he was told. He chose Gomer the daughter of Diblaim as his bride. Some try to find symbolic meanings in the names Gomer and Diblaim. The woman's name means something like "consumption [in sin]" and her father's name means "compressed fig-cakes" which supposedly points to the sweetness of sensual indulgence (Given). The fact, however, is that the text gives no symbolic meaning to either of these names as it gives to Hosea's children. Therefore these are real names of real people. No symbolism is intended at this point in the narrative (1:3a).

Gomer conceived and bore for Hosea a son. Nothing in the text suggest that this was an illegitimate birth in any way (1:3b).

A SYMBOLIC FAMILY
Hosea 1:4-9

The Lord directed Hosea to give symbolic names to the three children which Gomer bore for him. Each of those names had an ominous significance.

A. The Name Jezreel (1:4-5).

Yahweh directed Hosea to call the name of his new son

"Jezreel." In a negative sense this name means "God scatters." In a positive sense it means "God sows." In Hebrew the name Jezreel sounds very much like the name Israel. The paronomasia is probably intended. Israel, the "prince of God," would become Jezreel, "scattered by God" (1:4a).

The name Jezreel had prophetic significance. In a very short time something ominous would happen. Yahweh would "visit," i.e., punish, "the house of Jehu." Jehu was a military captain who slew King Jehoram of Israel in 841 BC and founded a new dynasty. Jehu was followed on the throne of Israel by four descendants—Jehoahaz, Jehoash, Jeroboam II and Zechariah. Jeroboam was the ruler on the throne when Hosea began his ministry. The last representative of this dynasty was assassinated in 752 BC.

The Jehu dynasty would be punished on account of "the blood of Jezreel," i.e., the blood shed in Jezreel. This is not referring to the blood of Naboth (1 Kgs 21:19ff.) for his blood was not shed by the house of Jehu. The reference must be to the blood shed by Jehu when he massacred the house of Ahab. While it is true that Yahweh had commanded the elimination of the wicked house of Ahab, Jehu did not execute the command in the right spirit. The captain was motivated by personal ambition rather than religious zeal.

The punishment for the blood shed by the house of Jehu in the village of Jezreel would be punished most severely. Yahweh declares that he would "put an end to the kingdom of the house of Israel." The northern kingdom would come to an end. This prophecy was fulfilled in 722 BC (1:4).

The name Jezreel had yet another significance. In the day of Israel's judgment Yahweh would "shatter the bow of Israel in the valley of Jezreel." The "bow," principal weapon of war in Israel, here symbolizes the entire military force. The Jezreel valley was the favorite battlefield of the region. Here the Assyrians would crush the army of Israel. No information has come to light regarding the location of the decisive battle between the Assyrians and Israelites (1:5).

B. Lo-ruhamah (1:6-7).

Hosea's second child was a daughter. No significance attaches to the sex of the child. Again Yahweh directed him in the naming of the baby. The names in this chapter do not reflect the cleverness of the prophet. Lo-ruhamah means "she has not obtained mercy." This name signified that Yahweh would no more "show compassion on the house of Israel." He had been showing compassion to the northern kingdom during the reign of Jeroboam, but no longer. A special kind of compassion is in view here, viz., the forgiveness of sin. Yahweh would not overlook or forgive their sin any longer (1:6).

Judah was exempt from the judgment which the northern kingdom would face. This is the first of several side glances toward Judah. Some of these "Judah notes" are favorable, some are unfavorable. Judah would face the same Assyrian armies which destroyed Israel. In Judah's case, however, the Lord promised to "save them in Yahweh their God." The deliverance would not be by bow, sword, war, horses or horsemen. This is clearly a prediction of the deliverance of Judah from Sennacherib in 701 BC (2 Kgs 19; Isa 37).

C. Lo-ammi (1:8-9).

Eastern mothers nurse their babies some two or three years. After Lo-ruhamah was weaned, Gomer bore her third child, another son. No particular significance is assigned to the weaning (1:8).

Again Yahweh named the child. The name Lo-ammi means "not my people." This name signals the climax of Israel's doom. The Lord would no longer recognize Israel as his people. They would be as Gentiles to him. If they were no longer his people, then Yahweh declared "I am not your God." They would no longer have any claim on God (1:9).

D. Reversal of the Names (1:10-2:1).

"Nevertheless," in spite of the impending doom for the northern kingdom, Israel as a people would still achieve her purpose in God's program. "The number of the children of Israel shall be as the sand of the sea which cannot be measured or numbered." The promise of numerous posterity made to Abraham, Isaac and Jacob would not fail even though the northern kingdom would be destroyed. The predictions of rapid multiplication of Israel in the Old Testament have messianic implications. This multiplication would be due to the influx of Gentiles in large numbers into the family of God through faith in Christ (1:10a).

In the exile in foreign lands it would be said to Israel, "You are not my people." Is this the opinion of their captors? Of God? Or themselves? In any case, "*there*"—in those lands of exile—in the future "it will be said to them, sons of the living God." Those regarded as Gentiles would become God's people. Paul (Rom 9:25-26) quotes this verse in reference to the conversion of Gentiles through the Gospel (1:10b).

In those distant lands God would gather both the children of Judah and the children of Israel. This presupposes that Judah would find herself in the same condition as Israel, i.e., cast off into captivity. Some former citizens of the northern kingdom may have joined Jews when they returned from Babylon under the leadership of Zerubbabel. The true significance, however, is much deeper. Those regarded as Gentiles (northern Israel) would be joined with the children of Judah (Jews). This prediction was fulfilled when Jew and Gentile were made one in Christ (Rom 9:25-26; 1 Pet 2:10).

The unity between Jew and Gentile would be effected because both would recognize the same leader. "They shall set for themselves one head." Their common allegiance to the head of the church would erase the distinctions among them. Later (3:5) Hosea would identify that leader as "David," i.e., a descendant of David. The reference must be to Christ, the greater son of David.

The one head would lead his people "up from the land." The language is taken from the Exodus. This future leader would be a second Moses. Jesus Christ leads his people out of the bondage of sin to the Promised Land, i.e., heaven.

That day of victorious march out of bondage is called "the day of Jezreel." The negative connotation in which this name was used in 1:4-5 is now dropped. God's scattering in judgment now becomes God's sowing for growth. The allusion is to the previous verse and to the great growth of the people of God in the messianic age (1:11).

The unit concludes with a command: "Say to your brethren, Ammi, and to your sisters, Ruhamah." To whom is this command addressed? Not to Hosea, for the verb is plural and so is the possessive "your." Apparently the members of Messiah's united people are encouraged to recognize their spiritual relationship to one another. "Lo-ammi"—not my people—now becomes "Ammi"—my people. All who follow the future Davidic ruler would recognize their unique relationship with God. "Lo-ruhamah"—she has not obtained compassion—now becomes "Ruhamah"—she has obtained compassion. All of those who follow Messiah know that they have been recipients of divine grace (2:1).

AN EXTENDED METAPHOR
The Adulterous Wife
Hosea 2:2-7

One of the major contentions of Hosea was that idolatry was equivalent to spiritual harlotry. This theme is developed in Hosea 2.

A. Her Shameless Profligacy (2:2).

Individual Israelites are urged by Yahweh to "contend," i.e., reproach or upbraid or reprimand, their "mother," i.e., their motherland or the nation as a whole. The nation should be told that she had lost her status with the Lord. The Sinai marriage (covenant) between Yahweh and Israel had been dissolved. She was no longer his wife and he is no longer Israel's husband (2:2a).

Yahweh's marriage to Israel had been dissolved because the nation had committed "whoredoms." Those citizens who had remained faithful to the Lord should plead with their motherland to give up her adulteries, i.e., idolatries. To "remove her whoredoms from her face" may refer to the painted face of a prostitute (cf. Jer 3:3; Prov 7:13). To remove "adulteries from between her breasts" may refer to a harlot's embrace of her lover. Others think the allusion is to the ornaments which prostitutes sometimes wore on their exposed breasts (2:2b).

B. Her Certain Punishment (2:3-4).

Should the wayward wife (Israel) fail to separate herself from her whoredoms, Yahweh threatened to "strip her naked." Some evidence suggests that women who broke marriage vows were first stripped naked before they were executed.[1] The Lord would "set Israel as in the day of her birth." In the beginning of her history Israel was a homeless wanderer in the wilderness. The threat here is that Israel would return to that condition (2:3a).

Israel would be stripped of property, prosperity, population and privileges. Yahweh would set her "as a wilderness" and "dry land." He threatens to "slay her with thirst." This figure means that all blessings would be withheld from Israel. The people as well as the land would be laid waste. The Lord would no longer show compassion on the sons of Israel. This threat was contained in the name of Hosea's daughter Lo-ruhamah (2:3b).

The reason for the absence of divine compassion is clearly stated. All the citizens of the north were "children of whoredom" because they were part of an apostate nation. No individual had any grounds to think that he might escape the punishment which would befall the nation (2:4).

C. Her Disgusting Behavior (2:5).

The citizens of Israel were children of whoredom because "their mother has committed harlotry." Harlotry throughout Hosea is a metaphor for flirtation with foreign nations and their gods. The individual citizens had been conceived by a mother who lived shamefully. The reference is to the gross immorality of the Baal cult which promoted drunkenness and sexual immorality. The profligate mother had declared, "I will go after my lovers," i.e., the Baal gods. To these fertility gods Israel attributed the provision of necessities and luxuries: bread, water, wool, flax, oil and drink.

D. Her Future Repentance (2:6-7).

Because of her unfaithfulness, Yahweh had a shocking announcement for Israel. The Lord would "hedge up" Israel's current path of unfaithfulness. The apostate nation would no longer be able to go after her lovers, the Baal gods. At the same time Yahweh would "wall up her wall." The expression is difficult. Perhaps it means to increase the size of her walls so that she could not see over them. As a result Israel would not "find her paths," i.e.. the various ways in which she was pursuing idolatry. The Assyrian oppression of Israel, the fall of the northern kingdom, and the exile are here in view (2:6).

The immediate reaction to the pressure of the Assyrian invasion would be to increase Israel's pursuit of idolatry. "She will pursue her lovers." The Hebrew Piel form points to the eagerness of the pursuit. Israel, however, would not "overtake them," i.e., make contact with her gods. In her desperation she would seek the idols, but would not find them. In that experience Israel would learn that idols could bring no help (2:7a).

Failing to find help from her idols, Israel would determine to "return to my first husband," i.e., Yahweh. Their sad and desperate experience awakened within them the desire to return to the faithful God of the covenant. "For it was better for me then than now." They would acknowledge that all good things had come to them as a nation from Yahweh, not Baal. In the exile Israel was cured of idolatry. The captives returned to the Lord (2:7b).

A CONCRETE ILLUSTRATION
Perverted Prosperity
Hosea 2:8-13

Another major theme in Hosea is introduced at this point, viz., the misuse of material blessings. Because Israel had ignored the source of their prosperity, that wealth would be cut off.

A. The Source of Prosperity Ignored (2:8).

At the time Hosea spoke, Israel was in a state of willful spiritual ignorance. That ignorance was sin. Constantly that people had been reminded by Moses that the produce of the land would be a blessing of Yahweh. The ceremonial offering of the firstfruits to the Lord was designed to remind them annually of this fact. Thus through revelation and ritual if not through reason Israel was taught that material blessing was a gift from her divine husband Yahweh (2:8a).

Yahweh declared through Hosea that he was the one who gave Israel her chief agricultural products: grain, new wine, and oil. In Canaanite theology the rains and hence the abundance of field and tree were attributed to Baal, the weather god. When Israel left the desert and settled in Canaan about 1400 BC the people quickly learned the techniques of the sedentary population. Unfortunately they also learned their religious myths.

The reign of King Jeroboam was the most prosperous since the days of Solomon. Israel traded her abundant crops to neighboring nations for precious metals. Since Yahweh gave the abundant crops he was also the one who "multiplied for her silver and gold." Yet Israel took these precious metals to make idols of Baal or to purchase sacrifices for use in the Baal cult (2:8b).

B. The Removal of Prosperity Threatened (2:9-11).

Since the divine gifts had been misused and unappreciated, God threatened to reverse his policy toward Israel. National wealth would be forfeited. "I will take away my grain in its time and my new wine in its season." The emphasis on the possessive pronoun should be noted. Men own nothing. They are merely stewards of what God lends them for their temporary use (2:9a).

"My wool and my flax," i.e., clothing as well as food, would also be removed. The verb "snatch away" suggests a sudden and unexpected calamity, even a violent act, which could not be anticipated weeks ahead. Deprivation of food and clothing would leave the nation destitute and hungry. At the same time, these dire straits would remind the people how dependent they were on Yahweh (2:9b).

The consequence of the deprivation of food and clothing is that Yahweh would uncover Israel's "shame" or "lewdness" (NASB). The word (*nabhlut*) seems to refer to the shameful sexual offenses which the nation, God's wife, had committed with the Baal gods. This stripping would take place "to the eyes of her lovers," i.e., false gods and foreign nations. In the eyes of both her deities and her allies God would strip Israel of her national wealth. Israel would be exposed to the derision of those who once admired her. "And none shall deliver her out of my hand." Neither god nor ally would make any difference when Yahweh acted to remove Israel's wealth (2:10).

The loss of material wealth is devastating in a materialistic world. So by removing Israel's wealth, Yahweh would "cause all her mirth to cease." The religious festivals, celebrated with great joy in Israel, would be no more. The new moon which was celebrated either monthly or quarterly, would pass away. The sabbaths—both the weekly sabbaths and the special sabbaths associated with festivals—would no longer be observed. Other "appointed seasons" would be a thing of the past. When God got through pouring out his wrath on Israel there would be nothing left to celebrate! (2:11).

C. The Abuse of Prosperity Reiterated (2:12-13).

Yahweh threatens to "lay waste" Israel's vine and fig tree. Again the verb suggests a violent action. These two trees, the principal fruit trees in Palestine, represent God's material blessings on his people. God's wife Israel regarded the grape and fig harvest as "a payment" (*'etnah*) which her "lovers" (the Baal gods) had bestowed upon her. The Hebrew term refers to the wages of prostitution (Deut 23:18). Israel's religious loyalty was purchased by the abundant crops which she attributed to blessing by Baal. Thus here the fruit crop would be treated just like the bread, water, wool, flax, oil and drink of verse 5 (2:12a).

God would turn that bountiful land into "a forest." The carefully cultivated fruit trees would become a tangled mass of brush wood. "The beast of the field" would devour what fruit survived. The picture here is of an uninhabited land overrun by wild beasts (2:12b).

The devastation of the land would be the result of an act of judgment by Yahweh, the God which Israel had betrayed. He would "visit," i.e., punish, his wayward wife "for the days of the Baalim." Were these special festivals in honor of Baal in addition to the special days of verse 11? Or had the Israelites turned Yahweh's feasts into celebrations of Baal? In either case the veneration of Baal is being condemned. The plural "Baalim" is used because each local shrine had its own version of the god Baal (2:13a).[2]

Israel was enthusiastic in the pursuit of Baal. First, she burned incense to this fertility deity. The verb (*qatar*) may have a more general meaning, to cause sweet smoke to ascend, or simply to sacrifice. Second, she "adorned herself with her ring and her jewels." The popular religion of the Canaanites required gala dress for holy days (cf. Exod 3:18-22). Both nose rings (Gen 24:47; Isa 3:21) and ear rings (Gen 35:4) were worn by women in Old Testament days. Some think that these rings were worn to honor the god Baal, but this is not certain. Third, she "went after her lovers." The figure here is of a woman trying to attract admirers, i.e., the nation Israel wanted to get involved with other nations and their gods. Fourth, in her zeal to pursue foreign gods "me she forgot." The order of the words emphasizes the enormity of the offense. Perhaps a modern equivalent would be leaving Christ out of Christmas (2:13b).

A TRIUMPHANT ANNOUNCEMENT
Love Wins Out
Hosea 2:14-23

After Israel finds herself stripped and abandoned, Yahweh in his grace would approach her again. The word "behold" announces something unexpected. Eventually Yahweh's love for his people would be rewarded. Love would win out. Israel would experience a new (1) courtship, (2) response, (3) covenant, (4) marriage, (5) prosperity, and (6) privilege.

A. A New Courtship (2:14-15a).

In the light of the ugly unfaithfulness of Israel the movement of God to rekindle the old relationship is shocking, but wonderful. "I shall allure her." The verb (*patah*) is a Piel participle. It suggests gentle persuasion through loving words. Yahweh would bring his wayward bride back into the "wilderness." The rejection of Israel throughout Hosea is represented as an expulsion from Canaan to Egypt, the land of bondage. Leading Israel into the desert was not punishment, but redemption out of bondage. In the relationship between God and his bride the wilderness was the old honeymoon grounds. That was a time when Israel was totally dependent on God. Now he would take his wayward wife into a metaphorical wilderness. There he would "speak upon her heart," i.e., speak tenderly to her. He would woo his wife! He would treat her as a chaste virgin even though she was an adulteress (2:14).

Out of that wilderness honeymoon God would lead his people anew into the Promised Land. Israel immediately would come into possession of rich blessings such as "vineyards." There Israel, as their ancestors had done, would walk through the "valley of Achor." In that valley Achan had been executed in the days of Joshua because he had troubled Israel with transgression. Here that valley of trouble has become "a door of hope." The valley is a symbol of fertility. Though the restored nation might have to walk through a troublesome valley, it would only be the beginning of a series of wonderful blessings. Stripping this prediction of its metaphor, this passage speaks of God's rapprochement to Israel in the captivity and the restoration of Israel to their homeland during the postexilic period (2:15a).

B. A New Response (2:15b-17).

The once wayward wife would respond positively to the wooing of her husband. She would "answer," i.e., respond, "as in the days of her youth, as in the day she came out of Egypt." The verb ('anah) could be translated "sing" (NASB) as well as "answer." The point would be that Israel would rejoice as once they had done upon leaving Egypt. In the days of Moses Israel loved Yahweh enough to follow him into a trackless wilderness. That ancient love would be rekindled in the remnant of the future (2:15b).

In that day when the relationship between Israel and Yahweh was restored, Israel would call Yahweh "Ishi," i.e., "my husband." Though the title "Baali" means essentially the same as "Ishi," the former term would not be used because of its pagan associations. Thus the verse points to a purification of Israel (2:16). Yahweh's love and blessing would lead to this total rejection of the Baal cult. The Lord would remove the names of the Baalim from Israel's mouth. All traces and memory of the Baal cult would be destroyed. Not even their names would be mentioned. After the exile even the proper names of earlier Israelites were changed to avoid the use of the name Baal (2:17).[3]

C. A New Covenant (2:18).

Yahweh promised to "make for them a covenant." This covenant *for* them is not to be confused with the covenant *with* them (Jer 31:31). The covenant here is with "the beast of the field, the fowl of the heavens, and the creeping things of the ground." It guarantees peace between restored Israel and the animal world. The time frame is "in that day," i.e., in the day when God reestablishes his relationship with Israel, after he has brought them back to the Promised Land. The reference may embrace the messianic age. The "beast of the field" refers to ferocious wild beasts. The point here, as in Isaiah 11:6-8, is that the future Israel would be a peaceful kingdom (2:18a).

Yahweh explained the meaning of the covenant with the animals by further declaring: "And bow and sword and war I will shatter from the land." Other prophets also emphasize the peaceful nature of the new Israel led by Messiah (Isa 2:4; Mic 4:3; Jer 23:6; 33:16). In Old Testament language the peace that passes all understanding (Phil 4:7) is being described. The absence of war means that Yahweh would cause his people to "dwell safely" in the land. The security of the believer in Christ is being described in Old Testament language (2:18b).

D. A New Marriage (2:19-20).

God promised to "betroth" Israel. The term is never used of the restoration of a wife who had been divorced; it refers only to the wooing of a maiden. A new marriage to the once unfaithful wife is in view. The threefold use of the word "betroth" underscores permanence, depth of affection and solemnity of the new relationship. Shameful adultery had severed the old marriage bond. Now, however, that old adulterous wife is being treated as a chaste virgin. The passage does not anticipate the patching up of the old marriage, but the establishment of a new marriage. Marriage here is a metaphor for the new covenant which the prophets associated with the coming of Messiah (2:19a).

Yahweh would shower his bride with five gifts worth more than rubies or gold. The new marriage would be founded upon "righteousness and justice," i.e., the right relationship with God and with one's fellows. The new marriage will also be based on "lovingkindness and compassion," two Old Testament words which point to grace. The marriage is also founded on "faithfulness." In the faithfulness of God his people have a certain pledge that the covenant would stand forever. In this new relationship God's people would come to "know" by experience the true nature of Yahweh (2:19b-20).

E. A New Prosperity (2:21-22).

In that day of the new marriage (covenant)—the messianic age— Yahweh would supply all the needs of his people. The heavens, as it were, ask Yahweh for permission to send the rain on Israel and he would respond positively. The heavens would respond to the cry of the earth for rain. The earth would respond to the cry of the grain, the new wine and the oil. These products in turn would respond to Jezreel, i.e., the new Israel of the messianic age. The point is poetically made that nature is attentive to the needs of the new covenant Israel. Yahweh would pass the orders down the ranks for all the needs of his people to be met. The God of the new covenant would hear the prayers of his people.

F. A New Privilege (2:23).

Continuing the agricultural metaphor, Yahweh declared his intention to "sow her," i.e., Jezreel, "in the land." The name "Jezreel" means "God sows." The faithful remnant returning from exile would be the seed which would eventually lead to a wonderful harvest of the faithful. The new crop would include Gentiles. "Lo-ruhamah," she who had not obtained compassion, would then experience Yahweh's compassion. "Lo-ammi," not my people, would be designated as "my people" in that day. This verse goes beyond 2:1. Not only would members of the covenant community regard themselves as God's people, they would in fact be God's people, acknowledged by none other than Yahweh himself!

AN ACTION PARABLE
Love Risks All
Hosea 3:1-5

Having looked forward to the remote future—the messianic age—Hosea now returns to the more immediate future. He performs an action parable involving an unnamed woman—most likely his estranged wife—to dramatize the tremendous love of God for Israel and the potentially healing power of that love.

A. Love for a Fallen Woman (3:1).

Hosea was commanded by Yahweh to go "once more" (cf. 1:2). He was to "love," i.e., openly demonstrate his love, for a woman. What woman? Two phrases are given by way of identification. First, she was a woman "beloved of her friend." A "friend" is an intimate companion. The "friend" of a woman must either be (1) her husband or (2) her lover. The word is used of a husband in the Old Testament, but never of an adulterous lover. Therefore, the "friend" must be her husband.

Second, the woman is described as "an adulteress." The participles indicate that the love of the "friend" (husband) and the adultery of the woman were contemporaneous. Most commentators see in this woman Gomer, Hosea's wife and the mother of his children. Though some (e.g., McGarvey) have questioned this interpretation, it does seem to be the most reasonable.

The conclusion follows that Gomer must have been unfaithful to Hosea. She must have deserted the home at some point. Or perhaps Hosea had been forced to expel her because of her immoral activities. She may have become a temple prostitute at the Baal temple or the slave concubine of another man. In either case, eventually she was compelled to sell herself into slavery. Here was where Hosea would demonstrate his love for her.

Hosea's marriage to Gomer illustrated the great love which Yahweh had for his wife Israel. Her unfaithfulness illustrated Israel's adultery with the Baal gods. Yet just as Hosea still loved his unfaithful wife, so Yahweh still loved his faithless wife Israel. What marvelous love! In spite of the fact that Israel turned from her legitimate husband to pursue other gods, yet God loved them. In spite of the fact that the children of Israel were "lovers of raisin cakes" which were used in pagan worship rituals. Yet Yahweh loved them. The sweet raisin cakes symbolize the sensual service which was part of the Baal cult (3:1).

B. Loving Discipline (3:2-3).

Hosea carried out the command of Yahweh. He reports autobiographically that he bought the woman for himself "for fifteen pieces of silver and a homer and a half of barley. The price of a slave in the Old Testament world was thirty pieces of silver. Apparently Hosea paid half the price in silver and half in kind. A homer equals ten ephahs and an ephah equals about a bushel. Hence, Hosea paid about fifteen bushels of barley for the woman in addition to the fifteen pieces of silver (3:2).

"Many days you shall sit for me," he told his wayward wife. Before the normal husband/wife relationship could be restored she must be subjected to a period of discipline. Gomer must learn to control her passions. She must *choose* to be restored to the status of Hosea's wife. During that period of discipline she would be prohibited from practicing her harlotry. She would be restrained from sexual association with any man, including Hosea. "Yes, even I will be thus unto you," he told her. As slave owner he could have forced himself on her. He chose, however, to impose this discipline upon Gomer to reform and train her (3:3).

C. Symbolic Significance (3:4).

In Hosea's dealings with his wife the Lord had a message for Israel. The children of Israel would also experience a period of discipline. The reference is to the exile in a foreign land. During that period Israel would dwell "without king and without prince," i.e., she would be deprived of her civil polity as she came under the authority of a foreign king. She also would be deprived of her religious privileges—sacrifice in particular—just as Gomer was deprived of her conjugal rights (3:4a).

Three other much beloved items would disappear from Israel during the days of the discipline (captivity). First, they would be without "pillar." The pillar was a monument connected with Baal worship. The use of this object was forbidden in the law of Moses (Exod 23:24); but pillars were common in Israel and even in Judah under the idolatrous kings.

Second, they would be without "ephod." This was a garment worn by the high priest in which or on which the Urim and Thummim were attached. God communicated with Israel through these stones, though exactly how they functioned is not known. The ephod mentioned here may refer to some idolatrous use of this garment as in Judg 8:27.

Third, they would not have Teraphim in exile. These were the household gods so common in that period. Teraphim may have been connected with ancestor worship. These were apparently consulted for oracles even outside Baalism (cf. Ezek 21:21).

The point in 3:4 is that Israel during the exile would be deprived of both legitimate and illegitimate forms of government and worship. The former would be abandoned out of necessity since the apparatus of Yahweh worship could not function outside the land of Israel. That which was illegitimate would be abandoned because the people would learn to abhor idolatry.

D. Prophetic Anticipation (3:5).

Whether or not the discipline of Gomer brought the woman to her senses is not stated in the book. Hosea correctly anticipated, however, that the divine discipline of Israel in exile would produce positive results.

First, Hosea announces that the children of Israel "shall return." In this context the word is probably the equivalent of the verb "repent." The return, then, is to Yahweh.

Second, the children of Israel would "seek Yahweh their God." Seeking Yahweh meant (1) humble and contrite worship; and (2) practical application of the principles of justice reflected in God's law (cf. Amos 5:4,6,14-15).

Third, the children of Israel would seek "David their king." A true return to God must involve a return to David their king since Yahweh had promised the kingship to David and his seed forever (2 Sam 7:13,16). This "David" must be the Messiah.

Fourth, the children of Israel would "fear Yahweh." They would turn to the Lord in trembling realizing at last the magnitude of their sins. To fear the Lord is equivalent in the Old Testament to worshiping him.

Fifth, the children of Israel would also fear "the goodness of Yahweh." The goodness of God is equivalent to his gifts (cf. Jer 31:12; Zech 9:17). The point is that they will reverently seek blessings from Yahweh and not from the Baal gods.

Two time notes mark the period when these anticipations would be realized. First, this turning to the Lord would come "afterward," i.e., after the exile. Second, the conversion of Israel is set "in the latter days." The New Testament identifies the latter days as the Gospel age.[4]

ENDNOTES

1. On the execution of adulteresses see Lev 20:10; Deut 22:22; Ezek 16:40; John 8:5.

2. Two examples of the tendency to localize the god Baal are Baal of Peor (Num 25:3) and Baal-berith (Judg 8:33).

3. In two prominent examples of deliberate name changes the term *"bosheth"* (shame) was substituted for Baal: Meri-baal to Mephibosheth (2 Sam 9:6); and Ishbaal to Ish-bosheth (2 Sam 2:8).

4. See Acts 2:17;1 Cor 10:11; Heb 9:26; Jam 5:3; 1 Pet 1:5,20; 2 Pet 3:3; 1 John 2:18.

CHAPTER SIXTEEN

The Lack of Knowledge
Hosea 4:1-6:3

Hosea 4-14 contains sayings rather than sermons of the prophet. The train of thought is difficult to follow in these chapters. Laetsch has proposed that 4:1 is intended to outline in broad categories the three main areas of concern in these chapters.[1]

Hosea calls upon his countrymen to "hear the word of Yahweh." This prophet was very conscious of being a spokesman for God. The "house of Israel" should pay careful attention to what is about to be said because "Yahweh has a controversy with the inhabitants of the land." The term "controversy" (*ribh*) refers to what scholars have called a covenant lawsuit. Yahweh, as it were, takes his people into court to prove that whereas he had been faithful to the terms of the covenant, his people had not (4:1a).

Three main charges are leveled against Israel in this covenant lawsuit. These are taken up in reverse order in the rest of the Book of Hosea: (1) lack of truth or faithfulness (chs. 11:12-14:9); (2) lack of mercy or kindness (6:4-11:11); and (3) lack of knowledge of God

(4:2-6:3). Each unit is marked off by an appeal for repentance at its conclusion.

In developing the theme of the lack of the knowledge of God Hosea treats (1) the sin of the land (4:2-19); (2) the judgment on the land (5:1-15); and the appeal to the land (6:1-3).

THE SIN OF THE LAND
Hosea 4:2-19

In discussing the sins of the land, Hosea focuses on three areas: (1) the sins of the people (4:2-5); (2) the sins of the priests (4:6-10); and (3) the sin of idolatry (4:11-19).

A. The Sins of the People (4:2-5).

The first five words of the indictment against Israel use a Hebrew form which enhances the vividness of the description. Here is a black catalog of sins: swearing, lying, killing, stealing, and adultery. These sins are violations of the ninth, sixth, eighth and seventh commandments of the Decalogue. "They break in," i.e., they resort to violent acts against another's property.[2] "Blood touches blood," i.e., one bloody deed follows on the heels of another (4:2).

Nature testifies to the sin in the land for it has been made to suffer on account of the sins of man. "The land mourns and everyone who dwells in it languishes" because of a lack of rain. All the animals—beast, fowl, fish—suffer. That the fish suffer too is indicative of the severity of the drought (4:3).

In spite of the divine judgment manifested in nature, the people prove themselves to be incorrigible in their sins. Reproving them is a waste of time, "for your people are as those who strive with priests." The priests were the last judicial authority (Deut 17:12). To rebel against them was to give the nation over to anarchy and lawlessness (4:4).

Yahweh warns his wayward people: "You shall stumble by day." The pronoun throughout this unit is masculine singular. The citizenry collectively is here regarded as male offspring, while the nation as a political entity is regarded as the "mother" of the citizenry. They would "fall" in the sense of perish. The light of day would not aid them in their escape. The professional prophets would similarly "stumble," i.e., perish. The darkness of night would not hide them. Israel, the motherland of these wicked people (cf. 2:2), would be destroyed (4:5).

B. The Sins of the Priests (4:6-10).

The reason the people of Israel were perishing was because they lacked "the knowledge," i.e., the knowledge of God, the only knowledge which really matters. The reference is to knowing God experientially and knowing his word factually. The people lacked this knowledge because collectively the priests had rejected it (4:6a).[3]

Since the priests had rejected the knowledge of God, Yahweh would "reject you from being priest for me." Spiritual leaders who do not personally know God, who do not love his teaching, are doomed to lose their standing. Rejecting the knowledge of God is further explained in the accusation "you have forgotten the Law of your God." Again the punishment corresponds to the crime. Yahweh threatened: "I also will forget your children." Not only would the present priesthood be rejected, but their sons after them would likewise be excluded from this honor (4:6).

The priests sinned in ever increasing measure. During the reign of King Jeroboam the priesthood grew in prosperity and power. The more they increased in power, the more they sinned against the Lord. They forsook the ideals of their office. God threatened: "I will change their glory into shame," i.e., the dignity of their office would become ignominy (4:7).

Yahweh charged: "The sin of my people they eat." The reference seems to be to the sin offering of which the priests were to eat the most part. The noun can mean either "sin" or "sin offering." Perhaps the word is used here in a dual meaning. The more the people sinned, the more the priests got to eat the choice meat of the sin offering. For this reason, "unto their iniquity they lift up their soul," i.e., they cherish or long for the people to commit iniquity because they prospered from the abundance of sin offerings brought to the temple (4:8).

These corrupt priests would not escape the punishment of the people of Israel. "And it shall be, like people, like priest." Their sacred office would not give them a waiver from judgment. They would receive no clergy pass out of the impending calamity. Yahweh threatened: "I will punish them for their ways." They would be rewarded "for their deeds," i.e., they would receive the wages of sin (4:9).

Even before the national judgment these priests would experience frustration in their lives. First, "they shall eat, but not have enough." The reference is probably to the sin offerings. Their lust to consume more and more of these offerings would be punished by unsatisfied hunger. This type of punishment was threatened many years before in the law of Moses (Lev 26:26).

Second, the priests "shall commit harlotry, but not increase." This has been taken to mean that the priests would (1) multiply wives and concubines; (2) engage in literal harlotry; (3) engage in idolatry; and (4) participate in temple prostitution. Perhaps they had introduced the Mesopotamian practice where every woman was to prostitute herself in the temple with a priest. These "sacred" rituals of the Baal cult were in reality nothing but "harlotry." All this sexual activity would not produce any "increase." The harlotry would not affect nature and result in a more abundant crop as promised in the theology of the fertility cult.[4]

The frustration experienced by the priests was due to the fact that "they have ceased obeying Yahweh." When God is ignored, all the zest goes out of life. The life more abundant is found along the path of submission to the will of the Creator (4:10).

C. The Sin of Idolatry (4:11-14).

In a general accusation Hosea charged that "harlotry, wine, yea new wine, take away the heart." The licentious lifestyle encouraged by the Baal cult had an intoxicating effect upon the lives of the Israelites (cf. Num 25:1). Drunkenness and debauchery of the pagan temples also had a devastating effect on the heart and intellect. In Hebrew psychology the heart was the seat of discrimination and reflection. In this context the "heart" is basically "the understanding" (4:11).

Idolatry results in superstitious practices. "My people ask counsel from their wooden idols," i.e., they seek after a divine revelation from their wooden idols (cf. Jer 10:3; Hab 2:19). The reference to their "staff" informing them probably denotes a mode of divination called rhabdomancy. Two rods were held upright, then allowed to drop while incantations were being uttered. The oracle was inferred from the way the sticks fell whether forward, backward, to the right or to the left (4:12a).

Why would intelligent people seek guidance from wooden idols or walking staffs? Hosea explained: "the spirit of harlotry has caused them to stray." The term "spirit" (*ruach*) is often used of an uncontrollable impulse which cannot be accounted for and leads a person whither he knows not (cf. Num 5:14; Isa 19:14; Zech 13:2). Harlotry or idolatry is here compared to a demoniacal power which had seized the nation. This "spirit of harlotry" had caused Israel to "play the harlot" against Yahweh. Like Gomer leaving Hosea, Israel had played the harlot "from under their God," i.e., from under his authority (4:12b).

The Canaanite custom was to sacrifice "on every high hill and under every spreading tree" (Deut 12:2). The tops of mountains were chosen as being closer to the heavens. On the "high hills they offer incense." The reference may be to the "high places" or artificial mounds mentioned so frequently in the Book of Kings. Shady places whether on the mountains (Brown) or in the valleys (Keil) were considered "good" for indulging in the immoral rites of the Baal cult (4:13a).

The immorality sanctioned and encouraged as religious magic spread like an infectious disease throughout Israel. While the men were visiting the temple prostitutes, their daughters and daughters-in-law were committing "harlotry" and "adultery." Immorality could not be confined to the cult (4:13b).

For their sinful conduct, however, God would not punish the young women of Israel because their elders did worse. The husbands and fathers of the land "consort with harlots" and "offer sacrifices with temple prostitutes." These were women dedicated to the service of Ashtaroth. This "sacrifice" involved immoral acts. When it comes to sexual sins the God of the Bible does not have a double standard (4:14a).

A true knowledge of God includes an understanding of sexual standards. "The people who do not understand will be trampled." Sexual impurity leads to national ruin. The verb "trampled" suggests foreign domination (4:14b).

D. A Warning to Judah (4:15-19).

In a side glance to the southern kingdom, Hosea warned Judah not to follow in the footsteps of Israel. First, Judah should not "become guilty" in committing harlotry, i.e., getting involved in idolatry. Second, Judah should not "come to Gilgal." Gilgal was an idolatrous shrine of the northern kingdom located about one mile from Jericho (4:15a).[5]

Third, Judah should not "go up to Beth-aven." Beth-aven seems to be another name for Bethel itself (cf. Amos 4:4; 5:5). The name means "house of nothingness" and is an opprobrious substitute for Bethel which means "house of God." The name "Bethel" is here changed either (1) to indicate what the place had become in the sight of God (Brown); or (2) because the place had become a house of idols on account of the golden calf.[6] Fourth, Judah was not to make a mockery of a solemn oath in the name of Yahweh. "As Yahweh lives" was a standard oath formula in ancient Israel. Swearing by the name of Yahweh was commanded in the Law (Deut 6:13; 10:20). This oath, however, was to have its roots in the fear of the Lord. It was not to be used by idolaters. Going to idolatrous shrines and swearing by the name of Yahweh were incompatible (4:15b).

The reason Judah should not follow in the path of Israel is now made clear.

1. Ephraim was a stubborn heifer. The heifer was a symbol of obstinacy (cf. 11:4; Deut 32:15; Jer 31:18; 46:20). Because of Israel's obstinacy Yahweh would feed them "as a lamb in a wide field." Such a lamb quickly becomes the prey of wolves and wild beasts. Untended by the shepherd, unguarded from the wild beasts, the lamb is doomed eventually to destruction.[7]

2. Ephraim was joined to idols. Ephraim was the most prominent tribe in northern Israel. Hosea often uses the name of this tribe for the entire nation. One who is "joined to idols" is so involve with idols that he cannot give them up. The figure is that of a wife's relation to her husband (cf. Mal 2:14). Ephraim was married, as it were, to idols. "Let him alone!" Literally, "let him rest," i.e., from exhortations, remonstrations, reproofs, etc. The sarcastic command underscores how hopeless the condition of the northern kingdom really was. These words were probably still addressed to Judah. The basic idea is that

Ephraim was too far gone; do not associate with him (4:17).

3. *Ephraim was morally degenerate.* "When their liquor is gone," i.e., when one orgy is over, "whoring they have committed whoredom." The drinking parties led to the sexual immorality at the Baal shrines. G.A. Smith has a colorful translation of these words: "their orgies over, a-whoring they go." In these despicable rituals "her shields have deeply loved dishonor." The clause is extremely difficult and is capable of various renderings. The "shields" are probably princes, the natural protectors of the state. These leaders loved the sin which actually brought shame to them (4:18)

4. *Ephraim was doomed.* "The wind has wrapped her up in its wings." This is a figure for the violence with which the conqueror would sweep Israel, here represented as a woman, into exile. In that day of national judgment "they shall be ashamed because of their sacrifices." They would be ashamed of their hypocrisy in offering sacrifices to idols while at the same time professing loyalty to Yahweh. They would also be ashamed because the deities which they worshiped could not deliver them from their enemy (4:19).

JUDGMENT ON THE LAND
Hosea 5:1-15

Having documented the sin in Ephraim, Hosea now describes in detail the impending judgment. He speaks of the impartiality, basis, necessity, and certainty of the divine sentence. This is followed by several portraits of what that judgment would be like.

A. Impartiality of the Sentence (5:1).

Hosea issues a threefold, climactic summons to his fellow countrymen to "hear this," "hearken," and "give ear." He addresses all classes of the population: priests, house of Israel, and house of the king. Whereas the priests and the people have previously been rebuked, the king and his court are here denounced for the first time. Determining which king is intended is impossible (5:1a).

All should pay careful attention because the prophet is about to announce a judgment of universal proportions. The focus here, however, is on the rulers. They have been "a snare at Mizpah," i.e., a trap to entice people into a net of destruction. Mizpah was in Gilead (Judg 10:17; 11:29). Here this town represents the territory east of the Jordan river. They had "spread a net upon Tabor." Here Mt. Tabor, the famous hill rising out of the plain of Esdraelon southeast of Nazareth, represents the land west of the Jordan. Thus throughout the land, on both sides of the river, the leaders had entrapped people. The entrapment might be economic, judicial or even religious. The point is that Israel's leaders were deceiving and enslaving the citizens (5:1b).

B. Basis for the Sentence (5:2-3).

The citizens of Ephraim are called "apostates," lit., those who have turned aside. They had "gone deep in making slaughter." These words could refer (1) to rampant murder or (2) excessive sacrifices, especially to false gods. In any case, Yahweh declares "I shall be a chastisement to them all." God would punish all of the citizens in the north—the priests and rulers as well as the people (5:2).

The judgment is based on the omniscience of God. "I surely know Ephraim." The pronoun is emphatic in the Hebrew. The irony here is that while Israel does not know God, he knows them intimately (cf. Amos 3:2). Nothing which the apostates did was hidden from the Lord. "Now," even as the prophet was speaking, the whoredom (apostasy) of Ephraim was a fact lying before them and was therefore undeniable. "Israel was defiled." This is the inevitable consequence of apostasy (5:3).

C. Necessity of the Sentence (5:4-5).

Sin had gained such a hold on the citizens of Israel that they had lost their power to repent (cf. Prov 5:22f.). "Their deeds will not allow them to return to their God." The "spirit of harlotry" was "in their midst," i.e., enthroned within their hearts. This evil spirit expelled the knowledge of the true God (5:4).

Israel's sinful pride in prosperity "testifies to his face." By its arrogance and self-reliance Israel stood self-condemned (cf. Amos 6:8).[8] "Therefore Israel and Ephraim will stumble in their guilt." Ephraim was the leading tribe of the north. "Israel" would embrace the other tribes of the northern kingdom. Because of pride the nation would stumble to destruction. "Judah also stumbles with them" because the southern kingdom was guilty of the same sins (5:5).

D. Certainty of the Sentence (5:6-10).

No amount of religious zeal could avert the judgment of God. In desperation akin to deathbed repentance, the northern citizens would attempt to "seek Yahweh" with their flocks and herds. Increasing sacrifice was always the solution Israel had to national jeopardy. These efforts, however, would fail. They would not find Yahweh by increasing the number of sacrifices. Either (1) their repentance came too late; or (2) when it came it was insincere; or (3) it was prompted by the wrong motives, viz., the fear of approaching calamity; or (4) their sacrifices were defiled through unclean and idolatrous rites. The unvarnished truth was that Yahweh had "withdrawn himself from them." He therefore did not hear their prayers or acknowledge their sacrifices (5:6).

Israel had dealt "treacherously" with Yahweh. The verb is used frequently of the infidelity of a wife against her husband (e.g., Mal 2:14). The treachery was that the Israelites had "strange children," i.e., illegitimate children (cf. Deut 25:5). Israel had begotten an adulterous generation of children whom Yahweh could not acknowledge as his own. They were "children of harlotry" (cf. 2:4). This explains why God had withdrawn from them. The special festivals (e.g., New Moon) with their hypocritical worship would not bring salvation, but would "devour them," i.e., be the ruin of the nation. Those phony worship occasions would devour "their portions," i.e., their ancestral inheritance in the Promised Land. In the judgment they would lose their land (5:7).

No amount of military preparation would avert the judgment. Hosea urged them sarcastically to "blow the trumpet," i.e., sound the alarm of invasion. Two types of "trumpets" were used in Israel: (1) the curved horn of a cow or ram; and (2) the long straight metal instrument. The alarm was to be sounded in the hill towns of Gibeah, Ramah and Beth-aven (Bethel). The location of these three towns a few miles north of Jerusalem may be intended to suggest that an enemy from the north had almost reached the southern border of Israel. Judah too was in danger! The words "Behind you, O Benjamin" are difficult. They could be (1) an ancient tribal battle cry; or (2) a note of warning—the judgment is coming to Benjamin after desolating Israel (5:8).

The sentence against Israel was certain because Hosea had spoken infallible words of truth. In spite of religious zeal and military preparation "Ephraim shall become a desolation," i.e., a waste land without inhabitant. The day was coming when Yahweh would rebuke sin by punishing it. "In the tribes of Israel I do make known that which shall surely be." The threats spoken by Hosea were not idle. All would come to pass. Fulfillment of these threats can be assigned to the Assyrian conquest of Israel in the years between 745 and 722 BC (5:9).

Judah too would experience that judgment. The princes of Judah were "like those who remove boundaries." This was considered the lowest form of wickedness in the ancient world. Upon these wicked princes Yahweh would "pour out like water my wrath" (cf. Ps 69:24; 79:6; Jer 10:25). The reference is probably to a stormy blast. Judah is not threatened here with utter desolation as was Ephraim. No lasting devastation was inflicted upon Judah by the Assyrians (5:10).

E. Portraits of the Judgment (5:11-15).

Hosea now gives four vignettes of the judgment: (1) the guilty defendant, (2) the moth and worm, (3) the incurable wound, and (4) the rampaging lion.

1. The defendant (5:11). Ephraim is pictured as a defendant justly facing severe punishment. "Oppressed is Ephraim, broken in pieces by judgment." The Hebrew uses participles to indicate a lasting condition. Ephraim should be condemned "because he willingly walked after the commandment." The reference must be to some human statute (cf. Isa 28:10,13). Probably the reference is to Jeroboam's commandment to worship Yahweh by means of the golden calves.

2. The moth and worm (5:12). Hosea pictures Yahweh like a moth and a worm in respect to Ephraim. The moth destroys cloth slowly over time. The worm (NASB "rottenness") does the same to wood. Both Ephraim and Judah slowly would be consumed in Yahweh's wrath.

3. The incurable wound (5:13). Ephraim had an incurable

wound. Eventually Ephraim (the northern kingdom) recognized the disease which was threatening the life of the nation. Judah also realized that the southern kingdom had a wound, lit., "that which is pressed out," i.e., a festering wound or abscess. The sickness and the wound are metaphors for the political mess in which both nations found themselves. The real disease of both kingdoms was apostasy from Yahweh. Idolatry and immorality were eating at the vital marrow of the sister kingdoms (5:13a).

Ephraim "went unto Assyria" looking for a political solution to what was basically a spiritual problem. The reference is probably to the tribute which King Menahem of Israel sent to Assyria in 738 BC (2 Kgs 15:19f.). Under King Ahaz Judah made the same mistake, but that is not the focus of what Hosea had to say. "King Jareb" is a nickname for the ruler of Assyria. The name means something like King Contentious, or King Combative, or perhaps King Pick-Quarrel (G.A. Smith). The king of Assyria, of course, had no cure for the disease of apostasy but on the contrary made the problem worse by demanding allegiance to Assyria's gods. Thus Hosea is indicating that seeking alliances with pagan powers was not only wicked, it was useless (5:13b).

4. *The rampaging lion (5:14-15).* Assyria could not help the two kingdoms because God himself, like a ferocious lion, was coming against both Ephraim and Judah. "I, even I, will tear" the sister kingdoms like a lion ruthlessly tearing the prey in preparation for eating it. The emphasis on the personal pronoun makes this truth all the more ominous. "And I will go away" like a lion carrying off his prey. So the God of judgment would carry off his people into exile. "I will take away and there will be no deliverer." A lion was a frequent symbol in Assyrian art. The Assyrian lion, however, would not be able to deliver Israel or Judah from the divine lion (5:14).

"I go, return to my place until they become guilty." As the lion withdraws to its cave, so God would withdraw himself from Israel until the people feel guilty about their sin. In their repentance they would "seek my face," i.e., seek me or turn to me. "In their affliction they will earnestly seek me." The exile would make them feel a sense of guilt. Their suffering would awaken within them the need for mercy (5:15).

AN APPEAL FOR REPENTANCE
Hosea 6:1-3

Hosea's sayings clustering around the theme of the lack of spiritual knowledge conclude with an earnest appeal for repentance.

A. First Exhortation and Incentive (6:1-2).

"Come! Let us return unto Yahweh." The prophet includes himself as one who stands in need before the Lord. The exile would drive Israel back to the Lord eventually. Hosea here is suggesting that repentance would be appropriate now as a preparation for the judgment. Perhaps God would even be merciful to them and spare those who turned to him from the judgment which has been described in this section (6:1a).

The incentive for repentance is the wonderful mercy of Yahweh. "He has torn" the nation just like the lion in the closing metaphor of chapter 5. This is a recognition that their national disintegration was a judgment from God. While Hosea acknowledged that Yahweh has already set in motion the judgment, still "he will heal us." Yahweh is the great physician. King Jareb cannot heal, but Yahweh can! Though Yahweh had "smitten" his people, "he will bind us up" (6:1b).

Hosea assured his people that Yahweh would "revive us" (NASB) after two days. This is a Hebrew idiom to express "after a short while." "On the third he will raise us up." The reference is to the moral and spiritual restoration of Israel. Ezekiel (37:1-10) used a similar figure. There is no direct allusion here to the death of Jesus. Nonetheless, Jesus was the second Israel as Hosea himself will later argue (cf. 11:1). What Hosea promised in metaphor to ancient Israel was re-enacted literally in the life of Jesus. Thus the third day was prophetically, typically and ideally the time for resurrection. For Hosea repentance would lead to resurrection and new life: "that we may live before him," i.e., under his sheltering protection and grace (6:2).

B. Second Exhortation and Incentive (6:3).

In view of the fact that Yahweh was the great healer who was bound to raise them up after repentance, Hosea again urged his countrymen to turn to the Lord. "Let us know, let us pursue to know

Yahweh." The knowledge here urged is not theoretical or even factual, but experiential. This is a practical knowledge consisting of obedience to divine commandments and growth in the love of God with all the heart (6:3a).

Again the incentive for repentance is a gracious promise of how the Lord would respond to their actions. "His going forth is certain as morning." Just as morning certainly follows night, so God surely comes to the help of them who repent. He goes forth out of his place (heaven) to aid those who seek to know him. "And he shall come as the rain to us." The rain here is a symbol of moral and spiritual refreshment. The Lord would revive his people f they would but turn to him. Yahweh would "water the earth like the latter rain." The produce of the soil depended on the early and latter rain falling in later autumn and in the spring. To those who seek him Yahweh truly provides the water of life (6:3b).

ENDNOTES

1. Theo. Laetsch, *Bible Commentary; The Minor Prophets* (St. Louis: Concordia, 1956), p. 41.
2. Following NASB and Keil. Others understand the verb in 4:2 to mean "they break all restraints."
3. Keil argues that the entire nation, not just the priests, had rejected the knowledge of God in 4:6.
4. The Septuagint reads, "They shall commit harlotry, but they shall not find satisfaction."
5. Gilgal was Joshua's headquarters during the conquest. At this spot Samuel proclaimed Saul to be Israel's first king. Gilgal is also mentioned as a center of idolatry in Hosea 9:15; 12:11; Amos 4:4; 5:5. Keil and Given argue that a northern Gilgal in the mountains is meant, but this is unlikely.
6. Abraham and Jacob erected altars at Bethel in the Patriarchal Period. When the kingdom divided in 931 BC Jeroboam I placed one of his golden calves in Bethel. The city was located on a small hill about ten miles north of Jerusalem.
7. Others understand the last half of 4:16 to be a question with the meaning: If Israel rebels against the Master's yoke, how can the nation expect to be treated as gently as a lamb?
8. Some take Ephraim's pride in 5:5 to be God himself as in Isa 2:10; 24:14; Mic 5:4; Amos 8:7. In that case, then God testifies to the face of Israel about the nation's sins.

CHAPTER SEVENTEEN

The Lack of Mercy
Hosea 6:4-8:14

The second cluster of the sayings of Hosea is loosely grouped around the theme of a lack of mercy or kindness (NASB). What God wants most from his people is mercy, not what he was getting. This contrast between what God wanted and what he was getting is the theme of this chapter.

MERCY, NOT SUPERFICIAL RELIGION
Hosea 6:4-11

One of the greatest dangers facing believers is the tendency to define religion in terms of formal acts of worship. This was the problem in Ephraim and Judah in the days of Hosea. The temples were overflowing with worshipers. These worshipers, however, showed no inclination to implement moral principles in their everyday lives. God did not want superficial religion.

A. The Charge (6:4-5).

The Lord had already tried various punishments to bring Israel and Judah to repentance. All efforts were in vain. The love of this people was like "a morning cloud, like the dew which quickly passes away." Israel and Judah had morning cloud religion. The metaphor stresses how quickly their love for the Lord was forgotten. Though God's people from time to time might show some signs of piety, these times of religious fervor quickly vanished away (6:4).

Because their love vanished again and again, God had to perpetually punish his people. "I have hewed them by the prophets." Through the prophetic message the Lord had carved out this people. "I have slain them by the words of my mouth." The prophets often proclaimed death and destruction. The judgments inflicted upon Israel "went forth as light." Yahweh's judgments on his people were obvious, as clear as the sun itself. Everyone should have observed this fact and laid it to heart (6:5).

B. The Contrast (6:6-7).

Religion in both Israel and Judah centered around temple rituals. There were two things which Yahweh wanted more than sacrifices and burnt offerings. First, he wanted "love." The word used here (*chesed*) is love to one's neighbor manifesting itself in righteousness; love which has its roots in the revelation of God. The word has been defined as obligatory love. *Chesed* is very similar to the *agape* love commanded in the New Testament. Sacrifices were never an acceptable substitute for *chesed* (6:6a).[1]

The second thing which God desired more than religious ritual was "the knowledge of God." By hypocritical sacrifices wicked men thought that they could hide their sin. The words of Hosea demand sincerity in religion. Religious ritual apart from a personal walk with God is worthless (6:6b).

Instead of giving Yahweh what he wanted, Israel "transgressed the covenant like Adam."[2] Adam ignored all the bounty which surrounded him to disobey the one requirement which God had placed upon him.

C. The Confirmation (6:8-11).

The presence of morning cloud religion in Israel is confirmed by the recitation of several examples of what was taking place there. First, Hosea charges that "Gilead is a city of evil doers." Gilead was a region east of Jordan, not a city. Either Hosea is again speaking metaphorically, or he has in mind specifically one of the leading cities of Gilead like Ramoth or Jabesh or Mizpah. In any case, Gilead was "foot-printed with blood," full of the traces of murder and bloodshed. When men are not right with God, society will be filled with violence (6:8).

Second, Hosea charges the priests with violence. They organized in bands to waylay and murder those who were traveling to religious shrines like Shechem. Shechem was a Levitical city of refuge (Josh 20:7; 21 21) on the road from Samaria to Bethel. Pilgrims going to the feasts would be traveling this road carrying with them offerings to be presented to the Lord. The priests, who were supposed to be sanctified to the service of God, had "committed lewdness" (*zimmah*). The word refers to unnatural crime. The word often has sexual connotations (cf. Lev 18:17; 19:29). Here, however, the term seems to refer to deliberate and premeditated violence (6:9).

Third, Hosea bears witness (as Yahweh's spokesman) to "a horrible thing" (lit., that which makes the hair stand up) which he had seen in Israel. The nation was "defiled" by "harlotry." Probably literal as well as spiritual harlotry is intended because in the Baal cult the latter involved the former (6:10).

Fourth, Judah itself was guilty of the same sins as Israel. Therefore "O Judah, a harvest is appointed for you." This is not a harvest of blessing (Hadjiantoniou), but of judgment (cf. Joel 3:13; Jer 51:33). This judgment would befall Judah "when I turn the captivity of my people." The expression never means to bring back captives to the Promised Land, but is a figurative way of saying, reverse the fortunes, i.e., from good to bad or from bad to good If Judah was currently riding the crest of prosperity that situation would be reversed (6:11).

MERCY, NOT VIOLENCE
Hosea 7:1-7

Sin is a malignancy which even the divine physician cannot heal without the cooperation of the patient. The dangerous nature of some diseases is often brought out by the attempt to heal them. God had attempted to heal Israel of her moral disease by prophetic reproof and by chastisement; but such efforts only revealed more clearly the enormity of the iniquity of Ephraim the nation and the wickedness of Samaria the capital (7:1a).

Two sins were especially prevalent in Ephraim. First, "they practice falsehood," i.e., lying and deception both in word and deed towards God and man. Second, violent robbery was the order of the day. "A thief comes in, a troop of robbers plunders on the outside." Both individual criminals and organized gangs plagued the land (7:1b).

These sinners did not take into consideration that Yahweh remembered all of their wickedness, i.e., he held them accountable for it. "Now their deeds have surrounded them," i.e., either as witnesses against them, or so as to entangle them. "They are before my face," i.e., the sins had come to the notice of God. The greatest sin of sinners is to deny the omniscience of God (7:2).

Sin acts in the most audacious manner. Sinners do not fear the rulers. "With their wickedness they make the king rejoice," i.e., the king got his cut from all the unlawful activities. The princes of the land rejoiced over the "lies" of the sinners. They had sunk to such a low level that they took delight in the unlawful activities of the people (7:3).

Sinners are persistent in their wickedness. The citizens of Israel were "adulterers." Literal adultery seems to be in view here. Hosea likens the lust of these men to an oven heated by a baker. The evil desires burned constantly within their hearts just as the baker's oven which is continually stoked. Between kneading the dough and its leavening, a baker would rest. Similarly the men of Israel rested temporarily after each indulgence before being overcome by lust again (7:4).

Sinners mock authority. On "the day of our king," i.e., the king's birthday or coronation day, the princes "make him sick with the heat of wine, i.e., they get the king drunk. The king thought that these princes were his friends. In reality "he stretched out his hand with scoffers," i.e., they had no respect for their king. They mocked him in his drunken state. As an oven is fired for baking, so the conspirators made their preparations for a coup. The whole night "their baker," i.e., the one who instigated the conspiracy, slept. He rested until the opportunity arrived for carrying out the plan. As a baker stirs up the

244

fire in the morning, so at the precise moment the insurrection was launched (7:5-6).

The princes were "all red-hot like an oven," i.e., they were hot with the passion for revolution. They "consume their judges," i.e., their rulers. "All of their kings have fallen." The period of anarchy after the death of Jeroboam II is in view. Four regicides are recorded in this period: Zechariah, Shallum, Pekahiah, and Pekah. Earlier in Israel Nadab, Elah, Zimri, Tibni and Jehoram were also assassinated. Yet in this political turmoil "none among them calls to me." They did not realize the causes and ultimate consequences of such activity. They did not recognize that Yahweh alone could bring peace to their land (7:7).

MERCY, NOT POLITICAL INTRIGUE
Hosea 7:8-16

From superficial religion and ungodly violence, Hosea next turned his attention to the political turmoil in Israel. The policy there was (1) ruinous, (2) futile, (3) disastrous, and (4) ungrateful.

A. A Ruinous Policy (7:8-10).

Yahweh had separated Israel from the nations that it might be holy unto him (Lev 20:24,26). Now Ephraim had "mixed himself among the nations." The northern kingdom was learning the ways of the Gentiles and serving their gods. Ephraim had become "a cake not turned." Cakes of bread were baked on hot ashes or red-hot stones. If the cake was not turned, it burned on the bottom side, and was gooey on the top side. The point is that the citizens of Israel were neither true worshipers of Yahweh, nor out-and-out followers of Baal. In religion they were mongrels—inconsistent and worthless hybrids. Such half-baked commitment was ruinous to the nation (7:8).

Due to the disastrous foreign policy Ephraim was prematurely aged. "Strangers have devoured his strength, and he knows it not." The reference is to the devastating wars and heavy tribute at the hands of the Syrians and later the Assyrians More than material and military strength is involved, however. In adopting the heathenish ways of her neighbors, Israel had sapped her spiritual vitality. Yet the citizens of Israel were not aware of the decadence which followed from the intercourse with foreign nations. "Gray hair is also sprinkled on him." Ephraim had become prematurely old. The gray hair here is a symbol of decrepitude and approaching death (7:9).

Arrogance blinded Israel to the fate which was rapidly approaching. "And the pride of Israel bears witness to his face" (cf. 5:5). Nothing that had happened in their dealings with foreign nations had brought these sinners to their senses. "They are not converted to Yahweh their God." They were obstinate in sin. "And for all this they seek him not." Amid calamities and miseries of the kingdom, both within and without, they did not turn to the Lord. They tried by political intrigue to extricate themselves from the dangers which were facing them (7:10).

B. A Futile Policy (7:11-12).

In its futile foreign policy Ephraim was like "a simple dove without understanding." The picture here is of a bird which leaves its nest and flies aimlessly here and there. So Israel's foreign policy shifted back and forth from pro-Egypt to pro-Assyria. In both Israel and Judah there was a strong pro-Egypt policy. Hoshea, the last king of Israel had an alliance with King So of Egypt. Egypt, however, proved utterly unreliable. This was a policy of hesitation and indecision, of reliance on balance of power rather than on the Lord (7:11).

Neither Israel nor Judah could preserve their independence through political intrigue. Yahweh addressed this foreign policy with this threat: "I spread my net over them." Just as the dove in its silliness falls into the net set by the fowler, so Israel runs into the net of destruction in seeking help from Egypt and Assyria. With the net of Assyrian power God would bring Israel down to the ground. Thus Yahweh would "chasten them according to the tidings in their assembly." The reference is probably to the public proclamations of the prophets, and the threats contained in the Law which were annually read before the assembly (7:12).

C. A Disastrous Policy (7:13).

The foreign policy followed by Ephraim was disastrous. Hosea pronounced a prophetic "woe" on them, i.e., an announcement of doom. In their anxiety to get help from either Egypt or Assyria they had taken flight from the Lord. The "woe" included the "devastation" of their land. That would be the fate of Ephraim because "they have fallen away from me," not accidentally, but by choice (7:13a).

In spite of the apostasy of Ephraim, Yahweh still desired to "redeem them." The Lord is always looking for an excuse to rescue his people from the consequences of their own stupidity—in this case, to rescue them from the disastrous consequence of their own foreign policy. Yahweh could not rescue them from the clutches of Assyria, however, because "they speak lies concerning me." The "lies" would include a denial of Yahweh's sole divinity and his power to protect or punish (7:13b).

D. An Ungrateful Policy (7:14-16).

Ephraim's foreign policy demonstrated ingratitude to God for material blessings. "They did not cry to me in their heart," i.e., they did not manifest any repentance. On the other hand, like spoiled brats, they "howl upon their beds." These howlings were the expression of unbelief and despair, not by any means evidence of faith. "They crowd together for corn and new wine."[3] It is not clear where they "crowd together." Possibilities include (1) the market place; (2) an idolatrous temple; (3) the type of huddling together which occurs when disaster has struck. This much is clear: their only concern was to fill their bellies. This meant that their howling and crowding together was tantamount to rebellion against God (7:14).

Ephraim's foreign policy also demonstrated ingratitude for Yahweh's instruction and strength. The Lord had "instructed" or trained their arm, i.e., by showing where and how strength was to be acquired. He "strengthened their arms" by giving them power over their enemies. In spite of all this, "they think evil against me." They regard Yahweh as but one deity among many. They think he cannot redeem them from their political turmoil (7:15).

Ephraim's ingratitude had disastrous consequences. "They turn everywhere but upwards." They look in all directions for help except to their God. "They have become like a false bow." By failing to turn to God they missed their own true destiny. They thus resemble a bow whose string did not have the elasticity to propel the arrow to the object at which it was aimed. "Their princes will fall by the sword." Those who instigated the assassination of kings and the "silly dove" foreign policy would die (7:16a).

The princes of Israel would fall by the sword "for the defiance of their tongue." Their defiance refers to the lies of v. 13 and the wickedness of v. 15, both of which were directed against Yahweh. These men wanted a clear separation of church and state, political policy uninformed by the directives of God's written and spoken word. "This is their derision in the land of Egypt." Egypt would fail to rescue them from Assyria. Then the Egyptians would take malicious delight in the downfall of the very princes who had formulated the pro-Egyptian policy (7:16b).

MERCY, NOT LAW BREAKING
Hosea 8:1-14

Hosea received a directive to put "the trumpet to your mouth," to act as a herald of judgment. The enemy, like an eagle or vulture, was about to swoop down on the house of Yahweh. The reference is not to the temple of Jerusalem or to the temple at Samaria, but either to (1) the land of Palestine (Brown) or (2) to the congregation of Israel (Keil). The reason for this judgment is plainly stated: "because they have transgressed my covenant and trespassed against my Law." They had violated the Sinai covenant. When covenants were violated in those days the vassal incurred the penalties which had been stipulated in the covenant or treaty with the Great King (8:1).

When the disaster fell the citizens would cry to the Lord. Desperate individuals would cry "My God" in an effort to secure special intervention. "We know you!" This is the cry of the whole nation. The verb suggests intimate association. "We are Israel!" This was the grounds of their appeal to Yahweh. The name "Israel" recalled God's past association with the Patriarch by that name as well as the centuries of involvement with the descendants of that Patriarch (8:2).

Yahweh had a sharp retort to the desperate cry of the individuals and the nation as a whole. "Israel loathes good." The verb is very strong. It means "to detest." "Good" is everything which Yahweh stands for as well as Yahweh himself (Harper).[4] Since Israel despised everything that was good, Yahweh ordered "Let the enemy pursue him." He turned Israel over to the enemy, especially the Assyrians (8:3).

Having stated generally the conditions which prevailed in Israel, Hosea then identified seven specific ways in which the nation had broken God's Law.

A. Illegitimate Rulers (8:4).

"They have set up kings but not from me." The reference may be to the schism of Jeroboam (Keil). Others think the verse refers to kings not ordained by prophets, or kings who gained the throne through violence. "They have set up princes and I know it not." In these words Yahweh disassociates himself from the political establishment of Israel (8:4a).

These illegal dynasties produced illegal religion in the northern kingdom. "Their silver and their gold they made into idols." This is further proof that Israel had rejected the Lord. Although silver was not used in making the calves, it was employed in maintenance of the cult. The words "that it may be cut off" describe the consequences of their idol making which was not intended but was nevertheless inevitable just as though it was intended. The singular "it" could refer to the nation itself, or to the golden calf which was the symbol of worship in the north (8:4b).

B. Illegal Religion (8:5-6).

"Your calf is loathed, O Samaria!" As Israel felt disgust for what was good, so did Yahweh feel disgust for the golden calf. The verb literally means "to smell bad." Samaria may represent the entire northern kingdom. There is no reference elsewhere to a calf being set up in Samaria itself. "My wrath is kindled against them" on account of the calf worship (8:5a).

A parenthetical question expressed Yahweh's exasperation with the religious life in the northern kingdom. "How long are they incapable of purity?" The noun refers to purity of walk before the Lord as contrasted to the abominations of idolatry. Hosea regarded idolatry not only as a false way of worship, but as an immoral way of life (8:5b).

"For this also is of Israel." The calf was man-made as well as the dynasties in the northern kingdom. Thus Hosea places side by side man-made kings and man-made gods. Those idols were constructed by a "workman." Consequently they could not be God. The prophetic polemic against idolatry was based on this premise: Nothing made by man can be God.[5] The calf of Samaria was doomed to destruction. It would become "splinters." The word occurs only here. "Splinters" is the Talmudic rendering which is adopted by many modern scholars. If this translation is correct, it suggests that the calf image was made of wood and only overlaid with gold (8:6).

C. Reckless Sowing (8:7-8).

Israel was playing a dangerous game. They were sowing "the wind." The reference is to the vanity and unprofitableness of their present ways, their foreign policy, their religion, and their human efforts. For this "wind" they would reap "the whirlwind," i.e., destruction.[6] The harvest answers to the sowing (8:7a).

Using a play on words Hosea indicates what he meant when he spoke of reaping the whirlwind. In English this might be rendered: "Stock without shoot shall never yield fruit." The basic idea is that the seed they sow never grows up to its full size. If here and there it does grow up, either it brings forth no grain or what grain it produces falls into the hands of an enemy (Brown). The point Hosea is trying to make is this: Israel's policies will never be successful and any wealth which by which the nation might acquire would be seized by other nations (8:7b).

In the whirlwind of judgment Israel would be "swallowed up." This threat was literally fulfilled. The ten tribes have disappeared from the scene of history and their identity is now only a subject for farfetched conjecture (Lehrman). Again Hosea uses the word "now" to introduce the theme of judgment. "Now have they become among the nations like a vessel wherein there is no delight." Israel would be held in dishonor among the nations. A vessel wherein there is no delight is one that is neither useful or ornamental (8:8).

D. Disastrous Foreign Policy (8:9-10).

Hosea charges that Israel "went up to Assyria like a wild ass alone by himself." The picture here is of a stubborn ass leaving the herd to go its own willful way in search of a mate. "Ephraim has hired lovers." Here is prostitution in reverse. Love gifts have been given to bribe Assyria to be the ally of Israel (8:9).

In spite of efforts to avert national destruction by paying the wages of prostitution among the nations, yet Yahweh declares: "Now I will gather them," i.e., gather them into exile and/or death. "And they will begin to diminish on account of the burden of the king of princes." The idea is that Israel would diminish in number in consequence of the Assyrian oppression. The "burden of the king of princes" is probably the yearly tribute required by the Assyrian king. Others, however, think that the "burden" is oppression in exile (8:10).

E. Multiple Altars (8:11-12).

Israel was required by the law to have only one altar (Deut 12:5-14). The law of the central sanctuary had been grossly violated in northern Israel. "Ephraim has multiplied altars for sin." The popular idea seems to have been that if the the Lord was pleased with sacrifice from one altar, he would be even more pleased with multiple sacrifices. The multiplication of altars was an act of defiance, rebellion against revelation, and sin. "The altars have become to him for sin." So the altars were motivated by sin. They had become the occasion for innumerable sins. Every sacrifice offered on those altars was in fact sinful (8:11).

Israel's sin resulted not from ignorance of God's will, but from neglect of God's commands. "I wrote for him the fullness of my law."[7] Israel was without excuse. Yet the law was "counted as a strange thing," i.e., like something foreign which does not concern them at all (8:12).

F. Worthless Offerings (8:13).

Not only did they multiply altars, they also increased the number of sacrifices. Gifts of slain offerings were presented to Yahweh continually. Their offerings, however, were no more than "flesh," i.e., meat which they slay and eat. "Yahweh has no delight in them." The consistent teaching of Scripture is that God is not pleased merely with religious ritual. Sacrifices which do not delight God do not atone for sin (8:13a).

"Now will he remember their transgressions and visit their sins."

Since their sins had not been covered by the blood of sincere sacrifice, their sins must be visited or punished. That punishment would involve a return to "Egypt." No actual captivity in Egypt is in view. The idea is that they would be driven into the land of bondage. "Egypt" here is a symbol of that land of bondage (8:13b).

G. Neglect of God (8:14).

The root sin in Israel was neglect of Yahweh. "For Israel has forgotten his maker." Once men rule God out of the universe, they begin to deify their own power. In Israel this manifested itself in the construction of palaces and other such buildings. Judah no less than Israel had forgotten God. Judah trusted in fortified cities instead of the God of the covenant. The punishment for this willful spiritual amnesia is forthrightly stated: "I will send a fire against his cities, and it will devour its castles." Here Hosea is using language very similar to that of Amos chapter 1.

ENDNOTES

1. The secondary importance of sacrifices is stressed in the following passages: 1 Sam 15:22; Isa 1:11-17; Mic 6:8; Ps 40:6-8.
2. Thus is 6:7 understood by the Targum, Talmud, Vulgate, Keil and others. Some take the reference to be to the place called Adam mentioned in Joshua 3:16. Still others think the phrase should be understood "like [ordinary] men," or "like men who have transgressed the covenant."
3. The Septuagint, Syriac and some Hebrew MSS read: "they cut themselves," i.e., so as to make their prayers more effective.
4. Cf. Amos 5:4f. Keil thinks "good" is the salvation which Yahweh had guaranteed to the nation through his covenant of grace, which God gives to those who keep that covenant.
5. On the prophetic polemic against idolatry see, for example, Isa 37:19; 40:19f.; 41:7; 42:17.
6. The whirlwind as a metaphor for judgment is found several times in the Old Testament. See, e.g., Hos 10:13; 12:2; Job 4:8; Prov 22:8.
7. Following the Masoretic text. Another reading is: "the ten thousand things" or "myriads" of the Law. KJV reads "the great things of My law." The verse bears witness to the existence of written directions which were viewed as authoritative.

CHAPTER EIGHTEEN

The Consequences of Sin
Hosea 9:1-11:11

The second major division of the sayings which began in 6:4 continues in this chapter. Here the focus is on the consequences of the sin of northern Israel. The unit concludes with a touching call for repentance.

SIN RESULTS IN GREAT LOSS
Hosea 9:1-9

Sin results in great loss. Hosea specifies four great losses which Ephraim would experience because of sin.

A. Loss of Joy (9:1-2).

Hosea urged Israel not to rejoice over the plentiful harvest like the nations. The heathen considered the harvest to be the gift of the gods in return for their sacrifices. Thus they made the obtaining of material blessings the aim and object of worship. Since Israel believed that material blessings came from the Baal gods, they had given themselves over to the debased worship of their local Baal shrine. They had "committed whoredom" against Yahweh. There could be no true joy in the harvest because Israel had been unfaithful to the Lord. Hosea charged: "You have loved the harlot's hire upon every grainfloor." Each act of Baal worship is compared to whoredom in which the harlot (Israel) received her hire (corn, wine, etc.) from her paramour, the local Baal (9:1).

The unfaithfulness to Yahweh would be punished by diminished harvest. "The threshing floor and the vat shall not feed them, and the new wine shall fail her." The vat is probably the oil vat rather than wine vat since wine is mentioned next. The Lord would take away the produce that Israel attributed to the Baal gods. This would not be by crop failure, but because the Israelites would be carried into exile as the next verse indicates (9:2).

B. Loss of Spiritual Privileges (9:3-5).

Because of apostasy, Israel would lose its freedom. "They shall not remain in Yahweh's land." This explains why all of their revelry and all their sacrifices (legitimate or otherwise) would cease. The land of Canaan was Yahweh's, not Baal's. Israel was merely a tenant permitted to dwell in that land on the condition of remaining faithful to the Lord. Since they had not met the conditions of tenancy, "Ephraim shall return to Egypt," not the land of the Pharaohs, but a new Egypt. "They shall eat unclean things in the land of Assyria." Assyria was the new Egypt. Since they would not be able to observe dietary laws, their food would be unclean in exile. They would also have to eat food which had not been sanctified by the offering of firstfruits to Yahweh (9:3).

Second, Israel would lose its worship privileges. "They shall not pour out wine to Yahweh" while in that foreign land. "Their sacrifices will not be pleasing to him." Israel could only offer sacrifices to God at a place where the Lord had made known his name, i.e., had revealed himself. Hence in exile proper sacrifice would be impossible (9:4a).

In exile "their bread shall be like the bread of mourners." Their food would defile them even as the funeral meal defiled those who partook of it. A person so defiled was unclean for seven days (Num

19:14). Their bread shall be "for their themselves alone," i.e., for their appetite, to satisfy their physical hunger. It would be mere bread and nothing more. Here is an irony. While in their own land they had eaten the sacrifices for their own appetite, forgetting Yahweh; in exile they would not be allowed to eat for any other reason but their appetite.[1] That bread in the foreign land would be common because "it does not come into the house of Yahweh." It therefore would not be sanctified by the offering of a token portion in Yahweh's temple (8:4b).

The loss of worship privilege would be felt most keenly on the festival and feast days. The exiled Israelites would miss the joyous worship of those occasions. If any difference is to be assigned to the words "festival" and "feast day" it would be this: The first term may refer to the three great annual festivals, while the second term refers to other special occasions, e.g., new moon celebrations (9:5).

C. Loss of Inheritance (9:6).

The Israelites would be forced to leave their desolate homes and land. "Egypt shall gather them together." For the third time Hosea used Egypt as a symbol of exile and bondage. "Memphis shall bury them." Vast burial grounds of Egypt were located in this ancient capital of Egypt. The point is that the Israelites would die in exile. "Their precious treasures of silver" would be overrun with nettles. Thorns would spring up in "their tents," i.e., their dwellings. The "precious treasures" have been taken to be (1) idols, (2) sacred vessels; or (3) ornamented houses. The growth of thorns and thistles presupposes the utter desolation of the land.

D. Loss of Hope (9:7-9).

Hosea announced the certainty of the coming "days of visitation," i.e., punishment and the "days of recompense," i.e., retribution. In that day Israel would come to realize that "the prophet" was a fool. The reference is to the false prophets who deceived themselves and the people with promises of peace and prosperity. The more charismatic type of prophets who had misled the nation by their antics would be regarded as madmen (9:7a).

The reason for the visitation of judgment was because of "the greatness of your guilt." The reference is to their attraction to false gods and foreign nations. A second reason for the visitation was "the great enmity," not merely against their fellow man, but against God and his true servants (9:7b).

In contrast to the false prophets, "the watchman of Ephraim was with my God" (NKJV). The sentence is very difficult. Probably the "watchman of Ephraim" is Hosea himself. He was "with my God" in the sense of being on the side of God.[2] "As for the prophet," i.e., the false prophet, "a fowler's snare is in all his ways." The false prophet laid snares in the paths of all God's people. Furthermore, he fomented "enmity in the house of his God." The false prophet was motivated by hostility toward God and toward true prophets like Hosea. He engendered hatred among God's people. "The house of his God" could refer to the temple of Yahweh or to an idol temple (9:8).

Led by their false prophets, Israel had fallen into terrible corruption. "They have deeply corrupted themselves as in the days of Gibeah." The reference is to the terrible immorality committed against a Levite's concubine (Judg 19). Because of this corruption, Yahweh would "remember" their iniquity and "visit" their sins. The false prophets have led the people to their own destruction (9:9).

ISRAEL'S SPIRITUAL BIOGRAPHY
Hosea 9:10-17

Hosea now outlines the spiritual biography of Israel from the days of the wilderness to the eighth century. There are four chapters in this biography.

A. An Early Fall (9:10).

The biography starts on a happy note. "I found Israel like grapes in the wilderness." To find grapes in the wilderness would bring a weary traveler great joy. That was how God felt about his people early on. "I saw your fathers as early fruit on the fig tree in the first shooting," i.e., at its first season, when it first began to ripen. The first ripe fig was proverbial for its sweetness. This figure denotes the pleasure which God found in Israel when he led the Israelites out of Egypt, and chose them for his very own (9:10a).

THE CONSEQUENCES OF SIN   HOSEA 9:1-11:11

The happy early relationship between Yahweh and his people ended when "they came to Baal-Peor" in Moab east of Jordan, near Mount Pisgah. On the very first encounter with the nature religion of the Canaanites, Israel fell into sin (Num 25). "They consecrated themselves to shame." While Israel was supposed to be consecrated to Yahweh, the nation instead chose to dedicate itself to Baal. "Shame" is here the name given to the idol of Baal-Peor. The result was that they "became an abomination like their lover." People become like the things they worship. The sexual immorality of the Baal cult was an utter abomination before God (9:10b).

B. A Terrible Punishment (9:11-14).

Ephraim faced a terrible judgment. "Their glory shall fly away like a bird." The "glory" here seems to refer to the population of the nation. The punishment for Ephraim's sins against chastity is childlessness. "No birth, no pregnancy, and no conception." The nation would lose its source of vitality in a catastrophic fall in the birth rate due to miscarriage and sterility. In a culture which prized large families, this would indeed be a terrible calamity (9:11).

"Yea, though they bring up their sons, yet I will bereave them without a man." Even if the sons did grow up, they would be swept away. The reason for this population disaster was that the nation had come under a divine "woe" because the Lord had departed from them (9:12).

God had selected Ephraim for himself to be a Tyre—a wonderful, prosperous land. He planted his people "in a pleasant place," i.e., he gave them an ideal geographical situation—in soil adapted for growth and prosperity. God intended that Ephraim should bloom and possess the glory of rich and powerful Tyre. Sin had changed all that. "Ephraim shall bring forth his children to the slayer." The nation would be compelled to send forth her bravest sons to repel the attack of the invader. They would perish in the tumult of battle (9:13).

Hosea interjects a prayer at this point: "Give them, O Yahweh, whatsoever you will give them." He goes on to add: "give them a miscarrying womb and dry breasts." This is an appeal to God to execute the threatened judgment. Holy indignation on the part of the prophet toward the abominations of Ephraim is being manifested here (9:14).

C. An Infamous Career (9:15).

Gilgal in the Jordan valley was the scene of many past mercies of God. Now "their wickedness is at Gilgal." The place had become the center of idolatry and iniquity. It was a seat of Baal practices (cf. 4:15; 12:11; Amos 4:4; 5:5). Their conduct at Gilgal evoked God's wrath: "For there I hated them." Because their deeds were so wicked, Yahweh announced: "I will drive them out of my house," i.e., either (1) the land of Israel; or (2) the congregation of the Lord (9:15a).

The expulsion of the sinners from God's house would take place because Yahweh declared: "I will not any more love them." All favor and mercy had been withdrawn from Israel. The reason is that "all of their princes are rebellious." In Hebrew this is a play on words which several writers have tried to capture in English. Thus "all their nobles are rebels" (G.A. Smith); all their rulers are unruly" (Box); "all their princes are prancers" (Horton); "all their rulers are revolters" (Brown).

D. A Final Rejection (9:16-17).

Israel is compared to a tree which has been so smitten by the sun (or perhaps a worm) that it dries up. "Ephraim is smitten; their root is dried up." The dead tree can produce no fruit. Even if they do beget offspring, Yahweh threatened: "I will slay the treasures of their womb." Their children would face the ravishes of war which Yahweh would send against Ephraim (9:16).

"My God will cast them away because they have not hearkened to him." By referring to Yahweh as *my* God, Hosea underscored Ephraim's alienation from the Lord. Ephraim would be rejected because of their refusal to obey God's will. "And they shall be wanderers among the nations." They would be banished from their land to wander about like Cain of old (9:17). The fulfillment of this threat is found in the deportation of thousands of citizens of the northern kingdom beginning about 745 BC.

GOD'S JUDGMENT ON APOSTATE RELIGION
Hosea 10:1-11

The focus on Ephraim's sin is followed by a renewed focus on the impending judgment. Hosea speaks of Ephraim's (1) sin, (2) sorrow, (3) shame, (4) suffering, and (5) sentence.

A. Israel's Sin (10:1-2).

At one point Israel had been "a running vine," lit., a vine pouring itself out. The picture here is of an overflowing and thus luxuriant vine. The vine "put forth fruit for itself." Ephraim's abundant fruit was only for himself, i.e., wasted on self or sin. "As his land became rich, he enriched his pillars." Prosperity was prostituted to the purposes of idolatry. The pillars were symbols of the goddess Asherah (cf. 3:4). The term "enriched" suggests carving or ornamentation of the pillars. The more God caused Israel to prosper in Canaan, the more Israel fell into idolatry (10:1).

In the words "their heart was smooth" the wickedness is traced to its fountainhead. Their heart is not right. The term "smooth" means deceitful or hypocritical. The term is usually applied to the tongue. That it is here the heart which is deceitful suggests that a false kind of Yahweh worship is being condemned. "Now they shall bear their guilt," i.e., shall be found guilty, or perhaps, "shall bear their punishment." Yahweh would "break in pieces their altars." The verb literally means, break the neck of their altars. The term may allude to the breaking off of the horns of the altar. At the same time the Lord would "desolate their pillars," i.e., ruin or destroy them (10:2).

B. Israel's Sorrow (10:3-5).

The day of judgment would bring to Israel a rude awakening. "Surely now they shall say, We have no king." Perhaps a period of anarchy is being described. "For we feared not Yahweh." They confessed their irreverence to their God. "And the king, what can he do for us?" They admitted the impotence of their man-made kings. Perhaps the reference is specifically to Hoshea who reigned by the grace of Assyria. Thus the loss of the ruler is first deplored, but, on second thought, even if there were a king, what would he do for the nation? (10:3).

The king and his ministers had "spoken words." The idea is that the leadership was guilty of vain talk and promises. They had "sworn falsely, made treaties." They had made solemn covenants without any intention of living up to the stipulations contained therein. Since covenants were sworn in the name of the deity, the false oaths were blasphemy against Yahweh. "Thus judgment springs up like hemlock in the furrows of the field." Israel had plowed her field, only to receive in its furrows the hemlock of divine judgment (10:4).

In the day of judgment "the inhabitants of Samaria shall be afraid for the calves of Beth-aven" or Bethel. All the calf worship in the north was under the jurisdiction of the priesthood at Bethel. The plural "calves" probably included the calves at Bethel, Dan, and possibly Samaria. The people would "mourn" over their calf. Far from being a help to its devotees, the calf would be a source of the greatest anxiety to them. Even the priests "shall tremble" for that calf. The term here translated "priests" is *kemarim,* a term that is used elsewhere only of idolatrous priests. The use of the term here expresses contempt. The term translated "tremble" (*gil*) has the basic meaning "to twist or whirl one's self." It can be applied to any violent emotion (10:5).

C. Israel's Shame (10:6).

The golden calf, the symbol of the northern cult, would "be carried unto Assyria for a present for King Jareb." On King Jareb see 5:13. The golden calf, discredited and stripped of glory would be taken as tribute to the king of Assyria. Thus "Ephraim shall receive shame, Israel shall be ashamed of his own counsel." This could be a reference to the policy of Jeroboam in setting up the golden calves originally. On the other hand, the prophet could be alluding to some more recent political policy which did not save Ephraim from destruction.

D. Israel's Suffering (10:7-8).

The monarchy of Israel would be easily swept away "like a splinter upon the water." This translation follows the Septuagint. The rabbis preferred to render the word "foam." In either case the point is the same (10:7).

At the same time that the monarchy is swept away, "the high places of Aven shall be destroyed." Aven is short for Beth-aven or Bethel. "Aven" means "iniquity." The Baal altars were often on hills, hence the terminology "high places." Such high places were "the sin of Israel." A major failing of both of the sister kingdoms was permitting these illegal high places to operate. "Thorn and thistle shall come up on their altars" (cf. 9:6). Those abandoned religious shrines would be forever forsaken (10:8a).

In that day of retribution "they shall speak to the mountains, Cover us! And to the hills, Fall on us!" The people of Israel would pray for swift death so as to avoid the pains and terrors of Assyrian conquest and captivity (10:8b).

E. Israel's Sentence (10:9-11).

The sentence against Israel was justified "Since the days of Gibeah you have sinned." The reference is the the gang rape of the Levite's concubine in Judges 19. This is now the second allusion to that ugly episode (cf. 9:9). Hosea saw the people of his day as still morally men of Gibeah. "There they stood." The idea seems to be that the current generation persevered in the sin which had been committed by their ancestors at Gibeah. Yet "the war against the sons of wickedness did not overtake them at Gibeah." While they persisted in the sin of Gibeah, they had never experienced the punishment which had come against the sinners in Gibeah in Judges 19. As the tribes once rose up against Benjamin at Gibeah, so now the nations would rise up against Israel (10:9).

That Ephraim should now experience chastisement or punishment was God's will. "According to my desire I shall chastise them." Yahweh would gather "the nations" against them. The Assyrian forces included contingents from many nations. The clause "when they are bound to their two transgressions" has received a wide range of interpretations. Among the more likely interpretations of the two transgressions are these: (1) apostasy from Yahweh and from the Davidic house (Keil); (2) man-made gods and man-made kings (Brown). The Ephraimites would be yoked to their sins, so to speak. In this there is an irony. They will exchange places with the beasts of burden which they have made into their gods! (10:10).

The animal metaphor continues in the next sentence. "Ephraim is a heifer that is taught which loved to thresh." Such an animal was treated with every kindness by its owner. The only task required of her was the pleasant and easy one of walking round and round the threshing floor, a task which carried with it the privilege of eating as much as the animal wished. For a beast this was the ideal job (10:11a).

Ephraim's situation was about to change dramatically. "And I, I have passed over upon her goodly neck." The idea is that God would now pass over that fair neck a heavy yoke of hard circumstances. "I will yoke Ephraim," thus equipping the heifer for the hard work of drawing the plow. What Hosea said of Ephraim was also true of Judah. "Judah shall plow, Jacob will break his clods." The hard work of plowing replaces the easy work of threshing. "Breaking clods" is a metaphor for the hard life under a foreign master (10:11b).

A CALL FOR REPENTANCE
Hosea 10:12-15

The second main division of Hosea's sayings began in 6:4. This unit concludes, as did the first collection of sayings, with a call for repentance.

A. The Exhortation (10:12).

Hosea urged his countrymen to "sow for yourself righteousness." This is an appeal to practice right relationship with their fellow man. To the appeal a promise is attached. "Reap according to mercy." When two imperatives are joined in Hebrew the second one indicates a promise. If they sow righteousness, they will reap (divine) mercy (10:12a).

A second appeal couched in agricultural metaphor is for Ephraim to "break up your fallow ground," i.e., unplowed ground. This imperative implies a change in the old ways of this people and the commencement of a new course of life. Before seed can be sowed or harvest reaped, the ground must be prepared. Weeds must be removed. This again is a metaphor for repentance.

The agricultural metaphors are explained in the words "for it is time to seek Yahweh." This may mean that it is high time to seek the Lord (Keil) or that there is still time to seek him (Brown). In any case, seeking the Lord involves reestablishing a relationship with him. "Till he come and rain righteousness upon you." In this context "righteousness" means salvation or deliverance.³ Keil, however, understands: God will give the strength to secure righteousness just as he gives rain for the growth of the seed (10:12b).

B. The Explanation (10:13).

Why was this national repentance necessary? Because "you have plowed wickedness." Heretofore their conduct had been the exact opposite of that which is exhorted in the previous verse. "You have reaped iniquity," i.e., the reward of iniquity. In this case the consequences of their iniquity was oppression at the hand of their enemies (10:13a).

The litany of accusation continued: "you have eaten the fruit of lies." The Hebrew refers to that which deceives, disappoints or fails one. Present national policies would lead to utter disappointment "because you have trusted in your way." They had put their confidence in their prudent plans and wise counsels rather than in the Lord. They also had trusted "in the multitude of your mighty men." They trusted in the strength of their armies and perhaps in the armies of those who were their allies (10:13b).

C. The Urgency (10:14-15).

Hosea's call for repentance was urgent. Ephraim soon faced a terrible judgment. "Therefore a tumult shall arise against your people." As in Amos 2:2, "tumult" is war. All of the fortifications of Ephraim would be "laid waste as Shalman laid waste Beth-arbel in the day of war." Shalman is probably a contracted form of the name Shalmaneser.⁴ The reference could be to the Assyrian king Shalmaneser IV (783-773 BC) or Shalmaneser V (727-722 BC). The former made an expedition to Damascus in 773 BC and may have invaded the country east of Jordan. The latter's campaign is mentioned in 2 Kings 17:3,5. Beth-arbel is west of the Sea of Galilee. Whenever it took place, that Assyrian campaign must have been extremely cruel. "Mother along with sons was dashed to pieces." This is a proverbial expression denoting inhuman cruelty (10:14).⁵

What happened at Beth-arbel would happen in Israel. "Thus shall Bethel do unto you because of your great wickedness," lit., the wickedness of your wickedness. The idea is that Bethel, the center of impure worship, is the source and cause of the coming disaster. "At daybreak is the king of Israel utterly cut off." In the very time of brightness and hope, the time when prosperity is once more about to dawn, the monarch in Israel would be cut off (10:15).

D. The New Beginning (11:1).

Even though the monarchy of Israel would come to an end, that would not be the end of Israel. "Nevertheless, Israel is a lad and I love him." Hosea clearly expected a future king after the exile, one that he called "David." Just as Hosea expected another David, so here he expects another Israel, one who would be called as a child by God. Matthew sees in this verse a reference to Christ (Matt 2:15). "And from Egypt I have called my son." Just as God called Old Testament Israel out of Egypt, so he would call this future lad— this future Israel—out of Egypt.[6]

THE GOD OF LOVE
Hosea 11:2-11

Nothing is a greater incentive to true repentance than exposure to the love of God. Hosea concludes his second call for individual repentance with a powerful portrayal of Yahweh's love for his people.

A. The Pain of God's Love (11:2).

God's love compelled him to do everything in his power to bring the people of Israel to repentance. He sent the prophets to call the people back to the old paths. However, the more God tried to communicate with his people through the prophets the more the people went in the opposite direction. They responded to God's call for obedience by plunging all the more into idolatry. "They sacrificed unto the Baal gods and offered incense to the idols."

B. The Picture of God's Love (11:3-4).

The love of God for Israel is placed in juxtaposition to the anti-love of Israel. "And I, I taught Ephraim to walk." Yahweh, the loving Father, guided Ephraim's tottering footsteps. "He took them upon his arms." When Ephraim was weary Yahweh carried him in his arms

(Deut 1:31; 32:11; Isa 63:9). The sudden shift from the first to the third person is not uncommon in Hebrew. "But they did not know that I healed them." When the child fell and bruised himself, the loving Father healed him. The first two clauses refer chiefly to the care and help afforded to God's people in the wilderness period when the nation was in its infancy (11:3).

The figure changes in 11:4. "I drew them with bands of a man." Here is the picture of a team of bullocks in charge of a kind driver. Thus God the Lord used cords with which one might lead a child, not a bullock. In fact he used "cords of love." There was no need for the rough ropes by which frisky animals are usually kept to their work. Perhaps the master used a gentle hand or simply words of encouragement to draw the animals after him. "And I was to them as the lifter up of a yoke upon their jaws and gently towards him I gave food." A merciful master lifts the yoke above the cheeks so as to make it easier for the animals to eat their food in comfort. Evidently in those days the yoke was connected with the jaws in such a manner that the animal was unable to eat with comfort when wearing it. The basic idea in this verse is this: The Lord made the yoke of his Law which was laid upon his people light and easy by his many merciful deeds which would induce the people to obey (11:4).

C. The Punishment for Rejecting God's Love (11:5-7).

The statement "he shall not return to Egypt" seems to contradict statements to the contrary in 8:13 and 9:3,6. In the former passages, however, Egypt was merely a type of bondage while here the literal Egypt is in view.[7] Though Israel would not return into the bondage of Egypt lest God's efforts in bringing them out seem futile, yet they would be brought into another bondage—that of Assyria. Why? "Because they refused to return," i.e., repent, to come back to God (11:5).

Again Hosea announced an impending invasion of Israel. "And the sword shall fall (lit., whirl about) on his cities. The "sword" symbolizes the power of war. The sword would "consume his bars and devour them." The reference is to the cross poles with which gates were fastened.[8] This disaster would befall Israel "because of their own counsels," i.e., the religious and foreign policy which is defined more precisely in the following verse (11:6).

The people of Israel seemed incorrigible. "My people is bent upon apostasy from me." The verb (*telu'im*) literally means "suspended, hung." The idea seems to be that they are impaled or fastened upon apostasy as upon a stake so that they cannot get loose. The prophets continually call the people "upwards" to the way of righteousness (cf. 11:2). "None will lift themselves up." Harper lists ten different translations and/or interpretations of this phrase. The basic idea seems to be that no one would respond to the call of the prophets (11:7).

D. The Perplexities of God's Love (11:8-9).

The thought of executing judgment upon Israel is a painful one to the Lord. "How shall I give you up, O Ephraim? How shall I surrender you, O Israel."[9] Here is the dilemma of the conflict between divine mercy and divine justice. The first two agonizing rhetorical questions are followed by two more: "How can I give you up like Admah? How can I make you like Zeboiim?" These were two cities of the plain overthrown with Sodom and Gomorrah (Gen 14:2; Deut 29:23; Jer 49:18). The prospect of the complete destruction of Israel was almost more than the Lord could bear: "My heart is turned within me, together my passion is kindled." The idea is that all of Yahweh's feelings of compassion have gathered themselves together, i.e., his whole compassion has been stirred within him. These, of course, are anthropomorphic expressions which are used to help humankind understand the agony which judgment brings to the Lord (11:8).

Suddenly Yahweh resolved the conflict between mercy and justice in favor of mercy. "I will not execute the burning anger of my wrath." If he were to do so, nothing would remain of Ephraim. "I will not destroy Ephraim again." Judgment must take its course, but it will be tempered with mercy. Yahweh must punish, but he will not exterminate (Brown). Once the heart of God has changed, it will not return to wrath to destroy Ephraim (11:9a).

Why did the Lord give this promise of tempered judgment? "For I am God and not man, the Holy One in the midst of you." Holiness requires absolute justice, and at the same time, grace and mercy. The basic idea of "holiness" is apartness. God is not like man in the way he administers punishment. "And I come not in burning wrath" but rather in wrath tempered with mercy (11:9b).

E. Predicted Results of God's Love (11:10-11).

God's love would eventually win out. "After Yahweh they shall go" in obedience to his summons to return to their land. "Like a lion he shall roar" and thus call his people to return to their land. The simile denotes the loudness of the call, and the awful majesty of the Lord. It may also signify the terrible judgments on Israel's enemies when he calls his people to return. When Yahweh roars "sons will tremble from the west," lit., from the sea, i.e., the distant islands and lands of the west (11:10).

They shall "tremble like birds out of Egypt and like doves out of the land of Assyria." The comparison with birds suggests the swiftness with which they return. Egypt here represents the lands of the south. Assyria represents the regions to the east of Israel. Thus from all over the world the sons of God hear the Father's call to return to their land. The fulfillment is to be assigned to the last days, the Gospel Age (Heb 1:1-2). The true Israel of God hears the call to come to the heavenly kingdom through Christ. "And I will cause them to dwell in their houses." They will succeed in coming home to the Father and they will settle down to live their daily lives in the kingdom of his grace (11:11).

ENDNOTES

1. R.F. Horton, ed., "The Minor Prophets" in *The New Century Bible* (New York: Henry Frowde, 1906), p. 49.

2. NASB renders "Ephraim was a watchman with my God, a prophet." NIV renders: "The prophet, along with my God, is the watchman over Ephraim."

3. The term "righteousness" means salvation or deliverance in Isa 46:12; 54:17; 32:16; 33:5.

4. Another possibility is that Shalman is the Moabite king Salamanu described in Tiglath-pileser's annals as one of several Syrian and Palestinian rulers who paid him tribute in 732 BC. (ANET, p. 282). See N.K. Gottwald, *All Kingdoms of the Earth* (New York: Harper & Row, 1964), p. 128.

5. Others take the clause "mother along with sons was dashed to pieces" to refer to what would happen in Israel rather than a description of what happened at Beth-arbel.

6. For a defense of the messianic interpretation of Hosea 11:1, see James E. Smith, *What the Bible Teaches About the Promised Messiah* (Nashville: Nelson, 1993), pp. 238-42.

7. Others understand this clause to refer to the longing of the people for help from Egypt; or they make this a question; or they remove the *lo'* ("not") and place it at the end of the previous verse. This in effect makes the prophet say that Israel would return (in exile) to Egypt.

8. Lehman thinks "bars" is metaphorical for the nobles and princes of the land.

9. Keil prefers to make these clauses exclamations yielding this sense: "How thoroughly I could give you up if I were to punish your rebellion as it deserves."

CHAPTER NINETEEN

Lack of Faithfulness
Hosea 11:12-14:9

Hosea's sayings have been grouped around the concepts of the lack of the knowledge of God (4:2-6:3), the lack of mercy (6:4-11:11), and now finally, lack of truth or faithfulness.

A SIN AGAINST ANCESTRY
Hosea 11:12-12:6

One of the interesting features in the Book of Hosea is the prophet's frequent references to Israel's early history. In the final unit of the book Hosea contrasts the life of the patriarch Jacob with his descendants.

A. Description of Degenerate Jacob (11:12-12:2).

Ephraim is accused of surrounding Yahweh with lies and deceit. The reference is to the hypocrisy with which Israel still claimed to be the people of God in the midst of their idolatry. They pretended to worship Yahweh under the image of a calf. Judah too was "wayward" in respect to God.[1] While his people were wayward, the Holy One—Yahweh—was faithful (11:12).[2]

The wind is a figure for what is empty, vain or of no real worth or practical benefit. "Ephraim grazes wind and pursues the east wind!" To feed on wind is to take pleasure in or draw sustenance from what can really afford neither. The east wind is a figure of destruction. Ephraim's course was not only idle, but injurious; not only delusive, but destructive; not only fruitless, but fatal (12:1a).

The disastrous course of Ephraim was on a parallel track. Socially "all day he multiplies lies and violence." This refers to man's conduct toward his fellow man (cf. Amos 3:10; Jer 6:7). Politically "they make a covenant with Assyria." King Menahem paid tribute to Assyria and entered into an alliance with that nation. When relations with Assyria soured, oil was sent to Egypt in order to secure an alliance. This took place in the reign of King Hoshea (2 Kgs 17:4). Thus socially and politically Ephraim was pursuing an unproductive and even dangerous policy (12:1b).

The Lord must rebuke, reprove and chastise Judah as well as Ephraim. "Yahweh has a controversy with Judah," i.e., a legal action, a lawsuit. Eventually Jacob—the entire covenant people—must experience a judgmental visitation. God would recompense both kingdoms for their rebellious deeds (12:2).

B. The Example of Historical Jacob (12:3-5).

The patriarch Jacob is set before his descendants as a good example. "In the womb he grasped the heel of his brother." Here is Jacob's eager attempt to secure his birthright. He was ambitious for God's blessing even before his birth. "And in his strength he strove with God." The reference is to what took place at Peniel (cf. Gen 32:25-29) when Jacob wrestled with a stranger near the River Jabbok (12:3).

The contest with God is further explained in the words "he wrestled with the angel and prevailed." The stranger with whom Jacob wrestled on the banks of the Jabbok was none other than the angel of Yahweh who appeared so often in Old Testament history as a visible manifestation of God—a theophany. Jacob "wept and prayed to him at Bethel." The language shows that at some level the conflict with the angel of Yahweh became spiritual. The weapon Jacob used was prayer. This weapon was also available to the Israel of Hosea's day (12:4a).

Jacob found God at Bethel. Thus a spiritual victory was won. This seems to refer to the second Bethel experience mentioned in Genesis 35:9ff. when God confirmed his name "Israel" and renewed the promise of his blessing. "And there he spoke with us." Perhaps the easiest of many interpretations is this: What God said to Jacob in that second Bethel experience still applied to the Israel of Hosea's day. He spoke to Israel in the person of their ancestor Jacob (12:4).

The promises of Yahweh to Jacob were still valid if only Israel would repent and seek the victory through prayer just as their sinful ancestor had done so many centuries earlier. This is what is suggested by the words: "And Yahweh, God of hosts, Yahweh is his remembrance." The name "Yahweh" signifies the unchanging one. He was the same to Jacob's posterity as he had been to the patriarch himself. He is God of "hosts." The term could refer to the heavenly bodies, heavenly beings, the armies of Israel or any combination of these (12:5).

C. The Appeal to Degenerate Jacob (12:6).

Since Yahweh is the same yesterday, today and forever—the same God who yielded to the prayers of the patriarch Jacob—Hosea called upon his countrymen to "therefore surely turn in respect to your God." The verb means to turn as to enter into a vital fellowship with God; to be truly converted (Keil). The preposition could also be understood as instrumental: by the help and power of God (Harper). That turning to God would require them to "keep mercy and justice" in respect to their fellow man (cf. Mic 6:8). It would also require them to "hope continually unto your God." Absolute trust in God is another of the conditions of returning to the Lord (12:6).

A SIN AGAINST FAITHFULNESS
Hosea 12:7-14

Hosea appealed to Israel's early history to prove his charge of unfaithfulness on the part of his people. Yahweh's faithfulness rebuked the faithlessness of Ephraim.

A. Rebukes for Sin (12:7-8).

Degenerate Israel was no better than a Canaanite (cf. Ezek 16:3). Israel was a deceiver whose highest aim was to become rich. "In his hand is the scale of cheating." The Canaanites (who were also known as Phoenicians) were the merchants of the ancient world. Apparently they had a reputation for dishonesty. "He loves to oppress," i.e., defraud a laborer or dependent of his due. Israel, like a fraudulent merchant, strove to become great by oppression and cheating. Israel was no longer Jacob who became great by striving with God for spiritual victory (12:7).

Ephraim did achieve wealth. This wealth, however, was attributed solely to national effort rather than divine blessing. Ephraim said, "Surely I have become rich." The emphasis in the clause is on the personal pronoun. "I have found wealth (or strength) for myself." Ephraim boasts of his riches though they had been procured by fraud and violence. He further maintains that he has not sinned in acquiring this wealth so as to expose himself to punishment or to be deserving of severe reprehension. Rather he had earned his wealth through "labors." Here is an unbelievable self-righteousness. When fraud and deception become business as usual a nation has surely reached rock bottom (12:8).

B. A Long-standing Relationship (12:9-11).

God replies to the delusion that Israel had acquired wealth by their own efforts. "But I am Yahweh your God from the land of Egypt." From the time of the Egyptian sojourn—more than seven hundred years—he had been their God. To him they owed all prosperity past and present. Because of their ingratitude they are threatened with being driven out of their good land into the wilderness. "I will still cause you to dwell in tents, as in the days of the appointed season." The feast of Tabernacles lasted for seven days during which Israel was to dwell in huts or booths. This verse is best regarded as a threat with an implied promise (Keil). While they have before them the prospect of being driven from their homeland, they also have set before them the repetition of divine guidance through the desert (12:9).

What is the proof that the Lord had been their God since the

Exodus from Egypt? "I have spoken to the prophets, and I have multiplied visions and spoken similitudes through the prophets." He had shown continual care for the spiritual welfare of Israel. He graciously had made known his will for them through the prophets. He communicated with those prophets in three ways: (1) word; (2) vision; and (3) parable (12:10).

"If Gilead is worthless, they shall be only nothing." This clause is obscure. "Worthless" suggests the moral decay of Gilead, the eastern half of the nation. "Nothing" refers to the physical deterioration of the nation which resulted from the moral decay. In Gilgal—the western half of the nation—"they offer bullocks." Gilgal, near Jericho, had become a center of idolatrous worship (cf. 4:15; 9:15). "Also their altars shall be as stone heaps in the furrows of the fields." With this play on words—Gilgal and "heaps" come from the same root—Hosea explained what he meant in the opening clause of the verse. The land would be abandoned (12:11).

C. An Illustration of God's Faithfulness (12:12-13).

"Jacob fled to the land of Aram." The reference is to the flight of Jacob from Esau (cf. Gen 28). This episode is cited (1) to stress God's providential care for his people; or (2) to contrast the flight of Jacob across the desert and the later guidance of Israel through the wilderness by a prophet. In any case, while in Padcan-aram "Israel served for a wife, and for a wife he did keep sheep." In order to pay the expected *mohar* for his two wives Jacob shepherded fourteen years for Laban (12:12).

Though Jacob had to flee for his life and labor for his wife, later the Lord brought up his descendants from Egypt "by a prophet." The prophet who led Israel out of Egypt was Moses. "And through a prophet was he guarded." The guarding of cattle by Jacob is contrasted to the guarding of Israel by God through Moses. The purpose of these verses is to call to Ephraim's remembrance that elevation from the lowest condition which God's people completely had forgotten (12:14).

D. Retribution Threatened (12:14).

"Ephraim has stirred up bitter wrath." Instead of thankful appreciation to Yahweh, Ephraim provoked God to anger by his sins. "Therefore he shall leave his blood upon him," i.e., his blood-guiltiness. Leaving his blood-guiltiness upon him means that he remained unforgiven and inevitably would be punished. "And his reproach shall his Lord return to him." The dishonor which Ephraim had done to the Lord by sin and idolatry would be repaid (12:14).

FROM LIFE TO DEATH
Hosea 13:1-8

Hosea now begins to focus on the theme of death. Ephraim was spiritually dead; Ephraim would shortly be politically dead. This divine sentence was just. The process of death, however, would be severe.

A. Present Spiritual Death (13:1-2).

There was once a time when the other tribes treated Ephraim with reverence and respect. "When Ephraim spoke there was terror." Hosea is probably thinking of the days of the Judges. "He exalted himself in Israel." The prophet has in mind the attempts made by Ephraim to seek the rule among the tribes which led eventually to the secession of the ten tribes. Through Baal worship Ephraim incurred guilt before God. Baal worship was introduced in Israel during the days of Ahab and Jezebel. Possibly Hosea also has in mind the introduction of the golden calves by which Yahweh was virtually turned into a Baal. In any case, when Baalism was introduced in Israel the nation died morally and spiritually. Baal worship sapped and undermined the strength of Ephraim. The nation began to die politically (13:1).

"And now they continue to sin." Baalism was not a passing fancy, but a continuing commitment in the north. "They have made for themselves molten images out of their silver, idols according to their understanding," i.e., their proficiency in art. Israel of Hosea's day was no better than Ephraim of old for they persisted in the worship of idols. These idols were "all the work of craftsmen," i.e., merely the product of human genius. "About them they are saying, those who sacrifice, Let them kiss calves." The custom seems to have been to kiss the hand toward the deity (cf. Job 31:27; 1 Kgs 19:18). Hosea is mocking the absurdity of human beings giving homage to calves (13:2).

B. Imminent Political Death (13:3).

Because Ephraim clung to irrational idolatry, the nation would perish quickly. Three figures follow. First, "they will be as the morning cloud and dew that early passes away." This figure, which appeared earlier in 6:4, is here given a new significance. The nation would disappear from the scene as quickly as the morning dew disappears from the ground. Second, they would be "as chaff which is stormed away from the threshing floor." They are as helpless in the face of the the blast of judgment as the weightless chaff is before a violent wind. Third, Ephraim would disappear from the scene "like smoke out of the window" or chimney (KJV; ASV). The chimney was in reality only a hole in the roof through which the smoke escaped from the house.

C. The Justice of the Death Sentence (13:4-6).

Yahweh had been the God of Israel since he had led them out of the land of Egypt centuries earlier (cf. 2:15; 9:3; 11:1; 12:9). "And you know no God besides me, and besides me there is no savior." The only God who had ever been a helper and savior to Israel was Yahweh (13:4).

Yahweh "knew' Israel in the wilderness, "in the land of drought." The verb (*yada'*) connotes favor and intimate relationship (cf. Amos 3:2). It is one of the key words in the vocabulary of election. Again Hosea looks back on the wilderness period as the ideal time in the relationship between Yahweh and his bride Israel (13:5).

In the wilderness Israel depended totally upon Yahweh. But "when they fed, they became full." Once in the Promised Land they had all they needed and wanted. They no longer felt dependent upon the Lord. "They became full and their heart was lifted up." Prosperity resulted in their being led away from God (cf. Deut 8:11ff.). "Therefore they have forgotten me." Here again is one of Hosea's major themes. Israel entered Canaan, prospered, and forgot God (13:6).

D. The Severity of the Death Process (13:7-8).

In the previous verse Israel was compared to a flock made full by pasture. Now Hosea depicts the chastisement of the people as the tearing in pieces of the fattened flock by wild beasts. Instead of a shepherd, Yahweh had become "like a lion" to Israel. More than that, Yahweh would "lie in wait" like a leopard by the wayside. The thought is that the Lord was awaiting the moment to pounce against his people in judgment (13:7).

The imagery of ferocious beasts reaches a climax in verse 8. Yahweh would encounter Israel in judgment "like a bear robbed of young." He would "rend the enclosure of their heart," i.e., their chest cavity. That would mean certain death. Then that which the bear had killed the lioness would eat. "The beast of the field will tear them." These beasts symbolize their enemies (13:8).

FROM DEATH TO LIFE
Hosea 13:9-16

The theme of restoration after destruction is common in the prophets. Hosea proclaimed that Yahweh would effect a resurrection after the political death of his people.

A. Israel's Rebellion (13:9-10).

Apostasy inevitably leads to destruction. Thus Yahweh declared: "It is your destruction that you are against me." The Lord had been the true help of Israel through the years. Now, however, his people had turned their backs on their true help and looked to man-made kings for help (13:9).

None of the weak kings who ruled Israel in the closing days of that nation's history could save the country from the Assyrian foe. "Where now is your king that he may save you in all your cities?" Hosea mocked the folly of trusting in these weak monarchs. After the death of Solomon the ten northern tribes had demanded "a king and princes." The royal family, however, would be of no help to them against Assyria (13:10).

B. Israel's Retribution (13:11-13).

God punished the desire for a king and princes by giving the people exactly what they wanted. "I give you a king in my anger and take him away in my wrath." It is possible here to take "king" as a collective. The imperfects denote an action that is repeated again and again. God permitted them to have kings and then punished them through those kings. During the twenty-one decades of northern kingdom history there were nine dynasties. Bloody regicides and civil wars were the rule in that kingdom. This political turbulence was viewed by Hosea as the divine punishment for the rebellion of the northern tribes (13:11).

Over the years the Lord had "bound up" the iniquity of Ephraim so as to preserve it. Literally the text says that Ephraim's sin was hidden away, i.e., carefully preserved so as not to be lost. Every sin of the nation would be recompensed in the judgment (13:12).

Hosea likens the judgment to come on Ephraim to "the pains of a travailing woman." Thus upon Ephraim would come an inevitable period of affliction which no power could turn aside. This is a picture of the sufferings and calamities connected with the judgment upon the northern kingdom (13:13a).

Suddenly the picture changes. Now Ephraim is no longer the mother, but the unborn child. "He is an unwise son that at the time does not place himself at the breaking forth place of children," i.e., in the opening of the womb. Thus the birth is retarded, and the life of both mother and child endangered. In the figure here the mother and child both represent Ephraim. The nation is "unwise" because even under the chastening judgment he still delayed his conversion and would not let himself be born again (13:13b).

C. Israel's Resurrection (13:14-15a).

Sudden changes of thought are characteristic of this section of Hosea. Elsewhere Hosea held out the promise of ultimate redemption (cf. 1:10f.; 2:15f.. 3:5; 14:4-8). So here Hosea looked beyond the judgment he had just pictured. "Out of the land of Sheol will I redeem them." The ancient versions and Paul in the New Testament understand this sentence as a promise. Sheol is the abode of the dead. The verb "redeem" (*padah*) means to redeem by payment of a price. "From death I will set them free." The verb *ga'al* means to redeem by right of kinship. The two verbs in this verse in their strict sense describe what Jesus did, buying men with a price and becoming their near kinsman by his incarnation (13:14a).[3]

Two triumphant questions proclaim Hosea's hope of victory over death. "Where are your plagues, O death? Where your destruction, O Sheol?" These two questions affirm more than just deliverance from the danger of death. They affirm the conquest of death itself. Death is being challenged to do its worst. It will not be victorious. The only meaning which this verse had for the Israelites of Hosea's day was that Yahweh possessed the power even to redeem them from death, and raise Israel from destruction into newness of life. The full and deeper meaning of these words was only brought to light by the resurrection of Jesus.

Two considerations underscore the certainty of this promise of victory over death. First Yahweh declares: "Repentance is hidden from my eyes." The purposes of salvation would be irrevocably accomplished. God would not repent of the promise. Second, Ephraim would "bear fruit among his brethren." The name "Ephraim" means "double fruitfulness." In its very name Ephraim possessed a pledge of blessing. The Lord would not let his people be annihilated in the coming judgment. There is an allusion here to the patriarchal blessing of Genesis 48:4,20; 49:22f. (13:14b-15a).

D. Israel's Ruin (13:15b-16).

Having glanced beyond the judgment to the distant redemption of God's people, Hosea returned to the national judgment which would shortly befall Ephraim. Yahweh would send against them "an east wind." Normally the winds were off the Mediterranean Sea. Occasionally, however, winds would shift and the wind would come off the eastern desert. This blistering wind is a figure of the judgment. While there is promise for true Ephraim—those who repent and turn to God—there is here judgment on Ephraim which went after the ways of Canaan.

The east wind of judgment would be devastating to Ephraim. All sources of water would become dry. "He shall plunder the treasures of all precious vessels." Here the figure has merged with fact. The pronoun refers to the Assyrian who would plunder all the treasures and valuables of the kingdom (13:15b).

Samaria will "bear her guilt," i.e., the punishment for her sin.

The city was guilty of having rebelled against her God. This was the root sin in the northern kingdom. Therefore the inhabitants of Samaria would "fall by the sword." "Their infants shall be dashed to pieces and his pregnant women shall be ripped up." Assyrian soldiers committed terrible atrocities such as these against those they conquered (13:16).

FINAL APPEAL FOR REPENTANCE
Hosea 14:1-8

The Book of Hosea concludes with a final call for repentance. The prophet paints a beautiful picture of what God would do for his penitent people.

A. The Call for Repentance (14:1-3).

Hosea cries out to his countrymen: "Return, O Israel, to Yahweh your God." The Hebrew uses a preposition which means more than merely turning *to* Yahweh. It means complete conversion. The salvation of God must be preceded by genuine repentance. "For you have stumbled through your guilt." Sin is represented as a false step. The words could be describing something which had happened already. On the other hand, the prophet's words could also be taken as predictive of the forthcoming national judgment (14:1).

Hosea then spelled out the method by which a return to God could be effected. When Israel returns to God they must not be empty-handed. Instead of Canaanitish sacrifices they must bring with them words expressing true repentance and contrition. "Take with you words and return to Yahweh." They needed (1) to beg for divine forgiveness; and (2) to ask Yahweh to "accept what is good," i.e., accept the only good thing which we are able to bring, viz., the sacrifice of our lips. "That we may offer our lips as bullocks." The sacrifice which God desires most is the acknowledgement of sin (14:2).

Turning to God requires renunciation of the world, of its power, and its gods. Thus the penitent must say first: "Assyria will not deliver us." They will no longer rely on political alliance to solve their national problems. Second, they must declare: "We will not ride upon horses." They would no longer trust in military power. The reference may be to Egypt, the country which supplied Palestine with horses. Third, the contrite one must denounce idolatry: "Neither will we call the work of our hands our God." Foreign gods as well as foreign alliances are renounced by those who wish to get right with God. Fourth, the penitent must recognize that Yahweh is a merciful Father: "For with you the fatherless find mercy." Because of his compassion, the penitent can be assured of forgiveness (14:3).

B. The Immediate Results of Repentance (14:4-5).

Repentance would have immediate and pleasant results. First, Yahweh promised: "I will heal their backslidings." Apostasy is regarded as a disease which would be healed by God. On the other hand, the picture is healing from wounds which had been inflicted upon them because of their apostasy. Second, Yahweh declared: "I will love them freely," i.e., with perfect spontaneity. Third, God explained that Israel's repentance would cause a change of attitude on his part toward them: "For my anger is turned aside from them." The ominous threat of 8:5 is reversed. Repentance averts God's anger (14:4).

Fourth, with his anger assuaged, Yahweh could again become beneficent toward his people. "I will be as the dew to Israel." In 6:4 and 13:3 dew is used as a simile of what is transitory; here it is used of a beneficent provision of nature whereby vegetation is preserved against the scorching effect of the east wind in a rainless season. Fifth, because of this grace of God, Israel would "blossom like the lily." The lily is the image of beauty and profusion. At the same time, Israel would "put forth roots like Lebanon." The forests of Lebanon are symbols of stability (14:5).

C. Long-range Results of Repentance (14:6-7).

In additional to the short range and immediate results of repentance, Israel would experience some long-range consequences. First, Israel would experience an increase in population. "His branches shall go forth." The people of God would not merely be a tree; they would be a garden. Second, Israel would be attractive to other peoples. Hosea compares the splendor of that restored nation to an olive tree, a symbol of lasting beauty and glory. The beauty to the eyes is more than matched by the aroma of the garden. "Its smell shall be like

Lebanon," i.e., like the famous cedars of that place (14:6).

Third, individual Israelites would prosper in the shade of that glorious olive tree (the nation). They would flourish "like the vine." Fourth, that blossoming vine would have a renown like the wine of Lebanon which has been celebrated from time immemorial (14:7).

D. Final Appeal (14:8).

God addressed Ephraim with a declaration. "O Ephraim, What have I further with idols?" Yahweh is saying that he would have nothing more to do with idols. The implication is that Ephraim should have nothing more to do with idols either. He promised his people that he would care for them, i.e., respond to their needs. He promised to be "a leafy cypress" providing shelter for them. He indeed is the true tree of life on which Israel finds its fruits. "From me is your fruit found." The fruit which God supplies nourishes the spiritual life of his people (14:8).

EPILOGUE
Hosea 14:9

The Book of Hosea closes with a warning. The moral of the entire book is summed up in this concluding verse. Wise and understanding readers would easily discern it. Yet because some are willfully obtuse, Hosea states in plain language what the book has tried to enforce. First, "the ways of Yahweh are straight" in contrast to the crooked ways of evil. The ways of Yahweh are revealed in his word. Second, "the righteous walk" in those straight paths. They live by the clear precepts of God's word. Third, "transgressors stumble in them to their own destruction." Those who ignore God's word would not see life more abundant or life eternal.

ENDNOTES

1. The meaning of the verb is in dispute. Some translate "rule." Keil and Brown trace the verb back to a root which means to be restless, to ramble about or be wayward.

2. In the Hebrew the word "faithful" is a singular adjective; the noun "holy one" is plural. In this form the term is used of God in Prov 9:10.

3. Those who insist that 13:14 must be interpreted as threat render the clauses in this verse as questions.

CHAPTER TWENTY

The Coming Judgment
Micah 1

Micah claimed up front that his message was "the word of Yahweh." The phrase stands first in the sentence because this prophet wants to stress the divine origin of his words. This message "came" to Micah. It was independent of the spokesman. Yet at the same time that word was very much a part of Micah. It was articulated in his own style and vocabulary. The formula with which this book begins is found in the superscriptions of four other prophetic books, and in slight variation, in yet four more.[1]

Micah says that he "saw" the word of Yahweh. This verb is a technical term embracing all divine revelation. In this case the revelation may have been more auditory than visual. The idea is that the prophet inwardly perceived certain facts through the influence of the Holy Spirit.

The divine word which Micah saw concerned "Samaria and Jerusalem."[2] Micah names Samaria first because its cup of iniquity was nearly full. Samaria's judgment would precede that of Jerusalem.

Actually the book contains only one oracle against Samaria—the first one in the book. What is important here that Micah saw Yahweh's judgment on Israel and Judah as a unified action.

A SUMMONS TO THE NATIONS
Micah 1:2

The book of Micah opens with a court scene. God is Judge, Plaintiff and Witness. The entire earth is called upon to witness the case against the covenant people of God. "Hear O peoples, all of you. Listen O earth, and its fullness." The language is reminiscent of Old Testament hymnic passages which underscore the universal kingship of Yahweh (cf. Deut 33:16; Isa 34:1; Ps 24:1). That which is about to be adjudicated in the court of heaven is (or at least should be) of interest to everyone. Later Micah describes the blessings which will come upon those nations which heed God's summons (4:1-4), and the catastrophes which befall those who do not give heed (5:15).

In keeping with the majestic scene of this opening paragraph, Yahweh is called Lord (*'adon*) or Sovereign. He is the authoritative ruler of the entire earth. The earth and its fullness is subject to him. The God of Micah is not some provincial deity. He is the King to which all nations are accountable. As Lord of the earth he is also the ultimate Judge. In his capacity of Judge, Yahweh makes pronouncements which impact upon all nations.

The Sovereign Yahweh is said to make his pronouncements "from his holy temple." In the Hebrew language one word indicates both temple and palace. At least in the case of God, deity and kingship are intertwined. Here the royal residence of the Sovereign Lord is sanctified as a temple by his holy presence. The reference here most likely is to the heavenly temple.[3]

The nations are called upon to allow the Sovereign Yahweh to "be a witness against you" (lit., "be against you for a witness"). In the passages which speak of God as a witness against something he acts as both a giver of evidence and accuser.[4] God's dealings with Israel and Judah are a witness to all nations. God was about to judge his people. In this judgment the nations should perceive the holiness and righteousness of Yahweh. Judgments upon Israel and Judah should also warn nations far more guilty that they too must soon face the wrath of heaven's holy Judge. The restoration of Israel after judgment bore testimony to the wonderful grace of God to those who renounce sin and seek his face. Both of these themes—judgment and restoration—are developed in the first five chapters of the book.

THE INTERVENTION OF YAHWEH
Micah 1:3-5

Micah now indicates the reason earth's inhabitants should pay attention. Yahweh was coming to earth in a mighty manifestation of his divine majesty.

A. The Announcement of His Coming (1:3).

With the interjection "Behold!" Micah points to the unexpected, sudden and surprising action of Yahweh. The Witness who speaks from the heavenly temple to and against the nations was about to intervene in the affairs of earth. "Yahweh is about to go out." The verb is frequently used of going out to war. Yahweh is said to have gone out against ancient Israel's enemies (cf. Judg 4:14; 2 Sam 5:24). The participle indicates the nearness of the action. Now he would "go out" in a judgment war against his own people. The sins of Israel have aroused him to action (1:3a).

Yahweh is said to go out "from his place." In some theophanies "his place" is Sinai (Judg 5:4; Hab 3:3; Deut 33:2). Here, however, "his place" is his throne in heaven. "He will descend" from that throne to come to earth. So great is this God that he must get down from his throne in order to walk upon the highest mountains of the earth. Scripture uses the anthropomorphic expression "go down" to depict divine investigation (Gen 11:5; 18:21) or intervention in the affairs of men.

Coming down from heaven to earth Yahweh touches first the mountains. Treading upon the high places of the earth denotes the victorious march of a conqueror. Israel is depicted poetically as walking on the high places of her enemies (Deut 32:13; 33:29; Isa 58:14). Possession of the heights ensured victory in battle. So Yahweh is said to march victoriously on the high places of the earth (cf.

Amos 4:13).[5] The implication of this description is this: Yahweh is infinitely greater than the created universe (1:3b).

B. The Effects of His Coming (1:4).

In highly poetic language Micah describes the awesome results of Yahweh's descent to the earth. "The mountains shall melt under him" as a mountain melts in a volcanic eruption. The imagery is based on the phenomena at Mt. Sinai following the Exodus (cf. Exod 19:18; Judg 5:4). The language conveys God's coming in power and action. "They shall cleave asunder into the valleys."[6] The earth virtually disintegrates before the force of Yahweh's coming. The mountains melt "like wax before a fire," i.e., spread in all directions. The crumbling debris would look like "waters rushing down a steep cliff."[7] How could mere man stand in the presence of such a God when the most substantial of earth's topography cannot endure his coming?

C. The Reason for His Coming (1:5).

Micah now explains the reason for theophany which he has just described. Yahweh is descending from heaven to earth "because of the transgression of Jacob and the sins of the house of Israel." The term "transgression" points to rebellion, breaking free of obligations to an overlord. "Sin" (*chata'*) refers to missing the mark, i.e., falling short of the moral ideal outlined in the law. The terms "Jacob" and "house of Israel" refer to the entire nation, northern and southern kingdoms. The irony here is that those who had been delivered in the past by the mighty intervention of God now face his wrath (1:5a).

In the second half of verse 5 the two kingdoms are separately designated as "Jacob" (northern kingdom)[8] and "Judah" (southern kingdom). Micah asks four rhetorical questions. First, "What[9] is the transgression of Jacob?" The prophet is asking, What is the center of the rebellion against Yahweh in the northern kingdom? Micah answers his first question with a second rhetorical question: "Is it not Samaria?" The capital—the seat of the government—was the headquarters of idolatry. Through Ahab and Jezebel, Baalism entered the northern kingdom at Samaria. That great city became a cesspool of moral corruption.

Third, Micah asks: "What is the high place of Judah?" The term "high place" is often linked with idolatry in the Old Testament. The use of the term here hints that the chief transgression of Judah was idolatry. Contrary to the law of God (Deut 12:11-14), idols were erected throughout the land in conspicuous places. Even the best kings of Judah were not able to remove these high places (cf. 2 Kgs 12:3; 14:4). Micah answers his third rhetorical question with a fourth: "Is it not Jerusalem?" The capital of the southern kingdom was no longer the Lord's sanctuary. The city was filled with "high places" (Jer 32:35). These unauthorized or idolatrous shrines virtually made all of Jerusalem a "high place." This passage probably antedates the heroic efforts of Hezekiah to remove those high places (cf. 2 Chr 31:1).

To summarize the reason for the intervention of Yahweh: the major sin of the northern kingdom was apostasy and rebellion. In the southern kingdom the major sin was unauthorized worship centers. For the following paragraphs Mays offers the catchy title "capital punishment for the capital cities."[10]

THE FATE OF SAMARIA
Micah 1:6-7

Micah now takes up the fate of Samaria, that almost impregnable capital of the northern kingdom. He describes the fate of the city and then the fate of the false religion practiced there.

A. The Fate of the City (1:6).

Four specific statements are made about the fate of Samaria. First, Yahweh threatens to make that great city "a heap," i.e., a pile of stones, "of the field." The language of verse 6 finds parallels in Assyrian monuments where cities are made into rubbish heaps.[11] As is frequent in such threats, no mention of the agent by whom Yahweh would effect this destruction of the city. The destructive work is to be understood as the effect of the theophany portrayed in verses 2-4. The fate of Samaria parallels that of Jerusalem in 3:12.

Second, Samaria would become "planting places for a vineyard." The city would remain so long in ruins, that vineyards would be laid out upon it. Visitors to the ruins of Samaria can observe for themselves the fulfillment of this prediction. The point is that the great urban metropolis would revert to rural countryside.

Third, Yahweh threatens to "pour down her stones to the valley." Like most ancient cities, Samaria was built upon a the brow of a steep hill. When the walls were destroyed, the stones would tumble into the surrounding valley some three hundred feet below. The slopes of that mound are strewn with the ruins which bear mute testimony to the splendor of that once proud city.

Fourth, Yahweh announces that he will "lay bare" Samaria's "foundations." The palaces and bastions of the city would be destroyed to their very foundations (1:6).

B. The Fate of False Religion (1:7).

Three statements are made regarding the fate of the paraphernalia of Samaria's false religion. First, "all her sculptured images shall be crushed." The same terminology is used of the smashing of the golden calf at Mt. Sinai (Deut 9:21). The sculptured images (*pesilim*) would be those adorning the temple in Samaria, especially the golden calf which was the major icon in the northern kingdom. These kinds of images were to have been destroyed by Israel when they entered the land (cf. Deut 7:25; 12:3). Yet in Samaria such images were cherished and venerated.

Second, "all her prostitutional wages shall be burned by fire." Hosea stressed that the northern state religion was idolatry (4:10-15). That northern prophet used the term "harlot's fee" for sacrifices offered to fertility gods to ensure fertility (2:12; 9:1). Micah suggests that the worshipers regarded the crops and other material blessings as wages paid by the fertility gods. All of that would be burned with "fire," i.e., in the conflagration created by an invading army. The torches of enemies may ignite that fire, but Yahweh directed them against Samaria.

Third, Yahweh threatens to make all her images desolate, i.e., without worshipers. The prophet does not indicate what would become of those worshipers. Thousands were slain; tens of thousands were carried away into captivity.

Fourth, their idols would return "to the wages of a prostitute." Samaria gathered her idols "because of a prostitute's wages." The gold and silver paid for religious prostitution had been melted down to make decorative coverings for idols. Enemy soldiers, however, would tear away the gold and silver leaf and spend it as currency for further prostitution.[12]

The prophecies against Samaria began to be fulfilled in 722 BC. After a siege of three years Samaria fell to the Assyrian king Sargon. The excavations show that at least part of the city was burned at that time. Assyrian records indicate that Sargon deported 27,290 persons from Samaria. Over the centuries which followed many conquerors marched through the city. The most devastating destruction of Samaria was administered by the armies of the Jewish high priest John Hyrcanus in 107 BC.[13]

LAMENT OVER APPROACHING JUDGMENT
Micah 1:8-9

The judgment of Yahweh initiated by Yahweh's descent from his heavenly throne moves southward from Samaria to Judah and ultimately to Jerusalem. "On account of this," i.e., the announced destruction of Samaria and the implicit judgment on Judah, Micah declares his intention to enter into a period of public lamentation.

A. Description of the Lament (1:8).

Three phrases describe his lamentation. The three verbs he employs are in a form expressing determination. He feels compelled by the circumstances to engage in such mourning. First, Micah says he must "mourn and wail." To "wail" (*yalal*) was to intensify mourning to the ultimate extreme. Wailing was usually accompanied by the pounding upon the breasts. Through this unrestrained display of grief Micah underscored (1) the desperate plight of his people; and (2) his compassion for those people.

Second, the circumstances compelled Micah to go "stripped," i.e., spoiled, plundered,[14] and "naked." The expression does not mean nude, but half naked, poorly dressed, without the upper garment. To dress in this fashion symbolized defeat and humiliation.

Third, Micah determines that he will make "lamentation like the jackals." Coming as he did from rural areas, Micah was quite familiar with the piercing, high-pitched howls and jarring yelps of the jackals in the night. He also likens his lament to the gruesome, agonizing screech of the ostrich (not owl as in NIV) which has abandoned her eggs. These similes indicate that mourning for an Israelite was not a quiet affair but a noisy expression of anguish (1:8).

B. Explanation of the Lament (1:9).

The hint in verse 8 as to the basis for the prophet's boisterous lamentation is amplified in verse 9. He cites three reasons. First, "her wounds are incurable." The reference must be to Samaria. The "wounds" (makkot) could be a reference to the deteriorating effects of transgression and idolatry. More likely, however, the "wounds" refers to the damage administered (or about to be administered) by God.[15] If it had not already happened, Samaria was about to receive a fatal flogging, a punishing devastation at the hands of God.

Second, Micah laments because "it has come unto Judah." The wounds, i.e., devastation, experienced (or about to be experienced) by Samaria would also come to Judah. The wounds were infectious, hence incurable. The fall of Samaria signaled doomsday for Judah for the sin of the southern kingdom was as bad as that of the northern sister. The "it" here could also be translated "he," referring to God. In either case the meaning is that judgment is approaching Judah.

Third, Micah weeps because with his prophetic eye he can see that "it" (the judgment) or "he" (God) "has reached unto the gate of my people." This terminology is used in Obadiah 13 of Jerusalem, the capital of Judah. Jerusalem is to Judah what a gate was to an ancient town, i.e., the seat of government. The prophet could see the judgment approaching the capital. This country prophet had genuine feelings for the fate of the capital of his nation. The expression "my people," used nine times in the book, indicates the empathy which Micah felt for his countrymen.

DEVASTATION CAUSED BY JUDGMENT
Micah 1:10-16

Micah now calls upon several towns to join him in his lamentation over the impending devastation of Judah. In each of the eleven lines of this unit the prophet names a city and develops a word play on its name. Micah saw a correspondence between the meaning of the names of these towns and the fate which they shortly would experience.

Concerning these towns these general remarks may be made. First, five of the towns are mentioned only here. Micah aimed to select names which lent themselves to his purpose of warning of judgment. Second, four of the towns mentioned were fortified cities protecting Jerusalem from attack from the coastal plain. Third, the unit is bracketed by anonymous exhortations (vv. 10a, 16). Fourth, the prophet alludes to five cities prior to Jerusalem and five after. Jerusalem is called "the gate of my people" (v. 12). This is the center of the chiasmic structure. Obviously Micah was focusing on the destruction of Jerusalem.

A. An Anonymous Exhortation (1:10a).

The prophet exhorts an anonymous auditor: "Tell it not in Telltown (Gath)." This is a quotation from a lament over the death of Saul (2 Sam 1:20) in which David did not wish the heathen adversaries of Judah to hear of the tragedy which had befallen Israel's king. So here Micah could not bear the thought that the Philistines would gloat over the defeat of Judah. The words "weeping, weep not" further define what Micah did not wish to happen in Gath. He did not wish men to proclaim in Gath the destruction of Judah with weeping.[16]

B. Towns North of Jerusalem (1:10b-12).

The exact location of the five towns mentioned next is not known. Micah seems to be describing a judgment which sweeps from north to south. This makes it probable that the towns lie north of Jerusalem.[17]

First, he urges those in "Dust-town" (Beth-le-aphra) to roll themselves in dust. Rolling in dust or sprinkling it upon the head was an act of mourning. In the face of the coming calamity even those in outlying villages would suffer devastation beyond imagination (1:10b).

Second, Micah urged the inhabitants of "Fair-town" (Shaphir) to "pass over," i.e., leave their town, "in shameful nakedness" (lit., in nakedness and shame). This means that they should remove their upper garment and dress as one who was a fugitive or a prisoner (1:11a).

Third, the inhabitants of "March-town" (Zaanan) have not

marched forth. This failure would be because (1) the cause was hopeless; (2) the village had been destroyed; or (3) they were afraid.

Fourth, "Neighbor-town" (Beth-ezel) would no longer be able to be neighborly. She would not be able to stand by Zaanan because she herself had experienced the calamity (1:11b).

Fifth, though the inhabitants of "Bitterness-town" (Maroth) were waiting anxiously "for good," i.e., some sign of relief, none would be forthcoming. Their prayers would not be answered. Only "evil calamity" would come down upon them "from Yahweh." There would be no relief from the bitter ordeal which Maroth must experience from Yahweh. This disaster would reach "unto the gate of Jerusalem." A play on the name Jerusalem may be intended. Jerusalem was the city of peace (cf. Ps 122:6ff.). If the city of peace must suffer, how much more Bitterness-town. Micah does not here affirm the destruction of Jerusalem. The calamity would come only to the gates of the city (1:12). This is exactly what happened in the Assyrian invasion of 701 BC. The outlying cities of Judah were captured by Sennacherib while King Hezekiah was shut up in Jerusalem "like a bird in a cage."[18]

C. The Towns South of Jerusalem (1:13-15).

The judgment would sweep south from Jerusalem into the Shephelah, the rolling hills between the hill country of Judah and the coastal plain. First, the inhabitants of Horse-town (Lachish) some 30 miles SW of Jerusalem sarcastically are exhorted to harness the chariot to the horses. They were to prepare for flight (1:13a). Lachish was the most important urban center in Micah's list. This was the headquarters of Sennacherib in 701 BC.

Lachish is said to be "the beginning of sin to the daughter of Zion," i.e., to the inhabitants of Jerusalem. Most likely the reference is to Judah's reliance on horses and chariots which later Micah lists first in a catalog of false supports which the Lord would cut off (cf. 5:9).[19] In Lachish were found "the transgressions of Israel," i.e., the same sins which tainted the northern kingdom had been adopted in Lachish (1:13b). The reference is to the idolatrous calf worship which was prominent in the northern kingdom (cf. Amos 3:14).

Second, "The Betrothed of Gath" (Moresheth-gath) would be given her farewell gifts (*shilluchim*) by the daughter of Zion. Micah's hometown was near the ancient Philistine capital of Gath. The picture is of a woman about to leave her home to go under the authority of another. In this case, Moresheth was doomed to come under the authority of an enemy (1:14a). Possibly the figure finds fulfillment in the indemnity which Jerusalem had to pay to Sennacherib in addition to the loss of this town, an indemnity which was paid at Lachish (cf. 2 Kgs 18:14ff.).

Third, the houses of "False-town" (Achzib) become a deceitful stream (*'achzabh*) to the kings of Israel. The idea is that the town would prove unreliable in the defense of Judah. The houses would disappear from this town as surely as winter waters disappear from a wadi in the summer months. The point is that the town, located in the plains of Judah, would be lost to the enemy (1:14b).

Fourth, "Inheritance-town" (Mareshah) near Lachish would pass into other hands. Yahweh declares: "I will still bring you the heir (*hayyoresh*)." The reference is to the right of inheritance by conquest. The "heir" here is the Assyrian. By conquest the enemy would inherit Mareshah (1:15a), one of the main fortresses of Judah (cf. 2 Chr 11:6-10).

Fifth, to "Refuge-town" (Adullam) the "glory of Israel" would take refuge. David once took refuge in the caves of this area (1 Sam 22:1). Adullam was later made a military bastion of Rehoboam (2 Chr 11:7). The "glory of Israel" might be the nobility of Judah. On the other hand the reference may be to the wealth of the nation. Some understand the clause figuratively meaning that Judah would sink into poverty and humiliation (1:15b). In any case, the fulfillment came in 701 BC with the invasion of Sennacherib.

D. An Anonymous Exhortation (1:16).

Zion, the mother of Judah, is called upon "make yourself bald and shear yourself." To signal a calamity the ancients would shave a bald spot on their head. The worse the calamity, the greater the bald spot. Here Zion is told to enlarge her bald spot "as the eagle." The reference is probably to one of two species of vultures which were common in Egypt and Palestine. The Percnotperus vulture is bald in the front of the head and neck. The Fulvus or Griffin vulture has a bald head and neck. Though shaving such bald spots was forbidden in the law (Deut 14:1; Lev 21:5), the practice was common (cf. Isa 3:24).

This extreme mourning is urged on Zion because of what would happen to "the sons of your delight." This has been taken to refer to (1) the pampered children of the palaces; (2) the cities and villages which were regarded as "children" of Zion; and (3) the armies of Judah. The sons of Zion "have gone captive from you," i.e., from Zion. Massive deportations are in view. Micah is using a so-called prophetic perfect verb tense in which what is future is so certain that it can be described as already past. In 701 BC Sennacherib claims to have taken captive 200,150 citizens of Judah.

ENDNOTES

1. Cf. the superscriptions of Hosea, Joel, Zephaniah, Malachi; Jeremiah, Jonah, Haggai, and Zechariah.
2. Only two other prophets (Isaiah and Amos) mention in the superscription the subject matter of their message.
3. The heavenly temple is referred to in Ps 11:4; Hab 2:20; Isa 63:15; Zech 2:13. The Jerusalem temple was the earthly counterpart of the heavenly temple. Hence sometimes the terminology "his/your holy temple" refers to that earthly temple. See Pss 5:7; 65:4; Jonah 2:4,7.
4. On God as witness see Jer 29:23 and Mal 3:5.
5. Some Jewish commentators explain "high places" metaphorically as the ground, and "mountains" (v. 4) as princes and rulers.
6. NASB "And the valleys shall be split." The translation proposed here is based on the rendering of the *Interpreter's Bible*.
7. Trembling mountains are often associated with the announcement of the coming of Yahweh: Exod 19:18; Judg 5:5; Isa 64:1; Hab 3:6. Mountains melting "like wax" specifically is found in Ps 97:5. Elsewhere the enemies melt like wax before the Lord (Ps 68:2).
8. This is the only place in the Book of Micah where "Jacob" refers to the northern kingdom.
9. The Hebrew actually uses the interrogative *mi* = "who?" Sometimes *mi* is used for *mah* (what) when the underlying idea is that of persons rather than things. See GK 137a.
10. J.L. Mays, *Micah, A Commentary* in "The Old Testament Library" (Philadelphia: Westminster, 1976), p. 38.
11. W.J. Deane "Micah" in vol. 14 *The Pulpit Commentary* (Grand Rapids: Eerdmans, 1963 reprint), p. 2.
12. NIC on 1:7. Another view is that idols would be carried away to be placed in pagan temples (Laetsch).

13. Josephus states that the city was so thoroughly destroyed at this time no sign of it remained (*Ant.* 13:10,3). A Roman city called Sabaste was built on the site by Herod the Great beginning in 30 BC. The exact date of the demise of the Herodian city is not known, but notices after the fourth century AD suggest that its destruction had already taken place. *Cyclopedia of Biblical, Theological, and Ecclesiastical Literature,* ed. John McClintock and James Strong (Grand Rapids: Baker, reprint 1981), s.v. "Samaria" 9:277-282. See also Andre Parrot, *Samaria the Capital of the Kingdom of Israel* (London: SCM, 1958), pp. 84-119.

14. Following NKJV and ASV. NASB and NIV follow LXX in rendering "barefoot." David went "barefoot" (*yacheph*) when he left Jerusalem in humiliation (2 Sam 15:30). Isaiah went "naked" (*'arom*) and "barefoot" (*yacheph*) as a symbol of Egypt's defeat and humiliation. In the present passage, however, Laetsch argues persuasively for the rendering "stripped."

15. For the term *makkah* used in reference to damage inflicted by God through an enemy see Isa 1:6; Jer 14:17; 19:8; 30:12; Nahum 3:19.

16. Following Keil, the phrase "weeping, weep not" is a further explanation of how they are not to tell the sad news of Judah's destruction in Gath, i.e., they were not to do so with weeping. Some prefer to follow the lead of the LXX in seeing in the word "weeping" (*baco*) a contraction of Acco, a Canaanite city belonging to Sidon in this period. This would yield the sense: "in Weep-town do not weep." For the technical arguments against this understanding of the clause, see Keil and Delitzsch, *Old Testament Commentaries: Ezekiel XXV to Malachi* (Grand Rapids: Associates, n.d.), p. 1119.

17. A more common view is that these towns lie between Jerusalem and the sea in the Shephelah or Philistine plain near to Moresheth, Micah's hometown

18. James Pritchard, ed. *Ancient Near Eastern Texts Relating to the Old Testament;* 3rd ed (Princeton: University Press, 1969), p. 288.

19. Traffic in horses was condemned in Deut 17:16f. Some violated the law in this regard (1 Kgs 10:28f.). Reliance on horses and chariots was regarded as an offense against Yahweh by Hosea (14:3) and Isaiah (2:7; 30:16; 31:1). Others think that Lachish was the seat of some form of idolatrous worship which had been adopted by the people in Jerusalem.

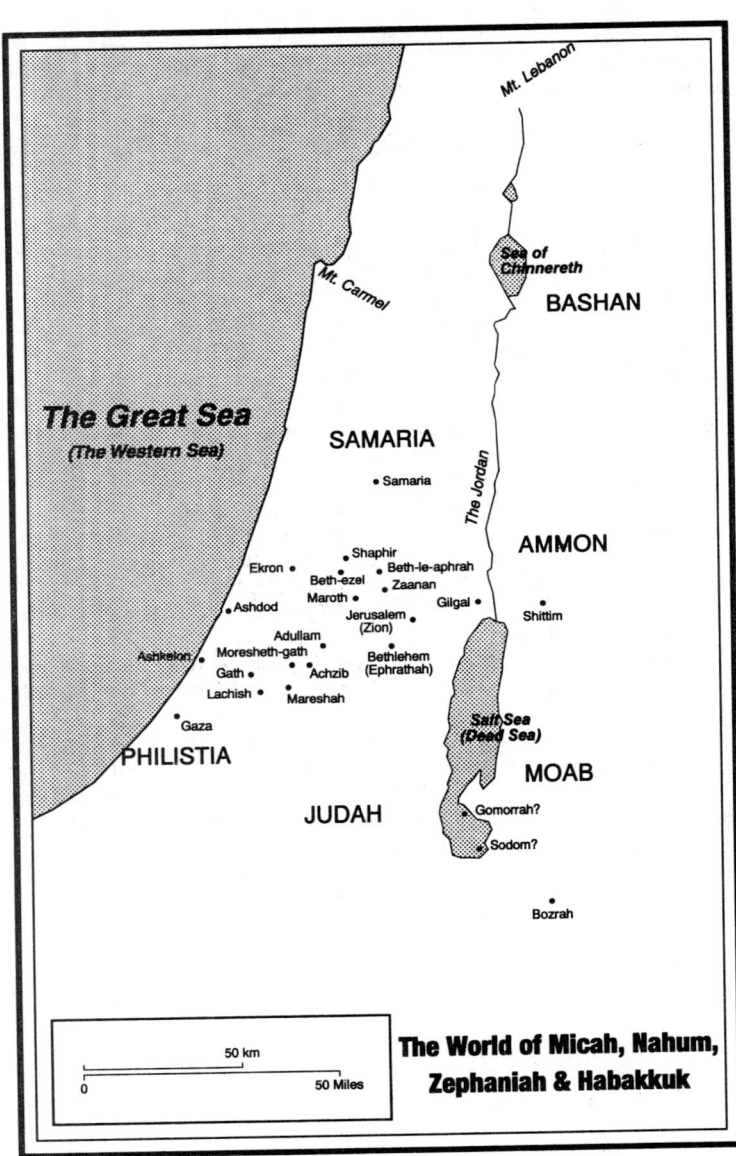

CHAPTER TWENTY-ONE

Present Corruption Condemned
Micah 2

If chapter 1 announced an imminent judgment, chapter 2 explains the reason for that judgment. Here Micah pronounced a general "woe" of the sinners of Judah. He then zeros in on various groups which were the center of the corruption of the nation.

WOE TO SINNERS IN JUDAH
Micah 2:1-13

Micah begins his exposure of the sinners of Judah with a "woe" saying. "Alas!" is the normal expression of shocked sorrow at somebody's death. The word comes from the vocabulary of lamentation. In prophetic literature it is frequently used sarcastically to announce the doom of sinners.

A. The Indictment (2:1-2).

Micah first condemns the diabolical plans of the upper class. They "devise iniquity." They "plan evil upon their beds." Thus these were not people who were victims of sudden temptation, deceived by the wiles of the Evil One. Rather these were people who were set in their sinful ways. They were constantly contemplating new crimes against their fellow citizens. "Iniquity" refers to actions which undermine the principles which God has established for the well-being of society (2:1a).

Next Micah condemns the execution of those evil plans. "In the light of the morning they do it," i.e., at the earliest opportunity. When criminals execute their crimes in the light of day they fear neither God nor man. In the case of these sinners, Micah notes that "it is in the power of their hand," i.e., they have the power to carry out their wicked deeds. Their philosophy was that might makes right. Under cover of unjust laws and corrupt courts they were able to carry out their designs for self-enrichment (2:1b).[1]

As the indictment unfolds Micah becomes more specific about the actions of the upper class nobles. First, in violation of the tenth commandment, "they covet fields." Sin begins in the heart. Second, they then "seize them," i.e., the fields. Such land-grabbing, even if by "legal" means, was a violation of the relation between neighbors ordained by God. Third, they take away "houses." They had no qualms of depriving a family of the roof over their head (2:2a).

Fourth, "they oppress a man and his household." The word for "man" (*gever*) indicates a person of some influence. To "oppress" (*'ashaq*) means to take something away from another through an advantage of position or power. Such oppression was condemned in the law (Lev 6:2; 19:13; Deut 24:14). Fifth, the oppression extended to "a man and his inheritance." In this case the word man (*'ish*) means one of the common people. The land barons were not respecters of persons. Land ownership gave a man social standing in the community. God's law required government officials to guard the property rights of the common citizen. Frequently, however, only the prophets showed any concern for the seizures of these family estates (2:2b).

B. The Punishment (2:3-5).

The word "therefore" links the announcement of judgment to the indictment of the guilty. Micah uses the messenger formula "Thus says Yahweh" for he speaks here as an agent of Yahweh. The first person pronoun refers to God.

1. Yahweh's plan (2:2). While the evil men plot upon their beds, God too was planning "evil," i.e., destruction, against them. What irony! Micah often stresses the poetic justice of God's judgment upon the wicked. The target of this divine planning is "this family," i.e., this crowd of crooks. The land barons were partners in crime, a malevolent Mafia.

2. The calamity (2:3). The nature of the calamity which Yahweh had planned is not here indicated. Micah gives three hints of the dimensions of the disaster. First, it would be like an iron yoke (Deut 28:48) from which they would not be able to extricate themselves. Those who had ruthlessly oppressed others would now become the oppressed. The language is generally used of submission to a foreign power.[2] Second, no longer would they be able to hold their heads high in haughty defiance of God's law. They would suffer the same feeling of helplessness which they had brought on others. Third, that time of judgment would be "an evil time," a prolonged period of disaster (2:3).

3. A lament (2:4). That day of judgment would be a time of lamentation. "One will take up a taunt song over you." A "taunt song" (*mashal*) is a poetical composition which points to the fallen ones as an object lesson. The fallen nobles would serve as an example to be shunned, a lesson not to pursue the same course. Probably the little people who had been so wronged would be the source of the taunt song (2:4a).

The taunt song would be accompanied by a bitter lamentation sung by either (1) those who where the victims of the judgment; (2) in parody by those who mocked the fall of the nobles; or (3) by professional mourners.

Four elements of that lament are cited. First, "we are utterly ruined." These words express (or mock) the indignation of the now landless landlords. Second, "he changes the portion of my people," i.e., the deed to the assigned territory of Israel has been handed over to another. Third, "how he takes it away from me!" God had given their land over to the conqueror. Fourth, "to the rebel he divides our fields." The heathen invaders are here contemptuously referred to as rebels or religious renegades. The "fields" are the great estates which had been unjustly acquired. These would be allotted to the armies of the conqueror (2:4b).

4. *Ominous prospects (2:5).* The lands confiscated by the enemy would never be restored to those land barons. "Therefore, you shall not have one who stretches the measuring line in the congregation of Yahweh." Land redistribution was the essential aspect of the year of Jubilee every fifty years. The point here is that certain families would have no representative left to stake their claim in any future land redistribution. Lacking land ownership these families would have no legal standing in "the congregation of Yahweh," i.e. the covenant community (2:5).

REFUTATION OF FALSE PROPHETS
Micah 2:6-7

Micah did not receive a warm reception when he carried his message of condemnation and punishment to Jerusalem. The people, and especially their prophets, considered his message theologically offensive.

A. Preaching of False Prophets (2:6).

The Jerusalem ministerial association kept preaching to Micah "Do not preach!" The term "preach" (*nataph*) here may have the derogatory sense of "to drip" or "to prattle." To those who are living ungodly lives the word of Yahweh is like a annoying faucet drip. The command is in the plural. It must, therefore, include other prophets who were preaching a message like that of Micah. The issue in this passage is not the hostility toward Micah personally, but the rejection of the messengers of God generally (2:6a).

"They" (the false prophets) "should not preach these things." The Hebrew grammar suggests absolute prohibition.[3] What is it that the false prophets were not to preach? "He will not carry us away with reproaches."[4] "Reproaches" refers to an humiliating catastrophe which would leave Judah exposed to the insults of those who witnessed the calamity. God would never allow such a thing to happen to them, they thought. That was the message of the false prophets. They were optimistic to the core (2:6b).

B. Acceptance of False Prophets (2:7a).

By means of a rhetorical question Micah forces his audience to admit that they warmly have embraced the optimistic forecasts of the false prophets. "Is this what is said by the house of Jacob?" The name "Jacob" means "heel grabber." God gave the patriarch Jacob a new name—Israel or "he who struggles with God"—when he experienced a spiritual transformation in his life (cf. Gen 32:28; 35:10). Using the title "house of Jacob" rather than "house of Israel" paints the picture of a people who were worldly and unconverted (2:7a).

The two rhetorical questions illustrate what the people were saying or at least were permitting to be said in their midst. First, "Is the Spirit of Yahweh cut off?" The concept of short of spirit is the opposite of slow to anger. That Yahweh was "slow to anger," i.e., patient, compassionate, eager to forgive, was a basic element in Israel's theology.[5] Any notion of imminent judgment was viewed as contrary to this basic tenet. Second, "Are these his deeds?" i.e., Is this the way Yahweh acts? The people of Judah could not reconcile threats of judgment with a God of love.

C. Response to the False Prophets (2:7b).

Yahweh responded to those who questioned his willingness to bring judgment with a rhetorical question of his own. "Do not my words do good to him who walks uprightly?" God's favor is conditional. Judgment can be averted by a change of conduct on the part of those who heard the judgment threats. God does "good," i.e., brings blessing, on those who "walk uprightly," i.e., live in harmony with the law of God.

SOCIAL VIOLENCE
Micah 2:8-9

While it is true that Yahweh rewards the upright, recent events indicated that Judah was anything but upright "My people rise up for an enemy." Their conduct had placed them outside the category of the chosen people. They were not upright; they were at enmity with God. The language is reminiscent of Hosea's name for his third child—Lo-ammi, not my people (2:8a).

What kind of conduct would make a people an enemy of their God? Micah now addressed this question with three illustrations. First, "from the front of a garment you have stripped a mantle from those passing by in safety." The picture here is of someone being forcibly stripped down to his underwear by either a robber or a creditor. The people being attacked by court bailiffs were "those passing by in safety," i.e., innocent, trusting people who were going about their daily business. Highway robbery was tolerated in Judah! The crime was even worse because it was against "those who have returned from war." Men who had laid their lives on the line for their nation were ruthlessly treated by the powerful land barons (2:8b).

Second, they had mistreated "the wives of my people." Probably the widows are in view here (cf. Exod 22:22). The powerful had "dispossessed" (*tegareshun*) these women. The verb is a military term. They had made war on the widows by evicting them from them "their pleasant houses," their cozy, happy homes (2:9a).

Third, they had attacked "her children," i.e., orphans, the children of each widow. These innocent and helpless ones had been evicted from their homes. The ruthless land barons had taken from upon them "my ornament" (*hadari*), i.e., the ornament, splendor, glory which God had given to these children. The preposition "from upon" (*me'al*) suggests that Micah is sarcastically referring to the outer mantle worn by these orphans. Even something of relatively small value was regarded by the powerful creditors as an ornament to be seized. This mantle they kept "forever" in open violation of the law of Exodus 22:26f. (2:9b).

EXPULSION FROM THE PROMISED LAND
Micah 2:10-11

The divine judge now pronounces sentence upon this people who had become his enemy. Just as he disinherited the filthy Canaanites in the days of Joshua, so Yahweh would now take the Promised Land away from his people.

A. A Stern Message (2:10).

"Arise and go!" The powerful land barons would be evicted from the Promised Land just as they had evicted the helpless from their homes. The Lord hands these men their marching orders just as they on numerous occasions had dispatched court bailiffs to execute their wicked orders against widows, orphans and the poor. The sinners would no long have a "resting place," i.e., a place where they could enjoy God's protection and peace. The term resting place (*menuchah*) is a synonym for "inheritance" (cf. Deut 12:9; 1 Kgs 8:56). The sinners would no longer have a place in the Promised Land (2:10a).

The expulsion from the Promised Land would take place "because of uncleanness." The Canaanites had defiled that land, and God had taken it from them (Lev 18:25). "Uncleanness" in the prophets is frequently idolatry.[6] Here, however, the mistreatment of the less fortunate seems to be in view. In any case, since they had defiled their land, it would now destroy them "with terrible destruction." The "destruction" here is the expulsion from the land (2:10b).

B. An Unpopular Message (2:11).

Such a message would be unpopular with the wealthy land barons of Judah. They had demanded that Micah cease his preaching (cf. v. 6). If, however, "a man walking in wind," i.e., a windbag, came along, they would readily embrace him and the lies which he spun. The implication in this description is that the message of the false prophets was nonsense and a tissue of falsehoods (2:11a).

The people of Judah loved those who promised to preach (lit., drip) to them "about wine and liquor," i.e., prosperity. Such preaching had an intoxicating effect on those who listened. It freed those auditors from responsibility. It impaired sound judgment.[7] Yet such a one would be the preacher (lit., dripper) for "this people." The language has a derogatory ring to it (cf. Isa 8:6,11f.). The text thus distinguishes between the oppressors ("this people") and the oppressed ("my people;" vv. 3f.). "Promise-box religion" has been the bane of every generation (2:11b).

A NOTE OF HOPE
Micah 2:12-13

The first section of the Book of Micah is rounded off with a note of hope. The abrupt transition here has raised doubts about the genuineness of these verses. These words were indeed spoken by Micah, but probably not at the same time as the previous verses. Micah arranged his book so as to make an important point. Judgment is not God's final word to his people. Sinners must be punished. Redemption, however, was the ultimate goal.

A. The Good Shepherd (2:12).

Yahweh declared that "I will surely assemble, O Jacob, all of you." The reference is to "the remnant of Israel," i.e., the whole number of those who were faithful to the covenant. Even in this note of hope, however, the word "remnant" rings ominous. The faithful must share the temporal judgment of exile to foreign lands with the wicked. For the faithful, however, there was hope. Someday the Good Shepherd would gather them together (2:12a).

The assembling of the remnant began with the work of Zerubbabel (Ezra 1-2) and Ezra (Ezra 7). Those gatherings, however, were but types of the Gospel gathering which is still going on today. While the focus here is on Jewish sheep, Jesus emphasized that he had other sheep which were not of this fold (cf. John 10:16).

Three phrases describe the condition of this flock of the faithful. First, "I will place them as sheep of Bozrah."[8] Bozrah was a city in Edom noted for its large flocks of sheep (cf. Isa 34:6). The phrase depicts the *safety* of the flock. Second, the remnant would be "like a flock in the midst of its pasture." The phrase depicts the *satisfaction* of the flock. The sheep are well-fed. Third, the flock of the faithful would "hum with men," i.e., by reason of men. This phrase depicts the *size* of the flock. A great multitude would raise their voices in prayer and praise to the Creator (2:12b).

B. The Glorious King (2:13).

The leader of the remnant of the faithful receives three titles in this passage. First, he is called "the Breaker." The general import of this title is clear. The leader breaks through all barriers which confine or impede the march of his people. Second, the leader is called "their king." He is one of them and one with them. The reference must be to the Messiah. Third, the leader is called "Yahweh." This name emphasizes the role of God as redeemer of his people. Parallelism requires that the King and Yahweh be one and the same person. This passage, as other Old Testament messianic prophecies, requires that the Messiah be regarded as a divine person.

The work of this future leader is indicated in three phrases. First, "he has gone up before them." This is a military idiom which means "to lead into battle" (cf. 1 Sam 29:9). Second, he has "gone on before them," i.e., he continues to lead them even after he led them victoriously through the ranks of their enemies. Third, he is "at the head of them," i.e., in total control of every situation.

What does this future Liberator do for the remnant? First, because their leader had battled through the ranks of the enemy, "they have broken through and have passed through the gate." The reference is to the gate of the prison in which these people were held captive, Satan's stronghold of sin and death. Second, "they have gone out thereat," i.e., into the freedom of Christ (cf. Gal 5:1).

ENDNOTES

1. The clause "for it is in the power of their hands" has also been translated in these ways: (1) "their hand is for God," i.e., they know no power except their own; (2) "their hand is to God,"i.e., lifted up against God.
2. See Isa 9:4; 10:27; 47:6; Jer 27:8; 28:14; Ezek 34:27.
3. Mays understands the false prophets to be saying that the true prophets should not preach. The following clause then denies the essence of what the true prophets were saying. Others render the clause as hypothetical: "But if they do not speak out concerning these things, reproaches will not be turned back" (NASB).
4. The Hebrew verb is difficult both as to root and form. The experts are divided as to how it is to be rendered in English. Probably Allen is correct in regarding the verb *yissag* as an orthographic variant of *yassig*, a Hiphil imperfect 3ms of the root *sug* = to remove or displace. The plural *kelimmot* ("reproaches") may be a plural of magnitude (the greatest of disgrace) used here as an accusative of specification. Hence, "he [God] will not remove [us] with reproaches."
5. On Yahweh being "slow to anger" see Exod 34:6; Num 14:18; Pss 86:5; 103:8; 145:8; Joel 2:13; Nahum 1:3; Jonah 4:2; Neh 9:17; Jer 15:15.
6. For idolatry as uncleanness see Jer 19:13; Ezek 22:5,15; 24:13; 36:25,29; 39:24.

7. Others take the wine and liquor to be the payment to the prophet (or dripper) rather than the promise of the prophet.

8. Following KJV and ASV. More recent versions render "pen" (NIV) or "fold" (RSV; JB; NKJV; NASB).

CHAPTER TWENTY-TWO

Man's Justice and God's
Micah 3

Micah 3 contains three oracles on the theme of justice addressed to the heads of the nation and the prophets who supported them.

The first words of the chapter "And I said," connect this section with the foregoing. The idea is "I continued to speak." Those addressed here are the same as in the previous chapter. Here, however, Micah makes clear that the government itself is the object of his denunciation, especially in its role as the guardian of justice.

FIRST PRONOUNCEMENT AGAINST THE RULERS
Micah 3:1-4

Micah first turned his attention to the rulers of the nation. After painting a graphic word picture of the corruption in high places, the prophet again announced the divine retribution.

A. Indictment of Corruption (3:1-3).

Micah calls upon "the heads of Jacob" to hear his prophetic word. These "rulers of the house of Israel" were those who administered the affairs of state. They also served as judges and magistrates.[1] The terms "Jacob" and "Israel" are usually applied to the northern kingdom. The context here suggests that Micah refers to Judah in general and Jerusalem in particular. The northern kingdom probably had already fallen (cf. 1:13; 2:12). The pairing of the two names here reminds Micah's audience of their roots as the people of God, a people with obligations to submit to the Lordship of Yahweh (3:1a).

1. A sin against knowledge (3:1b). Micah asked the leaders of Israel this question: "Is it not for you to know justice?" Yahweh is the ultimate lawgiver. As his representative Micah was concerned about justice *(mishpat)*. The point is that they, of all people, should know justice! To "know" means to know factually the legal traditions and to be skilled in applying those legal principles in contemporary society. "Justice" in this context is the even-handed and faithful implementation of the principles set forth in the law of Moses (3:1b).

2. A sin against society (3:2). Far from knowing justice, these leaders were "haters of good and lovers of evil." They loved everything God's law condemned, and hated everything that law encouraged.[2] To illustrate the monstrous perversions of divine justice Micah introduced a lengthy metaphor of savagery. "Who tear off their skin from upon them and their flesh from upon their bones." Here is a picture of the general public as a flock at the mercy of wild beasts. The verb "tear off" *(gazal)* is part of the Old Testament vocabulary of oppression. The peasants were being skinned of money and property by those who should have been their protectors. The courts were being run by a band of butchers who manipulated the legal processes to rob, cheat and defraud (3:2).

3. A sin against compassion (3:3). The heartless cruelty of the rulers is likened to cannibalism. They strip the skin from the carcass, break the bones, chop them up in pieces, and spread them out like meat in the pot. They cook and then "eat the flesh of my people." Eating people or their flesh is a common figure for oppression.[3] The rulers were particularly hostile toward "my people," i.e., God's people or Micah's people, the faithful, who were trying to live upright lives.

Micah has only one weapon to use in defense of these suffering citizens, viz., his scathing rhetoric (3:3).

B. Announcement of Judgment (3:4).

In the day of judgment these cannibalistic rulers would cry out to Yahweh for mercy. The Lord, however, would no more listen to their appeals than they had listened to the widows and orphans who had cried out to them so many times before. The term "cry out" here is the technical term for appeal to a judge for help against oppression (3:4a).

Far from hearing the appeal of these ruthless leaders, Yahweh would "hide his face from them in that time." The Lord makes his face to shine upon people when he blesses their lives and hears their prayers. To hide the face means to forget about, to ignore, to consciously cast one off.[4] God's actions were fitting retribution for the wickedness of these rulers. He would treat them thus "because they have made their deeds evil" (3:4b).

PRONOUNCEMENTS AGAINST THE PROPHETS
Micah 3:5-8

The upper classes of Judah were supported in their ruthless schemes by the ministerial association (cf. 2:6-11). Micah had a word of Yahweh for "the prophets," i.e., the false prophets.

A. Indictment of the Prophets (3:5).

Prophets were men called by God to communicate the divine will for his people in specific situations. In every generation, however, men arose who claimed this calling, but their message encouraged evil and contradicted the ancient Scriptures. Micah made four charges against the prophets of his day.

First, the prophets were "causing my people to go astray." How dare these men in the name of Yahweh misdirect "my people," i.e., God's people! Micah's blast against other prophets was not based on professional jealousy but on this man's compassion for those who had been misguided.

Second, the prophets were accused of selfish expediency. They were "biting with their teeth." One could purchase a tailor-made oracle with promises to wine and dine the prophet. Their god was their belly. What went into their mouths determined what came out of their mouths.

Third, the message of the prophets was always "peace" (*shalom*). The word means total well-being. Everything will be all right! They were optimistic to the core. No message of condemnation came from their lips, no call for repentance. Like their later counterparts, they cried "peace, peace when there is no peace" (cf. Jer 6:14).

Fourth, against one who refused to offer a bribe, the prophets would "prepare war." This is a powerful figure for persecution. They would declare God's wrath on the non-cooperative. They would stir up hatred toward those who disagreed with their Pollyanna preaching. Those who ooze love and liberality will often stop at nothing to silence the mouths of those who disagree with their viewpoint.

B. Announcement of Judgment (3:6-7)

The judgment against these perverted prophets is introduced with "therefore." Those who had abused their prophetic gifts would be deprived of them. "It shall be night for you without vision." The darkness indicates intellectual confusion. When the sun set on the nation of Judah they would no longer see, or claim to see, visions of peace. The change to direct address in this verse indicates that Micah was speaking to a group of these prophets (3:6a).

If visions of peace would be absent in that dark day, how much more would "divination" (*qisom*) be missing. The term includes magic, soothsaying necromancy. It is never used of genuine prophetic activity. In that day of judgment divination would yield no result.

Micah stresses four times in 3:6 the darkness of the coming day (cf. Amos 5:18f.). The future was not *shalom*, peace. Disaster loomed on the horizon. The ministerial association would not escape. "The sun shall go down upon the prophets." As an order they would cease to exist (cf. Zech 13:2-5).

So how would those prophets cope with that day of disaster? "The seers shall be ashamed." The term "seer" is an ancient title for a prophet (cf. 1 Sam 9:9). The title was based on the practice of acquiring oracles by means of visions. The seers who had published visions of *shalom* would be totally discredited by events. The diviners—the word has a pejorative sense—would be "confused." As God hid his face from them, so they would "cover their lips." They would be dumbfounded and shocked. They would have nothing to say "for there is no answer from God" to their prayers for help (3:7).

C. Micah's Credentials (3:8).

Following his announcement of the discrediting of the prophets, Micah presents his credentials. "But I, on the other hand, am filled...." The Hebrew expresses forcibly the contrast between Micah and the false prophets. Micah mentions four things with which he had been filled.

First, Micah was filled with "power" (*khoach*). He had the inner strength of conviction to persevere in the face of opposition. This "power" is something with which he had been filled, i.e., the power came to him from an external source, viz., God. Like other great prophets of the Old Testament, Micah felt a divine compulsion to preach, a compulsion which no amount of opposition could squelch (3:8a).

Second, Micah was filled with "the Spirit of Yahweh." The Holy Spirit enlightened the mind of the prophets and empowered them to communicate the divine message inerrantly (cf. 2 Pet 1:21). The endowment of God, not the pursuit of money, should be the motivating force within the proclaimer of God's word.

Third, Micah was filled with "judgment" or "justice" (*mishpat*). He had the ability to recognize what was right and wrong. He had moral conscience. He saw clearly the issues between God and his people. He received no monetary reward for preaching as he did. The burden of his heart compelled him to expose injustice and announce the just retribution of the flagrant sinners of Judah.

Fourth, Micah was filled with "might" (*gebhurah*), i.e., manly courage. The term is used of the courage which equips warriors in dangerous battle (cf. Judg 8:21; Isa 3:25). He could not be intimidated by threats, nor bought by bribes. He boldly proclaimed what he knew to be true.

The divine infusion of knowledge, wisdom and power enabled Micah "to declare to Jacob his transgression and to Israel his sin. The combination of the words transgression/sin has already appeared in 1:5 as the reason for the coming of Yahweh in judgment. The combination of Jacob/Israel has already appeared in 3:1. Declaring transgression and sin involves both the *denouncing* of that conduct and the *announcing* of judgment upon it. By so preaching Micah courted danger and death from his contemporaries (3:8).

SECOND PRONOUNCEMENT AGAINST THE RULERS
Micah 3:9-12

Again Micah called upon the the "heads of the house of Jacob and rulers of the house of Israel" to hear his words. These are the same leaders to whom 3:1-4 is addressed. The combination Jacob/Israel is a way of saying all Israel. At this time all that was left of Israel was Judah, the southern kingdom. By challenging these powerful rulers and condemning their conduct Micah was demonstrating the courage which he had just professed in the preceding verse.

A. The General Indictment (3:9b-10).

Both in attitude and actions the rulers of Judah failed in their responsibility to be the guardians of justice.

1. The disposition of the leaders (3:9b). The rulers of Judah regarded justice (*mishpat*) as loathsome and abominable. This attitude they demonstrated in their judicial decisions. Through his law Yahweh had established norms for protecting the rights of the powerless in disputes over life and property. Those norms had been despised and therefore disregarded. Even worse, the leaders "twist everything that is upright," lit., "they twist the straight way." They knowingly departed from a course of action that was marked out by the law as good and right. Regardless of the justice of a case, they knew how to twist it around so that the innocent were condemned and the victims were further victimized. They tolerated and practiced crookedness rather than righteousness.

2. The deeds of the rulers (3:10). The prophet from the village of Moresheth was not impressed with the architectural splendor of Jerusalem. The powers that be in Jerusalem "build up Zion with blood." This expression could be taken physically or metaphorically.

The eighth century building boom in Judah rested upon the foundation of the sweat, toil, and even blood of the lower classes. Innocent blood was the mortar which held together the walls of their palaces of hewn stone. On the other hand, Micah may be saying that the reputation of Jerusalem among the nations of that time had been built up by ungodly means. They had put Jerusalem on the map by bloody crimes and gangsterism (3:10a).[5]

What was true of the temple area of Zion was also true of the residential areas of Jerusalem. These were built up with "iniquity" ('avlah). Little people were crushed through evictions, confiscations of property, forced labor and the like. The rich got richer by unscrupulous and inhuman oppression of the weak. This was urban renewal with a vengeance.[6] The blood of the innocent slain cried out to heaven for justice so loudly that the Lord could no longer hear the hymns and prayers rising from the temple mount (3:10b).

B. Specific Indictment (3:11).

Jerusalem was dominated by a tyrannical triumvirate of rulers, priests and prophets. Each group was controlled by greed. First, "her heads judge for reward," i.e., the rulers took bribes. For a price the legal edicts were stamped with "satisfaction guaranteed." They knew no higher ambition than silver. They were completely money-mad.

Second, "her priests teach for hire." This is the only mention of priests in Micah. The "teaching" is probably the rendering of legal decisions (cf. Mal 2:7). The priests were no doubt lax in enforcing moral standards as conditions of admission to temple rituals.

Third, "her prophets divine for silver." These religious leaders had both the wrong methods and the wrong motives. Their methods were borrowed from pagan neighbors. Divination involved the use of external objects in the attempt to predict the future. The law strongly condemned the use of all such pagan paraphernalia (cf. Deut 18:9-13). As to motives, the prophets were no different than rulers or priests. Their god was their pocketbook (3:11a).

All the while the leaders fleeced the people "they leaned upon Yahweh." They were actually looking to the Lord to undergird the corrupt system. The term "lean" (sha'an) is part of the vocabulary of faith. It is used, for example, for depending on divine help in a military situation (cf. 2 Chr 13:18). Their motto was "in God we trust." Religion was for them a security blanket.

A rhetorical question expressed the grounds upon which the criminals in Zion built their shaky faith. "Is not Yahweh in our midst?" The temple was on a prominent hill within the city. The ark of God was in the holy of holies of that temple. That was proof enough that Yahweh was in their midst. Israel was his chosen nation. He had obligations to defend and protect them from enemies. Therefore, "evil shall not come against us."

Micah announced that God in fact had decreed "evil" (*ra'ah*) against Jerusalem (cf. 2:3). Here is the direct response to that announcement. With what they considered irrefutable logic they argued that "evil," i.e., disaster, could not come upon them since Yahweh himself was in their midst. The miraculous rescue of Jerusalem from Sennacherib in 701 BC may have fueled this false theology. The fallacy of their argument is that when people abandon God he is no longer in their midst (3:11b).

C. Announcement of Judgment (3:12).

Again the word "therefore" introduces the word of judgment. On account of these rulers, "Zion shall be plowed as a field." Zion was the most sacred section of Jerusalem. Those who built up Zion by unscrupulous means were those who were responsible for the demise of the city. The plowing of Zion would be by engines of war. No agent of this disaster is here named. Nonetheless, those who plowed Zion would be functioning as God's demolition crew.[7]

The disaster would leave Jerusalem in "heaps," i.e., total ruins, nothing but a pile of rubble. The temple could not guarantee their safety for the sacred mount would become "as the high place of a forest," i.e., overgrown with thorns and brambles. This announcement of judgment is a direct rebuke to the false theology which was so firmly entrenched in Judah in the eighth and seventh centuries. In challenging the unchallengable tenets of popular theology Micah was again demonstrating that courageous manliness with which God had endowed him (cf. 3:8).

An interesting sidelight on this prophecy is found in Jeremiah 26:18. The prophet Jeremiah was on trial for his life for daring publicly to preach that God was about to destroy Jerusalem. In his defense the elders cited verbatim this prophecy from Micah. They noted that King Hezekiah did not execute Micah for preaching much the same thing as Jeremiah.

ENDNOTES

1. Others think that the "heads of Jacob" were heads of father's houses representatives of whom formed an ancient court.
2. The pairing of love/hate is common in antithetical proverbs (cf. Prov 1:22; 9:8; 12:1). The pairing of good/evil appears in two wisdom psalms (cf. Pss 34:14; 37:27). Amos called upon his contemporaries in the northern kingdom to hate evil and love good (Amos 5:15; cf. Isa 1:17).
3. The cannibalism metaphor is used also in Pss 14:4; 27:2; Prov 30:14.
4. The idea of hiding the face implies forgetfulness (Pss 10:11; 13:1; 44:24); to be unmindful (Ps 22:24; 69:17; 102:2; Isa 59:2); to consciously cast off (Ps 27:9; 88:14; Deut 31:17f.; Isa 8:17); to leave one at the mercy of enemies (Isa 64:7; Jer 33:5; Ezek 39:23f.,29); to be in angry opposition (Ps 89:46; Isa 54:8; 57:17; Job 13:24); to cause terror (Ps 30:7); to cause death (Pss 104:29; 143:7).
5. Theo. Laetsch, *Bible Commentary; The Minor Prophets* (St. Louis: Concordia, 1956), p. 261.
6. J.L. Mays *Micah, a Commentary* in "The Old Testament Library" (Philadelphia: Westminster, 1976), p. 88.
7. Mays would make Micah say that Jerusalem would become a mound which would then be used for agricultural purposes. History, however, records no period of time when Jerusalem was deserted to this extent.

CHAPTER TWENTY-THREE

Hope for a Better Day
Micah 4

Micah 3 was an amplification of the condemnation of the upper classes which was introduced in chapter 2. Likewise Micah 4-5 is an amplification of the note of hope with which Micah 2 concluded.

ZION'S FUTURE GLORY
Micah 4:1-5

Both Micah and his contemporary Isaiah (cf. Isa 2) looked beyond the temporal judgment on Jerusalem to the "last days," i.e., the messianic age.[1] They could see the glory of that day beyond the gloom of Judah's judgment day.

A. Zion Exalted (4:1).

"The mountain of Yahweh's house," i.e., the mountain occupied by God's temple, would be established "in the top of the mountains." Mountains often symbolize kingdoms in prophecy. The temple mount here indicates that God's kingdom is spiritual. That kingdom would one day be exalted over all kingdoms of this world. The passive verbs of the verse are an indication of divine activity (4:1a).

The elevation of Zion is not physical. The text explains the elevation to mean that Gentiles would "stream" to that holy mount. In the language here there is perhaps a conscious play on the thought that in the future age streams would issue forth from the holy mount to water the earth (4:1b).[2]

B. Gentiles Converted (4:2).

Why would so many Gentiles stream toward Zion? Three reasons are suggested. First, "many nations shall go and say." A restless spirit among the Gentiles creates a yearning for the spiritual values of Zion, the church of Christ. Second, the Gentiles would hunger to know the ways of Israel's God. They would desire to go up unto the mountain of Yahweh because "he may teach us some of his ways." In that holy place they would learn enough of the ways of Yahweh to find salvation (4:2a).

Third, the Gentiles would desire to live their lives by Yahweh's precepts. They wished "to walk in his paths." Fourth, Gentiles would stream into Zion because "from Zion shall instruction go forth." From the kingdom of Christ the word of God would go forth into all the world. The inflow to Zion is followed by the outflow of missionaries. The point is that messianic Zion would focus on missions, and spreading God's word (4:2b).

C. Results of Gentile Conversion (4:3-4a).

Wonderful changes would result from the conversion of the Gentiles. First, Yahweh would "judge between many peoples." Converted Gentiles would make the word of God the standard for settling disputes among themselves. Second, through his word the Lord would "render decisions for strong nations afar off." At the feet of Zion's King the problems of the world would be placed for just solutions. The decisions of this Judge would be recognized as righteous and binding (4:3a).

Third, the hostility between nations would cease as a result of their common allegiance to Zion's King. Instruments of war—swords and spears—would be transformed into instruments of commerce—plowshares and pruning hooks. The prophecy envisions one greater than Solomon who would rule a peaceful kingdom where ancient hostilities would be erased. Fourth, those weapons would no longer be needed because "nation shall not lift up sword against nation, neither shall they learn war any more." Micah was not speaking of political peace but of the spiritual peace within the kingdom of God's grace (4:3b).

Fifth, in the absence of war, the citizens of Zion would enjoy the gifts of peace and happiness. "They shall sit each under his vine and under his fig tree." Micah is speaking of the spiritual gifts enjoyed by members of the church of Christ. In that kingdom there is freedom of hunger and want. To own property and to expend labor in cultivating that property is the Old Testament way of describing personal investment of time and energy in the work of the Christ's kingdom. Resting after labor is a picture of the satisfaction which comes to those who labor for the glory of Zion's King. Sixth, Zion's citizens enjoy perfect security. "There shall be no one to terrify them." Their godly fear casts out fear of any man (Matt 10:28). Their conviction that he that is within them is greater than he that is in the world (1 John 4:4) generates this sense of security.

Micah's prediction regarding Zion's future has received two very different interpretations. Some see this as a description of the millennial reign of Christ—a thousand years of peace with Christ ruling from the throne of David in Jerusalem. Others see in these verses a picture of the New Testament Zion, the church of Christ (Heb 12:22; Gal 4:25f.). In any case, where Christ's government prevails, peace follows.[3]

D. Certainty of the Hope (4:4b-5).

The hope of a glorious future for Zion is based on two factors, viz., the *promise* of God and the *provision* of God. First, these visions of the worldwide prominence of Zion were not idle dreams or wistful aspirations. "The mouth of Yahweh of hosts has spoken it." God himself signs a promissory note to bring these things to pass. What is here recorded by Micah is spoken by the one who commands all forces in heaven and on earth. Believers could therefore be certain that Zion's future was secure (4:4b).

Second, Zion's future was secure because God himself would provide the strength for his people to live the pilgrim life. Other peoples would continue to walk in the name of their God. The "name" is the revelation of one's nature, what one knows about another. For this reason some take the verse to affirm that Israel is expressing a commitment to regulate their conduct according to the nature of God. Walking in the name of God, however, refers to walking in the strength of God (cf. 1 Sam 17:45; Zech 10:12). The gods of the nations are worthless non-entities, without life or strength. Yahweh of hosts, however, is the Almighty. Therefore the heathen cannot disturb the peace or security which Yahweh would create for all those who embrace his saving word.

Two further implications of Micah 4:5 are worth noting. First, in Micah's day there was no sign of the nations turning to Yahweh in great numbers. There were some, however, who had already made that firm commitment to walk "in the name of Yahweh." Nations and their gods come and go. Yahweh, however, would always have a people who would faithfully follow his revelation. "We will walk in the name of Yahweh our God for ever and ever." Thus Micah 4:5 should be viewed as a commitment as well as an explanation of the promises just stated.

Second, even at the time when many nations stream toward the mountain of Yahweh, there would still be nations which would not seek Yahweh or his word. The heathen kingdoms are coterminous with the kingdom of God, at least for a time. These opponents will not be able to interfere with the salvation which God has prepared for those who love him.

ZION'S FUTURE RULER
Micah 4:6-8

The two phrases with which the next salvation oracle is introduced should be noted. The first—"in that day"—has both a literary and a chronological function. It ties this oracle to the one which precedes and it establishes the prophetic context of the following predictions as being the messianic age. The second phrase—"oracle of Yahweh"—is the strongest possible declaration of divine inspiration. These same two formulae introduce the prophet's oracle in 5:10.

A. The Action of God (4:6).

The focus is first upon God as the Good Shepherd gathering his sheep. The verb is imperfect, suggesting that the gathering is an ongoing process. Those who are gathered are described in three ways. First, the people of God are likened to limping sheep. This language may be an allusion to Jacob's limp (Gen 32:31). That limp was a reminder to the patriarch of his weakness after his encounter with the Lord at the river Jabbok. A limping people are a people who have been disciplined. Jesus looked on the crowds which followed him about as harassed and helpless sheep without a shepherd (Matt 9:36).

Second, the sheep of this gathering are described as "driven away" (*hanniddachah*), i.e. "exiles" (NIV) or "outcasts" (NASB). The term may have a legal background (2 Sam 14:13f.) referring to those who have been banished from the presence of the king because of treason.[4] The rescue of the flock from banishment is something which only the Good Shepherd, Zion's King, can do. It is an act of his compassion and grace.

Third, those who are rescued are those previously "afflicted" by Yahweh himself. The Old Testament used the figure of a wound to depict the result of divine discipline. The people suffered punishment at the hand of God. Only the one who wounded them can bind them up. The Good Shepherd is also a gracious Healer (cf. Deut 32:39; Hos 6:1; Job 5:18).

B. The Transformation of the Flock (4:7).

The gathering of the flock would be followed by a marvelous transformation effected by the grace of God. This transformation is set forth in three pictures.

1. The crippled are collected (4:7a). The ingathering of the flock by the Good Shepherd would lead to its total transformation. In the term "limping one" (*hattzole'ah*) those who are to be gathered are envisioned as afflicted, lame, wounded and helpless. Micah may have in mind the crippling effect of sin upon ancient Judah. In 586 BC Jerusalem was destroyed, the temple leveled, and the population deported. Thus were the people of God crippled by the results of their own sin. The prophecy, however, establishes a principle regarding the messianic age which has wider application. The most miserable, helpless and despised will not be excluded from the great salvation which God would bring about in the future.

The lame one would become "a remnant" (*she'erit*). This term is sometimes used in threats to indicate that only a small number of the inhabitants of a place would survive (e.g., Amos 5:3; Isa 7:3). In other passages the term is used as a promise. At least a remnant would survive God's judgment (e.g., Isa 37:31f.). Here in Micah the remnant is not created by judgment but by the saving activity of Yahweh. The remnant has in fact become the very object of God's great plan of redemption.[5] The Lord chooses that which is weak in which to manifest his mighty power.

2. *The banished gathered (4:7a).* The "limping one" is further described as "her that is far removed." The prodigal daughter is brought home. Sin scatters, banishes and expels from the presence of the Lord. A concrete example of this principle is the exile of both Israel and Judah. Salvation, on the other hand, gathers and empowers. The return of the Jews from exile beginning in 538 BC is an illustration of this principle. At the same time, the return from exile is a type, foretaste, or guarantee of the gathering of God's people out of the world which would be effected by the preaching of the Gospel. Paul later would declare that those who formerly were far off have been brought near by the blood of Christ (Eph 2:13). Those distant from God by choice, by ignorance or by judgment would be brought together to form "a strong nation." If those peoples who come to messianic Zion to worship are called "strong nations" (4:3), Israel itself—the people of God—would be no less strong—strong in the Lord and in the power of his might (cf. Eph 6:10).

3. *The leaderless governed (4:7b).* Yahweh would not only gather and transform the flock, he would "reign over them." This promise in no way contradicts the numerous Old Testament references to the rule of a descendant of David in the messianic era (E.g., Hos 3:5; Jer 33:17). At the very least this passage indicates that God would be the founder of that future Davidic kingdom. Yet much more is probably involved. That future Son of David—Jesus of Nazareth—would at the same time be Yahweh incarnate among his people. God governed the Old Covenant kingdom by the hand of David and his successors.

Yet at its best, that old system interposed a sinful and frail human being between God and his people. In this the messianic kingdom would far surpass the glory of the old. The Davidic ruler would himself be deity.

In and through the glorious Davidic King Yahweh would rule over his people "in Zion." The reference here is to that spiritual Zion of Hebrews 12:22, the Zion in which all Christians are citizens. If one is to make any sense out of Hebrews 12:22 Zion must be regarded as an Old Testament designation for the New Testament church. Thus Micah points to the establishment of a perfected monarchy such as never existed in Micah's day or in any age preceding his day.

Yahweh would reign over his people in Zion "from henceforth, even unto forever." Once the theocracy has been established by the Davidic God-man that reign would never cease. In this particular the Old Testament monarchy differs from that spiritual kingdom of New Testament teaching. The rule of the sons of David in physical Zion was interrupted by the banishment of the nation on account of sin. Two points must be stressed here. Since the Messiah was sinless (1) his kingdom would never be taken from him and (2) since he is eternal, his kingdom or reign must also be eternal. From the time he ascended in the cloud to the right hand of the Ancient of Days he has been enthroned on that eternal throne (Dan 7:13f.).

C. Restoration of the Monarchy (4:8).

At the very least Micah 4:8 affirms the restoration of Jerusalem as a royal city after its destruction by the Babylonians (cf. 3:12). Possibly much more is involved in this somewhat cryptic verse. Micah addresses "the tower of the flock." This is further described as the "hill (Ophel) of the daughter of Zion." The "daughter of Zion" is the city of Zion (Jerusalem) personified as a virgin. The "Ophel" seems to have been the royal fortifications which defended Zion from attack.[6] What is here called "the tower of the flock" was that prominent feature of the Davidic fortifications of Zion elsewhere called "the tower of David" (cf. Song 4:4).

The tower which was elevated high over the city is used as a symbol for the restoration of the house of David to power. The tower is here called "tower of the flock" or "flock tower" for three reasons.

First, David rose from a shepherd of a flock of sheep to shepherd of the nation Israel. Second, in the present context God's people have been compared to sheep. Third, the title may be a play upon the fact that Jacob once pitched his tent by a flock tower (cf. Gen 35:21). Both the tower and Ophel convey the idea of security for the flock of God.

Unto the Tower of the Flock "it shall come," viz., "the former dominion." The prepositional phrase (*'adecha*) is significant. It connotes the conquest of every obstacle which stands in the way of the goal. Thus no matter what, "it shall come" to the Tower of the Flock.

What is it that will come to the Tower of the Flock? The reference is to the glorious reigns of David and Solomon. The implication is that that dominion had been lost, or soon would be. The division of the kingdom in 931 BC weakened the rule of the house of David. The destruction of Jerusalem in 586 BC would totally remove dominion from David's descendants. The glory days, however, were still ahead when dominion would be exercised over the daughter of Zion by the Tower of the Flock.

The former dominion is further described as "the kingdom." That kingdom would come "to the daughter of Jerusalem." In 931 BC Jerusalem lost sovereignty over a large portion of the people of God, viz., the ten tribes of the north. In the messianic age Jerusalem in its spiritual counterpart, the church of Christ, would be the center of Messiah's rule over a kingdom which would extend to the ends of the earth.

In Micah 4:8 it is hard to escape the conclusion that "Tower of the Flock" and "Ophel of the daughter of Zion" are prophetic titles for the Messiah personally and not just geographical landmarks of ancient Jerusalem. In Christ the rule of a greater than Solomon commenced. He is the one who ever watches over his flock. He is the fortress which protects his subjects in time of attack.

ZION'S FUTURE VICTORY
Micah 4:9-13

Before the glorious future outlined thus far in chapter 4, Jerusalem must experience the most wrenching ordeal. This salvation oracle is divided into three sub-units each of which begins with the word "now." The term here is rhetorical or logical rather than temporal.

A. Zion's Distress (4:9).

Zion is depicted as a woman laboring in childbirth. The expression "pangs have seized you like a woman in childbirth" is a metaphor depicting reaction to bad news. It usually is used for the terror before an irresistible military assault. The expression became characteristic of Jeremiah.[7]

Micah addressed three rhetorical questions to the daughter of Zion. The second person pronoun is feminine singular. The three questions satirize the failure of human leadership. He asked first, "Why do you cry out aloud?" The dramatic interrogative is used to depict an astonishing situation. The term "cry aloud" (*rua'*) normally refers to the shout of joy or victory. Here, however, the term refers to the agonizing of the woman about to give birth (4:9a).

Second, "Is there no king in you?" This question ridicules the efforts of the kings of Judah to extricate the nation from the oppression of the great powers. In essence he is asking, "Can not your king save you now?" Some take the reference to be to the Lord himself, but in the light of the following question this is unlikely.

Third, "Has your counselor perished?" Zion's "counselor" is her king. He was supposed to have the political wisdom to guide the ship of state through the most treacherous waters. Why should there be such consternation in the nation if they really trusted their royal counselor? (4:9b).

B. Zion's Destruction (4:10a).

The crying of the previous verse is indeed justified. "Writhe and bring forth, O daughter of Zion, as a woman in travail." A fate more dreadful than any could imagine awaited Jerusalem. What the city was about to experience is likened to a terrible, agonizing and long-enduring labor and childbirth.

Leaving metaphor behind, Micah describes in three clauses the fate of the daughter of Zion. First, "you shall go out from the city." Obviously only a calamity of monumental proportions could force these people from their beloved city. Jerusalem was the city of the

Great King, the guarantee of Israel's security, the center and ground of their hope and faith.

Second, "you shall dwell in the field." Micah is depicting the long, slow journey into exile. The comfort of city life would give way to the rigors of camp life. Jerusalem could afford them no protection any more.

Third, "and you shall go unto Babylon." More than a century before it occurred, Micah was predicting the Babylonian exile. To minimize the force of this prediction some have argued here that Babylon is being used of Assyria, the contemporary world power. The Assyrian King Sargon did in fact deport people to Babylon (cf. 2 Kgs 17:24). Isaiah, however, also foresaw Babylon as the ultimate conqueror of Jerusalem (cf. Isa 39:3-6). One must conclude, therefore, that the God who knows the end from the beginning revealed to his two eighth century prophets the ultimate fate of Judah.

C. Zion's Deliverance (4:10b).

Micah looks again beyond the exile to the glorious future of Zion. In Babylon "you shall be delivered." This prophet could see a light at the end of a long dark tunnel. The prophets were consistent in regarding the exile as a terrible, but temporary setback for God's people. The exile would lead Israel to repentance. Repentance would be followed by restoration to fellowship with God and to their beloved homeland.

The deliverance from Babylon would be effected by Yahweh himself. "There Yahweh will redeem you." A kinsman redeemer in ancient Israel had the responsibility of paying the redemption price for relatives sold into slavery or property lost during financial duress. In the psalms and prophets Yahweh is frequently depicted as Israel's redeemer who will stand up for his people and vindicate them. The basic idea of the verb is to recover what is lost and to restore it to its original status. When Yahweh is depicted as Redeemer no redemption price is usually mentioned. Judgment upon the enemies, however, is sometimes identified as the price paid for Israel's deliverance (cf. Isa 43:1-3). Micah hints at that idea when he says that "Yahweh will redeem you from the hand of your enemy."

D. Zion's Ultimate Victory (4:11-13).

Zion (the people of God) redeemed from Babylonian captivity is a type or foreshadowing of Messiah's kingdom. That kingdom would come under vicious assault by enemies. "Many nations have assembled against you." Obviously these are those nations which refused to go up to Zion to learn of the ways of God (cf. vv.1-4). Yahweh on various occasions had assembled nations to use as instruments of judgment against ancient Israel. Here God's purpose is to break the power of those adversaries in a final way (4:11a).

The intention of the nations is twofold. First, the nations intend to defile the holy city and thus render it unsuitable as the chosen place from which God could exercise his rule in this world. Zion would be desecrated when heathen hoards overran the place. Second, they intended to gloat in triumph over the disaster they would inflict on Zion. "Let our eyes gaze on Zion!" The very existence in this world of a holy people is a rebuke and a restraint to the pride of the ungodly. The latter are gripped with a compelling need to silence the word of God and destroy the people of God (4:11b).

Yahweh, however, has other plans. The heathen cannot begin to imagine that their actions fall within the permissive will of God. In that all-out attack they would meet their doom. Yahweh "has gathered them like sheaves to the threshing floor." This agricultural metaphor is elsewhere associated with ruthless warfare (cf. Amos 1:3). What irony! The nations which march to the assault on Zion march to their own annihilation (4:12).

Yahweh urges the daughter of Zion—the citizens of the messianic Jerusalem—to "arise and thresh." They should resist the assault with the assurance that Yahweh was fighting by their side. Threshing is a process which separates the grain from chaff. Perhaps the idea here is that even in the effort to destroy Zion some of the enemy would be converted by the power of the Gospel. The rest of the enemies would be swept away as easily as chaff is blown from the threshingfloor.

How can Zion thresh her enemies? God would turn the threshing ox into a fighting bull. "I will make your horn iron and your hoofs brass." The daughter of Zion has as her mission to smash the pretensions of all those who plot the desecration of the city of God (4:13a).

In language derived from the ancient holy war, Micah pictures the wealth of those invading nations "devoted" (*hacharamti*) to Yahweh. This technical term denotes the destruction of enemy property and the dedication of metal objects to the sanctuary. Thus the individual citizens of Zion would not be enriched by the destruction of the attacking nations. The victory is the Lord's. His cause would be enriched by the overthrow and/or conversion of his enemies. This would testify to the fact that Yahweh was and is "Lord of the earth" (4:13b).

ENDNOTES

1. See Acts 2:17; Heb 1:2; Jas 5:3; 1 Pet 1:5,20; 2 Pet 3:3; 1 John 2:18. Cf. Leslie Allen: "The term is used of chronological sequence. It refers . . . to an important turning point within history when Yahweh will bring about his will among men as never before." *The Books of Joel, Obadiah, Jonah and Micah* in "The New International Commentary on the Old Testament" (Grand Rapids: Eerdmans, 1976), p. 324.
2. On the stream issuing forth from the temple mount see Ps 46:4; 65:9; Isa 33:21; Joel 3:18; Ezek 47.
3. On the spread of peace through the growth of Christ's kingdom see Acts 10:36; Rom 5:1; Eph 2:14,15,17.
4. On the banishment of Israel from the land due to sin see Deut 30:4; Zeph 3:19; Neh 1:9; Isa 56:8.
5. James L. Mays, *Micah, a Commentary* in "The Old Testament Library" (Philadelphia: Westminster, 1976), p. 101.
6. For a discussion of the terms employed in Micah 4:8 see Keil and Delitzsch *Old Testament Commentaries; Ezekiel XXV to Malachi* (Grand Rapids: Associated, n.d.), pp. 1143f.
7. See Jer 4:31; 6:24; 13:21; 22:23; 30:6; 49:24; 50:43. Isaiah used the expression of Babylon in 13:8; 21:3.

CHAPTER TWENTY-FOUR

The Glory of Bethlehem's Ruler
Micah 5

The glories of the messianic age continue to be described in Micah 5. The theme here is Zion's glorious king and the ultimate triumph of his kingdom.

ZION'S GLORIOUS KING
Micah 5:1-5a

In this unit the reader enters the Holy of Holies of Micah's prophecy. This is a prominent peak in a whole range of glorious promises to ancient Israel. Here, as so often in Micah, the prophecy moves from grief to hope.

A. Zion's Desperation (5:1).

A time of deep degradation would precede the messianic age. As in 4:9 and 4:11 this oracle begins with the logical "now." The daughter of Zion is urged to "gather in troops." She is figuratively called "daughter of troops" so as to produce assonance with the imperative. The figure means that the daughter of Zion is a lady under attack. The term troops (*gedud*) means a band of raiders. The term is used poetically for the Babylonian army (Jer 18:22). This prophecy was probably uttered after the 701 BC invasion of Judah by Sennacherib. The thrust here is that once again the daughter of Zion would come under attack.

The reason the daughter of Zion was to gather in troops was that "a siege he has set against us." The one who sets the siege is not identified here. The term *matsor*, however, is used especially of the siege of Jerusalem by Nebuchadnezzar.[1] Thus the siege of Jerusalem by the Babylonians in 587-86 BC is probably in view.

A second terrible condition would befall Israel. "With the rod he has smitten upon the jaw the judge of Israel." The enemy would humiliate the "judge" or ruler of Israel. The use of the term here suggests a shameful contrast with the heroic Judges of the past who smashed the enemies which came against ancient Israel. The irony here is that the one who should smite evildoers with his scepter is himself smitten by the rod. This is the ultimate humiliation which could befall a nation. Micah is probably not thinking of any particular judge or king. Humiliating subservience to foreign powers characterized the reigns of Manasseh, Jehoahaz, Jehoiakim, and Zedekiah. Others see here a reference to the bloody persecutions of Antiochus Epiphanes in the second century or the pompous pretensions of Herod the Great. The basic idea is that at the time of deepest degradation the Messiah would come.

B. The Coming Ruler (5:2-3a).

Micah speaks of the coming Ruler who would liberate God's people from the oppressor. He speaks of the place, purpose and significance of the birth of this Ruler.

1. The place of his birth (5:2a). Yahweh now addresses Bethlehem Ephrathah, the scene of a dramatic development in the divine program. The older name Ephrathah ("fruitful") is added to Bethlehem ("house of bread") to distinguish the southern town of this name from the town of the same name in the region of Zebulun (cf. Josh 19:15). Bethlehem is addressed with a masculine pronoun to establish a contrast with the helpless daughter of Zion in the preceding verse. Something powerful will happen in Bethlehem. In that village the hope of national recovery lies.

The smallness of Bethlehem is stressed. The village was too small "to be among the thousands of Judah." Bethlehem is not even named among the more than one hundred cities allotted to the tribe of Judah (cf. Josh 15:21-63). From this unlikely quarter Yahweh would bring forth a deliverer for his people.

2. *The purpose of his birth (5:2b).* From Bethlehem "he shall go forth to be ruler over Israel." A glorious Ruler would again come out of Bethlehem. Strictly speaking the words do not denote a birth, but the context strongly points in this direction. The chief priests and scribes when consulted by Herod the Great correctly interpreted this verse to refer to the birthplace of the Coming One (cf. Matt 2:1ff.). The belief that Bethlehem would be the birthplace of Messiah was widespread in the days of Jesus (cf. John 7:42). Bethlehem, which is referred to here with masculine pronouns, is regarded as the father of the coming Ruler.

The Coming One would go forth from Bethlehem "for me," i.e., Yahweh. Just as Yahweh provided for himself a king from among the sons of Jesse (1 Sam 16:1), so God would again provide a Ruler for his own redemptive purposes. Bethlehem's Ruler would be devoted to the will of the Lord. He would in a special way belong to the Lord. Yet at the same time he would be "ruler over Israel." His authority would be over all to which the term "Israel" could legitimately be applied. Under the New Covenant Israel consists of all those who have put their faith in Jesus as Messiah (Gal 6:16; Rom 9:6-29). Over the church of Christ Jesus is absolute Ruler (Eph 1:22; 5:23).

3. *The significance of his birth (5:2b-3c).* The Bethlehem Ruler would be one who had prior existence. "His goings forth are from of old." He was active on behalf of his people long before he appeared at Bethlehem. Jesus did not hesitate to affirm his preexistence (cf. John 8:58). This prophecy, however, does not merely assert that the Bethlehem Ruler came forth from heaven, but that he had been actively involved in the leadership of his people in the distant past. The terms "from of old" (*miqqedem*) and "from ancient days" (*mime 'olam*) are used of the Patriarchal age (Micah 7:14,20) and even of

eternity prior to creation (Prov 8:22f.). The reference is probably to the revelations of Messiah as the Angel of Yahweh throughout the Old Testament. This Ruler who would go out from Bethlehem had already gone out of heaven on many occasions to lead his people (5:2b).

In view of the fact that Bethlehem must eventually produce the glorious Ruler, it follows that the judgment threatened in 3:12, 4:10 and 5:1 must in some sense continue until the day of his appearing. The fact that Messiah would be born in Bethlehem and not in Jerusalem, the city of David, presupposes that the family of David would have lost the throne. Such could only be the case if Israel had been overrun by her enemies. The expression "he (Yahweh) will give them (Israel) up" points in this direction. The verb "give up" (*natan*) is elsewhere used to refer to the surrender of Israel into the power of her enemies as a punishment for sin (cf. 1 Kgs 14:16).

Yahweh would give his people over to the power of their enemies "until the time when she who is with child shall have given birth." God's abandonment of Israel would only be temporary. Israel's oppression would continue until the birth of Messiah. "She who is with child" must be the virgin who would conceive and bear a son called Immanuel (Isa 7:14). The Immanuel promise was uttered about thirty years prior to the present passage. Thus the future king's birth would signal the beginning of the end of the nation's oppression (5:3a).

C. A Glorious Reign (5:3b-5a).

Numerous blessings would follow the birth of Messiah in Bethlehem. The first blessing is that of conversion which Micah expresses by use of the verb "return." The returnees consist of "the sons of Israel" and "the remnant of his brethren." Israelites were his brethren according to the flesh. They were the first to receive the blessing of Messiah's coming. The "remnant of his brethren" must be his brethren spiritually, those who put their faith in Messiah (Heb 2:11; Matt 12:50; John 11:51ff.). The "remnant of his brethren" must be converted Gentiles, the other sheep which were not of the fold of physical Israel (John 10:16).

Second, Bethlehem's Ruler would "stand and shepherd" the flock of the Lord. The term "shepherd" in the ancient Near East embodies the ideal of kingship. In Israel the term may recall the fact that David was taken from the flock to care for God's people. The term "stand" signals vigilance, active involvement in his shepherding role.[2] New Testament theology frequently uses the shepherd imagery of Jesus.[3]

Third, the Ruler would be endowed with "the strength of Yahweh." He is worthy of the throne. This Ruler is not subject to human weakness. Though put to the test, his strength is irresistible.

Fourth, the Ruler reflects "the majesty (ge'on) of the name of Yahweh his God." He would possess the same glory in which Yahweh manifests his deity on the earth. He is in fact the Mighty God of Isaiah 9:5.

Fifth, this Ruler's authority is delegated to him by "his God."[4] Since he was born of a human mother, Yahweh can be called "his God." While in the flesh the Son was subordinate to the Father (cf. Matt 27:46; John 20:17). The language points to a special relation between this Ruler and Yahweh.

Sixth, the Ruler's power would provide security and stability for God's people. "They shall sit," i.e., dwell in safety. The original promise to David was that under his descendants Israel would never again be oppressed by wicked people (2 Sam 7:10). This ideal was not realized in Old Testament times. Under Messiah's powerful reign, however, the people of God would enjoy perfect security.

Seventh, the future Ruler would rule over a universal kingdom. "And now he will be great unto the ends of the earth." The term "now" introduces the contrast between the former time when he gave them over to the enemy (cf. v. 3), and the time presently in view when he would shepherd them. This explains why his subjects would dwell securely under his reign. He would be known and feared to the very ends of the earth. This universal sovereignty is also the subject of other personal messianic prophecies.[5]

Eighth, the future Ruler would be the hope of deliverance. "And this one will be peace." "Peace" (*shalom*) is salvation in its most comprehensive sense. It involves deliverance from danger, security and prosperity. The future Ruler would build upon the model of Solomon who brought *shalom* to ancient Israel (1 Kgs 4:24). In other personal messianic prophecies the concept of *shalom* is also associated with the appearance of this glorious Ruler (cf. Isa 9:5,7; 11:6-9). The Apostle Paul (Eph 2:14) sees the unification of Jew and Gentile in the New Covenant Israel as the fulfillment of this aspect of Micah's prophecy (5:5a).

ZION'S ULTIMATE VICTORY
Micah 5:5b-15

Messiah, the Prince of Peace (Isa 9:6), brings peace with him and gives it to his people. The remaining verses of Micah 5 develop the theme of messianic peace. He brings this peace to his people in four ways, viz., (1) by defending Israel against external attack; (2) by empowering his people to overcome the enemy; (3) by destroying all false supports upon which people tend to lean; and (4) by executing vengeance upon those who refuse to be converted.

A. Defense of Zion (5:5b-6).

Micah uses Assyria, the major power of his own day, to symbolize all the hostile forces which might attack Messiah's kingdom. At times those enemy powers might even "tread in our palaces," i.e., meet with some measure of success in their attack. Against this enemy God's people would set up "seven shepherds and eight princes of men." These spiritual leaders function as subordinates of the chief Shepherd. In prophetic symbolism seven is the perfect number, the number which points to the completed work of God. The idea is that seven would be enough to defend God's people, eight would be more than enough. The phrase "princes of men" means literally those anointed, appointed or installed from among men. Messiah selects from among men those who will assist him in shepherding the flock and protecting it from enemies (5:5b).

The shepherds appointed by the Chief Shepherd would "shepherd," i.e., rule, "the land of Assyria with the sword." That Assyria is used here symbolically is indicated by the parallel phrase "the land of Nimrod." Nimrod was the founder of the first empire in Mesopotamia (Gen 10:8ff.). He was an anti-God tyrant who built his empire with slave labor. The use of his name here suggests the nature of the kingdom of the world which opposes the people of God. The point here is that the church of Christ not only repulses the attack of her enemies. She also attacks the enemy in his own territory (5:6a).

The missionary activity of the church is here depicted, as frequently in Old Testament prophetic literature, as a military conquest of enemy territory (cf. Amos 9:12). While many nations will go up to Zion to learn the ways of the Lord (4:1f.), others will persist in hostility to the kingdom of God. These hostile kingdoms are here called "Assyria" and "land of Nimrod." The soldiers of Christ will surge even into the "gates" of the land of Nimrod, i.e., the centers of power and government. Perhaps Jesus had this passage in mind when he declared that not even the gates of Hades would not prevail against his church (Matt 16:18).

Before moving on to yet more glorious promises for messianic Israel, Micah reminds his readers that all which would be accomplished against Assyria would be the work of Messiah. "And he will deliver from the Assyrian when he shall come into our land and when he treads in our border." The "he" here is obviously Messiah, the Ruler who would be born in Bethlehem (5:6b).

B. Empowerment of Zion (5:7-9).

A second way Messiah would prove himself to be peace for his people is by empowering them to overcome their enemies. The "remnant of Jacob," i.e., the saved—the redeemed, those who embrace Messiah—"will be in the midst of many peoples." Those who have come to Zion for divine instruction would then spread out into the world to share the message of Messiah with all who would listen. Two figures are used to convey the result of the work of the redeemed among the unbelieving nations.

1. The refreshing dew (5:7). The message of salvation falls like dew or showers from heaven on the barren hearts of the heathen. In these words the promise to Abraham ("bless them that bless you") is projected into the age of Messiah. Those who treat the spiritual descendants of Abraham sympathetically and listen to the word which they preach will find refreshment and life. The message of the redeemed remnant is of divine origin, not human invention. These showers of spiritual blessing "are not looked for my men, nor awaited by the sons of men."

2. The rending lion (5:8-9). The remnant may bring a refreshing message to the nations, but that remnant would be anything but feeble. The redeemed of the Lord would be "like a lion among the beasts of a forest, like a young lion among the flocks of sheep." The picture is one of invincible power. The relationship between the people of God and the nations would be like that between a powerful lion and weaker wild and domestic animals. When this lion passes by he "treads down and tears." Here is the reverse side of Genesis 12:3, viz., "I will curse those who curse you." Those who attempt to resist the victorious march of God's church will be crushed. Believers are more than conquerors (Rom 8:33-39). Strongholds of sin, unbelief and superstitution are overthrown by the powerful proclamation of the Gospel (2 Cor 10:4). Those who do not believe the message of saving grace will be condemned (Mark 16:16). From this condemnation "there is no deliverer" (5:8).

The unit promising the empowerment of Zion concludes with a wish. The context suggests that the addressee is Zion. "May your hand be lifted up over your adversaries and all of your enemies be cut off." A hand is said to be high when mighty deeds are being performed and when the foe is being vanquished (cf. Isa 26:11). Before Zion can enter the work of peace she must deal with those who oppose her beneficent work (5:9).

C. Destruction of Props (5:10-14).

All the political and religious props upon which ancient Judah leaned for support would be removed in the age of Messiah.

1. Horses and chariots (5:10). The triumphs of Zion would not be accomplished by conventional instruments of war. Indeed, in that messianic day (cf. 4:1,6) Yahweh would cut off from Zion "your horses." Christ's kingdom is not of this world. God would purge his people of misplaced trust in carnal weapons. The background of this prediction is the trade with Egypt in horses and chariots. This trade was obnoxious to Micah and Isaiah (cf. Isa 30:15-17; 31:1-3). The verb "cut off" is used in the law of Moses to refer to the removal of persons who had violated the holiness of Israel (e.g., Lev 17:10). By cutting off the offenders Yahweh would bring pressure on the entire nation to shun that which was offensive to his holiness.

2. *Cities and strongholds (5:11).* Just as Yahweh would cut off horses and chariots, so would he also "cut off the cities" and "cast down . . . strongholds." God's people would not need the protection of walled cities (cf. Zech 2:4f.). The background of this prediction may be the capture of the forty-six cities by Sennacherib during his invasion of Judah in 701 BC.

3. *Sorceries and soothsayers (5:12).* In the religious realm, Yahweh would cut off from messianic Zion "sorceries" (NASB) or "witchcraft" (*keshaphim*) and "fortune tellers" (*me'onenim*). The precise distinction between these two classes is not clear. Apparently the reference is to people who practice divination using omens derived from natural or manipulated signs. Both groups are mentioned together and condemned in the law and prophets (Deut 18:10f.; Jer 27:9). Once the Prophet like unto Moses appeared (Deut 18:15), God's people would no longer have any desire to be involved with anything which offends their God.

4. *Idolatrous paraphernalia (5:13-14).* Yahweh would also cut off in that future day "graven images" (*pesilim*) and "pillars" (*mattsebhoth*). Worship of the God of the Bible is supposed to be aniconic, i.e., no images (cf. Exod 20:4; Deut 7:5,25). The use of these pagan pillars is condemned throughout the Old Testament (e.g., Deut 16:22). These objects are scornfully called here the work of men's hands (cf. Hosea 14:3; Isa 2:8). Perhaps Hezekiah's campaign to rid the land of such pagan paraphernalia forms the background of this prediction. The point is, messianic Israel would no longer desire to worship anything made by man. Their allegiance would be completely devoted to the Lord (5:13).

In that future day Yahweh would "pluck up" the Asherim which were such a prominent part of the apostasy recorded in the Old Testament. Asherim were emblems of the female deity Asherah, the consort of Baal (cf. Judg 3:7). The prophets of this goddess were driven from northern Israel by Elijah (1 Kgs 18:19). As time went on the term Asherim came to be applied to any wooden post or tree which symbolized the female deity at sanctuaries (2 Kgs 23:4). Since the object was fixed in the ground it is said to be plucked up or uprooted (5:14a).

Finally, Yahweh declares that he would destroy their "cities." In verse 11 Micah declared that the Lord would cut off their cities as defensive fortresses. Here the cities are destroyed as centers of idolatry (5:14b).[6] In this passage the gross heathen idolatry of Old Testament times is a figure denoting that more refined idolatry which will exist in the world until the coming of the Lord. The extermination of every kind of heathen idolatry is simply a prophetic way of expressing the purification of the church of Christ from everything of ungodly nature.

D. Vengeance on Enemies (5:15).

God's promise of peace would be realized because he would "execute vengeance." "Vengeance" (*naqam*) is a legal term for the action of a royal suzerain against rebels who do not acknowledge his sovereignty. The reference is to the exercise of legitimate sovereignty in a punishment which must occur if the rule of God is to be maintained in the midst of hostile humanity. The ultimate manifestation of the vengeance of God will be at the second coming of Christ (2 Thess 1:8).

The vengeance would be executed "in wrath and anger." This is not the irrational anger of a wounded ego, but the measured, appropriate, and just response to transgression in a moral universe. Both terms are anthropomorphisms used to express the inexorable and irresistible certainty of the divine response to human rebellion. Here there is an added dimension. The just retribution against transgression serves to rescue God's people from oppression by their enemies. The complete enjoyment of God's peace can only take place when God deals finally and conclusively with the wicked.

The victims of God's vengeance here are "the nations which do not hearken," i.e., obey the word of God (cf. JB). Yahweh is sovereign over all nations. Whether they realize it or not, the nations of the world are subject to the sovereign will of their heavenly King. As they witness the great acts of salvation which God would perform for his people, the nations should give heed to the claims and demands of Yahweh. If they do not submit to his sovereignty by acknowledging his Son, he will take vengeance on them.

ENDNOTES

1. On the term *matsor* used of the Babylonian siege see 2 Kgs 24:10; 25:2; Jer 52:5; Ezek 4:3,7; 5:2. It can either refer to a siege (Ezek 4:2) or to a siege rampart (Deut 20:20).

2. Leslie Allen thinks the term "stand" is an allusion to the traditional coronation ceremony, in which the royal prince stood beside a pillar in the Temple to be anointed (cf. 2 Kgs 11:14). *The Books of Joel, Obadiah, Jonah and Micah* in "The New International Commentary on the Old Testament" (Grand Rapids: Eerdmans, 1976), p. 346.

3. On Jesus as shepherd, see Heb 13:20; 1 Pet 2:25; Rev 7:17; John 10:11,16.

4. The phrase may go beyond the concept of authority. Micah may mean that Yahweh's name, i.e., his character or essence, would be in this Ruler. He would be the name of Yahweh personified. See John 1:14; 10:30; 14:9; Eph 1:20ff.

5. On the universal reign of Messiah see for example Pss 2:8; 72:8; Zech 9:10. Cf. Luke 1:32 which seems to be based on Micah 5:4.

6. Some argue that the term *'arekah* translated "cities" (NIV; NASB; RSV; ASV) must be rendered "enemies," "idols" or "obelisks" (ASV margin) because it is parallel to Asherim. Cf. BDB, p. 786 col. a.

CHAPTER TWENTY-FIVE

Present Repentance Pleaded
Micah 6:1-7:6

Having announced the imminent judgment, and promised the ultimate blessing, Micah now earnestly pleads for repentance on the part of his contemporaries. In so doing he points out the way of salvation.

THE CASE AGAINST JUDAH
Micah 6:1-8

Micah urges his contemporaries to "hear what Yahweh is about to say." The prophet is introducing what follows as the language of Yahweh himself. When God speaks, the highest duty of humankind is to listen, i.e., obey (6:1a).

A. The Opening of Court (6:1b-2).

The prophet is called upon to "arise" and present Yahweh's case against his people. The verb (*qum*) has a technical meaning. It signals preparation for speech (cf. Judg 20:8; Jer. 1:17), especially in the context of a court (cf. Deut 19:15f.).

Micah is to "contend," i.e., make a complaint, "with the mountains." The language does not make clear whether the mountains are (1) the judges, (2) the witnesses, or (3) the accused. Perhaps Micah is to condemn the mountains as the locale for much of the idolatrous practice in ancient Judah. More likely, however, the mountains and hills are viewed as the witnesses against the defendant Judah. The mountains had witnessed the original covenant between God and his people. They had witnessed the faithfulness of Yahweh toward his people, and their faithlessness in regard to him. Were they able to speak, these witnesses would bear testimony which would seal the doom of Judah (6:1b). In similar passages it is the heavens and earth which are called upon to bear witness (cf. e.g., Deut 4:26).

The prophet obeyed God and addressed the mountains. The mountains are called the "enduring ones." They had stood where God had stationed them at the "foundations of the earth," i.e., the creation. The mountains are alerted that the great King had a legal case with his people. Thus the litigants are introduced. Yahweh is the plaintiff and his people collectively the defendant. The term "case" (*rib*) is the technical name for a formal controversy between two parties. The point of such controversy was to submit to judgment as to which party was in the right. The language "his people" suggests that this is special covenant litigation. In covenant lawsuits God refers to Israel with terms of endearment (cf. Hos 4:1).

Yahweh is about to "argue" (*yitvakkach*) or "litigate" with Israel. The Hebrew form suggests a process in which the defendant would be given the opportunity to speak in his own defense. The root of this verb is used in the court vocabulary of the Old Testament for one who upholds what is right (cf. Amos 5:10; Isa 29:21). Thus God champions what is right in his case against Judah. Truth must come out in this formal trial (6:2b).

B. The Plaintiff's Question (6:3).

The direct address of Yahweh begins in 6:3. He addresses, not the mountains, but his people. "O my people, what have I done to you?" In paraphrase the Lord is asking, What have I done to deserve your neglect. He is quite ready to hear any credible evidence against him if

Judah can produce such. The tone here is not that of an outraged plaintiff, but one of a wounded spouse or parent. Many years later the Lord Jesus would ask his auditors, "Which of you convicts me of sin?" (John 8:46).

Some hint of Judah's complaint against Yahweh is found in the second question which Yahweh's asks his people. "How have I wearied you?" The verb "wearied" *(la'ah)* suggests to weary the patience of a person by demands of too great severity (cf. Isa 43:23), or by failing to perform one's promises (cf. Jer 2:31). A derived noun describes a condition of hardship and oppression (e.g., Exod 18:8; Num 20:14). People can become so beaten down and distressed that they lose hope. Perhaps the recent invasion by Sennacherib had discouraged many. While Jerusalem was spared miraculously, the countryside was devastated. Many had been carried off into Assyrian captivity. Judah was exhausted. The people held Yahweh responsible for their condition.

Yahweh calls upon Judah to "answer against me," i.e., produce evidence to support their grievance. Had the Lord really deserted them, or had they in fact deserted God? In 3:11 Micah alluded to the false trust in Yahweh manifested by the crooked leaders. Is the prophet speaking here at a different time and under different circumstances? Is he addressing a different audience? Or is he suggesting that the trust proclaimed in 3:11 was false, a misuse of faith to justify corruption? Probably the latter is the correct interpretation. The people had departed from the Lord in attitude and action and did not even know it. They were "weary" with the demands of true faith.

C. The Plaintiff's Case (6:4-5).

In defense of himself Yahweh appeals to history. God's people are called upon to "remember" what Yahweh had done for them in the past. This verb *(zachar)* is often used for reflection on Yahweh's saving activity (e.g., Ps 77:11; 119:52). Far from affording any excuse for complaint, God's treatment of Israel should have been the ground for national gratitude. God's people are not to live in the past. They must recognize, however, that past events have forceful implications in the present and for the future. Four gracious acts of Yahweh are mentioned here.

1. The Exodus (6:4a). Micah mentions first, the redemption from Egypt. "I brought you up from the land of Egypt." The Exodus event was at the center of Old Testament faith much like the cross and resurrection are at the heart of New Testament faith. In Hebrew the verb "brought up" (*he'eleticha*) is similar in sound to the verb "wearied" (*hel'eticha*) in the previous verse. This deliberate play on words places in juxtaposition the grace of God and the ingratitude of his people (6:4a).

The Exodus was not merely the migration of people from one land to another such as was common in the ancient world. The coming out of Egypt was an act of redemption. "From the house of bondage I redeemed you." The verb "redeem" (*padah*) means to free someone who is bound by legal obligation by the payment of a price. The word is frequently connected with the Exodus (e.g., Deut 7:8; 13:5). No redemption price, however, is named other than Yahweh's manifestation of grace and power (e.g., Deut 9:26).

2. Wilderness leadership (6:4b). Yahweh mentions a second gracious act which he had performed for his people. "I sent before you Moses, Aaron and Miriam." The redeemed people were not left leaderless. The ancient Targum on this passage suggested that Moses taught them the law, Aaron showed them the way of atonement, and Miriam taught the women. The "sending" of Moses and Aaron is mentioned in three other passages (Josh 24:5; 1 Sam 12:8; Ps 105:26). The joint leadership of Moses and Aaron is celebrated in Ps 77:20. The leadership role here assigned to Miriam may be based on her actions at the Red Sea (Exod 15:20).

3. Frustration of Balak (6:5a). The third historical event which Yahweh bids his wayward people to remember occurred just before the entrance into Canaan. God's people should remember "what Balak king of Moab devised and what Balaam the son of Beor answered him." The reference here is to that last desperate plot to prevent Israel from entering the Promised Land. Balak intended to use magic spells to cripple the fighting ability of the armies of Israel. God turned Balak's curses into blessings through the mouth of Balaam (Num 22-24). The triumph of Yahweh over the powers of magic is regarded as one of the great saving acts of God in Old Testament theology (cf. Josh 24:9f.).

4. Entrance into Canaan (6:5b). The words "from Shittim to Gilgal" point to the successful entrance into the Promised Land. Shittim was the last encampment before crossing Jordan. There God punished Israel severely for falling into idolatry, but did not reject them. Thus the term "Shittim" recalled the grace of God extended to a sinful people. Gilgal was the first encampment in Canaan. In spite of their sin, God brought them in—into that land he had promised to Abraham, Isaac and Jacob.

The purpose of remembering these past events is "that you may know the righteous deeds of Yahweh." The past deeds of Yahweh are called "righteous" because in them he demonstrated his faithfulness to the ancient promises made to the Patriarchs. The "deeds" of the Lord are one means by which God reveals his identity. The recitation of all that God had done in the past proved that he had not wronged his people in any way. Thus Yahweh is vindicated before the covenant court which was convened in 6:1.

D. The Question of the Defendant (6:6-9).

Micah places questions in the mouths of his listeners. They ask how they can discharge their obligation to God. The four questions become increasingly sarcastic. This suggests that the prophet's auditors were in essence denying that there was anything wrong with their relationship with Yahweh.

1. The basic question (6:6a). "With what shall I come before Yahweh, bow myself to God on high?" The question presupposes that one must come before God with something. The question also presupposes that God is the problem. Something must be done to change his attitude toward Judah. What appalling spiritual ignorance! They actually thought that they could bribe God with gifts to change his attitude toward them! At least they realized that they must "bow before him." God is "on high," i.e., in heaven. From "on high" (*marom*) Yahweh hears, and heals and helps those who come before him in the proper spirit (cf. Isa 58:4). Creatures of the earth must humble themselves before him. The problem was that the people of the eighth century defined humility in terms of sacrificial ritual rather than daily righteousness. Humility before God requires obedience to his word. Without that ritual humility is a sham.

2. *The value question (6:6b).* "Shall I come to him with whole burnt offerings, with calves of a year old?" Burnt offerings were voluntary sacrifices which were made when a worshiper wished to reestablish his relationship with God. Multiple burnt offerings would mean that the worshiper had offended God in the worst way. The fact that no sin offering is mentioned may suggest that these people recognized no failing on their part, at least none that they could identify. A calf might be offered to the Lord after it was eight days old (Lev 22:27; Exod 22:30). "Calves of a year old" would be much more valuable as an offering. Did Yahweh want from them more numerous and more expensive sacrifices? The very question indicates that they had not really listened to what the prophets like Isaiah and Micah had been saying.

3. *The impudent question (6:7a).* "Will Yahweh delight in thousands of rams, with ten thousand rivers of oil?" This question implies that Yahweh is greedy, unreasonable, even blood-thirsty. The term "delight" (*ratsah*) belongs to the technical vocabulary of the priest whose job it was to examine sacrifices and declare them fit for presentation to God. If God through the priest accepted the offering, then the worshiper was accepted for the purpose which he had in view when he made the offering.[1] Oil was used in connection with the meal offering (cf. Exod 29:2; Lev 2:1).

4. *The ultimate question (6:7b).* "Shall I give my firstborn for my transgression, the fruit of my belly for the sin of my soul?" Here for the first time the people mention their sin and transgression. They do so in such a way, however, as to mock the notion that they really had a sin problem.

These people must surely have been aware of the episode in which Abraham was commanded to offer up Isaac (Gen 22). They must surely have known the law of the firstborn sons (Exod 13:12f.). In both cases Yahweh was teaching his people that he wanted the surrender of the spirit, not the flesh. Human sacrifice was an abomination to Yahweh (Lev 18:21). By raising this question these people at the very least were demonstrating that they did not know the will of Yahweh. In reality the question mocks God. It assumes that if their sin was all that bad, human sacrifice would be required. But since everyone knew that human sacrifice was not acceptable, their sin must not be all that bad.

E. The Declaration of the Prophet (6:8).

The people had directed their sarcastic questions to Micah. He answered them sternly and plainly. God had not left anyone in doubt with regard to his expectations. "It has been declared to you, O man, what is good." The language here transcends ancient Israel. The fundamental expectations which follow are addressed to "O man," i.e., any man or humanity in general. "Good" is what Yahweh requires, what brings his blessing. The Lord looks for three qualities in all mankind.

First, Micah says that Yahweh requires all men to be practicing "justice" (*mishpat*). Perhaps justice heads Micah's list because social injustice was the great sin which scarred the society of his day (cf. 3:1,8). Practicing justice means to uphold what is right according to the will of Yahweh. Thus God requires the sacrifice of life, not the sacrifice of multitudes of animals to make things right with him. Upholding what is right often requires the sacrifice of personal aims and ambitions.

Second, Micah mentioned "loving mercy." The justice which God wants is based on kindness and mercy (*chesed*). The Hebrew word points to conduct which is becoming those who are covenant brothers. "Loving mercy" is an active quality. It is translating "mercy" into deeds.

As the last requirement Micah listed "make yourself humble to walk with your God." The Hebrew verb "make yourself humble" (*hattsnea'*) is used elsewhere only in Proverbs 11:2. The term refers not so much to self-abasement as to measured and careful conduct. One who would please God must not presume to go his own way. Rather he defers to the way and will of God as revealed in the word.

Without the three qualities mentioned in 6:8 sacrificial ritual had no significance.

A WARNING TO JUDAH
Micah 6:9-16

Having set forth clearly to an arrogant people what God required of them, Micah next warned his auditors of the consequences of rejecting the word of God.

A. Opening Exhortation (6:9).

Before the actual warning, Micah introduced the speaker. The "voice of Yahweh" is now speaking through his prophet to "the city," i.e., Jerusalem. This gives greater emphasis to the warning that follows. "Wisdom" (*tushiyyah*) or common sense would "keep your name in sight."[2] The "name" here is God's revelation of himself in nature, history and the word. In view of the fact that Yahweh was speaking, the city had best focus on his name. They needed to come to grips with the true nature of God. False theology is at the root of loose living (6:9a).

The citizens of Jerusalem are further exhorted to "hear the rod." The "rod" (*matteh*) is a symbol of judgment. Thus the people are called upon to listen to the message of judgment with which Yahweh was threatening them. In the eighth century BC the rod of judgment was Assyria (cf. Isa 10:5,24). Though Judah found it hard to believe, Yahweh himself had appointed that rod to discipline his people (6:9b).

B. Prevailing Sin (6:10-12).

The exhortation to heed the revelation of God is followed by a review of the prevailing sins of his society. Four areas of corruption are identified.

1. Contraband in the house (6:10). Micah uses the question form to sharpen the accusation and solicit self condemnation. "Yet is there in the house of the wicked the treasures of wickedness, and the ephah of leanness which is cursed?" No one could deny that at the very time Micah was speaking the fruit of ill-gotten gain was found in the houses of the wicked men of Judah. An "ephah" was essentially the size of a bushel. A "lean" ephah would be a false measure which could be used to cheat unsuspecting customers. Micah calls such a false measure "cursed" (*ze'umah*). Similar language is found both in the law (Deut 25:14-16) and in the wisdom books (e.g., Prov 20:10). God cannot stand any gain which is achieved by dishonest means (6:10).

2. Fraud in the shop (6:11). Apparently the businessmen in Judah saw no connection between their perverse practices and their relationship with the Lord. They graduated from the school which taught "Let the buyer beware." So Micah asked another question designed to prick the conscience: "Can I be pure with wicked balances and with a bag of deceitful weights?"[3] The reference here is to having a set of small weights for the purpose of selling goods, and a large set for use in making purchases. Thus the sharp businessman would cheat both in the buying and in the selling. Certainly the victims of such chicanery would not regard such a merchant as "pure" or innocent. Could they really believe that the Lord would overlook such practices? (6:11).

3. *Oppression in the courts (6:12a).* The rich men of Jerusalem "are filled with violence." The term "violence" (*chamas*) may refer to the crooked business practices of the preceding verse. The noun, however, seems to go beyond fraudulent merchandising. The term *chamas* seems to refer to the arbitrary and autocratic appropriation of what belongs to God or one's neighbor. Often the term involves physical assault. Thus the charge is that the rich men were attacking the less powerful such as widows, orphans and poor. Most likely they were employing the courts and perversion of the law to accomplish this (cf. 3:1-3).

4. *Falsehood among the citizens (6:12b).* The whole population was characterized by deceit. "Her inhabitants speak a lie and their tongue is deceitful in their mouth." The oppressed were as wicked as the oppressors. They would be acting the same as the rich men were they in a position to do so.

C. Impending Doom (6:13).

Already the effects of divine judgment were being felt.[4] "And I also have made you sick with your smitings." God's punishment against Judah is the consequence of, or retribution for, the sins just enumerated. To make a nation sick is to deprive that nation of its civic well-being. The idea is that God has made Judah incurably sick. The "you" is masculine singular, but it represents the population of the entire kingdom of Judah (cf. v.16). God's response to their sin is already evident even as the prophet delivered this oracle. With the rod of verse 9 Yahweh had smitten Judah with many blows. The reference is to the hardships, cruelty and destruction inflicted by Sennacherib in his invasion of Judah in 701 BC. Those "smitings," however, were only the beginning. Ultimately the smitings of God would "make desolate," i.e., lead to the total destruction of Jerusalem (6:13).

D. Increasing Futility (6:14-15).

In the language of the so-called futility curse of the law (cf. Lev 26:26; Deut 28:30-31, 38-40) Micah depicts the consequences of the administration of Yahweh's discipline. He cites five examples of labor or effort expended with no results, or at least no satisfying results.

First, they would experience painful hunger. "You shall eat and not be satisfied." No matter how much they ate they would still experience a gnawing hunger. Some take the reference to be to physical hunger experienced when they were under siege. Others see here the point that those who are motivated by greed to corrupt practices will never have enough, i.e., they continually go deeper into sin. Still others see in these words the truth that without God's blessing men experience a spiritual hunger which can never be satisfied. In any case, this hunger is clearly a result of the administration of God's punishment (6:14a).

Second, their possessions would be given to the enemy. Their efforts to remove their possessions and dependents to a place of security would be futile. "To the sword I will give it," i.e., Yahweh would give all that they possessed into the hands of their enemies. The irony here is that all that they had stolen from others through fraudulent dealings would be taken from them forcefully (6:14b).

Third, they would be deprived of their harvest. "You will sow and not harvest." The enemy would invade the land after the time of planting and before the harvest, thus frustrating all their labor in planting the crop (6:15a).

Fourth, they would lose the comforts of life. "You shall tread olives, but not anoint yourselves with oil." Olives were normally crushed in a mill. Better grade olive oil was beaten (cf. Exod 27:20). This is the only place in the Old Testament which speaks of the treading of olives. Oil was used as a medicine for wounds (Luke 10:34), for cosmetic purposes (Ps 104:15), and for anointing of priests and kings. In the hot climate oil lubricated the skin and made life tolerable. Anointing of the head of a guest was expected of a host (Luke 7:46). Thus deprivation of oil would make life more difficult. Yet Micah predicts that under the administration of God's punishment they would not be able to anoint themselves with the oil which they had trodden out so laboriously. The implication again is that the stores of oil would fall into the hand of the enemy.

Fifth, they would be deprived of life's joys. "You will possess, but you shall not drink wine." Probably the word "vineyards" is to be understood as the object of the verb "possess." Here again is the frustration of expending labor for years on cultivating a vineyard only to be deprived of the fruit of that labor. Some in ancient Israel abstained from wine. Priests when on duty were not allowed to drink wine (Lev 10:9), nor were Nazirites (Num 6:3,20), and Rechabites (Jer 35:6). In everyday life, however, wine or the fruit of the vine (*yayin*) was associated with joy. The Scriptures abound with warnings about the misuse of wine. Yet to plant a vineyard and not be able to enjoy the fruit of it was considered by the ancients one of the worst tragedies which could befall a man (cf. Zeph 1:13). That, however, would be the fate of Judah under the administration of God's judgment (6:15b).

E. Disastrous Policies (6:16a).

Why had Yahweh unleashed his disciplinary blows against Judah? Why did he threaten to destroy Jerusalem completely? The root cause of the prophetic threat is that Judah had followed in the path of her northern sister kingdom. "For the statutes of Omri are kept." Not much is related about Omri in the Book of Kings except that he was worse than all his predecessors on the throne (1 Kgs 16:25). The four kings of the Omri dynasty (885-841 BC) practiced oppression and injustice as no kings before them. These kings considered themselves to be above the law of God. The confiscation of Naboth's vineyard by the crown after a trumped up charge of treason (1 Kgs 21) is an example of what must have been practiced on a daily basis.

"All the works of Ahab" were also found in Judah. Under the sinister influence of Jezebel, the wife of Ahab,[5] Baalism made a bid to become the official religion of the land (1 Kgs 16:31f.). As a part of this process, the government launched a vicious persecution of the prophets of Yahweh (1 Kgs 18:4; 22:27). Through Athaliah, the daughter of Ahab and Jezebel, that same ruthless opposition to the true faith passed over into Judah (cf. 2 Chr 22:2-4).

The accusation becomes more pointed as Micah switches from third person description to second person accusation: "and you walk in their counsels." Judah in Micah's day was following the policy of these corrupt kings of the north. The same "might makes right" philosophy of business and justice, the same toleration if not promotion of Baalism here stands condemned (6:16a).

F. Final Disasters (6:16b).

Following the policies of Omri (godless oppression) and Ahab (pagan toleration) would prove disastrous. The word translated by NIV and NASB "therefore" (*lema'an*) literally means "in order that." The prophet regards the punishment of Judah as intentionally brought about by the sinners themselves. The word underscores the daring with which men live on in godlessness and unrighteousness. Micah points out three disasters awaiting Judah.

First, Yahweh would give Judah over to "desolation" (*shammah*). The emphasis of the word is on depopulation of a place. The "you" who would be made a desolation is a reference to the inhabitants of Jerusalem. They were the principal sinners targeted by Micah. Thus, the first disaster to befall Jerusalem would be depopulation.

Second, the inhabitants of Jerusalem would be given over to "hissing" (*shereqah*). The Hebrew term refers to the audible sound—whistle or hiss—expressed by those who passed by the ruins of a once proud city (e.g., Jer 19:8; 25:9,18). The sound was one of shock, amazement or perhaps derision (NIV; NASB). Not only would Jerusalem be depopulated, those citizens of that great city would be subjected to ridicule and mockery over the fate of their beloved capital.

Third, the inhabitants of Jerusalem would "bear the reproach of my people." This has been taken to mean the reproach which is threatened to my people if they are unfaithful, a reproach which is greater in scope because they are God's people. The term "reproach" (*cherpah*) often carries the connotation of casting blame or scorn on someone (cf. Job 27:6; Ps 74:10). Those who are the victims of reproach experience shame, disgrace, and dishonor. For the people of God to be given over into the power of a heathen enemy would be the ultimate disaster.

A LAMENT OVER JUDAH
Micah 7:1-6

The opening words—"Woe is me!"—of chapter 7 signal a lament. The subject of the unit is the corruption of society. What is not clear is the identity of the one doing the lamentation. Is the city itself responding to the announcement of 6:29? Is Micah here giving vent to personal frustration? Or is this God himself expressing his anguish over the condition of his people? Perhaps Micah here is acting as a spokesman for the believing remnant, those who were truly concerned about the direction of their country. In any case, the lamentation serves as (1) a confession of national sin, and (2) a justification for the forthcoming judgment.

A. The Absence of the Godly (7:1-2a).

In his preaching Micah felt frustrated. He used an illustration to express his frustration. He felt like those who came to the vineyard expecting the find the choice fruit of summer. All he found, however, were the inferior gleanings. The idea is that the good people were all gone; only the worthless were left in the land. "There is no cluster to eat." The vineyard had been stripped. The figure now changes a bit, but the same point is being made. "My soul desired the first-ripe fig" which was noted for being sweeter than those which ripen later in the year. He longed to discover even one who displayed in his life the sweetness of God's righteousness.[6]

The mini-parable of verse 1 is immediately interpreted. "The pious one has perished from the land." The "pious one" (*chasid*) is one who displayed in his life covenant faithfulness both to God and to other covenant brothers. The context here suggests that Micah had in mind humanitarian activities. One displays loyalty to God by consistently respecting the rights of all of God's people. Specifically, Micah has in mind "the upright" (*yashar*) among men, i.e., those who were absolutely honest. Such men "are not," i.e., they have departed from the land. The language usually refers to death (7:2a).

B. Corruption in the Public Sphere (7:2b-4).

So if the good guys are all gone, who is left? The scoundrels! "All of them lie in wait for blood." This is the antithesis of *chesed*, covenant faithfulness. The picture is that of an ambush, passively waiting for some innocent party to happen along. While not excluding murder itself, these words have a broader meaning. These men set their minds on treachery that they might rob their neighbor of his means of existence so that eventually he must die. Even covenant brothers were not exempt. "Each man hunts his brother with a net." The language suggests a more active pursuit. If no one happened along, they would go out looking for the prey! No hope exists for a society which treats brothers as animals (7:2b).

Again Micah interprets his metaphors with blunt prose. "Both hands are upon evil to do it well," lit., to make it good. The leaders of the land skillfully dabbled in all kinds of evil. The meaning may be that they were able to give evil such a form that it appeared to be good.

Specific examples of what Micah had in mind are now cited. The prince was constantly asking (Heb. participle) for a reward. The judge requested bribes of those who appeared before him.[7] The "great man," i.e., the rich and powerful, would make his "desires" known to the judges. Those schemes would then be implemented by the courts. Thus "they weave it." These princes, judges and great men were confederates in crime. They wove their ungodly schemes into the cord of justice so as to give them the appearance of legitimacy (7:3).

Micah's assessment of the society of his day is that "the best of them is like a briar," i.e., painful, ensnaring, worthless and easily consumed. The "upright one," i.e., one who appeared upright or who was upright by comparison to others, "is from a thorn bush." If the best of them is no better than this, then judgment was in order (7:4a).

In view of the total corruption which he saw in Jerusalem, Micah announced the judgment. "The day of your watchmen" has come.[8] A "watchman" (*metsappeh*) was a faithful prophet of God. The "day of your watchmen" refers to that judgment day of which the prophets had warned since the beginning of the prophetic movement in Israel. This time of judgment is also called "your visitation." God was about to visit them in or with his wrath. When this blow finally falls, the people of Judah would not be able to explain it. "It shall be their perplexity." Nothing flattens the inflated egos of clever schemers more than the unexpected intervention of God in the affairs of men (7:4b).

C. Treachery in the Private Sphere (7:5-6).

A series of imperatives underscores in yet another way the extent of the corruption in Judah. First, "do not trust in a neighbor" (*rea'*). People must constantly be on guard against treachery and deception. Second, "do not put confidence in an intimate friend" (*'alluph*).[9] One must be careful what he says in pillow talk with his wife. "From her that lies at your bosom keep the doors of your mouth." Thus blood ties, marriage ties, economic ties were being trampled underfoot. The most basic ligaments of society had been torn asunder (7:5).

Why must one be careful in what he says even within his own home? Because "a son dishonors his father" (lit., treats his father as a fool) thus violating the fifth commandment. "A daughter rises up against her mother." In a perverse society children are in open rebellion against their parents. The extended family was also affected, for the daughter-in-law would be against her mother-in-law. As a matter of fact, "the enemies of a man are the men (i.e., servants) of his house" (7:6). Jesus used the words of this verse to describe how his Gospel would have the effect of turning members of families against one another (Matt 10:35f.).

ENDNOTES

1. James L. Mays, *Micah, A Commentary* in "The Old Testament Library" (Philadelphia: Westminster, 1976) p. 140.
2. Most modern versions including NIV, NASB and RSV follow the ancient versions in rendering the verb in this clause "fear your name." Others take "wisdom" to be the object of the verb rather than the subject: "Your name shall keep in view wisdom."
3. NASB apparently regards God as the speaker in 6:11: "Can I justify wicked scales and a bag of deceptive weights?" NIV has approached the verse similarly. This requires reading the verb as a Piel rather than a Qal. Yet even in the Piel the verb does not carry the idea of acquittal or justification.
4. As recognized in the NIV translation. NASB renders the verb as a prophetic perfect, a future so certain that it can be described as already past.
5. Jezebel was the wife of Ahab and the mother of the next two kings, Ahaziah and Jehoram. In the revolution of 841 BC Jehu made reference to the tremendous influence of this devotee of paganism (2 Kgs 9:22).
6. Leslie Allen thinks Jesus may have been acting out a reference to this verse in the cursing of the fig tree (Mark 11:12-14; 20-22). *The Books of Joel, Obadiah, Jonah and Micah* in "The New International Commentary

on the Old Testament" (Grand Rapids: Eerdmans, 1976), p. 385.

7. Others interpret the text to say that the prince was asking the judge for a favorable decision, i.e., telling the judge how to rule. In this case there would have been no independent judiciary.

8. NASB finds another meaning in the verse: "The day when you post a watchman, your punishment will come."

9. The term *'alluph* is used of a woman's husband (Prov 2:17; Jer 3:4).

CHAPTER TWENTY-SIX

The Outlook and the Uplook
Micah 7:7-20

The Book of Micah concludes with some of the most magnificent material in prophetic literature. These positive words have lifted the spirits of God's people through the centuries. A confession of faith and final prayer are followed by a Handel-like explosion of praise to the Lord.

A CONFESSION OF FAITH IN THE FUTURE
Micah 7:7-13

The problem arises here as in 7:1 as to the identity of the first person speaker. If the nation is speaking, then the idea is that in spite of the circumstances Judah had not lost her faith in the Lord. Perhaps Micah continues to speak here as the representative of the faithful remnant. In any case, the words which follow constitute a confession of trust in the Lord. The opening words, "as for me" emphasize the contrast between what has just been described in society at large and the stubborn faith of Micah and kindred spirits.

A. Confidence in God (7:7).

In the midst of the corruption of godless society, Micah declared "I watch in the Lord." The prophet was following the maxim, when the outlook is bleak, try the uplook. Here Micah portrays himself as the faithful watchman who is attentive and untiringly alert to what the Lord might say. He waited expectantly as a city watchman might watch for the first signs of news from a battle front. He declares his intention to "wait on the God of my salvation," i.e., the God from whom all my salvation comes. The Lord could be trusted when no one else could be. In a present full of violence and betrayal Micah turned his attention to a future in which he could hope. Though love and faithfulness had vanished from Judah, Micah's confidence in the Lord could not be shaken. Waiting is the most powerful form of action by the helpless (7:7a).[1]

Why was Micah watching and waiting for Yahweh? This man of God (and perhaps the faithful he represented) was absolutely certain of two things. First, he was certain of his relationship with God, for he refers to him as "my" God. This is not the "my" of possession as though God in some sense belonged to him, but the "my" of commitment. He knew that he belonged to God because he had committed his life to him. Second, he was certain that "my God will hear me." When God hears, he helps! (cf. Ps 4:3).

B. Confidence in Victory (7:8).

Certainly Zion is the speaker in 7:8. Zion is placed by the prophet in the setting of the judgment which had been previously predicted (3:12; 6:16). "Rejoice not against me, O my enemy." The "enemy" here is the heathen power of the world, represented in Micah's day by Assyria. Celebration over the demise of Zion is premature. Zion defied the derision of her foes. Why? Because she was confident that after the judgment she had a future. "For I fall, I arise." The verb "fall" (*naphal*) is used here to denote the destruction of the kingdom of Judah (cf. Amos 5:2).

Heathen nations would fall to rise no more (Jer 25:27). Not so Zion! Zion knew that she must "sit in darkness," i.e., go through a period of sorrow, shame and persecution (cf. Isa 9:1; 42:7). Yet even in such a time she was sure that Yahweh would "be a light to me." In times of great darkness the believer finds in the word of God a light for his present path and a spotlight on a glorious future. Even in his wrath God does not violate his mercy nor break any promise which he has made to his people.

C. Confident of Vindication (7:9-10).

God's people confidently can face whatever judgment might be in store for Judah. Their strong faith in the Lord enables them to accept adversity as a manifestation of "the indignation of Yahweh." Unbelievers might explain Zion's plight as being due to the power of her enemies. Yet the faithful knew they were in reality in the hands of the God of the covenant. Thus she does not blame God. She determines to humbly "bear" Yahweh's indignation. She knows full well that the punishment was justified, for she declares "I have sinned against him" (7:9a).

Though willing to endure patiently the righteous judgment of Yahweh, Zion was confident of better things to come. In four first person declarations she boldly proclaims her expectation. First, she would bear the indignation of the Lord "until he shall plead my case" (*yaribh ribhi*). Keil attempts to capture the alliteration of the Hebrew with the translation "he shall fight my fight."[2] The day would come when Zion's Judge would become her Advocate and Defender. Believers ever live and cope with painful present circumstances "until" the glorious day of deliverance.

Second, in that day Yahweh would "execute justice for me" or "secure my right" (*'asah mishpati*). That would include the punishment of all powers which had oppressed Zion and the restoration to their homeland following the Exile. Third, at that time Yahweh would "bring me out to the light." Light here represents freedom and restoration to favor and blessing. The verb form is used of the great Exodus from Egypt. It would suggest to the minds of the Israelites another and even greater Exodus from darkness to light. Fourth, Zion declares: "I will see his righteousness." Here the term righteousness refers to the actions which God takes to vindicate his elect. Forgiveness and restoration to their land are examples of such actions. God is said to be righteous when he unfailingly keeps his glorious promises (7:9b).

How will the transformation of Zion affect her enemies? First, "then my enemy will see." See what? See (1) all the glorious changes which Zion would undergo; and (2) see that it is not vain to trust the Lord. Second, "shame will cover her who said unto me, Where is Yahweh your God?" When Jerusalem was devastated heathen neighbors heaped insult upon the God of Jerusalem (cf. Joel 2:17). If he really was the only true and living God as his devotees declared, why had he not intervened to save his temple and his people from destruction? Third, Zion would witness the tables turned on the enemies. "Now she shall be for an object of trampling like the clay of the streets." The enemies of Zion are ultimately doomed to be crushed by Yahweh's judgment. The term "now" (*'attah*) is not chronological but logical. While Zion rebuilds and increases, the enemies would be trodden down in utter contempt (7:10).

D. Confident of Expansion (7:11-13).

While the enemies go down to utter defeat, Zion flourishes. Micah anticipated a new era to begin with the rebuilding of the walls (*gederim*). The term refers to vineyard walls. A flourishing vineyard must have walls to protect it, and walls upon which the vines can grow. Whereas Isaiah (Isa 5:1-5) foresaw the destruction of God's vineyard (7:11a), Micah predicted its reestablishment. Jesus also saw his followers as branches of a new vine, i.e., a new vineyard (John 15:1-5).

The expansion and growth of Zion would be made possible by this fact: "that is the day the statute shall be removed." The term "statute" (*choq*) is rendered "boundary" by NIV, NASB and RSV, and more appropriately "decree" in ASV. The reference is to that which made Israel God's special people among the nations (Exod 19:5f.). Israel was set apart from all other peoples by land, laws and liturgy. Daily rituals and ceremonies, eating habits, and the like made them a distinct nation. The occupation of a particular land which had been given to them by divine decree also distinguished them. Micah, however, foresaw the day when this decree of separation would be removed. He foresaw the Gospel age when the wall of separation between Jew and Gentile would be abolished (Eph 2:11-22; Col 1:18-29; 2:16-23). Whereas the Mosaic law was exclusive, the Gospel is inclusive. Whereas that law focused on the separation of the redeemed, the

Gospel focuses on the salvation of the enslaved (7:11b).

Once the decree of separation is removed, Gentiles would flock to Zion. Micah expresses this thought first in nationalistic terms: "And unto you he shall come from Assyria and the cities of Egypt."[3] Assyria and Egypt were the two mightiest empires in the days of the prophet. Those who come to Zion would come from the "cities" of Egypt. This is no token delegation representing the government, but a grass-roots movement from all segments of the population. In this representation of the conversion of Egypt and Assyria Micah is echoing the thoughts of his contemporary Isaiah (cf. Isa 19:18-25).

Next the prophet states the same truth in geographical terms. The Gentiles will come "from Egypt even unto the River," i.e., the Euphrates river. The phrase is more encompassing for it includes all the lands lying between these two terminal points. From Africa to Asia they come to Zion.

Finally, Micah expands his description to a universal dimension. The Gentiles would come "from sea to sea and from mountain to mountain." Seas and mountains formed the boundaries of most countries in the ancient world. Micah had no particular seas or mountains in view. This very general expression must be given the widest possible interpretation. From every land situated between seas and mountains people would flock to Zion. This is but a further development of the glorious picture of 4:1f. (7:12).[4]

So far Micah has said that Gentiles in the future would be able to come to Zion, and that in fact they would come from all over the world. Yet he has not indicated why the Gentiles in such great numbers flock to Zion. That he does in 7:13. "The land will become a desolation on account of her inhabitants." In the very time when Zion is being built up, the earth gradually would become a devastated wasteland (*shemamah*).[5] This punishment would be inflicted on the Gentile world "on account of her inhabitants," i.e., as punishment for the sins of its inhabitants. The "fruit of their deeds" included rebellion, violence, immorality and such. For those gross sins the world would perish. In Zion, however, salvation would always be available. The idea here is that unbelievers are doomed under the sentence of death. Believers thrive in the kingdom of light and life (7:13).

PRAYER AND RESPONSE
Micah 7:14-20

The Book of Micah concludes with one of the sweetest prayers in prophetic literature. The notion that God himself would shepherd his people following the exile is a familiar theme in prophetic literature (e.g., Jer 50:19; Ezek 34:12). The prayer here calls upon God to fulfill those promises.

A. The Request (7:14).
Micah's initial petition is twofold. He asked for (1) protection and (2) provision for the flock of God.

1. The request for protection (7:14a). Micah called upon Yahweh to "shepherd your people with your staff." This is a request primarily for protection, but also for prodding and guidance. In Biblical literature Jacob was the first to address God as Shepherd (Gen 49:24). David thought of God in that metaphor as well (Ps 23:1). The shepherd/flock concept was one of the important ways ancient Israel described its relationship to the Lord. Surrounding nations frequently alluded to their kings as shepherds. Thus Yahweh is being recognized as the true King of Israel in contrast to Gentile rulers who would attempt to exert their authority over this people. The prayer is certainly related to the promise in 5:3ff. that a ruler would go forth from Bethlehem to shepherd the flock of God. This prayer, then, is a petition that Messiah might come (7:14a).

Micah offered two reasons for his petition. First, Israel was "the flock of your inheritance." This people had a long standing relationship to Yahweh. They were his flock. They were totally dependent on him. An "inheritance" is a possession which needs management and supervision. The term expresses an obligation on God's part to care for this people.

Second, Micah noted that Israel "dwells alone" (cf. Num 23:9). A flock without a protector was doomed to total extinction (cf. Hos 4:16). Third, Israel was like "a forest in the midst of Carmel." Some think this figure depicts the moral and spiritual isolation of Israel from surrounding nations. More likely Micah intended the figure to describe the plight of Israel. This flock was isolated in grazing ground overgrown by scrubby thickets. It cannot enjoy the good pasture of Carmel, i.e., a fertile land. Others were in possession of the good ground.[6]

2. *The request for provision (7:14b)*. Since the flock has no access to fruitful Carmel land, the second petition is appropriate. "Let them feed in Bashan and Gilead as in days of old." Bashan and Gilead east of Jordan were the best pasture regions of greater Canaan. Perhaps the hidden agenda of this petition is the restoration to Israel of the totality of her ancient territory. More likely, however, the prophet is only asking for adequate provision for the flock of God. The expression "as in days of old" refers to the times of Moses and Joshua when God himself was Israel's leader, and when the tribes first occupied Bashan and Gilead.

The prayer, while focusing on provision for the flock, has implicit in it another petition. Carmel was west of the Jordan; Bashan and Gilead were east of Jordan. Together the three areas represent the totality of the area once occupied by the people of God when they emerged from the wilderness wandering. In 931 BC the northern tribes which possessed Carmel, Bashan and Gilead, broke away from Judah. Perhaps the prayer is asking for a reunification of the flock under the one shepherd. Certainly this is a promise which other prophets emphasize (cf. e.g., Ezek 37:15ff.; Isa 11:13).

B. God's Answer (7:15-16).

The Lord answered the prayer by promising to do more than was even asked. First, he promised that he would show "him," i.e., the flock, "marvelous things" (*niphla'oth*). This term is used of the marvelous events which transpired during the Exodus from Egypt (Exod 3:20; Ps 78:11). The plagues against Egypt, the crossing of the Red Sea, and the theophany at Sinai were some of the wonders which led to the formation of national Israel. Similar wonders would precede the formation of messianic Israel, viz., the resurrection, ascension, and falling of the Spirit on Pentecost (7:15).

Gentiles would "see," i.e., recognize or perceive, the mighty works which God would perform for his people. The nations would "be ashamed of all their strength." They would be ashamed that his power was so much greater than any deity which they revered. Their national strength becomes impotence before his awesome power. They would be ashamed (1) that they had mistreated his people; and (2) that they had not previously recognized and submitted to the omnipotent power of Israel's God (7:16a).

The shame which the Gentiles experienced within their heart would be expressed outwardly. First, "they shall put a hand over their mouth." In the Near East placing the hand over the mouth is a gesture of reverential silence resulting from astonishment and admiration (cf. Judg 18:19; Job 21:5). They would be overawed by power of God's miracles on behalf of his people. They would not have adequate words to express their thoughts.

Second, at the same time, "their ears shall be deaf." Does the text refer to physical deafness? Is he suggesting that the mighty acts of God on behalf of his people are accompanied by thunderous and deafening noise. While this interpretation is possible, it is difficult to find in the Exodus analogy, Old Testament history, or prophetic tradition any support for this view. More likely the deafness here is spiritual, not physical. Overawed by God's great miracles the Gentiles no longer would wish to hear words of self-exaltation or the claims of other deities. Having found the pearl of great price they want nothing more. Every competing gospel is rejected out of hand (7:16b).

C. Micah's Amplification (7:17).

God's answer to the prayer of his people glides almost imperceptibly into a word from God's prophet. Building upon the wonderful promises made directly by Yahweh, Micah adds yet four more. First, the heathen "shall lick the dust like a serpent." In the modern idiom, they will bite the dust. The language here depicts total surrender to the Lord. In similar words the Lord announced the humiliation of Satan after the temptation in Eden (Gen 3:14).

Second, the Gentiles "shall tremble from their strongholds like creeping things of the earth" (*zochale 'erets*), i.e., snakes (cf. Deut 32:24). The picture here is of snakes being driven out or charmed out of their hiding places. The stunned Gentiles would recognize that their strongholds, whether physical or spiritual, would ultimately fall before the power of Yahweh. Hence they would desert these fortifications as quickly as snakes which come under attack.

Third, the nations would come "unto Yahweh our God with fear." This is not the fear of the criminal who seeks refuge from discovery, but the fear of one who has experienced a narrow escape. Converted sinners realize that apart from the grace of God they face eternal condemnation. By humbly coming to the Lord in obedient faith they have been snatched like a brand from the fire.

Fourth, the converted Gentiles "would continue to fear before you." The initial fear would be translated into a god-fearing lifestyle. To fear God in Scripture means to serve and worship him.

CONCLUDING PRAISE
Micah 7:18-20

Praise in the Bible comes in two forms, viz., praise to God and praise about God. These two types of praise might be labeled as prayer praise and proclamation praise. In the former the believer addresses his comments directly to the Lord. The latter is intended for others to hear. Proclamation or confessional praise might be likened to bragging on the Lord. Both types of praise mingle in the closing verses of Micah. The prophet begins with prayer praise, drifts into proclamation praise, and then returns to his direct address to God.

A. Prayer Praise (7:18a).

When it comes to dealing with sin, the Lord is incomparable. "Who is a God like you?" In this prayer the three main Old Testament words for sin are used. "Iniquity" (*'avon*) is perverseness or crookedness which makes a person guilty before God. "Transgression" (*pesha'*) is deliberate rebellion against God's word. "Sins" (*chatta'ot*) are all actions that fall short of God's glory whether intended or unintended, whether by commission or omission.

Yahweh is a specialist in dealing with the human sin problem. First, he "lifts up iniquity," i.e., he removes the perverseness which taints the character of man. Second, "he passes by the transgression of the remnant of his heritage." The "flock of your inheritance" of v. 14 will at some point become a "remnant" (*she'erit*), i.e., a small portion of what once existed. Only then would their transgression be passed over. The verb suggests the night when God passed over the houses of the firstborn of Israel. If God does not pass over the transgression, the transgressor is doomed.

B. Proclamation Praise (7:18b-19a).

Micah, speaking for the believing remnant, begins to make assertions about God rather than to God in the middle of verse 18. The theme is still the masterful manner in which the Lord deals with the human sin problem. Micah makes four assertions which build on what has just been said in the context of prayer.

First, Yahweh does not "seize," i.e., retain, "his anger forever." If he continually clung to his anger no one would escape destruction. Micah is declaring that Yahweh's anger last but a short time.

Second, Yahweh "delights in covenant faithfulness." Even when his people are unfaithful, Yahweh is faithful to his covenant commitment. He delights in keeping his program of redemption on track. To that end he is anxious to forgive. He looks, not for reasons to condemn and destroy, but for reasons to forgive and build up (7:18).

Third, since Yahweh delights in covenant faithfulness, "he will again have mercy on us." The verb "to show mercy" (*racham*) refers to the tender care which one who is stronger lavishes on one who is in need.

Fourth, Yahweh "will subdue our iniquities." Our sins are God's enemies. He will vanquish those enemies, i.e., he will give his people victory over sin.

C. Prayer Praise (7:19b).

Once again Micah addressed God directly in prayer praise. He continued to extol the gracious way in which God deals with the sins of his people.

Micah praises God for the completeness and finality of divine forgiveness. "You will cast all of their sins into the depths of the sea." Just as he destroyed the army of Egypt which pursued ancient Israel (cf. Exod 15:5), so Yahweh would destroy any sin which continued to hound his people.

The possessive "their" should be noted. Throughout the prayer Micah speaks of Israel in the first person. He reserves the third person for the nations (cf. vv. 16-17). The possessive suffix "their" in the midst of v. 19 suggests that now Micah is praising God that his forgiveness extends even to Gentiles who come trembling before him. Thus verse 19 affirms that God treads underfoot "our" iniquity, i.e., Israel's iniquity. At the same time he casts "their" sins, i.e., the sins of penitent Gentiles, into the sea.

D. Final Petition (7:20).

The verb which opens verse 20 is optative,[7] and should be rendered as a prayer form: "May you give . . . ." The closing petition of the book asks that forgiveness be followed by the fullness of heaven's blessing. Three such blessings are mentioned.

First, "may you give faithfulness to Jacob," i.e., to Jacob's descendants, Israel. "Faithfulness" (*'emeth*) is a characteristic of God's nature (Exod 34:6) and God's words (Ps 119:142). The word carries the underlying sense of certainty or dependability. God bestows this gift upon penitent people. The powerful deeds of divine mercy and grace are so tremendous that the sinner is persuaded to remain faithful to the Lord. For this faithfulness, however, God receives the glory, not man.

Second, Yahweh is asked to give "covenant faithfulness to Abraham." This is the only use of the name "Abraham" for the people of God corporately. Covenant faithfulness is a gift to the penitent in the same sense that faithfulness is a gift. Genuine love and gratitude are such powerful forces that the entire direction of lives can be changed permanently by them. Those who had been unfaithful through sin, become faithful. Those who were disloyal to the covenant through transgression, begin to live up to their obligations to God and fellow man. Again, Yahweh is the giver, because he provides the incentive to change through his grace.

The final petition is grounded in the Patriarchal promise made some thirteen hundred years earlier. Yahweh keeps the oath which he swore "to our fathers from days of old." All of the promises which God made to Abraham, Isaac and Jacob he has kept. Not the least of those was that in which Yahweh promised to bless all peoples of the earth through seed of Abraham, even Jesus. That oath to the fathers had created a special relationship which "obligatory love" (*chesed*) fulfilled and "faithfulness" (*'emeth*) maintained (7:20).

ENDNOTES

1. James L. Mays, *Micah, a Commentary* in "The Old Testament Library" (Philadelphia: Westminster, 1976), p. 157.

2. Keil and Delitzsch, *Old Testament Commentaries; Ezekiel XXV to Malachi* (Grand Rapids: Associated, n.d.), p. 1178.

3. The term translated "Egypt" (*matsor*) is translated by some "fortified cities" or "fortresses." The term *matsor* seems to be a poetic name for Egypt (cf. Isa 19:6; 37:25).

4. Some think that Micah is referring to scattered Jews returning to Zion. In the light of 4:1f. and the previous verse the reference seems to be to the Gentiles who become part of messianic Zion.

5. Others interpret 7:13 to be saying that the land of Israel must experience devastation prior to the coming of the glorious messianic age.

6. Mays, *op. cit.*, p. 164.

7. Keil and Delitzsch, *op. cit.*, p. 1183.

PART THREE

THE SEVENTH CENTURY PROPHETS

NAHUM
ZEPHANIAH
HABAKKUK

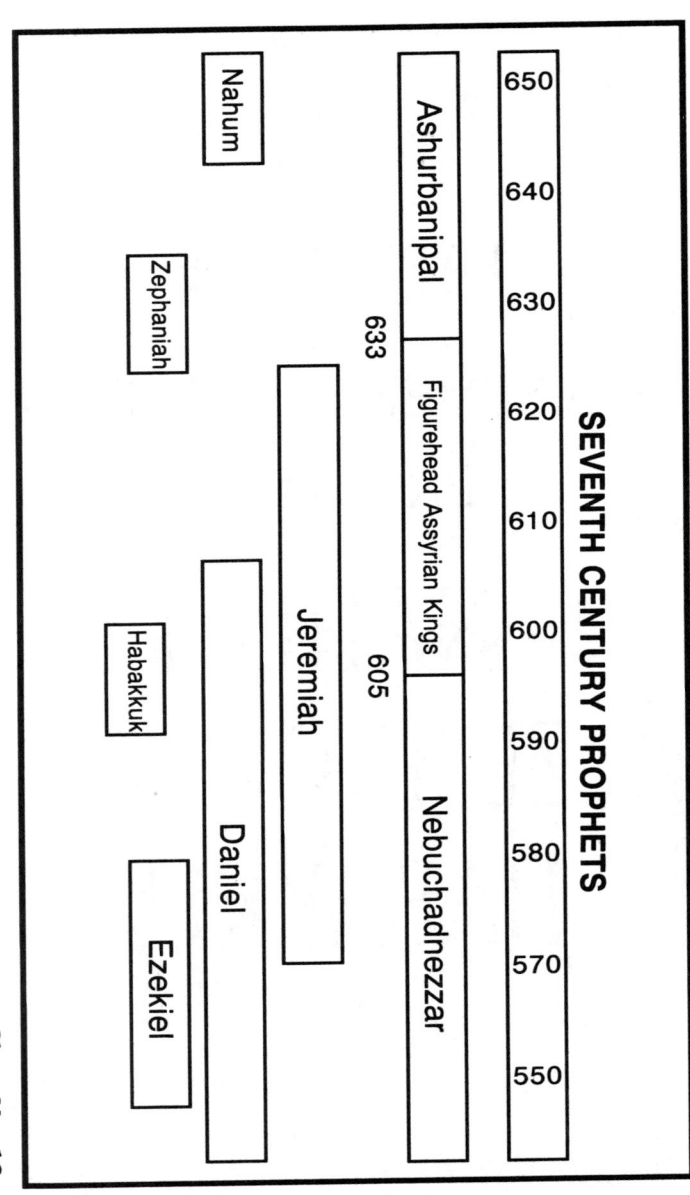

CHAPTER TWENTY-SEVEN

The Seventh Century Prophets
An Introduction

The seventh century BC has been called the silver age of Hebrew prophecy. Jeremiah was the dominant prophetic figure of this century. Preceding him, however, were three other prophets whose writings are part of the Minor Prophets.

BACKGROUND

The third triad of Minor Prophets prophesied during the dying days of the great Assyrian empire. Under Ashurbanipal (669-633 BC) the empire had reached its zenith. On the second of his two Egyptian campaigns this king had conquered Thebes (663 BC). In his annals he names King Manasseh of Judah as having rendered vassal assistance to him on that campaign. Though Ashurbanipal was a king of outstanding administrative capabilities, the vast empire, composed as it was of heterogeneous peoples, was virtually impossible to govern.

After his death, Ashurbanipal's two sons engaged in a disastrous civil war. At the same time, fierce mountain tribes were pressing into the empire from the north. Assyria's ancient rivals to the east—the Medes and Babylonians—were joining in military alliance.

A. Reign of Josiah (640-609 BC).

When King Amon was assassinated in 640 BC, his young son Josiah was put on the throne of Judah. In his eighth year of his reign Josiah cautiously began to lead Judah in a religious reformation. In the Assyrian empire a religious reformation was tantamount to rebellion against the central government. In his twelfth year (628 BC), after Ashurbanipal had died, the reformation in Judah accelerated.

In his eighteenth year Josiah ordered the high priest Hilkiah to cleanse the temple from the pollutions which had accumulated during the wicked reigns of Manasseh and Amon (2 Kgs 22:3-7; 2 Chr 34:8-13). In the course of this work, a lost scroll of scripture was discovered (2 Kgs 22:8; 2 Chr 34:14-15). The king was distraught when he heard the curses which this book pronounced against those who fell into idolatry. The prophetess Huldah confirmed that Judah had come under the condemnation of God because of the blatant apostasy of Manasseh's reign. Nevertheless, God had granted a reprieve to Judah because of the dedicated efforts of Josiah to restore the Mosaic faith. The lost scroll jolted Judah into an even more determined reformation.

While Josiah was leading Judah step by step out of the Assyrian orbit, the empire was rapidly crumbling. In 612 BC the great city of Nineveh, one of the Assyrian capitals, fell to the Medo-Babylonian coalition. By 609 BC the coalition was ready to crush the remnants of the Assyrian army. Pharaoh Neco sensed that the balance of power in the Near East was shifting. Though he had been a bitter enemy of the Assyrians, the Pharaoh calculated that Egypt's best interest would be served by militarily propping up what was left of the Assyrian government. To this end he led his forces up the coastal plain of Palestine to confront the upstart Babylonian prince Nebuchadnezzar.

B. Battle of Carchemish (605 BC).

For some reason unexplained in Scripture, Josiah felt it necessary to attempt to resist the advance of Neco along the coastal plain of

Palestine. The Judean chose Megiddo, a narrow pass through the mountains which jutted across the plains, as the location for the showdown. Neco appealed to Josiah to stand aside. Nevertheless the battle was joined. Josiah was mortally wounded (2 Chr 35:21-24). With the death of the godly king the reformation in Judah was rescinded.

Neco marched on to Carchemish on the Euphrates. There in one of the greatest battles of all history Nebuchadnezzar crushed the Egyptians. He literally chased the armies of Neco back to Egypt. Now the young crown prince and soon-to-be king of Babylon was the ruler of the world. The Neo-Babylonian empire would dominate the Near East for the next seven decades.

C. Reign of Jehoiakim (609-598 BC).

After the death of Josiah, the "people of the land" put his son Shallum on the throne. Shallum took the throne name Jehoahaz. In so doing the people passed over an elder brother, probably because of his pro-Egypt leanings. After reigning only three months, Jehoahaz was summoned by Pharaoh Neco to Riblah in Syria. He was deposed, put in chains, and deported to Egypt. There Jehoahaz spent the rest of his days.

Pharaoh Neco installed Eliakim, the elder brother of Jehoahaz on the throne of Judah (2 Kgs 23:30-45). He took (or was given by Pharaoh) the throne name Jehoiakim ("Yahweh sets up"). Neco put the land of Judah under heavy tribute.

Jehoiakim has been called the Solomon of the last days of Judah. He was an irresponsible spendthrift even in a time of national poverty. He conscripted laborers to build for himself a magnificent new palace, though the country was hard pressed to make its annual payments to Neco (Jer 22:13-14). This king was a bigot, an arrogant and irreverent tyrant. He had one faithful prophet extradited from Egypt and executed (Jer 26:21). He destroyed the first scroll produced by Jeremiah, and placed that prophet under an arrest warrant (Jer 36:23-26).

When Neco was soundly defeated at the battle of Carchemish in 605 BC, the way to Syria and southward lay open to Nebuchadnezzar. The death of Nebuchadnezzar's father temporarily delayed the Babylonian advance in this area. After being enthroned in April 604

BC, Nebuchadnezzar returned to the area of Syria-Palestine, the Hatti land as he calls it. By the end of 604 BC the Babylonian army had conquered Ashkelon in the Philistine plain. In connection with this invasion, or one the following year, Jehoiakim surrendered Jerusalem. He was put in chains to be carried away to Babylon (2 Chr 36:6). The Babylonian king, however, reversed himself and decided to leave Jehoiakim on the throne of Judah as his vassal.

Jehoiakim served Nebuchadnezzar for three years. When the Babylonians experienced heavy casualties on the borders of Egypt late in 601 BC, Jehoiakim seized the opportunity to revolt. The main Babylonian army was in no position to return to deal with the rebellious king. Nebuchadnezzar, however, did dispatch such Babylonian units as were available in the area. These units were assisted by mercenary bands of Ammonites, Moabites and Arameans (2 Kgs 24:2).

D. Reign of Jehoiachin (597 BC).

By December 598 BC Nebuchadnezzar was able to bring his main force back into Judah. Jehoiakim died that very month, most likely by assassination. He was given no burial. No one lamented his departure (Jer 22:18-19). His eighteen year old son Coniah assumed the throne, taking the throne name Jehoiachin (2 Kgs 24:8).

During Jehoiachin's reign of three months the huge Babylonian army was preparing for a siege of Jerusalem. The young king finally decided to surrender the city to Nebuchadnezzar. Perhaps he held out that long in anticipation of Egyptian help. In any case, on March 16, 597 BC the king, queen mother and ten thousand of the leading citizens of Jerusalem were deported to Babylon along with enormous booty from the temple and city (2 Kgs 24:12-16). Among the captives was a priest who was destined to become a great prophet. His name was Ezekiel (Ezek 1:1-3). The king's uncle Mattaniah—another son of Josiah—was put on the throne of Judah as a Babylonian vassal. Mattaniah took the throne name Zedekiah (2 Kgs 24:17).

THE PROPHET NAHUM
Prophet of Nineveh's Doom

Nahum is the seventh book in Minor Prophets. Its placement after

Micah in the English Bible follows the order of the Hebrew manuscripts as well as that of the Syriac and Latin Vulgate versions. In the Greek Septuagint, however, Nahum follows Jonah. In all forms of the Old Testament Nahum precedes Habakkuk.

Because of the subject matter of his book, Nahum has been called "the prophet of Nineveh's doom" (Huffman) and "the critic of Nineveh" (Ward). His skill as a poet has earned him the designation "the tragic poet" (Scofield) and "poet laureate of the Minor Prophets" (Patterson and Travers). A theologian might designate Nahum as "prophet of God's sovereign righteousness."

A. The Man.

Little is known about the prophet Nahum. He was "little more than a voice" (Robinson) in the history of Israel. Some regard his name, which means "compassionate," to be a misnomer. He certainly had no compassion upon Assyria. His message of doom on Nineveh, however, would demonstrate Yahweh's compassion for his people Judah. Though this name was common in the ancient Near East, this author is the only individual in the Old Testament to wear the name Nahum.[1]

Nahum is called in verse 1 "the Elkoshite." Unfortunately the location of Elkosh is disputed. The village has been located (1) on the Tigris near Nineveh; (2) in the region of Simeon south of Jerusalem; and (3) near Capernaum which means "village of Nahum." The fifth century scholar Jerome claimed that he visited a village in Galilee named Elkesi which a guide identified as the home of Nahum. Modern scholars tend to identify Elkosh with the town of Beit-jebrin in Judah. If this identification is accurate, Nahum lived in the same area as Micah of Moresheth.

B. The Mission.

Dating the ministry of Nahum is difficult. Obviously he lived during the period of Assyrian supremacy in the Near East. No king, however, is mentioned in the book. He prophesied after the fall of the Egyptian city Thebes (No-Ammon) in 663 BC, for he alludes to that event (3:8). On the other hand, the fall of Nineveh in 612 BC is clearly future. Thus Nahum's ministry should be dated between 663 and 612

BC. Rationalistic scholars[2] tend to date the book of Nahum as close as possible to 612 BC so as to eliminate the supernatural prediction.

Duane Christensen has suggested a link between Nahum's message and King Manasseh's rebellion against his Assyrian overlord (2 Chr 33:10-13). This revolt would fall between the years 652 and 648 BC. The assurance that Nineveh's fall had been decreed by Yahweh might have induced this king of Judah to join the rebellion against Assyria.[3]

Nahum may have known Jeremiah. He was a contemporary of Habakkuk and Zephaniah. It is also possible he knew Ezekiel prior to that priest's deportation to Babylon.

C. The Message.

The Book of Nahum appears in the English Bible in three chapters containing a total of forty-seven verses. The Hebrew and English numbering of chapters and verses do not always agree.

The immediate purpose of Nahum is to pronounce the doom that was about to fall on Nineveh. The ultimate purpose of the book is to set forth God's vengeance and sovereign righteousness.

Critics have been harsh in their evaluation of Nahum. He is regarded as a prophetic lesser light because he has no word of condemnation of Israel's sins and no call for her to repent. Pfeiffer declares that "there is nothing specifically religious in this exultant outburst of joy over the inevitable downfall of the Assyrian empire."[4]

Chart No. 20

THE STRUCTURE OF NAHUM		
The Verdict of Vengeance	The Vision of Vengeance	The Vindication of Vengeance
Judgment on Nineveh Declared	Judgment on Nineveh Described	Judgment on Nineveh Defended
Ch. 1	Ch. 2	Ch. 3

Others represent Nahum as malicious and proud. Sandmel, for example, describes this poem as "a blood-curdling song of rejoicing that Nineveh has fallen. . . . The paradox of the book is that the literature is as good as the religion is bad."[5] Patterson accuses Nahum of writing in order to express his personal delight and satisfaction over the destruction of Israel's enemies."[6] Nahum, however, was writing to express the relief and gratitude of the entire body of God's people over the prospect of the fall of an oppressor who had humiliated them and mocked their God for decades.

Some scholars have gone so far as to represent Nahum as one of the "false prophets" who opposed Micah and Jeremiah.[7]

Ample documentation exists of the ruthlessness and moral bankruptcy of the Ninevites. The annals of Assyrian kings boast as to how they dragged women and children off into captivity as the booty of war. They took pride in the absolute devastation of their enemies. The pictures which these kings put on the walls of their palaces are full of sickening gore. If any people deserved an outpouring of divine wrath the Assyrians did.

G. Campbell Morgan has a most appealing outline of the three short chapters of Nahum: (1) the verdict of vengeance; (2) the vision of vengeance; and (3) the vindication of vengeance. Chart No. 20 displays the structure of the book.[8]

According to Payne,[9] some seventy-four percent of the book of Nahum is predictive. All but one of the predictive verses are devoted to the single subject of the future fall of Nineveh. This makes Nahum the most single-focused of all the prophets. The Babylonian Chronicle for the fourteenth year of King Nabopolassar contains the contemporary record of the fulfillment of Nahum's prophecy.[10] Thirty-four verses are devoted to this main theme. The one other prediction is that Judah would recover after the demise of Assyria (2:2).

THE PROPHET ZEPHANIAH
Prophet of God's Wrath

Zephaniah has been called "the orator" (Robinson), "the zealous" (Ward), and "the prophet of all nations" (Scofield Bible). G. Campbell Morgan dubbed him the prophet of "the severity and goodness of God." He certainly was the "prophet of the wrath and mercy of God" (Elliott).

A. The Man.

The name Zephaniah means "he whom Yahweh has hidden or protected." Commentators strain to find some connection between the meaning of the name and the message of the book. Although Zephaniah mentions the possibility of being "hidden" from the terrors of the day of Yahweh, the word is not the same as is used to form the name Zephaniah. Three other Zephaniahs appear in the Old Testament (1 Chr 6:36-38; Jer 21:1; Zech 6:10-14). The prophet is said to be "the son of Cushi" who was a descendant of good King Hezekiah (1:1). Thus Zephaniah was of royal lineage. Most likely he lived in Jerusalem.

B. The Mission.

Zephaniah prophesied "in the days of Josiah...king of Judah" (1:1). The dates generally assigned to Josiah are 640-609 BC. The book certainly was penned before the fall of Nineveh (cf. 2:13) and most likely before the great religious reformation of 621 BC. A date of about 630 BC for the ministry of Zephaniah would not be far off. Most scholars conclude that his ministry was very short.

Some think that Zephaniah was written on the background of a supposed Scythian invasion of Palestine. The Scythians were a ruthless horde from the mountains of Anatolia. They drank the blood from the skull of the first victim slain in battle and made napkins out of their skin. Other scholars, however, are not convinced that the Scythians had anything to do with the writing of this book. No solid evidence exists that the Scythians ever came in the direction of Palestine.

The times in which Zephaniah prophesied were rotten. Judah was characterized by self-complacent pride, shameless falsehood, flagrant iniquity, merciless extortion and senseless idolatry. The guilty transgressors were unabashed. They knew no shame.

C. The Message.

The immediate purpose of the Book of Zephaniah is to warn Judah of approaching doom. The ultimate purpose is to warn all sinners and give encouragement to those who repent. While the book focuses largely on the theme of God's wrath, it does hold out the promise of redemption and salvation for those who believe.

According to Payne, of the fifty-three verses in the book, forty-seven (89%) are predictive. These statistics make Zephaniah the most predictive book of the Bible. Payne counts twenty separate predictions the most prominent of which (about half the predictive verses) is that of Jerusalem's fall to Babylon.[11]

The theme of the book is the day of Yahweh. Zephaniah emphasizes the imminence (1:2,3; 2:4-15; 3:8), universality (1:14ff.) and terror of that day (1:17). He depicts the great day of Yahweh as a day of judgment upon the wicked (2:3; 3:9ff.), but mercy for the remnant.

Chart No. 21 depicts the structure of the Book of Zephaniah.

Chart No. 21

THE STRUCTURE OF ZEPHANIAH		
LOOKING WITHIN	LOOKING AROUND	LOOKING AHEAD
The Sin of Judah	The Sentence against the Nations	The Salvation of the Remnant
1:2-2:3	2:4-3:8	3:9-20
Day of Wrath		Day of Joy

THE PROPHET HABAKKUK
Prophet of the Watchtower

Habakkuk has been called "the prophet of faith" (Elliott), "the optimist" (Ward), "the philosopher" (Robinson), "philosophic prophet" (Scofield Bible), and "the prophet of persistent faith" (Tesh). The character of this prophet and the nature of his prophecy are sadly misrepresented in such designations as "the father of speculation," "the skeptic," "the father of modern religious doubt," or "the freethinker among the prophets." Without question the assessment of Pusey is correct: "Habakkuk is eminently the prophet of reverential and awe-filled faith."[12]

A. The Man.

Virtually nothing is known about the personal history of Habakkuk. Older scholars suggested that his name means "embraced." Nothing is said of his parentage or hometown.

Many legends grew up around Habakkuk. He is a prominent character in one of the Greek additions to the Hebrew Book of Daniel, the so-called story of Bel and the Dragon. According to this legend, Habakkuk was carried by the hair of his head to take food to Daniel in the lion's den.

B. The Mission.

Dating the ministry of Habakkuk is difficult. No king is mentioned in the text. He probably is to be placed after the fall of Nineveh in 612 BC and before the battle of Carchemish in 605 BC. That chronological window probably can be narrowed to the reign of King Jehoiakim who began to reign in 609 BC. A few scholars argue for an earlier date of about 625 BC when the Chaldeans broke away from Assyria and began their rise to power.

C. The Message.

The immediate purpose of the Book of Habakkuk is to foretell Judah's punishment and pronounce doom on the Chaldeans. The ultimate purpose of the book is to teach the grand truths that the just shall live by faith and that the wicked shall not go unpunished.

The Book of Habakkuk is a dramatic dialogue between the prophet and God which reaches its climax in a prayer of praise by the prophet. Chart No. 22 indicates the structure of the book.

Payne found only four distinct prophecies in the Book of Habakkuk, but these prophecies occupy twenty-three of the fifty-six verses (41%). The four prophecies are these: First, the expansion of the Babylonian empire through the ancient Near East (1:5-11). Second, the Babylonian attack on Judah and the fall of Jerusalem in 586 BC (1:12; 3:16b). Third, the fall of Babylon in 539 BC (2:6-13, 15-19; 3:16a). Fourth, the new heavens and new earth (2:14).[13] To Payne's list at least one additional important prophecy should be added. Habakkuk foresaw the day when Satan would be pierced through with his own staves (3:13-14).

Chart No. 22

THE STRUCTURE OF HABAKKUK		
A BURDEN	**A VISION**	**A PRAYER**
Habakkuk Complains	Habakkuk Listens	Habakkuk Prays
Punishment of Judah	Punishment of Babylon	Power of God
Ch. 1	Ch. 2	Ch. 3
Faith Faces a Problem	Faith Finds a Solution	Faith Full of Assurance

ENDNOTES

1. Ralph L. Smith, *Word Biblical Commentary*, vol. 32 "Micah-Malachi" (Waco: Wood, 1984), p. 63. Another Nahum is mentioned in the genealogy of Luke 3:25.

2. Robert Pfeiffer alleges that the book of Nahum was wrongly understood by the organizers of the canon as a prophetic oracle. "To judge from his one extant poem, Nahum was not a prophet...." *Introduction to the OT*, p. 595.

3. Duane L. Christensen, "The Acrostic of Nahum Reconsidered," *Zeitschrift für die alttestamenliche Wissenschaft* 87:1975:29.

4. Pfeiffer, *op. cit.*, p. 594.

5. Samuel Sandmel, *The Hebrew Scriptures* (New York: Knopf, 1963), pp. 112-13.

6. C H. Patterson, *The Philosophy of the Old Testament*, p. 305.

7. J.M.P. Smith, *A Critical and Exegetical Commentary on Micah, Zephaniah and Nahum* in "International Critical Commentary" (Edinburgh: T. & T. Clark, 1911), pp. 273-274. Smith was followed by W.C. Graham in *The Abingdon Bible Commentary* (1929) and others.

8. G. Campbell Morgan, *The Analyzed Bible* (Old Tappan, NJ: Revell, n.d.), p. 314.

9. J. Barton Payne, *The Encyclopedia of Biblical Prophecy* (New York: Harper & Row, 1973), pp. 436f.

10. See James Pritchard, *Ancient Near Eastern Texts Relating to the Old Testament*. Third edition (Princeton: University Press, 1969), pp. 304-305.

11. Payne, *op. cit.*, pp. 440-443.

12. E.B. Pusey, *The Minor Prophets; a Commentary* (Grand Rapids: Baker, 1957 reprint) 2:165.
13. Payne, *op. cit.*, pp. 438f.

BIBLIOGRAPHY
Seventh Century Prophets

Allen, Roland B. A *Shelter in the Fury* (Zephaniah). Portland: Multnomah, 1984.

House, Paul R. *Zephaniah; a Prophetic Drama.* Sheffield: Almond, 1988.

Kennedy, James F. *A Commentary on the Prophecy of Habakkuk.* Chambersburg, PA: Franklin, 1896.

Lloyd-Jones, D. Martyn. *From Fear to Faith; Studies in the Book of Habakkuk.* 1953. Grand Rapids: Baker, 1982.

Marbury, Edward. *Obadiah and Habakkuk.* Sovereign Grace, 1960 reprint.

Maier, Walter A. *The Book of Nahum; a Commentary.* 1959. Minneapolis: Klock & Klock, 1977.

Robertson, O. Palmer. *The Books of Nahum, Habakkuk, and Zephaniah.* "The New International Commentary on the Old Testament." Grand Rapids: Eerdmans, 1990.

Stoll, John. *The Book of Habakkuk.* "Shield Bible Study Series." Grand Rapids: Baker, 1972.

Szeles, Maria E. *Wrath and Mercy; A Commentary on the Books of Habakkuk and Zephaniah.* Trans. G.F. Knight. "International Theological Commentary." Grand Rapids: Eerdmans, 1987.

Ungerer, Walter J. *Habakkuk, The Man with Honest Questions.* Grand Rapids: Baker, 1976.

CHAPTER TWENTY-EIGHT

The Verdict of Vengeance[1]
Nahum 1

The Book of Nahum focuses on the concept of vengeance. Biblical "vengeance" does not refer to malicious retaliation for inflicted wrongs. The Hebrew term *naqam* would be better translated by words that suggest punitive vindication in a judicial sense as Mendenhall has clearly shown.[2] Only God is capable of unerringly executing judicial discipline against sinful men (Deut 32:35,41). God takes vengeance with regard to his people in two ways. First, he becomes the champion of his people against a common foe (cf. Ps 94). Second, he punishes those who violate the covenant which they have with him (Lev 25:24-25). The "vengeance" or just recompense in Nahum is of the former kind.

THE TITLE OF THE BOOK
Nahum 1:1

The Book of Nahum opens with a double title which sets forth four facts about the book. First, the prophet refers to the form of his work. It is a "burden" (Heb. *mashal*). This word became a technical term for a prophetic oracle in which sense it is used at least ten other places in the prophetic literature (e.g., Isa 13:1). Among the Minor Prophets Habakkuk (1:1), Zechariah (9:1; 12:1) and Malachi (1:1) use this term to describe at least a portion of their writings. A "burden" was an oracle of denunciation in which God makes an object lesson out of a wicked subject. In a "burden" the haughty are humbled, the oppressed are liberated, the cursed are blessed and vice versa.

Second, the heading also points to the subject of the book, viz., Nineveh. This great city was located on the banks of the Tigris river above its confluence with the Greater Zab, opposite the site of the modern Mosul in Iraq. Nineveh was one of the oldest cities of the world. The tyrant Nimrod built the place as part of the second stage of his empire building (Gen 10:11,12). King Sennacherib spent twenty-five years enlarging, fortifying and beautifying the old city. Nineveh was the capital of the Assyrian empire during its golden age. About 623 BC Cyaxares, king of the Medes, attacked the great city. In the years that followed the Medes joined with the Babylonians in waging almost yearly assaults on the Assyrians. Finally in 612 BC the city was destroyed.

Third, the title points to the nature of the composition as a "book" (*sepher*). This is the only prophetic work in the Old Testament which describes itself as a book. This word suggests that this material appeared from the first as a literary composition rather than in the oral form. In other words, Nahum was probably not a preacher like Micah or Amos. He was a writer or composer, and a brilliant one at that. He may have intended his composition to be read or sung in worship services.

Fourth, the title points to the origin of the contents of the book. Nahum claims the material is a "vision" or revelation from God (cf. Obad 1). The prophet mentally saw the scenes which he so graphically describes in his book.

Finally, the heading identifies the servant used by God to announce the doom of Nineveh. He is identified as "Nahum the Elkoshite," Mr. Compassion who hailed from the town of Elkosh. On the location of this village, see Chapter Twenty-seven. Three other

THE VERDICT OF VENGEANCE

Old Testament prophets are identified by their hometown: Amos from Tekoa; Micah from Moresheth; and Jeremiah from Anathoth.

THE GREAT JUDGE
Nahum 1:2-8

The vision proper begins with a description of the sovereign Ruler of the world. This first paragraph is constructed as a psalm. Scholars recognize here a partial acrostic involving roughly the first half of the Hebrew alphabet. Many scholars attempt to rearrange the text so as to perfect the acrostic. Bible students, however, should not take such liberties with the text.

The paragraph serves as a backdrop against which the oracles concerning the destruction of Nineveh must be judged. These verses do not mention Nineveh specifically. Rather here are set forth basic theological principles of eternal validity. The paragraph is theologically rich. It focuses, not so much on the attributes of God as on his actions. By using a number of participles Nahum has succeeded in making God's intervention in human affairs very vivid. The hymn has three major divisions. Nahum celebrates (1) the disposition (2) manifestation and (3) power of Yahweh.

A. The Disposition of Yahweh (1:2-3a)

First, Nahum stresses that God is jealous (1:2). He cannot tolerate any rival to the love, fear and trust which he demands from all mankind. Nahum echoes the description of Moses: "Yahweh, whose name is Jealous, is a jealous God" (Exod 34:14).

Second, God is an avenger. As such Yahweh avenges and takes vengeance (1:2). The redundancy serves to emphasize the point. In his posture as avenger, Yahweh is "full of wrath," lit., he is a lord or master of fury. His enemies, who are also the enemies of his people, are the object of his fury. Jealousy, wrath and vengeance are a cluster of closely related concepts in the Old Testament. The attribute of jealousy causes God to act by pouring out his wrath with the result that vengeance—judicial recompense—is accomplished.

Third, God is patient (1:3). He is "slow to anger." He is not capricious, arbitrary, nor hasty in the exercise of his wrath. He is not like one who strikes out without rhyme or reason. His wrath is well planned and well placed.

Fourth, God is powerful (1:3). He is "great in power." He thus is in a position to execute any threat no matter how unlikely or difficult.

Fifth, God is just (1:3). He will by no means "clear the guilty," lit., declare the guilty to be innocent. He cannot acquit the wicked. No amount of bribery or flattery will deflect his judgment. His demand for perfection is absolute.

B. The Manifestation of Yahweh (1:3b-6).

The appearance of Yahweh is often depicted in the Old Testament as accompanied by a storm or whirlwind (e.g., Exod 19:16). Nahum sees him traveling through the tornadoes. He walks across the clouds as though they were dust beneath his feet (1:3b).

Yahweh "rebukes" the sea thereby making it dry just as he created a path through the Red Sea during the Exodus (Exod 14:16ff.). He dries up rivers as he did the Jordan when Joshua led the Israelites into Canaan (Josh 3:13ff.), or when two prophets were making their way into Transjordan (2 Kgs 2:8,14). Hills and mountains as well as rivers and seas are under the control of Yahweh. Fertile regions (Carmel, Bashan, and Lebanon) wither at his touch. Great mountains quake and "melt" before Yahweh, i.e., pour forth lava (1:4-5).

C. The Power of Yahweh (1:6-8).

By means of two rhetorical questions Nahum presses his point that no man can stand before God when he comes for judgment. The fierceness of his anger is irresistible. The fire (probably lightning) he pours out from on high smashes massive rocks. Therefore, what mortal can stand before his wrath (1:6).

The power of God is manifested positively as protection for his people. He has good will toward the oppressed. Therefore he provides a refuge or stronghold "in the day of trouble," i.e., in the time of physical or spiritual need, even in the time of death itself. Yahweh "knows" (participle indicating continuous action) "those who take refuge in him," i.e., trust in him. The word *know* suggests intimate knowledge and more. It suggests divine approval, selection and even care (cf. Ps 1:6; Am 3:2). He is *for* his people (1:7).

God's power is demonstrated in the total overthrow of the greatest power of that day. He would make a "full end" of "her place," i.e., Nineveh would be destroyed never to be reoccupied. Yahweh would use a "destructive flood" to accomplish this end.[3] While most likely this phrase is used figuratively of the series of disasters and assaults which pounded Nineveh, an ancient historian alludes to floods which hit that city in the third year of siege.[4]

THE VERDICT OF THE JUDGE
Nahum 1:9-14

The great Judge who was described in the opening paragraph now speaks definitively and decisively. He alternatively addresses the oppressor and the oppressed.

A. Address to Nineveh (1:9-11).

Nahum uses a rhetorical question to point out how vulnerable Nineveh would be in a confrontation with Yahweh: "What do you devise against Yahweh?" Assyrian political literature frequently attributes to neighboring nations such evil plotting and scheming.[5] What they attributed to others was in reality the essence of their own foreign policy. The royal advisers constantly were plotting how they might tighten the noose about the neck of smaller vassal states, including Judah. To plot against Judah was in effect to plot against Yahweh. The Lord would "make a full end" of any nation which had the audacity to engage in such plotting. The Assyrians cannot successfully withstand the God of Israel. Nineveh would never again be able to oppress the people of God: "affliction shall not rise up the second time." One blow from the mighty Yahweh would suffice to forever seal the doom of Nineveh (1:9).

Nahum uses three similes to describe the disaster which was approaching Nineveh. First, Nineveh was "entangled like thorns." This may refer to the confused defense policy. Another possibility is that the simile refers to the city's massive walls which would no more deter Yahweh than would a pile of thorn bushes. Second, Nineveh's defenders were "drunken with their drink," i.e., confused and incapable of mounting a credible defense. Third, the defenders of Nineveh would be consumed utterly "as dry stubble" (1:10).

Why this judgment on Nineveh? Nahum charges that "one who devises evil against Yahweh" had gone forth from Nineveh. The reference may be to Sennacherib who devised evil against Yahweh in his attack on Judah in 701 BC. More likely, however, this "wicked counselor"(or counselor of Belial)[6] is not any single individual, but a personification of the spirit of hostility (1:11).

B. Address to Judah (1:12-13).

While still a powerful city with numerous inhabitants, Nineveh would be cut down and disappear from the stage of world history. God had used Assyria as a tool to discipline his people. Now, however, the affliction of Judah by Nineveh would cease forever. Yahweh would break the yoke of oppression which had rested so heavily upon the shoulders of his people for more than a hundred years. The Jews had been forced to pay tribute and submit to all sorts of indignities. Attempts to re-establish independence had been brutally suppressed by the Assyrian army. Now Yahweh would set free those who were in political bondage to Assyria.

C. Address to Nineveh's Ruler (1:14).

Since the Hebrew forms are masculine in v. 14 the one addressed is probably the Assyrian king. Yahweh had issued a "commandment," a judicial order, regarding the great king. This divine decree was threefold. First, the king's "name" would no longer be "sown," i.e., his descendants would be no more.

Second, the king's temples where the patron gods of Assyria were housed would be emptied. These gods provided the theological foundation of the ruling dynasty's claim to power. The temples would be ransacked. The graven and molten images worshiped by the Assyrians would not be able to save themselves, let alone the shrines where they were housed. The judgment on Nineveh would expose the impotence of the gods which the Assyrians had required captive peoples to honor for decades.

Third, the king would be deprived of his royal mausoleum. Yahweh would dig his grave. The king would have neither the time nor strength to build his own tomb, as was the custom of great rulers.

Furthermore, Yahweh would treat the corpse of the king as "vile" (ASV; NIV) or "contemptible" (NASB). The burial would not be accompanied with pomp and pageantry. This king, contrary to his own self-estimate, was of little consequence. He would be buried in a muddy grave, not a rock mausoleum.

Not only did Yahweh dig the grave for the king of Assyria, he buried his capital as well. The once proud metropolis was so thoroughly "buried" by Yahweh that for many centuries the very location of the place was forgotten. Only beginning in 1843 were the ruins of Nineveh recovered by two intrepid archaeologists, Botta and Layard.

THE REACTION TO THE VERDICT
Nahum 1:15

The news of Nineveh's fall would be relayed toward Judah by messengers. Nahum uses the word "behold" to introduce the unexpected announcement. Using language borrowed from Isaiah 52:7, Nahum pictures the bearer of the good news racing along the mountain ridges. The report of Nineveh's fall in 612 BC would truly be "good news," for both Isaiah (10:5-27) and Micah (5:4-5) regarded the overthrow of Assyria as a prelude to the messianic age. In the fall of the oppressive superpower the faithful in Judah would discern the ultimate destruction of all enemies of God's people. While Nahum does not mention the Messiah, the promise of this good news is certainly messianic in connotation. For this reason Paul used the language here to describe Gospel preachers (Rom 10:15).

In the light of the fall of the oppressor the faithful are exhorted (1) to celebrate their feasts and (2) to perform their vows. Apparently joyous religious celebrations had been suspended during the Assyrian hegemony over Judah. The "vows" may refer to commitments which had been made to God if he would grant his people relief from the oppressor. Perhaps restrictions on temple worship during the Assyrian period made fulfillment of vows virtually impossible. Nahum is not here gloating over the destruction of the enemy so much as he is rejoicing over the restoration of pure worship of Yahweh. God's honor, not Israel's national pride, is the issue in this book. Nahum does not justify hymns of national or racial hatred.

Only in the last clause of verse 15 does Nahum mention the reason for the peace, joy and religious liberty which he has been celebrating. The "wicked one" (lit., Belial) i.e., the oppressor, "shall no more pass through you." "The champion of Nineveh's might and Ishtar's power has been overcome by the word of the Lord."[7] Assyrian armies would never again march through the length and breadth of Judah. The great enemy of God's people had been "utterly cut off," i.e., completely destroyed.

ENDNOTES

1. The outline of Nahum has been adapted from G. Campbell Morgan, *The Analyzed Bible* (Old Tappan, NJ: Revell,n.d.), p. 314.

2. G.E.Mendenhall, "The Vengeance of Yahweh," in *The Tenth Generation* (Baltimore: John Hopkins, 1973), pp. 69-104.

3. Isaiah compared the Assyrian invasion of Judah to a flood which would sweep through Judah. See Isa 8:5-8.

4. Diodorus Siculus, *Library of History* 2:27. Cited by Theo. Laetsch, *Bible Commentary, The Minor Prophets* (St. Louis: Concordia, 1956), pp. 298f.

5. Edward R. Dalglish, "Nahum" in vol. 7 *The Broadman Bible Commentary* (Nashville: Broadman, 1972), p. 239.

6. Some see Belial as a proper name virtually equivalent in meaning to Satan. See J.D.W. Watts, *The Books of Joel, Obadiah, Jonah, Nahum, Habakkuk and Zephaniah* in "The Cambridge Bible Commentary" (London: Cambridge University Press, 1975), p. 106.

7. *Ibid.*, p. 109.

CHAPTER TWENTY-NINE

The Vision of Vengeance
Nahum 2

Now that he has announced the verdict of the Great King regarding the fate of Nineveh, Nahum offers a poetic description of the judgment upon Nineveh. His purpose is not so much to celebrate the calamity of this enemy, but to reinforce the prediction which was made in chapter 1. After making a preliminary declaration, Nahum unfolds his vision of vengeance on Nineveh in three scenes. He then sketches the response to this vision on the part of God's people.

PRELIMINARY DECLARATION
Nahum 2:1-2

The second chapter begins with another direct address to Nineveh. The great city is warned that "he that dashes in pieces," i.e., the Smasher, has come up "against you." The reference is to Yahweh himself. In the agency of the Medo-Babylonian forces he would approach Nineveh to smash the power of that city.

Next Nahum used four rhetorical imperatives to exhort the city to prepare for the decisive battle: (1) "keep the fortress;" (2) "watch the way;" (3) "make your loins strong;" and (4) "fortify your power mightily." This rapid fire series of emergency commands does not grow out of charity on Nahum's part. Rather this is the prophet's way of underscoring the futility of Nineveh's defensive efforts (2:1).

The reason for the impending destruction of Nineveh is now stated. Yahweh was in the process of "restoring the splendor of Jacob as the splendor of Israel." Jacob the patriarch was once sinful, homeless and a fugitive. The name "Jacob" here points to the recent humiliation which Judah had received at the hands of the Assyrians. The Assyrians had blasphemed Yahweh and deported his people. They had demanded that the altar of their god be erected in the Jerusalem temple (2 Kgs 16:10-16). "Israel" was Jacob's spiritual name. In this context the name represents the full blessings which God had promised to his people.

Such intervention on the part of God to change the fortunes of his people was necessary. Assyria had gathered the fruit of Yahweh's vineyard, had poured out that fruit, and had destroyed the branches. The modern equivalent of this ancient metaphor would be, Assyria has run roughshod over the people of the Lord.

VISION OF THE CONFLICT
Nahum 2:3-5

In scene one of the vision Nahum sees Nineveh's enemies—the Medes—approaching. Their shields are painted red (cf. Ezek 23:14). They are clothed in scarlet uniforms. The polished metal parts of the attack chariots flash in the sunlight. Cypress-handle lances are brandished, i.e., placed in battle mode (2:3).

Nahum envisioned chariots racing in the broad streets which led to the city walls. The polished ornaments of those chariots reflected sunlight. Standing still they reminded Nahum of flashing torches. When they raced from one spot to another they flashed like lightning. The popular interpretation that Nahum is here predicting the modern automobile is too ludicrous to deserve refutation (2:4).

The interpretation of 2:5 is difficult. Some take the verse to be descriptive of the defenders of Nineveh; others think that Nahum here depicts the invaders. The latter are probably correct. The Smasher of 2:1 "remembers" (ASV), i.e., "summons" (NIV) his "nobles" (ASV) or "picked troops" (NIV). They stumble beneath the load of dirt and debris which they haul to the wall in order to construct siege works. They set up their "mantelet," a formation of defensive shields which protected the besieging army when they approached the walls (2:5).

VISION OF THE CONQUEST
Nahum 2:6-10

Nineveh was situated on the east bank of the Tigris river, and the river Husur ran through the city. Nahum foresaw the river gates of Nineveh opened by the enemy. The resulting flooding undermined the foundations of the city's buildings so that they "dissolved," i.e., washed away. Reports of flooding in connection with the fall of Nineveh are found in ancient literature (2:6).

Nahum gives to the besieged city, the national goddess or the queen a symbolic name. She is called "Huzzab" (KJV), she who is fixed.[1] Nineveh was ready for the attack by the enemy. Nonetheless, the proud city would be stripped, and then carried away captive. Her handmaids—lesser cities of the empire—would mourn over the harsh treatment of their mistress. Their plaintive moan is likened by Nahum to the sound produced by doves; they beat upon their breasts in a gesture of agony common in the Near East (2:7).[2]

Prior to her fall Nineveh had been like a pool overflowing with people. Now these "waters" flee away The Assyrian commanders urged their troops to stand fast against the onslaught of the enemy. The fleeing soldiers, however, do not even pause to look back upon the battle scene (2:8).

Meanwhile, the enemy is within the city. Nahum hears them urging one another to take the spoils of war—the silver and the gold. The stores of the great city seemed to the invaders to be inexhaustible. The "wealth of all goodly furniture" probably refers to precious stones, metals and ivories with which ancient furniture was often inlaid (2:9).

While the enemy plunders Nineveh, the population of the city huddles helplessly. The great city is "empty, and void, and waste," i.e., she has been stripped of all her wealth. The Hebrew here exhibits paronomasia which in English might be captured by the translation: "she is desolated, she is devastated, she is destroyed!" The citizens of Nineveh are incapacitated. Their hearts "melt," i.e. quake with fear. Their "knees smite together." They experience anguish in their "loins," i.e., a sick feeling in the pit of their stomach. Their faces are pale. They cannot lift a finger to prohibit the ransacking of their homes and temples (2:10).

RESPONSE TO THE VISION
Nahum 2:11-13

Nahum, speaking for all the peoples who had been oppressed by Assyria, employs mocking questions to underscore the fate of the former tyrant. He likens Nineveh to a lions' den where powerful beasts lived unmolested. The prey from distant lands was brought into the den. The members of that den were unafraid of any adversary. The Assyrian lion was able abundantly to provide for his lionesses and whelps. His caves and dens were filled with that which he violently had torn from others. Nahum's figure for Nineveh is most appropriate in view of the propensity for lion imagery in Assyrian statuary (2:11-12).

Yahweh hurls a challenge formula at the Assyrian lion such as one champion might hurl at another before mortal combat: "Behold! I am against you!" The title "Yahweh of hosts" underscores the inexhaustible power of the Lord. The chariots of Assyria which struck such fear into the peoples of the ancient Near East would be burned with fire. The enemy "sword," i.e., army, would "devour" the "young lions," i.e., the Assyrian infantry. All the prey accumulated through years of effortless campaigning would be cut off by God. Throughout the ancient Near East the voice of Assyrian ambassadors making their unreasonable demands upon hapless vassals would no longer be heard (2:13).

ENDNOTES

1. ASV, NASB and NIV regard *hutztzabh* to be a passive form of the root *natzabh*, to stand. Thus "it is decreed" (ASV; NIV) or "it is fixed." Some scholars think the term refers to the pedestal which supported the national idol. ASV recognizes in the marginal reading that the word could be taken as a proper name.

2. If Huzzab is the national goddess Ishtar, the maidens might well be the temple prostitutes which were an important part of the Ishtar cult. Normally they would dance in the temple; now they were being led away with gestures of grief.

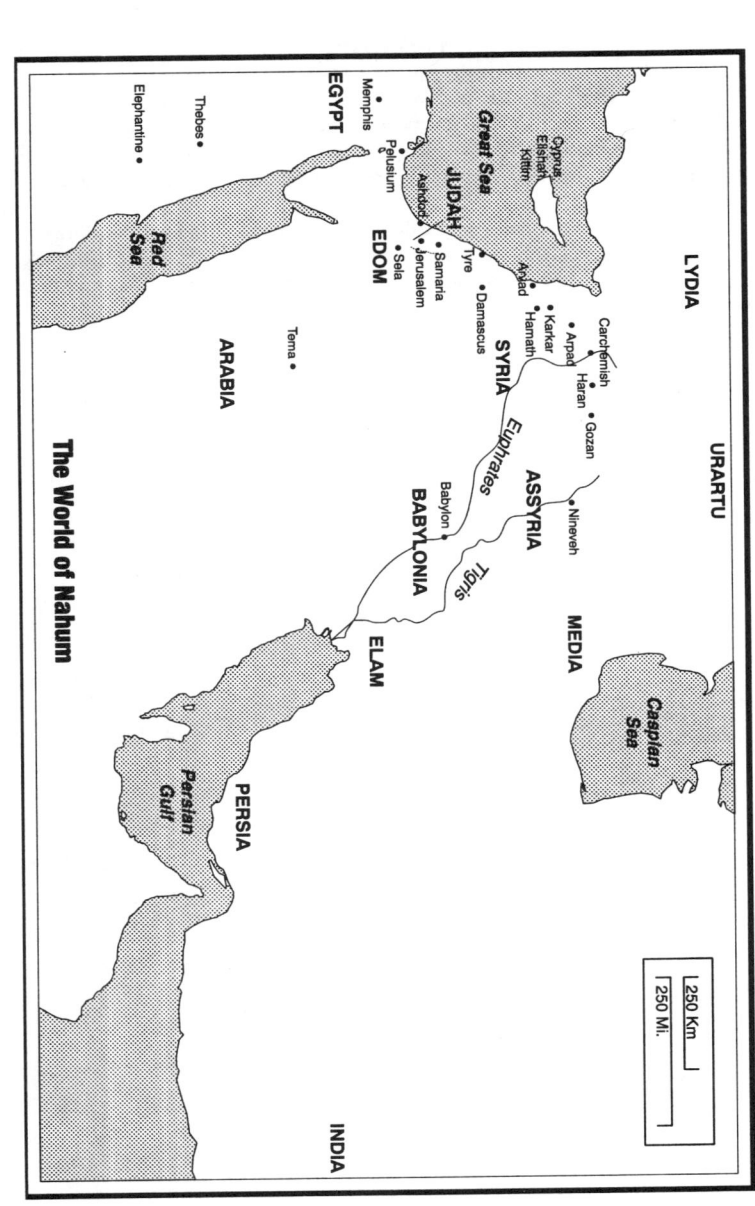

CHAPTER THIRTY

The Vindication of Vengeance
Nahum 3

In chapter three Nahum defends the judgment on Nineveh. He declares the wickedness of the city, describes that wickedness, and then dissects it.

EVIL DECLARED
Nahum 3:1-3

A prophetic "woe" is pronounced against Nineveh. The word signals an ominous future of devastating judgment from Yahweh. Nineveh was a "bloody city," i.e., a city which was built up through war and cruel oppression. The wealth of the place was due to (1) lies, i.e., fraud, deception both in business and government; and (2) rapine (ASV), i.e., robbery which takes away by violence that which rightfully belongs to another (3:1). Nations built upon the foundation of force and fraud are headed for ruin. Man is living in a moral universe. He cannot escape responsibility and accountability.

The content of the "woe" against Nineveh is a further description of the attack against the place except that the imagery is more gruesome than before. Nahum with masterfully descriptive phraseology helps his readers both hear and see the scene. The prophet can hear "the noise of the whip" cracking over the backs of the war horses; the noise of the rattling of the chariot wheels; the prancing horses thumping the ground with their hoofs and neighing with excitement and fear; chariots bounding first one direction, then the other (3:2).

Nahum sees the cavalry mounting for the attack, their polished swords and spears flashing in the sunlight. The assaulting army is glorious. Then, however, Nahum sees the result of the onslaught—a multitude of slain, corpses without number, a tangled pile of the bodies of attackers as well as defenders. Waves of fresh troops hurled into the battle by fearless commanders stumble over the bodies of those who had fallen earlier in the day. The scene is horrible. The resulting carnage underscores the fact that there is no glory in war (3:3).

EVIL DESCRIBED
Nahum 3:4-7

Nineveh was deserving of the "woe" pronounced against her. Nahum likens the city to a beautiful harlot. She had charmed the nations with her wealth, religion, art, commerce, and science. Her well-disciplined armies enticed lesser peoples to seek alliance with Assyria. She used her seductive powers to lure the nations into her arms (cf. Ezek 23:5-13). Even more, Nineveh was "the mistress of witchcrafts," i.e., she knew the art of politically mesmerizing other nations. Yet when these "lovers" failed to obey her slightest whim, the harlot sold out her allies—turned against them, enslaved them. King Ahaz of Judah was lured into the orbit of Assyrian allies (2 Kgs 16:10-19). In time, however, he paid a heavy price in terms of religious compromise and economic oppression.

For the second time Yahweh hurls a challenge formula at Nineveh (cf. 2:13): "Behold I am against you!" The seductive harlot would be punished in a manner appropriate to harlots (cf. Isa 47:3; Hos 2:3). First, Yahweh threatens to "uncover your skirts upon your face," i.e., strip the wayward woman. The harlot's nakedness would be put on public display before the kingdoms of the earth. She would thereby be disgraced before the nations. In this metaphor clothing symbolizes all the outward trappings of Assyria's power—her palaces, her gold and silver, her art, music, weaponry, etc. These would be stripped away by war and looting.

After stripping the harlot, Yahweh would "cast abominable filth" upon her. Thus the once arrogant harlot would be made "vile." Nineveh would become "a gazing-stock" (ASV) or "spectacle" (NASB; NIV). All who observed the humiliation and defilement of Nineveh—former allies and even enemies—would flee away in shock over the fact that the greatest city on the face of the earth "is laid waste." No one would mourn the death of Nineveh. No one would seek to comfort Nineveh in its hour of humiliation (3:6-7).

EVIL DEFEATED
Nahum 3:8-13

To demonstrate how the evil of Nineveh would be defeated Nahum resorts to historical analogy. The fall of such a mighty, well fortified city as Nineveh is not incredible, Nahum argues. Just look at what has happened recently. The city of No-amon (Thebes)[1] in southern Egypt had been captured by the Assyrian army of Ashurbanipal in 663 BC.[2] The great city, one of the wonders of the ancient world, had a strategic location on a large bend of the Nile river where that river is closest to the Red Sea. The waters which protected the approaches to the city are poetically called by Nahum "the sea." No-amon was the capital of a mighty empire at the time she fell. Egypt and Ethiopia were joined together. Put and the Lubim were allies of the ruling dynasty. Yet this powerful city was "carried away" by the Assyrians (3:8-9).

No-amon "went into captivity." Young children were "dashed in pieces at the head of all the streets." The attacking Assyrians had no respect for even the most helpless. The soldiers "cast lots" for the most honorable men of No-amon. These former diplomats and government officials were carried away in chains to become slaves. If such a disaster could befall such a powerful and influential city as No-amon, it could happen also to Nineveh (3:10).

Under pressure of attacking forces Nineveh would reel and totter like a drunk. She would attempt to hide, to flee to some other stronghold. The fortresses of Assyria, however, would become "like fig trees with the first-ripe figs." The enemy has but to shake the tree, and the figs drop into the mouth of the eater. Early ripe figs were a delicacy. They were easily shaken from the branches of the tree. So would the fortresses which guarded the approaches and escape routes for Nineveh fall easily to the enemy (3:11-12). Nineveh's defenders would become like women. They flee the fortresses which guarded the approaches to Nineveh. This was tantamount to throwing open the gates of the land to the enemy. Where fortresses did attempt to resist, the bars which reinforced the gates would be burned with fire (3:13).

EVIL DISPARAGED
Nahum 3:14-18

Nahum addresses Nineveh in 3:14. He calls upon the city to prepare for a protracted siege. They should (1) draw water for the siege; (2) strengthen the city's defenses; (3) and make more bricks to reinforce vulnerable places around the gates and walls. The Ninevites, however, would be cut down by the sword before their preparations were complete. The "fire" of war would consume all their defenses.

Nahum uses the figure of locusts in several ways to make his point regarding the fall of Nineveh. First, he argues that even if the defenders of Nineveh multiply like grasshoppers they would be destroyed (3:15b). For men to fight against God is utter folly.

Second, Nineveh had "multiplied" merchants "above the stars of the heaven," i.e., they had as many merchants as there were visible stars in the sky. This great commercial activity of Nineveh would suddenly stop as though consumed by a locust plague (3:16).

Third, Assyrian officials are likened to locusts sitting on a fence on a cold day. They are immobilized because of the cold. Just as locusts flee their perch in the heat of the day, so will the Assyrian officials flee in the heat of battle. The pesky insects disappear to parts unknown. So also one would be hard pressed to find Assyrian leaders when the attack began to unfold (3:17).

EVIL DESTROYED
Nahum 3:18-19

The Book of Nahum concludes with a graphic picture of the aftermath of Nineveh's destruction. For the first time in the book the mighty king of Assyria is addressed. He is informed that his "shepherds," i.e., secondary rulers, slumber in death. The nobles of the land are "at rest." The king's subjects are scattered across the mountains. No one ever would be able to reassemble these peoples. Only the king is left, the solitary survivor of the empire which once ruled the world (3:18).

Even the king of Assyria has received a grievous wound. No one could relieve the hurt or heal the wound. All who hear the report of the dying tyrant would clap their hands in glee. The wickedness—violence, idolatry, arrogance—which emanated from the palace of the king of Assyria had affected all peoples of the Near East "continually." One king followed another, but each was as bad or worse than his predecessor (3:19). Sin when it is full grown brings forth death! (James 1:15).

The Assyrian monarchy survived the fall of Nineveh for three years. With the loss of his capital and most of his army, the tyrant had been wounded with a mortal wound. In 609 BC Nebuchadnezzar attacked the remnants of the Assyrian army which was reinforced by a large army from Egypt. The Assyro-Egyptian coalition was soundly defeated, and the last claimant to the throne of Assyria met his death.

ENDNOTES

1. The city of No-amon (Thebes) is mentioned four other times in the Old Testament: Jer 46:25; Ezek 30:14,15,16.
2. For Ashurbanipal's account of his conquest of No-amon, see James Pritchard, *Ancient Near Eastern Texts Relating to the Old Testament*; 3rd ed (Princeton: University Press, 1969), p. 295.

CHAPTER THIRTY-ONE

The Coming Day of Yahweh
Zephaniah 1

The Book of Zephaniah opens with a claim that what follows is "the word of Yahweh." Zephaniah thus claims to be part of that unique fellowship of individuals to whom God revealed his word and through whom that word was made known to God's people. What follows, then, is not human speculation, opinion or prognostication. Yahweh was using this man to communicate to his people. In written form this document properly belongs with the sacred Scriptures. It deserves respect as that which is sacred, authoritative, infallible and inerrant.

Zephaniah identifies himself by means of a genealogy which traces his ancestry back four generations. He was the son of Cushi, the grandson of Gedaliah, the great-grandson of Amariah, and the great-great-grandson of Hezekiah. The recording of such an extensive genealogy is unique in prophetic literature.[1] The purpose must be to focus attention on the fact that he was a descendant of good King Hezekiah. His ancestry would have provided Zephaniah with access to the royal court and would, perhaps, have added weight to his utterances.

Zephaniah prophesied "in the days of Josiah son of Amon king of Judah." Josiah was the greatest king of the Old Testament period from the standpoint of his works. His dates are roughly 640 to 609 BC. For a more precise dating of Zephaniah's ministry within the reign of Josiah, see Chapter Twenty-seven.

JUDGMENT ON THE WORLD
A General Threat
Zephaniah 1:2-3

The coming day of Yahweh is the theme of Zephaniah. The prophet begins with a preface which sets the tone for the entire book. Then he focuses his attention on the more immediate threat against Judah.

A prophetic discourse could not begin on a more somber and shocking note. God was about to sweep the earth clean. He would "utterly consume" all things from off the face of the ground. A judgment having an impact like the great flood (cf. Gen 6:7) in scope is in view (1:2).

Using the technique of emphasis by enumeration, Zephaniah breaks down the universal statement of verse 2. He lists in reverse order of their Genesis creation the objects of God's judgment. First comes man and then beast. Yahweh then would consume the birds of the heavens and the fish of the sea. Fish were able to survive the great flood. They would not survive the judgment which Zephaniah envisions.

God had promised Noah that never again "so long as the days of the earth" continued would he destroy all flesh from the face of the ground (Gen 8:21). Zephaniah, however, envisions a judgment which comes at the end of earth's days, a judgment that ends time and ushers in eternity. He speaks of the final judgment.

All of creation is characterized by Zephaniah as "stumblingblocks" (ASV) or "ruins" (NASB). Sinful mankind has taken all that God created as good and turned it to evil purposes. The word describes the ruined state of every social and political institution. The blunt truth is that man has made a mess of both his physical and social environment. Religion, government, education, family have all been crippled by human sin. Specifically Zephaniah may have had in mind idols which were made in the form of created beings (cf. 2 Chr 28:23). Man who was given dominion over the creatures of earth perverted the order of nature by worshiping those very creatures he was to rule.

The stumblingblocks or ruins would be removed along with "the wicked" who created them. While Zephaniah pictures the judgment in universal terms, he focuses on the destruction of wicked humanity. Yahweh's solemn announcement is that 'I will cut off man from off the face of the ground."

Zephaniah's combination of "stumblingblocks" and "wicked" finds an echo in the announcement of Jesus: "The Son of man shall send forth his angels, and they shall gather out of his kingdom all things that cause stumbling, and them that do iniquity" (Matt 13:41 ASV). This statement confirms that Zephaniah is describing the final judgment.

JUDGMENT ON JUDAH
A Specific Application
Zephaniah 1:4-18

The character of world and the condition of the world require a final judgment. Individual and national temporal judgments all point toward the ultimate destruction of the wicked. Zephaniah argues that if God ultimately would deal with the wicked world at the end of time, he also would bring judgment on men and nations in the interim, before the end of time. The justice of God requires that unforgiven sin be punished.

If the announcement of universal judgment in verses 2-3 was shocking, it was not nearly so shocking as the next announcement made by this prophet. The citizens of Judah viewed themselves as the chosen of God. Ever since 701 BC when God had rescued Jerusalem from the onslaught of the Assyrian army, the theologians of Judah argued that God could never permit his city and his temple to be destroyed. Yet Zephaniah is emphatic in his announcement that Judah, laden down as it was with a burden of unforgiven sin, must face the wrath of Yahweh.

A. Cause of the Judgment (1:4-6).

The ultimate cause of the judgment is that Yahweh would "stretch forth" his hand. This metaphor suggests that God would move against them with all the forces at his disposal. Yahweh stretched out his hand in judgment against Pharaoh's Egypt and thereby brought against that land devastating plagues (Exod 7:5) and a crushing defeat at the Red Sea (Exod 15:12).[2] Now that same power which brought mighty Egypt to her knees would be directed against tiny Judah.

That hand of judgment would alight upon Judah. The inhabitants within the well-fortified city of Jerusalem would not escape. They would be "cut off." In the approaching judgment all forms of idolatry would be removed "from this place," i.e., from Jerusalem. The Holy One of Israel had established his earthly dwelling in Jerusalem. For that reason the purity of that place needed to be maintained (1:4a).

First, "the remnant" of Baal would be cut off. The old Canaanite Baalism virtually had been eliminated in the reform efforts of King Josiah. The judgment would root out that degrading nature worship once and for all.

Second, Yahweh would remove "the names of the Chemarim with the priests." The Chemarim were the idolatrous priests of the high places. Even the names of these once-influential priests would be forgotten (1:4b). The judgment against the remnant of Baal and the Chemarim began under King Josiah (2 Kgs 23:5,8) and was completed during the exile.

Third, those who worshiped the host of heaven would also be cut off. The worship of astral deities became popular during the period of the Assyrian hegemony over Judah (cf. 2 Kgs 21:3,5). King Ahaz introduced the worship of "the queen of heaven" (Jer 7:18). Under the law of Moses the worship of the host of heaven was a capital offense (cf. Deut 4:19; 17:3-7). Even after the destruction of Jerusalem by the Babylonians, the Jews who took refuge in Egypt continued to offer sacrifices to the host of heaven (Jer 44:19). Astrology is a modern adaptation of this ancient paganism.

Apparently the devotees of these deities had shrines to the sun, moon, stars or planets upon the roofs of their houses. This may suggest that astral worship did not have official status in Judah, yet with the masses it was very popular. Cuneiform texts from Ras Shamra contain a ritual which was to be performed "when offerings were made on the rooftops to astral deities and celestial luminaries."[3] Such "do it yourself" religion made a mockery of the priestly role of the people of Israel (Exod 19:6) and stands condemned by the Living God.

Fourth, the judgment would fall on those who "bow down and swear to Yahweh and also swear by Malcam." Malcom or Milcom is an alternative spelling for Molech, the chief god of Ammon. Normally a person in antiquity swore by the name of the deity he regarded as supreme. Israelites were to swear by the name of Yahweh (Deut 6:13; 10:20). By swearing in the name of two deities these worshipers were engaging in syncretism. They were placing a pagan deity on the same level as Yahweh (1:5).

Fifth, another group which would be removed in the judgment were "those that have turned back from following Yahweh." Sins of omission are as detestable to Yahweh as sins of commission. Apostate Yahweh worshipers—backsliders—would fare no better than idolaters in the day of judgment (1:6a).

Finally, those who had never sought Yahweh at all would also fall in the judgment. The two words used here "seek" (*baqash*) and "inquire" (*darash*) refer to a conscious effort to experience divine fellowship and guidance. Self-worship for some replaces the worship of the deity. These fall under the condemnation of Yahweh's judgment (1:6b).

B. Nearness of the Day (1:7).

Zephaniah called for quiet submission before Yahweh. "Hold your peace at the presence of Lord Yahweh." All manner of opposition must stop immediately. This is Zephaniah's way of calling for national repentance.

As an incentive to this repentance Zephaniah offers two considerations. First, he declares that "the day of Yahweh is at hand." This declaration means that the day was both inevitable and imminent. The grace period was over. Time had run out. Judgment was at hand.

To the prophets the day of Yahweh involved a theophany in which God would manifest his powers in a dramatic way. On that day Yahweh would manifest his sovereignty over all men. On that day he would enforce the sanctions of his covenant with his people.

Second, Zephaniah describes the day of Yahweh. He paints a gruesome picture. The destruction of Judah and Jerusalem is likened to a "sacrifice." In the Mosaic peace offering the worshipers sat down in the temple precincts to consume the meat of the offering. Only the fat portions were actually burned on the altar as a token that the entire animal belonged to God.

Those who ate of a sacrificial meal had to be ritually purified. Such was necessary because of the holiness of the divine Host at such a meal, God himself. For example, before coming into the presence of the Lord at Sinai, Moses sanctified the people and they symbolized such by washing their clothes (Exod 19:10). The covenant was actually ratified when the elders of the people "ate and drank" in the presence of Yahweh on the mount (Exod 24:11). So now Yahweh already had consecrated "his guests," i.e., those who would be instruments of Yahweh in the execution of the judgment. All was in readiness for the great "sacrificial" destruction of Jerusalem to begin.

C. Extent of the Destruction (1:8-13).

Zephaniah continues to develop the theme of the day of Yahweh. He now focuses on the devastating consequences of that day of judgment. He speaks first of the classes of the people and then the sections of the city which would be affected.

1. Judgment on all classes of people (1:8-9). In the day of Yahweh's sacrifice no sinners within the nation would escape. Those first in rank are the first to be named as victims of the disaster. The Lord would punish "the princes," i.e., national leaders, and even "the king's sons." Rank and riches would be no protection against what was coming. Why does Zephaniah not mention the king? Perhaps because the current king was Josiah, who was trying his best to bring about reform within the kingdom (1:8a).

Yahweh would "visit," i.e., punish another category of sinners, those that were "clothed with foreign apparel." Some think that the wealthy and powerful were refusing to wear the distinctive garments which were to set God's people apart from the heathen (cf. Num 15:38f.; Deut 22:11f.). By adopting the dress of neighboring nations the princes were abandoning the faith of their fathers. What one wears is a testimony to one's values, one s standards and one's faith. Others think that the reference is to the distinctive garb of the devotees of foreign cults. Those who wore "foreign apparel" were devoted idolaters (1:8b).[4]

Foreign superstitions as well as foreign garb had crept into Judah. Yahweh would also "visit" in that day those who "leap over the threshold." This was a Philistine practice (cf. 1 Sam 5:5). Superstitious acts are diametrically opposed to faith in the sovereignty of Yahweh for they imply that some force exists in the universe—luck, fate, fortune—which is not subject to the oversight of the Lord (1:9a).

Pagan standards as well as superstitions guided the actions of the princes of Judah. Among the people of God the political leaders were to be under the law, subject to its principles. In pagan society the royal family had unrestricted power to seize property. The princes of Judah are said here to "fill their master's house with violence and deceit," i.e., with objects taken by unscrupulous means. Money was the god of these men. Their creed was 'might makes right!" While they scrupulously observed superstitious practices, they willfully ignored the fundamental principles of the law of Yahweh (1:9b).

2. *Judgment in all sections of the city (1:10-11).* The coming judgment would affect the entire city of Jerusalem. First, Yahweh announces that the "noise of a cry" would arise "from the fish gate," an entrance on the north side of the city. This would be the first area attacked by an enemy. Second, he announces "a wailing" from "Mishneh," the second quarter of Jerusalem (cf. 2 Kgs 22:14; 2 Chr 34:22). The location of this part of the city is uncertain. Third, the Lord speaks of a "great crashing" from the hills. This may refer to breaking down of idols on the hills surrounding Jerusalem (1:10).[5]

Yahweh calls upon the inhabitants of "Maktesh." This seems to be the Old Testament name for the shallow valley to the west of Jerusalem called in later times the Tyropoeon valley.[6] Here is where "the people of Canaan" gathered. This phrase is further defined as "those laden with silver." Thus the Canaanites here must be a derogatory term for merchants. The Jews had become adept at shrewd and sometimes dishonest business practices like their Canaanite neighbors. These unscrupulous merchants would be "undone" and "cut off" in the day of Yahweh. Thus the commercial leadership as well as the political and religious leadership would face the wrath of Yahweh on his day. Jerusalem would cease to be a center of trade and commerce (1:11).

3. *Judgment on all sinners (1:12-13).* In that day of judgment the Lord would "search Jerusalem with lamps." Sinners would not be able to find a hiding place where they would be safe (cf. Amos 9:2-4). Yahweh would punish those who had "thickened" or "settled on their lees." The "lees" refers to the the solid matter allowed to settle to the bottom of a jar of freshly made wine. Wine would be left on the lees for awhile to pick up flavor and strength before being strained. If left too long the wine thickened, hardened. It became syrupy, bitter, unpalatable. Wine settled on its lees is a figure for undisturbed peace (1:12a).

Among the leaders of Judah spiritual complacency prevailed. They were saying in their hearts, "Yahweh will not do good, neither will he do evil." To them neither the promises nor the threats of God meant anything. God was a non-factor in all their planning. Yahweh to them was irrelevant (1:12b).

Wealth caused those leaders to think that they did not need Yahweh. That wealth, however, would be taken as spoil by an enemy. The magnificent homes in which these wealthy men lived would become a desolation. Yahweh would not allow these arrogant and spiritually autonomous barons to enjoy for long the fruit of their wealth. They might build houses, but they would never live in them. They might plant beautiful vineyards, but they would not live to taste the wine from those grapes. Those who stand under God's condemnation are doomed to absolute frustration (1:13).

D. The Terror of God's Judgment (1:14-18).

God pronounced his judgment on Judah in terms of his final judgment of the last day. All temporal judgments anticipate the final day of the Lord.

Zephaniah announced that the great day of Yahweh was near (cf. v.7). Not only so, but the prophet adds that the day was hastening toward fulfillment. In that day even mighty men would cry out in terror. Temporal judgments, such as the destruction of Judah by the Babylonians, are here called "the voice of the day." Temporal judgments herald the final judgment. They warn men and nations to prepare for that final confrontation with the Creator (1:14).

The great day of Yahweh is further described as a day of "wrath." Using the technique of emphasis by enumeration, Zephaniah mentions three pairs of descriptive adjectives to describe that day. The Hebrew reflects here the poetic device of paronomasia, i.e., the joining together of words with similar sounds. First, it would be a day of "trouble and distress." Both terms reflect extreme physical and psychological pressure. Second, it would be a day of "wasteness and desolation" (ASV). Judah would be left in utter ruin. Third, it would be a day of "darkness and thick darkness" (*apelah*), the same kind of darkness with which God afflicted the Egyptians (cf. Exod 10:22). Fourth, it would be a day of "clouds and thick darkness." The appearances of God during the Mosaic dispensation are often associated with such dark clouds (cf. e.g., Exod 20:21) (1:15).

The fifth pair of nouns becomes more specific as to the nature of that great day of Yahweh's wrath. That would be a day of "trumpet and alarm," i.e., a military invasion of Judah. The attack would be directed against "the fortified cities" and against "the high battlements." Every human defense would crumble on that day (1:16).

What do the figures of darkness and gloominess mean? Yahweh declares his intention to "bring distress upon men." The calamity would cause those men to "walk like blind men," i.e., in total confusion. In the case of Josiah's son Zedekiah, the last king of Judah, this prediction received a physical fulfillment. After forcing him to witness the execution of his sons, Nebuchadnezzar had Zedekiah's eyes pierced. He spent his last years in blindness in Babylon (1:17a).

In explaining this national calamity Zephaniah uses a generality: "because they have sinned against Yahweh." No further explanation was really necessary. To violate the will of Yahweh inevitably would bring upon Israel all the curses of the ancient covenant (1:17b).

The sinners in Judah faced a terrible future. Their blood would be poured out like dust, i.e., the ground would be covered with the blood of the slain. Their "flesh," i.e., corpses, would be left like dung upon the earth (1:17c).

Often nations would pay off an invader and avoid destruction. From that horrible fate, however, wealth would not be able to furnish escape. "Neither silver nor gold" could purchase for them deliverance in the day of Yahweh's wrath. The whole land would be devoured by "the fire of his jealousy." Yahweh's name is Jealous (Exod 34:14). He demands the exclusive allegiance of all his people. The worship of other gods leads inevitably to outpouring of his wrath (1:18a).

The Lord was determined to make an end of "of all those who dwell" in the land of Judah. That would be a "terrible end"—terrible in its suffering, in its cause, and in its consequence. Here Zephaniah is predicting the end of Judah as a political entity (1:18b).

ENDNOTES

1. Eight writing prophets have no family record. Six record the name of their father. One lists his grandfather as well as his father.

2. Moses frequently referred to the liberation of Israel from Egypt as being due to Yahweh's "mighty hand" and "outstretched arm." Cf. Deut 4:34; 5:15; 7:19; 9:29; 11:2; 26:8.

3. R.K. Harrison, *Jeremiah and Lamentations*, "Tyndale Old Testament Commentaries" (Downers Grove, IL: InterVarsity, 1973), p. 112.

4. O. Palmer Robertson cites the reference to the "keeper of the wardroom" and the donning of special vestments by the Baal cult in the days of Jehu (2 Kgs 10:22). *The Books of Nahum, Habakkuk, and Zephaniah* in "The New International Commentary on the Old Testament" (Grand Rapids: Eerdmans, 1990), p. 276.

5. *Ibid.*, p. 278.

6. Robertson (*op. cit.*, 279) thinks that the Maktesh (lit., pounding place or mortar) is a symbolic name for the entire city of Jerusalem. "Encircled by higher hills, Jerusalem itself may be compared to a mortar, a pounding place."

CHAPTER THIRTY-TWO

A Call for Repentance
Zephaniah 2

Having described the terrible dimensions of the great day of Yahweh's wrath, Zephaniah now appealed to his people to repent. He addressed to them five urgent admonitions for humility before God. Then he announced the fate of surrounding nations in an oblique call for repentance.

A DIRECT CALL FOR REPENTANCE
Zephaniah 2:1-3

Chapter 2 opens with five urgent admonitions to repentance. Faced with the prospects of the day of Yahweh's wrath, no other response was appropriate.

A. An Appeal for Humility (2:1).

In his first two admonitions Zephaniah calls upon his people to "gather together" (ASV). The verb root *qashash* means literally to stoop down as if to gather straw. This is not so much a call for assembly as for humility. By doubling the imperative Zephaniah reinforces this appeal for humility. Judah is worth no more than stubble. Judah's populace is called upon to bunch together in a manner "that acknowledges this utter worthlessness."[1] Those who refuse to humble themselves even to the dust before the holiness of God are doomed to be beaten into the dust by his judgment (2:1a).

The appeal for humility is addressed to, literally, "a nation not paled." The verb (*nichsaph*) means "to become pale." Translations and commentators offer two explanations: (1) "not paled (by shame), hence shameless; (2) "not paled (by longing)," i.e., they did not long after God. The former understanding is the basis for the ASV, NIV and NASB. The latter understanding is the basis for the ASV and NASB marginal readings (2:1b). The phrase is difficult, and either translation would conform to the context.

The need for repentance was urgent. Three times in 2:2 Zephaniah uses the word "before" (*beterem*) to stress the urgency of repenting prior to the beginning of the day of Yahweh. In two of these cases Zephaniah strengthens the "before" by adding a negative (*lo'*) which is untranslatable in English. Repentance must take place "before the decree" of judgment against Judah took effect. As early as the law of Moses the Lord had decreed a day of judgment against an apostate people (cf. Deut 28:15ff.). The day of God's grace was swiftly passing just as chaff was swiftly blown from a threshing floor (2:2a).

The urgency of repentance is underscored by mention of the terrible alternative. They must humble themselves immediately "before the fierce anger of Yahweh" (lit., the burning of Yahweh's anger). This expression occurs some thirty-three times in the Old Testament.[2] To emphasize this point Zephaniah repeats the threat virtually verbatim. Failing to take advantage of the day of grace would mean facing unprepared "the day of Yahweh's anger." The day of Yahweh was in essence the occasion when his fierce wrath was made manifest on earth (2:2b).

B. An Appeal for Action (2:3).

Three admonitions call for definite actions to be taken in the light of the coming day of Yahweh. The appeal is addressed specifically to the "meek (i.e., humble) of the earth." The reference is to those who acknowledge God's justice, who cling to his mercy, and who believe in the promise of redemption. These people needed reassurance that they were moving in the right direction. Perhaps they also needed to be motivated even to a more intense pursuit of that which was right.

The imperative "seek" (*baqqeshu*) sums up what God expects of these people in the light of the announced judgment. The plural imperative is used three times in the verse. This "seeking" is something that should be done corporately, perhaps in a context of worship. The word implies wholehearted commitment to the effort, persistence in the pursuit, and faith that the goal would be worth pursuing. Three objects of this required seeking are named.

First, they must "seek Yahweh," for he alone can be a refuge in the coming day of judgment. The basic reason for the judgment in the first place was that the nation did not seek the Lord (cf. 1:6). The promise that those who seek him will in fact find him is no less certain in the Old Testament than in the New (Jer 29:13).

Second, they must "seek righteousness." This refers to the proper treatment, as judged by the law, of one's neighbors. Justice in the courts, and civility in everyday life is in view here.

Third, they must "seek meekness." They must cast away every trace of self-righteousness and pride. Meekness is strength under control. It is a quality most clearly demonstrated in the life of Jesus (Matt 11:28-30).

Such action was the only hope. "Perhaps" (*'ulay*)—Zephaniah would offer no guarantees—they would find safety in the day of Yahweh's anger. Is Zephaniah saying that even the righteous and penitent could not be sure they were part of the remnant? Not at all. The point is that even the remnant may have to experience, along with the wicked, the temporal judgment upon Jerusalem. Zephaniah could not offer more assurance than the Lord had revealed to him (2:3).

AN OBLIQUE CALL TO REPENTANCE
Focus on the Nations
Zephaniah 2:4-15

Like most of his prophetic colleagues, Zephaniah recorded Yahweh's word regarding several surrounding nations. The point of this survey is to offer to Judah another incentive to repentance. The devastation of these neighbors should make the citizens of Judah take warning as they face the day of Yahweh's wrath. God must punish unrighteousness wherever it is found. Judah would derive benefit from these Gentile judgments. That too should make Judah turn to God out of gratitude. Finally, the revelation that Gentiles would one day share in the blessings of God's people was calculated to stimulate in Zephaniah's auditors a determination to so live that they would share in the blessings of that day. All of these elements are present in the oracles regarding foreign nations.

Zephaniah selects one nation in each of the four directions of the compass to illustrate his point: the Philistines in the west, Moab and Ammon in the east, Cush in the south and Assyria in the north.

A. In the West: Philistia (2:4-7).

The four remaining cities of the Philistine Pentapolis[3] would face the wrath of Yahweh. Gaza, the southernmost Philistine city, would be "forsaken." The oracle then moves north along the coast to Ashkelon and Ashdod. Ashkelon would become a "desolation." The enemy would "drive out" Ashdod "at noonday." Either a surprise attack—during the afternoon siesta—is intended, or else the notion that the city would be captured in only half a day. Ekron, an inland Philistine city, "shall be rooted up." The verbs used here have the cumulative effect of depicting a total destruction (2:4).

Zephaniah pronounced one of those ominous prophetic "woes" on "the inhabitants of the seacoast." Philistia was located along the Mediterranean coast. These people are here called "Cherethites," which appears to be an earlier name for the Philistines or for a closely related people. The word of Yahweh was against "the land of the Philistines" (2:5a).

Zephaniah addressed Philistia as "Canaan" because that region was destined for the same fate as ancient Canaan. The "land of the Philistines," the consummate enemy of God's people during the period of the Judges and the early monarchy, faced total destruction. Yahweh had declared: "I will destroy you, that there be no inhabitant." The first person direct address adds weight to the announcement (2:5b).

The results of the devastation of the Philistine city states is further sketched. The area would lose its significance as an important commercial area through which great trade routes passed. Philistia would become pasture lands for shepherds and their sheep (2:6).

A new and dramatic consideration now comes to the forefront in the book. For the first time Zephaniah introduces the concept of a remnant for Judah. The "perhaps" of verse 3 becomes a promise in verse 7. A community of God's people would survive the ordeal of judgment. Zephaniah does not further identify this remnant. Apparently they are the "humble" who "sought" the Lord in accord with the previous appeal of Zephaniah in verse 3 (2:7a).

The spiritual remnant would one day take full possession of the land of promise. In the conquest under Joshua the Israelites were unable to possess the land of the Philistines (Josh 13:2-3). This remnant, however, would even possess the territory of the Philistines. As Yahweh's flock the remnant would find pasture there. In the evening they would lie down in the unoccupied houses of Ashkelon.

Two reasons are given for why the remnant of God's people are able to occupy the territories of the Philistines. First, Yahweh their God would "visit them." In Scripture divine visitations can either be positive or negative. Earlier Zephaniah had spoken of a visitation for judgment (cf. 1:8-9). In this case a positive visitation is intended, a visitation for salvation. Second, Yahweh promises to "bring back their captivity." The idiom is common in the prophets. It means that God would reverse the fortunes of his people. For the Philistines there was no hope beyond judgment. For God's people, however, there was hope. Such was the assurance given as early as the time of Moses (cf. Deut 30:1-3).

During the intertestamental period Philistia was conquered by the Maccabean Jewish rulers.[4] The reference probably refers, however, to the messianic age. The shepherds would be the leaders of the Christian faith (John 21:15ff.; Acts 20:17,28ff.; 1 Pet 5:2ff.) and the sheep would be those who followed their teaching (John 10:2-30). During the first Christian century the region of Philistia was Christianized. For centuries it was the center of vigorous Christian activity.[5] Occupation of the territory of the Philistines is but a specific application of the general promise made by Jesus that the meek shall inherit the earth (Matt 5:5).

B. In the East: Moab and Ammon (2:8-11).

The second foreign nation oracle is directed against the blood relatives of Israel. It goes beyond the first in several respects. Here Zephaniah specifies the reasons for the judgment. Rather than passively occupy the ruins of the enemy, here the remnant would spoil the enemy. Finally, this oracle anticipates the day when Gentiles worldwide would offer their worship to the God of heaven.

Yahweh himself pronounces the judgment upon Moab and Ammon. Both of these peoples were descendants of Lot, the nephew of Abraham. At the time of the Exodus the king of Moab hired Balaam to pronounce a curse on Israel (Num 22:3-6). Under the compulsion of the Spirit Balaam revealed that a future king—the star and scepter—would one day crush through the forehead of Moab (Num 24:17). Zephaniah now renews that threat against Moab.

The Ammonites attempted to take advantage of Israel throughout the parallel histories of the two peoples. King Nahash attacked Jabesh-gilead and made the most outrageous demands of its inhabitants (1 Sam 11:1-2). His son Hanun humiliated David's ambassadors by shaving half their beards and cutting off their garments so as to reveal their buttocks (2 Sam 10:1-4). Amos had condemned the Ammonites for "ripping open the pregnant women of Gilead" (Amos 1:13). Even after the time of Zephaniah the Ammonites would continue to mock and harass God's people (Jer 40:14; Neh 4:3).

The Moabites and Ammonites are condemned for doing what they had done through the centuries, viz., heaping reproach upon the people of Judah. These neighbors had reviled them in the day of their calamity. From their homelands in Transjordan these cousin nations had "magnified themselves" against the border of Judah, i.e., they were guilty of border incursions. They had their sights set on possessing the inheritance which God had given to his people. This sin was all the worse because Israel, under divine directive, had always respected the borders of Ammon (2:8).[6]

A divine oath seals the doom of Moab and Ammon. "As I live" introduces an oath formula in Hebrew idiom. As certainly as Yahweh is the Living God, so certain is the utter devastation of Moab and Ammon. The deity identifies himself with two appropriate titles. He is "Yahweh of hosts," i.e., the God of irresistible power; and he is "the

God of Israel," i.e., he had a special relationship with Israel (2:9a).

Moab and Ammon would face the same fate as Sodom and Gomorrah (cf. Deut 29:23). Those geographical regions would be possessed by "nettles" and "salt pits." The region would become "a perpetual desolation." The comparison to Sodom and Gomorrah is most appropriate because the ancestors of these two nations were born shortly after the destruction of those cities. The traditions regarding the destruction of those two sinful cities must have been widely circulated among the Moabites and Ammonites.

Suddenly Zephaniah changes the metaphor. He now turns from the lands of Moab and Ammon to the people. The Ammonite and Moabite people would become "a prey' of "the residue of my people." The remnant of Israel would "inherit" these peoples (2:9b).

This prophecy, like that which pertained to Philistia, began to be fulfilled in the intertestamental period when some of the Maccabean rulers launched campaigns in Transjordan.[7] Yet since the terms "residue" and "remnant" often seem to have a spiritual connotation in prophetic literature, the Christianization of the Transjordan area probably is in view.

At this point the oracle shifts from the first person pronouncement by Yahweh, to Zephaniah's discourse about Yahweh in the third person. National arrogance mixed with a sense of religious superiority was at the root of the divine opposition to Moab and Ammon. Both Isaiah (16:6) and Jeremiah (48:29) also reference the pride which was so characteristic of these peoples. These eastern nations had "reproached and magnified themselves against" the people of Yahweh of hosts. That was tantamount to mocking Yahweh himself (2:10).

The point that Zephaniah is trying to make is this: If Yahweh would humble the arrogance of neighboring nations, would he not also humble the arrogance of Judah? At the outset of this chapter the prophet had made the point that only in humility and meekness was there any hope of survival in the day of Yahweh's wrath. Though the world mocks the virtue of meekness, still it is only those who possess such a quality who can stand before the Lord. God will break those who are not broken before him.

In the day of judgment Yahweh would be "terrible," i.e., awesome, unto them. He would come to them in a judgment which would be great beyond human imagination. Human pride would quickly dissipate in the face of that awesome manifestation.

In that day of judgment Yahweh would "famish [make lean] all the gods of the earth." This means that he would bring idolaters to such straits that they would no longer be able to bring the sacrifices required by their gods. Without their daily sacrifices those idols would starve to death! Prophetic sarcasm oozes from these words. By mentioning the humbling of the gods in juxtaposition to the pride of Moab and Ammon the prophet may be suggesting that the source of the pride of those people was their national religion (2:11a).

At some point after the cutting off of the gods of Moab and Ammon people all over the world would worship Yahweh. Earlier in this chapter Zephaniah had indicated that only a remnant of his people would survive the judgment. This remnant would possess the land of promise. Now he expands on that picture. Great throngs of Gentiles would come to know Yahweh. Every one would worship "from his place," even in the distant coastlands of the nations, i.e., the most distant nations (cf. Isa 66:19). Zephaniah thus joins the great prophetic chorus in joyfully proclaiming the day when Gentiles as well as Jews would love and serve the true and living God (2:11b).

Zephaniah in no way contradicts the picture painted by Isaiah of throngs of Gentiles marching up to Jerusalem for worship (Isa 2:3). Isaiah also knew of a future in which Gentiles would worship the Lord in their own lands (Isa 19:19,21). People would have no need to travel to geographical Jerusalem, for true Jerusalem (Heb 12:22) would be worldwide in scope. Jesus may have had such passages in mind when he told the Samaritan woman that the day was fast approaching when the geography of worship would no longer matter (John 4:21-23).

C. In the South: Ethiopia (2:12).

In the south Zephaniah selects Ethiopia for his example of judgment. Why does he not use Egypt, that far more powerful southern neighbor? No satisfactory answer to this question has been proposed. From 715-664 BC Egypt and Ethiopia were united under the twenty-fifth dynasty. Perhaps Zephaniah is in fact referring to Egypt under the derogatory term Cush or Ethiopia. Juxtaposing Cush and Assyria (in the following verse) suggests that Zephaniah was in fact referring to the great power of the south under the name Cush. One, however, cannot be certain of this.

The extreme brevity of this oracle sets it apart within this section of foreign nation pronouncements. Zephaniah elaborates neither on the judgment itself nor the reasons for it. The direct address to the Cushites also is distinctive. The mere mention of the Cushites seems to be sufficient to establish the need for judgment and the severity of it. Zephaniah need say no more! Obviously both the prophet and his audience had information about Cush which is not available to the modern reader.

Yahweh now warns the Ethiopians that they too would be slain by the divine sword. The point is that Yahweh would be directly involved in executing this judgment. The fountainhead of the theme of Yahweh's sword are the words spoken by the Lord through Moses in the covenant renewal ceremony of the plains of Moab (Deut 32:40-42). In the battles of the settlement period that sword was wielded against the enemies of God's people (Josh 5:13; Judg 7:20). The sword is spiritualized in the New Testament as the "sword of the spirit" (Eph 6:17). In the Revelation John again saw that sword smiting the nations (e.g. Rev 1:16).

If Zephaniah was referring to Ethiopia (rather than Egypt under the name Cush), then no fulfillment for this oracle can be documented. Before Zephaniah's day the Cushite dynasty which ruled Egypt suffered greatly at the hands of the Assyrians. After the battle of Carchemish, Ethiopia probably suffered as an ally of Egypt at the hands of Nebuchadnezzar (Ezek 30:4). With the Medo-Persian ascendancy came a fresh series of calamities. Cambyses, the successor of Cyrus, reduced the country to a condition of vassalage in 525 BC; and in the time of Xerxes the Ethiopians had to furnish a contingent for the Great King's invasion of Greece.[8]

The previous oracles directed to Philistia, Moab and Ammon have as their climax the eventual conversion of Gentiles to the worship of Yahweh. Possibly that is also the thrust of the brief oracle regarding Cush (Ethiopia). The Gospel came to Ethiopia through a government official who was converted while making a trip to Jerusalem for worship (Acts 8). Yahweh may well smite the Cushites with the sword of the spirit as well as the sword of judgment.

The point is that if God's sword can smite distant Cush, should not Judah take warning? That sword which was poised, as it were, over Cush should have reminded Zephaniah's auditors of another time when that same sword hovered over Jerusalem (2 Sam 24:16-17). Thus the brief oracle against Cush, like the two oracles which preceded it in this section, is a call for serious contemplation and reconsecration.

D. In the North: Assyria (2:13-15).

Yahweh would also stretch out his hand against the north. Assyria, which had ruled the world from about 1100 to 612 BC, would face his wrath. Though the Assyrians had passed their imperialistic heyday at the time Zephaniah wrote about 621 BC, they still were a major player in the politics of the Near East. The verb forms in verse 13 express the prophet's personal wish or desire. Perhaps Zephaniah had personally witnessed atrocities for which the Assyrians were deservedly infamous in the ancient world. In any case, the standard English versions do not reflect the thrust of the Hebrew when they render these verbs as simple futures.

Zephaniah expressed his desire that Yahweh would "stretch out his hand" . . . "destroy" . . . and "make desolate." The focus of these verbs progressively narrows: "the north" . . . "Assyria" . . . "Nineveh." Nineveh was the cultural capital of the world when Zephaniah wrote. Yet that great city would "dry up like the wilderness." The place was already in ruins at the time Xenophon traveled through the area about 400 BC (2:13).[9]

Where once a proud people assembled, "every kind of beast of a nation" would lie down. Zephaniah seems to be designating the new inhabitants of Nineveh as a "nation." Herds of cattle would graze there. Wild desert birds would roost in the decorative columns and sing in the windows of the once-great cities. Rubble would make entrance to the deserted buildings virtually impossible. Yahweh would lay bare "the cedar-work" of the city, i.e., the foundations of the walls which often contained rows of wood to lessen the impact of earthquakes. The picture here is of total destruction of the great cities of Assyria (2:14).

The great city of Nineveh was once joyous. She "dwelt carelessly," i.e., she was proud and secure. She said in her heart, "I am, and there is none besides me." The Ninevites regarded their city as supreme in the earth. She had no rivals commercially, militarily, culturally. The city virtually deified herself! This national arrogance called forth the wrath of Yahweh (2:15a).

That once proud city would become a desolation. The ruins of the place would be the habitation of beasts of various kinds. Travelers in the area would express their amazement over the fate of the place by a whistle or hiss, and by a wag of the head (2:15b).

CONCLUSION

Thus Zephaniah pled with his people to repent, first directly with admonitions to humility and meekness, then indirectly by surveying the fate of surrounding nations. The God of the Bible punishes wickedness wherever it is found. He is no respecter of persons when it comes to judgment. Only those who humble themselves before him have any chance of escaping temporal judgment, not to mention eternal judgment.

ENDNOTES

1. O. Palmer Robertson, *The Books of Nahum, Habakkuk, and Zephaniah* in "The New International Commentary on the Old Testament" (Grand Rapids: Eerdmans, 1990), p. 290.
2. J.M.P. Smith, *A Critical and Exegetical Commentary on the Books of Micah, Zephaniah and Nahum* (Edinburgh: T. & T. Clark, 1911; reprint 1974), p. 214.
3. Gath is here omitted (as in Amos). This city had been laid low by King Uzziah prior to the time of Zephaniah (Cf. 2 Chr 26:6).
4. On the conquest of Philistia in the intertestamental period, see 1 Macc 5:68; 10:67-89; 11:60ff.; 13:43ff.
5. Theo. Laetsch, *The Minor Prophets* (St. Louis: Concordia, 1956), p. 368.
6. G.E. Wright and F. V. Filson, *The Westminster Historical Atlas to the Bible,* pp. 70-81; see Plate XII:A, p. 80.
7. Deut 2:19. Judg 11:14-28. This irony is pointed out by Robertson, *op. cit.,* p. 304.

8. A.C. Jennings, "Zephaniah" in vol. 5 of *An Old Testament Commentary for English Readers* ed. Charles John Ellicott (New York: Cassell, 1901), p. 541.
9. Xenophon, *Anabasis* 3.4. pp. 10-12.

CHAPTER THIRTY-THREE

The Results of the Great Day
Zephaniah 3

The final chapter of Zephaniah weaves the threads of facts previously related about the great day of Yahweh into another picture of that event. The day of Yahweh brings destruction to those who have refused to repent and purification to the remnant. On that day both God and his people will be able to celebrate the result of Yahweh's intervention in the affairs of man.

In chapter 2 Zephaniah directly and indirectly pled for humility and meekness before the Lord. Chapter 3 opens with a unit describing what will happen to those who do not heed that call. The focus throughout the unit is on the city of Jerusalem although the name is never used. First the prophet pronounces a "woe" on the city; then Yahweh himself speaks directly to the city.

A WOE ON THE CITY
Zephaniah 3:1-5

In the previous chapter Zephaniah pronounced a "woe" (*hoy*) on the Gentiles who lived in the coastal area (2:5). Now he utters that ominous word against the city, i.e., Jerusalem. The word comes from the vocabulary of lamentation. It suggests an impending funeral, in this case, the funeral of Jerusalem. Destruction is the fate of those who fall under a "woe" of Yahweh.

A. The Addressee (3:1).

Three participial forms here indicate the conditions for which the city stands condemned: "rebellious," "polluted" and "oppressing." First, Jerusalem was "rebellious" (*more'ah*). The place was living in open revolt against the principles of God's covenant. Like spoiled brats, they had abused the privilege of their special relationship to Yahweh. They felt that they were not bound by his law. Their disposition toward the word of Yahweh was both obstinate and defiant.

Second, Jerusalem was "polluted" (*nig'alah*). Their state of being in rebellion against God defiled them. They could no longer carry on the distinctive responsibilities of a priestly nation because of their defilement (cf. Ezra 2:62; Neh 7:64). They were disqualified from drawing near to the Lord as his special people. Zephaniah has in mind more than the ceremonial pollution so common under the Mosaic law. He is not thinking of moral pollution, but of bloody deeds of violence which splatter the perpetrators with blood (Lam 4:13-14). Killing the innocent, especially the little ones, is the moral outrage which had polluted Jerusalem (3:1a).

Third, Jerusalem is designated as "the oppressing city." The reference is to the mistreatment of the poor and helpless in the judicial system. From the earliest times Israel had been charged not to oppress the stranger (Exod 22:21; Lev 19:33), a brother (Lev 25:14) or a slave (Deut 23:16). Now the city collectively is charged with oppression. Mistreatment of the unfortunate was a way of life there (3:1b).

B. The General Indictment (3:2).

The indictment consists of four terse charges. First, Judah is charged with not obeying "the voice." Hearing the voice of Yahweh had been a unique privilege of Israel (Deut 4:32-33). Yet that privilege had been abused (cf. Num 14:22). Every covenant curse was directed against those who would not hear the voice of God (Deut 28:45,62). So the accusation made by Zephaniah is indeed ominous. The reference is probably to the voice of the prophets who spoke as God's ambassadors to his people during the monarchy period.

Second, Judah would not receive correction. She disregarded the corrective discipline—the *musar* judgments—which God sent upon her. Yahweh had chastened them again and again throughout their history, but they had paid no mind. Famine, drought, war, and pestilence had all failed to bring Israel to her senses and to her knees (cf. Amos 4:6-12).

Third, Judah did not trust in Yahweh during national emergencies. Unbelief was the bedrock sin of this city. All other sins of the place resulted from this fundamental failure. Like King Ahaz Jerusalem typically had sought a political solution to her difficulties rather than a spiritual one (cf. Isa 7:3-17).

Fourth, Jerusalem did not draw near to God. This implies true worship. What a bold accusation to make against a city where morning and evening sacrifices were offered each day in the temple of Yahweh! To draw near to God requires faith, a contrite heart, loving gratitude, and exclusive devotion. Truly drawing near to Yahweh excludes any dalliance with other deities. On all counts Jerusalem failed. The place was devoid of true worship (3:2).

C. The Specific Indictment (3:3-4).

Next Zephaniah takes up the corruption of Judah's leaders. He condemns the princes, the prophets and the priests.

1. The princes (3:3). Zephaniah likened Judah's princes to "roaring lions" lusting for more prey. Second, the judges were like "evening wolves." These vicious animals would go about under cover of darkness. They "leave nothing until morning," i.e., they utterly devour their victims. Leaders of God's people should model after shepherds. Too often they are vicious beasts.

2 The prophets (3:4a). Even the religious leaders of the nation stood under God's condemnation. Judah's prophets were "reckless" in their proclamation of God's word. They presumed to speak in Yahweh's name even when he had not spoken. They presented personal opinion as divine oracle. Such conduct under the law of Moses was a capital crime (cf. Deut 18:20). Those prophets were also "treacherous persons." They did not bring their own lives into conformity with God's word. They abused the trust of God's people. They used their sacred office to further their own agenda.

3. The priests (3:4b). Against the priests two charges are made. First, they had "profaned the sanctuary," i.e., defiled it by permitting ritually and morally unclean persons to come to its courts. Second, they had "done violence to the law," i.e., they had twisted and perverted the law to make it support unjust decisions. On difficult cases the priests would assist the courts in rendering judicial decisions (Deut 17:8-9). Because of bribery or prejudice the priests of Zephaniah's day had abused this responsibility. By their sophistry and bungling these priests had brought the law of God itself into disrepute.

D. The Efforts of Yahweh (3:5).

Yahweh, the God of unchanging righteousness, continued to dwell in the midst of this corrupt people. Every morning he would "bring his justice to light" without fail. The reference is probably to the morning sacrifice which illustrated his wrath against sin. Still "the unjust knows no shame." They failed to learn from the sacrificial system that the wages of sin is death. So they continued to engage in the most despicable conduct. How much longer could an eternally righteous God dwell in the midst of such a corrupt people? (3:5).

A WORD TO THE CITY
Zephaniah 3:6-8

Yahweh had a personal word for the city of Jerusalem, a word of justification and a word of encouragement.

A. Word of Justification (3:6-7).

He reminds the citizens of Jerusalem how he had judged the wicked in other nations. Yahweh had "cut off" nations, i.e., brought them to political extinction. Even as Zephaniah spoke, the battlements of those nations were desolate, the streets of their cities empty. Travelers no longer visited those once proud places. A conspicuous example of Yahweh's judgment would be Israel, the former northern kingdom, which had been carried into captivity about a century before Zephaniah (3:6).

Throughout the years when he was unleashing his wrath on neighboring nations, Yahweh had appealed to Jerusalem time and again. He urged his people to "fear him," i.e., reverently serve him. He urged them to receive "correction" or "instruction." Only thus would they be able to postpone the "cut off" of their nation. Repentance was the only means by which Judah might escape all that God had "appointed" concerning her (3:7a).

Judah gave no heed to all of God's efforts to salvage them as a nation. They ignored his judgments. They rose up early[1] to corrupt their deeds, i e., they were eager to corrupt their ways. Their actions fulfilled a prediction of Moses in Deut 31:29 (3:7b).

B. Word of Encouragement (3:8).

Yahweh urged believers in Judah to "wait on me." When the wicked prosper the righteous can only trust that in his own time God will bring judgment on them. God's day was coming! In that day he would "rise up to the prey." The picture here is of a hunter (or perhaps a ravenous beast) rising up from his camouflage to seize the victim which had been ensnared in the trap (3:8a).

God had determined to gather the nations and kingdoms for judgment. In that day he would pour out on them his "indignation" and "fierce anger." All the earth would one day be devoured with the fire of divine jealousy. No sinner would be able to stand before him (3:8b).

SALVATION OF THE REMNANT
Zephaniah 3:9-13

The fire of judgment must fall upon Jerusalem. That, however, would not be the end of the story. In the previous verses Zephaniah has assumed the destruction of Jerusalem and the scattering of her citizens. In this unit the prophet anticipates the reconstitution of the people of God.

A. A United People (3:9).

Another reason for patient hope on the part of believers is that eventually Gentiles would turn to the Lord. After the judgment God would "turn to the peoples," i.e., show them mercy. The peoples or Gentiles would then have a "pure lip," i.e., a language free of the names of idols, a language of appropriate respect for Yahweh. Lips speak out of the abundance of the heart. Thus purified lips point to purified hearts, or conversion (3:9a).

These converted Gentiles would then "call on the name of Yahweh," i.e., address him in prayer. Earlier Joel (2:32) similarly had anticipated a calling on the name of Yahweh for salvation. The Apostle Peter interpreted what transpired on the day of Pentecost in AD 30 as the fulfillment of the predictions of Joel. Now Zephaniah uses the same language of the nations. These Gentiles would serve Yahweh "with one shoulder" or "shoulder to shoulder" (NASB). They would cheerfully join Jews in putting their shoulder to the task of carrying out the will of God (3:9b).

B. An Evangelistic People (3:10).

Specifically, that to which these converted Gentiles would put their shoulder is the task of evangelism. Beyond the rivers of Ethiopia the gospel of God's grace would have its impact. Converted Gentiles there would bring precious souls as an offering to Yahweh.[2] The offering would consist of "my suppliants," i.e., those who would make supplication of him, who would call upon him for salvation (3:10a).

Those who are brought as an offering to Yahweh are further described as "the daughter of my dispersed." Such language implies a previous assembly which has been dispersed. The allusion is most likely to the dispersion of Israel after the fall of the northern and southern kingdoms. The "daughter" of Yahweh's dispersed people would be the offspring of the dispersed remnant of Israel. Thus the beautiful picture here is that of converted Gentiles evangelizing Jews and bringing them back to the Lord as an offering. The greatest offering that one can bring to God is another soul (3:10b).

C. A Purified People (3:11-13a).

"In that day," i.e., the New Testament age, Zion shall be glorious. Physical Zion (Jerusalem) was earlier condemned because she knew no shame (cf. 3:5). New Testament Zion shall not be put to shame for her deeds. Zion's citizens will serve the Lord sincerely, faithfully, morally. Past transgressions will have been forgiven (3:11a).

The community of faith is pictured without shame because God had removed all those who are resolute in sin. Proud and arrogant transgressors will have been purged from New Testament Zion. The New Jerusalem would be characterized by humility. Recognition that salvation is by grace and not of works produces humility in the hearts of the redeemed (3:11b).

Those who remain in Zion after the purging will be "an humble and poor people." These terms—basically synonyms—in this context are best regarded as spiritual rather than social categories. The humble and poor are those who have heeded Zephaniah's call to humble themselves as stubble (cf. 2:2), i.e., to regard themselves as worthless as stubble and as vulnerable to God's fiery wrath as a pile of straw. They know their sinfulness. They know they have nothing to offer with which to make amends for that sin. These people put their whole trust "in the name of Yahweh," i.e., in his revelation, his word (3:12).

The remnant of Israel, i.e., those who are saved, "shall not do iniquity." The reference is to willful transgressions oft repeated, the kind of sin which kills faith and trust in God's word. Yahweh does not do iniquity (cf. 3:5). Thus the thought is that the redeemed adopt the character of their God. They reflect the image of God (Col 3:10) in their daily walk (3:13a).

The remnant would not "speak lies." To emphasize this point Zephaniah added, "Neither shall a deceitful tongue be found in their mouth." The redeemed would not be hypocrites, saying one thing while doing another. Their purified lips cannot speak what is untrue for their mouths reflect the purity of their hearts.

D. A Content People (3:13b).

Using a scene taken from the life of shepherds, Zephaniah depicts the blessing which would come upon the purified remnant. They would find contentment in a holy and godly life. Like sheep they shall feed and lie down safely in a pasture prepared by the Good Shepherd. The prophets of God expected God to shepherd his flock after the exile (Ezek 34:11-19). In the more distant future they expected a Davidic ruler who would be the Good Shepherd (Ezek 34:23-24).

When Jesus claimed to be the Good Shepherd he was making a messianic claim (John 10:11).

Under the care of the Good Shepherd the flock would not be afraid. Later prophets would use this same language to depict the status of God's people after the exile (Jer 30:10; 46:27; Ezek 34:28; 39:26). Moses had promised that obedience to the covenant would result in just this kind of security (Lev 26:5-6; Deut 28:1-14). So the new Israel of God—Jew and Gentile together—would inherit the covenant promises of the law of Moses (3:13b).

CELEBRATION OVER THE OUTCOME
Zephaniah 3:14-20

If Zephaniah opened his book with one of the most blunt descriptions of the wrath of God, the book closes with one of the grandest depictions of his love. Beyond the temporal judgment on national Judah would come the day of great happiness. Thus the redeemed are encouraged to "sing," "shout,"[3] "be glad," and "rejoice with all the heart." Zephaniah piles up the verbs which express joy to serve as stepping stones from the present gloom to the future glory. Knowing what the future holds and how the battle with evil shall terminate, believers can live confidently even in the midst of despair. God intends for his people to enjoy life in the here and now. In the darkest hour Biblical hope casts joyous rays of light on the believer's path.

A. Terms of Endearment (3:14).

Zephaniah bestows three honorable names upon those who are the elect of God. First, they are "the daughter of Zion." New Zion would consist of converted Jews and Gentiles who through humble faith have committed their lives to the Lord. New Zion would not be a dot on the map, but a universal kingdom to which all the redeemed have come (Heb 12:22).

Second, the people of God are called "Israel." The remnant of the old Israel (v. 13) plus the converted Gentiles would constitute the New Israel (Gal 6:16). Messianic Israel would be a nation based on grace not race, on faith, not biological descent (Matt 21:43; 1 Pet 2:9).

Third, the people of God are called "daughter of Jerusalem." The geographical Jerusalem was a type of the New Jerusalem, the center of God's activity. The church of Christ is the heavenly Jerusalem (Gal 4:25.26; Heb 12:22).

B. Confidence in Forgiveness (3:15-16).

Why does Zephaniah encourage such joy on the part of true believers? First, Yahweh would take away all judgments. Having been forgiven of their sin, citizens of the New Testament Zion no longer stand under the condemnation of God (Rom 8:1). Second, Yahweh would "cast out" all of Zion's enemies. Defeat of enemies was a promise which God made to Abraham and Judah (Gen 22:17; 49:8). The promise was repeated as part of the Mosaic covenant (Deut 28:7). Third, the King of Israel, even Yahweh himself, would dwell in the midst of that New Jerusalem. Jesus promised: "Lo I am with you always" (Matt 28:20). Fourth, the people of God would have no need to fear any evil, i.e., disaster, in the future (3:15).

In that messianic age Jerusalem would be told not to fear. With Yahweh dwelling in their midst and all their enemies defeated what would there be to fear? Fear is the opposite of joy. Fear also hinders effective service. So New Testament Zion would be told "let not your hands be slack." (cf. Heb 12:12-13). The point is that believers must not yield to discouragement. They must not let fear intimidate, or in any way hinder the work of God's people. Believers have been saved to serve, not sit! (3:16).

C. The Presence of God (3:17).

Fear can be banished because of the presence of Yahweh in the midst of Zion. The name "Yahweh" brings to mind all the mighty acts which the Lord performed on behalf of ancient Israel. Yahweh is "your God," i.e., the God who claims this people and is in turn claimed by them. The words suggest a new relationship between Yahweh and his people. The Lord is also called here "a mighty one" (*gibbor*). The term is used of a warrior who is able to overcome all his foes. Yahweh can and will save his people from all dangers. His presence brings confidence and courage (3:17a).

When he sees his people joyfully and confidently serving him, Yahweh would rejoice over Zion "with joy." The last phrase underscores the intensity of the rejoicing of the Lord. At times he would "be silent in his love," i.e., he would contemplate with satisfaction his people in their service. At other times he would burst forth "with singing" in his joy over his people (3:17b).

FINAL ENCOURAGEMENT
Zephaniah 3:18-20

The Book of Zephaniah concludes with a first person word of encouragement for the believers from God himself. Those living in the dark days preceding the Babylonian destruction of Jerusalem needed much encouragement.

A. Consolation (3:18).

After the judgment would come consolation. All the sorrows associated with that judgment would be forgotten. Yahweh promises to gather his people. The promise assumes they had previously been scattered. Those who participate in this gathering are said to be those who "sorrow." God has at his disposal the most delightful ways of wiping away the tears of the faithful.

The sorrow here envisioned is of a very specific kind. Yahweh would gather those who sorrowed "for the solemn assembly." The fall of Jerusalem would mean the destruction of the temple and consequent cessation of all formal worship. Not all, as it turned out, lamented the loss of Yahweh's temple and the worship system it represented (cf. Jer 44:15-19). The focus here is on those who formerly lived in Jerusalem ("who were of you," i.e., Jerusalem) who shared the feelings of the author of Lamentations. Those who sorrow when deprived of worship are acknowledged as being part of Zion; they are still God's people.

Western peoples have a difficult time understanding the deep love which Jews had (and still have) for Jerusalem. The ridicule of the Gentiles added to the physical suffering which they experienced in the fall of the holy city. The "shame" of Jerusalem's destruction was "a burden" for these people. First, they were ashamed of their sins which brought about the disaster. Second, they had to bear up under the reproach of enemies who mocked their continued faith in God. Such as experienced this shame would be gathered by God to that place once again (3:18).

B. Vindication (3:19).

These burdened souls are assured that God would one day deal with all those who afflict the people of God in any way. Four times in verse 19 Yahweh speaks in the first person. He would take the initiative in the deliverance of his people. The word "behold" suggests the shocking, unexpected nature of this positive turn of events. The time frame for this deliverance is indicated by the phrase "at that time." At the time when the destruction of Jerusalem and the sin which caused it would be lamented, Yahweh would intervene to change the fortunes of his people (3:19a).

First, Yahweh promises to "deal with all those that afflict you." Israel's oppressors themselves would be humiliated. Since it was Babylon which destroyed Jerusalem and took captive the Jews, the fall of Babylon in 539 BC must be the fulfillment of this prediction.

Second, God would save "the lame" and gather "the outcast." Zephaniah is envisioning a return from exile. True believers who may be scattered and injured in the fall of Jerusalem to the Babylonians would still have a glorious future. The Lord would regather them and reconstitute them as a nation.

Third, God would "make them a praise and a name." In the ancient world such a promise would imply the overthrow and defeat of national enemies (cf. 2 Sam 7:23). Throughout the earth those who formerly had cast aspersions on Israel and her God would stand in awe at the spectacle of the restoration of this nation (3:19b).

C. Restoration (3:20).

God promises, "I will bring you in." God is the Good Shepherd who brings his people into the fold of Zion. The words include the physical return of the remnant to the Promised Land. Those words point to bringing the saved into the spiritual Zion of which the Old Testament Promised Land was but a type. The phrase "at that time" used twice in the last verse of the book is a point of light at the end of a black tunnel. At some point after the exile God would gather his people and "bring them in" (3:20a).

For emphasis God repeats the promise to make his people "a name and a praise." This time, however, the scope of this promise is expanded. The fame of Israel would not simply be in those places to which they had been carried away in shame. Now Zephaniah foresees a day when "all the peoples of the earth" shall recognize Israel's glory. Messianic Israel is in view here.

Yahweh promises that he will "bring back your captivity." The words point to a radical transformation in the status of God's people. No matter what present conditions may be, the hope of the remnant is always for the great transformation. Yahweh effected the transformation from physical captivity to freedom; from geographical Zion to spiritual Zion. The final transformation of God's people is yet future (Phil 3:21).

The great transformation which is here anticipated would be done "before your eyes." Few, if any, of Zephaniah's generation would live to see the restoration from Babylon. None of them would live to see the transformation of Israel from a physical to a spiritual entity. In the resurrection, however, all of God's people will see the fulfillment of all the promises which God has made—the end of suffering and chastisement and the fullness of redemption.

Zephaniah began with a description of universal judgment and the destruction of the earth. Properly understood, the concluding verses of Zephaniah reach out to the new heavens and new earth in which righteousness dwells.

ENDNOTES

1. The phrase "rising up early" is used frequently in Jeremiah of God's efforts to reach the hearts of his people through the preaching of the prophets. See Jer 7:13,25; 11:7; 25:3; 26:5; 29:19; 32:33; 35:14-15; 44:4. Thus while God was doing his best to reach his people, they were doing their best to corrupt their ways.

2. NIV, NASB, NKJV and RSV understand 3:10 to be saying that the suppliants/dispersed ones bring an offering to Yahweh (cf. Isa 18:7). ASV margin and BV understand the text to say that the suppliants/dispersed ones were the offering brought by the converted Cushites.

3. The word for "shout" (*hari'u*) is frequently used of the shout at the outset of a battle (Num 10:9). The actual words of the battle shout are sometimes recorded (e.g., Judg 7:20).

CHAPTER THIRTY-FOUR

Faith Out of Focus
Habakkuk 1:1-2:1

The heading to the Book of Habakkuk stresses two points. First, the word "burden" describes the nature of what follows. The word came to have the connotation of an oracle announcing the demise of foreign nations. In this case the word is even more appropriate. Habakkuk is concerned throughout with an intellectual and emotional burden which only the revelation of God can alleviate.

Second, the authority of the book is indicated in the mention of the office of the writer. He is called "a prophet." He was one who had been called of the Lord to proclaim to his generation the message of God.

Third, Habakkuk "saw" the contents of this book. They do not represent human speculation, but are in fact divine revelation.

A PRAYER OF COMPLAINT
Habakkuk 1:1-4

Habakkuk was a devout believer, a man of deep faith. Like many such individuals through the ages he was puzzled as to how a righteous and holy God could permit wickedness to triumph on the earth even briefly. Two expressions introduce the complaint of the prophet: How long? and Why?

A. Complaint about Prayer (1:2).

Habakkuk complained about unanswered prayer. Chafing under the arrogant pretensions of the wicked, Habakkuk often had cried out to Yahweh, but the heavens were silent. When God neither gives answers nor takes action he is said not to hear a prayer. Thus Habakkuk cried out, "How long shall I cry, and you will not hear?"[1] The thought that God did not seem to be nearly as upset about the situation in the land as was Habakkuk made this man of God even more distraught (1:2a). Prayer is the framework in which all the burdens of the people of the Lord may be poured out. Therefore prayers expressing perplexity are appropriate as long as they are expressed in the context of faith.[2]

Habakkuk complained to the Lord about the violence in the land. Here Habakkuk is using the same word (*chamas*) which was used to describe the deplorable conditions which existed on the earth prior to the Flood. In his prayers he described to Yahweh this violence. Yet the Lord did not lift a finger to save the righteous from the oppression of violent men. Habakkuk seems to be describing conditions in Judah as they existed during the reign of wicked King Jehoiakim who came to the throne in 609 BC. He is speaking as a mediator on behalf of the righteous members of the community who were suffering at the hands of violent men.

B. Complaint about His Vision (1:3).

Habakkuk complained about his vision. What Habakkuk saw in the land is spelled out in three couplets. He had seen "iniquity and wickedness." He had observed "destruction and violence." He had seen "strife and contention" rising up. So Habakkuk's disgust with conditions in society were based only partly on personal experience. Through divine revelation he had seen the thorough corruption of his people as well as the consequences of that corruption.

Habakkuk complained about the lack of law enforcement. Because the violence was so pervasive, "the law is slacked," i.e., not enforced. "Justice" never seemed to "go forth" like a warrior to battle the corruption. The wicked outnumbered the righteous and forced their will on them.

C. Complaint about Injustice (1:4).

The prophet complained about the lot of the righteous. "The wicked compass about the righteous," i.e., surround them. The "righteous" here are those innocent of wrongdoing. They are attacked and punished. The power of the government was used to victimize the innocent. The only justice which did go forth from courts of law was perverted by bribes and prejudice.

GOD'S ANSWER
Habakkuk 1:5-6a

The silence of the heavens was broken. Yahweh answered the complaint of his prophet and those who felt as he did. He does not answer the "why" of Habakkuk, nor does he explain why he delayed so long in answering the complaint of the prophet. On the other hand, the Lord does not rebuke the prophet for his complaint, nor dispute the accuracy of the facts as Habakkuk had articulated them. In fact, Yahweh agreed that the corruption of the land was terrible.

The revelation of God's plan and the demonstration of God's power does not follow any program designed by man. God is sovereign. He responds to prayer at the time and in the manner he deems best. Believers must cease to think of prayer as the tool by which they can force the Lord to follow their agenda and schedule.

A. Preparation for the Revelation (1:5).

The divine answer is addressed to the people of Judah as well as Habakkuk. It begins with "behold," a word which always introduces something unexpected if not shocking. Whether men know it or not God is at work behind the scenes of history to straighten out the mess made by sinful men in society.

Those who might complain of Yahweh's inactivity should look "among the nations," i.e., the Gentiles. God's agent of chastisement would appear on the international horizon. Only the wisdom of God could design a plan which would address the corruption in Judah by performing a work among the nations.

Those who did comprehend what God was doing among the nations could not help but "wonder marvelously." His way is not the way of man, and consequently it evokes constant amazement. It is in fact incredible. So dramatic and decisive is God's action that the righteous would find it difficult to believe the reports of it.

People of faith in every generation must hear the declaration of Yahweh: "I am working a work in your days," literally, "a worker is working in your days." The redundancy produced by the cognate accusative in the Hebrew serves to underscore the activity. The participle suggests either current action or imminent action. In essence Habakkuk was about to threaten the destruction of Jerusalem. For this reason the Apostle Paul could appropriate these words to warn the Jews of another shocking work of God in their days, viz., the destruction of Jerusalem by the Romans (Acts 13:41).

B. A Shocking Announcement (1:6a).

A second "behold" statement defines the divine work and illustrates why people would be so incredulous at the report of it. "Behold, I am about to raise up the Chaldeans." The Neo-Chaldean or Neo-Babylonian kingdom was founded in 626 BC by Nabopolassar. The Chaldeans, however, had inhabited the region of southern Mesopotamia since at least 1000 BC. They were not a new people on the stage of history.

Since it is impossible to pinpoint the exact year in which Habakkuk received this revelation, the political status of the Chaldeans at the time is hard to determine. From 626 to 612 BC—the fall of Nineveh—they were persistent and pesky adversaries of the Assyrians in southern Mesopotamia. From 612 to 605 BC the long term success of the Chaldean kingdom must still have been in doubt. After all, it was only with the help of the Medes and the Scythians that major Assyrian fortresses had been conquered. After 605 BC, however, mastery of the world was clearly in the hands of Nebuchadnezzar, the greatest of the Chaldean rulers.

God is explicit in his identification of the agent which he would use to bring judgment upon Judah. Yahweh is sovereign over all nations. He raises up kings, and brings them down. In his marvelous wisdom, God dispersed his people among the nations so that they might bear witness to him among their captors. This was part of the grand preparation for the coming of the Promised One in the fullness of time. Yet the timing was such that this spreading of the knowledge of the true God coincided with the need to discipline the covenant people.

GOD'S AGENT DESCRIBED
Habakkuk 1:6b-11

Having identified his special agent, Yahweh next describes this instrument of judgment. Some twenty features are noted, several of them in couplets. The focus is first on the Chaldean infantry, then their cavalry, and finally their leader.

A. The Infantry (1:6b-7).

Yahweh describes the Chaldeans as a "bitter and hasty" people, i.e., angry and impetuous. The adjectives are explained by the speaker himself: "they march through the breadth of the earth." People who are bitter lash out irrationally in all directions. Those who get in their way suffer great injustices.

The Chaldeans would march "through the breadth of the earth." The picture here is of an army which advances swiftly, even recklessly, in all directions. Throwing military caution to the wind, they would spread out in all directions so quickly that those in their path would have no time to escape. The Chaldeans would have the boldness to take on the whole world. The early years of Nebuchadnezzar were devoted to conquest. Nineveh fell in 612 BC. Pharaoh was crushed in 605 BC. Jerusalem was destroyed in 586 BC. Nebuchadnezzar even invaded Egypt in 568 BC.

Through their conquests the Chaldeans would come "to possess dwelling places which are not theirs." These words are reminiscent of the promises made to Israel on the eve of the Conquest (cf. Deut 6:10-11). Whereas Israel had once been God's instrument to dispossess the idolatrous Canaanites, now idolatrous Chaldeans would be the agent to dispossess rebellious Judah (1:7).

Another duo of adjectives is used to describe the Chaldeans. They are said to be "terrible and dreadful." The first term (*'ayom*) occurs elsewhere only in Song of Solomon 6:4,10 where it refers to the awe-inspiring character of an army with banners. The second term (*nora'*) indicates the feeling of foreboding one might experience when crossing a danger-infested wilderness (Deut 1:19; 8:15) or by witnessing one of the mighty acts of God (Exod 34:10). Those who would experience the terror are the people of Judah.

Wherever they marched they imposed their "judgment," i.e., they demanded submission to their will and obedience to their laws. They are totally self-sufficient, or so they think: "their judgment and their dignity proceed from themselves." They derive standards from no one. They ascribe honor to no one, least of all God. They are a monument to themselves (1:7). The irony here is that Yahweh would deign to use as an agent a people who render unto him no honor.

B. Their Cavalry (1:8-9).

The cavalry units made the Chaldean military a formidable force in the Near East. Habakkuk describes them swiftly sweeping over a country. He likens their horses to leopards in their speed and to ravenous wolves in their fierceness. Proud and determined riders from distant lands press those fearsome mounts forward. They swoop down upon the unsuspecting like vultures hastening to the carrion.[3] Distance would be no barrier to those forces. Flight would be impossible. Potential allies would be in no position to help (1:8).

The "set of their faces is forward," i.e., they are eager to press on in their work. Their goal is "violence." That of which Habakkuk had complained in his own nation (cf. 1:2) would be punished by the ruthlessness of this invader. They never avoid confrontation. They never look back. "Irresistibly, inevitably, uninterruptedly, this horde of warriors moves toward the land of God's covenant people."[4]

The speed and determination of the Chaldeans would enable them to "gather captives as the sands." The figure emphasizes first the vast number of captives. At the same time the language hints at the inhumanity of the invaders. They would have no sympathy for the plight of their captives any more than one might feel sympathy for a pile of sand (1:9).

C. Their Leader (1:10-11).

The focus now shifts to the leader of the Chaldeans. He scoffs at other royal figures. He holds them in contempt because they are unable to offer any effective resistance to his forces. He "derides every stronghold" for he knows they will fall easily to his troops. "He heaps up dust," i.e., builds siege works, and captures every fortress. Tiny Judah can expect no help from any quarter. Nations geographically situated between Judah and Chaldea would not block the westward march of the fearsome foe (1:10).

The conqueror shall "sweep by as a wind," i.e., as soon as he finishes one conquest, he is off to another. Eventually, however, he "transgresses" both in attitude and action and thereby becomes "guilty." The particular sin of which the Chaldean conqueror would be guilty is self-deification. He would begin to worship his own power. His "might" would be "his god." In his mind might makes right. He regarded himself as incapable of doing wrong (1:11). This oracle hints that the Chaldean would thereafter meet his doom.

To summarize the book this far: Habakkuk had asked "How long?" God had responded, "Not long." The prophet had asked, "Why is there no justice on earth?" The Lord had responded, "My vengeance is swift and terrible. It will fall even upon my own people!"

A SECOND COMPLAINT
Habakkuk 1:12-17

If the first complaint focused on the inactivity of God in the face of the apparent triumph of evil in society, the second complaint concerns God's actions. Not only do believers want God to do something about evil, they want the Lord to follow their agenda. Habakkuk now became exceedingly bold. Cautious at the outset, the prophet actually challenged Yahweh's intention to punish Judah by means of the ruthless Chaldeans.

A. His Confidence in God (1:12).

Like the first complaint, the second also opens with a rhetorical question addressed to "Yahweh, my God, my holy one." Habakkuk obviously felt a close relationship to God. His complaints should not then be viewed as the mockery of a skeptic, but as the sincere questions of a believer.

The prayer acknowledges immediately that the divine perspective is not the earthly perspective. God is "from everlasting," i.e., eternal. He is Yahweh, the God of covenant. He is *'elohim*, the transcendent Creator. He is the holy one, i.e., totally set apart form all things sinful.

The prayer continues with an affirmation of understanding. Habakkuk states what he understands Yahweh to have declared in the previous oracle. "We shall not die." The Chaldeans would not totally destroy the Jewish people. Rather Yahweh had ordained these foreigners to exercise "judgment" and "correction" upon Judah. This affirmation of understanding contains two names for God. The name Yahweh is repeated in order to emphasize the covenant relationship which God had to Judah. The affirmation underscores the nature of God as a "Rock," one who is immutable, unchanging, inviolable (1:12).

B. His Questioning of God (1:13).

The announcement of chastisement was not what bothered Habakkuk. He himself had suggested in his first prayer the necessity for such judgment. Simply stated, Habakkuk's complaint is this: How can a holy God use such a wicked people to accomplish his purposes? God's eyes are pure, i.e., he can only look with favor on things that are pure. He cannot bear to gaze upon "evil" or "perverseness." That being the case, how can God look with favor "upon those that deal treacherously," i.e., underhandedly?

How can God remain silent when "the wicked swallow up the man that is more righteous than he." In the past God had swallowed up the wicked on behalf of Israel (cf. Exod 15:12; Num 16:30). Now God's people face the prospects of being swallowed up by their enemies. Habakkuk may mean that the Jews, as bad as they had been, by comparison are much better than the Chaldeans. On the other hand, he may be saying that if the wicked Jews are punished by the Chaldeans the righteous remnant would suffer along with the masses. In the light of the subsequent verses, the second interpretation is superior (1:13).

So Habakkuk's puzzlement grows out of two basic concerns: a

devastation of Judah which he perceives to be disproportionate to the sin being punished; and God's employment of an agent who was more wicked than those being chastised.

C. His Challenge of God (1:14-17).

Habakkuk emphasizes four characteristics of the Chaldeans which he believed made it impossible that the holy, gracious and merciful God could use them to punish Judah.

1. Chaldean ruthlessness (1:14). Habakkuk argues that should God carry through on his threat to bring the Chaldeans against Judah, he would be treating men like fish or small creeping things "who have no ruler over them," i.e., they are not organized like human societies. God created men in his image, to have rule over the creatures of the world. Chaldean oppressions would dehumanize people, would reduce them to the level of a mess of fish. By sending the Chaldeans, God, in Habakkuk's view, was directly involved in their atrocities. This for the prophet was a major concern.

2. Chaldean brutality (1:15). The brutality of the Chaldeans also was part of Habakkuk's protest. The fish illustration of the preceding verse triggered Habakkuk's next charge. Each Chaldean comes after potential captives with a "hook" in his hand. Monuments from Mesopotamia document the custom of literally driving a hook through the lower lip of captives. Long lines of captives with hooks through their lips are depicted being hauled off to Babylon (1:15a).

In a second figure of Chaldean brutality, Habakkuk pictures the Chaldeans dragged along in a "net." The figure is apropos. In one relief from this period the major Babylonian deities are depicted dragging a net in which their captives squirm.[5] The fishing apparatus mentioned by Habakkuk in this verse is symbolic of the Chaldean war machinery (1:15b).

Brutality is an inevitable ingredient of all war. With the Chaldeans, however, brutality was part of their strategic planning. The Chaldeans actually boasted of their ruthlessness. They gloated over the misery which they inflicted on others. The oppression would be made that much worse by the sting of mockery. How could God permit this? How could he employ such a vicious power to punish anyone, especially the covenant people? (1:15c).

3. *Chaldean sensuality (1:16).* Chaldean sensuality was part of Habakkuk's complaint. This conqueror "sacrifices" and "offers incense" to his "net" and "drag," i.e., he worships his military ability, his instruments of torture. He attributes his "fat portion," and "plenteous food" not to the blessing of deity, but to the success of his war machine. The prophet pictures the Chaldeans worshiping that which brought them prosperity and temporal pleasure. Thus they sanctified brutality and deified greed. They regarded as righteous whatever horrible actions might perpetuate their sensuous lifestyle. How could Yahweh tolerate such perversity? Worship properly belongs only to God, not to things made by man.

4. *Chaldean relentlessness (1:17).* Habakkuk expressed his concern for the relentlessness of the Chaldeans by means of a rhetorical question. "Shall he therefore empty his net, and spare not to slay the nations continually?" The picture here is of the Chaldean dumping out the prey he had captured in one conquest in order to hurry forth to collect more victims. Habakkuk can hardly grasp the dimensions of this disaster. Not individuals, but whole nations became victims of Chaldean cruelty. Would God continue to allow the Chaldeans to sweep up one population after another? Would God permit the ruthless slaughter of the nations to continue indefinitely?

HABAKKUK'S WATCH
Habakkuk 2:1

Habakkuk has boldly challenged the plan of God to punish Judah by means of a Chaldean invasion. The prophet knew that God would respond to the challenge. The response, however, was quite different from what Habakkuk expected.

Habakkuk depicts himself standing "upon my watch" and "tower" to await a divine response to his complaint. This is a way of saying that he would be alert, like a city watchman, for any sign of response on God's part. At reason's end one must wait on revelation. Sometimes prophets searched the Scriptures (cf. Dan 9:2,11,13; 1 Pet 1:10-12). One has no right to expect a special revelation when general revelation in the Bible has already provided the answer. This verse should not be interpreted as an arrogant demand that God would address his questions. Rather Habakkuk wished to know what God would say, so that he, as God's spokesman, would know what to say. He anticipated being challenged with the same kind of complaints when he announced God's plan regarding the Chaldeans to Judah. A preacher must resolve within himself unanswered spiritual questions before he would presume to preach to others.

ENDNOTES

1. Habakkuk was not the first in Scripture to ask "How long?" God asked that same question concerning Israel in Exod 16:28 and Num 14:11.
2. O. Palmer Robertson, *The Books of Nahum, Habakkuk, and Zephaniah* in "The New International Commentary on the Old Testament" (Grand Rapids: Eerdmans, 1990), p. 138.
3. Cf. the threat in the Mosaic covenant. Unfaithfulness would bring an enemy from a distant land "like an eagle swooping down" (Deut 28:49).
4. O. Palmer Robertson, *The Books of Nahum, Habakkuk, and Zephaniah* in "The New International Commentary on the Old Testament" (Grand Rapids: Eerdmans, 1990), p. 154.
5. Theo. Laetsch, *Bible Commentary; The Minor Prophets* (St. Louis: Concordia, 1956), p. 326.

CHAPTER THIRTY-FIVE

Faith in Corrected Focus
Habakkuk 2:2-20

Habakkuk has stated his concerns about the society of Judah. He has learned that God was about to bring against Judah a powerful army of chastisement.

YAHWEH'S GENTLE WORD
Habakkuk 2:2-5

Habakkuk triumphantly announces that "Yahweh answered me." He did not have to answer the prophet. He is not bound to debate the mysteries of life with those he created. Yet he answered Habakkuk. That he does so here is evidence of his marvelous grace. Yahweh's gentle but firm response was probably far different from what Habakkuk expected.

A. The Importance of the Vision (2:2).

The response was not secret and mysterious. It was not to be shared only with a select few who were on the inner circle with God. Rather Habakkuk was to "write the vision," i.e., preserve it for a wider audience. The written word was viewed of having greater authority then the word merely spoken.

Second, He was to "make it plain upon the tablets." The use of the plural and the definite article in the Hebrew suggests that an allusion is being made to the tablets upon which the Sinai covenant was recorded (cf. Exod 24:12). "The vision revealed to Habakkuk compares in significance with the original giving of the law to Moses."[1] For this reason Jewish rabbis declared that the 613 individual statutes of the Pentateuch are reduced to one principle in Habakkuk 2:4-5.[2] Others consider the tablets to be the equivalent of the modern billboard. Even to this day in eastern lands the public bulletin board is an important means of communicating information to the public.

Third, He was to write the message so "that he may run who proclaims it." The need to publish this vision was urgent. Prophets are often depicted as "running" with their message (Jer 23:21; cf. 2 Kgs 4:26; Zech 2:4). Another interpretation is that Habakkuk was to make the letters so large that one who was running by would not even have to pause to read the message (2:2). A similar command was given to Isaiah (8:1).

B. The Character of the Vision (2:3).

The message concerned "the vision." Most likely the reference is to what the New Testament calls "the hope of Israel," i.e., the glorious messianic age when God's people would enjoy peace and security. The cryptic message contained four parts.

1. Declaration. "The vision is for the appointed time." It was on God's calendar. Whatever hardships and discipline they might experience in the present, the future looked bright.

2. Encouragement. "It hastens (lit., pants) toward the end, and cannot lie." The "appointed time" toward which this vision pointed is further defined as "the end." The reference must be to what the New Testament calls "the last days" (Heb 1:1-2), the Christian dispensation. The vision—the messianic hope—will not be delayed. Like a runner pressing toward the finish line, the vision hastened toward fulfillment. God himself has a longing to see the fulfillment of this word of prophecy. The statement that the vision "cannot lie" indicates that circumstances will often suggest that the hope of believers is nothing but wishful thinking. Sometimes faith would contradict experience. In such times believers must remember that God cannot lie.

3. *Exhortation.* "Though it tarry, wait for it." Believers should not get discouraged and give up on the vision. It would be worth waiting for. The Greek Old Testament—the Septuagint—rendered this verse in such a way as to suggest a personal messianic allusion. "If he tarry, wait for him.' The Hebrew text could be understood in this way. Several rabbis gave a messianic interpretation to these verses.³ All the hope of the believer is wrapped up in a person, the Messiah. The writer of Hebrews (10:37) embraced this personal interpretation of the vision of Habakkuk.

4. *Assurance.* "It surely will come, it will not delay." God surely would bring to reality the glorious messianic vision. From the human perspective the hope may appear to tarry. From God's perspective, however, events are right on schedule.

C. The Substance of the Vision (2:4-5).

The term "Behold!" introduces the substance of the vision. It pertains to two groups: the proud who rely on themselves, and those who rely on God.

1. *Regarding the proud (2:4a,5).* The proud were "puffed up," i.e., conceited. Such people—whether the proud within Judah or the invading Chaldeans—are not, nor can they ever be, "upright" (lit., straight). Consequently they stand in jeopardy in respect to God (2:4a).

The Lord traces the arrogance of the Chaldeans to their addiction to wine. That beverage is "treacherous" in the way it deceives those who drink it. They think of themselves more highly then sober assessment would permit. The announcement of the end of the Chaldean kingdom occurred while Belshazzar was drinking himself drunk at a banquet of his lords and ladies (cf. Dan 5). Strong drink unleashes all the ugliness of human pride (2:5a).

Spurred on by pride, the Chaldean would not stay at home. "He enlarges his desire as Sheol." Sheol (New Testament Hades) is the abode of the dead. No matter how many people die, death is never satisfied. So also the Chaldeans. Like a political vacuum cleaner, the king of the Chaldeans (Nebuchadnezzar) "gathers unto him all nations." He is never satisfied. "He heaps unto himself all peoples," i.e., linguistic and ethnic groups which may not have been politically defined as nations (2:5).

2. *Regarding the righteous (2:4b)*. The "righteous" in the Old Testament are those in the right standing with God. The word has a legal flavor. The righteous are those who have been adjudged innocent by the heavenly Judge. One is regarded as righteous because of faith (Gen 15:6). In this context the righteous are the exact opposite of the proud.

One who has been justified by faith must continue to live "by his steadfast trust" (*be'emunato*). The structure of the Hebrew sentence requires this understanding of the phrase. The steadfastness is not a life of works, for that would lead to the pride which is condemned in the first half of the verse. Those who become righteous by faith must continue steadfastness in faith. This steadfastness in faith manifests itself outwardly in praise, worship and godly works. This was Paul's understanding of Habakkuk, and the Apostle adopted it for the theme of his Roman letter.

The righteous man, however, "shall live by his faith." Faith expresses itself in faithfulness. The two concepts can scarcely be separated. This great statement to Habakkuk has both a temporal and an eternal significance. In trying times a righteous person must trust God to handle the situation appropriately. Paul (Rom 1:17; Gal 3:10ff.) saw something more in these words from Habakkuk. Eternal life is also appropriated through faith (2:4).

Thus Yahweh's response to Habakkuk offers hope. In the end the proud will receive their due. They will be cut down. Meanwhile, believers must expect the wicked to continue in their violence and brutality. Those who have been justified by faith must continue to live a life of trust in the trying times which precede the day of Yahweh.

A DESCRIPTION OF GOD'S JUDGMENT
Habakkuk 2:6-20

Humble believers live by faith. Haughty unbelievers face the wrath of God. Doomsday for the Chaldeans was coming. Captive peoples and nations would one day take up against the king of Babylon "a parable" or a "taunting proverb." They would mock the fallen king and derive joy from his overthrow. Thus as the world watches, Yahweh would humble the proud Chaldeans. Publicly shaming the wicked is one way in which God vindicates the righteous.

"All" of the nations brutalized by Babylon would join in the mockery of the once mighty mistress of the world. Even the smallest nation would join the chorus of those who sing the taunt song. No people would fear any reprisal. From the overthrow of Babylon the inextricable moral principles which govern the conduct of humankind would be evident. Those principles are stated in the form of five "woes."

The term "woe" (*hoy*) which is used five times in Habakkuk 2 was part of the vocabulary of lamentation in ancient Israel. In prophetic literature it introduces invective utterances. The word *hoy* is usually followed by a description of the reprehensible conduct of people toward Yahweh. Often that description is followed by a threat.[4] Sometimes, as here in Habakkuk 2, the invective appears without the accompanying threat.[5] The *hoy* oracles, however, are ominous. Judgment is always implied. In essence the prophet was singing a funeral chant over those who were at odds with their Creator.

The "woe" oracles of Habakkuk are brilliantly constructed. A number of literary devices are used to make these utterances memorable. Most of these (e.g., assonance, alliteration, double entendre, rhyming phrases) are lost in translation.[6]

A. The Plunderer Plundered (2:6b-8).

The first "woe" is pronounced on the one who increases that which is not his own. " He makes himself rich with loans," i.e., he is living royally off that which he has "borrowed" from other people. "How long?" the prophet asks parenthetically, will such abuse of the rights of others be tolerated (2:6b).

The tables would soon be turned. Those who have been "ripped off" suddenly rise up to "bite" (lit., exact usury) the one who confiscated their wealth. Those who had been docile before the oppressor would "awake" to "vex," (lit., toss to and fro) their tormentor. The plunderer of nations would himself be plundered by others. Why?

First, he had shed blood in the process of piling up wealth. Second, he had done violence to the land. Third, he had done violence to the city and its inhabitants (2:7-8).

Thus the first "woe" emphasizes that those who brutally mistreat their fellow man will one day experience the same treatment which they have meted out to others. Evil men will reap what they sow, often in this life, most surely in the life to come.

B. The Secure Exposed (2:9-11).

The second woe is pronounced on the unholy ambition of one who "gets an evil gain for his house." The Chaldean king was concerned about his dynasty or family as well as himself. The reference is to profiteering. His evil gain is intended (1) that he may "set his nest on high," i.e., on the peak of a rocky crag. The king wants to establish an unassailable dynasty. The language may also apply to covetous people in general who by hook or crook attempt to move from the apartment to the penthouse. (2) The covetous person wants to live on high in order that "he may be delivered from the hand of evil." He will have the wealth to shield himself from any negative circumstance (2:9).

The covetous person in general (and the king of Babylon in particular) discovers that the results of his actions are just the opposite of what he intends. He has "devised shame" to his house, i.e., his actions would be recompensed by shame upon his descendants. What actions? " He was guilty of "cutting off many peoples." Price gouging causes great suffering, even death in extreme cases. By inconsiderate treatment of his fellow man the sinner has in fact "sinned" against himself. How so? He has created a circumstance in which he must experience God's judgment (2:10).

In spite of his efforts to establish a lasting dynasty the "house" of the king of Babylon (and all covetous people) will crumble. "The stone shall cry out of the wall" in agony and "the beam out of the timber shall answer it." The prophet uses the collapse of a physical structure to illustrate the fall of the dynasty of the Chaldean king (2:11).

C. The Expansionist Thwarted (2:12-14).

The third "woe" is pronounced against one who would "build a town with blood, and establish a city by iniquity." Oppressive policies of the Chaldeans are the focus of this woe. The reference may be to forced labor—the corvée—where conquered peoples were forced to labor under oppressive conditions (2:12).

The Chaldeans boasted of their building works. Other nations and peoples throughout history have built their cities without regard for the laborers or for those displaced by the construction. All of those structures would come crashing down. Yahweh would see to it that these builders labored "for fire," i.e., destruction. They had wearied themselves "for vanity," i.e., without satisfying and lasting results. The point here is that evil empires will eventually topple. Although directed specifically to Babylon, this "woe" embraces nations and people of all generations (2:13).

The "city" here is the apex of humanistic culture. Every culture prides itself on working hard to build up that city. In the end, however, human culture will fail. Men labor in vain to build who labor without the Lord.

While the kingdom of darkness is frustrated in its attempt to expand throughout the earth, the kingdom of God quietly extends its boundaries. "The earth shall be filled with the knowledge of the glory of Yahweh, as the waters cover the sea." Through Great Commission preaching the knowledge of the true God as revealed in his Son Jesus is gradually spreading across the earth even today. Yet not until the designs of the wicked have been finally frustrated, and the haughty have received their just recompense will the knowledge of God's holiness completely fill the earth. Thus the words of Habakkuk have an eschatological thrust to them. Ultimately the wicked will fail and the gospel will triumph throughout all the earth (2:14).

D. The Shameless Defamed (2:15-17).

The shameless actions of the king of Babylon are in the foreground here. Yet in the background stand all in every age who resort to shameless deeds of treachery to advance their personal agenda. Ever since Eve brought the forbidden fruit to Adam, the psychology of sin is such that those who wish to live wicked lives are determined to drag others down with them. The king of Babylon delights in luring others into the debauchery for which he was famous (2:15a).

Yahweh here condemns a person who would get a neighbor

drunk in order to "look upon his nakedness." He even "spikes" the drink with "venom"[7] so as to totally incapacitate the victim. The point here is getting a person in a helpless condition so as to humiliate and take advantage of him. The phrase "to look upon nakedness" sometimes has the connotation of committing sexual immorality (cf. Lev 20:17,18). Robertson suggests that the Chaldean wished to get his neighbor drunk so that he might commit a homosexual act with him.[8]

Such a wicked one will experience a most appropriate recompense. First, the perpetrator would experience the shame of his victim. Second, just as he had compelled others to drink his cup of booze, so now the king must drink from the cup that is in the right hand of Yahweh. That cup of God's wrath would "come around" to all who take advantage of the helpless and ignorant. Jeremiah later would develop this figure at length (Jer 25:15-29; 51:7). Jesus prayed in the garden that this cup of God's judgmental wrath would pass from him (Matt 20:22; 26:42). The figure reappears in the final book of the New Testament (Rev 14:8; 17:4).

Third, as a result of drinking from that cup the nakedness of the king would be exposed (lit., "let your foreskin be uncovered"). Uncircumcision indicates lack of submission to the will of God. Thus in the Old Testament era shame attached to that status. The nakedness of the king is a way of indicating that he would be stripped of all his royal trappings and paraphernalia. Fourth, "foul shame," i.e., shame of the worst sort,[9] would be heaped upon the glory of such a one. The picture here is of the king of Babylon lying drunk and naked in his own vomit (2:16).

The Chaldeans would fall to such shame for three reasons. First, they had done violence to Lebanon. They had stripped those beautiful mountains of their forests[10] and frightened and destroyed the wild beasts. Concern for the well being of animals is considered in Israel's wisdom literature as the mark of a righteous man (cf. Prov 12:10). Even Yahweh himself always has the well being of the animals at heart (Jonah 4:11). In their lust for conquest the Babylonians needlessly had done violence to both tree and beast.

Second, they were responsible for "the blood of men," i.e., bloodshed. Third, they had done violence to the land, the city and those who dwelled within. This "violence" will "cover" Chaldea, i.e., their land will be treated with the same ruthlessness which they had used in denuding the forests (2:17).

E. The Idolatrous Powerless (2:18-20).

The condemnation of idolatry stands last in this series of "woes" on the evils of the Chaldeans. Peoples who create their own gods invent their own moral standards. The root sin of Babylon was idolatry. Their religious orientation led to all the other atrocities which are cited in this section of Habakkuk. Furthermore, this blast against the idols removes any hope the Chaldeans may have had that their gods would protect them from the judgments which have been threatened in the preceding verses.

The fifth woe is structured differently. It begins with a rhetorical question before the "woe" is uttered. Yahweh inquires about the benefit of an idol. Two types of idols are mentioned. A "carved idol" (*pesel*) refers to images sculpted from wood or stone. A "molten image" (*massekah*) was made of melted materials such as silver or gold. In Israel the making of such images was strictly forbidden (Exod 20:4). Such images were an abomination which brought down the curse of God on the one who made them (Deut 27:15).

The impotence of idolatry is indicated by Habakkuk in several ways. First, an idol is only the creation of a mere man. How can one who fashions a graven or molten image put his trust in that which he has created? Second, an image is a "teacher of lies" in that it stands for unreality. Since in reality God is invisible, omnipresent, and articulate he cannot be represented by an image which is visible, stationary, and dumb. Furthermore, an idol gave the appearance that it had the power of a supernatural being. The elaborate rituals associated with idolatry seduced people into putting their trust in lifeless images. Third, idols are "dumb." They cannot communicate. They are "speechless nothings" (2:18).[11]

Those who treat lifeless idols as though they were living beings come under the woe of Yahweh. Idolaters awakened their idols each morning, bathed them, fed them and pretended that they were living beings. The image was overlaid with precious metal. Outwardly the idol was splendorous. The image, however, could not teach, i.e., communicate. It had no "breath," i.e., life in it. The glittering gold could not conceal the lifelessness of the idol any more than an ornate burial mask can conceal the lifelessness of a mummy (2:19).

In contrast to the idols, Yahweh "is in his holy temple." The reference is to his heavenly temple high above the earth. He is transcendent. He does not need the doting of devotees concerned about his health. The only response to his awesome rule is "silence." The idea is that those who oppose him, those who would instruct him, those who would question him should submit to his majesty. "Let all the earth keep silence before him!" (2:20).

ENDNOTES

1. O. Palmer Robertson, *The Books of Nahum, Habbakuk, and Zephaniah* in "The New International Commentary on the Old Testament" (Grand Rapids: Eerdmans, 1990), p. 169.
2. Strack and Billerbeck cited by Robertson, *op. cit.*, p. 169.
3. Talmud, *Sanhedrin* 97b.
4. In the Minor Prophets *hoy* followed by a description of sin and a threat appears in Amos 6:1; Mic 2:1; Nah 3:1; Zeph 2:5; 3:1.
5. Other examples of *hoy* without accompanying threat are Isa 5:18,20,21,22; 29:15; Amos 5:7.
6. Robertson, *op. cit.*, pp. 186-188.
7. The term *chamatekah* often means "anger, fury" (about 80 times). In Deut 32:24 and Ps 58:4 the word means "poison."
8. Robertson, *op. cit.*, p. 202.
9. The term translated "foul shame" (*qiqalon*) occurs only here in the Old Testament. It appears to be a compound word constructed by Habakkuk to indicate the magnitude of the disgrace which the Babylonians would experience. The word literally means something like "vomit-like shame." See Robertson, *op.cit.*, p. 204.
10. Lebanon was synonymous with beauty in the ancient world. See Deut 3:25; 1 Kgs 4:33; 2 Kgs 19:23; Ps 104:16.
11. Robertson, *op.cit.*, p. 209.

CHAPTER THIRTY-SIX

20/20 Faith
Habakkuk 3

The last chapter of Habakkuk contains a prayer for God's intervention and a vision of the Lord coming in vengeance against evil doers. Habakkuk then acknowledged God's ultimate victory. The chapter concludes with a description of the prophet's reaction to the mighty display of divine power.

A PRAYER FOR GOD'S INTERVENTION
Habakkuk 3:1-2

Habakkuk 3 is designated "a prayer."[1] This prayer is closely related to the concluding observation of chapter 2. Solomon urged Yahweh to respond to the prayers of his people when those prayers were directed toward his temple. Having recognized that Yahweh is in his holy temple (2:20), Habakkuk then addressed a prayer to that temple in full confidence that the Lord would hear that prayer.

A. Introduction to the Prayer (3:1).

In his office as a prophet, Habakkuk offers this prayer to Yahweh in his temple. The cliché that priests represented the people before God while prophets represented God to the people is only a half truth. Intercessory prayer was an essential responsibility of the prophetic office (cf. Gen 20:7). This prayer is offered as a model for God's people in the face of what might appear to be the injustice of circumstances. In his dialogue with the deity Habakkuk came to have a new perspective on God's program in this world. The prayer reflects the submission of the believer to the ultimate justice of God.

This prayer was to be "set to *Shigionoth*," i.e., it was designed to be sung in the temple by the Levitical singers. *Shigionoth* appears to designate a song that was to be sung with great emotion.

Habakkuk's prayer outlines God's plan for the future of his people until the end of time. Faith grows as it is publicly expressed. Through the dark years which Judah was about to experience, this prayer-song would serve to express and strengthen the faith of God's people. Yahweh fortified Israel against temptation in the land of Canaan by means of a song (Deut 31:19-21), so now Habakkuk fortifies his people for the trauma of Chaldean judgment (3:1).

B. The Prayer Proper (3:2).

The prayer is addressed to Yahweh. Old Testament worshipers did not hesitate to use the covenant name of God. During the intertestamental period Jews superstitiously avoided pronouncing God's name. They would substitute the the word *'adonay* (Lord) for the name Yahweh. That custom survives among the Jews even to this day.

The vocative is followed by narrative prayer. Habakkuk reports: "I have heard the report of you." The reference is to all the great works which God had done in the past. This report or record made Habakkuk "afraid," i.e., filled him with reverent awe.

The prayer contains three petitions. First, Habakkuk asked for a revival of God's work. "Revive your work." Revived work would imply a repetition of the mighty works which were equal to or superior to those which were part of the record of Yahweh's dealing with his people prior to the time of Habakkuk. The prophet desires for Yahweh's work to be revived "in the midst of the years," i.e., in present time, not at the end of time.²

Second, Habakkuk asked for understanding. "In the midst of the years make it known." He wants the Lord to make clear to believers his program and purpose in this world. Job agonized in his lack of understanding. So did Habakkuk until God gave him a revelation. This model prayer which was designed to sustain faith in the face of terrible national calamity now calls upon the Lord to make clear to all believers what he had revealed to Habakkuk.

Third, Habakkuk asked for God to be merciful in the midst of the discipline administered by the Chaldeans. The word translated "wrath" (*rogez*) in 3:2 by KJV, NIV, and NASB actually connotes agitation or disturbance. Judah faced a time when the very foundations of her faith in Yahweh would be shaken. Jerusalem would be destroyed, the temple burned, and her citizens carried away into captivity. In such a time Habakkuk asks for divine mercy, for only assurance of Yahweh's compassion will be able to sustain his people through the national ordeal.

A VISION OF GOD'S COMING
Habakkuk 3:3-7

A theophany is a visible manifestation of God's presence. Habakkuk sees a theophany in vision. He describes the fact of Yahweh's coming as well as the glory and effects of that coming.

A. The Fact of his Coming (3:3a).

Habakkuk could see in prophetic vision Yahweh in all of his glory approaching Judah. Here Habakkuk uses an ancient title for God, Eloah.³ In difficult times believers always have expressed their renewed faith in the coming of God. Such was certainly the instruction of the Hebrew writer to the early Christians who were facing persecution within the Roman empire (Heb 10:37).

God is said to have come from the direction of Teman and mount Paran. Teman is associated with Edom (Obad 9). Paran designates the vast desert of the Sinai peninsula on the southern border of Judah (Num 13:26; 1 Sam 25:1). These geographical terms, then, mark the route by which Yahweh brought his people from Sinai to Canaan in the days of Moses. Then God came with Israel to dispossess the Canaanites. Now he was coming to bring judgment to dislodge Israel from the same land.

The God who is coming from Paran is "the Holy One." He requires his people to be holy as he is holy (Lev 11:44-45; 19:2). He must deal with sin. He can show no partiality in judgment. First he will bring the ungodly within Judah to the bar of justice. Then he would turn on the godless Chaldeans. By these actions he would show himself to be the Savior of the faithful (3:3a).

B. The Glory of His Coming (3:3b-4).

The glory of the approaching Holy One blankets the heavens. His "praise," i.e., the attributes of God which are worthy of praise, fill the earth. This is not the glory of God as it is reflected in creation (Ps 19:1), but the greater glory of God which is displayed in grand acts of deliverance. In all acts of past salvation God revealed his glory to his people. The ultimate display of divine glory will accompany the return of Jesus in his role as judge of the wicked and deliverer of his people (3:3b).

Habakkuk, like all Biblical writers, gropes for words to describe the glory of God. He, like David before him (cf. 2 Sam 22:13) uses light to depict the intervention of God. "Horns" or rays of light come forth from his hand. These laser-like beams can penetrate the darkest recesses, the strongest fortresses. This concentration of light in the hand of God signals his readiness to act on behalf of his people. He has the power to deliver the faithful from the clutches of oppressors.

The visible rays of light streaming from God's hand were only a shield for the invisible and awesome power of the Coming One. The human eye cannot even stare directly into the brilliant light of the sun. Yet it is this light which shields the glory and power of God! No wonder, then, that it must be veiled from human sight! (3:4) Paul later would declare that the God of the Bible dwells in unapproachable light (1 Tim 6:16).

C. The Effects of His Coming (3:5-7).

The prophet saw a pestilence going before Yahweh slaying all who were before him. "Plague" (NASB) was "at his feet." Habakkuk sees the Lord bringing destruction with him as he comes. This idea was nothing new. Ancient covenant curses (Lev 26:25; Deut 28:21-22) threatened such a judgment if Israel were unfaithful (3:5).

Before the battle Yahweh "stood," i.e., he paused before the battle to survey the scene. The earth trembled (ASVmar) in anticipation of what was about to happen. His mere gaze "drove asunder the nations," i.e., the united opposition was disrupted and scattered. The eternal mountains were "shattered" and the ancient hills "collapsed" (NASB) before him. Since the earliest hours of creation (Gen 1:9) these massive land formations had silently performed their assigned task of binding together the earth (Ps 104:9). Now the hills and mountains are flattened before the majesty of God (3:6a).

Yahweh's ways are "everlasting" (ASVmar). The passage makes a deliberate contrast between the destruction of the eternal hills and the execution of the eternal program of God. In the past God had demonstrated his wrath against the enemies of his people again and again. Egypt, Philistia, Assyria, and Babylon, to mention but a few, were demolished in his judgments. Habakkuk sees the Lord coming again to smash his enemies and rescue his faithful ones from their oppression (3:6b).

Habakkuk reports that he saw the habitations of Cushan and Midian trembling as Yahweh passed by. Cushan is probably an abbreviation for Cushan-rishathaim, the first foreign invader to punish Israel during the period of the Judges (Judg 3:8-11). The Midianites were also foreign oppressors of that period (Judg 6:1).[4] The point is that after bringing judgment upon wayward Israel, these famous foreign oppressors were themselves smashed by Yahweh. The figure of trembling tents suggests how vulnerable these powerful peoples were to the actions of Yahweh. Habakkuk had learned through revelation that the Chaldeans were about to unleash another disciplinary invasion of Israel. Their fate would be that of Cushan and Midian (3:7).

AN ACKNOWLEDGMENT OF GOD'S VICTORY
Habakkuk 3:8-15

In the middle of verse 8 Habakkuk began to address Yahweh in the second person. Yahweh had now completed his journey from Sinai to Israel.

A. Impact on Nature (3:8-11).

Habakkuk envisions rivers and the sea affected by the coming of Yahweh. In the interest of his people in the past the Lord had smitten the Red Sea, the Jordan, and the Kishon. The particular rivers which now face the wrath of God are not here named. Since the immediate concern was the coming of the Chaldeans, Habakkuk may have had the Tigris and Euphrates rivers in mind. The Revelation depicts great acts of judgment against river and sea in terms of similar actions which God took in the past (Rev 16:3-4,12). The point here in Habakkuk is that no geographical barrier can protect an adversary from the wrath of God when he begins to act on behalf of his people (3:8a).

The storm clouds which Habakkuk envisioned approaching Judah were "chariots of salvation." The imagery of God riding as a mighty warrior in a chariot to conquer his enemies appears frequently in the Old Testament (3:8b).[5]

Yahweh was coming to rescue his people. To do so, however, would require a titanic battle. Yahweh would empty his bow, i.e., exhaust his arsenal of destructive arrows, in the course of that battle. "Sworn were the chastisements (lit., rods) of your word." The threats which Yahweh had made over the years to recompense evil were solemn oaths which now Habakkuk sees him fulfilling. Another view of these words is that Yahweh is pledging every weapon at his disposal to the destruction of his enemies (3:9a).

Again Habakkuk saw the judgment of Yahweh affecting the realm of nature. The earth would melt into rivers of volcanic lava. The mountains saw Yahweh and quaked in pain. The mighty "tempest of waters," i.e., hurricane, saw what Yahweh was about to do and lifted up its hands in petition to the Almighty. The flashing of Yahweh's arrows and spears stunned the sun and moon. They "stood still," i.e., ceased to function, to give light, since they could not compete with the dazzling glory of Yahweh's weaponry (3:9b-11).[6]

B. Explanation of the Disaster (3:12-15).

Why the upheaval in nature? Was God expressing irrational anger against his own creation? Is this why mountains and rivers, sun and moon experience such trauma? Is this a depiction of nature gone haywire? No, Yahweh was marching through the earth in indignation. All nature trembles under the weight of his footsteps (3:12a).

In his anger he would trample the nations of the world, the Gentiles who know him not. As Micah before him (Micah 4:13), Habakkuk uses the strong figure of threshing to describe what Yahweh would do to the enemies of his people (3:12).[7]

This coming of Yahweh is seen again (cf. v. 8) as a rescue mission for God's people. Salvation would be accomplished "with" (Heb. *'et*) God's anointed one (*mashiach*) or Messiah.[8] Habakkuk seems to be anticipating the coming of that great Davidic king anticipated by his prophetic predecessors (cf. Amos 9:11; Hos 3:5; Isa 9:7). Christian theology teaches that the salvation of the elect was effected by the work of Christ on the cross and by his glorious resurrection victory over death (3:13a).

How would the rescue of Messiah and his people be effected? Yahweh would "strike through (*machats*) the head of the house of the wicked." The expression "head of a house" is used frequently in the Old Testament to refer to the head of a family. The head of the household of the wicked would be that one who leads the forces of evil against God's people and God's purposes in this world. Balaam envisioned a future king in Israel smiting through (*machats*) the corners of Moab, a type of the wicked (Num 24:17). David prophesied that this king would strike through (*machats*) the head of many countries (Ps 110:5-6). What Habakkuk envisions is a battle similar to that announced in the Protevangelium (Gen 3:15). A singular champion of God's people wins the ultimate victory over the leader of the wicked opposition. To state the matter plainly, Christ the anointed one par excellence would one day defeat Satan the head of the household of the wicked.

The results of the struggle between the anointed one and the chief of the wicked ones is set forth in a graphic metaphor. He will lay bare "the foundation even unto the neck." The "foundation" appears to be the legs of the chief of the wicked. "Laying bare" those legs suggests exposing them to attack, undercutting them. All that supports the kingdom of darkness will be smashed. The expression "unto the neck" suggests a total assault which utterly destroys the chief of the wicked (3:13b).

The picture changes in 3:14. The leader of the kingdom of darkness is called "the head of villagers" or "warriors" (ASV). Satan commands vast unfenced areas as well as walled cities. Yahweh pierces with his own staves the head of this army. Sin and death were the staves of the devil. By becoming sin for sinful man, and dying on the cross, and rising victoriously from the grave, God pierced Satan with his own staves (2 Cor 5:21). In Jesus' resurrection Satan was forever crushed.

Before his final overthrow the "head of villagers" will lead forth his throngs to attack the godly. The wicked hordes would come out like a whirlwind with devastating power. They would come out "against me." Apparently Habakkuk had felt the brunt of Satan's attack. His enemies were as confident of victory as those who devour the poor in secret (3:14).

Under this brutal attack, Habakkuk recalls past deliverances of Yahweh. The Lord rode through the Red Sea for the deliverance of his people (Exod 15:3-12,19). So Habakkuk was confident that the Lord would ride with his chariots through waters of opposition and persecution. Thus, Yahweh is ultimately victorious, his people are finally rescued. Past deliverances bolster Habakkuk's faith in the final victory of the righteous (3:15).

A COMMITMENT TO GOD
Habakkuk 3:16-19

Habakkuk had seen Yahweh drawing near in judgment upon the wicked and with deliverance for the righteousness. In the concluding verses of his book the prophet records his response to this vision.

A. Present Anguish (3:16).

Habakkuk acknowledged that he had "heard" what the Lord was communicating to him through vision and word. Earlier he had been quite willing to protest to the Lord. As a result of his dialogue with God, the prophet was speechless. He could not respond. He has been physically traumatized by the reception of the divine revelation.

Habakkuk's encounter with God had a profound effect upon him physically. First, his body trembled. Second, his lips quivered at the thunderous voice of God (cf. Ps 29:3-5 7-9). Third, he felt that his bones were rotting away within him, i.e., his frame did not seem to be strong enough to hold him up. Fourth, his legs were trembling under him.

Habakkuk was deeply anguished that he must wait for the day of adversity. The enemy was coming—the day of trouble—when the Chaldeans would invade the land. Habakkuk was now resigned to the invasion which God announced in chapter 1. The knowledge, however, that Yahweh would ultimately crush Satan and all his hosts enabled Habakkuk and all other believers to maintain their faith even in the face of temporary triumphs of the enemy. Deliverance was certain, but it would come only after judgment.

B. Anticipated Adversity (3:17).

Terrible devastation would come to Judah as a result of the Chaldean invasion. Habakkuk is not contemplating mere hypothetical possibilities. He recognizes that the ravages of war on Judah would be dreadful. The fig trees, the vineyards, the olive groves and grain fields would not yield their crops. Flocks and herds would be cut off. Neither luxuries nor necessities of life would be available. Habakkuk imagined the worse possible scenario (3:17).

C. Resolute Commitment (3:18-19).

Habakkuk could accept the coming judgment now that he had seen the ultimate manifestation of God's justice. Yet even though all material comforts be removed, as long as he had life in his body, Habakkuk resolved to rejoice in Yahweh. His joy was in the person of God, even when he could no longer rejoice in the physical gifts of God (3:18a).

Habakkuk calls Yahweh "the God of my salvation." He could rejoice in the person of Yahweh because he understood that ultimately the Lord would accomplish his purpose for his people. He would deliver the faithful from their oppressors. He would restore the prosperity of his people. The concept of "salvation" in the Old Testament included material well-being as well as a new relationship with the Lord (3:18b).

The revelation of the ultimate victory of God gave spiritual strength to Habakkuk. He may have stumbled for a time over the issue of God's dealings with the world. Now, however, God had made his feet "like hinds feet." The Lord would help him walk on "high places" conquering one obstacle after another. The revelation of ultimate victory enables believers to live triumphant lives (3:19a).

Habakkuk's personal faith in God and his firm commitment to remain faithful to him are the best illustrations of what was meant in 2:4, "the righteous shall live by his faith." He would keep on trusting in God despite any calamity which might befall him and his country.

SUPERSCRIPTION
Habakkuk 3:19b

At the end of the book either the prophet himself or the editor has added a note: "For the chief musician upon my stringed instruments." This superscription suggests that Habakkuk's psalm of submission to God was utilized in the temple music program.

"To the chief musician" is an expression which occurs some fifty-five times in the superscriptions of the Psalms. This is the only place where this expression occurs at the conclusion of a poetic piece. Apparently the purpose of this language is to alert the temple music conductor to the note that follows.

The poem was apparently designed to be sung to the accompaniment of "stringed instruments." The highest function of humankind is rendering praise to the Creator. Singing songs of praise is integral to life (cf. Isa 38:18-20). In the darkness of doubt and despair songs of praise renew life, celebrate life, and look forward to life.

By the use of the singular possessive pronoun "my" with "stringed instruments" Habakkuk affirms that he himself would furnish the accompaniment for the singing of this psalm. From this the conclusion seems justified that the prophet himself was qualified to take part in the public performance of such pieces of music in the temple worship. He must, therefore, have belonged to one of the Levitical clans to whom this responsibility was entrusted.

ENDNOTES

1. The term "a prayer" is found in the heading of five psalms: Pss 17, 86, 90, 102, 142.

2. O. Palmer Robertson suggests that "the midst of years" refers to the time between the two acts of judgment previously revealed, viz., the purging judgment on Judah and the consuming judgment which would vindicate God's people. *The Books of Nahum, Habakkuk, and Zephaniah* in "The New International Commentary on the Old Testament" (Grand Rapids: Eerdmans, 1990), p. 217.

3. *'Eloah* occurs 41 times in the Book of Job, and 16 times in the rest of the Old Testament.

4. Others take Cushan and Midian to be desert tribes which Yahweh passed over en route from Sinai to the Promised Land.

5. For discussion of the various passages involving Yahweh's use of horses and chariots see Robertson, *op. cit.*, pp. 232f.

6. Some see in the sun and moon "standing still" an allusion to the Battle of Beth-horon (Josh 10). In answer to Joshua's prayer the sun and moon "stood still" enabling Israel to win a great victory over the enemy.

7. Gideon threatened to "thresh" (*dush*) the men of Succoth, who had positioned themselves with the enemies of Israel by failing to aid their brethren in time of war. This Gideon later did. He "taught" them with thorns and briers (Judg 8:7,16).

8. Most English versions take the Hebrew *'et* to be the sign of the direct object. Hence, "you went forth . . . for the salvation of your anointed." Robertson argues persuasively that the *'et* here should be recognized as the preposition "with." The common translation, however, would still yield the same sense, viz., that the salvation or rescue of God's people is wrapped up in the deliverance of God's land. For a discussion of the use of the term *mashiach* in the Old Testament, see James E. Smith,*What the Bible Teaches about the Promised Messiah*, (Nashville: Nelson, 1993), pp. 1-3.

PART FOUR

THE POSTEXILIC

PROPHETS

HAGGAI
ZECHARIAH
MALACHI

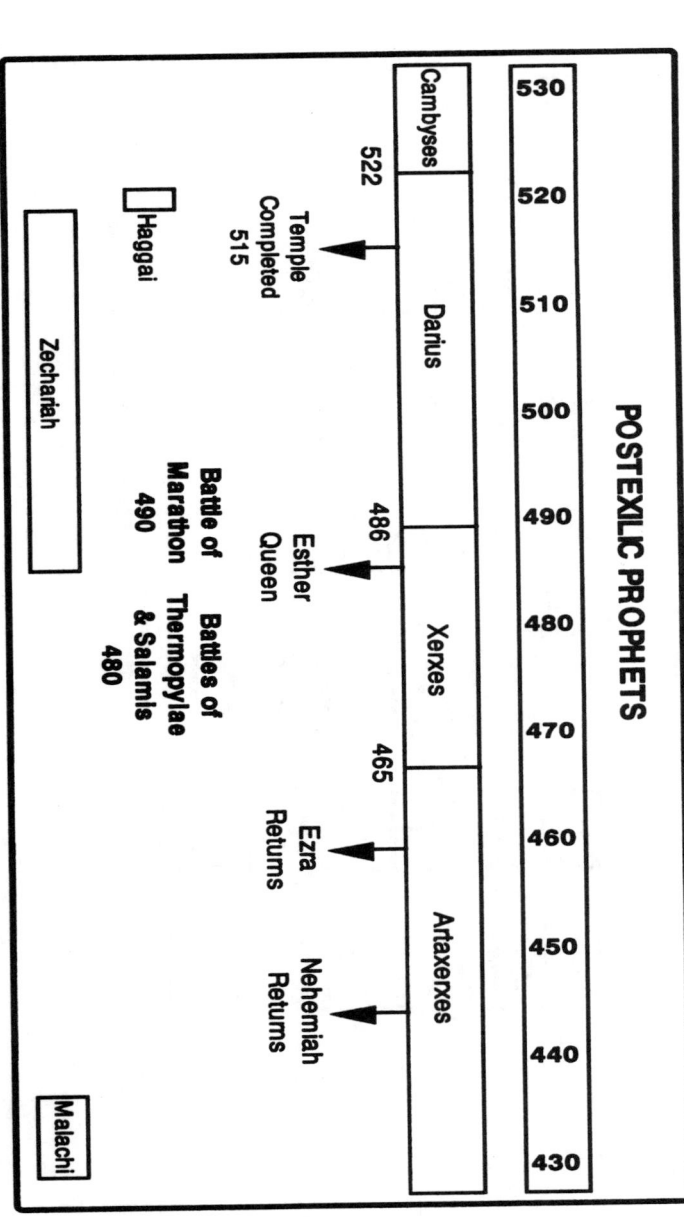

CHAPTER THIRTY-SEVEN

The Postexilic Prophets
An Introduction

The postexilic period of Biblical history (586-400 BC) was one of the most important periods in world history. This was an era of religious ferment. Zoroaster (Zarathustra), the founder of a religion which still has adherents in the East, lived during this period. Laocius (Laotse, "the Old One"), the founder of Taoism, and Confucius (K'ung-futse, "Master K'ung") flourished in China in this same period. Gautama Buddha was born in India about 550 BC. The Upanishads, the sacred writings of Hinduism, were written about 500 BC.

This period was also an era of cultural flowering. This was the period of the great lyric poets Sappho, Archilochus, Anacreon, and Pythermus. The enlightened code of the lawgiver Solon emanates from this period. The golden age of Pericles in Greece was one of the greatest cultural advancements in all history. Great thinkers such as Socrates (469-399 BC) and Plato (427-347 BC) were on the scene at this time.

HISTORICAL BACKGROUND
586-400 BC

The postexilic period was also a time of political upheaval. Judah fell to Babylon in 586 BC. Babylon was overthrown by the Cyrus the Great in 539 BC. Egypt was conquered by the Persians in 525 BC. Greece struggled heroically to repel the Persian invasion. Toward the end of this period Persia was tottering.

A. The Fall of Babylon.

During latter years of his long reign of forty-seven years Nebuchadnezzar devoted his attention to building projects around Babylon. He was succeeded by his son Amel-Marduk in 562 BC. In the Bible this king is called Evil-Merodach. He was responsible for releasing the Judean king Jehoiachin who had been taken captive to Babylon in 597 BC. Amel-Marduk was followed on the throne by Neriglissar (560-556 BC), Labashi-Marduk (556 BC) and Nabonidus (556-539 BC).

Nabonidus was more interested in archaeology than in governing the empire. He spent a great deal of time out of the capital, thus neglecting the sacred rites by which his kingship was received annually from the god Marduk. Belshazzar his son was de facto king in his father's absence. The Book of Daniel calls Belshazzar "king" although the Babylonian sources found to date suggest that he occupied a secondary position under his father Nabonidus. The Biblical writer refers to Nebuchadnezzar as the "father" of Belshazzar because he was the greatest predecessor on the throne.

In 550 BC Cyrus revolted against his overlord Astyages the Mede. He conquered Ecbatana the same year. By 546 BC Cyrus had pushed his conquests to Lydia in Asia Minor. In 539 BC he determined to challenge Babylon for the rule of the world.

According to Daniel 5, Belshazzar was engaged in a desperate attempt to regain the favor of Babylon's gods as Cyrus approached his capital. Exactly how Cyrus gained access to the city is not clear. Accounts by the Greek historians Herodotus and Xenophon suggest that his troops diverted the Euphrates river which ran through the city.[1] The Persian troops then waded through the river gates to surprise the defenders within. The cuneiform sources, however, declare that the Babylonians opened the gates of the city to welcome Cyrus as a liberator from the hated Nabonidus and his son Belshazzar.[2]

So that he might press on to other conquests in the east, Cyrus appointed a certain Gubaru as king over the now fallen Babylonian empire. The Jews knew this ruler as Darius the Mede. Daniel held a position of great honor in this Medo-Persian administration.

B. The Edict of Cyrus (539-530 BC).

During his reign of ten years Cyrus established a reputation as the great liberator. He permitted all peoples who had been deported to Mesopotamia by the Assyrians and Babylonians to return to their native lands. The Jews benefited from this policy. The edict allowing them to return to Judea is contained in Scripture in two versions, the official Aramaic form (Ezra 6:3-5) and the popularized Hebrew version (Ezra 1:2-4).

Under the leadership of Zerubbabel (Sheshbazzar)[3] a group of some fifty thousand Jews returned to the Promised Land in 538 or 537 BC. Many chose to remain in Babylon because during the exile there they had become prosperous merchants. Only the most spiritually committed desired to return to the ruins of Palestine to rebuild their nation and their temple.

The first order of business upon their return was the rebuilding of the altar on the site of the ruined temple in Jerusalem. To these devout Jews worship was central. As soon as they had settled in their homes, the foundations of the temple were prepared. Materials were gathered for the immediate reconstruction of the house of the Lord. At that point, however, difficulties set in. Opposition arose from the peoples of the land. The builders became discouraged. The temple work ceased. Not one stone was set on that foundation for over fifteen years.

C. The Reign of Darius the Great (522-486 BC).

Cambyses succeeded his father Cyrus as ruler of the Persian empire. This king is not mentioned in the Bible. Nothing of significance happened as far as the Jews were concerned during his reign. Cambyses died under mysterious circumstances while on a campaign to Egypt in 522 BC. One of his generals, Darius, claimed the throne.

From 522-520 BC Darius had to crush rebellions against his rule in various parts of the empire. The famous Behistun inscription records his successful efforts to assert his rule throughout the empire.

In 520 BC God raised up two prophets, Haggai and Zechariah. In August of 520 BC Haggai preached a blistering sermon in which he challenged the people of Judea to build God's temple. The work resumed immediately. Three other messages of Haggai are recorded. All were delivered before the end of the year 520 BC. Just before Haggai delivered his last oracle, Zechariah was called to deliver his first message. He too focused on the work of temple building.

In spite of opposition, the temple work concluded by March 515 BC. The hands of Zerubbabel which had commenced the work back in 538 BC also completed the work.

D. The Reign of Xerxes (485-465 BC).

The death of Darius triggered new rebellions, especially in Babylon and Egypt. Xerxes was finally able to consolidate his power. He then determined to expand his empire into Europe. A great assembly was called to plan the invasion of Greece. Esther 1 probably alludes to that planning session.

In 480 BC the expedition to Greece was undertaken. Xerxes met with devastating defeats in a sea battle at Salamis, and in land battles at Thermopylae and Plataea. The Persian king then retreated to his capital at Shushan (Susa) to rebuild his forces. As a diversion for the shattered ego of their king, Xerxes' advisors suggested that a new queen be selected to replace Vashti who had been deposed prior to the invasion of Greece when she refused to obey the command of her husband.

In 478 BC, after a lengthy search process, the Jewess Esther was selected to be Xerxes' queen, i.e., the leading wife of his harem. Some five years later Esther was able to use her influence with the king to foil the plot of the prime minister to exterminate the Jewish people.

In 466 BC Xerxes made one last attempt to invade Greece. This effort was even more disastrous than the first. The following year Xerxes was assassinated.

E. The Reign of Artaxerxes (465-424 BC).

In his seventh year of rule, Artaxerxes commissioned Ezra, a Jewish scholar, to be secretary of state for Jewish affairs in the entire region "beyond the river," i.e., west of the Euphrates. He was given the authority to enforce the law of God among his people even to the extent of executing those who resisted him.

After a perilous journey of four months, Ezra and a group of returnees arrived in Judea in July of 457 BC. The reformer discovered almost immediately that several of the leading Jewish men had cast aside their Jewish wives to marry heathen women. Ezra organized a procedure for investigating and resolving all alleged cases of religious intermarriage.

Apparently Ezra also attempted to rebuild the walls of Jerusalem (Ezra 4:11-23). Since this was not part of his commission the effort failed. Under pressure from the people of the land Artaxerxes ordered that the work cease until he ordered otherwise. Ezra, somewhat discredited by this failure, disappeared from the scene.

Thirteen years after Ezra's mission, Nehemiah became governor of Judea. He had royal permission to rebuild the city. In spite of a determined effort by the people of the land to stop the project, the walls of Jerusalem were rebuilt in fifty-two days. Completion of the walls was celebrated with a dedication service in which two groups of leaders walked the walls in opposite directions. Nehemiah led one of those groups; Ezra led the other.

Jerusalem was then repopulated to further protect it from the local enemies. At the same time Nehemiah instituted other reforms designed to bring the postexilic community into compliance with the law of God.

After twelve years Nehemiah returned to the Persian court perhaps to have his commission as governor renewed. In his absence many of the abuses which Nehemiah and Ezra had corrected reappeared. Most likely the ministry of Malachi should be assigned to this period of Nehemiah's absence from Jerusalem.

About 420 BC Nehemiah returned to Jerusalem. He dealt decisively with the problems of sabbath abuse and intermarriage with the heathen. In his absence Tobiah, the Ammonite leader who had so bitterly opposed the rebuilding of Jerusalem, had been assigned a chamber in the temple courts where he could reside when visiting the city. Nehemiah threw Tobiah out of those chambers. Thus Old Testament history concludes with a dramatic effort by Nehemiah to purge Jerusalem of the corrupting influence of non-believers.

THE PROPHET HAGGAI
Prophet of Temple Building

He has been called "the prophet of divine shaking," "the matter-of-fact prophet" (Box); "the master builder" (Ward); and "the prophet of relative values" (Morgan). Perhaps the most picturesque title which has been bestowed upon him is found in the Harper Study Bible: "the goad of God." The sharp-pointed messages of this man were used of God to provoke his people to frenzied action in rebuilding the temple of the Lord.

A. The Man.

The name Haggai means "festive" or "festival." The name suggests that Haggai may have been born on one of the great Old Testament holy days. Though no other person in the Bible has this name, it has turned up in a fifth century BC tablet at Nippur. The name also appears frequently in the Elephantine papyri from the same period.

Not much is known about Haggai, not even the name of his father. From 2:3 students have inferred that he had seen the first temple. This would mean that in 520 BC he would have been about eighty. Jewish tradition states that he spent most of his life in Babylon. Scripture contains no clue as to when he returned to Judea.

Early Christian tradition considered Haggai to be from the priestly family. In the light of 2:10-14 it can be said that this prophet knew the finer points of the ceremonial law. He also was knowledgeable about political events and agricultural practices.

Tradition connected Haggai's name with the Book of Psalms. He is mentioned in the headings of several psalms in the ancient versions.[4] Haggai may have arranged these psalms for temple worship. Later tradition also regards Haggai as one of the founders of the Great Synagogue, a deliberative body which was the fountainhead of Pharisaic oral law. Along with his fellow postexilic prophets, Haggai is also said to have introduced into the Hebrew alphabet the five terminal letter forms.

B. The Mission.

Haggai's ministry lasted only four months, from late August to mid-December of 520 BC. He had a single-track mind. His focus was on the building of the temple of God. For some fifteen years no work had been done on the temple. The community leaders, Zerubbabel and Joshua the high priest, were discouraged. Under the preaching of Haggai and his younger contemporary Zechariah (Ezra 5:1; 6:14) Yahweh stirred up the hearts of the postexilic community. In six months Haggai accomplished more than any other Old Testament prophet. He was "a steam-engine in trousers" (Pfeiffer). By the time he retired or died, the work of reconstructing the house of God was well under way.

C. The Message.

The Book of Haggai contains only thirty-eight verses. It is second only to Obadiah in the brevity of its contents. The book consists of four oracles delivered on three different occasions. These oracles are precisely dated in terms of the year, month and day of the reign of Darius the Great. Since the chronology of this period is on solid ground, these dates can be converted to the modern calendar rather easily.

Chart No. 24

THE STRUCTURE OF HAGGAI			
A Call to ACTION	A Call to COURAGE	A Call to PATIENCE	A Call to HOPE
Reproof	Encouragement	Blessing	Promises
Ch. 1	2:1-9	2:10-19	2:20-23

Besides precise dating, the book also articulates most forcefully the prophet's claim to be inspired of God. The formula "the word of

Yahweh came" appears five times, as does also the messenger formula ("Thus says Yahweh"). The oracular formula ("oracle of Yahweh")[5] is used eleven times. The strongest claim to inspiration is found in 1:3: "Then spoke Haggai, Yahweh's messenger in Yahweh's message unto the people."

The key exhortation in the book is "consider your ways," (lit., "set your heart upon your ways"). This challenge appears twice in the complete form (1:5,7) and three additional times in an abbreviated form (2:15,18). The use of the imperative "be strong" three times in 2:4 also should be noted.

Haggai is certainly less poetical than his prophetic predecessors, yet parallelism is not altogether lacking in the book. This book contains, however, what might be called "elevated prose," "unadorned, but hard-hitting."[6] The use of the rhetorical question is a favorite device of this prophet. He uses it five times in the book. Haggai "is not wanting in pathos when he reproves, or in force when he exhorts."[7]

Payne regards fifteen of the thirty-eight verses (39%) in the book as predictive. The main predictions are the shaking of the present order so that the kingdom of Christ might be ushered in (2:6-7; 21-22); the coming of the Desire of Nations (2:7); the greater glory of the temple in the messianic age (2:9); and the elevation of Zerubbabel (i.e., one of his descendants) to authority in the messianic age (2:23). Only the first of these predictions is cited and explained in the New Testament (Heb 12:26,27).

The structure of the Book of Haggai is displayed in Chart No. 24.

THE PROPHET ZECHARIAH
Prophet of Night Visions

Zechariah has been called "the temple builder" and "the seer" (Robinson). Patterson referred to this prophet as "the idealist" while Ward branded him "the enthusiast." Since such a large part of his book centers on eight visions which he received in one night Zechariah might appropriately be called "the prophet of night visions."

A. The Man.

The eleventh of the minor prophets had a very common name. At least thirty individuals in Scripture were called Zechariah. The name means "Yahweh has remembered."

The prophet is said to be the son of Berechiah the son of Iddo (1:1,7). In the Book of Ezra (5:1; 6:14) he is called simply the son of Iddo. Berechiah may have died young leaving Zechariah to be raised by his grandfather. In Nehemiah (12:4) a priest named Iddo is named among those who returned from Babylon with Zerubbabel in 538 BC. This Iddo is said to have had a son named Zechariah (Neh 12:16). It is probable but not certain that the author of the Book of Zechariah is being named in Nehemiah 12:16.

Concerning Zechariah's personal life little is known. That he was a contemporary of Haggai is clear from the date assigned to his first oracle. Assuming that he is mentioned in Nehemiah 12, he functioned as a priest and head of a father's house in the days of Joiakim who succeeded Joshua as high priest (Neh 12:12,16). Zechariah was probably born and educated in Babylon. This may account for his frequent use of visions and allegories.

In tradition Zechariah is associated with Haggai in the titles of certain Psalms. He is also is said to have made a contribution to the liturgical worship of the restored temple. Tradition regarded him as a member of the so-called Great Synagogue, a law-making body which supposedly guided the people of God in postexilic times.

In Patristic tradition Zechariah is said to have exercised his prophetic office in Babylon where he worked miracles. He returned to Jerusalem at an advanced age where he discharged the duties of the priesthood. He supposedly was buried beside Haggai. A careful study of the chronology of the book, however, indicates that Zechariah was a young man when he began to preach.

In Matthew 23:35 Jesus referred to a Zechariah son of Berechiah who was slain in the courts of the temple. The phrase "son of Berechiah" does not appear in the parallel passage in Luke 11:51. It is also absent from some manuscripts of the Gospel of Matthew. Most commentators think Jesus was alluding to the death of Zechariah son of Jehoiada (2 Chr 24:17-22). One tradition stated that the author of this prophetic book also died in the temple like his earlier name-sake. Of course Jesus may have been referring to some other Zechariah.[8]

B. The Mission.

Haggai had been preaching in Judea since August 29, 520 BC when Zechariah joined him sometime in October or November of that same year (1:1). The last dated message in the book is assigned to December 4, 516 BC. No doubt he lived to see the temple rebuilt and dedicated (March 12, 515 BC). His ministry, however, probably continued much longer. Zechariah would have been in his sixties when the Persians were defeated in their attempted invasions of Greece in 490 and 480 BC. He would have seen Greece rising steadily on the horizon as a potential enemy of his people.[9]

C. The Message.

The Book of Zechariah in its entirety can be classified as apocalyptic literature. Here there is a progression from the local scene to the world scene; from a point in time to the end of time. Visions are prominent along with an angelic interpreter of those visions. Angels are featured prominently. The book reflects a certain determinism. God had already worked out his purposes in heaven, and all that remained was for him to initiate those purposes on earth. Here there is animal symbolism as well as the use of symbolic numbers.[10]

The Book of Zechariah is one of the most difficult of the prophetic books to interpret. Much here is obscure and difficult to fit into any system of eschatology. The conflicting interpretations of modern scholars are not just limited to individual words or verses, but to the entire structure of the book.

The Book of Zechariah consists of fourteen chapters. The book falls naturally into two divisions. The first part (chs. 1-8) is generally regarded as the work of the postexilic Zechariah who is mentioned with Haggai in Ezra 5:1 and 6:14. The second part (chs. 9-14) differs from the first in both style and subject matter. For this reason critics have argued that the last six chapters must have been written by a different person. Some even regard these chapters— sometimes dubbed Deutero-Zechariah—as having been written prior to the exile! Conservative scholars, of course, have defended the unity of the book ably. No insurmountable difficulty stands in the way of accepting the entire fourteen chapters as the work of one prophet, Zechariah son of Berechiah.

Chart No. 25

THE STRUCTURE OF ZECHARIAH				
Message During the Construction of the Temple			Message After the Completion of the Temple	
Introduction	8 Visions + a Symbolic Action	Four Messages	Cycle One	Cycle Two
1:1-6	1:7-6:15	Chs. 7-8	Chs. 9-11	Chs. 12-14

Payne finds seventy-eight predictions in the Book of Zechariah involving some 144 verses or sixty-nine percent of the book.[11] The book is rich in personal messianic prophecy.

The structure of the Book of Zechariah is displayed in Chart No. 25.

THE PROPHET MALACHI
Herald of the Messianic Dawn

Because he was the last of the Old Testament prophets Malachi has been dubbed "the seal of the prophets," or more poetically, "the last flush in the sunset of Hebrew prophecy" (Farrar). The style which is manifested in this book has caused others to call Malachi "the prophet of didactic-dialectic," or "the lecturer" or "the Hebrew Socrates" (Robinson). The message of this man of God has earned him the title "the prophet of universal worship" or "the prophet of the coming and the return of the Messiah."

A. The Man.

The name Malachi means "my messenger." Malachi is not mentioned in the New Testament or Josephus. Another by this name is not found elsewhere in the Old Testament. The name stands alone in verse one without any further definition as to family or hometown. For these reason a tradition arose in ancient times that "Malachi" was not a proper name. The Targum, for example, attributed the authorship of this book to Ezra. Jerome echoes this opinion. Other traditions attributed the book to Nehemiah or Zerubbabel or Mordecai. Because Mal 1:1 parallels Zech 9:1 and 12:1 some modern scholars have suggested that Malachi originally may have been a third appendix to the Book of Zechariah. This idea is surely incorrect. The content and style of Malachi have nothing in common with the style and content of Zechariah 9-14.

On the other hand, none of the above arguments for the anonymity of the last book of the Minor Prophets has that much weight. Other prophets, for example, also are mentioned without further definition in the opening verses of their books. If there was a Jewish tradition that this book was written by someone other than Malachi, there was also a parallel tradition that Malachi was a personal name. Malachi appears as a proper name in 2 Esdras 1:40, the Talmud, and the heading of the Septuagint. Epiphanius and other church fathers accepted Malachi as the name of an individual.

Probably Malachi should be taken as the proper name for the last Old Testament prophet. It would be very strange if the last book of the prophetic canon were the only book not to have the name of its author in the opening verse. In the final analysis there is no valid reason for rejecting Malachi as a proper name.

Nothing is known of the life of Malachi except what can be deduced from the book itself. He was an excellent teacher. He was deeply devoted to sincere worship of the Lord. Tradition held that Malachi was a Levite who was born at Supha and who lived in the region of Zebulun.

B. The Mission.

The Book of Malachi fits the situation amid which Ezra and Nehemiah worked "as snugly as a bone fits its socket."[12] Yet no uniformity of opinion exists as to the precise relationship between the prophet and the governor. Five different positions have been proposed. Malachi prophesied (1) before the coming of Ezra in 457 BC; (2) between Ezra and Nehemiah's coming in 445 BC; (3) as a co-worker with Nehemiah; (4) between the two governorships of Nehemiah, i.e., after 432 BC; and (5) just after Nehemiah's return to

Jerusalem for his second governorship.

Only one small piece of evidence exists to help narrow down the range of possibilities. Malachi challenged his audience to present an offering to their governor (Mal 1:8). Yet the Scriptures declare that Nehemiah did not require gifts from those he governed (Neh 5:15,18). Therefore one might conclude that Malachi ministered at a time when Nehemiah was absent from Jerusalem. On this solitary piece of evidence the position has been taken here that Malachi ministered between the two governorships of Nehemiah, some time between 432 and 425 BC.

Malachi's mission was to correct the abuses and attitudes of the Jewish community in the last half of the fifth century before Christ. He furthermore was commissioned to announce the coming of the Sun of Righteousness and the day when men throughout the world would worship God in spirit and in truth.

Jerusalem in Malachi had just been rebuilt and repopulated, but the temple had been functioning for almost a century. The Persians ruled the world at the time. Their philosophy generally was to grant religious freedom to subject peoples. While some of the neighboring peoples made life difficult for the Jews, for the most part during this period the Jews were free to practice their faith as they saw fit.

Spiritually the Jews of the fifth century had lost the joy of their salvation and their zeal for the Lord. The priesthood was degenerate. The people would bring faulty sacrifices, and the priests would approve them for presentation before God. Religious apathy and skepticism were widespread. Tithes were neglected. Divorce was common. Yet the people and priests refused to admit that anything was wrong. Into this environment Malachi marched. With these hypocrites and apostates he engaged in public debate. When he was finished he had laid bare the rotten foundation upon which their relationship to God rested.

C. The Message.

In his message Malachi reaches back to clasp the hands of Moses, and reaches forward to clasp the hands of Messiah and his forerunner. The fifty-five verses which constitute the Book of Malachi are arranged in three chapters in the Hebrew Bible. The ancient versions, however, organized the same material into four chapters. The English translations have followed the four-chapter arrangement.

Chart No. 26

THE STRUCTURE OF MALACHI			
Introduction Yahweh's Sovereign Love	The Priests Sin Against Love	The People Sin Against Love	Final Exhortation
1:1-5	1:6-2:9	2:10-4:3	4:4-4-6

Malachi is more prosaic than any other prophetic book. The parallelism is less pronounced. The imagery lacks force and beauty. Perhaps this is the reason that at least one liberal writer sees in Malachi "the hardening of the spiritual arteries of the prophetic faith which reached its apex in Pharisaism."[13] Malachi was not, however, a formalist; the book breathes the genuine prophetic spirit. Here is an incisiveness which is unequaled by any other.

The method of this prophet has been called didactic-dialectic or dialogistic. Seven times in the book this pattern recurs. Malachi will make an affirmation or assertion about some sin or problem in the community. The people would then object to the charge by interrogating Malachi. They would demand in effect that Malachi explain the charge and present his evidence. Thus the dominant pattern in this book is assertion, objection and refutation. To put the matter another way, the literary pattern in Malachi is affirmation, interrogation and rebuttal. The prophet would then refute the objection by presenting his case. Certainly this is the most argumentative of all Old Testament books. A courtroom atmosphere prevails throughout the book.

The theme of Malachi is "the sovereign love of God" (1:1-5). Both the priests (1:6-2:9) and the people (2:10-4:3) had sinned against that love. Chart No. 26 displays the structure of the Book of Malachi.

ENDNOTES

1. Herodotus, *Persian Wars*, 1:190-91; Xenophon, *Cyropaedia* 7:5.
2. The cuneiform accounts which allude to Babylon's fall are (1) the Nabonidus Chronicle (ANET, p. 306); (2) the Persian Verse Account of Nabonidus (ANET, pp. 312f.); and (3) the Cyrus Cylinder (ANET, p. 316).
3. Scholars are not in agreement as to whether Zerubbabel and Sheshbazzar were two names for the same person, or two different persons.
4. Haggai's name is found in the headings of the following psalms: In the Latin Vulgate alone: Ps 111 (112); in the Syriac Peshitta alone: Pss 125, 126; In the Greek Septuagint alone: Ps 137; in the Septuagint and Peshitta: Pss 146-148; in the Septuagint, Peshitta and Vulgate: Ps 145.
5. The Hebrew noun *ne'um* is invariably translated by the English versions as a verb: "says" or "declares."
6. Richard Wolff, *The Book of Haggai* in "Shield Bible Study Outlines" (Grand Rapids: Baker, 1967), pp. 17f.
7. George L. Robinson, "Haggai" in *The International Standard Bible Encyclopaedia* (Grand Rapids: Eerdmans, 1956), 2:1318f.
8. Cf. Josephus *Wars* 4:5,4. J. Barton Payne, "Zechariah who Perished," *Grace Journal* 8 (Fall, 1967): 33-35.
9. Eli Cashdan, *The Twelve Prophets* (London: Soncino, 1961), pp. 269-70.
10. Joyce Baldwin, *Haggai, Zechariah, Malachi* in "The Tyndale Old Testament Commentaries" (InterVarsity Press, 1975), pp. 70-74.
11. J. Barton Payne, *Encyclopedia of Biblical Prophecy* (New York: Harper & Row, 1973), p. 450.
12. J.M.P. Smith, *A Critical and Exegetical Commentary on the Book of Malachi* in "The International Critical Commentary," 1912 (Edinburgh: T. & T. Clark, 1971), p. 7.
13. W. Neil, "Malachi" in *The Interpreter's Dictionary of the Bible* (New York: Abingdon, 1962), Vol. K-Q, p. 231.

BIBLIOGRAPHY
Postexilic Prophets

Baldwin, Joyce G. *Haggai, Zechariah, Malachi* in "The Tyndale Old Testament Commentaries." InterVarsity, 1972.

Barnes, W. Emery. *Haggai and Zechariah.* "The Cambridge Bible for Schools and Colleges." Cambridge: University Press, 1917.

Baron, David. *The Visions and Prophecies of Zechariah.* 1918. Grand Rapids: Kregel, 1975.

Coggins, R.J. *Haggai, Zechariah, Malachi.* "Old Testament Guides." Sheffield, England: JSOT Press, 1987.

Delaughter, Thomas J. *Malachi: Messenger of Divine Love.* New Orleans: Insight Press, 1976.

Dods, Marcus. *The Post-Exilian Prophets* in "The Cambridge Bible for Schools and Colleges." Cambridge: University Press, 1956 reprint.

Gill, Clinton R. *Minor Prophets: Micah, Nahum, Habakkuk, Zephaniah, Haggai, Zechariah, and Malachi.* Joplin, MO: College Press, 1971.

Heater, Jr., Homer. *Zechariah* in "Bible Study Commentary." Grand Rapids: Zondervan, 1987.

Isbell, Charles D. *Malachi.* Grand Rapids: Zondervan, 1980.

Kaiser, Jr. Walter C. *Malachi; God's Unchanging Love.* Grand Rapids: Baker, 1984.

Laney, J. Carl. *Zechariah* in "Everyman's Bible Commentary." Chicago: Moody, 1984.

Leupold, H.C. *Exposition of Zechariah.* Grand Rapids: Baker, 1965.

Logsdon, S. Franklin. *Malachi, or Will a Man Rob God?* Chicago: Moody, 1961.

Luck, G. Colman. *Zechariah.* Chicago: Moody, 1957.

Moore, T.V. *A Commentary on Zechariah.* 1856. London: Banner of Truth, 1968.

Morgan, G. Campbell. *"Wherein?"* New York: Revell, 1898.

MacFadyen, D. *The Messenger of God.* London: Elliot Stock, 1910.

Perowne, T.T. *The Books of Haggai and Zechariah* in "The Cambridge Bible for Schools and Colleges." Cambridge: University Press, 1908.

Peterson, David. *Haggai and Zechariah 1-9, a Commentary.* "The Old Testament Library." Philadelphia Westminster, 1987.

Verhoff, Pieter A. *The Books of Haggai and Malachi.* "The New International Commentary on the Old Testament." Grand Rapids: Eerdmans 1987.

Wolf, Herbert M. *Haggai and Malachi; Rededication and Renewal.* "Everyman's Bible Commentary." Chicago: Moody, 1976.

Wolff, Hans Walter. *Haggai, a Commentary.* Trans. Margaret Kohl. Minneapolis: Augsburg, 1988.

Wolf, Richard. *The Book of Haggai* in 'The Shield Bible Study Outlines." Grand Rapids: Baker, 1967.

Wright, C.H.H. *Zechariah and his Prophecies.* 1979. Minneapolis: Klock & Klock, 1980.

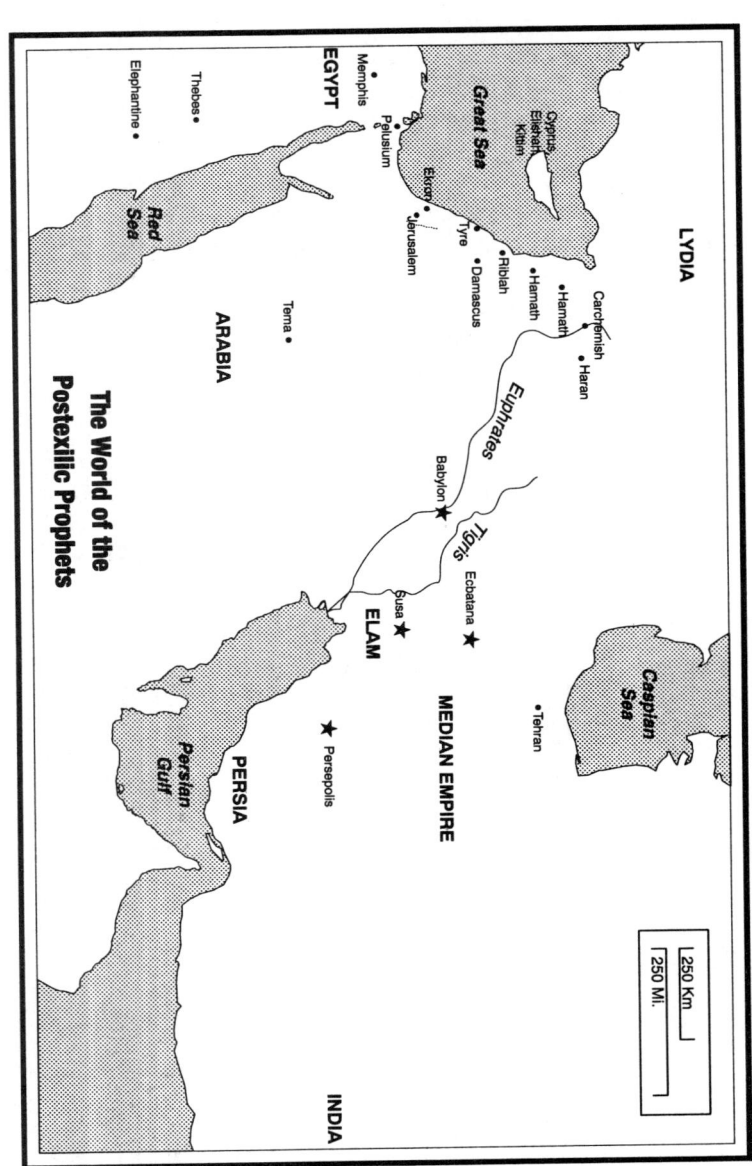

CHAPTER THIRTY-EIGHT

A Call to Action
Haggai 1

The postexilic community in Jerusalem had become complacent. The temple foundations had been laid back in 537 BC. No further work, however, had been done. In 520 BC God addressed the complacency by a prophetic word through an old man named Haggai.

THE PREFACE
Haggai 1:1

The opening verse has the function of dating the oracle, credentialing the speaker, and naming the recipients.

A. The Date of the Oracle (1:1).

The Book of Haggai begins with a date. Chronology was very important to this prophet. He began to speak to his countrymen in the second year of Darius Hystaspes (522-486 BC). That was a time of international uncertainty. The king was still in the process of putting down rebellions all over his empire.

Haggai numbered rather than named the month in which his ministry began. His younger contemporary would use the Babylonian month names as did Nehemiah and Esther. Perhaps Haggai, being older and more conservative, could not bear to use the month names which were associated with Babylonian religion. In any case, the message of the Lord came to him in the sixth month of the year.

The first day of that sixth month was the fateful day when the God of the covenant spoke to Haggai. On a lunar calendar the first day of the month was always a new moon. At least every quarter, perhaps every month, the new moon was celebrated as a religious holiday. He whose name means "festival" first received divine revelation on a festival day!

Converting the chronological data supplied by Haggai, scholars have computed that this prophet's ministry began on August 29, 520 BC.

B. The Credentials of the Speaker (1:1).

Haggai was not bashful about claiming that he was the recipient of divine revelation. "The word of Yahweh" came to him, and by him to the people. "For the first time in the postexilic era, the authentic voice of prophecy was heard."[1]

This divine word came literally, "in the hand of Haggai," i.e., into his care, his stewardship. Haggai's right to speak came not because of his family status. His father's name is omitted. That did not matter. What was really important is that he had received the divine word.

Haggai, like Habakkuk, refers to himself as "the prophet." He was the spokesman for Yahweh, the instrument by whom the divine word would be presented to the postexilic community. Five times—more than any other Biblical prophet—Haggai refers to himself as "the prophet." This man was very conscious of his responsibility to proclaim what God had placed in his hand.

C. The Recipients of the Oracle (1:1).

The first oracle is addressed to two leaders of the postexilic community. First, Haggai names Zerubbabel. His name means "seed of Babylon," or perhaps "begotten in Babylon." Zerubbabel was "the son of Shealtiel," the grandson of King Jehoiachin. Young King Jehoiachin had been deported to Babylon in 597 BC. The king had been released from prison by Amel-Marduk the son of Nebuchadnezzar about 560 BC. Though he was descended from the royal family, no evidence exists that the Persians, much less Zerubbabel himself, ever expected that he would sit on the throne of his ancestors as king.

A problem arises regarding the father of Zerubbabel. Whereas the text here says he was the son of Shealtiel, 1 Chronicles 3:19 lists him as the son of Pedaiah, the brother of Shealtiel. Probably he was the son of Pedaiah by birth. His father died while Zerubbabel was young. His uncle Shealtiel adopted him as his own son. Both Matthew (1:12) and Luke (3:27) regard Shealtiel as the father of Zerubbabel.

Zerubbabel was the governor of Judea. No doubt he was appointed to that office by the Persians, but the circumstances of that appointment are not narrated. In the structure of the Persian empire, the governor of Judea reported to the governor of the Trans-Euphrates province, who in turn reported to the satraps of the Persian empire (cf. Ezra 5:3).

Some question exists as to the precise relationship between Zerubbabel and Sheshbazzar (Ezra 1:8,11; 5:14,16). While some think that these are two separate individuals, the best view is that these are two names for the same person.

The second addressee is Joshua, also spelled Jehoshua and Jeshua. Translated into the Greek version the name became Jesus. Joshua was the son of Jehozadak. Seraiah, his grandfather, had been slain by Nebuchadnezzar in the aftermath of the fall of Jerusalem in 586 BC (2 Kgs 25:18ff.). His father Jehozadak had been carried into captivity by the same king (1 Chr 6:15). Joshua was the high priest. In the Persian period this was an office of considerable prestige. The Persians granted subject people religious freedom.

REPROOF FOR NEGLECTING GOD'S HOUSE
Haggai 1:2-6

Haggai's first oracle begins with a rebuke for neglecting the house of God. He first speaks of the reason for the neglect (1:2-4); then he spells out the results of that neglect (1:5-6).

A. The Reason for the Neglect (1:2-4).

The oracle begins with a messenger formula: "Thus says Yahweh of hosts." This formula is used five times in the book. Royal ambassadors who delivered written documents in the name of their king first delivered the message orally before handing over the written word. They introduced their oral word with this messenger formula.

The title "Yahweh of hosts" first appears in the Bible in 1 Samuel 1:3. The title is used some three hundred times in the Old Testament, 247 of those times in the prophetic books. The title is especially popular in the exilic and postexilic period. It is used fourteen times in Haggai, fifty-four times in Zechariah, and twenty-four times in Malachi. The title emphasizes the invincible might behind Yahweh's commands. He is Lord of all powers seen and unseen in the universe and in heaven (1:2a).[2]

The postexilic community was claiming "it is not time to come, the time for Yahweh's house to be built," i.e., it was not time to begin temple construction. Haggai seems to be placing in opposition his "thus says Yahweh" with "this people say." The language "this" people rather than "my" people suggests contempt for the indifference and lack of action in the community. Essentially the sin of the postexilic community was procrastination (1:2b).

The term "house" is used eight times in reference to the temple in Haggai. Twice the prophet uses the term *hechal*, meaning "palace" or "temple." The temple was viewed by Israelites as Yahweh's earthly dwelling, the palace of the Great King.

Why did the community feel that the time was not right to renew the construction of the temple? The times were tough. Resources were few. The Persians might not approve. The seventy years of temple devastation were not yet up. Neighboring peoples would resent the work. People can always find some plausible reason for failing to build up the house of God.

Why was the prophet so concerned about the rebuilding of the temple? The temple was the center of religious life for the Jews. It was a type of the spiritual temple of the future age. The rituals of the temple were designed to portray the need for redemption and the penalty of sin. The temple would be the mechanism to hold together as a people the covenant nation until the coming of Christ.

The word of Yahweh again came to Haggai directing him to use a rhetorical question to unmask the hypocrites of the postexilic community "Is it time for you, you I say, to dwell in your houses?" If they could build comfortable houses for themselves, their conditions could not be too bad. The truth was that their personal comfort ranked higher on the list of priorities than reconstructing the house of God. Furthermore, the houses which they were building were not just basic accommodations. They were "paneled" houses.³ Paneling a dwelling was a sign of ostentation (cf. 1 Kgs 6:9; 7:3,7). Nothing was too good for their personal dwellings. The paneling was probably of cedar wood, perhaps the same wood which had been gathered earlier (Ezra 3:7) for use on the temple. The construction delay may have tempted the people to use that cedar for their personal dwellings rather than let it go to waste (1:3-4a).

While the postexilic community enjoyed their paneled homes, "this house lies desolate." The temple site was still desolate save for the open-air altar upon which sacrifices were made to Yahweh. No work had been done since 537 BC when Zerubbabel had led in laying the foundations of the house. The attitude of this community is in stark contrast to the attitude of David. He could not bear the thought of his God dwelling in a tent while he lived in a palace. At least in David's day Yahweh had a tent! In Haggai's day the temple site was a desolation (1:4b).

B. The Result of the Neglect (1:5-6).

In view of the indifference which the community had shown for building the temple, Haggai calls upon his audience to "consider your ways." Literally the text reads, "set your heart upon your way." Honest evaluation would compel these people to admit that their lives were not being blessed. The Giver of every good and perfect gift cannot smile on spiritual indifference, convoluted priorities, laziness, and fear (1:5).

Haggai calls attention to three disturbing conditions which prevailed in the restoration community. First, they were experiencing inadequate harvests. "You have sown much, but to bring in little." The Lord was not giving them abundant harvests. Their labors were not being rewarded.

Second, they had inadequate supplies. They did not have enough food. They did not have enough drink to satisfy their needs, lit. to get drunk on, perhaps to drown out their misfortunes. Their clothing was not adequate to keep them warm. Apparently the people were afraid to use what they needed for fear of exhausting their supplies.

Third, they were receiving inadequate wages. "The wage earner earns wages unto a punctured bag." The cost of living was such that it seemed they were losing most of their money before they even spent it.

EXHORTATION TO BUILD GOD'S HOUSE
Haggai 1:7-11

Haggai was not merely a social critic. He was not content to merely gripe about what was wrong in his society. He had a plan. He now begins to motivate the restoration community to get busy.

A. The Appeal Presented (1:7-8a).

The appeal for action is reinforced by the messenger formula. It is Yahweh, the God whose house has been neglected, who is appealing to this people through Haggai. For the second time he urged self-examination (1:7; cf. 1:5).

Haggai urged his people to begin gathering materials for the temple project. "Go up to the mountain, and bring wood." The hill country around Jerusalem was well wooded at this time (cf. Neh 2:8; 8:15). Olive, myrtle and palm was available locally. This wood could be used for scaffolding. Heavier support beams would have to be imported from Lebanon. Ancient builders set wooden layers in rock walls to minimize earthquake damage. The emphasis is here on the wood rather than the stone for two reasons. First, the stone foundations of the new temple had already been laid. Second, additional stone was readily available right on the site from the ruins of the first temple.

Haggai urged that the work commence immediately: "build the house." Solomon used conscription to build the first temple. This prophet expected voluntary labor.

B. The Appeal Reinforced Positively (1:8b).

Two positive considerations reinforce the directive to get busy on the temple work. The first motive for temple building is "that I [Yahweh] may take pleasure in it."[4] The highest motivation for the believer is to please the Lord. To know that Yahweh would delight in that "house" would spur on a people discouraged by the realization that they would not be able to build a temple anything like as magnificent as the one built earlier by Solomon.

Why would the Lord take pleasure in a rebuilt temple? Of course he always delights in the fruit of labor done in love for him. More than that, however, is involved here. In that rebuilt house the sacred rites of Mosaic faith would be performed. The temple furnishings and the rituals associated with them were designed by God to set forth continually the greater glories of the Church Age. Thus the rebuilt temple was a preparation for the coming of Christ.

The second motive for temple building is "that I [Yahweh] may be glorified." At the very least these words mean that God would accept the work as done for his glory. Perhaps the idea is that by constructing the temple the Jews would be declaring to the world that their God was worthy of a dwelling place where he could be worshiped. Others think the idea is that God would display his glory in the new temple, perhaps by personal appearance. When the first temple was dedicated "the glory of Yahweh" filled the house. The priests were not able for a time to carry on their temple duties because of that glory (1 Kgs 8:11). Something even more wonderful would happen in that second temple. The Lord himself, incarnate in the flesh, would bring glory to the place by teaching in its courts.

Rabbinic exegesis is often curious and even humorous to western students of the Old Testament. The rabbis noticed that a letter—the letter *hey*—was missing from the verb "be glorified." Letters in Hebrew also serve as numbers. The letter *hey* is the number five. Operating on the assumption that nothing is omitted from the text without significance, the rabbis thought the absence of the *hey* indicated the five articles missing from the second temple: the ark, Urim, heavenly fire, Shekinah, and the Holy Spirit of prophecy (*Yoma* 21b).

C. The Appeal Reinforced Negatively (1:9-11).

The prophet offers some negative reinforcement to his appeal for temple building by further allusion to the plight of the restoration community. First, they were experiencing disappointing harvests. The yield was certainly less than expected, perhaps even less than was sown. Literally the text reads: "looking for (the) much, and behold for little." The Hebrew uses an infinitive to stress timelessness. Every time they looked for a great harvest they were shocked ("Behold!") to discover that it was meager.

Second, they were experiencing devastating blight. Whenever they brought that meager harvest to the barn, Yahweh "blew" upon it. The Hebrew construction suggests customary or repeated action. The reference here is probably to some sort of blight or decay which attacked the crop after it was housed. Others understand the text to be saying that God blew away the harvest as if it were mere stubble (1:9a).

Why was the postexilic community experiencing such agricultural disasters? "Because of my house that is waste." Unfinished building projects are ugly. They bear testimony to fear, lack of resolve, bad planning, or change of purpose. Their indifference to the things of God tainted and contaminated everything else which they attempted to do.

While the temple project had been abandoned over fifteen years earlier, the citizens of the postexilic community "run each man to his own house." The verb "run" has the connotation of being zealously concerned about something. The center of their interest was their own dwellings, not the house of God. These convoluted priorities rendered all their hard work useless (1:9b).

Because they cared more for their own houses than for God's house, "the heavens are restrained from dew." In the rainless summers of Palestine the growth of vegetation depended upon the dew. The absence of this moisture meant that the earth had "withheld its produce" (1:10).

Why had they experienced this drought? Their agricultural failures did not result from some natural change in weather patterns. Yahweh here reveals that he personally had intervened in the world of nature to turn off the supply of moisture. "I called for a drought!" The current drought was a *musar* judgment—a disciplinary disaster—designed to force God's people to reassess their priorities (1:11a).

The drought brought a chain-like devastation upon the entire nation. First to feel its effects were "the land" and "the mountains" where the crops were grown. Second, the crops—grain, new wine, and oil—were affected. The grain grew in the valleys. The grapes which produced the wine and the olives which produced the oil grew on the mountains. In fact all that the ground produced was affected. Third, men and cattle which depended upon vegetation for survival felt the effects of the drought. Fourth, "all the labor of their hands" was ultimately affected. Craftsmen, for example, could not concentrate on their labors because of the gnawing hunger pangs due to food shortages (1:11b).

THE RESPONSE IN BUILDING GOD'S HOUSE
Haggai 1:12-15

The last paragraph of Haggai 1 relates the response to the prophet's call to action. The work was resumed with the right spirit (1:12), with divine blessing (1:13-14), and with haste (1:15).

A. Work Resumed in the Right Spirit (1:12).

The temple work resumed with the spirit of unity. Zerubbabel the governor and Joshua the high priest were joined by "all the remnant of the people." What a gratifying sight it is when spiritual leaders have the wholehearted support of the congregation. This is the first use of the term "remnant" in the book. Only when the restoration community began to obey the Lord were they worthy to be called "the remnant of the people." Haggai regarded the small group of returnees as the fulfillment of Isaiah's remnant theme (1:12a).

The work resumed with the spirit of obedience. Zerubbabel, Joshua and the remnant "obeyed the voice of Yahweh their God." They accepted Haggai's first oracle as the very word of God himself. Thus in this situation to obey the voice of Yahweh meant to obey "the words of Haggai the prophet." A prophet was the mediator of God's word to man. They recognized Haggai as having that office. Their preexilic ancestors for the most part had rejected all those whom God raised up to deliver his word. The restoration community recognized that "Yahweh their God had sent" Haggai unto them. The grounds upon which they accorded him this recognition are not known (1:12a).

The work resumed with the spirit of reverence. "The people did fear before Yahweh." This verse points to genuine conversion, for the fear of God is the spirit of true faith. Theirs was not the unwilling obedience of terror, but the hearty service of godly fear. The voice of God through his prophetic messenger had awakened them from their indifference. The explanation of their present difficulties made them realize that worse awaited them if they failed to renew the temple work. The paralyzing fear of hostile neighbors was displaced by the energizing fear of the Lord. Obedience is the demonstration of one's fear or reverence for God (1:12b).

B. Work Resumed with Blessing (1:13-14).

The temple work was resumed with divine blessing. When the people got busy on the project the Lord sent them a message of consolation through his prophet. Haggai is called here "the messenger of Yahweh" (*mal'ach Yahweh*). This title usually refers to the special messenger—a manifestation of God himself—who visited Israel at different times (e.g., Gen 16:7). Haggai is the only prophet to use this title of himself.[5]

The word which Haggai was about to deliver was so important that Haggai emphasizes his credentials in yet another way. He referred to the office in which he functioned as literally "Yahweh's messengership." He had been commissioned by Yahweh as his messenger (1:13a).

After this double emphasis upon the authority of his word, Haggai delivered the message. In the Hebrew it is but two words: "I am with you." This is then followed by the oracular formula, "oracle of Yahweh." Thus a two-word oracle is surrounded by assertions of the authority of the utterance. Nonetheless the power of those two blessed words is not lost in the verbiage but rather is enhanced by it even as a beautiful frame enhances the beauty of a picture. Now that the remnant had resumed the work on the temple their God was with them, empowering, sustaining, blessing, observing. This is a word of commendation which was designed to uplift those who had so recently committed themselves to a tremendous task (1:13).[6]

Not only was Yahweh with his people in some passive or supportive sense; he was actively involved in the work. Yahweh was stirring up the spirit of Zerubbabel, Joshua, and "all the remnant of the people." The threefold use of the word "spirit" emphasizes God's work on the inner man. The same language is used to explain why so many decided to return to Judah in 538 BC. For the most part, those who were being stirred by God now were the same people who had felt that same stirring some eighteen years earlier.

How did Yahweh stir up the spirit of the temple builders? Primarily through the messages of Haggai. His call to action got the attention of the remnant. The oracle of assurance in the preceding verse supplied additional motivation when the enormity of the task was confronted. To know that the Lord is with his people in any enterprise would be motivation enough to make them want to do the work. If God used other means to stir these hearts those means are not indicated in the text (1:14a).

C. Work Resumed with Haste (1:14b-15).

As a result of the mighty stirring by the Lord, the restoration community came and "did work in the house of Yahweh of hosts." The reference is probably to that unglamorous site preparation which must precede any building effort. Materials would have to be gathered and moved to the site. Debris would have to be removed. No doubt spade, wood and rock work was available for even the most unskilled laborer. The professionals would have to be called in later. At the outset, however, 'all" the remnant joined in the project (1:14b).

The reconstruction efforts began on the twenty-fourth day of the sixth month. Only twenty-three days had passed since Haggai began to preach (cf. 1:1). After over fifteen years of indifference the mighty word of this mighty preacher stirred this community to resume this most important work (1:15).

ENDNOTES

1. Joyce Baldwin, *Haggai, Zechariah, Malachi; An Introduction and Commentary* in "Tyndale Old Testament Commentaries" (InterVarsity, 1975), p. 37.
2. *Ibid.*, pp. 39f.
3. The literal meaning of the word is "covering." This raises the possibility

that the complaint is that they had a roof over their head, while the Lord's house remained unfinished. See Herbert Wolf, *Haggai and Malachi; Rededication and Renewal* (Chicago: Moody, 1976), p. 17.

4. ASV and BV render 1:8 as a promise rather than an incentive: "and I will take pleasure in it and I will be glorified."

5. The title "messenger" (*mal'ach*) is used by Malachi to refer (1) to the priest (2:7); (2) the one who would prepare the way for God (3:1); and (3) the Messiah (3:1). The name Malachi itself means "my messenger."

6. Several others heard a similar assurance of God's presence: Jacob (Gen 28:15); Moses (Exod 3:12); Joshua (Josh 1:15); and Jeremiah (Jer 1:8). The theme reached a new level of significance in the words of Jesus: "I am with you always" (Matt 28:20). Ultimately believers will find that "the tabernacle of God is among men" throughout eternity (Rev 21:3).

CHAPTER THIRTY-NINE

The Great Shaking
Haggai 2

The second chapter of Haggai contains three oracles delivered on two different dates. In these oracles Haggai issues a call to courage (vv. 1-9), a call to patience (vv. 10-19), and a call to hope (vv. 20-23). The prophet's purpose was to bolster the temple builders. While it took the prophet only one message to restart the temple work, it took three oracles to encourage the builders to stay with the work.

A CALL TO COURAGE
Haggai's Second Oracle
Haggai 2:1-5

Haggai's call to courage was delivered almost a month after the temple work had begun, on the twenty-first day of the seventh month. On the modern calendar the date would be October 17, 520 BC. This was the last day of the feast of tabernacles. Temple progress had been interrupted by the holy days of the seventh month (2:1).

Haggai received another revelation from the Lord on this date. He was directed to deliver a message to Zerubbabel, Joshua and the remnant. The purpose of this oracle was to boost the morale of the builders and strengthen them in their resolve to complete the task. Haggai accomplished his goal by assuring the builders of divine blessing (2:3-5); and by sharing with them revelations of future glory (2:6-9).

A. Present Discouragement (2:3).

The oracle begins with this question: "Who is left among you that saw this house in its former glory?" The question presupposes that some were still living who had seen the first temple. The temple had been destroyed some sixty-six years earlier in 586 BC. Haggai may have been among those who had seen the first temple.

By referring to the temple as "this house" Haggai was identifying the building under construction with Solomon's temple. Scholars refer to the period from 520 BC to AD 70 as the period of the second temple. To the Jews, however, there was only one temple. "There is a unity to the Temple throughout history, whatever the outward form."[1]

"The former glory" of the temple refers to the way that structure appeared just before the destruction of Jerusalem. The temple had been refurbished several times. In the course of the centuries it had been sacked and stripped of much of its precious metals even before 586 BC. Even so that building and its surrounding courts were an architectural masterpiece.

To those who had seen the previous temple Haggai directed two questions: "How do you regard it now? Is not such a one as nothing in your eyes?" The people must have been discouraged with the work which was now taking place. Foundations generally do not inspire a great deal of enthusiasm. Back in 537 BC some of the community wept when they saw the foundations of the second temple (Ezra 3:12). Apparently some were thinking that the present effort was inferior to the previous temple.

B. Encouragement to Steadfastness (2:4).

The encouragement to steadfastness is emphasized by four techniques in the text. First, encouragement is emphasized by direct address to Zerubbabel, Joshua and the people of the land. Second, the use of a threefold repetition of the imperative "be strong!" also emphasizes encouragement. These are the same words spoken by David to Solomon before the building of the first temple (cf. 1 Chr 28:10). Third, encouragement is emphasized by the use of an explanatory imperative: "Work!" Positive action is the best antidote for timidity. Finally, the encouragement is emphasized by a promise: "for I am with you!" The personal presence of the Lord always gives courage, determination and the conviction that he will not permit his cause to fail.[2]

C. Encouragement to Fearlessness (2:5).

Yahweh calls upon his people to "Fear not!" The words are in the imperative, reminding believers that fearlessness is not a desirable option but rather a divine mandate. Fear would be banished from the temple builders when they realized that Yahweh was "with the word which I covenanted with you when you came out of Egypt." The idea is that God stands behind his covenant word.[3]

A second incentive to fearlessness is that "my spirit is standing firm in your midst" (KJV; RSV). God the Spirit would protect them from their adversaries and lead them in their work.

REVELATIONS OF FUTURE GLORY
Haggai 2:6-9

A major portion of Haggai's second oracle is devoted to revelations of future glory. The passage has messianic implications. This is the most difficult, yet most significant section of the book. The section begins with a 'Thus says Yahweh." Four times in these verses the solemn declaration "oracle of Yahweh" occurs. Haggai appreciated the staggering implications of what he was saying and thus undergirded his words with this concentration of claims to inspiration. Yahweh speaks about the preparations for the messianic age (vv. 6-7a); and promises for the messianic age (vv. 7b-9).

A. Preparations for the Messianic Age (2:6-7a).

A great shaking would prepare the way for the messianic age.

"Yet once, it is a little while, and I will shake the heavens, and the earth, and the sea, and the dry land." This statement sets forth four great truths.

First, the preparatory shaking would be a repetition of what had taken place previously. The word "yet" has the connotation of "yet again." The previous shaking was what took place at Sinai (Heb 12:26). Haggai envisioned a new era ushered in with great commotion.

Second, the shaking would occur but once again. Only once more in history would God reveal himself in the manner and significance of Sinai. The Septuagint and the Book of Hebrews render "once for all time." The Gospel dispensation will endure unto the end of time.

Third, the shaking would begin in a very short time: "it is a little while." Some think that the vicissitudes of the Persian empire are intended (Keil). Others think the shaking was to begin with the coming of Messiah (Pusey; Deane).

Fourth, the shaking would involve the entire universe: "the heavens, the earth, the sea and the dry land." At Sinai there was literal shaking.[4] Physical convulsions also accompanied the advent and ministry of Christ: the star, the angels, darkness at noon when he died on the cross; the earthquake at his resurrection, and the ascension; Pentecost. The introduction of Christianity also produced a moral and spiritual shaking.

Yahweh also announces that he would "shake all nations." Great political upheavals took place before the first coming of Christ. The Persian empire fell to Alexander the Great. The Greek empire divided after Alexander's death, and the fragments of that empire warred among themselves until the Romans conquered the world. As the gospel was carried out into the Roman empire the critics of Christianity exclaimed that the disciples had "upset the world" (Acts 17:6).

B. The Coming of Messiah (2:7b).

As a result of the great shaking, "the Desire of all nations shall come" (KJV). More recent English translations translate the noun as a plural: "the precious things of the nations shall come." The idea is that converted Gentiles would bring their wealth to the temple of God. Certainly this is a Biblical concept (cf. Isa 60:5), but that does not settle the issue here.

The noun (*chemdat*) is singular in the received text, though the same consonants could also be vocalized as a plural. The term certainly can have a personal reference. It was earlier used of Saul (1 Sam 9:20). All the desire of Israel—the hope for a successful monarchy—was fixed on Saul. The term may be used of the Messiah in Daniel 11:37. In the plural the word is used of Daniel (Dan 9:23; 10:11,19) and of Esau (Gen 27:15). On the other hand, the term in both the singular and plural can also refer to wealth, especially silver and gold (e.g. 2 Chr 32:27; 20:25).

Most commentators think that the plural verb used here prohibits a personal messianic interpretation of the phrase "Desire of nations."[5] It is true that normally in Hebrew when a plural noun specifies one person, a singular verb is used. The singular noun could have a collective sense and thus govern a plural verb.[6] The multi-faceted character of the Messiah might call for the plural verb in this passage.

C. Results of Messiah's Coming (2:7b-9).

Three promises are attached to the coming of the Desire of all nations: (1) the filling of the house, (2) the greater glory of the house, and (3) heavenly peace.

1. The filling of the house (2:7b-8). Yahweh promised that he would "fill this house with glory." The term "glory" can refer to material splendor (Gen 31:1; 1 Chr 29:12) or to the personal presence of God (Ps 26:8; 1 Kgs 8:10-11). In the days of Solomon the temple was filled with a visible cloud signifying Yahweh's presence (2 Chr 7:1). The temple which was under construction as Haggai spoke was beautified materially by the extravagances of Herod the Great. Material splendor alone, however, cannot fill God's house with "glory." The glory associated with the temple was the result of the Lord's personal presence, the Shekinah glory as it was called in Jewish tradition (cf. Exod 40:34-35). Yet Jewish tradition recognized that the Shekinah glory was absent from the second temple (*Yoma* 21b). Thus the promise that Yahweh would fill that house with "glory" is best taken as a reference to the presence of Christ in the temple. He filled that place with a glory which it never before had experienced (cf. Mal 3:1). When baby Jesus was brought to the temple by Joseph and Mary, the aged Simeon praised God that his eyes had been permitted to see "the glory of your people Israel" (Luke 2:32).

The promise of glory for the temple is reinforced by means of a declaration. "The silver is mine, and the gold is mine." Some were discouraged because what they were building was not as ornate as the temple their forefathers had known. They should not, however, worry about the poor offerings which were being brought for the temple project. Earth's riches already belonged to the Lord. More important to him than silver and gold is the faithful, obedient and loving service of his people (2:8).

2. *The greater glory of the house (2:9a).* Yahweh promised that "the latter glory of this house shall be greater than the former." The second temple never physically surpassed the first temple all the efforts of Herod the Great notwithstanding. This promise, therefore, must be interpreted spiritually of the messianic temple, the church of Christ. The temple which was under construction in 520 BC was but a type or shadow of the spiritual temple of the New Testament dispensation, a temple built up of living stones—the precious souls which obey the gospel (1 Pet 2:5). The messianic temple is superior to the material temple in its worship, its builder, its dimensions, its materials, its influence, and its duration.

3. *Heavenly peace (2:9b).* Yahweh promised: "and in this place will I give peace." Messianic prophecy is full of promises of an ideal peace (e.g., Ezek 34:25; Mic 4:3f.; Zech 8:12). The history of the material temple is filled with strife. Again the promise must relate to Christ's kingdom, the latter day Jerusalem and spiritual temple (Heb 12:22).

A CALL TO PATIENCE
Haggai's Third Oracle
Haggai 2:10-19

On the twenty-fourth day of the ninth month of that second year of Darius, Haggai received his third oracle from the Lord. This was just over two months after his second oracle, and about three months after the work on the temple had resumed. Converted to the modern calendar, the date of the third oracle would be December 18, 520

BC. By this date Zechariah had already started his ministry (2:10).

The third oracle explains past calamities (vv. 11-17) and promises future prosperity (vv. 18-19).

A. The Nature of Defilement (2:11-13).

Haggai was directed to ask the priests a question concerning a principle of law. The priests were the teachers of the law, and therefore he knew that they would be able to answer a simple question. Haggai's purpose was to elicit an answer which would explain why the circumstances of the people had not markedly changed even though they were now busy building the temple (2:11).

The hypothetical situation which Haggai posed was this: A person who had been offering sacrifice accidentally gets some consecrated meat caught in the "wing of his garment," i.e., in the border corner or fold of the breast. This portion of the garment then accidentally brushes against some non-consecrated food—"bread, pottage, wine, oil or any food." The question then which the priests are asked to answer: Would the holy meat impart holiness to the object accidentally touched? The priests answered the prophet's question with an emphatic "No!" According to Leviticus 6:27 their answer was correct. The "wing" or cuff of the garment—that which was directly touched by the holy meat—was holy, but not that which the cuff touched (2:12).

A second question makes the case that defilement is much more easy to transfer than holiness. "If one unclean by reason of a corpse touch any of these things, shall it be unclean?" The priests answered this question: "It shall be unclean." Again they were correct. According to Numbers 19:22 an unclean person communicated his uncleanness to everything he touched. Such uncleanness lasted seven days and, according to Numbers 19:11, could only be removed after elaborate ritual (2:13).

B. The Fact of Defilement (2:14).

Haggai then made an application of this legal principle regarding defilement. "Thus is this people and thus is this nation before me." The language "this nation" is language often used of heathen nations. It may be a sign of contempt. Just what had defiled the nation? Perhaps they were defiled by the wicked among them (Cashdan), or by their foreign contacts (Bloomhart). More likely, however, it was their fifteen years or so of indifference regarding the work of the temple which had caused the defilement (Baldwin).

In any case, just as in the case which Haggai posed to the priests, "everything they touch is defiled." "Every work of their hands" was unclean and even "that which they offer there," i.e., on the altar. These words probably were spoken by the prophet as he pointed to the provisional altar erected many years earlier (Ezra 3:2). "The faint aroma of sanctity coming from their altar and sacrifices was too feeble to pervade the secular atmosphere of their life."[7]

C. The Cause of Defilement (2:15-17).

Haggai now asked his auditors to "consider from this day and backward." "This day" is probably referring to the twenty-fourth day of the sixth month when the work on the temple resumed. In paraphrase Haggai was saying: Look back on the time before you began to rebuild the temple. What was their condition like in the time "before stone was laid upon stone in the temple of Yahweh?" (2:15).

Prior to the resumption of the temple work the situation of the remnant was desperate. "Through all that time" one would come to "a heap" of sheaves which should have yielded twenty measures of grain. That heap, however, only yielded about half what would normally be expected. The same was true of the vintage. They came to the wine vat expecting to find fifty vessels, but found only twenty. The wine vat was the receptacle into which flowed the juice forced from the grapes when trodden out by feet in the wine press (2:16).

To explain these disappointing harvests, Haggai repeated what he said in his first oracle some four months earlier (cf. 1:10-11). Yahweh declared: "I smote you with blasting, and with mildew and with hail." The "blasting" (*shiddaphon*) was the blight caused by the blasting of the east wind coming in from the hot desert. In a dream Pharaoh saw the grain of Egypt blasted by this wind (Gen 41:6). These divine judgments affected "all the work of your hands," i.e., God was frustrating everything they tried to do. These disciplinary disasters had not moved the people to repent. "Yet you turned not to me" (2:17).

D. Promises of Renewed Prosperity (2:18-19).

Haggai calls upon the builders to "consider" (lit., set your heart) from this day and backward." "This day" refers to the twenty-fourth day of the ninth month," the day on which he was delivering this third oracle. They should reflect on the period from the day Haggai was speaking back to the day "that the foundations of Yahweh's house were laid." Does he mean the time when the foundation of the temple was originally laid back in 537 BC? Or does he mean the more recent renewal of the work on the twenty-fourth day of the sixth month? Probably the latter (2:18).

In the three months since the temple work had been resumed, no improvement in the circumstances of the remnant had been experienced. "Is yet the seed in the barn?" It is not clear whether he anticipates a positive or a negative answer to his question. If negative, the seed already had been used for sowing or consumed and used up. The vines and fruit trees had not produced. Thus even while they were building the temple the builders had to worry about the adequacy of the food supplies. If the situation was desperate back in August, it was even worse in December (2:19a).

Yahweh promises that the blessing would begin immediately. "From this day I will bless." The reference must be to December 18, 520 BC, the date of this third oracle. Thus the workers needed to be patient. Their previous defilement due to indifference had affected all their previous work. Now, however, all that would change (2:19b).

Chart No. 27

HAGGAI 2:15-19				
Time before stone was laid to store (2:15)	Work Resumed 6/24	From the day the temple foundation was laid (2:18)		Haggai's 3rd Message 9/24
Conditions were bad before the work resumed		Conditions still bad, but shortly will improve		
About 15 Years		Three Months 520 BC		

A CALL TO HOPE
Haggai's Fourth Oracle
Haggai 2:20-23

Haggai delivered his fourth oracle on the same day he delivered his third oracle. See on 2:10. Two points are made in this final call for hope: the kingdoms of the world would be shaken (vv. 21-22); and the kingdom of God would be unshaken (v. 23).

A. World Kingdoms Shaken (2:21-22).
In closing his short book Haggai returned to the theme of 2:6. Yahweh announced: "I will shake the heavens and the earth." A new age would be introduced with a tumultuous shaking in the moral, spiritual, and physical universe (2:21). For the fulfillment, see on 2:6.

The shaking would especially include the political world. "I will overthrow the throne of kingdoms." The term "throne" is used distributively for various thrones of several kingdoms. Haggai is not just talking about a change of dynasty in Persia. The "strength of the kingdoms of nations" would also be destroyed. The term "strength" (*chozeq*) is used five times in the Old Testament, always with the sense of military prowess. Specifically Yahweh announces: "I will overturn the chariot and its riders and the horses and their riders," i.e., symbols of the military weaponry by which the nations had risen to power (2:22a).

Though Yahweh would orchestrate these political upheavals, he would use others to accomplish his purposes. The overthrow of chariotry and cavalry would be accomplished "each by the sword of his fellow." Internal revolutions and invasions by other kingdoms are in view here. Heathen powers would vanquish one another either in the panic that fell upon them or in the strife that would develop between them. Haggai seems to be echoing Daniel 2 and 7 which depicts symbolically the rise and fall of various empires which would precede the manifestation of the kingdom of God on earth (2:22b).

B. God's Kingdom Unshaken (2:23).
"In that day" when the kingdoms of the world were being shaken, Yahweh declared: "I will take you, O Zerubbabel." The language

implies special selection for a special mission. It also suggests that Zerubbabel would experience divine protection during those tumultuous times. Zerubbabel is called "my servant." This is a title given in recognition of past faithfulness, but also in anticipation of grater usefulness in the future. "My servant" is an honorable title used especially of David (e.g., 1 Kgs 11:13; Jer 33:21) and of the Messiah (Isa 42:1; 52:13; Ezek 34:23).

The Lord promised to make Zerubbabel "as a signet." A signet was worn on the finger or on a cord fastened round the neck. A signet was equivalent to a signature in a world where most people did not write. Thus Zerubbabel would be God's signature, his authoritative leader among the remnant. In similar words Yahweh had rejected Zerubbabel's grandfather, Jehoiachin, from the throne (Jer 22:24). Thus these words attest the reinstatement of the Davidic line. Zerubbabel would be Yahweh's pledge that all of the ancient promises made to David (2 Sam 7:12-16) would be fulfilled.

Finally, Yahweh assured Zerubbabel: "I have chosen you." This is not to be taken as a personal assurance only to Zerubbabel; he did not rise to any special prominence in the kingdoms of the world. The language reflects what was said of God's Servant in Isaiah 42:1. The fulfillment must be looked for in Christ, who was a descendant of Zerubbabel (Matt 1:12; Lk 3:27). Promises are often made in Scripture to individuals which are accomplished only in their descendants. Apparently the grand promises made to David are here passed on to Zerubbabel and to his line. From him would spring the Messiah in whom alone these wide predictions find their fulfillment.[8]

As the Book of Haggai concludes the temple had not yet been completed. Substantial work, however, had been done. Due to the motivational preaching of this grand old prophet the project was well on its way to completion.

ENDNOTES

1. Herbert Wolf, *Haggai and Malachi; Rededication and Renewal* (Chicago: Moody, 1976), p. 30.

2. Joyce G. Baldwin, *Haggai, Zechariah, Malachi* in "The Tyndale Old Testament Commentaries" (InterVarsity, 1975), p. 47.

3. The "word that I covenanted with you" may be the object of the imperative "do" or "work" in the previous verse. The intervening words would then be parenthetical.

4. Judg 5:4-5; Ps 68:8-9; 77:15f.; Exod 19:16-18. The plagues also may have been considered part of the shaking which introduced the Old Covenant.

5. The disagreement in number between the subject and the verb has caused the NASB to opt for an adverbial translation: "they shall come with the wealth of the nations." A disagreement in number between subject and verb is not that uncommon. In Haggai 1:2, for example, "this people" is singular, and the verb "says" is plural.

6. Herbert Wolf, "'The Desire of All Nations' in Haggai 2:7: Messianic or Not?" *Journal of the Evangelical Theological Society* 19 (Spring 1976): 97-102.

7. A.B. Davidson, quoted by George L. Robinson, "Haggai" in *The International Standard Bible Encyclopaedia* (Grand Rapids: Eerdmans, 1956), 2:1318.

8. W.J. Deane " Haggai" in *The Pulpit Commentary*; New Edition (New York: Funk & Wagnalls, 1909), p. 23.

CHAPTER FORTY

Opening Words and Visions
Zechariah 1-2

Haggai's ministry concluded before the temple project was completed. Perhaps the old prophet was taken away by death. In any case, God raised up a young visionary to continue the work begun by Haggai. Through sermons, visions, and symbolic actions Zechariah provided encouragement to the temple builders.

PREREQUISITE FOR SPIRITUAL BLESSING
Zechariah 1:1-6

In the eighth month of the second year of Darius the Great (October/November 520 BC) Zechariah received the first of many revelations from Yahweh. His opening message consists of an exhortation for the remnant to return to the Lord (vv. 2-3) followed by an example (vv. 4-6) which reinforces the need for the preceding exhortation.

A. An Exhortation (1:2-3).

Zechariah began by announcing how angry Yahweh was with the

generation of the captivity. He employs a strong verb and two grammatical devices to stress the acuteness of the displeasure: "Displeased has Yahweh been with displeasure concerning your fathers." Thus there was a desperate need for repentance (1:2).

God saw in the present generation the same root sin which he had so hated in the captivity generation, viz., disobedience. Therefore, Yahweh called upon these people to "return unto me." Repentance is always manifested in concrete ways. In this case the completion of the work on the temple would indicate their repentance (1:3a).

A change of conduct on the part of the people would induce a change of attitude on the part of God. "Return unto me in order that I will return unto you." The Hebrew reflects progressive action. God will ever and continually return to those who return to him (1:3b).

The divine origin of Zechariah's opening words is underscored in three ways: First, the messenger formula: "Thus says Yahweh." Second, the oracular formula: "oracle of Yahweh." Third, the declaration formula: "said Yahweh of hosts."

B. An Example (1:4-6).

Zechariah urged his people: "Do not become like your fathers." God's word had been spurned by the fathers. This is the first of four times Zechariah cites the fathers as an example of apostasy and warning. The fathers did not listen to "the former prophets," i.e., the prophets before the exile, especially Jeremiah. Those prophets forcefully, yet with tact and love, had urged the fathers to "turn please from your evil ways and your evil deeds." The fathers "did not hear, nor hearken unto me." Rejecting the prophetic word is equivalent to rejecting God himself (1:4).

God's word was fulfilled upon the fathers. To make this point Zechariah asks three questions of his audience. First, "Your fathers, where are they?" Of course they were dead. Second, "And the prophets, do they live forever?" Of course they do not. Zechariah now made his point: "But my words and my statutes which I commanded unto my servants the prophets, did they not overtake your fathers?" The divine threats spoken by those the prophets caught up with the disobedient. The point is that the message of God is infallible. The messengers and the original auditors may die, but the word lives on (1:5-6a).

God's word was eventually acknowledged by the fathers. So the fathers "turned." The turning here is probably not that of repentance but indicates a change of mind or opinion forced on one by circumstances. The judgment of exile forced the fathers to acknowledge the truth, accuracy and justice of God's word. "According as Yahweh purposed to do to us, according to our way and according to our deeds, so has he dealt with us" (1:6b).

VISION ONE
THE MAN AMONG THE MYRTLES
Zechariah 1:7-17

The series of eight visions is such an important part of the Book of Zechariah that the prophet carefully dates them in the second year of Darius. He refers to the month first by number (eleventh month) and then by its Babylonian name (Shebat). Converted to the modern calendar the day of Zechariah's visions is February 24, 519 BC. This was about three months after Zechariah's first address and Haggai's last address and about five months after the work on the temple had resumed (1:7).

A. That which the Prophet Saw (1:8-9).

Zechariah says that he saw his visions in the night. They all came in one night at short intervals. It is impossible to tell whether he sees with the bodily eyes or whether he was rapt in ecstasy.

The prophet's attention is first fixed on a man mounted upon a red horse. This "man" is no doubt an angel, probably the angel of Yahweh mentioned again in verses 10-11. The rider on the red horse is apparently the leader of the company of horsemen who follow him. He is not to be confused with the interpreting angel who also appears in this vision. No significance is assigned to the color red here.

The rider on the red horse had halted among the myrtle trees. These trees once were common in the vicinity of Jerusalem. Several commentators have suggested that these trees symbolize Israel. The trees were "in the bottom." This may be a reference to an ordinary valley near Jerusalem (Cashdan); others think the word is used to denote horrible, inescapable agony and hopelessness (Leupold). Thus

Israel was in a state of deep humiliation (1:8a).

Zechariah observed a troop of horses behind the rider on the red horse. Most likely these red, sorrel and white horses were being ridden by angels. Horses suggest the swiftness with which God carries out his purposes. The fact that the riders are not mentioned, but the color of the horses is mentioned suggests that the colors are symbolic. Commentators, however, are not in agreement as to what the colors symbolize. Either the colors represent the lands which these horses traversed (Keil) or the different tasks which had been assigned to them (Barnes). The important thing here is that God's agents were on the scene and they were about to move against the enemies of Israel (1:8b).

The prophet then addressed the interpreting angel who accompanied him throughout the visions: "O Lord, What are these?" He wanted to know the symbolic import of what he was seeing in this first vision. The interpreting angel responded "I will show you what these are." He did this by allowing Zechariah to overhear the conversation between the angelic riders. In other words, he turned on the audio for the moving picture which the prophet was observing (1:9).

B. That which the Prophet Heard (1:10-13).

The man on the red horse actually explained what the other horsemen had been doing. "These are they whom Yahweh has sent to walk to and fro through the earth." This was a heavenly reconnaissance troop. They had just returned from their mission and were ready to report to their commander. The phrase "to walk to and fro" is used in a military sense, to patrol (cf. Job 1:7), to make careful survey (1:10).

The riders of the various colored horses reported to their commander, the rider on the red horse who is now identified as "the angel of Yahweh." Whereas these riders had been sent forth by Yahweh, they report to the angel of Yahweh. This is another indication that the angel of Yahweh and Yahweh are one and the same (1:11a).

The report of the riders was that they had completed their mission. "We have walked to and fro in the earth." What did this reconnaissance patrol discover? "Behold, all the earth sits still and is at rest." The participle indicates continuous action. When used of a place it has a passive force, i.e., to be peacefully inhabited. To be "at rest" in this context means to have respite from war. From the standpoint of the postexilic community this was bad news. There was as yet no sign of Haggai's predicted shaking of the nations which would lead to the restoration of the Davidic dynasty in a descendant of Zerubbabel (Hag 2:20-23). Gentile nations were enjoying security while Judah was in a state of misery and oppression (1:11b).

Zechariah then heard the angel of Yahweh offering up an intercessory prayer on behalf of the postexilic community. In the passages where he appears in the Old Testament the angel of Yahweh is clearly presented as being deity. Yet here he prays to Yahweh. Here is the same mystery which New Testament students face when the Son of God—who is clearly presented as deity—is pictured praying to his Father. The revelation of the angel of Yahweh in the Old Testament is a preparation for the later revelation of the pluralistic unity of the Godhead.

The prayer is in the form of a rhetorical question which is in fact an oblique way of requesting aid. "O Yahweh of hosts, how long will you not have mercy on Jerusalem and on the cities of Judah?" Here the angel of Yahweh appears, not only as the representative of Yahweh, but as the advocate of Israel. He is identified with his people in their suffering, degradation and woe, i.e., he is standing among the myrtle trees in the deep valley. The present pitiful condition of the restoration community is regarded as evidence that God had not blessed his people (1:12a).

God had had indignation against his people for "seventy years." This is not the seventy years predicted by Jeremiah (25:11; 29:10) because that period ended with the fall of Babylon in 539 BC. This seventy years of indignation began with the destruction of Jerusalem in 586 BC. By the date of this vision that period had almost run its course. As yet, however, there was no sign that the divine indignation was at an end. Judah was still ruled by Persia. The temple was not yet complete (1:12b).

Yahweh gave an answer to "the angel that spoke with me," i.e., the interpreting angel. The answer was not given to the angel of Yahweh since, being a manifestation of deity, he already knew the answer.[1] The answer is described in two ways: (1) as "good words," i.e., a positive response; and as "comforting words." Here the text uses the plural of abundance. Yahweh had abundant comfort for the discouraged postexilic community. The essence of this comforting message is summarized in the words which follow (1:13).

C. What the Prophet was to Proclaim (1:14-17).

The interpreting angel ordered Zechariah to "cry" or proclaim the good news to Jerusalem. In this unit twice this prophet was told to "cry." Five times he was told to assure the people that his message was the word of God. Three times he was to remind them that the covenant God was the Lord of hosts with inexhaustible resources to carry out his pledges to Jerusalem.

Zechariah was to proclaim Yahweh's favor toward Zion. Yahweh declared: "I am jealous for Jerusalem and for Zion with a great jealousy." He had for this city an ardent love that cannot bear to see the object of love injured. Unger points out seven syntactical devices used here to express the intensity of God's love for his people (1:14).[2]

Zechariah was to proclaim God's hostility toward those who were Israel's enemies. "I am greatly displeased with the nations that are at ease." The participle indicates continuous anger. The particular nations in view here are those which had oppressed Israel. Why this divine displeasure with these nations which had been used as tools by Yahweh to punish Israel? "When I was a little displeased then they helped for calamity." The nations had exceeded their limitations as God's instruments of chastisement. They had wished to destroy Israel completely or to oppress them beyond measure (1:15).

Zechariah was to proclaim Yahweh's return to Zion. "I have returned to Jerusalem with compassions." The Hebrew uses the plural of abundance. "My house shall be built in it." The construction continued apace even as the prophet was speaking. "And a line shall be stretched forth over Jerusalem." The city eventually would be rebuilt as well as the temple. This was done when Nehemiah returned to rebuild and repopulate Jerusalem in 445 BC (1:16).

Zechariah was also to proclaim Yahweh's choice of Zion. "Yet shall my cities overflow with prosperity." During the intertestamental period many villages of Judea were very prosperous. "And I will comfort Zion." God's people would be comforted by the reconstruction of their temple, and the realization that they once again were playing an important role in God's program. "And I will yet choose Jerusalem." Jerusalem would yet play a role in God's program. That city would be the stage upon which the great drama of redemption would be performed—the crucifixion, resurrection and initial proclamation of the gospel (1:17).

VISION TWO
THE FOUR CRAFTSMEN
Zechariah 1:18-21

In the account of his second vision, Zechariah first describes what he saw. He then recounts what he was told when he inquired as to the meaning of the symbolism of what he had seen.

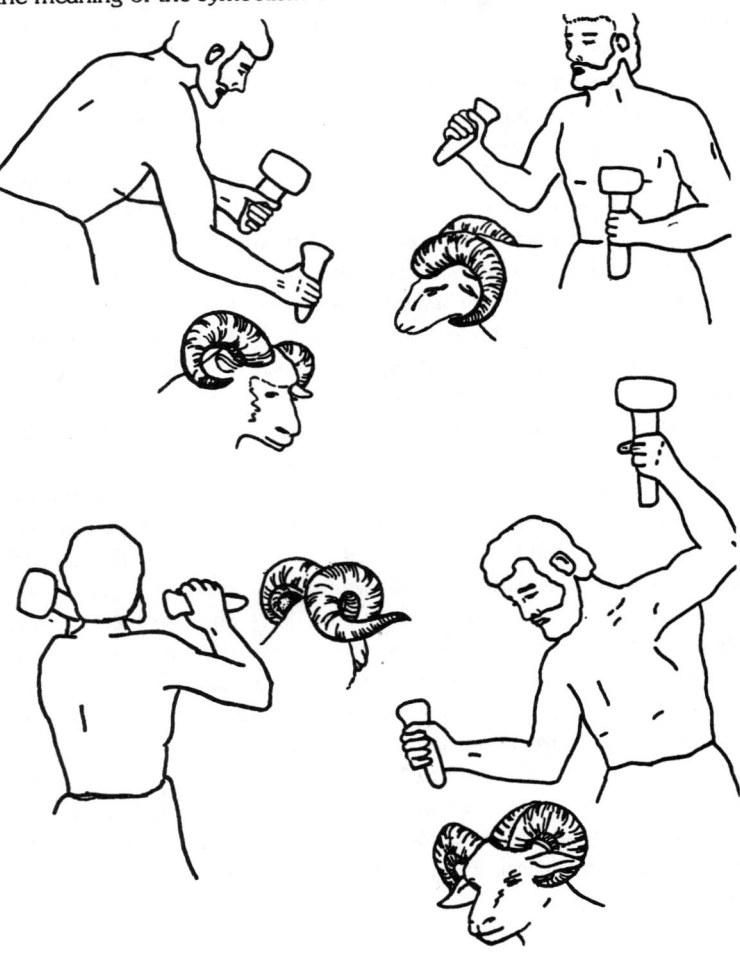

A. The Imagery of this Vision (1:18-20).

Zechariah lifted up his eyes and saw four horns. The text does not indicate whether or not these horns were attached to some object or floating loose in the air. Horns are symbolic of power (cf. Dan 8:3). These horns represented the nations which had "scattered" Judah, Israel and Jerusalem. The Hebrew uses a form which indicates how unmercifully the Gentile nations had sifted Israel. The term "Israel" could be a reference to the old northern kingdom. On the other hand, "Israel" here could be regarded as the ancient and honorable name for the entire nation. The basic idea is that the crime of the horns had been against Yahweh's people, and therefore against Yahweh himself.

Various meanings have been assigned to the fact that four horns are depicted. Four has been taken to be (1) the number of completeness (Deane); (2) the four directions of the compass (Cashdan); and (3) four specific national oppressors of Israel. Wright identified those powers as Assyria, Egypt, Babylon, and Persia.[3] More likely, however, the four oppressive powers are the same kingdoms represented by beasts in the Daniel 7: Babylon, Persia, Greece, and Rome.[4] The vision views the horns as having already been destroyed. Hence the Hebrew perfect ("have scattered") is the so-called prophetic perfect used of future things certain to be accomplished.

Zechariah saw four craftsmen or smiths. The term refers to artisans who work with wood, stone or metal. In this vision they represent the human agencies employed by God to overthrow the powers which were hostile to God's people. Some try to identify the craftsmen as four kings, e.g. Nebuchadnezzar, Cyrus, Cambyses, and Alexander the Great. Others see in the craftsmen a depiction of four spiritual leaders of Israel. e.g., Zerubbabel, Joshua, Ezra, and Nehemiah. Most commentators, however, think that it is best not to try to identify the craftsmen. They should be regarded as all saviors who arise to lead God's people to victory over their oppressors. The fact that "craftsmen" represent the conquerors of the oppressors may suggest the peaceful means by which God's kingdom eventually triumphs.

If Zechariah's second vision, however, is intended to correspond to history the horns and the craftsmen may overlap. The horns in turn, under the punitive hand of God, became craftsmen to destroy the previous empire. Thus, the Medo-Persian Cyrus was the craftsman who skillfully brought about the demise of the Babylonian empire. The incredibly brilliant strategist Alexander the Great was the craftsman who engineered the overthrow of the Medo-Persian empire. The power and policies of Rome led to the eventual overthrown of the last remnants of the Greek empire. In this approach, the fourth craftsman would be the kingdom of Messiah which peacefully but powerfully displaced imperial Rome as a worldwide empire.[5]

B. The Interpretation of the Vision (1:21).

Zechariah inquired about the meaning of the vision by asking what "these," i.e., both the horns and the craftsmen, had come to do. The interpreting angel identified the horns as the powers which "scattered Judah." Deane suggests the figure of a bull catching the prey on horns, tossing them into the air, and scattering them to the wind.[6] This certainly would include the Babylonians and probably any other nations which had taken advantage of the weakness of Judah. The people of God had been so crushed by these powers that "no person raised his head," i.e., no one could stand up to resist the horns.

The craftsmen had come "to frighten" the horns, i.e., to throw them into panic, to drive them away in terror. The craftsmen probably were carrying hammers with which they intended to shatter the horns. These craftsmen would "cast down the horns of nations." All opposition to God's people eventually would be overthrown.

VISION THREE
THE MEASURING OF JERUSALEM
Zechariah 2:1-5

Zechariah lifted up his eyes. The heavens themselves seem to have functioned as a screen on which the prophet saw his visions. Again the prophet recounts first what he saw. In this vision Zechariah interacts with the characters in the vision.

A. Presentation of the Vision (2:1-4a).

Zechariah observed a man with a measuring line in his hand. This "man" was probably an angel. The measuring line was a piece of

OPENING WORDS AND VISIONS   ZECHARIAH 1-2

equipment used by surveyors in preparing ground for building purposes. Once the enemies are destroyed (vision two), God's people can grow and develop until the time of their final glory (2:1).

Again Zechariah asked the man with the measuring line where he was going. This was an interactive vision in which the prophet could communicate with those he saw. The man responded that he was on his way to "measure Jerusalem," obviously in preparation for the reconstruction of the place (2:2).

At this point the interpreting angel "went out," i.e., he left Zechariah. Neither his direction nor his purpose is stated. A second angel appears in the vision. He brings with him a revelation from God. Zechariah then overheard a conversation between the two angels (2:3).

Zechariah heard one of the angels give the other an order to "run and speak unto this young man." Probably it was the second angel who gave the order to the interpreting angel. The "young man" who was to receive the message could be either (1) the man with the measuring line (Wright; Cashdan), or (2) Zechariah himself (Pusey; Deane). If the former, then the surveyor was making a mistake in attempting to define the limits of what would be unlimited (2:4a).

B. The Meaning of the Vision (2:4b-5).

The message for the "young man" was that the Jerusalem of the future would be "inhabited as villages without walls." In ancient times cities had walls, villages did not. The Jerusalem of the future would be so extensive that walls would no longer be able to contain its inhabitants and cattle. About seventy-five years after this oracle, the walls of physical Jerusalem were rebuilt by Nehemiah. Some take the point to be that physical Jerusalem would one day overflow his walls (Wright). Others think a millennial Jerusalem is in view (Unger). Most likely, however, the reference is to the messianic Jerusalem (Leupold), the Jerusalem of Hebrews 12:22. The church embraces all nations and is boundless. The "cattle" would represent the possessions and wealth of the city (2:4b).

A wall around the future Jerusalem would not only be impossible to build, it would be unnecessary. The church does not need walls of stone, for God himself would be her wall, a fiery wall that consumes all who might attack the place. Furthermore, God declares that he would be "the glory in the midst" of Jerusalem. Christ is in his church. The providential care for the church reflects his glory (2:5). When the Lord returns, he will be glorified in his saints (2 Thess 1:10).

AMPLIFICATION OF THE THIRD VISION
Zechariah 2:6-12

The third vision is amplified by means of an earnest appeal to the Jewish exiles in Babylon (2:6-9), and an announcement to the remnant in Palestine (2:10-12).

A. An Appeal to the Exiles (2:6-9).

A speaker who is as yet unidentified, addressed the distant exiles by means of a double exclamation: "Ho! Ho!" In some contexts the Hebrew term (hoy) is translated "woe." It contains an element of sympathy and pity. Here this term is designed to arrest attention. Thus, out of his great concern for what is about to happen in the land of the north, the speaker calls upon God's people to flee the scene.

The exiles of Judah had been spread abroad "as the four winds of the heavens."[7] A great number of exiles still remained voluntarily in "the land of the north," i.e., in Mesopotamia. They had become rich and prosperous. Zechariah now urged these exiles to "flee" lest they suffer the same fate which God had in store for Babylon. During the reign of Darius the city of Babylon was twice captured in brutal fighting. Since the context refers to the messianic Jerusalem, the land of the north may symbolize all the enemies of the church through the ages (2:6).

Those who dwelled "with the daughter of Babylon," i.e., the people of Babylon are urged to flee "to Zion." After 586 BC "Babylon" stood for all lands of the exile. Through the gospel God calls those who dwell in "Babylon"—the world—to flee the doomed city and enter into the blessed safety of Zion (2:7). God is always calling his people out of the world (cf. Rev 18:4-8).

The anonymous angel of 2:3 is finally identified in 2:8. Yahweh of hosts had dispatched the speaker "unto the nations which spoil you." The participle indicates that the plundering by the nations was continuing. Who else but the angel of Yahweh himself—that glorious Old Testament manifestation of the second person of the Godhead—would be entrusted with such a mission?

The angel of Yahweh had been dispatched "after glory." He has been sent to get glory or honor over the heathen by taking vengeance on them. The justification for this judgment is set forth in the words "he who touches you touches the pupil of his eye." Yahweh is injured by any harm which is done to his people. Thus he must vindicate himself in judgment upon those who oppose him (2:8). Here is an anticipation of the New Testament revelation of the Father sending the Son to glorify him (John 17:4).

The angel of Yahweh has but to wave his hand in a threatening gesture and his enemies shrink with fear. Those who had abused his people would "be spoil for those that served them." The proud masters would become servants. The fulfillment of such a prediction is to be sought in the spiritual realm. When hostile peoples are converted to the worship of the true God their resources then become "spoil" in the sense that they are devoted to the work of the Lord (2:9a).

The appeal to the exiles concludes with the certainty formula: "And you shall know that Yahweh of hosts has sent me." One view is that the fulfillment of these staggering promises would identify the angel of Yahweh and vindicate his mission. On the other hand, these may be the words of Zechariah speaking about himself. The prophet was certain that his word would be fulfilled. His prophetic ministry would be vindicated by the future conversion of peoples once hostile to Israel (2:9b).

B. Announcement to the Remnant (2:10-12).

While those still in exile were addressed in ominous minor key, the remnant in Judea is exhorted to exuberant praise. The "daughter of Zion"—the inhabitants of Zion or God's people—are urged to "sing and rejoice." This triumphant shout of victory is appropriate because, as shocking as it might now appear to be, Yahweh himself was coming to dwell in the midst of his people. The temple currently under construction would be his dwelling place. That temple, however, was but a type of the New Testament temple—the church of Christ—in which the Son of God continues to dwell with his people. The ultimate joy of every true son and daughter of Israel was that Messiah would come. The Christian testimony to the world is "Joy to the world, the Lord has come!" (2:10).

That day of Yahweh's coming in the person of Messiah would be a day of mass conversion of Gentiles. "Many nations shall join themselves to Yahweh in that day." Those who thus embraced Yahweh as revealed through his Son would be considered "my people," i.e., Israel. It is within this expanded version of Israel—this Israel of faith, the church of Christ—that Yahweh would dwell. Thus the poor and pitiful remnant of Zechariah's day are bidden to see with the eye of faith the glorious future of the people of God. When that glorious day arrived they would know for certain that Yahweh had sent his messenger—the Word—unto them (2:11).

In that day when Yahweh would come to his people in the person of his Son, he would "inherit Judah as his portion." The Judah here envisioned, as the context clearly shows, is that expanded Judah of faith which would include Gentiles who by faith embraced Yahweh. The church is the inheritance of Christ. Following his enthronement at the ascension Jesus Christ became head over all things to the church which is his body (Eph 1:22; 4:15).

Yahweh would inherit messianic Judah "in the holy land." This is the only place where the expression "holy land" is found in sacred literature. The term is not to be restricted to physical Palestine. Wherever God reveals himself, there is the holy land.[8] If "Judah" in this context consists of the remnant of Israel plus a mass of converted Gentiles, perhaps the "holy land" would be the glorious kingdom in which these saved ones dwell, the kingdom of Christ (Col 1:13).

Yahweh would once again "choose Jerusalem." All the decisive religious events of the future would take place in physical Jerusalem. Yet the context here bids the interpreter to look beyond the type—the physical city—to the antitype, the Jerusalem of the redeemed, the church of Christ (Heb 12:22; Gal 4:25f.). Thus in this passage the redeemed of the messianic age are viewed in three ways: as a nation ("Judah"), as a land ("the holy land"), and as a city ("Jerusalem"). The point is that the remnant would have a glorious future in a new relationship with their God (2:12).

The promises to the remnant conclude with an exhortation to "all flesh" to be "silent before Yahweh" (cf. Hab 2:20). Some take these words to be an encouragement for the people of God to be patient and to wait in awe for the great messianic day to arrive (Laetsch). More likely, however, is the view that these words are a warning to the nations that God was coming to execute judgment upon them

(Deane; Unger). Yahweh is "aroused out of his holy habitation." He was preparing even as the prophet spoke to fulfill all his promises to believers, and his threats to those who oppose him. Thus the concluding verse of chapter 2 harks back to the theme of the third vision, viz., the enemies of God's people must be smashed before the glorious day of promise could dawn (2:13).

ENDNOTES

1. W.J. Deane suggests that in 1:13 "Yahweh" is an abbreviation for "angel of Yahweh." "Zechariah" in *The Pulpit Commentary*; (Grand Rapids: Eerdmans, 1963 reprint), pp. 3f.
2. Merrill Unger, *Zechariah; Prophet of Messiah's Glory* (Grand Rapids: Zondervan, 1963), p. 30.
3. C.H.H. Wright, *Zechariah and his Prophecies*, 1879 (Minneapolis: Klock and Klock, 1980 reprint), p. 28. This is based on the mention of "Israel" which is taken to be the old northern kingdom, and the form of the verb which is thought to refer only to past action.
4. E.J. Young, *An Introduction to the Old Testament* (Grand Rapids: Eerdmans, 1960), p. 299; Merrill F. Unger also sees the reference to the four great empires of Daniel. Curiously he then names five empires: Babylon, Medo-Persia, Macedonia, Greece and Rome. *Zechariah; Prophet of Messiah's Glory* (Grand Rapids: Zondervan, 1963), p. 37.
5. Cf. Unger, *op.cit.*, pp. 40-41.
6. Deane, *op. cit.*, p. 5.
7. Cf. Keil, Wright and Leupold who take the clause "for I have spread you abroad as the four winds" as a promise of the future expansion of God's people.
8. Corresponding to the expression "holy land" are the terms "holy hill" (Ps 2:6; 15:1) and "holy mountain" (Pss 48:1; 99:9).

CHAPTER FORTY-ONE

The Visions Continue
Zechariah 3-4

Zechariah has related three visions so far. He saw the rider on the red horse among the myrtle trees. In that first vision the status of the world was peaceful. There was no sign as yet of the tumultuous shaking of the nations forecast by Haggai. The second vision—the four horns and four craftsmen—stressed that God would remove all the oppressors of his people. The third vision depicted messianic Jerusalem as a city without walls in which the Lord himself would reside. The visions now continue in chapters 3-4.

VISION FOUR
JOSHUA REINSTATED
Zechariah 3:1-7

The fourth vision centers on Joshua the high priest in his role as the representative of the priesthood and the people.

A. The Condition of Joshua (3:1-3).

The interpreting angel directed Zechariah's attention to Joshua the high priest. He was "standing before the angel of Yahweh." The setting of this vision is not indicated. The possibilities include (1) the heavenly temple, (2) the earthly temple, and (3) the city gate where trials were conducted. Also uncertain here is the sense in which Joshua was "standing" before the angel of Yahweh. Some think he is here viewed as a defendant on trial (Cashdan; Baldwin). Others think he was rendering priestly service in the temple (Unger; Laetsch). The mention of his garments suggests that this latter view is correct (3:1a).

In any case, Satan (*hassatan* = the accuser) was "standing at Joshua's right hand." As is common in the Old Testament, the author has appended a definite article to a common noun to form a proper name.[1] Satan standing there "to be his adversary," lit., to satanize him. The Evil One here is not so much a judicial accuser as an enemy who is trying to resist Joshua's efforts to intercede for his people (3:1b).

Yahweh addressed Satan in this vision. The reference is probably to the angel of Yahweh before whom Joshua was ministering. Since the angel of Yahweh is a manifestation of Yahweh, he is often simply called "Yahweh." In any case, he administered to Satan a stinging rebuke: "Yahweh rebuke you, O Satan." Unger points out several syntactical elements in the Hebrew which indicate that the rebuke of Satan was thorough, final, and authoritative (3:2a).[2]

The rebuke of Satan for attempting to hinder the ministrations of Joshua is based on two considerations. First, Yahweh had "chosen Jerusalem." The physical city of Jerusalem would not be reconstructed for another seventy years. The temple was currently under construction. The rest of the city would be rebuilt by Nehemiah in 445 BC. As noted above (on 2:12), all decisive religious events of the future would take place in physical Jerusalem. The term "Jerusalem" includes the inhabitants of the city as well as the walls and buildings. The point is that what was taking place in that place had God's blessing. The remnant was a chosen people performing a God-ordained work in a place which had been designated by God centuries earlier. Thus in opposing Joshua, Satan was in effect opposing the will of God himself.

The second basis for the rebuke of Satan is expressed in a rhetorical question: "Is not this a brand plucked out of the fire?" The proof that Joshua (and the people he represented) stood in God's favor is seen in the fact that he had been rescued from grave danger. God had rescued Israel from the fire of exile where they as a people might well have been destroyed. Therefore, Joshua, as the representative of this people, was not to be the victim of malicious slander on the part of the Evil Accuser (3:2b). For those who have been saved, there can be no condemnation (Rom 8:1).

While the rebuke was being administered to Satan, Joshua was standing silent "clothed in filthy (lit., excrement-soiled) garments." The high priest not only looked terrible, he stunk. The filthy garments are symbolic of the personal sin of Joshua and the entire nation. Satan had a point. What business did this man have ministering before Yahweh? The participle used here indicates a continuing state of moral and spiritual filthiness. Joshua could utter not one word in his own defense. He was aware of his unworthiness to serve as priest to his people (3:3).

B. The Cleansing of the Priesthood (3:4-5).

The Angel of Yahweh ordered subordinate angels to remove the filthy garments from Joshua. Only Yahweh himself can remove human sin and guilt. The significance of the removal of the filthy garments is explained by the Angel to Joshua himself: "Behold! I cause your iniquity to pass from you." The term "iniquity" here is the whole sinful disposition which leads to distress and guilt. Thus the removal of the garments is symbolic of the remission of sins or cleansing. Joshua had done nothing to deserve this cleansing. He merely had responded to the call of God to return to his land and his ministry. For Joshua (and the people he represented) God in his grace would provide forgiveness and cleanings (3:4a).

In this passage grace builds on grace. Reinstatement would follow cleaning. The Angel declares to Joshua: "And I will clothe you with festive garments," lit., a garment that is put off, taken off, before going to work; hence, a precious, costly, beautiful garment. Undoubtedly the "holy garments" of the high priest are intended (cf. Exod 28). These garments are symbolic of righteousness and glory (3:4b). The cleansing of the Old Testament priesthood here is a type or preview of that wonderful cleaning and ordination to service which the priesthood of all believers (1 Pet 2:5,9) experienced when they embraced the gospel of Jesus Christ (1 Cor 6:11).

Zechariah was so excited by what he saw in his vision that he gave vent to his emotions: "Let them place a clean miter upon his head." The miter or turban was the crowning headgear of the high priest. The miter declared the priest to be holy to Yahweh, and thus qualified to make intercession for the people. The request of the prophet was immediately carried out. While this was taking place "the Angel of

Yahweh was standing by" sanctioning, directing and approving what was being done (3:5).

C. The Covenant with the Priesthood (3:6-7).

In the vision Zechariah heard the Angel of Yahweh "solemnly testify" unto Joshua regarding the obligations which devolved upon him as a result of the gracious action of the Lord (3:6). First, Joshua had the personal responsibility to "walk in my ways," i.e., observe my commandments. Second, he had the ministerial obligation to "keep my charge," i.e., faithfully execute the official duties of priests (3:7a).

If Joshua was faithful in these personal and ministerial duties, he would experience a threefold blessing. First, he would "judge my house." Joshua would rule and order divine worship in the temple. He would govern the ministers in the sanctuary. Heretofore the kings had exercised a large measure of authority over temple worship. Now the rights of the high priest would be indisputable. Second, Joshua would also "keep my courts," i.e., guard them from desecration by ungodliness, frivolity and idolatry.

The third promise seems to reach beyond Joshua personally. Yahweh promised to give Joshua "free access 'lit., a walking path) among these that stand by." High priests of the old covenant had been admitted to the Holy of Holies once each year on the Day of Atonement. The promise here is that the high priest would be admitted to the very throne room of God himself. He would enjoy direct communication with God, like the angels (3:7).

MESSIANIC APPLICATION OF THE FOURTH VISION
Zechariah 3:8-10

Whatever application this promise may have had to Joshua, the ultimate fulfillment is in Jesus Christ, Joshua's ministerial successor. As the great high priest of the Christian era, Jesus sits upon the right hand of the throne of God where he makes intercession on behalf of his people (Heb 7:25). As is often the case in Old Testament prophecy, the promise made to an individual was fulfilled in someone who either was his descendant or successor in office. The messianic application of the promise made to Joshua is made clear in the verses which follow.

A. The Sign (3:8a).

Yahweh addressed a word of explanation to Joshua and his associates in the priesthood. These priests were "men that are a marvelous sign." The word can mean a special display of God's power, or a token of a future event (cf. Isa 8:18). The term is used of men rousing the attention of the people to a coming event. Thus Joshua the high priest and his fellow priests were to be regarded as types prefiguring the New Testament priesthood. In their persons, office and duties they foreshadow the good things to come. The restored priesthood was a sign of the advent of Messiah. The purification of Joshua prefigured the greater purification which would be effected by the Messiah.

B. Servant and Shoot (3:8b).

The reason Joshua and his associates were to be regarded as a sign is now stated: "For behold I will bring forth my Servant." Like Isaiah (e.g., Isa 52:13), Zechariah calls Messiah "my Servant." He is so called because of his willing, patient, and perfect obedience to his Father. The Servant is also called "the Shoot." Ancient interpreters, both Jewish and Christian, agree in explaining the Shoot as the Messiah. Zechariah makes this term a proper name. The title points to the miraculous origin of Messiah and to the mystery of his person. He was implanted by God in this world as a tender shoot (3:8b).

C. The Stone (3:9-10).

Zechariah's attention was now drawn to another feature of the vision. A stone had been set before Joshua. Leupold lists nine different interpretations of what the stone symbolizes. Among the more plausible views are these: the stone is the capstone of the temple (Cashdan), or the spiritual temple, the church (Leupold, Deane), or the Messiah himself (Wright, Pusey; Unger). Since "stone" in Old Testament prophecy is frequently used of Messiah,[3] the personal messianic interpretation is probably correct.

1. The seven eyes (3:9a). The "stone" was unique for it is described as "one stone." On that stone were "seven eyes" (*'enayim*). Some prefer to translate the term "facets," but it is doubtful that the word has this meaning. Furthermore, a stone with seven facets would be difficult to use either in the foundation or as the headstone of a building. Baldwin translates the word "wells." Moses struck a rock and brought forth water (Exod 17:6). So this stone would have seven wells, producing an abundance of water to bring cleansing to the land. In all likelihood, however, the traditional translation "seven eyes" is correct. The meaning would then be that the Stone—the Messiah—would have perfect wisdom and knowledge, i.e., omniscience (3:9a).[4]

2. *The engraving (3:9b).* A second "behold" statement introduces another unexpected quality of the Stone. "Behold! I will engrave the engraving of it." The text does not indicate what the engraving is. Is the engraving the "eyes" of the previous clause? Be that as it may, an "engraving" is that which is cut into a stone which makes a stone beautiful. If the Stone here is the Messiah, then the engraving must be that which was cut into his sinless humanity. The scars in his body are what make him beautiful to the believer.

The result of the engraving or deep cutting of the stone is that Yahweh would "remove the iniquity of that land in one day." That day when Jesus was pierced through to the death became the final Day of Atonement when the ultimate and perfect sin offering was made once and for all time (3:9b).

3. *Messianic peace (3:10).* The coming of the one known as Servant, Shoot and Stone would usher in a glorious new day for God's people. "In that day, says Yahweh of hosts, you shall call every man his neighbor under the vine and under the fig tree." The idiom signifies peace and prosperity (cf. 1 Kgs 4:24f.). Micah (4:4) used a similar figure to describe the messianic age (3:10).

VISION FIVE
THE LAMPSTAND AND THE OLIVE TREES
Zechariah 4:1-5

After the fourth vision Zechariah fell asleep. The interpreting angel then came to him to awaken him. Divine revelation was traumatic. Those who received such revelation were psychologically and physically exhausted. The opening verse of chapter 4 establishes that the visions which Zechariah received were not dreams. He had to be awakened in order to continue his education regarding the things to come (4:1).

A. A Lampstand (4:2).

The first four vision accounts began with the prophet reporting on the object or scene which he saw. In the fifth vision the interpreting angel begins his interrogation before Zechariah reports seeing anything. This format suggests that the interpreting angel is prodding the prophet to continue with his visionary activity.

Zechariah's attention is directed toward a lampstand. The configuration of this lampstand (*menorah*) is problematical. A seven-branched *menorah* illuminated the tabernacle built by Moses (Exod

25). The temple of Solomon contained ten such lampstands. Some commentators have tried to impose that form on this passage.[5] Zechariah's description of what he saw, however, simply does not fit the description of the Mosaic *menorah*. Thankfully, archaeological research has excavated some lampstands which are remarkably similar to that which Zechariah describes.[6]

Zechariah seems to have seen a tapered cylinder with a "bowl" mounted on the top. Around the rim of the bowl were seven "lamps," smaller bowls with grooves for wicks. Each lamp had seven (lit., seven and/even seven) "lips"[7] from which wicks dangled into the reservoir of oil. Thus each of the seven "lamps" contained at least seven wicks.[8] The lampstand gave forth abundant light.

The object was very precious for it was a "lampstand all of gold," i.e., solid gold. This is the only respect in which this visionary *menorah* resembled the tabernacle and Solomonic *menorot*. The former *menorah* is said to have been made of "pure gold" (*zahab tahor*), i.e., the gold of the finest quality (Exod 25:31). The ten *menorot* in Solomon's temple are said to have been made of "pure gold" (*zahab sagur*) or perhaps "beaten gold" (1 Kgs 7:49; cf. 6:20-21).

B. Two Olive Trees (4:3-5).

On either side of the lampstand Zechariah observed two olive trees. By means of two golden spouts (cf. v. 12) the trees emptied their oil into the large bowl which served as the oil reservoir. The emphasis here is on the automatic and spontaneous supply of oil without human agency (4:3).

General agreement exists among the commentators that the lampstand signifies the people of God. Israel was precious to the Lord, as precious as gold. The design of Israel, like the lampstand, was to give light in the world. In this ministry Israel would experience supernatural vitality as is indicated in the endless supply of oil. The oil itself probably signifies the Holy Spirit or perhaps the grace of God.

Zechariah did not grasp the significance of what he had seen. He asked, "What are these?" The angel thought that the symbols were so clear that the prophet should have grasped them. He therefore delayed answering the prophet. This action served to sharpen the prophet's question, and focus greater attention on the concluding verse of the chapter (4:4-5).

Rather than answer Zechariah's questions about the symbolism of the vision, the angel addressed two words of application to Zerubbabel. These two messages hint at the meaning of the vision symbolism.

A WORD TO ZERUBBABEL
Zechariah 4:6-7

The word of Yahweh is directed especially to Zerubbabel. Joshua the high priest had been given the special word in vision four, hence the concentration on the governor. The first word to Zerubbabel sets forth a general principle and a personal promise.

A. A General Principle (4:6).

An unusual Hebrew construction makes the words of Zechariah 4:6 a slogan of encouragement: "Not by might nor by power, but by my Spirit, says Yahweh of hosts." The term "might" (*chayil*) is a general word for human resources such as physical strength, ability, wealth, military power and force. In rebuilding the temple Zerubbabel would not have at his disposal the armies of workers and (literally) tons of wealth which Solomon employed in the first building of the temple.

The term "power" (*khoach*) is used of the strength of the burden bearers in the days of Nehemiah (Neh 4:10). The term again denotes human strength in all its forms—physical, mental, and material. The repetition of the negative emphasizes the complete insufficiency of human strength and resources to accomplish the work of God.

If human resources would be entirely inadequate to accomplish God's work, the Holy Spirit would be sufficient. The second half of the slogan is introduced by an emphatic exceptive or restrictive phrase (*ki 'im*). The point of connection with the vision is this. The lampstand was fed with oil not by man's hand and without human effort. So the temple would be restored not by the strength of Zerubbabel's hands but by the Spirit of God.

B. A Personal Promise (4:7).

The personal promise to Zerubbabel is introduced by a rhetorical question: "Who are you, O great mountain?" All difficulties impeding the progress on the temple are lumped together and figuratively called a great mountain. Those difficulties probably included lack of resources, lack of manpower, and government red tape. That hostile mountain would be leveled before Zerubbabel! The construction in the Hebrew is dramatic and emphatic: "Before Zerubbabel...a plain!" The language assumes that Zerubbabel will continue to pursue the work aggressively. As he goes about his work, God will go about his. The Lord is in the business of making molehills out of mountains! (4:7a).

Zerubbabel would have the privilege of completing the task which he had commenced some months earlier. "He shall bring forth the top stone" (lit., the stone of the head). This was the richly ornamented stone which crowned the building and signified its completion. That top stone would be put in position "amid shouts, Grace, grace unto it." The people would cheer the finished work. "Grace" in this context indicates loveliness or elegance. Thus the beauty of the top stone itself and that which it represented (i.e., the entire temple) would be praised by the people (4:7b).

ANOTHER WORD FOR ZERUBBABEL
Zerubbabel 4:8-10

Zechariah received a second revelation which removed any ambiguity which attended the first promise (4:8). Four words summarize this second word to Zerubbabel: declaration, vindication, intimation, and revelation.

A. The Declaration (4:9a).

The Lord declared: "The hands of Zerubbabel have laid the foundation of this house; his hands shall also finish it." The stress in the Hebrew is on the fact that Zerubbabel's hands and no one else would finish the work. It would have been enough had God merely promised that this work, which Zerubbabel had started, would be brought to a successful conclusion. Grace beyond grace stresses, however, that this faithful worker would live to see his beloved temple completed. Thus the project would be brought to a conclusion in the near rather than the distant future (4:9a). In the Old Testament world the inability to complete an important project in life was considered a terrible curse from God (cf. Deut 28:30-33; 38-42).

B. The Vindication (4:9b).

The recognition formula so common in this book is appended to the promise of successful completion of the temple work. "Then you shall know that Yahweh of hosts has sent me" (4:9b). The completion of the temple would vindicate either the message of Zechariah (Baldwin) or the mission of the angel of Yahweh (Unger; Laetsch).

C. The Intimation (4:10a).

A rhetorical question brings to light one of the difficulties which Zerubbabel was facing in his construction ministry. "For who has despised the day of small things?" Every great work for God started small, perhaps only as a vision in the mind of a great soul of faith. In the day of small things the critics are numerous, and the carping vicious. In kingdom work every dreamer faces ridicule, every doer mockery. A thousand times he will hear the pundits opine that the dream is undoable, the work impossible. In spite of such nay-sayers Zerubbabel pressed on with his work with the help of the few whose hearts God had touched. The glorious completion of the temple would put to shame all those who sneered at the meager beginnings of the work.

D. The Revelation (4:10b).

While critics derided Zerubbabel's efforts, the Living God looked down upon the progressing work with joy. How dare the doubters continue their campaign of ridicule! Zechariah refers to "these seven" who "shall rejoice." He interprets "these seven" as "the eyes of Yahweh which run to and fro through the whole earth." The idea that God's eyes roam throughout the earth in search of those who are willing to risk everything in bold expressions of faith was first introduced by the prophet Hanani in the days of King Asa (2 Chr 16:9).

God, who is a Spirit being, does not have seven eyes, nor any eyes for that matter. Eyes—as well as other body parts—are anthropomorphically attributed to God throughout Scripture so that earthbound and body-oriented humankind may come to have a warm and loving relationship with their Creator. Seven is the number of completeness or perfection. Thus the seven eyes of God would symbolize his perfect knowledge of all that transpires on this earth. To state the matter in theological terms, God is omniscient. He not only knows of the work which Zerubbabel had undertaken, he rejoices in every advancement of that work.

Specifically, the seven eyes of God rejoice when they see "the plummet in the hand of Zerubbabel." The plummet was a string attached to a weight which enabled a builder to determine a true right angle (cf. Amos 7:7). Zerubbabel was a "hands on" leader, not an armchair director, or a pulpit motivater. The plummet in his hands is a symbol of the ongoing work of temple reconstruction. The point is that God took pleasure in the sweat and toil of those few who were committed to seeing his house rebuilt in Jerusalem.

MESSIANIC APPLICATION OF THE FIFTH VISION
Zechariah 4:11-14

Zechariah sensed that his fifth vision had an application beyond Zerubbabel and the current temple reconstruction. In response to probing questions by the prophet, the interpreting angel explained the messianic significance of the vision of the eternal light.

A. The Prophet's Requests (4:11-13).

Zechariah still did not understand the significance of the olive trees in his fifth vision. Therefore, he asked: "What are these two olive trees upon the right side and upon the left side of the lampstand?" To this general question the angel gave no answer. Silence has a place in pedagogy. An keen student will perceive in the silence of his teacher that he has not precisely framed his question (4:11).

Zechariah reformulated his question to zero in on that which still perplexed him. "What are these two olive branches which by means of the two spouts empty from over them the gold?" Two spouts connected the fruitful olive boughs to the bowl or reservoir of the lampstand. Clear olive oil flowing through golden spouts might resemble liquid gold. Apparently the olives of the trees were automatically and miraculously processed into oil. The oil then accessed the lampstand by means of golden spouts (4:12a).

The angel responded to Zechariah's question with a question. The symbolic significance of the boughs which poured oil into the lampstand should have been obvious to the prophet. Students generally—including prophets—would rather have a teacher give a quick answer than to spend time analyzing possibilities and reflecting upon probabilities. Even those who are spiritually hungry are often intellectually lazy! Zechariah humbly confessed his ignorance of the meaning of the boughs and the trees from which they grew (4:12b).

B. The Angel's Explanation (4:13).

The boughs of the olive tree, the angel explained, represented "the two anointed ones" (lit., sons of oil). Joshua the high priest was certainly an anointed one. He figured prominently in the fourth vision. The second "son of oil" is most likely Zerubbabel. While it is doubtful that the governor had undergone an anointing ceremony, he was in fact a descendant of King David. Thus Zerubbabel was the representative of the royal family. The text avoids naming individuals so as not to limit the application of the vision to specific personalities.

The anointed ones are said to "stand alongside (lit., over) the Lord of all the earth." In ancient Near Eastern art kings are normally depicted sitting while their servants stand "over" them, i.e., about them. The idea here is that Joshua and Zerubbabel were servants of the most high God. They were available to carry out the wishes of their King. At the same time, these leaders had access to God on behalf of the people they represented. Through these special servants God carried out his work on earth. Through them he met the needs of his people.

If the olive boughs represent Joshua and Zerubbabel in particular, the trees must represent the royal and priestly offices. These offices empowered the people of God to give forth their light of witness in the world. In Christ the priestly and royal offices were combined. Christians are said to be both kings and priests because of their relationship with Christ. Through the witness of the church the oil of the Holy Spirit is conveyed to mankind.

ENDNOTES

1. On the doctrine of Satan in the Old Testament, see T.T. Perowne, *The Books of Haggai and Zechariah* in "The Cambridge Bible for Schools and Colleges" (Cambridge: University Press, 1908), Appendix B, pp. 153-157.
2. Merrill F. Unger, *Zechariah; Prophet of Messiah's Glory* (Grand Rapids: Zondervan, 1963), pp. 58f.
3. On the messianic stone, see Isa 28:16; Ps 118:22. Cf. Matt 21:42; Eph 2:20.
4. Another view is that the seven eyes of God are directed toward the stone in watchful care.
5. Cf. C.H.H. Wright, *Zechariah and His Prophecies* (Minneapolis: Klock and Klock, 1980), pp. 84f.
6. At Tell Dan and at Taanach lampstands have been unearthed which have all the essential structural attributes of the lampstand which Zechariah describes. See Robert North, "Zechariah's Seven-Spout Lampstand," *Biblica* 51(1970)183-206; David Petersen, *Haggai and Zechariah 1-8* in "The Old Testament Library" (Philadelphia: Westminster, 1984), pp. 216-224.
7. The term *mutsaqot* is rendered "pipes" (ASV), "spouts" (NASB), "channels" (NIV), "ducts" (BV), and "lips" (RSV; JB). The term seems to be derived from a root (*tsuq*) which means "to be in straits." In this context the *mutsaqot* referred to are pinched lips on a lamp rim which held the wicks. See Petersen, *op. cit.,* p. 221.
8. The exact number of the lips is in dispute. "Seven and seven" has been taken to mean (1) seven times seven (Leupold); (2) seven plus seven; and (3) seven even seven.

CHAPTER FORTY-TWO

Visions of Future Glory
Zechariah 5-6

The first five visions were designed to bring comfort to God's people. The last three visions constitute a stern warning that the Holy One of Israel cannot tolerate evil in any form. These visions are followed by a symbolic crowning of Joshua the high priest.

VISION SIX
THE FLYING SCROLL
Zechariah 5:1-11

The two visions in chapter 5 have an application to the restoration community. God must deal with unrepentant sinners before the period of blessing can dawn. In the account of the vision of the flying scroll Zechariah describes what he saw, explains it, and then applies the vision to the postexilic community.

A. The Vision (5:1-2).

The sixth visionary account begins as in the second and third visions: "And again I lifted up my eyes." Zechariah was shocked ("Behold!") to see a scroll flying like a banner for all to read. The use of the participle in the Hebrew indicates continuous action. The scroll was hovering in mid-air (5:1).

By means of a question the interpreting angel prodded the prophet to describe verbally what he had seen. In response Zechariah described the dimensions of the scroll. It was huge!—twenty by ten cubits, i.e., thirty by fifteen feet. That was as large as the holy place of the tabernacle (Exod 26:15-25) and the porch of the temple (1 Kgs 6:3). The material from which the scroll was made, whether papyrus or leather, is not indicated (5:2).[1]

B. The Meaning of the Vision (5:3).

The interpreting angel indicated that the scroll symbolized the curse of God against sinners in Israel. The law of Moses taught that those who kept the law would prosper; those who broke it would meet with disaster. God's word stipulates judgment and punishment for those who ignore what that word commands. The scroll represented the law with its specific curses on law-breakers within the covenant community. The subjects of the curse of God in this context are representative of all sinners (5:3a).

The scroll was inscribed on both sides. The one side contained the condemnation of sins against one's fellow man. A specific example of such a sin was stealing. Those guilty of violating the eighth commandment (and similar commands) would be "cut off" (ASV) from all covenant benefits. The reverse side of the scroll condemned sins against God. Swearing frivously in God's name is cited as a specific example of such sins. According to the scroll, these sinners also would be "cut off" (lit., "be cleansed out" or "purged from") from covenant benefits (5:3b).

C. Application of the Vision (5:4).

In the first person God dramatically declared his intention to "cause it (the curse) to go forth." Behind the written word is "Yahweh of hosts," Lord of all armies celestial and terrestrial. The sanctions, penalties and curses of his word are not idle threats or antiquated verbage. In Scripture God's words are often personified and depicted as going forth on errands assigned by the deity (cf. Ps 147:15; Isa 55:11).

In that day of judgment none would be able to hide from God. His word of judgment would find its way where civil judicial machinery cannot go, viz., into the homes of sinners. Again those who steal—the Hebrew suggests a professional thief—and those who swear to a lie in God's name are named as representative of all sinners. The house of the evil doer would be consumed "with its timber and its stones," i.e., the house would be utterly destroyed. The language points to the day when sinners would be purged from the midst of God's people.

All acts of divine judgment against sinners in history point forward to that final day of retribution at the coming of Christ. Jesus will return "with the angels of his power in flaming fire" to execute vengeance on those who do not know God and that do not obey the gospel. These shall suffer eternal destruction "from the presence of the Lord and the glory of his might" (2 Thess 1:7-10).

VISION SEVEN
THE WOMAN IN A BASKET
Zechariah 5:5-11

Vision six depicted the removal of transgressors from the land. Vision seven sets forth symbolically the removal of the principle of sin.

As in the fifth vision, the interpreting angel stepped forth from the background to arouse the prophet's attention. "Lift up now your eyes and see what this is that is going forth." The Hebrew participle indicates that the action was taking place before the prophet's eyes. Zechariah at first did not recognize the object which appeared to him, or at least he did not perceive the significance of that object (5:5-6a).

A. The Symbolism of the Vision (5:6b-7).

The symbolism of the seventh vision involves (1) an ephah, (2) a talent of lead, and (3) a woman.

1. The ephah (5:6b). In response to Zechariah's question the interpreting angel gave two responses. First, he identified the object that was going forth before the prophet as "the ephah." The ephah was the largest of the dry measures used in commerce by the Israelites (cf. Amos 8:5). It was about the size of a bushel.

Second, the angel said "this is their eye in all the land," i.e., their appearance.[2] The ephah points to godless commercialism as the besetting sin in the postexilic community (5:6b).

2. The talent of lead (5:7a). The second object was of unusual interest to Zechariah as is indicated by the interjection "behold!" He observed a talent being lifted up. Like the ephah, the talent is a symbol of commerce. It was the largest weight used by the Hebrews[3] to weigh out commodities (e.g., grain) and precious metals as a medium of exchange.

Two other details are noted about the talent. First, the talent was of lead. Lead was the most common heavy metal used to weigh out silver and gold. Second, the lead talent was "lifted up." It must have served as a lid to the ephah. That the lid of the ephah was made of heavy lead suggests that the effort was being made to hold secure the contents of that vessel.

3. *The woman (5:7b-8)*. The lid of the ephah was lifted so that the prophet could see what was within. In the ephah Zechariah saw a (lit., one) woman. An ephah of regular size could not have contained a woman, even a very small one! Therefore, like the oversized scroll

in the previous vision, this visionary ephah must have been of exaggerated dimensions. The woman was sitting in the ephah. The participle in this context suggests contentment. She was at home "in the midst of the ephah." She was accustomed to and nurtured by the godless commercialism symbolized by the ephah (5:7b).

The interpreting angel explained that the woman symbolized "wickedness." In Hebrew the noun "wickedness" is feminine, so it is appropriate that the woman should be given this significance.[4]

At this point the woman apparently attempted to climb out of the ephah. The verbs indicate a struggle took place. Apparently the woman sensed that her doom was at hand. The interpreting angel cast the woman back down into the midst of the ephah. That is where she belonged. That is where she must stay. To keep her there he cast the weight of lead upon the mouth of the ephah (5:8).

B. The Significance of the Vision (5:9-11).

Subsequent to the securing of the woman in the ephah, Zechariah lifted up his eyes a second time. Again he saw something of arresting significance ("behold"!). Zechariah observed two other women going forth. The women had wings. The prophet saw that "the wind was in their wings," i.e. they were moving swiftly (5:9a).

The wings of the women were large and broad such as those possessed by a stork. The Hebrew word "stork" literally means "faithful one." A play on words may be intended. Wickedness is to be removed by those who were faithful to the Lord. In any case those wings were adequate to support the weight of these two women and the heavy burden which they were assigned to bear. The ephah became airborne. The two women "lifted up the ephah between heaven and earth" (5:9b).

The symbolic import of the two women, if any, is not explained in the text. Some commentators think these two women had no symbolic significance. They were simply part of the visionary background. Others think that the women represent angelic agents of God. Still others see them as agents of evil who are trying to rescue the first woman from divine judgment. The main point seems to be the removal of evil from the land. God's people have always looked forward to a new heavens and new earth wherein dwells righteousness (cf. 2 Pet 3:13).

The prophet inquired as to the destination of the two women. The interpreting angel explained that the two women were en route to the land of Shinar. Since the days of the anti-God tyrant Nimrod, Shinar had been the archetypical land of evil. There they would build for the first woman "a house," perhaps a temple. When the house was established, the ephah would be set there "upon its base." In the land of evil, godless commercialism and wickedness personified become the focus of Satanic worship (5:10-11).

The basic point here is that all evil is removed from Zion to a land which is under the curse of God. Here is symbolically depicted that final discrimination between good and evil to which Jesus referred in his parables (Matt 13:36-43).

VISION EIGHT
THE CHARIOTS OF WRATH
Zechariah 6:1-8

The cycle of visions comes to a close with a symbolic portrayal of worldwide judgment. In the first vision the angelic reconnaissance force found the world to be at ease and the people of God humiliated. Now divine wrath is unleashed against these oppressors. The security of Zion, the people of God, is thus achieved.

A. The Vision Presented (6:1-3).

One last time Zechariah registered his shock at what he saw when he lifted up his eyes. The prophet observed some ominous chariots attached to multicolored horses.

1. The chariots (6:1). He observed four war chariots, the vehicles of judgment against the nations. Four is the number of universality in Biblical prophecy. Here the four chariots represent Yahweh's intervention on the world scene (6:1a).

The chariots came forth from between "the two mountains." The article may point to two well known mountains, perhaps Mt. Zion and the Mount of Olives. The valley between these two mountains is elsewhere in Old Testament prophecy associated with judgment upon the nations (cf. Joel 3:2). Thus the judgment against the oppressors of God's people emanates from Jerusalem and the temple.

The mountains are said to be "mountains of bronze." This signals that the mountains are not to be interpreted geographically. The two mountains seem to point to Jerusalem. The fact that those mountains were bronze suggests that the reference is celestial, not terrestrial. The heavenly Jerusalem, the throne room of the Most High, is the point from which the chariots of wrath are dispatched on their mission of judgment. These mountains guarded the approaches to God's heavenly throne. Thus the point is that no hostile power would be able to overwhelm the throne room of heaven (6:1b).

2. *The horses (6:2-3).* The horses are said to be "in" the chariots. The idea is that the horses were in position, hitched up to the draft pole or tongue of the chariot. This signals that the chariots were ready to proceed without delay on their mission.

Fastened to the first chariot were red horses. Red points to bloodshed and war (cf. Rev 6:4). The black horses of the second chariot symbolize famine and death (cf. Rev 6:5-6). The white horses of the third chariot probably point to victory and triumph (cf. Rev 6:2). Fastened to the fourth chariot were "spotted-strong horses" perhaps symbolizing plagues (cf. Rev 6:8). The various color horses, then, represent the various types of disasters with which God will destroy the nations which have opposed his people and his program in this world (6:2-3).

B. The Vision Explained (6:4-5).

Zechariah again asked the interpreting angel for an explanation of what he had seen. He was told that the four chariots were "the four winds" or "spirits" (*ruchot*). The latter interpretation is probably correct. These angelic spirits were commissioned to execute the judgment (6:4-5a).[5]

The spirits had been "standing before the Lord of all the earth." This confirms the interpretation that the four *ruchot* are in fact angels. It also confirms the interpretation that the chariots issued forth from the heavenly throne room. No mediation of the judgment through human agency is indicated. This final world judgment is ordered by God and executed by those spirit beings who do his holy bidding (6:5b).

C. The Vision Amplified (6:6-8).

Zechariah now learned that the chariot to which the black horses were attached was going out to the land of the north. This was the region where Israel's most terrifying enemies dwelled. The white horses "went forth after them."[6] Perhaps two judgment chariots were dispatched to the north to symbolize the crushing of the two ancient enemies of Israel, viz., Assyria and Babylon. The spotted horses moved southward toward Egypt, Israel's traditional enemy (6:6).

The text declares that "the strong horses went out." Some think that the strong horses are another designation for the red horses mentioned earlier. If this is the case, then two categories went to the south even as two went to the north. Others think that "strong" is epexegetical of the spotted horses of the previous verse. If this is true, then only one category of horses went south. The latter view is probably correct (6:7a).

Why then are the red horses omitted in this amplification of the vision? Perhaps they were being held in reserve until the judgment in the north and south was complete. Why is there no mention of the east and west in this vision? In the west Palestine bordered on the sea and in the east on the desert. From the viewpoint of people living in Palestine, a worldwide judgment would of necessity have to depart north and south.

Zechariah observed that the horses "sought to go," i.e., they pawed the ground awaiting the command to carry out their mission. They were anxious "to walk to and fro through the earth." Then Zechariah heard Yahweh give the fateful order: "Go! Go to and fro in the earth." The judgment of the world was underway. The affairs of the world are under the scrutiny the Sovereign Lord. He who is Lord of all the earth will one day send forth his vengeance against all evil doers (6:7a).

The interpreting angel speaking directly for the Lord of all the earth cried out to Zechariah. He had good news to share with the prophet. He pointed to the black and white horse chariots and said: "Those have quieted my spirit in the land of the north." To quiet the spirit means to cause anger or wrath to assuage. In vision one God's anger was aroused by the unjudged atrocities committed by the nations of the world against Israel. Here God proclaims victory over the powerful enemies of the north. If those enemies have fallen, by implication every foe has been vanquished (6:8).

A SYMBOLIC CORONATION
Zechariah 6:9-15

The crowning of Joshua is closely connected with the revelations of the eight night visions. The visions set forth the glorious destiny of Zion, the people of God, and the final doom of the Zion's enemies. Here the glorious reign of the King-Priest Messiah is set forth symbolically by the coronation of Joshua the high priest. This ceremony is not part of a vision. It is an actual historical event which appears to have taken place on the day following the night visions.

A. The Actions of Zechariah (6:9-11).

A delegation of Jews arrived from Babylon bringing with them gifts for the temple. Apparently those who remained in the lands of captivity sent offerings regularly to Jerusalem for use in the temple. Normally those temple gifts would be given to the temple personnel. On this occasion, however, Zechariah was told to take these offerings for another purpose (6:9-10a).

The names of the leaders of the Babylonian delegation were Heldai Tobijah and Jedaiah. These names all have meanings which express a relationship to Yahweh. Thus one would assume these Jews were men of faith on a pilgrimage of love. Zechariah was to meet the delegation at the home of Josiah the son of Zephaniah. In verse 14 Josiah is called Hen ("gracious") because of his hospitality (6:10b).

From the gold and silver which he took from the visitors Zechariah was to fashion crowns.[7] The plural indicates a composite crown made of entertwined circlets.[8] The mention of two kinds of metal suggests that the crown consisted of at least two circlets woven together (6:11a).

Zechariah was to place the interwoven circlets on the head of Joshua the high priest. The word "crowns" (*'atarot*) is always used of royal crowns and never for the headdress of the high priest, for which the word *gezer* is used. Under the Old Testament law, however, the high priest could not wear a royal crown. Thus this act of crowning Joshua must have prophetic or typical significance (6:11b).

No crown was placed on the head of governor Zerubbabel by the prophet. To have done so would have been misleading, pointing to the reestablishment of the Davidic kingdom. Liberal interpreters insist that Zerubbabel was crowned. In their view Zechariah anticipated the restoration of the Davidic monarchy. When that failed to materialize, some scribe changed the text of the prophetic book to make Joshua the recipient of the crown. Nothing could be further from the truth.

In the Mosaic system a rigid distinction existed between the royal and priestly offices. The former was confined to the descendants of David, the latter to the descendants of Aaron. King Uzziah attempted to usurp the office of priest and paid for it by losing his health and his throne (2 Chr 26:16-21). The prophet David, however, foresaw the coming of a mighty priest-king after the order of Melchizedek (Ps 110:4). Here at the close of Old Testament prophecy that hope is reaffirmed through this symbolic crowning.

B. Explanation of the Actions (6:12-13).

At the coronation of Joshua, Zechariah was to say to the high priest: "Behold! A man! Shoot is his name, and from his place he will shoot up." Joshua symbolized a man to be known as Shoot. As in 3:8 Shoot is a name for Messiah. The play on words is obvious: Shoot will shoot up. The language indicates the obscurity of his origin. He would come where and when there was little prospect of new life, like a root out of dry ground (cf. Isa 53:2).

The messianic Shoot would "build the temple of Yahweh." The reference is not to the temple then under construction, for that would be completed by Zerubbabel (cf. 4:9). The Shoot would build a future temple (6:12).

Zechariah was to use repetition to underscore the certainty of the future work of Messiah. "Yes, he shall build the temple of Yahweh." The priest-king symbolized by Joshua would be a temple builder (6:13a). What temple? Not "the third temple" which some students of prohecy believe will herald the second coming, for this temple is built *by* Messiah, not *for* him. Not some millennial temple built by Christ after his return, for his presence will render temples obsolete (cf. Rev 21:22). The priest-king Jesus is currently building his temple, the church of Christ (cf. 2 Cor 6:16; Eph 2:21; 1 Pet 2:5).

The priest-king of the future would "bear the glory." The word is used of majesty, honor, beauty. It is used almost exclusively of the divine splendor. The hint here is that the messianic priest-king would be divine.

Zechariah now makes explicit what was set forth symbolically in the coronation ritual. Shoot would "sit upon his throne." He would be king. Thus the royal crown in the symbolic ritual was very appropriate. At the same time, he would be "priest upon his throne." That a priest would sit on the throne of Israel is tantamount to an announcement that the Old Testament system would come to an end.

The declaration that "peaceful counsel shall be between the two of them" is difficult to interpret. Neither the numeral itself nor its masculine plural suffix is connected grammatically with a definite antecedent. The meaning here must be determined by implication and context. The reference must be to the concord existing bertween the offices of priest and king. Only when these two offices were combined in one person could such concord exist (6:13b).

Shoot would be a royal priest, like Melchizedek in the Patriarchal era (cf. Gen 14:17-20). As early as the days of David Yahweh revealed that a glorious priest-king would arise in the future. Already the prophet Jeremiah had used the term Shoot in a context where both kingly and priestly functions are mentioned (cf. Jer 33:15).

C. The Memorial to the Event (6:14).

The gold and silver brought from Babylon were designated for the temple. There in the temple the royal crowns—interwoven circlets of gold and silver—would serve as a memorial to the generosity of the guests from Babylon. Four individuals were thus honored. The names Tobijah and Jedaiah are repeated from verse 10. Helem ("strength") is substituted for Heldai ("mole") either because (1) the more dignified name was preferred for official purposes; or (2) because as a result of this incident, this man was given a more honorable name. Hen ("grace") is substituted for Josiah, the man who entertained the guests from Babylon because of his hospitality.

According to Jewish tradition the crowns were hung in the windows in the height of the temple. Placing them there not only honored the donors, but pledged the coming of the glorious priest-king.

D. A Final Messianic Note (6:15).

Zechariah saw in the generosity of the guests from Babylon another messianic pointer. People from distant lands—Gentiles—would bring their gifts to the future temple. They would come and "build in the house of Yahweh." While the messianic priest-king would be the ultimate builder or designer or that temple, he would accomplish his work through the agency of Gentiles. The priest-king builds the temple; the Gentiles build *in* the temple. The building of Zerubbabel's temple can hardly be intended because it was already well on the way to completion by this time.

The recognition formula is appended to this promise of Gentile assistance in temple building. "You shall know that Yahweh has sent me unto you." The fulfillment of the messianic predictions would corroborate the truth of Zechariah's word.

This messianic passage concludes with these words: "It shall come to pass if you surely hearken to the voice of Yahweh your God." Zechariah is not saying that fulfillment of the messianic prophecy was contingent upon the obedience of the Jews. Rather the idea is that in order to participate in the blessings of those distant days the community must continue to be obedient.

ENDNOTES

1. The largest papyrus scroll attested in the ancient world is the Harris Papyrus found in Egypt. It is 133 feet long and seventeen inches wide.

2. Joyce G. Baldwin argues for the rendering "their iniquity" which necessitates a slight emendation of the Hebrew text, but is supported by the Greek and Syriac versions. *Haggai, Zechariah, Malachi* in "The Tyndale Old Testament Commentaries" (InterVarsity, 1975), p. 128.

3. Estimates on the weight of the talent range from 75 to 108 pounds.

4. Some commentators go beyond the text in suggesting that the woman symbolizes all sinners collectively massed together as grain within an ephah for judgment (Keil); apostate religion, the ecclesiastical Babylon of Rev 17 (Unger).

5. In Revelation 7:1 four angels and four winds are associated with God's judgment. The angels are depicted restraining the winds of world judgment.

6. On the basis of a slight emendation of the text, Baldwin (*op. cit.*, pp. 131f.) renders "the white ones go toward the west country."

7. The Greek and Latin versions support the plural Hebrew reading. The Syriac version, however, has a singular here and the Greek has the singular in v. 14. Unger (*op. cit.*, p. 112) insists on emending the Hebrew plural to the singular.

8. Baldwin (*op. cit.*, 133) points out that eastern crowns were circlets which could be worn singly or fitted together to make a composite crown. The expression "many crowns" in Rev 19:12 probably refers to one of these composite crowns.

CHAPTER FORTY-THREE

Fasting or Feasting?
Zechariah 7-8

In the fourth year of King Darius, on the ninth day of the fourth month (Dec 7, 518 BC), a delegation arrived from Bethel, twelve miles north of Jerusalem, to pose a question about religious ritual. This provided the background for the next oracle of Zechariah. Again "the word of Yahweh" came unto the prophet (7:1).

The Bethel delegation was headed by Sharezer and Regemmelech. The first name is Babylonian and means "protect the king." The second name means "friend of the king."[1]

The purpose of the delegation was "to entreat Yahweh," i.e., to mollify, appease, or entreat the favor of Yahweh. In the postexilic community this expression meant to offer worship in the temple (cf. Mal 1:9). Before asking the question which was troubling them, the delegation engaged in temple worship. Perplexity in theological matters is best packaged in awe, surrender and praise to the Almighty (7:2).

The question was addressed to the priests and prophets at the temple. In the postexilic community the hostility which often characterized the relationship between priests and prophets before the exile seems to have disappeared. The priests were those who were experts in the law and religious ritual. The prophets from time to time received direct revelation from God to guide the community in areas where the law did not speak (7:3a).

The question posed to the religious leaders was framed in the first person singular: "Shall I weep in the fifth month being separated as I have done these many years?" Bethel here is personified and speaks as one person. The language suggests that the citizens of Bethel were weary with fasting and wished to be rid of it (7:3b).

Only one mandatory fast day was part of the religious ritual ordained in the law of Moses. On the annual Day of Atonement in the fall the people were told to "afflict" their souls (Lev 16:29,31). From time to time leaders called for national fasting, but these were not thereafter set. The question posed by the Bethelites pointed to a fast which had been observed annually through the years of the exile.

Zechariah's response to the question about fasting came in four oracles.

THE FIRST ORACLE
A More Basic Issue
Zechariah 7:4-7

The first oracle of Zechariah in response to the question regarding fasting is addressed to "all the people of the land, and to the priests." The revelation here related had implications for the entire population. On the basis of the written law the priests could not answer the inquiry of the Bethelites. They must yield to the inspired revelation of the prophet. The first oracle consists of three rhetorical questions.

First, Yahweh asked through the prophet: "Did you fast unto me, even me?" The fast of the fifth month commemorated the destruction of Jerusalem by the Babylonians. A similar fast in the seventh month memorialized the assassination of Gedaliah, the last governor of Judah. For seventy years these fasts had been observed. Now that the temple was nearing completion, the seventy years of temple desolation were coming to an end. A new era was about to dawn. In view of this fact the Bethelites wondered if they had to continue the ritual fasts (7:5).

The point of the first rhetorical question is that the fasts commemorating events associated with the fall of Jerusalem were man-made, not God-ordained. They were not being observed to please the Lord. Therefore, as far as the Lord was concern it was a matter of indifference whether these fasts were observed or not.

The second rhetorical question was this: "And when you eat, and when you drink, do you not eat for yourselves, and drink for yourselves?" The feasts of the people, as well as their fasts, were man-centered. The people of the postexilic community were indifferent to God in all aspects of their lives (7:6).

The third rhetorical question was this: "Should you not hear the words which Yahweh cried by the former prophets?" The real issue was whether or not the people would listen to the word of God. The "former prophets" were those who preached prior to the destruction of Jerusalem when all of Judah flourished. The Jews had lost their prosperity and land by failing to listen to those prophets. What God had said to the pre-exilic generation still was applicable. The implied warning here is that failure to listen to the current prophets would likewise lead to disaster (7:7).

SECOND ORACLE
Focus on the Word
Zechariah 7:8-14

In the second message Yahweh summarizes the message of the former prophets to which the postexilic community should listen. He then describes the attitude of the previous generation to that word.

A. Summary of the Divine Word (7:8-10).

In summarizing the message of the former prophets two positive and two negative commands are given. First, "with true judgment judge," i.e., make judgments, especially in courts of law, without partiality or bias. Second, "with covenant faithfulness and mercies deal each man with his brother." The form "mercies" is an intensive plural with a singular meaning, i.e., abundant mercy (7:8-9).

On the negative side God required that his people "do not oppress the widow, nor the fatherless, the sojourner nor the poor."

No one should take advantage of society's most helpless ones. The four categories are frequently grouped in the law as needing special consideration. Finally, God required even the thoughts of his people to be pure: "and evil of a man his brother do not think in your heart." The reference is to plotting or devising evil. Thoughts of revenge against a brother were forbidden (7:10).

B. Rejection of the Divine Word (7:11-12).

The pre-exilic people had "refused to hearken" to the divine word. They had "pulled away the shoulder" like an ox which refuses to have the yoke put on its neck (cf. Neh 9:29; Hos 4:16). The last thing these people wanted to hear was God's word. "They stopped their ears (lit., made their ears heavy) that they might not hear" (7:11).

The pre-exilic people were not open to the word of God because they had "made their hearts as an adamant stone, lest they should hear the law." An adamant stone was one which could receive no cutting or engraving. The diamond may be in view here. Yet the words which the former prophets had spoken were in fact "the words which Yahweh of hosts had sent by his Spirit." Here is a clear claim of inspiration (cf. Mic 3:8). Therefore, because they had snubbed God by ignoring his word, "there came great wrath from Yahweh of hosts." Disobedience always stirs God's wrath (7:12).

C. Results of Rejecting the Divine Word (7:13-14).

Through the former prophets Yahweh cried again and again to his people, urging them to repent. Israel, however, would not listen. So as a result, these people cried out to God again and again during the period of the great wrath, but Yahweh would not listen to them. Their prayers went unanswered. "And I scattered them among all the nations." The word "scattered" is a violent word associated with whirlwinds. The places to which God scattered them were "nations they did not know," i.e., people of a strange tongue (cf. Deut 28:33; Jer 16:13). Thus the exile was the punishment for not listening to the word of God. The passage hints that a similar fate will befall the post-exilic community if they refuse to listen to the new generation of God's spokesmen (7:14a).[2]

When Israel was taken captive to Babylon, the homeland "was

made desolate after them." Travelers no longer passed through that region. The responsibility for what happened to the land lay squarely on the shoulders of the previous generation. They were responsible for making the land of Canaan a desolation (7:14b).

THIRD ORACLE
The Potential for Blessing
Zechariah 8:1-17

The third response to the question of fasting contains a decalogue of promises each of which begins with the words "thus says Yahweh of hosts."

A. Yahweh's Zeal for Jerusalem (8:1-2).

Zechariah uses several syntactical devices to underscore how Yahweh's attitude toward his people had changed since the destruction of Jerusalem. "I am zealous for Zion with great zealousness." If because of the prior disobedience Yahweh had engineered the destruction of Judah and the deportation of her citizens, so now he was determined to do whatever was necessary to build up his people. In fact Yahweh declared that "with great fury I am zealous for her," i.e., Zion. One side of God's love for Zion is shown in the punishment of Zion's enemies (cf. 1:14-15).

B. Yahweh's Return to Zion (8:3).

Yahweh had deserted the city prior to the Babylonian conquest (cf. Ezek 10:18; 11:23). The restoration of the exiles, the rebuilding of the temple, and the voice of prophecy showed that God had returned to Jerusalem. Now Yahweh promises to settle down, abide and remain in Jerusalem (8:3a).

The coming of Yahweh to dwell in Jerusalem would inaugurate a new era. As a result of Yahweh's habitation Jerusalem henceforth would be called by three names. First, since Yahweh is the God who cannot lie (Titus 1:2), Jerusalem would be known as "the city of truth" (cf. Zeph 3:14) or "faithful city" (RSV; cf. Isa 1:26). Those who dwell in that messianic Jerusalem would be especially devoted to truth.

Second, Jerusalem would be called "the mountain of Yahweh of hosts." The Canaanite pantheon was reputed to assemble on Mt. Zaphon or Mt. Cassius in north Syria (cf. Isa 14:13). The Greek gods assembled on Mt. Olympus. Yahweh, however, would occupy messianic Zion as his mountain. That spiritual mountain would be exalted above the earth's mountains—governments, nations, religions—in the age of Messiah (cf. Isa 2:2).

Third, as the habitation of the Holy One of Israel, Jerusalem would be called "the holy mountain." The citizens of that spiritual city would be those who had been saved and sanctified, redeemed and cleansed. All within that city, even the most common objects, would be holy to the Lord (cf. Zech 14:20,21).

C. Jerusalem Peaceful and Secure (8:4-5).

To stress the peace and security of that future (spiritual) Jerusalem—the church of Christ—Zechariah paints two word pictures. First, elderly men and women, each with a staff in his hand by reason of years, would sit in the streets of Jerusalem. They would have no fear of thunderous chariots racing in those streets, throngs of invading armies, or any other danger. Second, the prophet portrays those at the opposite end of the age spectrum playing (lit., laughing) in the streets. That holy city would be a happy city, even for the little ones. Where there is peace and security children can truly enjoy their childhood.

D. Marvelous Promises (8:6).

The promises made to and about Jerusalem in the previous verses were truly marvelous in the eyes of those who dwelled in postexilic Jerusalem. Man's extremity is God's opportunity. Yahweh specializes in the impossible. After all, he is Yahweh of hosts! All power in heaven and earth belongs to him. What men regard as marvelous is routine in the workings of God.[3]

E. Gathering the Dispersed (8:7-8).

The fifth promise in the decalogue of blessings is introduced with "Behold!" which points to something unexpected. Yahweh promises: "I am about to deliver my people from the land of the east and from the land of the west." These two directions are symbols of the entire world. The participle denotes continuous actions (8:7).

Those who are gathered are brought to dwell in the midst of Jerusalem. As long as the Old Testament was in effect the passage referred to physical Jerusalem. In the New Testament era Yahweh continues to gather his people into Jerusalem—spiritual Jerusalem, the church of Christ (Gal 4:26; Heb 12:22; Matt 8:11). That the passage does not refer to the return from Babylon entirely is indicated by two facts. First, that return came from only one direction, usually designated north. Second, the bulk of the return from Babylon was already past at the time these words were written (8:8a).

Those who respond to the call of God to leave the world and set their course for spiritual Jerusalem enter into a new covenant relationship with the Lord. "They shall be my people and I shall be their God" (cf. Jer 31:31). This new relationship would be based "in truth and in righteousness." On the one hand, God would faithfully keep his promises. At the same time those who were rescued out of the world would cling to the Lord in faithful trust and obedience. Such is the status of those who have been translated out of the darkness of this world into the kingdom of his dear Son (8:8b).

F. Conditions Reversed (8:9-13).

The sixth promise in the decalogue of promises begins with an exhortation and a reminder. Those being addressed are described as "those who are hearing in these days these words from the mouth of the prophets who were in the day when the foundation of the house of Yahweh of hosts was laid." The reference is to the ministries of Haggai and Zechariah and perhaps others of kindred spirit. These are exhorted to 'Let your hands be strong," i.e., be of good courage. The point is that the same prophets who urged the commencement of the temple project are still present to offer encouragement to the builders (8:9).

1. Prior conditions (8:10). Zechariah next reminded his audience of the conditions which existed prior to the rebuilding of the temple. Those days were marked by three terrible conditions. First, there was economic depression. The crop yield was so small that laboring men or beasts were not needed to gather it in.[4] Second, the land was insecure. They could not go about their usual occupations or move from place to place with safety on account of the enemies that compassed them about (cf. Ezra 4:4). Third, the population was torn asunder by internal dissension. "And I set every man against his neighbor."

2. *Promises (8:11-12).* Things were about to change in Judea. Five promises are extended to the community. First, Yahweh would not deal with his people as in former days. Second, "the seed of peace, the vine, shall give its fruit." The basic idea here is that the crops would be safe and secure.[5] Third, "the land shall give its increase," i.e., they would have abundant harvests. Fourth, "the heavens shall give their dew," i.e., they would have the moisture essential in summer to produce crops. Fifth, Yahweh promises that he will cause "the remnant of this people to inherit all these things," i.e., the land, abundant harvest, and security.

3. *Vindication (8:13).* Attitudes toward Judea would change when God changed the circumstances of his people. The deplorable conditions of the postexilic community made the land "a curse among the nations." The fate of the Jews was used as a formula of imprecation among the heathen. When they expressed imprecation upon other peoples they would say something like, "May your fate be that of the Jews" (8:13a).

Yahweh, however, would deliver these people from those deplorable conditions. Yahweh declares: "I will deliver you!" The result would be that Judea would become a blessing. They would be used as a formula of blessing from henceforth. Thus God reverses the fortunes of his people (8:13b).

G. Promise of Good (8:14-17).

The recent captivity was no accident. This "evil" or disaster was a result of the deliberate, purposive divine planning. The previous generation had "provoked" Yahweh to anger. God did not "relent" concerning the threatened judgment. He carried out the dreaded decrees which the prophets had announced in his name to the apostate nation (8:14).

God had purposed evil for this people in this past. Now he purposed good for them. The past chastisement which happened as threatened was a guarantee of the fulfillment of the promised blessings. Yahweh's purpose now was "to do good to Jerusalem and to the house of Judah in these days." The change of divine attitude was due to the fact that the people had turned to the Lord (8:15).

The promises articulated in the previous verses of this chapter were conditional. God sets forth five expectations for his people. First, they must speak truth every man with his neighbor. All conversations and transactions with their fellow citizens must be governed by integrity. Second, they must judge with truth and the judgment of peace in their gates. There must be perfect equity in judgments. Such decisions would secure peace and concord between the parties concerned. In the ancient world the "gate" of the city is where the judges sat (8:16).

Third, no one was to devise evil in his heart against his neighbor (cf. 7:10). Fourth, they must love no false oath. The prevalent sin of the postexilic period was not idolatry, but lack of integrity. In the land of Babylon, the land of commerce, these people had sharpened their skills of cheating, lying, and injustice. Finally, they must hate all things which are hated by God. Sin is that which is absolutely repulsive to God (8:17).

H. Fasts to Become Feasts (8:18-19).

The original question of continuing the fasts which had been observed for almost seventy years is now addressed directly. Four fasts are named. The fast of the fourth month (cf. 7:5) commemorated the day when a breach was made in the walls of Jerusalem by the Chaldeans on the seventeenth day of Tammuz.[6] The fast of the fifth month (cf. 7:3) commemorated the day the Jerusalem temple burned in 536 BC on the ninth day of Av (8:18-19a).[7]

The fast of the seventh month commemorated the death of Gedaliah.[8] The fast of the tenth month—the tenth day of Tebeth—commemorated the beginning of the siege of Jerusalem.[9] In the future God would shower such blessings upon his people that they would forget past miseries. Those fasts would become "joy, gladness, and cheerful feasts." In the light of this glorious future, God's people should "love the truth and peace" (8:19b)

I. The Conversion of Gentiles (8:20-22).

The ninth promise in the decalogue of blessings would surely have lifted the spirits of the discouraged remnant. Instead of being despised and ridiculed by neighboring nations, the people of God would find themselves the envy of the world.

1. *Gentiles would seek Yahweh increasingly (8:20).* In the future Gentiles in large numbers—"the inhabitants of many cities"—would seek Yahweh. Why? Probably because they observed the wonderful blessing with which God would shower his people (8:20).

2. *Gentiles would seek Yahweh earnestly (8:21a).* "The inhabitants of one city shall go to another saying, Let us go speedily." Those who were saved would not be content to enjoy their salvation in solitude. Hebrew has a construction (an imperfect followed by an infinitive absolute) which implies "Let us go on and on continually."[10] This is the Old Testament way of describing the missionary compulsion of those who have embraced the Lord Jesus.

3. *Gentiles would seek Yahweh reverently (8:21b).* They would come "to pray before Yahweh and to seek Yahweh of hosts." Zechariah is not merely describing how Gentiles would attend the great pilgrim festivals in Jerusalem. Rather he indicates that they would desire to seek to know the Lord and worship him in an acceptable manner.

The expression "I will go also" is difficult. These words may be taken to be (1) the words of some straggler or doubter; (2) the city which is being exhorted in the first half of the verse; (3) Zechariah himself; or (4) those who give the exhortation. The last view is probably correct. Those who exhort others to turn to Yahweh in prayer and worship will set the example. Thus it is not "Do as I say" but "Do as I do!" (8:21b).

4. *Gentiles will seek Yahweh in Jerusalem (8:22).* For emphasis, several of the previous promises regarding the Gentiles are repeated. Not just "peoples" (cf. v. 20), but *many* peoples would come. Not just any nations, but *strong* nations would seek Yahweh. It is one thing when downtrodden people turn to the Lord as a last resort. It is quite another when nations in their strength humble themselves to acknowledge the God of a powerless nation to be supreme. Yet Zechariah foresees the day when earth's powerful peoples recognize the supreme power of "Yahweh of hosts," commander of all forces of heaven and earth.

In that day when Gentiles would turn to the Lord in great numbers, Jerusalem would be the center of the worship. The old geographical Jerusalem was but a type of the Jerusalem which is from above. During the intertestamental period some notable Gentiles did become Jewish proselytes. They would bring their sacrifices to the temple in Jerusalem. The reference here, however, is to the antitypical Jerusalem, the spiritual city in which all who embrace the gospel are citizens. Thus Zechariah is describing the present age in which Gentiles throughout the world by countless millions have turned to Yahweh of Hosts through his Son Jesus (8:22).

J. Prominence of the Jews (8:23).

"In those days" when the Gentiles in great numbers turn to Yahweh, Jews would occupy a prominent place in the divine scheme of things. "Ten men," i.e., a large number, from every language group would seek to come to Yahweh. "Ten" is symbolic of a large indefinite number (cf. Gen 31:7). Diversity of language would be no barrier to the unity of the faith (8:23a).

Those concerned Gentiles would "take hold" (lit., grasp, seize, grab) the robe of a Jew. The verb, which is repeated for emphasis, indicates the zeal of those Gentiles in their search for Yahweh. They would say to the Jew, "We will go with you." The picture is one of a Jew coming from some far country to celebrate the festivals in Jerusalem. That Jew would have a number of Gentiles clinging round him, asking permission to accompany him on his spiritual journey. Why? "Because we have heard God is with you!" The founder of the Christian faith was of the seed of Abraham. The twelve ambassadors sent forth to preach the gospel throughout the world were Jews by birth. All Christians, however, are true Israelites (Rom 4:11; Gal 3:7; 4:26). Through their evangelistic efforts and joyous lifestyle Gentiles find their way out of the kingdom of darkness and into the kingdom of Christ (8:23b).

ENDNOTES

1. The Hebrew word order allows for three interpretations of the verse: (1) Bethel sent . . (ASV; RSV; JB); (2) he, i.e., Darius sent . . . ; (3) Bethel-

Sharezer sent . . . (Baldwin). The Regem-melech who was sent to Zechariah is considered by Baldwin to have been a royal official on an official mission by Persian leaders who had become Jewish proselytes.

2. Some render the verbs in 7:13b-14a as futures: "so they shall cry, and I will not hear, said Jehovah of hosts; but I will scatter them with a whirlwind among all the nations..." (ASV). If this is future then what happened in the past is a sign of what shall befall them in the future in punishment of like obduracy (Deane).

3. The interrogative force of verse 6 is only indicated by the context. The unthinkable and theologically incompatable alternative is to regard God as expressing amazement regarding the promises which he has just made.

4. Another interpretation is that the poverty was so bad that the hired man could not be paid and the beast could not be given its share of the grain.

5. The "seed of peace" may be the vine (Wright; Keil; Leupold). Others think the reference is to seed time marked by absence of war (Unger, Perowne, Deane).

6. See 2 Kings 25:3; Jer 52:6,7; 39:2.

7. 2 Kings 25:8-9; Jer 52:12.

8. The third day of the seventh month was observed as a fast even though the Scriptures do not specify the day of the month when Gedaliah was slain. See 2 Kings 25:25; Jer 41:1,2,4,5. It is possible, but not likely, that the fast of the seventh month was the Day of Atonement.

9. See 2 Kings 25:1; Ezek 24:1-2.

10. C.H.H. Wright, *Zechariah and his Prophecies* (Minneapolis: Klock & Klock, 1980 reprint of 1879 ed), p. 192, n. 2; E.B. Pusey, *The Minor Prophets; a Commentary* (Grand Rapids: Baker, 1957 reprint of 1860 ed.), p. 392.

CHAPTER FORTY-FOUR

Yahweh's Triumphant Intervention
Zechariah 9:1-10:2

Zechariah 9-14 are some of the most difficult chapters in the Old Testament. The contrast with the first eight chapters is so sharp that critical scholars have alleged that chapters 9-14 were written by a different author. A strong case, however, can be made for the unity of the book. Similar expressions, some rather rare, are found in both sections. Similar concepts are also evident. In both halves of Zechariah there is a predilection for the number four. Earlier prophets are used in both units. There is no insurmountable obstacle to embracing the traditional view that the entire book was written by Zechariah the son of Berechiah.

Even though the last six chapters contain no dates, the conclusion that Zechariah 9-14 were written at a later time in the ministry of the prophet is probably correct. In the first eight chapters Zechariah addressed the problems of the Jews of the sixth century. The last six chapters take a wider range, focusing on the kingdom of Messiah. These chapters are intended for all people of all times.[1] They are the most quoted section of the prophets in the passion narratives of the

Gospels. Next to Ezekiel, Zechariah has influenced the author of Revelation more than any other Old Testament writer.²

Chapters 9-11 contain some of the grandest and most powerful passages in the book. These chapters are as fine as any in Hebrew poetry.³ The prophecies here seem to focus mainly on the period between the time of Zechariah and the revelation of the Messiah at his first coming.

THE COMING OF THE WORLD CONQUEROR
Zechariah 9:1-9

Yahweh would intervene in history by means of a mighty conqueror who would sweep down upon Palestine from the north.

A. Judgment on Syria (9:1-2a).

"The burden of the word of Yahweh," i.e., his weighty word of judgment, would first find its resting place in the "land of Hadrach and Damascus." Hadrach is not elsewhere mentioned in the Old Testament, but it is mentioned in Assyrian inscriptions. The place was situated between Hamath and Riblah. Damascus was one of the major cities of Syria throughout the history of that area. The point is that God's judgment would begin in Syria (9:1a).

The clause "for to Yahweh shall be the eye of mankind and all the tribes of Israel" has received various interpretations. Some see here an affirmation that God has seen all the evil that the nations have inflicted upon the tribes of Israel. Others think the text is here affirming that all people as well as the tribes of Israel would recognize God in the future (cf. 8:22). Probably the idea is that all peoples on earth would take note of the movements of the mighty conqueror who in fact is acting as the agent of Yahweh (9:1b).

The Syrian city of Hamath "also shall border on it," i.e., the city would share in the judgment of Hadrach and Damascus. The city of Hamath survives today under the name Hama with some 50,000 inhabitants (9:2a).

B. Judgment on Phoenicia (9:2b-4).

The mighty invader sweeps southward. Tyre was known in the

ancient world for its wisdom (cf. Ezek 28.3-4). The mention of Tyre's wisdom here is either sarcastic, or the wisdom is being condemned as worldly wisdom. Sidon is mentioned parenthetically. The focus is on the dramatic fall of Tyre (9:2b).

Tyre would not be able to resist the coming invader. Though they should build a stronghold[4] it would not save them (9:3a). The citizens of Tyre built a fortress on an island off shore which served them well in time of attack. Already the city had been besieged by the Assyrians for five years and by the Babylonians for thirteen years. Alexander the Great under great duress had his engineers construct a causeway to that fortress utilizing the debris from the mainland city which his army had leveled. The Macedonian was able to accomplish in a few weeks what the Assyrians and Babylonians had not been able to accomplish in several years (cf. Ezek 26:7-14).

Through her commercial enterprises Tyre had amassed great wealth. "Though she heap up silver like dust and fine gold like the mire of the streets" still she would not be able to escape destruction. Her enemies would not be deterred by bribery (9:3b).

The shocking truth ("Behold!") is that "Yahweh will dispossess her." The attack upon Tyre would be orchestrated by the Lord of hosts. The great commercial center would fall into the possession of the invaders. Yahweh would smite Tyre's wealth into the sea (cf. Ezek 26:4). Echoing the prophecy of Amos 1:10, Zechariah predicts that Tyre would be consumed with fire (9:4).

C. Judgment on Philistia (9:5-7).

The Philistine cities would be humbled by the coming invasion. Ashkelon would fear for her own safety when she saw what the invader did to Tyre. Eventually Ashkelon would not be inhabited, i.e., the city would fade from the scene. Gaza would be in anguish. Ekron also would be disturbed because "her trust," Tyre, had been put to shame. The king would perish from Gaza, i.e., Gaza would lose her independence (9:5).

In the once proud Philistine city of Ashdod "a bastard" would dwell. The term is often interpreted to mean one born of incest or adultery (cf. Deut 23:2). Here the term is probably being used in the broad sense of a stranger or foreigner (9:6a).

The four great cities named in this prophecy were the pride of the Philistines. When these cities capitulated to the enemy the "pride of the Philistines" could be said to be "cut off" (9:6b).[5]

At some time subsequent to the overthrow of Philistia by the coming invader, the Philistines would be converted to the Lord. Yahweh declares "I will remove his blood from his mouth." The reference probably is to the drinking of sacrificial blood as an act of worship or eating of victims used in sacrifice with the blood.[6] Yahweh would also remove "his abominations from between his teeth." These abominations could be animals forbidden by the Mosaic law (Deut 14:3ff.) or sacrifices offered to idols and then eaten (9:7a). During the intertestamental period the Maccabean rulers of Judea successfully annexed the Philistine territory.[7] Mosaic regulations were forced on those who lived in this area. The real fulfillment, however, is found in the conversion of Gentiles of that region to Christ (cf. Zeph 2:6-7).

Converted Philistines would be "a remnant to our God," i.e., they would no long be considered aliens, but members of the covenant community. "He (i.e., converted Philistines) would even become "as a chief in Judah," i.e., a leading citizen in the spiritual Israel. "And Ekron shall become like the Jebusite." The Jebusites were the ancient inhabitants of Jerusalem conquered by David and incorporated into Israel.[8] The basic idea which is being reinforced here is that Gentiles would in the future be incorporated into the people of God.

D. Protection for Jerusalem (9:8).

While the Syrians, Phoenicians, and Philistines would be overrun by the invader from the north (Alexander the Great), Yahweh promised to "encamp around my house," i.e., the temple, the family, the kingdom of Israel. This protection would be necessary "because of the one passing through and the one returning." Alexander bypassed Jerusalem on his way to Egypt in 332 BC. He later returned through Palestine without doing harm to the holy city.[9]

The clause "an oppressor shall not again cross over against them" is very difficult. Probably the best solution is to regard the reference to be to Alexander's invasion. The Macedonian would never again come into the land of Judah.[10] Why this promise? "For now I have seen with my eyes." During Israel's past calamities God had not looked upon them; but now he noticed their plight and intervened on their behalf.

The deliverance from their enemies without fighting in the times of Alexander was foretold as the pledge of Messiah's kingdom of peace. This is the subject which the prophet next takes up.

THE COMING PRINCE OF PEACE
Zechariah 9:9-11

The Messianic character of the following unit is established by the use of these verses in the New Testament. The gospel writers apply these words to Jesus (cf. Matt 21:5; John 12:15). Zechariah makes four points about the coming Prince.

A. The Promise of his Coming (9:9a).

Zechariah calls upon "the daughter of Zion" to "rejoice exceedingly." The daughter of a place is the population of that place personified as a female. Why this outburst of joy? The shocking announcement ("Behold!") is that "your king shall come to you." The coming Prince will be one of their own. While the oppressor of the preceding unit bypasses Jerusalem, the Prince of Peace comes to his people.

B. The Character of the Ruler (9:9b).

Zechariah describes the coming Prince in four ways. First, he is "righteous." He is just and impartial in judgment. In this context the term may mean "triumphant." Second, the Prince will be "showing himself a savior."[11] In his words and his actions he will demonstrate that he came to seek and save the lost. Third, the Prince is "lowly" (lit. afflicted).

Fourth, the Prince would come into Jerusalem "riding upon an ass." From the time of Solomon the ass was considered a lowly animal and a symbol of peace. The ass is further described as "a foal," i.e., a young animal, not yet ridden, but still running behind the she-asses. The youthfulness of the animal is again emphasized in the words "the son of she-asses." Jesus arranged for the precise fulfillment of this prophecy (Matt 21:1-7) because he wished to declare himself to be the Prince promised in this passage.

C. The Nature of the Kingdom (9:10).

The prophet sees three qualities of the kingdom of the coming Prince. His would be a peaceful, united, and universal kingdom.

1. A peaceful kingdom. In the day when Messiah enters Jerusalem Yahweh would "cut off the war chariot . . . the horse . . . the battle bow" from his people. All apparatus of war would disappear from the kingdom ruled by this Prince. Messiah's kingdom was to be established without physical force.[12]

2. A united kingdom. The people of God are designated as "Ephraim" and "Jerusalem." Thus the citizens of the former northern kingdom, cast off by God as "not my people," i.e., Gentiles (Hos 1:9), are joined with Jews in the messianic kingdom envisioned here. In the church of Christ the partition separating Jew and Gentile has been broken down (Eph 2:13f.).

3. A universal kingdom. Messiah will "speak peace to the nations." This statement makes clear what was implied in the combination of the terms "Ephraim" and "Jerusalem." Messiah's kingdom would not be limited to the Jews and to the Promised Land. It would extend to the nations as well. The advancement of this kingdom would be through the proclamation of peace by the ambassadors of the king—peace with God, peace within, peace with one's fellow man. The gospel of Jesus announces this peace and sets forth the terms upon which it may be obtained and enjoyed (9:10a).

The kingdom would be geographically as well as ethnically universal. "His dominion shall be from sea to sea and the River unto the ends of the earth." The "River" here is the Euphrates, the most remote eastern boundary of the Promised Land. The two seas may be the Dead Sea and the Mediterranean Sea. Thus Messiah's kingdom will incorporate all of the old territory of the Promised Land and more. It would extend to the ends of the earth. Such is the kingdom of Jesus Christ (9:10b).

D. The Redemption of the Coming Ruler (9:11).

In that glorious day when Messiah's kingdom would stretch to the ends of the earth, the Lord would redeem the daughter of Zion, i.e., the people of God. He would "send forth," i.e. free, her "prisoners." The figure of the "pit in which there is no water" reflects the desperate circumstances of Joseph (Gen 37:22) and Jeremiah (Jer 38:6). In such a pit a person would inevitably perish if he were not drawn out. Since the context here is messianic, the bondage here spoken of must be spiritual rather than physical. It is the bondage of sin and the snare of the Evil One which is being metaphorically described by Zechariah.

God would extricate the daughter of Zion from the pit of sin for the sake of "your covenant blood." The Sinai covenant was sealed with blood (Exod 24:5ff.); so also was the new covenant (Matt 26:28). The messianic context suggests that it is the latter which is in view. On the basis of the shed blood of Jesus, God would redeem his people from the bondage of sin.

THE COMING DIVINE WARRIOR
Zechariah 9:12-17

Great things would transpire prior to the coming of the messianic King. Zechariah describes for his people a glorious promise and a mighty intervention.

A. A Glorious Promise (9:12-13).

The unit begins with an exhortation addressed to the "prisoners of the hope." The hope of Israel is explained in the New Testament to be the gospel message, the spiritual kingdom of Christ (Acts 26:6-7; 28:20). Those who looked forward to the messianic kingdom are urged to "turn to the fortress." Some take the fortress to be Jerusalem, but that city was wall-less and essentially uninhabited in Zechariah's day. The "fortress" or "stronghold" (NASB) is God himself, or perhaps Messiah. During the difficult time of persecution which would be unleashed against the people of God during the intertestamental period they are urged to return in heart-felt commitment to their God. In times of intense suffering God alone can offer consolation and comfort (9:12a).

For those who turn to the Lord the promise is glorious. "Even today I declare, Double I will return to you." The Lord promises a double measure of blessing to compensate his people for past suffering (9:12b).

What exactly did Yahweh plan to do for those who put their trust in him during the persecutions of the intertestamental period? With his foot he would "tread Judah" as his bow, i.e., he would bend the bow. He would fill that bow with Ephraim. Zion (Judah + Ephraim) would be used as God's weapons in the battle against the invading armies of Greece. Yahweh would "stir up" the sons of Zion against the sons of Javan or Greece. In the second century before Christ the Seleucid kings sent huge armies again and again to put down the rebellions of the Jews in Palestine. The sons of Mattathias, known as the Maccabees, using guerrilla tactics inflicted enormous losses on these Greek armies (9:13).

B. A Mighty Intervention (9:14-15).

In the battles against the Greeks "Yahweh shall appear over them." He would fight for his people as he had down countless times in Old Testament history. The figure is of a storm cloud hovering over the battlefield. The lightning bolts going forth from the cloud are compared to the arrows of God's judgment. The accompanying thunder is compared to the blast of a trumpet. The storms of the south—the most violent kind—would serve as the chariots of God's wrath (9:14).

Yahweh of hosts would be a shield over his people in that day. The historical records are full of examples of God's special interposition on behalf of the Maccabees in their struggles against the Greeks.[13] Emboldened by the special help of Yahweh, the Jewish armies "would devour" their enemies. The figure here is of a devouring lion which consumes the prey (cf. Num 23:24). In holy boldness they would despise the missiles of their enemies. They would surge forward trampling under their feet the slingstones of their enemies. Like lions, the armies of God would drink the blood of the enemy, and the taste of that blood would spur them on to even greater efforts. Two figures underscore the amount of the blood which would be consumed by the lion of God's people. They would become sated on blood like the sacrificial bowls used at the altar and like the corners of the altar where the blood was smeared during the sacrificial rituals (9:15).

C. A Wonderful Relationship (9:16-10:2).

The mighty intervention narrated in the previous verses would be effected by "Yahweh their God." Whenever his people come under attack "he will deliver them in that day." Again the intertestamental wars with the Greeks are in view (9:16a).

Two figures underscore the new relationship which would exist between God and Israel. First, Israel is God's flock. He is the Good Shepherd who regards each sheep as exceedingly precious. Second, God's people are as precious to him as jewels in a crown. They are glittering upon his land. The idea is that the land is the crown in which the precious stones, the redeemed people, are placed (9:16b).[14]

Viewing the scene of the redeemed people in their own land, the prophet cries out in an exclamation of amazement: "How great is his goodness." The suffix "his" refers to Israel, rather than to Yahweh. The "goodness" is not moral goodness, but good appearance or prosperity. A second exclamation explains the first: "How great is his beauty." In that day God would bless the crops of Israel. "Grain shall make the young men flourish and new wine the virgins." The grain and wine are symbols of prosperity and great abundance (9:17).

The agricultural prosperity is attributed to a new relationship with Yahweh. In that day Yahweh would cheerfully respond to their prayer requests for rain "in the time of the latter rain," i.e., the spring rains which were essential to a successful harvest. Israel would realize that it was Yahweh, not Baal, "who makes the lightning and showers of rain." Their God would send the showers and the resulting vegetation for man and beast (10:1).

The prayers to Yahweh for rain come from a people who have repudiated idolatry. First, they have learned through bitter experience that "the teraphim have spoken vanity." The teraphim were images, sometimes in human form, and sometimes life size. They were kept at shrines, but were also found in private houses. Evidently they were among the instruments used by the pagan diviners.

Second, in their experience Israel had found that "the soothsayers have seen a lie." Divination employs external objects (e.g., crystal balls) in an attempt to predict the future. The optimistic forecasts of these charlatans were "dreams of deceit." They comforted their auditors in vain. Their promises of rain and prosperity, for example, were not fulfilled.

Third, involvement in soothsaying and idolatry had led to the straying of the sheep of God's flock. "Therefore they went their way like sheep." They wandered away from Yahweh, and as a result wandered into exile. They were continually oppressed by their enemies "because there was no shepherd." The reference may be to the heavenly King from whose love and protection they had wandered. On the other hand, the reference may be to the earthly king. The last king of Judah who lived up to the high standards of his theocratic office was Josiah. Those who occupied the throne of Judah after Josiah's death in 609 BC did not take seriously their responsibility as the shepherd of God's people (10:2).

ENDNOTES

1. Talbot W. Chambers, "The Book of Zechariah" in *Commentary on the Holy Scriptures* ed. John Peter Lange (Grand Rapids: Zondervan, 1960 reprint), p. 10.
2. Joyce Baldwin, *Haggai, Zechariah, Malachi* in "The Tyndale Old Testament Commentaries" (InterVarsity, 1972), p. 59.
3. W.J. Deane, "Zechariah" in *The Pulpit Commentary*, New Edition (New York: Funk & Wagnalls, 1909), p. xi.
4. In the Hebrew there is an obvious use of paronomasia which might be represented in English by this translation: "Though Tyre build a tower...."
5. The city of Gath—the fifth city of the Philistine Pentapolis—is not mentioned since it never fully recovered from the destruction in the days of Uzziah (cf. 2 Chr 26:6).
6. On the consumption of blood in pagan worship, see Ezek 33:25; Lev 3:17; 7:26; 17:10,12.
7. See 1 Macc 5:68; 10:84; 13:47f.
8. See 2 Sam 5:6; 24:22; 1 Chr 21:23.
9. On Alexander's campaign through Palestine, see Josephus, *Antiquities* 10:1:8. Others think the phrase "passing through and returning" merely indicates the overrunning of a land by an invading army (cf. Ezek 32:27; 35:7).
10. Others think that 9:8 is presently being fulfilled in the protection which God provides for his people whenever they come under attack. It will continue to be fulfilled until finally no more oppressors shall bother the people of God.
11. The Hebrew uses the Niphal stem in a reflexive sense. Others, however, think that here the Niphal has a passive sense. The Prince is "endowed with salvation" (Keil; Deane). Either sense would be appropriate in this context.

12. Other prophecies associating peace with the messianic era: Ps 72:7; Isa 2:4; 9:4-7; Mic 5:10-11.

13. On the divine interventions on behalf of the Maccabees, see 1 Macc 3:16-24; 4:6-16; 7:40-50; 2 Macc 2:21-22; 3:24; 5:2-4; 11:8; 12:11,15,22,28,37; etc.

14. Others think that the white sheep grazing under the brilliant oriental sun might be figuratively called jewels.

CHAPTER FORTY-FIVE

Messiah Is Coming!
Zechariah 10:3-11:17

The intertestamental victories over the Greeks and the reinstatement of the relationship between God and Israel would help prepare the way for messianic salvation. Zechariah now focuses on the coming triumphant savior and terrible consequences to physical Israel of the rejection of this savior.

PROVISIONS FOR MESSIANIC SALVATION
Zechariah 10:3-4

The coming of Messiah is a major theme of Scripture from Genesis 3:15 onward. In the present unit God makes provision for messianic salvation in three ways.

A. Old Leaders Removed (10:3).

Yahweh's wrath was kindled against "the shepherds." He would "visit" his wrath upon the "he-goats" (cf. Isa 14:9; Ezek 34:17). The reference is probably to the Greek rulers who dominated Israel during the intertestamental period. The defeat of the efforts of Antiochus Epiphanes to destroy the faith of the Jews is also a major theme in the Book of Daniel (cf. Dan 8:9-14, 22-26; 11:20-35).

Yahweh would defeat the ruthless shepherds and he-goats through his people. "For Yahweh of hosts shall visit his flock the house of Judah." He would visit the he-goats in wrath; he would visit his people in salvation. Yahweh would make his people "as a majestic horse in the battle." The shepherdless sheep would be transformed into a majestic war horse on which God would ride to battle against his foes. This brilliant figure accomplishes two things. First, it promises strength and courage to God's people. Second, it reminds them that the Lord can advance against the enemy only so far as they carry him in faith. God does not accomplish his work on earth without his people. The Maccabean victories over the Greek armies were a preparation for the coming of Messiah.

B. New Leaders Raised Up (10:4).

Once the victory over the Greek oppressors had been won, Yahweh would bring forth a prince from the tribe of Judah. Three titles are given to that prince here. First, he is the Corner (*pinnah*) or Cornerstone (cf. Isa 28:16). He would be the foundation for the entire edifice of God's house, i.e., his people, in this world (cf. Matt 21:42; Eph 2:20).

Second, that Prince is the Nail or Peg. The term *yated* is used of (1) the stake that fastens the cord of a tent; (2) a nail used in building with timber; (3) a peg used for hanging arms and utensils on a wall. Thus the Prince is one who holds or holds together the nation.

Third, the Prince is the Battle Bow. This King would be a warrior. Just as Yahweh led his people into battle against the Greek forces in the intertestamental period, so Messiah would do battle on behalf of his people against the forces of sin, Satan and death.

In addition to the Prince, Yahweh would bring forth from the tribe of Judah "every ruler." The term *noges* used here is elsewhere used in the Old Testament for a taskmaster or exactor. If the word has this meaning here it would indicate that the people of God shall subjugate their enemies, oppress them and exact tribute from them. But the term apparently is used here in a more general sense of a "ruler" (cf. Isa 3:12; 60:17). The reference would then be to the rulers who would assist Messiah in the administration of his kingdom. Each of the original Apostles came from the tribe of Judah. Paul came from the tribe of Benjamin, a tribe which often was subsumed under the larger tribal name of Judah in the Old Testament.[1]

MESSIANIC VICTORY
Zechariah 10:5-7

Zechariah portrays messianic salvation in terms of a military victory. He speaks first of the role of Judah, then of the role of Ephraim in achieving the great victory.

A. Role of Judah (10:5-6a).

The followers of Messiah would be "as mighty men treading down their enemies in the mire of the streets in the battle." Messiah himself declared that the gates of Hades itself would not prevail against his church (Matt 16:18). Even the cavalry of the enemy "shall be put to shame." Old Testament Israel's forces mainly consisted of infantry, while that of her enemies in the later period mainly consisted of cavalry. The point is that under Messiah God's people will prevail over those better armed (10:5).

As in the wars against the Greeks in the intertestamental period (cf. 9:13), Messiah would empower his people to gain the victory over their enemies. "And I will strengthen the house of Judah" (10:6a).

B. Role of Ephraim (10:6b-7).

The old northern kingdom—"the house of Joseph"—would join in the conflict and share in the victory. All of God's people north and south, Gentile and Jew, would be united in Messiah's kingdom. God would "save" them, not just from the onslaught of their enemies, but to a glorious land, i.e., heaven itself. "And I will cause them to dwell," i.e., in safety and comfort. This complete reinstatement of the citizens of the old northern kingdom would grow out of God's compassion for them. "And they shall be as though I had not cast them off." Ephraim would be fully restored. In the light of the teaching of Hosea, Ephraim was cast off to become "not my people," i.e., Gentile. Thus in the messianic context the restoration of Ephraim to covenant status is equivalent to the conversion of Gentiles (10:6b).

The men of Ephraim—former Gentiles—would prove themselves mighty heroes in the coming conflict. "And their heart shall rejoice as through wine." They would hasten to the battle like men refreshed and strengthened by wine. The children of these converted Ephraimites would be led to a joyful relationship with the Lord by the courageous actions of their fathers. The point is that converted Ephraimites—former Gentiles—for more than one generation would be fully integrated into the covenant people of God. In the church of Christ such prophecies find their ultimate fulfillment (10:7).

MESSIANIC LIBERATION
Zechariah 10:8-12

Zechariah now offers a second extended picture of salvation under Messiah. He envisions a great gathering of God's people. This picture is developed in three stages.

A. Promise of the Gathering (10:8).

Yahweh would gather his people by whistling like a shepherd might do to attract his sheep; or like a beekeeper might do to cause his bees to swarm (cf. Isa 5:26; 7:18,19). Those who are gathered are those previously redeemed by the power of the Lord. Most likely the reference is to the gathering of the people of God out of the world by the gospel. This body of redeemed people would "increase as they have increased." Just as the ancient Israel grew so much in Egypt (Exod 1:7,12), so would the New Testament Israel grow through the preaching of the gospel.

B. Prelude of the Gathering (10:9).

The redeemed are gathered into one body. Then, however, Yahweh would "sow them among the peoples." This is not the sowing to scatter, but the sowing for increase (cf. Hos 2:23; Jer 31:27). The church of Christ has been gathered out of the world of sin so as to be sent into the world of lost humanity to preach the gospel (10:9a).

The results of the evangelistic efforts of the church are set forth in three clauses. First, "in far distant places they shall remember me." Distant peoples who had suppressed the knowledge of the living God (cf. Rom 1:20-23) would again be brought to God-consciousness, i.e., a realization that only the Creator is worthy of man's devotion, adoration, fear and love.

Second, "they shall live." Remembering the Lord in obedient faith would bring spiritual renewal, a new birth and life. "They shall live" is the Old Testament way of announcing the New Covenant abundant life. This abundant life the redeemed would enjoy "with their children." The new relationship with God and all the attendant blessings would not be a momentary emotional outburst but a long-range commitment with would continue through the generations.

Third, "and they shall return." These words further explain the verb "remember." They shall return to the Lord from whom they had wandered into sin, idolatry and spiritual bondage (10:9b).

C. Picture of the Gathering (10:10-12).

Yahweh announces that he would bring his people "from the land of Egypt and from Assyria," i.e., out of the great historical lands of the captivity. In this context these lands symbolize the bondage of sin. The words point to a general reassembling and reorganizing of the people of God.[2]

Those who are gathered out of the land of bondage would be brought into "Gilead and Lebanon," i.e., the territories east and west of the Jordan. These were the areas which were depopulated in the fall of the old northern kingdom. In this context Gilead and Lebanon symbolize Christ's kingdom. Because the numbers of those redeemed from bondage are so great, "no place shall be found" for all of them. The point is that the old physical Promised Land would no longer be able to contain all those who have been redeemed. The kingdom of Christ is universal in scope and therefore cannot be geographically located (10:10).

Just as Yahweh led ancient Israel through the Red Sea to freedom, so he would again make a way for his people through the sea which is said to represent "affliction" (cf. Isa 11:15). In fact, Yahweh would "cross over the sea." Through suffering he would make a path to freedom for those held captive in sin. Through the suffering of the cross God made it possible for people to be set free from the bondage of sin and death (cf. Heb 2:14f.).

In a similar figure God would "dry up" the depths of the river. The Nile river held Israel captive in Egypt in the days of Moses. The Euphrates held the captives captive in Assyria and Babylon. So here the river represents the boundary of that land of bondage in which all sinners reside prior to redemption. The point is that the Lord would make it possible for those who are held captive to find freedom. The drying up of the river suggests the demise of the oppressors of God's people. "The pride of Assyria shall be brought down and the rod of Egypt shall be removed." In his resurrection Jesus won a smashing victory over the forces of sin and darkness. The devil and his host have been defeated (10:11).

While the forces of evil are overthrown in the resurrection, those who have been rescued from the bondage of sin would be a strong people. Their strength would lie in Yahweh himself and in his "name" (cf. Micah 4:5; Col 3:17). This means that the redeemed would live their lives by the principles and power symbolized by the name or attributes of God (10:12).

JUDGMENT ON NATIONAL ISRAEL
Zechariah 11:1-6

In rich poetic imagery Zechariah describes an enemy approaching Judah from the north. The inhabitants of the land would suffer great trauma as a result of this invasion. For the time being the prophet says nothing of the reason for this invasion. As the chapter unfolds it becomes clear that Judah falls under terrible judgment for rejecting the Good Shepherd.

A. The Approach of the Enemy (11:1-3).

Zechariah calls upon Lebanon to open her "doors," i.e., the passes which give access to Palestine from the north. Through those passes a judgment "fire" would come which would consume the cedars of Lebanon. The cedar trees probably are here a symbol of northern Palestine. The point is that a judgment would sweep into Palestine from the north (11:1).

The trees of southern Palestine are told to "howl" for two reasons. First, the fir trees of southern Palestine would soon suffer the same fate as the northern cedars. Second, "those which are mighty have been destroyed." The leaders of the Jewish nation would fall in the judgment.

The "oaks of Bashan" east of Jordan would not escape the judgment. Thus Zechariah exhorts these "trees" to "howl." If the inaccessible forest of Lebanon has been brought down, the open country of Bashan could not possibly escape (11:2).

As the judgment sweeps southward, Zechariah hears the howling of the shepherds. The "glory" of the shepherds is pasture lands. That glory now was "spoiled." The same is true of the "pride of Jordan," that jungle which lined the Jordan river from north to south. This tangled brush was the habitat for many wild animals. The fire of judgment, however, has now "spoiled" this habitat. Thus the fire of judgment has now reached the southern extremity of the land of Palestine. Zechariah probably is presenting here a poetic description of the Roman conquest of Palestine, especially the Roman war against the Jews in AD 66-70 (11:3).

B. The Punishment of the People (11:4-6).

Zechariah now received a prophetic commission to "shepherd the flock," i.e., to play the role of a ruler to national Israel. The nation is called the "flock of slaughter" because it is destined for destruction at the hands of their present shepherds (11:4). The commission authorizes Zechariah to perform his second action parable (cf. Zech 6:9-11).

The national leaders are compared to worthless owners of a flock of sheep. "Those who possess them, slay them." They make decisions which inevitably lead to the slaughter of the common people. Yet in spite of their gross negligence regarding the welfare of the flock "they consider themselves not guilty." These leaders sell out the flock, and then brazenly praise God for ill-gotten gain. The under shepherds who work for the owners of the flock have no compassion for those under their jurisdiction (11:5).

God would permit this mistreatment of the flock or nation. No longer would the Lord have "pity anymore upon the inhabitants of the land," i.e., upon national Israel. The idea is that the abuse of the leaders is a manifestation of God's anger with his people. They are here being punished for a terrible crime which will be illustrated in the verses which follow (11:6a).

In a shocking announcement ("Behold!") Yahweh declares his intention "to cause men to be found each man in the hand of his neighbor." God would permit national Israel to be rent by internal strife. During the war with Rome (AD 66-70) Judea was torn asunder by at least three factions. More died as a result of the three-way civil war then died at the hands of the Roman army.

Yahweh would also deliver each man of national Israel "into the hand of his king." In Pilate's judgment hall the crowd, spurred on by national leaders, cried out "We have no king but Caesar." As a result of that decisive decision the armies of the foreign king would "smite the land." God would not deliver the Jews from the power of this adversary, i.e., the Romans (11:6b).

MINISTRY OF THE GOOD SHEPHERD
Zechariah 11:7-14

In a series of symbolic actions Zechariah now presents the reason for the devastating judgment which he has just described.

A. The Ministry Portrayed (11:7).

"And I fed the flock of slaughter," i.e., Zechariah played the role assigned to him (cf. v. 4). The flock here is national Israel. Within the nation were "the poor of the flock," the remnant of true believers. These were those who would be abused by the rest of the flock and by the national leaders as well (11:7a).

To carry out the symbolism of shepherding the flock Zechariah took up two staves. A shepherd often carried "a rod and a staff" (Ps 23:4). With the rod he would ward off wild beasts. With the crooked staff he would guide his flock and rescue the straying. The prophet gave symbolic names to the two staves. The first staff was called "Delight" or "Beauty." This staff symbolizes the loving and gracious care of the Good Shepherd. The second staff was called "Bands."

This staff symbolizes the unifying mission of the Good Shepherd (cf. John 10:16). Using his two staves, Zechariah acted out the role of the Good Shepherd (11:7b).

B. Relationship with the Shepherds (11:8).

Zechariah symbolically "cut off three shepherds." The reference is to the national leaders. Many different interpretations have been offered as to the identity of the three shepherds. Perhaps the easiest one is to see here an allusion to the three classes of shepherds mentioned in 11:5—"the buyers," "sellers" and "shepherds."[3]

The shepherds were cut off "in one month," i.e., in a very short period of time (cf. Hos 5:7). The reference is to that brief period when the unbelief of the national leaders came to a head just before they demanded the crucifixion of Jesus.

The shepherds were cut off because of the mutual antagonism which developed between them and the Good Shepherd. "And my soul loathed them," declares the prophet in his symbolic role. The Good Shepherd became utterly disgusted with the national leader—the scribes and Pharisees and perhaps Herodians (cf. Matt 23:13-33). Reacting to his blasts against them, "their soul abhorred me." The leaders hated Jesus. Early in his ministry they began to plot how they might destroy him.

C. Reaction of the Flock (11:9).

Next the Good Shepherd abandons the flock (national Israel) to its fate. "The one that dies, let it die." The reference may be to those who died in the plagues which swept through Jerusalem during the Roman siege in AD 69-70. "The one that is cut off, let it be cut off." Many would die in violent conflict with the Romans. "And let the rest eat each one the flesh of another." Because of famine many in the besieged city of Jerusalem in AD 69-70 turned to cannibalism according to the accounts of Josephus.

D. Abandonment of the Flock (11:10).

After making his announcement about the fate of the shepherds and the national flock of Israel, Zechariah symbolically broke his first staff "Delight." God would withdraw his gracious protection of national Israel because the Good Shepherd was rejected by the flock. Just as that wooden staff was broken, so would God break his "covenant . . . with all the people." The reference is to the restrictions which God had placed on foreign nations regarding what they would be permitted to do to Jerusalem and the temple. Thus in breaking the first staff Zechariah is acting out the abandonment of the flock which he announced in the previous verse.

E. Reaction of the Remnant (11:11).

Zechariah symbolically acted out what God would do "in that day," i.e., in the day when the national leaders showed contempt for Good Shepherd. The "poor of the flock" who embraced the Good Shepherd "knew that it was the word of God." The disciples of Jesus knew that national Israel was doomed to be attacked by the nations, i.e., the Romans. In AD 66-70 the early Christians saw the abomination of desolation—the Roman legions—approaching Jerusalem. Following the instructions of Jesus (Matt 24:15-22; Luke 20:21), these Christians fled Jerusalem to safety in the Transjordanian city of Pella.[4]

REJECTION OF THE GOOD SHEPHERD
Zechariah 11:12-14

The action parable continues. Zechariah acts out the rejection of the Good Shepherd in three stages.

A. Request for Wages (11:12).

The Good Shepherd asks the flock to give him his wages. "If it is good in your eyes, give me my hire, and if not desist." The wages which the Good Shepherd desired were repentance, faith, and obedience. Unlike the wicked shepherds (national leaders), he puts no constraint on them. Here was the opportunity to show their gratitude for all God had done for them (11:12a).

The flock responded to the request of the Good Shepherd by weighing out thirty pieces of silver. He was of no more value to them than a slave (cf. Exod 21:32). By this act they mocked the Good Shepherd. Their evaluation demonstrated their ingratitude (11:12b).

The action parable finds fulfillment in the money paid by the chief priests to Judas for the betrayal of Christ (Matt 26:15).

B. Rejection of Wages (11:13).

The insult administered to the Good Shepherd is taken personally by Yahweh. So the Lord contemptuously rejected the sum. With biting sarcasm he refers to their wages as "the goodly price with which I was evaluated by them." So the Lord ordered, "Cast it unto the potter." The thirty pieces of silver for which Jesus was betrayed to the chief priests eventually were used to purchase a potter's field (Matt 27:7-9).

C. Rending of the Nation (11:14).

At this point Zechariah severed his second staff named "Bands." This symbolized the dissolution of all the bands that held the nation together. The "brotherhood between Judah and Israel" was broken. The nation would be shattered into factions as happened after the death of Solomon in 931 BC. Civil and social disunion paved the way for the Roman victory over the Jewish state in AD 66-70.

THE COMING FALSE SHEPHERD
Zechariah 11:15-17

Zechariah was commissioned to act out a second parable. "Yet take for yourself the equipment of a foolish shepherd." The equipment of a shepherd would include garb, rod, staff and other accessories. This time Zechariah was to assume the role of one who is the antithesis of the Good Shepherd (11:15).

The action parable is a prophecy of great significance. "For behold I am about to raise up a shepherd over the land." This "shepherd" must represent some leader or power which appears subsequent to the rejection of Christ by national Israel. In Christian theology this false shepherd is sometimes called antichrist.[5] All who oppose the Biblical doctrine of Christ are in fact antichrists (1 John 2:18-22). Yet the Scripture seems to point to one final leader who will oppress the people of God (Dan 7:21f.), assume divine prerogatives, and counterfeit Biblical miracles (2 Thess 2:3-9).

The foolish or false shepherd would display the most ruthless character. "The cut off ones he will not visit," i.e., he would not go after the straying sheep. Nor would he visit the young of the flock and those who were wounded. He would give no food to the starving animals. The sheep which stand still are those too feeble to move. The point is that he would be totally unconcerned about the flock of God. On the other hand, he would eat the flesh of the fat sheep. He would drive the sheep over places so rough that their hoofs would be broken. The flock which rejected the Good Shepherd would suffer much under the leadership of the foolish shepherd (11:16).

Because he had abandoned the flock, the foolish shepherd eventually would face the judgment of God. "A sword shall be against his arm and against his right eye." God would deprive him of the power and understanding which had been abused in his leadership position. "His arm shall be completely dried up and his right eye shall be utterly dimmed" (11:17).

ENDNOTES

1. Unger understands the text to say that the *noges* (oppressors) would depart from Judah under the reign of Messiah, i.e., there would be no more oppressor for the people of God. Cf. 9:8. Merrill Unger, *Zechariah; Prophet of Messiah's Glory* (Grand Rapids: Zondervan, 1963), pp. 179f.

2. Marcus Dods, *The Post-exilian Prophets* (Edinburgh: T. & T. Clark, 1956 reprint), pp. 104f.

3. An alternative suggestion is that the three shepherds are three orders of rulers in the Jewish state at the time of Christ—priests, teachers of the law, civil magistrates.

4. Eusebius, *Hist. Eccles.* 3:5.

5. Other identifications of the false shepherd: the Romans; King Herod; false Christs; and false prophets.

CHAPTER FORTY-SIX

The New Jerusalem
Zechariah 12-13

That a new literary unit begins with 12:1 is indicated by the introductory formula: "the burden of the word of Yahweh concerning Israel" (cf. 9:1). In the previous chapter Zechariah has predicted the rejection of physical Israel. The "Israel" addressed here is the Israel of the spirit, the church of Christ, the messianic theocracy—the people of God in contradistinction to the world of nations which is estranged from God (12:1a).

Zechariah delivers the message for Yahweh the all-powerful Creator of the heavens and earth. He it is "who stretches forth the heavens, and lays the foundation of the earth." He it is who "forms the spirit of man within him," i.e., he is responsible for human life and intelligence. When the Creator speaks, all creatures should listen (12:1b).

This unit describes a great siege, a great salvation, a great smiting, and the great day of Yahweh.

THE GREAT SIEGE
Zechariah 12:2-9

Zechariah depicts Jerusalem under siege. Yet here the prophet stresses the security of Jerusalem, the strength of the city, and the deliverance which God would provide in the day of attack. At the time Zechariah spoke these words Jerusalem had no walls, and hence was a small and despised city.

A. Security of Jerusalem (12:2-4).

In attacking Jerusalem the enemies of God's people encounter greater resistance than they expected. Their shocking discovery is indicated by the word "Behold!" The attackers make three discoveries.

1. Jerusalem a cup of staggering (12:2). Jerusalem's enemies may have looked on the city as a bowl of delicious wine from which they could drink with ease. They would discover, however, that Yahweh had made Jerusalem "a cup of reeling," i.e., a container whose contents produce stupefaction.[1] Hostile powers crowd about what seems to be a defenseless city. The experience, however, proves fatal to the attackers. What is said of Jerusalem applies to Judah as well. Those who attack any of God's people will experience disastrous consequences.

2. Jerusalem a burdensome stone (12:3). In that day of attack the enemies would find that Yahweh had made Jerusalem "as a stone of burden to all peoples," i.e., a burdensome stone. To attempt to move that immovable rock would result in frustration and injury. "All who burden themselves with her will surely be lacerated." The attack envisioned here is not that of the Greeks against physical Jerusalem, but that of "all nations" against the Jerusalem which is from above (cf. Heb 12:22). The world is constantly in battle array against the church of Christ. The world, however, shall never be able to budge that weighty rock.

3. Jerusalem a source of confusion (12:4). As in the battles of ancient Israel, Yahweh would intervene on behalf of his people. The cavalry units of the attackers would be quickly neutralized. The horses and riders would experience "confusion," "madness," and "blindness," i.e., bewilderment, consternation and panic. On the other hand, upon the people of "Judah," i.e., God's people, Yahweh would "open" his eyes. He would see their plight, experience compassion for them, and come to their rescue. The point is that attacks against spiritual Jerusalem ultimately would fail.

B. Strength of Jerusalem (12:5-6).

In the preceding verses the defense of Jerusalem is the work of Yahweh. Therefore the princes of Judah, i.e, the leaders of God's people, would face the attackers with quiet confidence. Each would know in his heart "that the inhabitants of Jerusalem are my strength." Leaders and people work together in marvelous unity. Spiritual Jerusalem is not a city of walls and gates, but of people consecrated to the service of God—men and women with unwavering faith "in Yahweh of hosts their God." This mighty commander of all armies in heaven and on earth is on their side. The survival of spiritual Jerusalem would be a token of divine favor (12:5).

Supported by spirit-filled citizens and by God, the leaders of spiritual Jerusalem would devour their enemies. "In that day[2] I will make the chiefs of Judah like a pan of fire in the wood and like a torch of fire in the sheaves." All those who attack spiritual Jerusalem would be vanquished. "And they shall consume upon the right and left all the people round about." During those desperate days "Jerusalem shall be inhabited yet in its own place even in Jerusalem." Spiritual Jerusalem would remain settled on her site as before, unshaken, unmoved, unconquered (12:6).

C. Deliverance of Jerusalem (12:7-9).

The deliverance of God's people from attack is further amplified in the verses of this unit. Three points are made.

First, Yahweh would intervene on behalf of the defenseless and less prestigious populace outside the walls of Jerusalem. He would "save the tents of Judah first." In Old Testament times open towns and villages could offer no effectual resistance to an enemy. God, however, would see to it that every citizen of his spiritual kingdom would have his divine protection. Not just those in prominent places, but those in distant and less prestigious areas would experience the same deliverance. This would be the case "in order that the glory of the house of David and the inhabitants of Jerusalem does not exalt itself over Judah." The point being made in Old Testament language is that the same salvation by grace is needed by all and experienced by all. No one of God's people can, therefore, lord it over others. There is nothing of which to boast, save the cross of Christ (12:7).

Second, the Lord would defend the inhabitants of Jerusalem and empower them for mighty deeds on their own behalf. For emphasis Zechariah repeats the promise that "in that day Yahweh will defend the inhabitants of Jerusalem." Empowered by the Spirit of the Lord, the weakest among the citizens of Jerusalem would be a hero such as David. In the strength of the Lord David had confronted Goliath and countless companies of Philistine soldiers. The "house of David" (leaders of spiritual Jerusalem) would be "like God," i.e., endowed with supernatural powers. Further explaining the phrase "like God" Zechariah adds: "like the angel of Yahweh before them."[3] They would lead God's people into battle like the angel of Yahweh led the ancient armies of Israel (12:8).

Third, Zechariah states plainly the bottom line of this unit: "And it shall come to pass in that day that I will seek to destroy all the nations which come against Jerusalem." Those who set themselves as enemies of the church of Christ have charted their course to destruction (12:9).

THE GREAT SALVATION
Zechariah 12:10-13:6

Having described the security of spiritual Jerusalem, the prophet next depicts in Old Testament language the process by which new covenant people came to be such. Here he relates how the church commences the Christian life and obtains the right to the divine protection mentioned in the preceding paragraph. The emphasis is upon the process of conviction, the provision for cleansing, the picture of consecration, and the proof of commitment.

A. Process of Conviction (12:10).

The process of coming under conviction as to one's lostness and need of salvation is viewed in three stages.

1. The outpouring of God's Spirit (12:10a). Under the Old

Covenant kings, prophets and priests were anointed with oil which symbolized the gift of the Holy Spirit. In the messianic age God would "pour out" his Spirit not only upon "the house of David," but also upon "the inhabitants of Jerusalem," i.e., both the leaders and the citizens. In this context the reference is to those who are members of the church of Christ, i.e., all believers. The verb suggests the abundant measure in which the Spirit would be given.

The Spirit is here called "the Spirit of grace" (cf. Heb 10:29) because his work in the heart of the believer is undeserved and because he uses the gospel of God's grace to persuade and convict sinners (cf. John 16:8). He is called "the Spirit of supplication" because he encourages sinners to call upon the name of the Lord (cf. Acts 22:16).

2. *The looking to the pierced one (12:10b).* As a result of the work of the Spirit through the word, sinners would come to "look unto me whom they have pierced." Without question God is the speaker in 12:10. Yet it is the speaker who is pierced! The verb "pierced" (*daqar*) means to thrust through, to slay by any kind of death whatever. Certainly the Jews pierced the Lord metaphorically by their rebellion and ingratitude throughout their history. At that place called Calvary, however, they pierced him literally (cf. John 19:37). To look on him whom they have pierced suggests more than merely observing the fact that someone has been slain. The implication is that they will recognize the person of the one they have slain.

An excellent example of how this works is found in Acts 2. In the first public proclamation of the complete gospel, Peter accused his audience of having nailed to a cross one accredited by signs and miracles, i.e., their Messiah (Acts 2:22f.). The Apostle then went on to demonstrate by Scripture and logic that Jesus had been raised from the dead, and that he had been enthroned at the right hand of the Father. This powerful preaching caused those assembled to be pierced to the heart. Through the gospel the Holy Spirit brought these sinners to faith in Christ and placed them under conviction for their sin.

3. *The mourning over sin (12:10b-14).* The realization that one's sins made necessary the piercing of the Lord leads to godly sor-

row and repentance (cf. 2 Cor 7:10). "They will mourn for him." The shift to the third person pronoun *him* is significant. The one who is pierced is Yahweh, but yet he is distinguished from Yahweh. The language suggests two persons who in fact are one (cf. John 10:30). Yahweh declares that to pierce *him* is to pierce *me*. The passage clearly teaches the deity of the one who is pierced.

Zechariah stresses the intensity of the sorrow over the piercing of the one who is deity. He uses three illustrations to make his point. First, "they shall mourn over him like the mourning over an only son." Among the Hebrews the preservation of the family was deemed of vast importance. The death of an only son would be the heaviest blow that could happen. Second, their bitter lamentation is likened to that which might be experience when a firstborn son died. The firstborn son was the leader of the ancient family. He was slated to receive a double portion of the family inheritance along with heavy family responsibility (12:10b).

Third, "in that day the mourning shall be great in Jerusalem like the mourning of Hadad-rimmon in the valley of Megiddo." At this place the most beloved king of the Old Testament met an untimely death. For years there was a national lamentation over this event (cf. 2 Chr 35:25). Such would be the intensity of the mourning for the pierced one (12:11). This prophecy of lamentation over the piercing of Messiah began to be fulfilled on the very day of his crucifixion (cf. Luke 23:47f.).

The mourning shall spread from Jerusalem to "the land" as men and women come to look with the eye of faith upon him whom they have pierced. Using the technique of emphasis by enumeration the prophet describes how various families would be affected by the message of the pierced one. The family of David in general, and the Nathan branch of that family would mourn over the pierced one. The priestly family of Levi and the Shimeite clan within that family would also be affected. "All the families that remain" would also mourn. Special notice is given to the mourning of the women of each of the families. The point of these verses is to stress that the mourning would be universal and continuous among the people of God. Whenever believers pause to look upon the pierced one they realize anew that their sin put him on the tree (12:12-13).

B. The Provision for Cleansing (13:1).

In the messianic age "a fountain shall be opened for the house of David and for the inhabitants of Jerusalem," i.e., the whole nation (cf. 12:10). Those who were brought to penitent mourning by the recognition of the pierced one have the opportunity of cleansing "for sin and for uncleanness," i.e., guilt and pollution. The latter word is used of ritual uncleanness (cf. Lev 15:20). In discussing the fulfillment of this prediction commentators are more influenced by the "fountain filled with blood" of the hymn writer than by the teaching of the New Testament. Fountains are not filled with blood, but with water. The proclamation of the gospel in the first century concluded with an exhortation to "repent and be baptized" (Acts 2:38; 22:16). To this grand act of submission to Jesus' Lordship Paul refers when he speaks of the "washing of regeneration" (Titus 3:5). As the sinner is baptized into the death of Christ (Rom 6:3) the blood of Jesus is sprinkled upon him (1 Pet 1:2). That blood continues to cleanse the believer who confesses his sins to the Lord (1 John 1:7). Thus in prophetic language, the passage is alluding to the gospel plan of salvation: faith (looking unto the pierced one), repentance (mourning over sin) and baptism (the fountain of cleansing).

C. The Picture of Consecration (13:2).

In that messianic age God would remove from the midst of his people the practice of idolatry. "I will cut off the names of the idols from the land." This the Lord would do through the powerful and persuasive message of the gospel. The idols so popular in ancient Israel would "not be remembered any more." The point is that those who experience the messianic cleansing of the preceding verse would have no association with idolatry (cf. Hos 2:16f.). The Lord sanctifies as well as saves his people.

Through that same gospel the Lord would remove "the prophets" from the land. The reference is to false prophets, those who preach in the name of other gods, or who proclaim falsehood in the name of Yahweh. Zechariah uses the term "prophet" because there is no word in the Hebrew language for the concept of "false prophet." God would remove "the spirit of uncleanness," the lying spirit which works in false prophets (cf. 1 Kgs 22:19-23), from the land.[4] Under the Old Testament theocracy false prophets were stoned. In the New Covenant era capital punishment is reserved for the government. The "death sentence" administered by the church is excommunication. Those who have committed their lives to the pierced one will not tolerate false doctrine (cf. Gal 1:8).

D. Proof of Commitment (13:3-5).

In the messianic era those who attempted to revive false prophecy would be dealt with most severely. One who would prophesy falsely would face the ultimate rejection of his own father and mother. Because their son dared to speak lies in the name of Yahweh the parents would thrust him through, i.e. put him to death (cf. 12:10) the next time he attempted to prophesy. The intimation here is that prophetic powers would cease. Those who claimed such powers, therefore, would be marked as false prophets. The Old Testament law required the execution of those who prophesied falsely (cf. Deut 13:6-10; 18:20). Parents were required by the law to stand with God and truth even against their own flesh and blood. The point is that people would be totally committed to the Lord in the New Covenant era. Jesus predicted that allegiance to him would in some instances divide families (Luke 12:53). This verse finds fulfillment in the supreme commitment of men and women to Jesus Christ (13:3).

Before the exile the false prophets were men who were honored in the community (cf. Isa 9:15; Jer 5:31; Micah 2:11). In the New Covenant age, however, those who engaged in false prophecy would come to realize the error of their ways. The false prophets would "be ashamed each because of his vision when he prophesies." So strong would be the popular feeling against false prophecy in the kingdom of Messiah that the false prophets would be ashamed to make any pretense to visions. No longer would they wear "a hairy mantle in order to deceive." Elijah had worn such a rough outer garment (cf. 2 Kgs 1:8). Apparently such garments had become the badge of prophets. The basic thought here is that some false prophets would be converted. Perhaps the conversions of men like Simon the sorcerer (Acts 8:9,13) or those practitioners of the occult arts in Ephesus (Acts 19:13-20) would illustrate the fulfillment of this prophecy (13:4).

That one converted from false religion by the power of the

gospel would cheerfully confess that he was not really a prophet. "No prophet am I." Rather he would admit to being just a farmer, and a hired hand at that. He was merely a nobody who used religion to attempt to gain followers and make a living. He was a first-class con artist. Those who embrace the truth do not hesitate to admit the hypocrisy and outright lies of their sinful past (13:5).

E. An Explanation (13:6).

The main theme of the one who is pierced surfaces again in the final verse of this unit. A question is addressed to "him," not the false prophet of the preceding verse, but the one whom they have pierced in 12:10. The pierced one is asked: "What are these wounds between your hands?" The wounds may be on the breast, but more likely they are on the back. "Hands" here probably refers to the arms. The pierced one explains: "Those with which I was wounded in the house of my friends." Jesus was wounded by those he loved, those he came to save. His own people turned against him and demanded his death.

THE GREAT SMITING
Zechariah 13:7-9

In the previous unit Zechariah prophesied the piercing of one is Yahweh, yet distinct from Yahweh. The present unit builds upon that thought. It further identifies the one who would be smitten and the tragic results of that smiting.

A. The Call for the Smiting (13:7).

The sword of of divine justice is directly addressed. "O sword, awake." Matthew (26:31) interprets these words to mean that God himself would smite the Shepherd. The term "sword" represents any kind of instrument which inflicts death (cf. Exod 5:21; 2 Sam 12:9). The term often has the connotation of judicial execution. The sword is commanded to "awake," i.e., go into action.

The one who is smitten is described in two ways. First, the sword would awake against "my shepherd." The reference is not to the foolish shepherd of 11:15-17, nor the national leaders who would oppress Israel (cf. 11:5). The smitten one is the Shepherd of Yahweh, the Good Shepherd introduced in 11:4. This Shepherd is none other than Messiah, the one who is identified with Yahweh in 12:10. Second, the smitten one is "the man that is my fellow." The word "fellow" (*'amiti*) occurs only here and in Leviticus where it is usually rendered "neighbor." It suggests one united to another by the possession of common nature, rights and privileges.[5] The language could refer only to Christ (cf. John 10:30). This identification is proved by the application of the following clause to Jesus in Matthew 26:31.

The smiting of the Shepherd would result in the dispersion of the Jews and their denationalization. The scattering due to the smiting began in the Garden of Gethsemane and at the cross when even his disciples forsook him and fled (Mark 14:50-52).

Though scattering would be the result of the smiting of the Good Shepherd, still the Lord promised: "I will return my hand over the little ones." The figure of returning the hand is used in both a positive and a negative sense in Scripture (cf. Isa 1:25; Amos 1:8). Here the expression seems to be used in the sense of protection. The "little ones" are the humble and meek, those who embraced Messiah, the disciples of Jesus (cf. Luke 12:32).

B. The Results of the Smiting (13:8-9).

The smiting of the Good Shepherd would result in terrible devastation, carnage and death "in all the land." Two-thirds of the population—the vast majority which rejected Messiah—would perish. Most likely the reference is to the war with Rome which broke out in AD 66 (13:8).

A third part of the population would escape the great tribulation which would come upon the land. This group represents all those who embraced the Messiah. Though spared from the devastation of the land, this group would also pass "into fire," i.e., persecution. Through the fire of persecution the Lord would refine his people as men refine silver or gold (13:9a).

In that time of persecution this remnant would "call upon my name." They would have full access to God. For his part, Yahweh would acknowledge this people as his very own. The remnant would respond by saying: "Yahweh is my God." They would bear testimony to everyone of their commitment to the Lord (13:9b).

ENDNOTES

1. The theme of the cup of Yahweh's wrath is developed in the following passages: Obad 16; Isa 51:17; Jer 25:15; 51:39,57; Hab 2:16.

2. The phrase "in that day" occurs fifteen times in Zechariah 12-14. The phrase serves to bind together into one time frame all that is being described in these chapters. In the previous eleven chapters the phrase appears but five times.

3. Thus the "angel of Yahweh" and Yahweh himself are equated. See comments on Zech 1:10f.

4. Hailey takes the "unclean spirit" to be a reference to demonic possession. "In the conquest of Christ over Satan and his forces, unclean spirits have ceased to control men as they did in the time of the ministry of Christ and the apostles." Homer Hailey, *A Commentary on the Minor Prophets* (Grand Rapids: Baker, 1972), p. 392.

5. W.J. Deane, "Zechariah" in *The Pulpit Commentary*; New Edition (New York: Funk & Wagnalls, 1909), p. 148.

CHAPTER FORTY-SEVEN

The Triumph of Spiritual Jerusalem
Zechariah 14

Zechariah 14 is one of the most difficult of prophetic Scriptures to interpret. The language is plain enough. The problem comes in finding the intended fulfillment of the predictions found here.

THE GREAT DELIVERANCE
Zechariah 14:1-7

The first unit in the chapter has much in common with 12:2-9. Jerusalem comes under attack and is dramatically rescued by the Lord at his coming. But which Jerusalem, geographical or spiritual? And which coming, the first coming of Christ or the second? These are questions upon which commentators are divided.

A. Antecedents of his Coming (14:1-2).
Before the coming of the Lord Jerusalem—probably the spiritual Jerusalem of Hebrews 12:22—would be ravished. The prophet first

sets forth this fact in general terms, then he develops that thought by specific details.

1. The general picture (14:1). Zechariah fixes the attention of the reader on the shocking situation which he is about to describe by using the interjection "Behold!" He then announces "a day of Yahweh is coming" (14:1a). The concept of the great day of Yahweh's intervention in the affairs of men dates to at least the time of Joel. Every judgment action of God in history was "a day of Yahweh." Each "day of Yahweh" was a type, preview and warning of the final day of Yahweh, i.e., the final judgment of the wicked.

The day of Yahweh here is preceded by a devastating attack against Jerusalem. The possessive pronouns in verse 1 are feminine and thus refer to the city. The enemy would feel so secure they would divide the spoils in the midst of the subjugated city. Commentators of the classic Protestant tradition argue that the papacy is being described here. Others point to modernism which captures congregations, colleges and parachurch organizations from Bible-believing constituents. Still others point to cults and false prophets, and religious charlatans who fleece the wealth of New Testament Jerusalem, the church of Christ (14:1b).

2. The detailed picture (14:2). Those who attack spiritual Jerusalem are now identified. "For I will gather all nations unto Jerusalem to fight." The church is being attacked by non-believers, those who are not citizens of Zion. The plural "nations" suggests that the attackers will be of varied backgrounds. They will share only one thing in common, viz., their hatred for God's people. Whether or not they have a supreme commander Zechariah does not state. Daniel depicted a similar attack against the saints of God just before the final judgment led by one whom he calls "the little horn" (cf. Dan 7:19-22). The Apocalypse also depicts a final attack against spiritual Jerusalem which would be destroyed by fire from heaven (Rev 20:7-9).

Before deliverance comes testing and refinement. The city would actually "be captured and the houses shall be plundered and the women raped." The suffering described here was the usual fate of a conquered city in antiquity. The point is that the enemy would come within the walls. "Half of the city shall go out into captivity." Satan's agents constantly seek to take captive the weaker citizens of Zion (cf.

2 Tim 3:6). The point is that the situation is desperate.

From the worldly standpoint, the prognosis is not good for the survival of the church of Christ. Yet the prophet assures his readers, "the rest of the people shall not be cut off from the city." A remnant would be left to Zion. The words cannot refer to the destruction of geographical Jerusalem in AD 70, for the city was razed at that time, and its inhabitants were slain or sold as slaves (Josephus *Wars* 6:9). The reference must be to spiritual Jerusalem. Though assaulted on every side, though her walls be breached, yet will a remnant remain faithful to greet their returning Lord (14:2).

B. Results of his Coming (14:3-5).

The results of Yahweh's coming is set forth in three wonderful pictures. In Old Testament prophecy the coming of Yahweh in an eschatological sense equates to the coming of Christ.

1. He will fight on behalf of his people (14:3). When things are the most desperate for spiritual Jerusalem the Lord will appear. He will fight against the nations (unbelievers) who are warring with great success against his people. He will fight "as in the day of his fighting in a day of battle." This is an allusion to the numerous times when Yahweh intervened on behalf of ancient Israel in Old Testament times, and especially at the Red Sea. Calvin was aiming in the right direction when he saw in these words a promise of divine intervention on behalf of the people of God throughout the course of their history. Probably, however, the prophecy points specifically to that deliverance which will come for the faithful when the Lord Jesus returns.

2. He will provide an escape (14:3-4). "And his feet shall stand in that day upon the Mount of Olives which is beside Jerusalem on the east." In the person of Messiah Yahweh would return to the same mount from which he ascended. The mountain is mentioned many times in the Old Testament, but only here by this name. From this height one can look down on the temple mount (Mt. Moriah) and on Mt. Zion across the deep Kidron valley.

The coming of the Lord to the Mount of Olives will result in a gigantic earthquake which triggers topographical changes. "The Mount of Olives shall be split in two." Half of the mountain moves to the north and half to the south. The result would be a very great east-west valley. Through that valley the beleaguered citizens of Jerusalem could flee to safety to Azel. The exact location of Azel is not known. It would be east of the Mount of Olives.[1] The desperate flight from Jerusalem is likened to the flight before the earthquake in the days of Uzziah king of Judah (cf. Amos 1:1).[2] The basic idea in this is that the Lord will rescue his people from attack.

3. He will be accompanied by angels (14:5b). Zechariah predicts that "all the holy ones" will come with Yahweh in that day.[3] This detail is another clue that the description here is of a rescue of the faithful at the second coming of Christ (cf. 2 Thess 1:7).

C. Time of his Coming (14:6-7).

When will this day of deliverance for the besieged saints of the Lord take place? Three points are made by the prophet.

First, his coming will occur during a gloomy day. "In that day there shall not be light." The luminaries "shall shrink." The verb (*qapha'*) denotes drawing together, thickening, solidifying, losing some of the characteristic attributes or functions. Thus the luminaries grow dim. This gloominess is symbolic of the plight and persecution of the people of God. It will be a dark day for God's people when the Lord of glory returns to rescue them (14:6).

Second, his coming will occur at a time known only to God. "And it shall come to pass in one day," i.e., a unique day, an unparalleled day (14:7a). That God alone knows the time of that day of intervention is specifically affirmed regarding the second coming (cf. Matt 24:36).

Third, his coming will occur just before the close of the day of mingled light and darkness. Zechariah describes the day of his coming as being "neither day nor night," i.e., neither wholly day nor wholly night, but a mixture of both. Perhaps this means that the day of his coming will not be entirely a time of consolation nor a time of affliction. "But it shall come to pass at evening time there shall be light." In the midst of trouble and danger, deliverance shall come for God's people (14:7b).

GLORY OF MESSIANIC JERUSALEM
Zechariah 14:8-21

Zechariah's prophecy concludes with a lengthy description of messianic Jerusalem. That spiritual city is said to be exalted, secure, and holy.

A. An Exalted City (14:8-11).

In the Messianic age Jerusalem—the kingdom of God—would be an exalted city. Zechariah outlines four dimensions of the glory of that city.

First, spiritual Jerusalem would be a source of blessing for the rest of the world. "And it shall come to pass in that day that living waters shall go out from Jerusalem." Living water is fresh, pure, flowing water. The stream of blessings would flow both toward the "eastern sea" (Dead Sea) and toward the "hinder sea" (Mediterranean Sea). That water would flow in summer as well as winter, i.e., it would not dry up in the summer as most brooks in that region do. Water here is probably symbolic of the Spirit (cf. John 7:38-39). The gospel would be preached until east and west meet each other, i.e., throughout the world (14:8). The theme of water issuing forth from Messianic Jerusalem is developed by Joel (3:18) and Ezekiel (47:12).

Second, spiritual Jerusalem would be a center of divine rule. "And Yahweh shall be king over all the earth in that day." The Creator would be universally recognized due to the influence of the living water (the gospel) from Jerusalem. "And there shall be one Yahweh and his name one." The idea is that the name of Yahweh would be in the mouth of all people (14:9).

Third, spiritual Jerusalem would be prominent. "And the land shall be turned as the Arabah." The Arabah is the flat Jordan valley, the deepest depression on the face of the earth. The idea is that the land becomes flat around Jerusalem so that the holy city becomes all the more prominent. This would be the case "from Geba" six miles northeast of Jerusalem "to Rimmon" near Beersheba in the south. "Jerusalem shall be exalted on its hill." This is a way of stressing the exaltation of the messianic kingdom. Isaiah (2:2) described messianic Jerusalem in similar manner (14:10a).

Fourth, spiritual Jerusalem would be an inhabited city. "And it shall be inhabited in its place," i.e., the city would occupy her ancient limits. Similar predictions are recorded by Jeremiah (31:38-40) and Ezekiel (48:15). Five geographical landmarks of the old Jerusalem are included in the area which would be occupied. The "Benjamin gate" was in the northern wall. The "first gate" was in the eastern wall. The "corner gate" was west of the Benjamin gate. "The tower of Hananeel" was the northeast corner of the wall. The "winepresses of the king" were probably near "the king's garden" (Neh 3:15) at the southeast extremity of the city. Zechariah is illustrating the growth and stability of the church by the figure of the earthly city of Jerusalem firmly ordered and built.[4]

Fifth, spiritual Jerusalem would be safely inhabited. "They shall dwell in it." In the days of Zechariah earthly Jerusalem was not inhabited. The thought of the habitation of Jerusalem would have been very precious to those who heard Zechariah preach. "And utter destruction shall be no more." The citizens of spiritual Jerusalem would not incur the curse which is inflicted on transgressors, idolaters and their cities by the old law (cf. Exod 22:20; Deut 7:2; 13:12-15). Perhaps this is the Old Testament way of saying that there is no condemnation for those who are in Christ (Rom 8:1). The point is that "Jerusalem shall be safely inhabited." Sin has been removed. There would be no more occasion for chastisement of the entire city for it would be the habitation of the redeemed. The spiritual Jerusalem would never be destroyed (14:11; cf. Zeph 3:12-15).

B. A Secure City (14:12-15).

Zechariah now amplifies the thought of the security of spiritual Jerusalem. That holy city would come under attack from time to time. The Lord, however, would protect New Covenant Jerusalem in three ways.

1. Protection by means of plague (14:12). God would send a contagious affliction upon all peoples (unbelievers) who fight against Jerusalem. The flesh of each one—Hebrew suffixes are singular to indicate that no one would be overlooked—would be consumed "while he is standing upon his feet." The flesh would putrefy and molder away while these enemies were in the very act of attacking Jerusalem. The eyes of the attackers "shall rot in their sockets and their tongue shall rot in in their mouths." Obviously a supernatural plague is in view. Both collectively and individually all attackers would be punished. This gruesome picture of the fate of the enemies of Christ is intended to give confidence to the citizens of spiritual Jerusalem, the church of Christ.

2. *Protection by means of mutual slaughter (14:13)*. In that day when spiritual Jerusalem would come under attack "a great tumult from Yahweh shall be upon them," i.e., upon the attackers. The enemy would be smitten with general panic or confusion as in some of the battles of ancient Israel (cf. Judg 7:22; 1 Sam 14:20). In this confusion the enemies would "seize each man the hand of his neighbor" but not in friendship. The enemies would fall upon one another with the weapons intended for use against the people of God. The hand of each man "shall go up against the hand of his neighbor" (14:13).

3. *Protection by the sword of Judah (14:14)*. Judah would rally to the defense of the capital. If Jerusalem here is spiritual, the church of Christ, then Judah must also refer to the church for a capital is but a specific location within a kingdom. Judah comes to gather "the wealth of all the nations round about," i.e., the spoil abandoned by the enemy in the confusion inflicted by God would fall to the people of God. This would include "gold and silver and garments in great abundance." The point is that the church would emerge victorious from persecutions. She would be enriched and adorned by the means of those who planned her destruction. The irony here is that the nations had come to spoil Jerusalem; now the wealth of those unbelievers would be gathered to requite God's people.

4. *Protection by total defeat of the attackers (14:15)*. A summary verse underscores the complete defeat of those who attack God's people. "And thus shall be the plague of the horse, the mule, the camel, and the ass and all the cattle which shall be in those camps as this plague." The devastating plague of 14:12 falls on the animals as well as the troops of the enemy. The basic idea is that the wealth which does not fall to God's people would be destroyed. Thus unbelievers would lose everything by attacking God's people.

C. A Worship Center (14:16-19).

Not all the heathen would be destroyed in the attack on Jerusalem. Those who survived the attack would "go up from year to year to worship the king, Yahweh of hosts." Where once they had striven to crush God's people, now the converted go to worship. One specific worship occasion is mentioned, viz., the feast of tabernacles. This was the last, and perhaps the most important, of the three prescribed annual feasts of the Mosaic system. It was *the* feast par excellence (cf. 1 Kgs 8:2). Tabernacles was an occasion for thanksgiving for harvest vintage. During temple times sacrifices were brought on this festival on behalf of the nations of the world. Prayers were offered for the fall rains. The feast also commemorated Israel's sojourn in the wilderness and divine protection there. Tabernacles was a more ecumenical feast than either Passover or Pentecost. The prophet depicts New Testament worship in Old Testament language. The point is that under Messiah the Gentiles would be converted to true religion. They shall worship God in regular, orderly fashion.[5]

Not all those who survived the attack on spiritual Jerusalem would be converted. Some "of the families of the earth" would not go up to spiritual Jerusalem "to worship the king, Yahweh of hosts." Upon that individual who refused to render homage to heaven's king "there shall be no rain." Failure of periodic rain in Palestine meant drought, famine, and distress. In a spiritual sense, rain represents the grace and blessing of God (cf. Ezek 34:26). These blessings are withheld from those who refuse to worship him (14:17).

The thought of the blessing attached to worship of Yahweh in the messianic age is amplified by a specific example. "And if the family of Egypt shall not go up and shall not come, neither upon them shall the rain come." Instead of the showers of blessing will come the "the plague with which Yahweh will plague the nations which do not go up to celebrate the feast of tabernacles." The reference is not to the devastating supernatural plague which would smite those who actively attack spiritual Jerusalem in verses 12 and 15. Rather here the plague is the lack of rain (blessing) of the preceding verse (14:18).

For her sin—missing the mark with regard to heaven's king—Egypt would be punished. So likewise would "all the nations which do not go up to celebrate the feast of tabernacles." Once again the Mosaic feast is symbolic of all the worship of spiritual Jerusalem (14:19).

D. A Holy City (14:20-21).

Zechariah concludes his description of the messianic Jerusalem by emphasizing the holiness of that city of the redeemed. He makes four distinct points about it in contrast to the old geographical Jerusalem which was its prototype.

1. *The previously unholy would be made holy (14:20a).* "In that day," i.e., the messianic age, the "bells of the horses" in Jerusalem will have inscribed on them "Holy to Yahweh." The reference is probably to small metallic plates suspended from the necks or heads of the animals for the sake of ornament and making a tinkling noise when striking against each other. These plates may have had the names of the owners inscribed on them. The inscription "Holy to Yahweh" was that which appeared on the miter of the high priest (cf. Exod 28:36) The basic idea here is that the ornaments of worldly pomp and warlike power would be as consecrated to God as the very miter of the high priest.

2. *The previously holy shall be made holier (14:20b).* "The pots in the house of Yahweh shall be like the bowls before the altar." The bronze pots were used to remove ashes (cf. Exod 27:3). They were of inferior sanctity. Those pots, however, would be like "the bowls before the altar," i.e., vessels of superior sanctity. These golden bowls held the sacrificial blood for sprinkling upon the altar and they were also used for other libations. The prophet is using comparisons which would be familiar to those who first heard him in order to make his point about the holiness of spiritual Jerusalem.

3. *The previously common shall be made holy (14:21a).* "Every vessel in Jerusalem and in Judah shall be holy to Yahweh of hosts." All distinction between sacred and secular shall be a thing of the past. Every vessel (possession) used throughout Messiah's realm would be devoted to the service of the king. Common, ordinary vessels would be suitable for sacrificial purposes. The basic idea here is that old Levitical distinctions in degrees of holiness in society (priests, Levites, people), temple (outer court, holy place, holy of holies), animals (clean, unclean) would disappear. All shall now be equally holy. Thus Zechariah is making clear that he was not anticipating a restoration of the Mosaic system in the messianic age. Rather he envisions an entirely new worship system.

4. *The irreclaimably profane will be forever shut out (14:21b).* In that messianic day "there shall be no longer a Canaanite in the

house of Yahweh." The term "Canaanite" here is best regarded as a proper name used symbolically of an unclean person, i.e., one who had not consecrated himself to the service of God. Such would be excluded from the house of God, i.e., the New Testament temple, the church of Christ or perhaps heaven itself (cf. Rev 21:27).[6]

ENDNOTES

1. Some take Azel to mean "union" and see here a union of law and gospel, Jew and Gentiles.
2. Josephus (*Antiquities* 10:4) connects this earthquake with the attempt of Uzziah to burn incense in the temple (2 Chr 26:19).
3. The standard Hebrew text reads: "the holy ones [shall come] with you." Jewish interpreters take "with you" as a reference to Jerusalem and give it the meaning "for your sake."
4. W.J. Deane, "Zechariah" in *The Pulpit Commentary*; New Edition (New York: Funk & Wagnalls,1909), p. 158.
5. *Ibid.*, p. 159.
6. Eli Cashdan proposes this alternative: "Canaanite" means "merchant." The money makers who exploited pilgrims with the sale of animals and vessels would be excluded from the future temple. For this use of "Canaanite" see Prov 31:24; Job 41:6. "Zechariah" in *The Twelve Prophets*; "The Soncino Books of the Bible" (London: Soncino, 1961), p. 332.

CHAPTER FORTY-EIGHT

Divine Love Slighted
Malachi 1:1-2:4

Malachi referred to his words as "the burden of the word of Yahweh." The term "burden" (*massa'*) is literally, "that which is lifted up." The word often introduces a prophecy of judgment, a weighty woe against the wicked. The NASB and NIV rendering "oracle" perhaps is too technical. A better translation would be "proclamation." Thus Malachi opens with the claim that what follows is a proclamation of the word of Yahweh (1:1a).[1]

The message of the final Old Testament book is addressed to "Israel" (1:1b). Since the fall of the northern kingdom of Israel in 722 BC this name was used for the entirety of the covenant people. The postexilic community was viewed as being comprised of former citizens of both Israel (northern kingdom) and Judah (southern kingdom). Malachi speaks of the privilege and pollution of this people.

THE PRIVILEGE OF ISRAEL
Malachi 1:2-5

Malachi lays the foundation for all that he will say in the four verses following the heading. He sets forth a proposition, and then offers the proof to sustain his proposition.

A. The Proposition (1:2).

The message begins with a grand assertion by Yahweh which can be translated either "I love you" (present perfect) or "I do love you" (perfect of certitude). In Hebrew the perfect can be used to express facts which were accomplished long before, or conditions and attributes which were acquired long before, but of which the effects still remain in the present. Hence the language underscores the unchanging love of Yahweh for his people. This grand announcement presupposes widespread skepticism regarding Israel's status with the Lord (1:2a).

Malachi verbalizes the doubts of the people in a question which he anticipates he will hear (or perhaps actually heard) in response to the assertion of Yahweh's love: "Wherein have you loved us?" The present trials apparently had caused them to forget all the past mercies of the Lord. Their doubt may have been rooted in several circumstances. They had returned from exile (as God had promised), and they had built their temple (as God had promised.) Yet the monarchy had not been re-established. As yet there was no sign of the glorious priest-king predicted by Zechariah. They were not a great and victorious people. Gentiles were not coming to worship at Jerusalem. Prosperity had not returned. Enemies had not been crushed.

Malachi answered the question of the people with a question. "Was not Esau Jacob's brother?" Every Jew would have known the answer to this question. Now the point: "Yet I have loved Jacob." God had treated the twin brothers very differently. By Esau and Jacob Malachi means the nations which were descended from these men. Compared to the lot of the Esauites, the Jacobites were most blessed.

B. The Proof (1:3-5).

Through the years Yahweh had loved Jacob, but he declared: "I have hated Esau." Compared to his love for Jacob the divine attitude toward Esau was hatred.[2] God had chosen or elected to use Jacob or Israel for his glorious purposes in this world as his special people. The choice was one of sovereign grace; it was undeserved. Esau was the eldest, the favorite son of his father. Yet Jacob was chosen. Jacob was not a righteous man in his youth, yet he was chosen. The choice here has nothing to do with eternal life for the Edomites are specifically included in messianic salvation (cf. Jer 49:11; Amos 9:12; Obad 19,21). God is simply contrasting here the history of two nations, the one blessed, the other unblessed (1:3a).

The evidence that God loved Esau less than Jacob could be observed in the condition of the nation Edom. "I have made his mountains a desolation." The inheritance of Esau, i.e., his land, had been taken over by "the jackals of the wilderness," i.e., the desert creatures. Malachi may be referring to the destruction of Edom by Nebuchadnezzar in the thirty-seventh year of his reign (Deane). On the other hand, the reference could be to the Nabataean invasion of Edom which resulted in the expulsion of the Edomites and their migration to the desert country of southern Judah. The exact date of this invasion is not known though it may have occurred during the lifetime of Malachi.

Edom's future prospects were as bleak as its present condition. The dispossessed Edomites boasted that they would reclaim the land and rebuild their country. Yahweh declared that they would never be able to make good on their boasts. Every time the Edomites attempted to rebuild, Yahweh would "throw them down." The Edomites were successively beaten down by the Nabataeans, the Macedonians, the Maccabees, the Romans and the Mohammedans (1:4a).

Because of the desolation of their once proud country men would call them "the border of wickedness," i.e., they would rightly conclude that Edom had been punished for some grave wickedness. The land of Edom would gain the reputation of being eternally condemned of God (1:4b).

Israel would observe from a distance, safe and secure in their own land, the tragedies which would befall Edom. Though Israel would have its share of setbacks, Edom's far more miserable circumstances would demonstrate God's watch care over his people (1:5).

Having established how God had displayed his love for Israel, Malachi charged first the priests and then the people with slighting that love. In this chapter the sins of the priests are considered. Malachi leveled several serious charges against the priests. They had polluted the altar, profaned the name, and perverted the covenant. For this the priests would experience punishment at the hands of their God.

THE POLLUTION OF THE ALTAR
Malachi 1:6-10

The most sacred duty which God delegated to priests under the law was their service at the altar of sacrifice. Here was where these priests helped sinful people find reconciliation with God. The ritual acts performed at that altar were rich in symbolism for Old Covenant worship. At the same time those rituals pointed forward to the perfect sacrifice of Christ. To officiate at that altar was a great honor and a solemn responsibility. Yet the postexilic priests polluted that altar both by their attitudes and by their actions.

A. Accusation and Denial (1:6).

The main body of the book begins with a double accusation against the priests and a double denial on the part of those same priests. The prophet accused the leaders of religion of despising God's name and desecrating God's altar.

To set up the accusation Malachi set forth a proposition: God is deserving of honor. A son honors his father and a servant his master. God was the father of Israel by creation, election, preservation and watchful guardianship (Deane). The Israelites were called in the law the children of God (Deut 14:1). Yet God did not receive the honor due a father. Nor did he receive the dread or fear (*mora'*) which a servant should feel for his master or king.[3] So in Malachi's day God was neither reverenced nor feared, just ignored (1:6a).

The disrespect for God was especially prevalent among the priests. Through Malachi Yahweh addressed these words to the priests "who despise my name." The Hebrew participle form denotes continuous manifestation of disrespect, a state of mind, a characteristic trait. The leaders of religion continuously mocked God and sneered at his name and will.

Malachi depicted the priests pompously denying that they had despised God's name. "Wherein have we despised your name?" They totally rejected the prophet's accusation (1:6b).

B. Unholy Offerings (1:7-8).

The priests were offering upon God's altar "polluted bread." Any sacrificial substance whether animal or vegetable which was presented to God was call "bread." These offerings were called "polluted" (*mego'al*) because God rejected them as unqualified or unfit. They were not being offered in accordance with the ceremonial law (cf. Lev 22 18f.).

The priests recognized the seriousness of the charge. They recognized that to offer polluted offerings was tantamount to polluting God himself. So with bluff and bluster they asked: "Wherein have we polluted you?" Malachi shot back the answer: "In that you say, The table of Yahweh is contemptible." Most likely the priests were not expressing this opinion audibly, certainly not publicly. Their actions, however, spoke louder than their words. Instead of regarding the temple service as an undeserved honor, they regarded it as a contemptible, miserable job. The altar here is called a "table" because there the sacrifices were "eaten" by fire (1:7).

The priests demonstrated their contempt for the altar of God by offering there unholy sacrifices. Blemished offerings were forbidden by the law; a sacrificial animal must be perfect (e.g., Lev 22:19-25). Yet these priests did not consider it "evil" to present blind, lame and sick animals as offerings to the Lord (1:8a).

Malachi challenged the priests to offer the same animals to the governor of the land. This implies that the governor in Judah during this period was accustomed to accept offerings from those he governed. Since Nehemiah refused to burden the people with such offerings (cf. Neh 5:14-18), this verse may indicate that Nehemiah was no longer governor. On the other hand, Malachi's challenge may be taken as hypothetical and general. In any case, such blemished offerings would not curry favor with an earthly ruler. On the contrary, a human superior would be insulted by such a present. Yet the priests thought that such animals were appropriate to present to the King of Kings as a sacrificial offering (1:8b).

C. Useless Intercession (1:9).

His voice oozing with sarcasm, Malachi urged the priests to "entreat the face of God." The verb (*chalah*) in the Piel stem means literally "to soothe or make sweet the face of anyone." The idea is to mollify, or entreat the favor of someone. In the case of God, this is done through worship and sacrifice. The basic function of priests was to seek a favorable hearing for the needs of God's people. If they succeeded in their ministry then Yahweh would "be gracious" to Israel (1:9a).

The expression "while this is being done by your hand" (lit., from your hand this has been) is difficult. The NASB renders "with such an offering on your part." The NIV is very similar. The idea seems to be that as long as they continue with their present sacrificial practices they need not expect any gracious response from the Lord. This is stated in the form of a question: "Will he accept any of your persons?", i.e., will he acknowledge you? Will he grant the favor to you? The implied answer, of course, is negative (1:9b).

D. Undesirable Service (1:10).

Verse 10 expresses a divine wish which is in effect also a threat. Malachi inserted a word (*gam*) which implies a thought wholly unexpected and shocking to the priests: "Oh that there were even one among you who would shut the doors!" The reference is to the doors of the inner court where the great altar stood. Rather than continue to insult God with their tainted sacrifices, it would be better, Malachi argued, to shut down the temple. Sacrifices were no longer accomplishing their purpose. They were lighting the altar fire "in vain," i.e., for nothing. The sacrifices were doing more harm than good. They angered God rather than pleased him (1:10a).

The reason God no longer desired temple worship is stated bluntly and personally: "I have no pleasure in you." Worship acts are not acceptable unless the worshipers are acceptable to the Lord. By their attitude the priests had forfeited their right to be worship leaders. Yahweh declared: "Neither will I accept an offering at your hand."

The term offering (*minchah*) is the general term for all sacrificial offerings, animal and vegetable (1:10b).

THE PROFANATION OF THE NAME
Malachi 1:11-16

The name of God—his character, reputation—was to be held in honor by all Israelites. One of the Ten Commandments proscribed taking God's name in vain (Exod 20:7). God's name can be profaned by actions and attitudes as well as words. The priests of Malachi's day were guilty of profaning the holy name in all three ways. Before, however, he made this case against the priests, Malachi announces a day in which God's name would be honored worldwide.

A. Future Honor of God's Name (1:11).

In contrast to the indifferent attitude and blasphemous actions of the postexilic priests, Yahweh announces a future day when he would be honored worldwide. "For from the rising of the sun even unto the going down of the same my name shall be great among the Gentiles." Some think that the context demands a present rather than a future tense. In this case the reference would be to the Jews who were scattered among the Gentiles in Malachi's day. More likely this is a prophecy of the conversion of the Gentiles in the days of Messiah. Among those Gentiles God's name would be "great," i.e., treated with the utmost respect (1:11a).

The worthy attitudes of the Gentiles would be demonstrated in worthy actions. "In every place incense shall be offered unto my name." The Hebrew participle implies habitual performance. Incense may symbolize prayer (cf. Rev 8:3-4). The incense would be accompanied by "a pure offering." This future devotion by those considered unclean and unworthy further rebukes the priests of Malachi's day and brands their actions as utterly reprehensible.

Under the Mosaic system any offering made apart from the temple was illegal and unclean. Yet this prophecy announces that all over the world such sacrifice would be offered by sincere worshipers and accepted by a holy God. The implication is that the Mosaic system would be replaced by a new worship system. In that day Gentiles would be included among the people of God. For emphasis the prophecy repeats the words: "my name shall be great among the Gentiles" (1:11b).

B. Present Dishonor of God's Name (1:12-14).

Following the brief glance into the glorious future, Malachi returns to the inglorious present. The same name which would be treated with great reverence by Gentiles was currently being profaned, i.e., treated lightly, irreverently, by the priests.

1. The priests regarded God's altar as polluted (1:12a). In verse 7 these priests denied that they had polluted God's table or altar. Their actions, however, indicated a contempt for the entire sacrificial ritual.

2. The priests complained about their compensation (1:12b). They regarded the "fruit" of the altar as "contemptible." Part of priestly compensation came from the offerings which were placed on the altar. Apparently the priests were complaining because God got the best part of the sacrificial animals while the priests were only getting the leftovers.

3. The priests regarded their work as irksome (1:13a). Concerning their ministerial labors the priests were saying "Behold, what a weariness it is!" The routine of sacrifice had become irksome to them. Slaying the animals, skinning them, gutting them and cutting them up was a filthy, bloody job. The material reward was simply not adequate. The priests "snuffed at it" as one might snuff at spoiled food with putrid smell. To put it bluntly, the sacrificial ritual stunk![4]

4. The priests brought unworthy sacrifices (1:13b). To that altar which they despised in their heart the priests brought "that which was violently taken." Some take the reference to be to animals stolen or obtained by fraud. Others think the sacrificial animals had been snatched from the jaws of wild beasts, hence mutilated and unfit for sacrifice. Sick and lame animals were also brought to the altar. Rhetorically God asked, "Should I accept this at your hand?" The obvious answer is, No!

5. The priests cooperated with hypocritical worshipers (1:14a). Perhaps influenced by the attitude of the priests, the worshipers were attempting to deceive or cheat God in numerous ways. The situation envisioned is that a worshiper had available that which fully met the requirements of a vow which he had taken. Once the emergency was past, however, he cheated God by offering a less valuable blemished animal instead. Apparently the priests winked at this religious charade.

6. *The priests failed to recognize the greatness of God (1:14b).* All of the failings of the priests could be traced to one fundamental theological error. Their concept of God did not remotely correspond to the truth about God. First, they did not recognize the position of God: "I am a great King." Second, they did not understand Yahweh's power. He was commander of all hosts of earth and heaven. Third, they did not recognize the prestige of Yahweh. One day his name would be "reverenced" (*nora'*) among the Gentiles.

THE PUNISHMENT OF THE PRIESTS
Malachi 2:1-4

Priestly disdain, dishonor and disrespect demanded punishment. In terms of its origin that punishment is called here a "commandment." In terms of content that punishment is here called a "curse."

A. The Threat of the Curse (2:1-2).

Because of their contemptuous attitude the priests merited punishment from the Lord. "And now, O priests, this commandment is for you." The threat or announcement of judgment is called a "commandment" because God ordained it and issued orders for its execution (2:1).

The priests would face the commandment of judgment if they did not "hearken" or "lay it to heart." The repetition of the idea in different terms serves to emphasize the importance of this conditional clause. What must the priests do to avoid the "commandment"? They must "give honor to my name." This was the primary function of priests. This honor would manifest itself in due regard for the proper forms and rules of sacrifice. Failure to conform to the requirements of Yahweh would bring down Yahweh's "curse" or wrath upon the offending priests (2:2a).

The curse would be sent, not only on the person of the priests, but upon their "blessings" as well. The reference could be (1) to the blessing which they had receive in being ordained to the priesthood; or (2) to the blessing which the priests would pronounce over the people (cf. Num 6:23-27). In fact, Yahweh asserts, "I have cursed it already!" The curse or wrath of God had already begun to work in the ministries of those priests. The singular suffix "it" may refer to each individual blessing of the many just mentioned.[5] Turning a blessing into a curse was considered the ultimate punishment (2:2b).

B. The Result of the Curse (2:3).

The results of the curse on the priesthood would be threefold. First, Yahweh declared "Behold, I will rebuke your seed." The meaning seems to be that God would forbid the seed to sprout and grow and bear fruit because of these disobedient priests. Consequently these priests would not receive their dues from the people.[6]

Dishonor would be the second aspect of the curse. "I will spread dung upon your faces." The "dung" is the undigested food and stomach juices in the sacrificial animal. The dung would be smeared upon them during the great festivals when the priests were the center of attention in their most splendid vestments. This action would render the priests unclean and unfit for the discharge of their functions. Most take this clause to be figurative for the contempt which the priests would come to have in the eyes of the people. The fact that the text uses the second person possessive "your feasts" and not "my feasts" is significant. The contemptuous disobedience of the priests nullified the spiritual value of the feasts.

The third penalty of the curse is this: "you shall be carried away unto it," i.e., unto the dung heap. According to the law the dung of the sacrificial animals was to be carried forth and burned outside the camp (Exod 29:14; Lev 4:12; 16:27). The priests would be treated as filth by the people. They would be swept out of office (2:3b).

C. The Design of the Curse (2:4).

The curse against the priests would be designed to accomplish two objectives. First, when they began to experience the effects of the curse the priests would realize that "I have sent unto you this commandment." They would recognize the source of their calamity and the reason for it. Second, the purging of the priesthood would fulfill the stipulations of the covenant with Levi. The reference is to the selection of the tribe of Levi for the ministry of the sanctuary (2:4).

ENDNOTES

1. In prophetic literature the term *massa'* is used about twenty times in reference to a prophetic utterance. The term previously has appeared in the headings of the books of Nahum and Habakkuk. Zechariah titled chapters 9-11 and chapter 12-14 respectively with this term. For this reason some have proposed that Malachi originally was an appendix to Zechariah. The style of Malachi is so different from that of the preceding book that it is difficult to think that it could ever have been a part of that book.

2. Leah was "hated" (*senu'ah*), i.e., unloved, by Jacob (Gen 29:31). The law of Moses anticipated a situation in which a man might have two wives (not necessarily simultaneously) and one of them be "hated" (*senu'ah*), i.e., unloved or loved less than the other (Deut 21:15).

3. The word "master" is a plural in Hebrew. This may be an example of a majestic plural denoting a king. Cf. 1 Kgs 22:17; 2 Chr 18:16; Isa 19:4.

4. Jewish tradition reads "snuffed at me," i.e., God. Possibly here is an intentional scribal alteration to remove the harshness from the passage. The scribes could not bear the thought that priests would "snuff" at God!

5. The Septuagint (followed by KJV) has a plural suffix.

6. The ancient versions follow a slightly different vocalization of the Hebrew which means "shoulder." Thus some scholars interpret the verse to mean that God would take away from these priests the "shoulder" or power of performing their official duties (Deane). Others think that the "shoulder" might be the portion of the sacrificial animal allotted to the priests (cf. Lev 7:31-32).

CHAPTER FORTY-NINE

Broken Covenants
Malachi 2:5-16

In a covenant two parties bind themselves with solemn oaths to perform certain responsibilities one to another. Socially a nation is in deep trouble when such covenants are broken. Spiritually the breaking of one's oath brings inevitably the wrath of God both in temporal judgment, and finally in eternal judgment. In the center section of his book Malachi describes how three covenants had been broken. In their sin against Yahweh the priests had corrupted the covenant with Levi. On the other hand the people had broken the national covenant by intermarrying with foreign women. In the process of doing this, solemn marriage covenants with Jewish wives were also being abrogated.

THE PRIESTLY COVENANT PERVERTED
Malachi 2:5-9

The covenant with the tribe of Levi involved certain privileges and responsibilities. Malachi first sets forth the ideal of that ancient covenant. He then points out how the priests of his day had shattered the ideal image of the priesthood.

A. The Ideal of the Covenant (2:5-7).

A covenant is an agreement between two parties. In the covenant with Levi God's part was to grant "life and peace." God granted to Levi the undisturbed enjoyment of life, abundance and prosperity. Along with the blessings of life and peace, God gave to Levi "fear." Some take this to be a reference to reverence imparted by God to Levi and through him to the priesthood. Another view is that God granted the blessings of life and peace so that he might fear. The very thought of losing the high privilege of priesthood by disdain or carelessness was horrifying to Levi (2:5a).

Levi responded on his part to the covenant in that "he feared me and before my name he was afraid." The proper response to God's gracious gifts is always reverence and humility. At Mt. Sinai God stipulated that the tribe of Levi, led by Aaron, be set aside for priestly service. The family of Aaron occupied the priesthood, and the remainder of the tribe had secondary sacerdotal responsibilities. Malachi is suggesting that those original priests took their responsibilities seriously and carried out their functions reverently (2:5b).

The priestly covenant envisioned a high standard. First, the priest was to be incorruptible in doctrine. "The law of truth was in his mouth." The term "law" *(torah)* embraces all forms of instruction. The priests were not to teach their own views, human theories nor speculations. They were to teach only the infallible and unchangeable truth as revealed in the written word.

Second, the priest was to be unwavering in judgments. "Iniquity (lit., crookedness) was not found in his lips." They were not to twist the law to fit their own fancies. Their legal decisions were to be made without prejudice.

Third, the priest was to be devout in conduct. "In peace and in uprightness he walked with me." His life as well as his teaching was to be pure and good. He was to be a friend of God, walking in "peace" *(shalom,* i.e., full harmony) with him. A personal walk of godliness and fellowship is in view.

Fourth, the priest was to be focused in labor. "And many they caused to turn from iniquity." Their faithful words and work would cause many to turn from sin (2:6).

Fifth, the priest was to be immersed in knowledge. "For the lips of the priest should keep knowledge." It was the duty of every priest to study the law and to teach it faithfully. This would include the knowledge of correct ritual and ceremonial rules. The knowledge here, however, is also the true knowledge of God that finds expression in a moral life and spiritual aspirations. The priest was the appointed interpreter of the law. The people should have confidence in their priest to teach the holy word accurately.

Sixth, the priest was to be honored in his office. "He is the messenger of Yahweh of hosts." The term "messenger" (*mal'ach*) is used historically in the Old Testament of (1) the prophet Haggai, (2) angels, and (3) the Angel of Yahweh. The term is used prophetically of (1) John the Baptist and (2) Messiah. This passage establishes the importance of the priesthood and the great honor which devolved on those who filled that office (2:7).

B. Betrayal of the Covenant Ideal (2:8-9).

The priests of Malachi's day had betrayed every standard of that covenant with the priesthood. First, they were perverse in life. "But as for you, you have turned from the way," i.e., the way of holiness. Their lives were the opposite of exemplary.

Second, they were pernicious in example. "You have caused many to stumble in the law." By their example and teaching they had made the law a stumblingblock, causing many to disregard and disobey it.

Third, the priests were unfaithful in commitment. "You have corrupted the covenant of Levi." They no longer paid God due reverence and obedience They were covenant breakers.

Fourth, the priests were contemptible in reputation. "Therefore I, even I, have made you contemptible and base before the people." They had despised the Lord, so he had caused them to be despised before the people. The verb could be regarded as a prophetic perfect and rendered as a future in English.

Fifth, the priests were negligent in duty. They had been punished because they had not "kept my ways." They had disregarded the priestly directives of the law.

Sixth, the priests had been prejudiced in judgment. They had "respect of person in the law." They had perverted judgment and shown partiality in the administration of the law.

THE NATIONAL COVENANT BROKEN
Malachi 2:10-12

Israelites were forbidden to marry those who were devotees of pagan gods (Ex 34:16; Deut 7:3). Yet intermarriage with unbelievers was a major problem in the postexilic community. A few years before the time of Malachi Ezra had forced those who had married heathen women to divorce them (Ezra 10:3-5). The problem had arisen again. Malachi points out three terrible truths about these unlawful marriages.

A. The Covenant Defiled (2:10).

God was the father of Israel. He had created this special nation at Mt. Sinai. The rhetorical question "Is there not one father to all of us?" does not teach the doctrine of the universal fatherhood of God. Rather here the text is stressing the uniqueness of Israel as a nation. The rhetorical question "Did not one God create us?" does not refer to the original creation, but to the creative act by which God chose Israel as his own people (2:10a).

If in fact Israel was a special creation of God, a holy family, "Why do we deal treacherously each man with his brother?" The prophet includes himself as a member of the sinful nation. The sin of the people, which Malachi has yet to identify, is a sin against brotherly love. Intermarriage defiled "the covenant of our fathers." The practice was a menace to the distinctive faith which was the basis of God's covenant with Israel as well as the national existence. God had often warned against marrying the daughters of unbelievers.[1]

B. The Nation Defiled (2:11).

In the midst of the covenant nation Israel, of which the postexilic community was the representative, an "abomination" had been committed. The term is used to describe pagan idolatry and immorality. In

Jerusalem, the site of the temple and capital of the nation, the abomination was evident. "Judah has profaned the holiness of Yahweh." Holiness is a fundamental attribute of God. Because Yahweh is holy, his people were to be holy (i.e., set apart from the world of sin) in all areas of their lives. Now, however, the holiness of the nation had been violated. The fact that God loved Israel so much aggravated the treachery of the national conduct (2:11a).

The men of Israel were guilty of the sin of intermarriage with unbelievers. "Judah . . . has married the daughter of a strange god," i.e., a woman who adhered to a foreign deity. Such marriages had always been condemned because of the danger of seduction into idolatry. The principle of holiness—separation from the world—had thus been violated (2:11b).

C. Judgment Announced (2:12).

Those who had disregarded God's command to refrain from marriage with the heathen would face a terrible judgment. "Yahweh will cut off to the man who does this awaker and answerer from the tents of Jacob." Some take this to mean that both the sinner and his kin would be exterminated. More probably, however, is the interpretation that the transgressor and his descendants would be deprived of their position as members of the covenant nation. The expression "awaker and answerer"[2] is probably a military phrase derived from the challenge of sentinels and the answer thereto. In time the phrase became a proverbial expression denoting all the inhabitants of a city (2:12a).

Even if those guilty of intermarriage were faithful in temple worship, they would still be "cut off" by Yahweh. Propitiatory offerings would not placate the Lord. One cannot hope to find forgiveness for sins deliberately committed without genuine repentance and cessation of the offensive act (2:12b).[3]

THE MARRIAGE COVENANT ABROGATED
Malachi 2:13-16

Marriage was instituted by God and governed by his law. In Malachi's day the people had forgotten the fundamental purpose of marriage. They also were disobeying the divine principles which governed that institution. Malachi charged them with unlawful divorces as well as unlawful marriages.

Divorce under the law of Moses was permitted. If a husband found some indecency in his wife he was permitted to send her away so long as he provided her with a legal document declaring her to be a free woman. Remarriage following such a lawful divorce was permitted (Deut 24:1-4). Unlawful divorce would be the casting off of a wife for any reason other than indecent behavior. Unlawful divorce was another sin against the covenant which had become common in the postexilic community. The prophet makes four observations about this sin.

A. Unlawful Divorce Hurts Innocent People (2:13).

"You cover the altar of Yahweh with tears, with weeping, and with sighing." Probably this lamentation comes from the wives who had been cast out in favor of the younger pagan women. They took their agony and anger to the temple altar.[4] Intermarriage with unbelievers had created a barrier—a barrier of tears—between the sinners and God. He could no longer regarded with favor any of their offerings (2:13).

B. Unlawful Divorce Violates a Covenant (2:14).

The guilty men denied responsibility for the agonizing wailing at the altar. So Malachi sharpened his indictment. First he noted that Yahweh had been a witness between each offender and the wife of his youth. Apparently God had witnessed their marriage vows. He likewise had witnessed how these same wives were being treacherously treated by their husbands. The expression "wife of your youth" is designed to evoke emotional recollections of happier days. Surely the passing of years should not weaken marital love but rather purify it, solidify it and deepen it (2:14a).[5]

The hardened sinners suppressed the memories of youthful joy and the solemn vows of marital commitment. They "dealt treacherously" against their Jewish wives. The one who initiates an unlawful divorce is a traitor! Only for the cause of fornication may a believer lawfully initiate divorce proceedings. All other grounds are unlawful.

The language indicates the seriousness of divorce. In the ancient world women were virtually destitute after divorce, especially if they had no male children to care for them. Casting off such a faithful spouse to satisfy the lust of the flesh is therefore considered by God a treacherous act.

The divorce of their Jewish spouses was especially reprehensible for two reasons. First, she was "your companion." The noun comes from a root meaning "to bind, join or unite." God joined together man and wife in a union which was to be severed only by death. Godly men were to cleave to their wives in love and affection (Gen 2:24). Second, she was "your covenant wife" or the wife of your covenant. The persons wronged were those with which these men had entered the solemn covenant of marriage.[6] Solemn vows of fidelity had been exchanged before God and men. Now those marriage covenants had been set asunder because of the lust of these men.

C. Unlawful Divorce Frustrates Divine Purpose (2:15).

Malachi 2:15 is the most controversial and difficult verse in the entire book. First, Malachi asked, "And did he not make one?" The reference seems to be the original marriage. Jesus may have been referring to this verse in Matthew 19:4. The first rhetorical question calls attention to the fact that in the beginning God created only one pair and made them one flesh.[7] "Although he had the residue of the Spirit," i.e., the life-giving spirit or creative power. The point is that God could have made several wives for Adam (2:15a).

A second rhetorical question further develops the accusation of the prophet. "And wherefore one?" i.e., Why did God make one flesh, one pair in the beginning? The answer: "He sought a godly seed." Marriage was designed by God to perpetuate a godly seed on earth. Ultimately that godly seed would include Messiah (cf. Gen 3:15).

Based on the implications of his two rhetorical questions Malachi sets forth a stern warning: "Therefore, take heed to your spirit," i.e., your spiritual life, your faith in and love for God. "Against the wife of your youth do not deal treacherously." Persistent disobedience in the matter of divorce can cause one to lose what spiritual life which he has. The warning is made even stronger by being addressed in the second person to the guilty parties.

D. Unlawful Divorce Angers God (2:16).

Another reason the actions of the men of the postexilic community stood condemned is now set forth in a first person declaration. "For I hate divorce, says Yahweh, the God of Israel." God hates divorce because it was not a part of his original plan. He hates divorce for what it does to women and children. The man who treacherously divorces his covenant wife "covers his garment with violence." The idea here is that divorce is like a filthy spot on a man's garment, on his reputation, his life.

ENDNOTES

1. E.g., see Exod 34:16; Deut 7:3; Josh 23:12,13. Ezra contended against the practice (chs. 9-10). Nehemiah fought it as well (Neh 13:23-28).
2. Other suggestions as to the meaning of the Hebrew phrase: (1) master and scholar; (2) son and grandson; (3) master and servant; (4) stranger and kinsman.
3. Some think that the "one who offers an offering to Yahweh" is the priest who attempted to offer an offering to atone for the sin of one who intermarried, rather than the sinner himself.
4. Others think that the tears are those of the men themselves who realize that their sacrifices are no longer being accepted by God.
5. Theo. Laetsch, *Bible Commentary: The Minor Prophets* (St. Louis: Concordia, 1956), p. 527.
6. Another interpretation: the divorced wife belonged to the covenant between God and Israel, i.e., was of Jewish faith as opposed to the daughter of a strange god.
7. Traditional Jewish interpreters offer this interpretation: The people are trying to justify divorcing their wives. "The one" is Abraham. He "divorced" Hagar. Yes, but he had a godly spirit; he was seeking godly seed. The RSV offers yet another interpretation: "Has not the one God made us and sustained us for the spirit of life?" The NASB renders the first clause as a statement: "But not one has done so who has a remnant of the Spirit." This seems to mean that no truly spiritual man would ever have divorced his covenant wife.

CHAPTER FIFTY

The People Sin Against Love
Malachi 2:17-4:6

The people of the postexilic community also stood guilty before God of terrible sins. Malachi has set forth the sin of the priests against their God. Now he identifies the four great sins of the populace.

THE SIN OF DOUBT AND SKEPTICISM
Malachi 2:17-3:6

Malachi addressed a complaint of the people which he saw as an evidence of doubt. He answered that skepticism with a dramatic announcement of the coming of Messiah.

A. The Complaint of the People (2:17).

Skepticism wearies God. "You have wearied Yahweh with your words." The Hebrew perfect tense describes the act in its completion. Again the people demanded proof. "Wherein have we wearied him?" Malachi offered as proof the fact that they were saying, "Everyone who does evil is good in the eyes of Yahweh." Here is the age-old complaint: the wicked prosper while the righteous are in low estate. The underlying assumption here is that prosperity always results from divine blessing and implies divine approval. God must "delight" in the wicked else they would not be so blessed.

The words "or where is the God of judgment" are not a second complaint, but the logical conclusion which the people had reached. Either evil is pleasing to God or there is no God of justice. Skeptics through the ages have echoed similar arguments against the God who has revealed himself as absolutely just.

B. The Promise to the People (3:1).

The God of judgment was nearer than any of the skeptics imagined. Malachi stressed that the coming of God would be both certain and sudden.

1. His coming is certain (3:1a). An announcement of supreme importance is introduced by the word "Behold!" The term suggests something shocking, yet certain to happen. Yahweh declared: "I will send my messenger." The New Testament identifies this messenger as John the Baptist.[1] This messenger would "prepare the way before me." The verb means "to turn aside, turn away," thus "remove or clear." John prepared the way for the coming of God by preaching repentance and removing sin which stood between God and his people. The first person singular pronoun clearly identifies Yahweh with Messiah.

2. His coming is sudden (3:1b). Following the work of the preparatory messenger (John the Baptist) "the Lord whom you are seeking shall suddenly come." The skeptics had asked, "Where is the God of judgment?" The Hebrew expression *ha-adon*, "the Lord," appears eight times in the Old Testament. In each of the seven other occurrences it is used alongside the proper name Yahweh (e.g., Exod 23:17; Isa 1:24; 3:1). Thus "the Lord" (Yahweh) is about to come, the God of judgment whom the skeptics were seeking. The term "suddenly" indicates that his coming would be unexpected. The announcement of his birth and the commencement of his ministry some thirty years after his birth were both unexpected.

The Lord would suddenly come "to his temple." The change in

persons from *me* to *his* should be noted. He who comes is the same one who authorized the temple to be built in the Old Testament. Jesus was presented as an infant in the temple (Luke 2:22ff.). He also visited the temple for teaching purposes (cf. John 2:13; 5:1ff.; 7:14ff.).[2]

The Lord who would suddenly come to his temple is further identified as "the messenger of the covenant." This is the only place where this title is employed. Apparently this "messenger of the covenant" is the same as "the angel of Yahweh" who appears throughout the Old Testament as a visible manifestation of God (cf. Heb 9:15). The "covenant" would be that New Covenant announced by Jesus and ratified by his shed blood (3:1b).[3]

C. The Purpose of his Coming (3:2).

The Jews expected Messiah to come to judge the heathen. Malachi warned the skeptics that they would be the first to be judged. "But who endures the day of his coming? and who stands when he appears?" None of the ungodly would be able to stand under the burden of this judgment (3:2a).

Two illustrations point to the judicial purpose of his coming. First, "he is like the fire of the refiner." The idea is that he would burn away all corrupt ingredients that were mixed in with the precious metal. Messiah is the great discriminator. At his coming he would sever good people from bad. Second, Messiah also would be "like the soap of clothes-cleansers." The term "soap" (*borit*) is lye, alkali, particularly vegetable alkali or potash, obtained by leaching the ashes of plants.[4] The cleaner massaged the clothes by treading upon them. Thus Messiah would be a cleanser, one who would purge sin from the lives of his people.

D. The Result of his Coming (3:3-6).

The result of the coming of Messiah is twofold. He would purify the priests and punish the wicked.

1. Purification of the priests (3:3-4). The coming one would sit "as a refiner and purifier of silver," i.e., he would sit as a judge. The prophet confines himself to the first of the two images presented in the previous verse. The process of purification would begin with the priests. Some think that the cleansing of the temple by Jesus is the focus here. Others mention the fact that the teaching of Christ was directed against the religious leaders of his day. Still others point to the conversion of many of the Levitical priests in Acts 6:7. Actually the Hebrew uses participles implying that the refining work would go on continually. Perhaps the fulfillment is in the continuous cleansing of the antitypical Levitical priesthood, the church of Jesus Christ (1 Pet 2:9; 1 John 1:9).

The purified priests would be to Yahweh "offerers of an offering in righteousness." Their offerings would then in every respect meet the requirements of the Lord (3:3).

"Then shall the offering of Judah and Jerusalem be pleasant (lit., a sweet savor) to Yahweh." The purified priests would offer pure offerings which would be acceptable once again "as in ancient days." The golden age of sacrifice—the days of Moses, or David, or Solomon or the Patriarchs—would be restored (3:4). The prophet does not necessarily expect that the Mosaic ritual would last forever and be maintained throughout the world. Rather he is using terms with which the Jews were conversant to express the worship of the new covenant. It is the church of the New Testament which Malachi here foresees. Every member of this church is a member of the purified priesthood (1 Pet 2:5,9). Each is capable of offering up sweet savor sacrifices to God (Phil 4:18).

2. *Punishment of the wicked (3:5-6).* Those the Lord cannot refine and purify come under his judgment. "I will come near to you to judgment." The Lord (in the person of Messiah) will be the judge. He will also be the prosecuting witness: "I will be a swift witness." Five classes of sinners are cited as examples of those who would stand condemned in that judgment. First, he bears witness against "the sorcerers," those who dabble in the occult. Second, the "adulterers" stand condemned. God has always warned about the consequences of sexual immorality. Third, Messiah bears witness against "the false swearers," i.e., those who misuse the name of God in solemn oaths by swearing to that which is untrue.

Fourth, oppressors will experience the divine judgment. The victims of these oppressors might be the hireling, the widow, the fatherless or the sojourner. The hireling's wages were to be paid at sundown. To withhold those wages constituted oppression. To deny the legal rights of the sojourner or resident alien also constituted oppression. Finally, God's judgment would fall on those who do not fear Yahweh of hosts. Obeying God is the supreme manifestation of godly fear or reverence (3:5).

The reason the Lord must come to purify the priests and punish the wicked is because Yahweh does not change. He cannot be satisfied with less than perfect holiness (cf. Lev 11:44f.). Thus at some point he must initiate judgment against those who transgress his law. Yet his absolute justice does not negate his boundless love and compassion. "Therefore you, O sons of Jacob, are not consumed" by his uncompromising holiness. The Jews here are called "the sons of Jacob" because they were so much like their ancestor. Like Jacob, the Jews of Malachi's day were guilty of deceit in respect to God and man (3:6).

THE SIN OF DISHONESTY AND THEFT
Malachi 3:7-12

The attention of Malachi now shifts to another sin of the people. First he presents his indictment for the sin of dishonesty. Malachi then indicates the predicament which had befallen the people because of this sin. Then the prophet offers an inducement to bring the people out of this sin.

A. The Indictment (3:7-8).

Disobedience was an ever recurring sin in Israel. "From the days of your fathers you have turned from my statutes" (cf. Zech 1:4). Divine blessing under the Old Covenant economy was contingent upon obedience to God's law. To turn aside from God's statutes in attitude leads to disregard of the law in practice. Therefore the charge is leveled against them: you "have not kept them," i.e., the statutes (3:7a).

In spite of the fact that they deserved to be rejected as covenant breakers, God graciously pleads with his people to return to him. Yet the impudent people respond: "Wherein shall we return?" This answer indicates how thoroughly depraved these Jews had become.

Their self-righteousness blinded them to their own need for repentance (3:7b).[5]

The specific charge is couched in the form of a rhetorical question. "Will a man rob God?" The verb *kaba'* occurs only here and in Proverbs 22:23. Jewish tradition took the word to mean *to rob, to take by force*.[6] Again the people vehemently deny the charge. They demanded proof of this indictment. "Wherein have we robbed you?" The Lord fired back the response: "with regard to tithes and offerings." The tithe was an annual contribution to the Levites of one tenth of the yield of the field (Num 18:21). The offering (*terumah*) may be offerings in general (Exod 25:2) or the heave offering which was given to the priests (Num 18:11). They had robbed God by withholding from his ministers those gifts which were rightfully theirs. The unfaithfulness of the priestly family was no excuse for failing to comply with the law of tithing (3:8).

B. The Predicament (3:9).

The disobedience of the people in respect to their tithes and offerings had brought a curse upon their land just as the unfaithfulness of the priests had brought a curse upon their ministry (cf. 2:2). The curse probably took the form of drought, poor crops and economic depression. Yet even while the curse was in progress and in evidence the people were continuing to rob God. The Hebrew word order stresses (1) the audacity of this theft: "and *me* you are robbing;" and (2) the universality of this despicable sin: "this whole nation" (3:9).

C. The Inducement (3:10-12).

As an inducement to repentance in respect to tithes and offerings, Malachi sets forth a challenge, a commitment, and a consequence.

1. A challenge (3:10a). God challenged his stingy people to "bring all the tithe into the storehouse," i.e., the temple treasury. A chamber in the temple court was set aside for the collection of the tithe and heave offerings (cf. Neh 10:38; 12:44; 13:5,12). Only if they were faithful in this respect would there be "meat in my house," i.e., food. Probably the reference is to the food of the priests and Levites. Another possibility is that the "food" is the sacrificial animals.

Yahweh then challenges these people to "prove me now herewith." If they bring the tithes into the temple storehouse they would see a change in their fortunes.

2. *A commitment (3:10b-11).* The Lord committed himself to respond to the faithful tithing of his people in five wonderful ways. First, he promised abundant rain. Yahweh would "open the windows of heaven," i.e., send abundant showers. This abundant rain would be the down payment on other blessings. Second, he promised to send "a blessing." While this may be a second allusion to the drought-ending rain, the expression also may include other abundant blessings as well. Third, God would continue to pour out this blessing "until there is no measure." They would be blessed superabundantly (3:10b).

Fourth, the Lord promised pest protection. "And I will rebuke the devourer for your good." The reference is to locusts which may have been ravishing the country in Malachi's day. Nothing would be allowed to injure the crops. Fifth, God promised crop maturity. "Neither shall the vine cast its fruit into the field on account of you." The reference is to premature production of unripe, undeveloped fruit. God would prevent such a waste of resources (3:11).

3. *A consequence (3:12).* The prosperity of Judah would be so conspicuous that the Jews would be the envy of all the nations. "And all nations shall call you blessed." The heaven-blessed Jews would become "a delightful land," i.e., a land in which God is well pleased; a fruitful and well nourished land. Here the personal pronoun is repeated for emphasis: "You, you yourselves" shall be a delightful land. Obedience was the key to blessing under the Old Testament economy.

THE SIN OF DISILLUSIONMENT AND CYNICISM
Malachi 3:13-4:3

The last accusation against the people revolves around the words of certain cynics, the words of the faithful, and the words of God.

A. Words of the Sinners (3:13-15).

Yahweh charges that the words of the people had been hard or harsh against God. They had used offensive language. Again the hardened sinners denied the accusation by means of a rhetorical question. So the Lord spelled out what those offensive words were (3:13).

First, the people were negative in their attitude toward serving God. "You have said, It is vain to serve God," i.e., serving God is unprofitable business. They thought that serving God demanded too much and returned too little! They saw no value in keeping the ordinances and ritual observations. "And what profit is it that we have kept his charge." They were observing his ordinances, especially the ritual observances. They fasted, mourned, lamented, and walked in sackcloth "before Yahweh of hosts." Worshiping God was as boring to them as a funeral ritual. When the people said "we have walked mournfully before Yahweh of hosts" most likely they were exaggerating in order to articulate their disgust for temple ritual (3:14).

Second, the people viewed the wicked as more blessed than the righteous. "And now we call blessed (or happy) the proud." The proud (*zedim*) in the Old Testament are the self-willed, malicious, unprincipled, and turbulent; those who defied God by disregarding his precepts. The skeptics also claimed that "the workers of wickedness are built up," i.e., they prosper in spite of their wickedness. In the opinion of the skeptics, those who arrogantly disregarded God's law were happy and prosperous. "Also they try God and are delivered." They seemed to challenge God and yet escape any punishment. Thus in the eyes of many, serving God was of no benefit, and disobeying him brought no punishment (3:15).

B. Word of the Saints (3:16).

Among the skeptics was a cadre of faithful, like the seven thousand in Elijah's day who had not bowed the knee to Baal. In the midst of national skepticism and unbelief they would encourage one another with their words. What they said to each other is not recorded, but it was certainly well-pleasing to God. Perhaps they argued with the impious skeptics; perhaps they warned others against them. If they questioned the circumstances of life it was in full faith that God does only that which is good (3:16a).

God did not forget the faithful within the nation. "A book of remembrance was written before him." The Lord had heard their words and those words were written before him. The book represents God's providence and omniscience, his ever-wakeful care, his unfailing knowledge (3:16b).[7] In this book of remembrance Yahweh would take note of "those who fear Yahweh" and "those who think on his name." The "name" of God is his self-revelation; his word. So the Lord assured believers, those who truly reverenced God and possessed God-consciousness, that they would not be forgotten.

C. Words of God (3:17-4:3).

Yahweh responded to the words of faith spoken by the saints in Zion. He spoke of four coming days.

1. A glorious day (3:17-18). A day was coming when God would acknowledge his own. "And they shall be mine, says Yahweh." On that day they would be a "special possession" (*segullah*), i.e., a possession exclusively belonging to Yahweh. At Sinai centuries before this term had been used for all Israel (Exod 19:5; cf. 1 Pet 2:9). Now it applied only to the faithful minority (3:17a).

The Lord would have pity on those who were his special possession "as a man has pity upon his son who serves him." The ultimate fulfillment of this promise is in heaven. While others are being punished the faithful will be spared in that day (3:17b).

In that day the faithful would "again discern between the righteous and the wicked, between him that serves God, and him that serves him not." In times past again and again they had abundant opportunity to observe, both in their national and individual lives, the different treatment of the saint and sinner. The day of final discrimination, however, was coming when all men would see virtue rewarded and vice punished. In that day all will have plain and convincing proof of God's moral government of the world (3:18).

2. A terrible day (4:1). For the wicked a terrible day was coming. "For behold the day comes, burning like an oven." Fire is often associated with the day of judgment in both testaments. It is a symbol of the holiness of God which consumes all impurity. It also represents the punishment inflicted on the wicked. In that burning day "all the proud and all who do wickedness shall be stubble." Those that the skeptics regarded as happy and blessed in this world would become "stubble," i.e., the worthless stubs that remain after the wheat has been cut and gathered into the garners (4:1a).

"The day that comes shall burn them up, says Yahweh of hosts."

Throughout the Old Testament the day of Yahweh is a day of judgment upon the wicked. The proud and wicked would be left neither "root nor branch." As far as this world is concerned, the wicked would be totally removed. This formula has also been found in Phoenician literature. The figure is of a tree given up to be burned so that nothing is left of it (4:1b). John the Baptist used this same figure (Matt 3:10).

3. *A healing day* (4:2). Those who continued to fear Yahweh's name, i.e., worship, honor and revere him, would experience a visitation of healing in that future day. These would be those who remained faithful in spite of the skepticism of the majority (cf. 3:16). "The Sun of Righteousness shall appear." This appears to be a title for the Messiah. That Messiah would bring light is a major theme of messianic prophecy.[8] Zacharias called him "the Dayspring from on high" (Luke 1:78), an apparent reference to this passage.[9] The figure points to Jesus as light after darkness, warmth after cold, beauty after bleakness, and joy after gloom (4:2a).

The Sun of Righteousness is said to have "healing in its wings." The rays of that Sun would radiate healing for broken hearts and perplexed minds. He would awaken the righteous to a new life as the sun in the spring awakens nature to a new life. The figure of the winged sun may have been suggested to the prophet by the winged solar disc of Egypt, Babylon, Assyria and Persia.

That Sun rise would usher in a joyous new day for the faithful. "And you shall go forth and leap as calves from the stall." An animal which has been penned up for some time expresses joyous abandon when first released. So the figure here expresses freedom after oppression, joy after gloom, vigor after vicissitudes. Paul may have had this verse in mind when he spoke about the "glorious liberty of the sons of God" (Rom 8:21).

4. *A victorious day (4:3).* In that day of liberty and light the faithful, empowered by their Lord, would "tread down the wicked." The picture here is of the treading of grapes in a winepress (cf. Rev 14:19-20). "For they shall be like ashes under the soles of your feet." The wicked would be reduced to ashes by the burning judgment of God. The basic idea here is that the oppressed will be victorious over the oppressor "in the day which I am making." God is currently

preparing that day when the righteous will be rewarded and the wicked will be vanquished.[10]

CONCLUDING WORDS
Malachi 4:4-6

The prophecy of Malachi concludes with an exhortation and a warning.

A. An Exhortation (4:4).

The Lord exhorted his people to "remember the law of Moses my servant." Malachi thus sets his seal of approval on the Pentateuch. This is a fitting climax to the entire Old Testament. The law of Moses after all came by divine command in the range of mountains called "Horeb." The particular peak where Yahweh entered into a covenant with his people was Sinai. The mention here of the place where the law was given would serve the dual purpose of (1) reminding the readers of the awful wonders that accompanied the giving of that law; and (2) underscore the divine origin of that law. The entire law of Moses is characterized as "statutes and ordinances." These terms include all the enactments, legal, moral and ceremonial.[11] The best way to prepare for the day which Yahweh was preparing was to give heed to God's law.

B. A Warning (4:5-6).

Malachi closes with the assertion that Yahweh would send "Elijah the prophet" to sound the final warning to national Israel. The traditional Jewish view is that the prediction refers to Elijah the Tishbite. Jews set a cup for Elijah at Passover and a chair for him at circumcisions. Traditional Catholic exegesis supports this view. The New Testament, however, seems to clearly indicate that John the Baptist is intended (Matt 11:14; Luke 7:27). John came in the spirit and power of Elijah (Luke 1:17).[12]

Elijah (John the Baptist) would come "before that great and fearful day of Yahweh." Some think the reference is to the final judgment. According to this view when John prepared the Jews for the first advent, the forerunner was preparing them for Messiah's second advent as well. More likely is the view that "the great and fearful day of Yahweh" refers to the destruction of Jerusalem in AD 70. This event figures prominently in Old Testament prophecy as well as in the teaching of Jesus.[13]

Elijah (John the Baptist) would "turn the heart of the fathers to children and the heart of the children to their fathers." A great chasm existed been the godly forefathers and the degenerate generation of John's day. The idea here is not the settlement of family disputes, but the conversion of the children so that they would be like their godly forefathers. To state the matter differently, John would lead in a mighty revival among the Jews. Thus did the angel interpret this passage in the announcement of John's birth (cf. Luke 1:16-17).

Those who listened to John followed Jesus. In following Jesus they escaped the tragedy of the Roman war which devastated Judea in AD 66-70. At that time the land of Judea was smitten with "utter destruction," i.e., the ban. Just as the Canaanites were devoted to destruction by the armies of Joshua, so the land of Judea would be subject to total destruction by the Romans. Christians heeded the warning of Jesus to flee Jerusalem when they saw the abomination of desolation—the Roman armies—approaching the city (cf. Matt 24:15).

Thus the last prophet of the Twelve announces the coming of the last prophet under the Old Covenant (cf. Matt 11:12-13). Some four centuries after Malachi the Elijah of prophecy arose to warn of impending judgment and to point his auditors to Christ.

ENDNOTES

1. See Mark 1:2; Matt 11:10; Luke 7:27. Another prophecy interpreted as pointing to John the Baptist is Isa 40:3.
2. Some take the "temple" to be God's people in a figurative sense rather than the physical temple in Jerusalem.
3. Keil thinks it is the Old Covenant which is intended. Packard applies the term to both covenants.
4. Theo. Laetsch, *Bible Commentary; The Minor Prophets* (St. Louis: Concordia, 1956), p. 534.
5. The words could mean "in what manner shall we return?" Most likely, however, the words mean, "In respect to what sin shall we return?"
6. The Septuagint renders: "shall a man heel," i.e., grasp the heel or deceive God?
7. The book of remembrance was common in the Persian court. See Ezra 4:15; Esther 2:23; 6:1. The same practice was common in Israel and Judah. Cf. 1 Kgs 11:41; 14:29. Names of public benefactors were inscribed in this book. On God's book of remembrance see Exod 32:32; Ps 56:8; 69:28; 139:16; Dan 7:10; Rev 13:8; 20:12-15.
8. On the association of light with the coming of Messiah see Num 24:17; Isa 9:2; 42:6; 49:6.
9. This chapter of Malachi has already been cited twice in the first chapter of Luke. (See Luke 1:17,76). This makes it even more likely that Zacharias' "Dayspring from on high" is based on Malachi 4:2. See also 2 Pet 1:19; Eph 5:14; Rev 21:23.
10. Laetsch (*op. cit.*, p. 541) interprets the verb here in the absolute sense, i.e., to act, do successfully.
11. Laetsch (*op. cit.*, p. 543) thinks the term *mishpatim* ("ordinances") refers to the decisions of judges which had been accepted as common law. The LXX places this verse (4:4) at the end of the book probably because they considered the original ending (4:5) as too harsh.
12. Other references pointing to John as the fulfillment of the Elijah prophecy are these: Matt 3:1-12; 17:11-13; Mark 1:2-8.
13. Joel 2:31; Dan 9:26-27; 12:1; Matt 24:1-28. Luke 21:1-21.